剑桥应用语言学年度评论 2004
Annual Review of Applied Linguistics

语言教育学的进展
Advances in Language Pedagogy

主编 〔美〕Mary McGroarty

导读 彭宣维

2016年·北京

Originally published by Cambridge University Press in 2004. This reprint edition is published with the permission of the Syndicate of the Press of the University of Cambridge, Cambridge, England.
原书由英国剑桥大学出版社于 2004 年出版。
本版经英国剑桥大学出版社授权出版。

This edition is licensed for sale in the People's Republic of China only (excluding Hong Kong SAR, Macao SAR and Taiwan Province). No part of this publication may be reproduced or distributed by any means, or stored in a database or retrieval system, without the prior written permission of the publisher.
本版仅限在中华人民共和国境内(不包括香港特别行政区、澳门特别行政区及台湾)销售。未经出版者书面许可,不得以任何方式复制或发行本书的任何部分。

剑桥应用语言学年度评论
专家委员会

主　任　　胡壮麟
副主任　　田贵森　朱永生
委　员　　曹　进　何　伟　靳　琰　赖良涛　李战子
　　　　　彭宣维　齐振海　孙迎晖　王振华　辛志英
　　　　　杨信彰　于　晖　张　辉　张　琳　张　薇
　　　　　郑　萱

CONTENTS

总序 ··· 胡壮麟　1
导读 ··· 彭宣维　11
EDITOR'S INTRODUCTION
·· Mary McGroarty　i

RESEARCH IN TEACHING LANGUAGE SKILLS

1. LISTENING TO LEARN OR LEARNING TO LISTEN?
   ··· Larry Vandergrift　3
2. RESEARCH IN THE TEACHING OF SPEAKING
   ························· Michael McCarthy and Anne O'Keeffe　31
3. RESEARCH ON TEACHING READING
   ·· William Grabe　53
4. RESEARCH IN TEACHING WRITING
   ························· Tony Silva and Colleen Brice　84

RESEARCH IN TEACHING LANGUAGE SYSTEMS

5. RESEARCH IN TEACHING PRONUNCIATION AND INTONATION
   ·· Jennifer Jenkins　131
6. CURRENT DEVELOPMENTS IN RESEARCH ON THE TEACHING OF GRAMMAR
   ························· Hossein Nassaji and Sandra Fotos　152
7. RESEARCH IN TEACHING VOCABULARY
   ·· John Read　176

TEACHING LANGUAGE IN SPECIFIC SETTINGS

8. TRENDS IN TEACHING ENGLISH FOR SPECIFIC PURPOSES
   .... Diane D. Belcher   199
9. TRENDS IN TEACHING STANDARD VARIETIES TO CREOLE
   AND VERNACULAR SPEAKERS
   .... Hazel Simmons-McDonald   226
10. RESEARCH PERSPECTIVES ON TEACHING ENGLISH
    AS A LINGUA FRANCA
    .... Barbara Seidlhofer   254

CURRICULUM, PEDAGOGY, AND TEACHER PREPARATION

11. CROSSING FRONTIERS: NEW DIRECTIONS IN
    ONLINE PEDAGOGY AND RESEARCH
    .... Richard Kern, Paige Ware, and Mark Warschauer   293
12. CONTENT-BASED INSTRUCTION: PERSPECTIVES
    ON CURRICULUM PLANNING
    .... Fredricka L. Stoller   315
13. ASPECTS OF COLLABORATION IN PEDAGOGICAL
    DISCOURSE
    .... Richard Donato   342
14. CONSTRUCTIVIST ISSUES IN LANGUAGE LEARNING
    AND TEACHING
    .... Dorit Kaufman   366
15. EMERGING RESEARCH AND PRACTICES IN
    IMMERSION TEACHER EDUCATION
    .... Tony Erben   388

CONTRIBUTOR BIODATA

总　　序

　　自2013年8月起,商务印书馆与剑桥大学出版社开始商洽在大陆出版《应用语言学年度评论》(Annual Review of Applied Linguistics)事宜,至2014年春末签约。此后,商务印书馆英语编辑室领导栾奇和马浩岚并责任编辑杨子辉博士先后来访,约我办三件事,一是代为组织国内学者为各卷写导读,二是承担导读的审稿任务,三是为商务版《应用语言学年度评论》写一个总序。作为对我的照顾,同意我邀请复旦大学朱永生教授[①]和北京师范大学田贵森教授[②]参加导读审定工作。就总序而言,多次思考之后,想谈以下四个方面。

一、刊物方针

　　《应用语言学年度评论》(以下简称《年度评论》)是美国应用语言

[①] 朱永生：复旦大学教授、博导,杭州师范大学钱塘学者,高校功能语言学研究会副会长,高校语篇分析研究会副会长,Linguistics and Human Sciences 编委及《中国外语》等杂志编委。曾任苏州大学外语系主任、复旦大学外文系主任和国际文化交流学院院长、国际系统功能语言学研究会执委、国务院学科评议组成员、全国高校外语教学指导委员会委员等职务。著有《系统功能语言学多维思考》《系统功能语言学再思考》《语境动态研究》《系统功能语言学概论》等。

[②] 田贵森：北京师范大学外文学院教授、博导,中国功能语言学学会常务理事、中国社会语言学学会理事。1976年河北师范大学外语系毕业后留校任教,1987年北京外国语大学硕士,1991年纽约市立大学硕士,1997年北京大学博士。曾任河北师大外国语学院院长、河北省高校外语教学研究会会长、中国教育学会外语教学专业委员会副理事长。著有《禁忌语的功能研究》《英语专业毕业论文写作教程》《新编英语词汇学教程》等。

学学会（American Association for Applied Linguistics，简称 AAAL）主办的一部书刊结合的出版物，自 1980 年起每年一卷，至 2014 年已出版 34 卷。该刊最初由 Newbury House 出版社出版，自第 5 卷起改为剑桥大学出版社出版，延续至今。美国南加州大学美国语言研究所主任 Robert B. Kaplan 教授筹划第 1 卷《年度评论》时，邀请犹他州布里格姆-扬大学日耳曼语系 Randall L. Jones 教授和华盛顿大学应用语言学中心主任 G. Richard Tucker 教授三人合作主编。在他们领导下的编委会对办刊宗旨确定这样一个基本认识：尽管 1941 年美国密执安大学率先成立了将语言学理论应用于语言教育的英语学院，1956 年英国爱丁堡大学成立了应用语言学系，1959 年美国华盛顿大学建立了应用语言学中心，1966 年 TESOL Quarterly 出版，1977 年美国应用语言学学会成立，《年度评论》编委会无意选定其中之一作为应用语言学界共同遵循的蓝图，而是决定走自己的路。在此基础上编委会确定的方针有如下特点：(1)《年度评论》不是杂志，因为它一年只出一本；它又被看作是一本杂志，因为它由出版社的杂志部负责编辑、发行事务。[①] (2) 该出版物不对应用语言学做面面俱到的报道，而是对应用语言学学科的现状进行专题评论、综述和文献式的归纳。(3) 应用语言学具有高度的跨学科性，因此该刊重点结合双语教育、语言教育学、心理语言学和社会语言学四个方面进行选题。考虑到这四个学科枝叶蔓生，年刊会对一个学科的某一领域做全面的综述和评论。(4) 即使上述四个学科也不是应用语言学的唯一研究领域，因为该刊遵循美国应用语言学学会所倡导的功能导向，着眼于具体应用更甚于理论。(5) 所有的文章由编委会组织某一领域的专家撰写，不转载已在其他刊物上发表的文章，也不采用在某个学术会议上已经宣读的论文，更不对某一部具体的学术著作进行评论。因此，《年度评论》的主要任务是收集和突出被学术界很少报道或研究的领域，不重复已有工作，更不企图贬低某一

[①]《应用语言学年度评论》问世后，受到国际学术界的高度重视，被权威的《社会科学引文索引》（SSCI）、《艺术和人文科学引文索引》（AHCI）和《科学引文索引》（SCI）所收录。

个方面,或对本学科内某项研究的价值进行排队。这样,《年度评论》对二语习得和语言干扰等内容谈得不多,因为这方面的研究成果已经发表很多。反之,微语言学、符号语言学、计算机辅助教学等受到重视。(6)《年度评论》本身应当正确面对来自不同领域实践者的认同或挑战。[①][②] 鉴于上述情况,《年度评论》每卷都有一个主题,如"语言和语言教育政策"(卷2)、"书面话语"(卷3)、"读写教育"(卷4)等。这些选题均具有学术性、实用性、时代性和独特性。与此同时,该刊每隔四五年会有一卷就应用语言学的整体研究从不同方面进行总结式的调研和讨论,内容涉及语言学习和教学、话语分析、教学创新、二语习得、计算机辅助教学、职场语境下的语言用途、社会语言学、语言政策和语言评估(如卷1、5、10、15、19等)。每年向读者提供500多个新的文献,以帮助本学科教学科研人员能深入掌握情况,点面结合。《年度评论》原计划的第1卷在1980年出版,由于组稿和印刷的原因,实际上在1981年问世。这一脱节现象直到1994年第14卷才得到扭转,即每卷标明的年度与出版年度取得一致。[③]

二、主编更迭

三十多年来,《年度评论》的总主编大约十年更换一次。美国南加利福尼亚大学美国语言研究所主任 Robert B. Kaplan 教授从创刊起任总主编,连续十年。Kaplan 曾任美国应用语言学会会长、英语作为第二语言教

[①] Rota, A. (1982). ANNUAL REVIEW OF APPLIED LINGUISTICS (ARAL). Robert B. Kaplan (Gen. Ed.); Randall L. Jones and G. Richard Tucker (Co-Eds.). *TESOL Quarterly*, *16*, 398–404.

[②] Kaplan, Robert B. (1980). Introduction. *Annual Review of Applied Linguistics*, *1*, vii–xi.

[③] Kaplan, Robert B. and William Grabe. (2000). Applied Linguistics and the Annual Review of Applied Linguistics. in *Annual Review of Applied Linguistics*, *20*, 3–17. Cambridge University Press.

学学会会长、《牛津应用语言学手册》总主编、《国际语言学百科全书》编委等。① 在 Kaplan 主编的《牛津应用语言学手册》中，他认为应用语言学家至少应该具备以下领域的一些知识：人类学、社会学、经济学、政治学、教育学、老年人学、历史学、国际关系、语言学习和教学、词典编纂学、政策研究、心理学和神经科学、公共管理、教师培训和文本生成等。此外，每一位应用语言学家都应精于计算机使用，能够对数据进行统计分析。②③

自第 11 卷起，William Grabe 任主编。Grabe 是美国北亚利桑那州大学负责科研的副校长，曾先后在该校英语系和应用语言学系任教。Grabe 认为应用语言学的核心是"试图解决人们在日常生活中遇到的与语言相关的问题"，是一种"研究现实世界语言问题的、实践驱动的学科"。④ 鉴于这个原因，应用语言学必然是一个交叉学科，涉及许多其他领域。这可见之于他对每卷的选题，如"读写教育"（卷 12）、"二语教学"（卷 13）、"语言政策和规划"（卷 14）、"技术和语言"（卷 16）、"多语现象"（卷 17）、"二语教育基础"（卷 18）、"应用语言学的学科性"（卷 19,20）。Grabe 任总主编至 2000 年卸任。在他最后一次负责的第 20 卷，他和 Robert Kaplan 合写了一篇回顾应用语言学和《年度评论》发展历程的总结性文章。

自 2001 年起任总主编的是北亚利桑那大学英语系的 Mary McGroarty 教授。她主要研究双语现象、语言政策、语言教育和课堂研究、社会语言学、二语教学的文化影响等。由于第一次出任主编，McGroarty 邀请了美

---

① Bruthiaux, Paul, Dwight Atkinson, William G. Egginton, William Grabe, Viadehi Ramanathan. Eds. (2005). *Directions in Applied Linguistics in Honour of Robert B. Kaplan.* Clevedon: Multilingual Matters Ltd.
② Kaplan, Robert B. (1999). *The Oxford Handbook of Applied Linguistics.* Edinburgh: Edinburgh University Press.
③ 刘海涛. 从比较中看应用语言学. 北华大学学报（社会科学版），2007, 8(2): 4.
④ Grabe, William. (2000). Introduction. *Annual Review of Applied Linguistics*, 20, 1–2. Cambridge University Press.

国著名外语教学法专家 Wilga M. Rivers 为第 21 卷"语言和心理学"写序，题为"沿着记忆巷道的漫长旅程"。此后，McGroarty 在她任期内主编了"话语和对话"（卷 22）、"语言接触和演变"（卷 23）、"语言教育学的进展"（卷 24）和"通用语语言"（卷 26）。《年度评论》第 27 和 28 卷的主题分别为"语言与科技"和"神经语言学和认知语言处理"，但未见到这两卷本应由总主编执笔的引言，在目录中也未出现，原因不详。作为总主编的 McGroarty 在第 29 卷"语言政策和语言评估"中再次出现，不过她邀请了著名学者 Bernard Spolsky 作为客座主编。Spolsky 教授长期在以色列的 Bar-Ilan 大学任教，曾任该校人文学院院长，并创建语言政策研究中心。在编辑业务方面，他曾任国际刊物 Language Policy（《语言政策》）的总主编，Asia TEFL（《亚洲英语作为外语教学》）杂志的出版部主任和总编辑。Spolsky 的专著都与语言政策和语言教育有关，如《教育语言学导论》（1978）、《二语学习的条件》（1991）、《社会语言学》（1998）、《以色列诸语言：政策、意识和实践》（1999）、《语言政策》（2004）、《语言管理》（2009）等。[①] 由此看来，Spolsky 无力全心投入《年度评论》的编辑工作，这次只是扮演一次客串角色而已。

自第 30 卷起，总主编一职由美国密执安州立大学的 Charlene Polio 教授担任。Polio 的主要研究领域为二语写作、二语习得、外语课堂话语、新技术和有经验教师之间的行为差异。她在编辑工作上有较多经验，除接受《年度评论》的总主编任务外，也是 Modern Language Journal（《现代语言杂志》）的编辑，此前曾为 Journal of Second Language Writing（《二语写作杂志》）和 TESOL Quarterly 杂志编委会委员。[②] Polio 为《年度评论》各卷确定的选题为"应用语言学专题"（卷 30）、"第二语言教育研究"（卷 31）、"公式化语言研究"（卷 32）、"多语现象研究"（卷 33）、"研究方法专题"（卷 34）。这体现了她作为总主编延续了该刊创办时的主导思

[①] Spolsky, Bernard. Homepage. http://www.biu.ac.il/faculty/spolsky/. 2015. 1. 3.
[②] Polio, Charlene. http://www.wsu.edu/~oikui/. 2015. 1. 5.

想,即每卷的稿子都是就某一领域的特定问题而精选的。

为《年度评论》写稿的作者中不乏名人,如 Henry G. Widdowson、James R. Martin、Bernard Spolsky、Alan Davies 等都是国际著名语言学家。

三、国人参与

我国大陆、港台地区和国际华人圈对《应用语言学年度评论》很为重视。

台湾学者郑锦全(Chan-chuan Cheng)在第7卷上发表"语言和计算机"一文。郑当时任台湾师范大学华语文教学研究所讲座教授、台湾地区研究院语言所研究员和人文社会科学研究中心通信研究员(Cheng, 2014)。[①]另一位是台湾清华大学培养的许静芬(Ching-fen Hsu)博士,现在台湾华梵大学人文学院师资培养研究中心工作,专攻威廉姆斯综合征(Williams Syndrome)发育障碍的语言习得研究,是第28卷"威廉姆斯综合征:基因型和认知表型描述"一文的第一作者。[②]香港教育学院语言教学研究中心主任的李楚成(David C. S. Li)教授在第26卷上发表"作为大中华通用语的汉语"一文。[③]在《年度评论》第30卷独立发表有关传承语学习的社会文化维度一文的何纬芸(Agnes Weiyun He)教授,早期毕业于北京外国语大学,现为 Stony Brook 大学应用语言学和亚洲研究专业的教授,筹建了该校多语和跨文化交际中心。何纬芸主要研究语言语境和语篇的结合,人们如何通过日常互动逐步构建和重构概念、社团和文化。近十年来,她专门研究不同时期和不同背景下汉语作为传承语的社会化。[④]在《年度评论》第27卷与 John Flowerdew 联名发表"多语制和二语写作在电

[①] Cheng, Chan-chuan(郑锦全). http://doc88.com/P-795557797523.html. 2014.12.9.

[②] Hsu, Ching-fen(许静芬). http://www.docin.com/p-2898691.html & key. 2015.1.5.

[③] Li, David, C. S.(李楚成). http://dfl.shufe.edu.cn/structure/xueshu-com-142410-1.htm. 2014.12.9.

[④] He, Agnes Weiyun(何纬芸). http://www.stonybrook.edu/commcms/asian/PROGRAMS.html. 2014.12.9.

子时代的关系"一文的李咏燕博士（Yongyan Li）任教于香港大学教育学院英语教育系，其研究范围包括专业写作、多语学者的研究和发表实践、言而有据的写作、科学文章的整篇抄袭现象、在职教育等。[①] 令人瞩目的是，上述学者与大陆高校和研究单位保持良好的学术联系，如郑锦全教授曾担任四川大学文学与新闻学院兼职教授、厦门大学嘉庚学院中文系兼职教授、北京大学汉语语言学研究中心兼职研究员；李楚成教授曾在上海财经大学举行关于中国外语学习者和使用者常见错误的纠正讲座；何纬芸教授与上海交通大学苗瑞琴副教授合作编写了"继承语之习得及其社会化"一文。[②]

大陆学者对《年度评论》也做出了应有的反应和贡献。早在 1981 年《年度评论》第 1 卷问世后，我国学者左焕琪教授便在国内语言学权威刊物《当代语言学》上作了报道，既介绍了编者 Kaplan 的背景，也对该卷四个部分作了近似导读的介绍。作者当时就以敏锐的眼光指出这是"近年来美国应用语言学领域引人瞩目的新刊物"。[③] 较近的可举 2012 年方秀才的"程式语面面观介绍"一文，对《年度评论》第 32 卷从认知视角、教学应用、社会学进展和未来展望四个部分深入介绍。作者特别注意到，为了从多种视角讨论程式语这一主题，总主编没有限定程式语的定义、内涵，也没有统一术语，让每篇文章的作者采用自己认同的术语和定义，[④] 这表明《年度评论》并没有因为总主编的变动而放弃原有的风格。

行文至此，有必要提一下以 Charlene Polio 为首的新编委会所作的一个重大决定，那就是她代表编委会聘请了我国广东外语外贸大学王初明教授从第 31 卷起任《年度评论》顾问委员会的委员。这是对我国应用语言

---

① Li, Yongyan（李咏燕）. http://www_researchgate.net/profile/Yongyan_Li/publications. 2014.12.9.
② 何纬芸, 苗瑞琴. 继承语之习得及其社会化. 载姬建国, 蒋楠主编：应用语言学（西方人文社会科学前沿述评）. 北京：中国人民大学出版社, 2007. 239–255.
③ 左焕琪. 应用语言学年度评述（1980）.《国外语言学》, 1983,（3）：46–49.
④ 方秀才.《程式语面面观》介绍.《当代语言学》, 2013, 15（4）：492–495.

学研究发展和水平的肯定。我与王初明教授结识于 1995 年 9 月，当时我是香港中文大学的访问学者，他是英语系的博士生。我们经常一起讨论学术问题。长江后浪推前浪，2011 年我从北京外国语大学中国外语教育研究中心学术委员会主任退下后，他接替了此职。王初明教授现在的学术兼职有国务院学位委员会外国语言文学学科评议组成员、中国高等教育学会外语教学研究分会副会长。他的主要研究方向为第二语言习得研究及其在外语教学中的应用，主要学术创见有外语写长法、语境补缺假说、外语语音学习假设、外语学习的学伴用随原则、读后续写的理论和应用价值。

四、"商务"特色

除保留剑桥版《应用语言学年度评论》的原有特色外，商务版《应用语言学年度评论》有它自己的特色。

商务版《年度评论》从第 20 卷开始，而不是从第 1 卷开始。我认为商务印书馆此举着眼于让读者以更多的精力把握应用语言学在新世纪的发展，急读者之所急。我们还应该看到，《年度评论》第 20 卷实际上起到承前启后的作用。在该卷中，为上世纪创刊时立下汗马功劳的 Robert Kaplan、William Grabe 和 G. Richard Tucker 分别对应用语言学和《年度评论》在二十年中的发展作了系统的总结，帮助读者对前二十年有个总体了解，又寄厚望于这门新学科在新世纪、新千年的发展，把握前进的方向。其次，商务版《年度评论》增加了满足中国读者需求的新内容，那就是每卷都有一篇 1.5 万字左右的中文导读。这便于帮助读者掌握每卷的基本内容和背景材料，特别是汉语界的教师、研究者和学生。

参与此任务的导读作者有国内外语界著名学者，也有新生代的中青年学者。这些专家学者对自己撰写的内容比较熟悉。作为此项目的组织者，我没有向他们摊派任务，而是让各位学者根据自己熟悉的领域自由选题。对各位作者的努力我在此谨表谢意。如前所述，导读初稿完成后均由上海复旦大学朱永生教授和北京师范大学田贵森教授分别先行审读。对两位教授退休后仍能不辞辛苦、鼎力相助的感激之情,难以言表。

由于《年度评论》涉及多个学科和领域,各卷原版的体例不全相同,而各位导读作者的学术生涯也不尽相同,我们对导读编写体例上只作大致要求,不强调绝对统一。总的印象是,每位导读作者对本卷各章内容都能做提纲挈领的介绍和解释,帮助读者理解和抓住要点,这是共同的优点。导读作者各自的特色则表现在:(1)能在正文之前对本卷的总主编、客座编辑做介绍,并对总主编的引言深入分析,起到画龙点睛的作用;(2)对本卷主题进行了解释;(3)对有关主题在20世纪的研究状况或《年度评论》已经发表过的专辑作必要回顾;(4)对每卷论文内容进行归纳,指出其特点;(5)坦率指出某卷内容的不足之处;(6)结合国内现状进行讨论,并进行反思;(7)在讨论中,引入当代先进理论;(8)向我国学界和领导部门提出今后有待深入展开研究的问题。

在结束本序之际,再次感谢各位导读作者,以及永生教授和贵森教授的共同努力,使本项艰巨任务得以顺利完成;祝贺商务版《应用语言学年度评论》正式出版;祝愿商务印书馆今后在应用语言学和理论语言学等领域为外语教育界和学术界做出更多更大贡献!

北京大学蓝旗营寓所
2015年元月

导　　读[*]

彭宣维 [①]

《应用语言学年度评论》（以下简称《年度评论》）2004 年第 24 卷的标题是《语言教育学的进展》(Advances in Language Pedagogy)，其关键词是"语言教育学"(Language Pedagogy)。按照《朗文语言教学及应用语言学辞典》，此术语本身是用来"描写第一语言、第二语言或外语教学"的(Richards et al, 1998: 253)；据此，本卷的议题则是对人们在与语言教学相关研究方面的进展给予的综论性描写；而具体情况正是如此，尤其大量涉及二语教学和外语教学的研究进展与相关问题。

关于语言教育学这一主题在《年度评论》1998 年第 18 卷已出现过。本卷的出版表明，在此短短六年中，语言教育学这个领域在理论和实践上出现了巨大发展，成为应用语言学的一个热门话题。

历史地看，语言教学的方法经历了传统的翻译法、直接法、听说法、视听法、自觉实践法、认知法、功能法、计算机技术辅助法、甚至发展到今天的计算机微课（慕课）这一以技术为主导的实践历程，教学材料已经从传统的单一语类选样（如注重经典语文的语言教学）跳出来、走向了基于语料库的多语类并重的阶段，探究内容从聚焦于听说读写等基本技能的提高、发展到同时对教学环境和技术手段的重视，从传统课堂以教师为中心的组织方法、到以学生为中心的观念转变、再到师生并重而阴阳互根的

[①] 彭宣维，广东外语外贸大学。中国英汉语比较研究会功能语言学专业委员会会长。国际系统功能语言学会国际委员；发表论文 120 余篇，著作 7 部；主研功能语言学理论及应用。

思路上来了（Haliday, 1988/2007, 1990/2007; Martin, 待出版），进而从教师教育本身挖掘语言教育教学潜力。从这个大的背景看，这里的进展报告不仅在听说读写四个传统的技能教学思考上有了实质性推进，对构成语言系统的语音语调、语法和词汇的教学探讨也可谓日新月异，而结合社会语言学路径的教学指导以及关注教学过程、教学设计与教师教育发展的教学法本身，研究成果也可谓汗牛充栋。因此，这些发展既体现在对相关目的探究的深广度方面，更有方法、手段和理念上的突破，可谓一日千里。

本卷《年度评论》由北亚利桑那大学 Mary McGroarty 教授主编。McGroarty 自 2001 年即开始负责主编第 21 卷《语言和心理学》，并继续担任 2002 年第 22 卷的《话语和对话》、2003 年第 23 卷的《语言接触和演变》的主编。本卷共组织 15 篇文章，分 4 个大类进行综述：听说读写教学研究，4 篇；语音语调和词汇语法教学研究，3 篇；社会语言学视野里的语言教学探讨，3 篇；对教学过程、项目设计与语言教师发展的探索，5 篇；前附主编对本书的扼要介绍。虽然本卷目录中没有按上述四个大类明确分栏，但主编的组织思想是清楚的。下面四大部分的标题是导读作者按各部分内容添加的。此外，行文将在相关部分结束之后分别给予简评；结语部分则从整体上总结相关发展思路，并指出今后研究值得关注的课题。

第一部分 听说读写教学研究的实质性推进

这就是传统上说的语言学习"四项技能"，也是早已为外语教学界认可的外语教学基本功。但从语言教学实践的专业研究与发展看，相关议题跟早先相比已经走出很远了，这体现在近年来人们在研究目的和研究方法的不断探索上。

我们先看听力教学研究，这是 Larry Vandergrift 在第 1 篇综述的基本内容："以听促学还是以学促听？"（Listening to learn or learning to listen?）。作者现任加拿大渥太华大学教授，曾在埃德蒙顿市克里斯琴高级中学教授法语 22 年，深受学生在日常法语会话中的焦虑和绝望状况触动。因此，在20世纪90年代中期攻读博士学位期间，该作者潜心研究二语听力教学，其成果很快被同行接受。Vandergrift指出，人们早先认为听力学习只是一个被动的倾听过程，基本指导方法就是听说法——先听，后口头复述；紧随其后的是"问—答理解"。这两种指导方式的更替都是有进步的，毕竟从传统的机械行为主义思路转到了以内容为导向的理解上来了。到上个世纪80—90年代，在交际教学法盛极一时之际，听力教学的思路又一次发生了实质性变化：人们大力提倡适时倾听真实生活中的真实话语，要求学习者重视交际任务，鼓励他们与操该语的本族语者交往，从而达到互动学习的目的。此时，听力指导不再局限于所听内容——为学而听（listening to learn），还关注听力过程——学会倾听（learning to listen）。总体来看，当时人们对听力教学的指导还不够。不过，相关研究毕竟为语言教师、教材编写者和课程发展者提供了一些有益的启示。第一，鉴于听力在四种语言技能中具有最不起眼的地位，也最难学，人们将注意力放到了倾听涉及的不同层次的生理与认知过程、相关语境和"具有社交意义的听觉线索"（socially coded acoustic clues）上面。早先的研究综述（Lynch, 1998, 2002; Mendelsohn, 1998; Oxford, 1993; Rost, 2002; Rubin, 1994）指出，二语听力教学的研究者们主张同时采取自上而下与自下而上相结合的理解策略：自上而下是运用语境和先前的知识，如主题、语类、文化以及长时记忆中的其他图式知识，为听力理解确立概念框架；自下而上是以语素到话语逐步结合的方式来建构意义的过程。但研究发现，二语听力练习者应该学会根据自己的倾听目的来有效使用两种过程，但学习者需要在实际话语交际中做出选择：通过互补策略、语境因素和其他任何可资利用的相关信息，对付没能理解的部分。第二，人们通过实证研究探索各种指导性技巧，以便帮助二语听力练习者处理语言输入，包括课前组织教学（advance organizer）、语境和内容性的视图支持（如观看带字幕的 DVD）、自下而上的词语识别理解、元认知策略的发展与有效运用。这些质性策略的探索为二语听力教学摸索出了一条以策略为进路的教学方法，但其长期效果如何还需深入探讨。第三，帮助学生发展技能以弥补理解空缺，教师需要深究学生得出有关答案，尤其是错误答案的原因，从而为缺乏技能的学生寻找有效策略。相关研究指出，指导学生如何学会倾听涉及的不同阶段：一是根据主题和语篇类别对即将倾听的、可能涉及的信息类别和词语做出预测；二是对预测进行核实，并给予反思；三是总结相关元认知策略，包括预测注意、监控调整与选择性注意、监控性调整与问题解决和评估、选择性注意与监控、终极评估，等等。在这里，自上而下与自下而上的方法并协工作，从而有针对性地给予补救性训练。在对语篇进行宏观分析的反思阶段，学习者可以通过扩展方式统摄对语篇的微观分析，从而将两种方法整合为一个有机体。第四，相关研究区分了学术性听力、双向性听力（关注适时输入信息、消除理解中没有把握的地方、批判性地处理已经理解的内容、并给予反馈）和窄式听力（为学习者提供大量可理解的输入），并从社会语言学维度给予相关指导。

我们再看口语教学研究。这是 Michael MaCarthy 与 Anne O'Keeffe 在第 2 篇"口语教学研究"（Research in the teaching of speaking）报道的研究成果。Michael MaCarthy 为美国宾夕法尼亚州立大学应用语言学教授，国际知名的英语教学专家，在过去 40 多年的学术生涯中，在口语教学、教材设计、词典编纂和语料库研究等领域均卓有建树。Anne O'Keeffe 是爱尔兰李默瑞克大学圣洁玛利亚学院的应用语言学讲师。两人多有合作，其中最有名的当数《Routledge 语料库语言学手册》（The Routledge Handbook of Corpus Linguistics, 2010）。两作者在本卷一开篇就指出，自上一次综述分析（Burns, 1998）之后，相关研究没有发生方法与实践方面的范式改变，但由于口语语料库的大量出现，人们对于口语的认识的确发生了变化，促使人们对口语教学内容与方法做出思考。同时，人们在基于本族语和非本族语口语语料库的口语材料标准上产生了分歧，出现了有关英语的"标准使用者"（expert users）和"成功使用者"（successful users）的术语分野，继而引发了关于自然口语材料与非自然口语材料的争论，更有人坚持对口语语法和词汇进行独立描述的主张。进而，作者综述了四种主要的课堂口语教学方法：话语分析（话轮互换结构在课堂口语教学中的应用及师生互动话语模式），会话分析（受任务设计与执行因素影响的会话结果，主张提高口语任务的设计与实施水平），关注产出的流畅性、复杂性与准确性的认知方法，以及以维果茨基的支架与趋近发展概念为代表的社会建构视角；一些学者也提到了采用系统功能语言学和语用学作为口语教材的描写框架。课堂口语材料的筛选还涉及不同语类的口语教学，如日常会话、讨论、叙事。值得一提的是，综述者提到了口语教学的发展，包括口语活动的社会语境化、口语能力与读写能力、计算机技术化与传统的读写分离、口语语料库在口语教学中的进一步应用等议题。

接下去是阅读教学。这是 William Grabe 在第 3 篇"阅读教学研究"（Research on teaching reading）归纳的研究内容。William Grabe 为北亚利桑那大学英语系教授，曾任英语系主任、美国应用语言学会主席，长期从事阅读教学研究，成果颇丰，享誉学界。作者首先明确本综述的两个初衷：1）主张跨越先前的综述关涉的阅读理论、阅读评估和阅读指导的范围；2）提醒读者注意 10 个指导阅读教学方法的研究成果，以提高二语阅读教学水平。这 10 种方法包括：1）通过训练确保单词识别的自动性与流畅性；2）强调词汇知识学习对阅读理解的作用；3）通过适当方式激活相关背景知识；4）确保有效的语言知识和通用阅读技能；5）教授语篇结构与话语组织模式；6）提高阅读技能而不是教授单一的阅读技巧；7）提升阅读的流畅性和速度；8）促进广泛阅读，扩大词汇量；9）发展阅读的内在动机；10）为学生阅读制定具有连贯性的课程规划。据此，作者总结了三个方面的研究发现：1）在过去 15 年间，英语作为第一语言的阅读教学研究取得了丰硕成果；这些成果对英语作为第二语言的教学也是有价值的，尽管后者存在语言水平、书写系统、流畅程度、加工能力以及受母语迁移和干扰的差别；2）早先的具体阅读能力对于良好的阅读者来说大有裨益，但整体阅读能力和具体阅读技能可能在很大程度上有相互促进作用；3）一些具体的阅读技能可以作为有效方式纳入连贯性阅读教学的课程体系。综述者指出，相关研究并不能保证有效阅读实践，但可以提供检验手段，寻找最佳效果，进而指出实践经验（practitioner knowledge）与具有说服力的研究成果的融合对有效阅读教学的指导价值。

　　本部分最后一篇综述是 Tony Silva 和 Colleen Brice 撰写的"写作教学研究"（Research in teaching writing）。Tony Silva 为美国普渡大学英语系二语研究生课程和写作课程负责人，在二语写作研究领域享有国际声誉；Colleen Brice 毕业于普渡大学，现为美国密歇根州州立大河谷大学副教授。他们与 Melinda Reichelt 合著的《1993—1997 年二语写作教学研究文献评注》（*Annotated Bibliography of Scholarship in Second Language Writing: 1993—1997*）一书于 1999 年由 Ablex Publishing Corporation 出版，是二语写作教学领域的必读文献。本篇聚焦于二语写作，关注应用研究，但同时间接指向写作教学法。作者概述了大量文献，基本要点包括：基础研究，含写作过程、对书面语篇的重点、语境、语类和层次的关注和评估；应用研究，即基于内容的写作指导、高层次的身份建构、写作与阅读的关联、计算机软件和当代网络技术的介入、词汇语法对提高表达准确性的作用、写作学习者之间的互动、剽窃问题、教师反馈、文学与电影的作用；一些影响二语写作教学的普遍问题与相关事项，诸如外语（而非二语）写作研究的发展、探究二语写作的特定方法、课程体系与教学设计、二语写作规划、二语写作面临的意识形态问题、二语写作的历史发展等。总起来看，早期的二语写作教师是指导方法的被动接受者，涉及有控制的作文、当时通行的传统修辞手段、过程法、学术/语类英语写作等。后来，教师的思想意识发生了实质性变化，教师成了富有经验的成熟职业人士，对二语写作现象的特点有自己的理解，熟悉相关理论和研究领域，他们有素养，从而有依据地针对学生需要发展课程设计，开发教材，对教学方式及其相关方面（如政治的、体制的和课堂的语境）都有清醒认识，在研究的深广度和复杂性上都有拓展和创新，并且具有更多的全局意识，在基础和应用研究之间有更为平衡的原则立场。这些研究一方面成就理论模型建构，另一方面鼓励学习者对政治和意识形态角色的深度把握。

我们看到，像听力教学研究那样触及正式性与非正式性的社会语言学视角、口语教学研究引入语言学的研究成果、阅读教学注重理论探讨与应用过渡的思考、写作教学还涉及二语环境下的意识形态问题，均已把各类分支技能的教学向前推进了一大步，涉及研究手段、研究方法、研究议题和范围以及研究目的；而语料库方法、科技手段和教学法意识则让它们在各自的领域内获得了广泛的价值空间。这在2004年之后的发展中有进一步体现，如近年来兴起的微课，从而使相关教学思想发生了革命性的变化。国内在这方面的文章可谓成果丰硕，但感想居多，真正研究意义上的论述很少。这一现象值得我们深思。

第二部分　语音语调和词汇语法的语言结构教学

这里的综述共3篇，分陈于第5、6、7篇，集中讨论语言核心部分的教学问题。

第5篇"语音语调的教学研究"（Research in teaching pronunciation and intonation）由 Jennifer Jenkins 撰写。作者为英国南安普顿大学全球英语中心教授和奠基人，著述丰硕，其代表作有《国际大学中的英语通用语》（*English as a Lingua Franca in the International University: The Politics of Academic English Language Policy, Routledge, 2013*）和《全球英语学生参考书》（*Global Englishes: A Resource Book for Students, Routeldge, 2014*；注：本书为 *World English: A Resource Book for Students* 第三版）等。作者认为，早先的语音教学研究集中采用对比分析技巧去处理一语和二语语音片段，甄别其间的差异，以此梳理从一语到二语可能出现的迁移错误。后来，语音研究的重点发生了两个转向：一是对过渡语语音系统更为精细的研究，涉及二语学习的迁移性、普遍性、发展阶段和其他过程；二是对切分尤其是超切分特征的兴趣。新近一些研究者不再把语音看作一种孤立自足的语言与教学法现象，而是把语音研究同其他研究成果联系起来，并尽可能采用技术发展的最新成果。这些研究成果正是本章讨论的基本内容，集中在两个方面：

一是语音教学跟语境的关系,二是技术进步的推动作用。对此,综述分三个议题介绍相关研究内容:1)语音语调在话语语境中的作用;2)未来社会语境下的语音教学思考,包括身份、态度和动机等社会心理因素;3)新技术在语音教学中的使用及其对先前相关研究的挑战。这里要特别提到话语语境视角下的语音教学研究。这是在伯明翰大学 David Brazil 教授提出的话语语调(discourse intonation)理论基础上发展起来的。Brazil 在 Halliday 和布拉格学派有关论述(如 Halliday,1970)的基础上,系统阐述了语法与语调以及语调与态度意义的表达两个议题。这对人们将态度与语法功能赋予音高变动(话语语调也关注后者)的研究思路来说,无疑具有超前性。"它既涉及会话控制(包括话轮、引入和结束主题),也以赋予显著性、调式和声调选择的方式关注社交意义与角色定位:降调传递非共享信息,降—升调表达说话人认定的共享基础信息。"(Brazil,1997)因此,它可以为师生提供分析和解释语调选择可资操控的工具。作者进而介绍了话语语调研究方法的可行性与局限性,以及对局限性的补救尝试。而在语言使用语境下,语调教学研究则有母语者语境、二语者和外语学习者语境以及国际环境下的语言使用之别。对于第三种情况,作者归纳了自己早先提出的一个五阶段语音学习法:1)为学习者的产出与接收资源库添加核心项目,包括通用语的核心项目;2)为学习者的接收资源库添加英语作为二语的一系列口音特征;3)添加调和技能;4)为学习者的接收资源库添加非核心项目;5)为学习者的接收资源库添加英语作为第一语言的一系列口音特征。上述过程涉及社会语言学、社会心理学以及可理解性要求,其中社会心理因素包括在相关文化语境中的语言态度、动机和身份问题(Jenkins,2000)。而应用于语音教学研究的计算机技术之前面对的主要是言语识别和单一音素的产出,如元音与辅音,最近则进行超切分段的语调教学。其他运用则包括编纂带光盘的词典、收集语音语料、研究语言节律模式,等等。显然,上述探索拓展了语音教学研究视野,会成为今后研究的一个重要议题。相对于其他方面的探索而言,这方面的思考尝试在国内最为薄弱,因此有大量观点可以借鉴。

对语法教学研究的综述是 Hossein Nassaji 和 Sandra Fotos 在本书第 6 篇"语法教学研究的现状"(Current developments in research on the teaching of grammar)陈述的基本内容。Hossein Nassaji 现任加拿大维多利亚大学语言学系应用语言学教授、系主任,研究领域除了语法教学,还有二语阅读、词汇教学、课堂角色互动等;Sandra Fotos 曾在日本专修大学英语与应用语言学系教学,退休后入加拿大维多利亚大学任教。二人合著的《在二语课堂教授语法》(*Teaching Grammar in Second Language Classrooms: Integrating Form-Focused Instruction in Communicative Context*, Routledge, 2010)一书简明易懂。上一个世纪 70 年代末,随着交际教学法的兴起,人们贬低语法教学在二语学习中的作用,甚至认为语法教学不仅无益,甚至可能有害:它顶多能发展语法结构的陈述性知识,但正确使用语言并不能发展程序性能力,因为两者位于大脑的不同部位,两种不同的知识之间没有接口,依据是英语的形态习得——一语的语法学习不需要正式指导,那么二语学习也就没有必要,类似声音也在普遍语法及其语言习得的应用中出现过。但近年来的大量研究表明,学习者要达到高水平的精确表达,仍然需要接受正式的语法教学指导,理由至少有以下四个方面。1)如果以为语言学习只关注语言形式就有理论问题,毕竟"关注"(noticing)是语言学习的一个必要条件;2)语法的"可教性假设"(teachability hypothesis)表明,人类语言的发展涉及一些固定的发展程序,不能更改,而其他一些结构的学习可在任何时间进行;3)以意义为中心的交际教学法教学使学习者长期面对意义输入(侵入式语法教学),导致他们无法正确表达某些语法形式,因此,学习者要想在目标语学习中获得表达的准确性,就必须聚焦于语法形式的教学;4)过去 20 年大量的实验研究、课堂观察和广泛的文献考察表明,明确的语法教学,无论是准确性还是学习效率,均有实质性效应。尽管有大量关于语法教学的实证支持,一些人仍然持反对态度,认为所教与所学并非直接关联,语法教学的效果带有"边缘性"和"脆弱性"(如 Krashen 1993: 245;也见 Truscott, 1996, 1998)。而另一些人比较谨慎,包括那些明确支持语法教学的学者也小心翼翼，语言学习本质上毕竟带有隐性特点（如 Ellis et al, 2002）。不过，这并不意味着语法教学一无是处。事实上，我们需要形式和意义并重的教学指导，而学生会同时接受显性和隐性的语法教学法，包括输入加工法、互动反馈法、侵入式语篇教学提升法、基于交际任务的任务教学法以及基于真实交际过程的话语教学法。目前，我们对语法学习过程还认识不足，不过学习者对语言形式的持续关注、对包含以意义为中心的形式的反复输入、增加输入和练习机会，则是习得语法形式、提高语言表达准确性的根本前提。

词汇教学跟阅读教学直接相关，但第 7 篇 John Read（新西兰奥克兰大学语言习得资源中心）的综述"词汇教学研究"（Research in teaching vocabulary）也有自己的侧重点。第一，人们区分了随意词汇学习与留意词汇学习两种方法；后者指没有实质性教学方法介入的词汇学习，虽然一度为某些人所追捧（情形与有人把听力教学看作非人为介入的观点相当），但这一点已不再受人青睐：对词汇形态和意义的加工水平是长期保存词汇信息的有效途径；心理语言学研究发现：对词汇做定期复述、死记硬背、词语自动识别训练等传统方法，有必要重新给予关注；当然，词汇学习的难度可以分级进行。第二，对于二语和外语学习者来说，前 2000 个常用词与高频词作用很大，所以出现了不少学习者词典。第三，区分口语词和书面语词汇也有助于听力和阅读理解；而在高频词之上区分特定学科的半专业词汇与专业词汇的主张，在当今世界范围内的大学教学中已经成为共识；在这里，词汇的语料库建设显得尤为重要。第四，学生有效使用为他们专门编纂的词典，尤其是电子词典，显得尤为重要。第五，课堂词汇教学，包括教师用语，对学习者的词汇习得需要也很重要。第六，计算机辅助词汇教学，特别是基于语料库的词汇教学，已经显示出它的优势。最后，词汇知识的测试在词汇知识的深广度把握上也是一个重要议题。不过，目前的词汇教学仍然存在问题：几乎所有的相关教学都采取孤立方法，需要特别关注。

笔者发现，相关研究跟人们对听说读写的探讨一样，均已突破了传统思路；而其中的语法教学研究因其发展的起伏性，特别值得留意。国内在这方面的研究成果最多,但要取得突破性进展还需要更为广阔的国际视野。

第三部分　社会语言学视野里的语言教学探讨

如今的语言教学法研究,或多或少受到了教育与社会因素影响。这些影响体现在专门用途英语教学的社会与关键性转向、语言使用的正式性与非正式性、英语在非母语环境下作为通用语教学的教学法诸方面。这是本部分 3 篇综述文章的主旨。

美国佐治亚州立大学教授 Diane Belcher 在第 8 篇 "专门用途英语教学的发展趋势"(Trends in teaching English for special purposes)一文中,从社会话语、社会文化与社会政治的理论探讨和应用分析角度,对专门用途英语教学的研究趋势做了概述。就社会话语的理论探讨看,有三股力量对专门用途英语教学产生了直接影响:一是发端于后现代理论与一语写作研究的芝加哥新修辞学派,二是派生于系统功能语言学悉尼学派的语类理论,三是语料库语言学。新修辞学派与悉尼学派均尊崇巴赫金的对话理论,将话语看作活动行为。但前者侧重于语言、个体与社会的关系;后者主要关注语篇,据此识别和恢复相关语境,并把语类知识看作一种社会权力资源。语料库语言学为学习者提供了浸入式教学材料。作者进而从专门用途英语教学中的学术英语教学与职业英语教学的角度,归纳了基于语类教学的实践探索,具体语类包括会议摘要、与编辑的通信、学术职位申请、医护病人用语、律师委托人用语、商务人员顾客用语、航空交通控制者和飞行员会话等。显然,职业用途英语中的一部分仍然属于学术英语。从社会文化角度看,学者们提倡完全融入目标语情景的浸入式教学法,但面对语言与读写问题时便显得力不从心,因此有人主张更为明确的、"导引性"的浸入式原则,并为学习者提供情感关注与社会物质环境(如职场实践);同时,机助学习拓展了现场教学的效果。而从社会政治的理论角度看,相关议题主要是批评某些教学法专家的如下主张:关注超语言实践,具体涉及权利、需求、身份等要素，以提升学习者的种族、阶层和性别意识；在实践中，他们以多种方式走进课堂，包括挑剔性地把传统的需求分析重新定义为"权利分析"的做法；超越合作式学习而采取的集体主义行动；不仅为语篇植入语境，还把它看作多种语境的杂合成品，即个体与社会身份的协定场所——家庭与学术或职业价值的协定场所。尽管经过了几代人的努力，对相关行动进行了研究和更为正式的学术探讨，但有关认识仍然远不尽人意。其原因也许在于人们刚刚开始理解各种不同的次语类；而伴随计算机介入的交际又生成了一组全新的语类，介于口语与读写之间，超越了视听范围，包括颜色、声音、画图和视频，这对研究者来说则是新的挑战。对语境而非语篇更感兴趣的一些研究来说，有大量研究领域尚未涉猎，包括家庭清扫、工厂工作和保育职业。据此考察中国国内的情况，我们才触及皮毛。笔者还发现，Martin 的积极/绿色话语分析主张，提出了更高的要求。因此，我们需要对语篇和语境有更为深入的了解，需要对学校、工作场所和其他交际场合有更加宽泛的认识。

中美洲西印度大学的应用语言学教授 Hazel Simmons-McDonald 在第 9 篇"克里奥尔语方言使用者的标准变体教学发展趋势"（Trends in teaching standard varieties to Creole and vernacular speakers）一文中，讨论了向克里奥尔语与说本地语的学生教授标准方言变体的方法问题，重点是帮助他们以使用克里奥尔语和本地语的方式培养二语读写能力（另请参阅 Halliday, 1978）。研究表明，克里奥尔语和本地语对提高二语和标准方言的读写能力大有裨益。事实上，彼此在词汇方面的相似点越多，对二语和标准语的读写能力的发展帮助就越大。而有二语学习经历则有利于三语的学习。总起来看，相对于其他各篇的研究文献，该部分涉及的内容最少，研究对象主要是加勒比海地区。在笔者看来，虽然跟我们的外语教学关系似乎不那么直接，但也很有启示，因为我们这个多民族和多方言国家，目前正处于国际化和城市化发展的关键时期，面临大量类似于加勒比海地区的标准语、二语甚至外语学习情形。我们该如何提出一套适合我国国情的相关教学法呢？这个课题意义重大。

维也纳大学语文与文化学部英语系教授 Barbara Seidlhofer 在第 10 篇以"英语作为一种通用语教学的研究概述"(Research perspectives on teaching English as a lingua franca)为题,揭示了作为通用语的英语是怎样以前所未有的速度深受影响的,指出了英语作为唯一一种世界语的独特功能。与前面各篇尤其是第 9 篇相比,本篇内容极为丰富。首先是英语作为世界语的定义,所用术语甚多,但一个不争的事实是:英语在全球范围内使用,不仅包括外围圈,也包括英语为母语者的内层圈,还有不同种类的英语。而作为通用语的英语,已经在相当程度上形成了由母语使用者确立的规范;事实上,它也有存在的权利。因此,我们质疑在一切语境中遵从英语本族语规范的做法,强调不使用社团英语变体的合法性,正视英语全球化扩散的态度价值和语言学意义,认可描写整理的必要性。不过,仅仅认可必要性还不够,关键是要落到实处——描写。迄今人们所做的工作主要是对作为通用语的英语的语音系统和语用交际进行描写,而对语法的研究还很少。前者关注相关语料库的建设,途径是实地观察、对不同母语者在交际中使用的英语的语音录制、不同母语者使用英语的调核重音研究,分析原则是可交流性与相对的可操作性。后者有所不同,所受限制小一些,但研究的可操作性也要小一些,而违背母语语用规则也很少受到关注。不过,这方面仍然出现了一系列成果。这些研究得以展开的前提是一些突出的语用特征(如长时停顿、言语重叠、话题突然转变)以及把语用学纳入跨文化交际的研究传统。因此,我们仍然可以归纳出一些共性:误解发生情况不多、受母语交际规则干扰的情况很少、遇到问题时则采取容忍态度,因此表现出明显的合作性与相互支持态度。不过,这种表面的认同现象会掩盖深层次的问题根源,需要严肃对待和进一步研究;此外,交际者易于表现出一种相对自我中心,各行其是,因而出现一种平行单语而非相互对话现象。对于通用语的语法研究,人们也发现了一些共同问题,容易引发交际障碍和误会,而缺乏足够的词汇在交际中就无法有效进行变换表达;而最大的问题可能还是相关用语不地道。随后,作者概述了英语通用语的使用场合,包括地域变体和特定领域变体。书面英语的使用也已经非常广泛，因此需要遵从某些既有规范，以便使用者能够自我调整，维系全球范围内的相互理解水平，这就可能涉及与母语规范有别的书面语形式，从而形成跟口语相当的区别性特征。相关研究则需要在母语变体与变化、本土化变体、语言接触、语言使用和教学法的简单化、早先英语作为国际语言的概念和实证工作等领域多下功夫。这里存在一个编纂国际英语学习者语料库的庞大规划问题。目前这项工作已经有人在尝试了。最后，英语通用语的教授有以下目标：确保可交流性，不强求正确性；帮助学习者发展互动策略，提高礼貌水准；培养语篇能力，为学习者选择有目的的阅读和写作技能。具体方法如：选择具有文化敏感性的教学材料；反思教学法的实施过程；尊重学习者的本土文化。接下去的工作是要对英语通用语概念化与描写发展的探讨，毕竟正是通用语自身构成了语言教学的实质性内容，放弃英语使用的母语化和完美交际这一不切实际的想法，可以放开人们的手脚，培养出具有通用语自身特点的能力，包括从超语言特点中提取有价值的要素、在共享知识的基础上进行特点识别和身份建构、评测和调整交际者的语言知识、维系性倾听、以不伤情面的方式提示无法理解的话语、要求重述、变换措辞之类的促动行为。类似特点的形成将促成评估方式、甚至教师教育的主体方向的改变。当然，这一过程会涉及一些问题，需要研究者做仔细观察与详尽分析。

笔者认为，本部分所涉及的研究在我们国内相对较弱，不过有一个重要因素值得我们关注：人们一方面容忍英语作为通用语使用中出现的自身特点与非习惯性表达，而另一方面有交际效果方面的考虑。就整个亚洲的英语教学看，中国大陆的师资力量在口头交际方面总体水平应该是最好的（胡壮麟，1997，2003），但我们不能就此放弃继续向本族语者学习的基本原则，毕竟我们目前面临着国际化和本土化的双重任务，缺乏地道表达方式的交际必然受限，不利于我们的发展。同时，专门用途英语应该加强而不是减弱，尤其是高层次人才培养，应该让语言学理论介入外语教育教学的整个过程，这也是我们正在积极探索的教改课题，以达到国家向我们外语教师提出的前所未有的要求。

第四部分　对教学过程、项目设计和语言教师发展探索的反思

　　本部分内容最多，从第11篇到第15篇，分别从课堂过程、项目设计与语言教育者的准备等不同角度综述了跟教学法有关的议题。

　　第11篇是加州伯克利分校法语系 Richard Kern 教授、德克萨斯州南卫理公会大学教学系系主任 Paige Ware 副教授与加州大学尔湾分校教育与信息科学 Mark Warschauer 教授三位作者以"跨越前沿：在线教育与研究的新趋势"（Crossing frontiers: new directions in online pedagogy and research）为题合作概述的相关研究成果。技术在指导语言教学过程中发挥的作用，已不再是要不要的问题，而是如何适应特定的教学语境问题。早期的网络化计算机应用于语言学习主要体现在三个方面：1）面对面的机助教学探讨；2）语言特征和语言功能；3）用于在线交际的学习资源的量化问题、情感和动机类型。如今这一领域已经将重点转向远距离合作研究，势头有增无减，尤其是在特定社交语境下对特定使用练习的描述与评估，这就是基于语言网络教学研究的社会认知转向，内容涉及语境、互动与多媒体网络化，跨越在线互动语篇，步入跟那些语篇相关但范围更为宽广的动态语境视野，从而从早先的质性方法转向课堂文化和语言使用。新近，关注重点不再局限于单一课堂，而是远距离合作，重视不同文化之间的交际能力以及文化学习与文化读写要素，关注局部场景之外的更为广泛的社交话语，探究交际和不同文化之间的交际能力自身。这又涉及三个相关方面的研究内容：1）语言互动，如意义协商和口头产出；2）不同文化之间的学习项目，包括教学方法、交际、跟交际和文化有关的文化接触；3）读写能力发展以及与之相关的身份建构。总之，人们已经把互联网作为一种真实的交际媒介加以利用，这对早期的说写互动方法提出了质疑，涉及互动本身，以及文化、身份与读写水平。据此，语言教育者就不再是使用互联网来教授同一种语言现象，而是帮助学习者进入一种合作探究与知识建构的新领域，把不同身份与交际策略作为一种资源来看待。

第 12 篇是北亚利桑那州英语系副教授 Fredricka L. Stoller 撰写的"基于内容的教学指导：课程规划诸视角"（Content-based instruction: perspectives on curriculum planning）。Spanos（1990）在本系列第 10 卷指出，20 世纪 80 年代，人们对"整合性指导"（integrated instruction）着迷，但也有不少质疑，包括语言与内容指导者的合作问题、行政支持、教材研发与项目评估。Crandall（1993）在第 13 卷中对美国的内容教学研究历史做了综述，涉及合作学习、以内容为基础和经验的学习、整体语言策略以及图像式思考辅助工具等成功的指导策略。但由于这些领域的个案研究不多，加之先前的调整，人们在实践中很难为整合性指导梳理出最佳条件，包括时间、不同项目模型的相对有效性，尤其是有用的策略、文本与评估方案。Snow（1998）在第 18 卷中考察了基于内容教学的指导性实践、评估和教师培训。与先前的综述不同，本卷（第 24 卷）关注基于课堂的相关研究，视野扩大到项目结果之外，包括不同学科的语言特点、培训之后相关部门在教学法方向上的转变、二语英语学习者在学术上的进步等。贯穿探索过程始终有一条不变的主线，这就是基于内容的教学指导，以便为学生提供一种继续学术发展的途径，提高他们的语言水平。在这一背景下，Stoller 在延续先前相关研究的基础上，侧重从以下几个方面考察了基于内容的教学指导：新近全球性的内容教学指导兴趣、相关课程结果对这一教学方法的支持及其课程体系水平级别的挑战、源自一语和二语语境的课程设置模型、为开发基于内容的课程体系而进行的实证研究，涉及侵入式语境、学习成功所依赖的诸多要素、语言和社会语境的内在关系、合作性的策略性阅读、教师的口头话语以及师生互动话语等一些常见因素。最后，Stoller 指出了需要进一步关注的课题，包括实证研究、相关语境下对评估的系统探索，而一些卓有成效的研究成果也需要进一步思考，同时需要让一线教师、课程体系与课程设计者、教学材料开发者以及评估者了解这些成果，最终让学生在内容和语言学习的能力方面都受益。

第 13 篇是匹兹堡大学教育学院 Richard Donato 博士综述的"教学法话语中的合作因素"（Aspects of collaboration in pedagogical discourse），

旨在全面考察合作教学,以便更好地了解教学法语境之下与共构活动有关的现象。合作活动源自认知、社交、历史和情感发展,在发展心理学与教育研究中被广泛接受。Donato 指出,自上个世纪 80 年代以来,互动研究的理论与实践在添加性语言习得领域文献丰富,但对学习者共建活动中的合作议题谈得很少。就语言教学法的发展情况看,这个话题很有必要。为此,作者演示了学习者的语言运用和学习效果有关的各种合作研究,尤其是合作研究与互动研究以及二语习得的差别,主张把社会文化理论作为合作学习的指导性解释框架,涉及三个方面。首先,作者梳理了合作的内涵,包括三个相互关联的角度。第一,如今的课堂教学合作(school-based collaboration)已经含有文化特点。合作文化会培育差异性,但能同时建立信任、引发焦虑并容纳焦虑、将隐性知识上升为线性知识、寻求群体内外不同观念的联系及其内在性;合作可以通过有意义和有目的的协作,在相关历史与文化语境(如学校和社团)中促成社会关系的改变;其结果便形成群体意识,促成群体新知识的产生与增长。第二,合作教学涉及的是一种"亲和群体"(affinity group),而不只是带有浪漫和善意色彩的"社团实践"(communities practice);亲和群体,不管在工作场所、社团之中、还是互联网上,始终处于实践状态,并共享某些特征,彼此依赖,采用关系网络中不同成员的知识来加以组织;亲和群体成员与特定符号领域相关,彼此易于以内部成员的身份获得认同。第三,合作是一种群体趋同的心理与行为,忽略个体:个体是群体的派生,有独特性;合作含多层次性——从合作努力、到中心活动、再到表面性的社交亲和关系。建构活动是集体的核心,其实就是心理层面的合作,涉及各个成员对相关活动的目的、赋予相关活动以社会和个体意义的态度。相关活动本身则调节人际关系,并构成所有成员的历史与文化背景,因而亲和关系是集体成员带有特定任务的理念与价值的表现。集体的表面特征主要由个人与情感产生,但可以在活动的集体目标面前获得消解。在厘清三种合作内涵之后,Donato 区分了合作与互动的内涵,确立了合作研究的概括性议题,概述了研究课堂环境下合作活动的代表性观点,诸如合作的整合作用——将离散的个体转变成各种社团网络关系的参与者与贡献者;合作使学习者不仅服从于任务,更要主动建构任务,促进语法、语用和话语能力的发展。Donato 还将研究发现与社交文化理论相关联,拟定了合作与课堂场景下语言学习的一些需要研究的关键领域。

第 14 篇是纽约州立大学石溪分校职业教育项目负责人 Dorit Kaufman 博士综述的"语言的学与教中的建构主义议题"(Constructivist issues in language learning and teaching)。建构主义有两个来源,一是侧重于认知发展的皮亚杰,二是强调社会认知的维果茨基。它认为,学习是一个发展过程,涉及跟先期学习经历有关的变化、自我生成与建构,是儿童通过读、听、探索与体验来进行理解建构的发生过程,有同化、调节与平衡三个各有特点但彼此关联的阶段:新的经验经过同化被整合进入当前图式,其结果便是平衡;对于儿童来说,思维与意义生成是社交建构的,源自他们同环境互动,学习过程受周围人的促动;他们具有一种潜在的学习能力,从而引导他们设计解决问题的任务,决定学习需要的支架水平与范围以便完成这些任务。这个过程需要明确的教学指导。建构主义的出现正好与从以教师为中心的模式到以学习者为中心的教学法的转型契合,在普通教育改革、在数学与科学教学的教学法发展领域是一个支配性的智力因素,也关乎语言教学;它在由技术促成的微观世界的发展与应用方面、在读写技能与叙事发展的语言研究领域,都产生了重要影响。

本卷最后一篇综述是南佛罗里达中等教育系 Tony Erben 教授的"浸入式教师教育中的新天地及其实践"(Emerging research and practices in immersion teacher education)。教师教育源自一种自上而下的教育教学理念:从研究教师行动出发,以此为基础进行实践操作。这里包括两个主要议题。一是教师教育模型研究,二是对浸入式教师教育过程进行分解的实证研究。就教师教育的设计模型看,它主要分几大块:1)基础研究:教育社会学、教育哲学和教育心理学;2)教师发展研究:规划、课堂处理、评估和课程体系;3)学科研究:浸入、双语、二语习得、应用语言学、外语教学法与方法论,文化研究;4)课程体系研究:数学、科学、社会研究、音乐、戏剧、艺术、健康与体育、一语语言艺术、外语语言艺术；5）实习经历：重点是通识基础、外语和浸入，具体方式有短期访问、街区实习和/或国内实地考察等。它涉及从职前培训到在职培训（职业发展和发展职业）的整个连续体；职前培训主要指本科和硕士研究生阶段的学习，一般需要3到4年的专业训练，主要是二语的浸入式教学，或者二语与一语结合浸入，大都以面对面的方式进行，将浸入原则整合到所有课程的学习中，还需要多期教学实践经历，目标定位，并结合二语水平的发展进行；在职培训的目的是提升与再培训，一般需要1年或少于1年的时间，对象主要是一语，或者结合二语，途径是技术，浸入作为独立课程进行教授，没有实习时间，顶多只有课堂演示，关注内容和知识，尤其是教学法知识。

除了教师教育模型研究，本篇的第二个重点是对浸入式教师教育过程进行分解的实证研究，也是本篇的重点，具体涉及五个领域：1）对浸入式教师教育项目的效果评估，结果有好有差；但从整体上讲，今后以英语为媒介的教师教育项目需要引入更多的交际教学方法，以提升学员的整体英语水平；2）二语使用水平的提高受师生互动影响，只是在某些文化环境下接受培训的教师受培训教师的影响大，而在另一些环境下不仅受特定任务影响，更受具体目标和互动方式影响；3）就教学实习的经历看，二语使用受两个因素支配：一是互动小组内更有经验的组员的行为，二是每个学员使用二语作为中介工具的可接受程度，但集体介入十分关键；4）以技术为中介的指导（这里特指以计算机为中介的交流与以计算机为中介的教学法）效果甚佳；5）语言学习不是一种孤立现象，最好同时涉及语言、文化、语境和内容知识的多维度对话。在上述两个基本议题之外，作者对浸入教师的能力与职业需求进行了描述性研究。总之，浸入式教师教育是一个具有多元目标的社会化过程，不仅受教育目标影响，更受相关政治、社会和文化因素左右。

就这一组概述涉及的研究内容看，技术在教学法推进中已经成为一个关键因素，可以全面介入逐渐复杂化的语言教学与社交场景的相互关系以及始终处于中心地位的师资培训。

本卷出版至今已届 10 年；而这个系列从开始到 2004 年，作为年度报告的研究回顾，也已经走过了 20 来年的历史，这样一个阶段性的总结值得我们细读。这不仅是针对语言教学研究 30 多年来突飞猛进的发展历史说的，也是针对广大的普通外语教育同行说的。不过，有一点需要提醒国内同仁，语言教育学的发展虽然在一些局部议题上走向了深入，也形成了自身的系统性，但撇开教育技术层面的问题不论，仅就教学内容涉及的整体视野看，它并没有超越 Halliday (2007) 论及的指导思想与操作原则，有兴趣者不妨一探真伪。此外，国内的绝大多数文章相对说来则缺乏应有的深广度。本人 2014 年 5—6 月集中浏览过国内不同层次的期刊上发表的 1000 多篇相关"研究"，大都以"浅谈"、"感想"、"思考"为题，既缺乏深度，也没有系统，这一真正意义上的费时低效现象让人忧虑和深思。

剑桥应用语言学系列每年按照某一专题的方式对相关各子领域给予年度分析，这在我们这个引进系列中也有一定程度的反映。这一举措对于我们来说具有极大的现实意义。我国的语言和外语教学研究、包括整个应用语言学甚至理论语言学探索，按照这一思路为后学提供便捷的学习方式、甚至为专题研究提供契机的总结性工作，目前已经做起来的还很少。可见，我们在整体上需要提升对相关学科的发展引导与设计规划意识。

此外，就本卷涉及的"语言教育学"这一整体议题来看，依据语言范畴开展的相关教学研究在国际上已经取得了可喜的成绩，但还远远不够。这对我国今后的外语教育教学改革来说，应该是一个可以解决关键问题的议题，毕竟我们面对的是某一门外语的整体系统，而缺乏全面的语言学范畴介入，无论在教育政策、大纲设计还是教材研制上，难免挂一漏万。这对于作为母语的汉语教育教学来说，同样值得重视。

* 本导读写作得到"中央高校基本科研业务费专项资金"的支持（项目编号：310400077）。

参考文献:

Brazil, D. (1997). *The Communicative Value of Intonation in English*. Cambridge: Cambridge University Press.
Burns, A. (1998). Teaching speaking. *Annual Review of Applied Linguistics*, vol.18.
Crandall, J. (1993). Content-centered learning in the United States. *Annual Review of Applied Linguistics*, vol. 13.
Ellis, R., H. Basturkmen, & S. Loewen. (2002). Doing focus-on-form. *System*, 30.
Halliday, M. (1970). *A Course in Spoken English: Intonation*. Oxford: Oxford University Press.
Halliday, M. (1978). Is learning a second language like learning a first language all over again? In D. Ingram & T. Quinn (Eds.), *Language Learning in Australian Society: Proceedings of the 1976 Congress of the Applied Linguistics Associations of Australia*. Melbourne: Australian International Press & Publications.
Halliday, M. (1998). Some basic concepts of educational linguistics. In V. Bickley (Ed.), *Languages in Education in a Bilingual or Multilingual Setting*. Hong Kong: Institute of Language in Education; reprinted in J. Webster (2007). (Ed.). *Language and Education, Volume 9 in the Collected Works of M. A. K. Halliday*. London: Continuum.
Halliday, M. (1989). On the concept of 'educational linguistics'. In R. Giblett & J. O'Carroll (Eds.), *Discipline-Dialogue-Difference: Proceedings of the Language in Education Conference, Murdoch University*. Murdoch: Duration Publications; reprinted in J. Webster (2007). (Ed.), *Language and Education, Volume 9 in the Collected Works of M. A. K. Halliday*. London: Continuum.
Halliday, M. (2007). Language and Education, Volume 9 in *The Collected Works of M. A. K. Halliday*. London: Continuum.
Jenkins, J. (2000). *The Phonology of English as an International Language*. Oxford: Oxford University Press.
Krashen, S. (1993). The effect of formal grammar teaching: Still peripheral. *TESOL Quarterly*, 27.
Lynch, T. (1998). Theoretical perspectives on listening. *Annual Review of Applied Linguistics*, vol. 18.
Lynch, T. (2002). Listening: Questions of level. In R. B. Kaplan (Ed.), *Oxford Handbook of Applied Linguistics*. Oxford: Oxford University Press.
Martin, J. R., forthcoming, Teaching/learning: the yin and yang of language development from home through school. In PENG Xuanwei & CHENG Xiaotang (Eds.), *Applications of Systemic Functional Linguistics*, special issue of *Linguistics and the Human Sciences*.
Mendelsohn, D. (1998). Teaching listening. *Annual Review of Applied Linguistics*, vol. 18.
Oxford, R. (1993). Research update on teaching L2 listening. *System*, vol. 21 (2).

Richards, J. C., J. Platt & H. Platt, *Longman Dictionary of Language Teaching & Applied Linguistics* (朗文语言教学及应用语言学辞典). London: Longman, 1992; 北京：外语教学与研究出版社, 1998。

Rost, M. (2002). *Teaching and Researching Listening.* London: Longman.

Rubin, J. (1994). A review of second language listening comprehension research. *Modern Language Journal*, vol. 78.

Snow, M. (1998). Trends and issues in content-based instruction. *Annual Review of Applied Linguistics*, vol. 18.

Spanos, G. (1998). On the integration of language and content instruction. *Annual Review of Applied Linguistics*, vol. 10.

Truscott, J. (1996). The case against grammar correction in L2 writing classes. *Language Learning*, 46.

Truscott, J. (1998). Noticing in second language acquisition: A critical review. *Second Language Research*, 14.

胡壮麟. 东亚人学英语——记国际"双语教育"电子论坛的一次讨论会.《福建外语》, 1997,（2）。

胡壮麟. 在中国环境下说英语.《大学英语》, 2003,（2）。

EDITOR'S INTRODUCTION

Mary McGroarty

Overview of Volume 24

Has language pedagogy advanced since the topics included here were last addressed in the *Annual Review of Applied Linguistics* in 1998 (Vol. 18)? Yes, in many directions, as a survey of these contributions reveals. Even with respect to the traditional "four skills," discussed in the first section, professional understanding of best practices is now more differentiated with respect to both purposes and means of language instruction, in part because of advances based on recent related research. Vandergrift's review gives some sense of the interrelationships and the differences between learning to listen and listening to learn in a second language and explores the directions pedagogy may take. Regarding instruction in speaking skills, McCarthy and O'Keeffe provide insights into the impact of corpus-based language research on materials available and related pedagogical options. Grabe uses current research in reading to derive 10 propositions with good potential for instructional improvement and further research as a basis for practice. Silva and Brice document the explosion of interest in and research attention to second language writing and identify many potential areas for future investigation.

Research on the long-established "four skills" is now complemented by related research on the systems of language that contribute to fluent and effective language use. Chapters in the second section reveal something of the breadth of recent applied research into the structural systems of language, whether phonological, grammatical, or lexical, that has provided insights of considerable potential for language pedagogy. Jenkins's distinction between core and non-core elements of pronunciation and intonation opens an avenue for empirically based pedagogy that can move beyond the debates regarding the relevance of native speaker models to better illuminate aspects of intelligibility. Nassaji and Fotos show that recent research on grammar teaching, long a staple activity in language classes, helps us to better grasp critical and variable roles of exposure to models, types of practice, and roles and types of feedback in influencing learner mastery. By identifying the directions taken by recent research in vocabulary teaching and learning, Read helps us appreciate once more how greatly setting and purpose for language study affect the relevance of lexical knowledge, now much more clearly illuminated through corpus-based research, and points out that vocabulary research is just beginning to grapple with issues of teaching word combinations as opposed to individual lexical items.

Setting of language study and purpose for language instruction determine many pedagogical practices, but formal and informal pedagogies invariably also reflect aspects of social relations as well as linguistic preoccupations in the larger social context. Chapters in the third section show how thoroughly many questions related to language pedagogy have also come to incorporate and reflect attention to additional educational and social issues, to a greater or lesser degree. Even in the design of language instruction developed for specific student groups, Belcher shows persuasively that the social and critical turn observed in many other settings has informed recent discussions of English for specific purposes. Simmons-McDonald illustrates key issues related to the teaching of standard varieties for creole and vernacular speakers and shows that there is a role for innovative methodologies that draw on traditional local genres (and even incorporate aspects of contrastive analysis) in supporting learner growth, particularly mastery of literacy in standard varieties. Seidlhofer's exploration of the question appropriate model (s) for language pedagogy draws on the growing awareness that English as a lingua franca brings with it consequential decisions about how a language used for communication among many groups of people, none of whom are native speakers, should be learned and taught.

Chapters in the final section also address matters of pedagogy through a variety of lenses, including classroom processes, program design, and the preparation of language educators. Kern, Ware, and Warschauer show that the questions related to the roles of technology in supporting language instruction are no longer *if* but *how* and *why* particular uses of technology may suit a particular instructional context. In reviewing the literature on content-based instruction, Stoller provides a sense of the breadth of models available and the wealth of research questions ripe for investigation. Classroom processes related to collaboration are the focus of Donato's paper, which offers insight into both varying definitions and results of collaborative work across several types of language classrooms and illustrates some of the many questions deserving further investigation. Many discussions of educational reform highlight the relevance of constructivism as a guiding philosophy for both classroom instruction and teacher preparation; Kaufman's discussion shows that this perspective, now common in academic considerations of general educational reform and of improvements in math and science instruction, also has relevance to language instruction that has yet been fully exploited. Finally, in considering issues related to the preparation of teachers for immersion language programs, Erben provides an account of the many innovative programs in which several of the trends mentioned by other scholars here, among them new uses of technology, optimal combinations of language and content teaching, increased attention to the nature and topic of collaboration, and questions related to overall instructional goals and philosophy converge as they shape programs to prepare immersion educators. Taken as a group, all the papers in this volume attest to the genuine advances in language pedagogy achieved in recent years, growing awareness of the many important applications of technology that can be integrated into language teaching, increased sophistication with respect to interrelationships between language instruction and social setting, and the continued centrality of issues of teacher preparation. In addition, each contribution outlines some of the many research directions needed to extend the relevant knowledge base and refine pedagogical practice. Future discussions of language pedagogy in *ARAL* will, it is hoped, build on some of the foundations set out here.

Procedural Notes

Although no single volume can capture the diversity of relevant research conducted worldwide, one of *ARAL's* continuing goals is to attest to the international nature of scholarship in applied linguistics. Hence, when inviting prospective authors, contributors from many geographic areas are regularly sought. In extending invitations to contribute, the Editorial Directors and members of the Editorial Advisory Board work with the editor to identify prospective authors, regardless of location, whose publication record demonstrates their command of current research on topics identified for review. With this volume, I am pleased to welcome Numa Markee, a renowned scholar who will serve as a representative of the American Association for Applied Linguistics, to the *ARAL* Editorial Directors. The collective wisdom of this group is largely responsible for the breadth of *ARAL* contributions.

Another purpose of *ARAL* is to serve as a research tool for specialist readers. Readers wishing to locate recent discussions of particular topics should consult the Contributor Index for Volumes 14–23, included at the end of this volume, to see which authors and topics have appeared in the last 10 years. Comprehensive indexes for author citations covering the last five years and for the subjects discussed in the last ten years can be consulted through the *ARAL* section of the Cambridge Journals Web site: http://journals.cambridge.org/jid_APL. These indexes should prove useful to *ARAL* readers in tracing some of the lines of influence in applied linguistics in recent years and in locating references related to particular topics.

Acknowledgments

Many individuals and institutions contribute to the successful publication of each volume of the *Annual Review*. The Editorial Directors and members of the Editorial Advisory Board offer wise counsel regarding appropriate topics and potential authors. Contributors to the volume, all active scholars, teachers (and often, also, administrators) have prepared insightful and comprehensive treatments of their topics and responded to queries quickly. Staff members of Cambridge University Press have also provided the full array of expertise required for production and distribution of *ARAL*. I am most grateful to Ed Barnas, Journals Manager; Ed Carey, Production Manager; Susan Soule, Journals Marketing Marketing Manager; Mark Zadrozny, Journals Editor; Rachel Adler, Editorial Assistant, and to the additional Cambridge staff members who assist these individuals for the prompt and professional support consistently provided.

Those more closely associated with the processes of turning a set of rather disparate manuscripts into a cohesive completed volume of *ARAL* have once again excelled. I am, as always, deeply grateful to Beth Yule, *ARAL* Editorial Assistant, for her tremendous efficiency, conscientious attention to all details of manuscript and index preparation, and ability to manage many different phases of work with aplomb. Julie McCormick, *ARAL* compositor, has, as usual, shown similar attention to presenting each chapter and the entire volume with the accuracy and clarity the discussion deserves; she has resolved the issues related to electronic modes of receiving, transmitting, and preparing final copy with technical ingenuity and insight. Our work has been greatly facilitated by Marc Lord, who maintains the server that enables electronic exchange of manuscripts during production, and by Patrick Deegan, who acts as courier when paper copies must be exchanged. On numerous occasions, members of the Reference staff at Cline Library, Northern Arizona University, have responded quickly and courteously to my sometimes-obscure questions and thus materially contributed to bibliographic accuracy. Teresa Barensfeld has provided meticulous copyediting; Paula Garcia and Camilla Vásquez have done repeated rounds of careful proofreading. (In working with authors, every effort to ensure bibliographic accuracy has been made. My sincere apologies in advance to contributors and to readers if any inaccuracies or discrepancies have remained.) Activities related to the planning and production of *ARAL* benefit from the continuing in-kind support received through the cooperation of Susan Fitzmaurice, Chair of the English Department, and Laura Huenneke, Dean of the College of Arts and Sciences, at Northern Arizona University. Many thanks to all who help to make each volume of *ARAL* a reality.

Mary McGroarty
Flagstaff, Arizona
March 2004

RESEARCH IN TEACHING
LANGUAGE SKILLS

1. LISTENING TO LEARN OR LEARNING TO LISTEN?

Larry Vandergrift

Listening is probably the least explicit of the four language skills, making it the most difficult skill to learn. This chapter begins with a brief overview of cognitive processes involved in listening and their implications for L2 listening instruction. Recent research (1998–2003) on a variety of instructional techniques to help L2 listeners process linguistic input is then reviewed, noting insights that can inform listening instruction, particularly techniques that can teach students how to listen. Two approaches to listening instruction are presented: an approach to raise metacognitive awareness about listening (favoring top-down processes) and an approach to develop lexical segmentation and word recognition skills (favoring bottom-up processes). An integrated model for L2 listening instruction is proposed. Finally, recent research on different types of listening (e.g., academic listening, bidirectional listening) and the sociolinguistic dimension of listening are reviewed. The chapter concludes with recommendations for future research. The basic premise underlying this chapter is that, given the critical role of listening in language learning, students need to "learn to listen" so that they can better "listen to learn."

The image of L2 listening instruction is changing. At one time, listening was assumed to be a passive activity, meriting little classroom attention. Now listening is recognized as an active process, critical to L2 acquisition and deserving of systematic development as a skill in its own right (Morley, 1999). The utility of listening instruction has been underscored by language learners who want to learn to understand spoken texts in the target language and to interact with native speakers (e.g., Kim, 2002).

The approach to listening instruction has also evolved. First was the "listening to repeat" approach of the audio-lingual period, followed by the "question–answer" comprehension approach. More recently, a common approach is real-life listening in real time, involving communicative tasks and/or interaction with native speakers (Morley, 1999). Furthermore, listening instruction is expanding from a focus on the product of listening (listening to learn) to include a focus on the process (learning to listen). Although research in L2 listening instruction remains limited, recent findings provide some useful insights for language teachers, textbook writers, and curriculum developers. Many questions still remain, however, to be explored by teachers and researchers.

This chapter will review the recent research in listening instruction. The first section will provide a brief overview of the cognitive processes involved in listening and their implications for L2 listeners. The next section will review recent research on a variety of instructional techniques to help L2 listeners process linguistic input, noting insights that can inform listening instruction. The third section will examine two approaches to listening instruction and consider an integrated model that might encompass both approaches. The next two sections will review recent research on different types of listening and research on the sociolinguistic dimension of listening. The final section proposes future research directions for listening instruction.

Cognitive Processes in Listening Comprehension

Listening is probably the least explicit of the four language skills, making it the most difficult skill to learn. It involves physiological and cognitive processes at different levels (Field, 2002; Lynch, 2002; Rost, 2002), as well as attention to contextual and "socially coded acoustic clues" (Swaffar & Bacon, 1993). Research on instruction in L2 listening must take into account the complex cognitive processes that underlie the listening construct.

Earlier reviews of research in L2 listening instruction (Lynch, 1998, 2002; Mendelsohn, 1998; Oxford, 1993; Rost, 2002; Rubin, 1994) call attention to the critical role of both bottom-up and top-down processes in comprehension. Listeners use top-down processes when they use context and prior knowledge (topic, genre, culture, and other schema knowledge in long-term memory) to build a conceptual framework for comprehension. Listeners use bottom-up processes when they construct meaning by accretion, gradually combining increasingly larger units of meaning from the phoneme-level up to discourse-level features. While these processes interact in some form of parallel distributed processing, the degree to which listeners may use one process more than another will depend on the purpose for listening. Admittedly simplistic and somewhat mechanistic in orientation, this description is nevertheless helpful for understanding how different types of knowledge interact in parallel fashion as listeners create a mental representation of what they have heard. Research on these cognitive processes suggest that L2 listeners need to learn how to use both processes to their advantage, depending on their purpose for listening. As pointed out by Mendelsohn (2001), in real-life listening we listen in different ways, depending on our purpose for listening.

The speed and effectiveness at which listeners carry out these processes, however, depends on the degree to which the listener can efficiently process what is heard. Native language listeners do this automatically, with little conscious attention to individual words. Beginning-level L2 listeners, however, have limited language knowledge; therefore, little of what they hear can be automatically processed. They need to consciously focus on details of what they hear, and given the limitations of working memory and the speed of speech, comprehension suffers. Either comprehension breaks down or listeners may use compensatory strategies, contextual factors, and any other relevant information available to them to guess at what was not understood.

An awareness of each of these processes and their relative contribution to comprehension in different contexts and at different levels of language proficiency is fundamental to a theoretically grounded pedagogy of L2 listening comprehension. Presently, there appears to be a general consensus in the literature that listening instruction has favored the development of top-down processes at the expense of developing bottom-up processes (e.g., Field, 2001; Hulstijn, 2003; Rost, 2002).

Empirical Studies on Listening Instruction

Much of recent research pays attention to teaching strategies that provide support to the listener for processing linguistic input to enhance comprehension. These studies examine the effect of advance organizers, visual support, captions, vocabulary knowledge, and listening strategy instruction.

Research on Advance Organizers

The importance of advance organizers to facilitate comprehension was affirmed by Herron, Cole, York, and Linden (1998) with beginning-level learners of French. One group, the declarative group, heard a six-sentence summary of the video clip, while a second group, the interrogative group, heard the same sentences transformed as questions, followed by three possible answers. As expected, both treatment groups outperformed the group with no advance organizer; however, the interrogative group did not outperform the declarative group. It was expected that the interrogative mode would foster a more active engagement with the text, thereby enhancing comprehension and retention. However, the mismatch between the questions of the advance organizers and the questions on the final comprehension measure likely encouraged the listeners to focus on the wrong parts of the video text. While this research demonstrates the value of advance organizers, the relative benefits of questions as advance organizers, particularly questions related to an authentic purpose for listening, need further research.

Visuals are another aid to listening. Ginther (2002) investigated the relative effect of two kinds of visuals on listening performance on the computerized TOEFL test. Context visuals (pictures that set the scene for the upcoming verbal exchange) prepare listeners for the text or verbal exchanges, whereas content visuals (pictures related to the actual content of the verbal exchange) support the text. Results indicated that content visuals slightly enhanced the comprehension of mini-talks, but context visuals decreased comprehension. It appears that advance organizers that provide no directly related information (e.g., context visuals) are not helpful to the listener. These visuals still require processing themselves, thereby consuming attentional resources and limiting the amount of working memory available to the listener for attending to the required information. This interpretation also provides theoretical support for the results obtained by Herron et al. (1998).

The important relationship between schema activation and comprehension has been established (e.g., Long, 1990). However, "mismatch" conditions between schema and text can occur when the schema activated by the first lines of a text is not completely congruent with the remainder of the text. In such conditions, listeners will need to resort to more bottom-up processing to reconcile the details with the schema. This prompted Tsui and Fullilove (1998) to investigate whether bottom-up processing might be the discriminating factor in listening test performance. They found that when schema met expectations, there were no differences between more skilled and less skilled listeners. However, when the schema did not meet expectations, the more skilled listeners performed better. It appears that when schema and input are consistent, less skilled listeners can rely on top-down processing; however, their bottom-up processing skills are inadequate for finding the answer in the "mismatch condition" in real time, or for answering global questions where they must draw conclusions and inferences. Tsui and Fullilove conclude that, while less-skilled listeners may initially benefit from a great deal of contextual support, they will need to develop rapid and accurate bottom-up processes to become skilled listeners.

Listeners with more language knowledge (and more automated processes) have more room in working memory to retain all information and make necessary revisions or inferences as they listen. These differences between native and nonnative speakers in use of working memory during listening comprehension were examined by Tyler (2001). When listeners had access to topic (as an advance organizer), differences in working memory consumption (assessed by a working memory index score) between the groups were not statistically significant. However, when the topic was not available, working memory consumption for nonnative speakers was much higher. This is likely due to inappropriate or inefficient bottom-up processing, because word recognition skills of nonnative speakers are not yet fully automatized. Tyler concludes that topic-familiar texts may inhibit development of bottom-up skills and recommends a differentiated approach for teaching listening: an emphasis on bottom-up work for long-term language retention but top-down training for quick acquisition by learners such as travelers. This recommendation is not consistent with Tsui and Fullilove's recommendation that less skilled listeners initially be provided with a great deal of contextual support since topic-familiar texts provide listeners with contextual information useful for compensatory strategy development. Furthermore, travelers, for example, also need to develop bottom-up skills for understanding the details they are likely to request (e.g., directions, information).

In sum, beginning-level listeners are limited by working memory constraints. Advance organizers that help listeners focus directly on the desired information are most useful for efficient processing. They free attentional capacity for focusing on desired details, which requires bottom-up processing skills. How best to teach bottom-up skills at beginning levels without encouraging online translation is another area for further research.

Research Using DVD with Captions

Widespread availability of DVD video with multilingual soundtracks and captions provides opportunities for written support to enhance listening comprehension. Markham, Peter, and McCarthy (2001) compared the effects of different captions on the listening performance of intermediate-level students of Spanish. They found that the English captions group outperformed the Spanish captions group who, in turn, outperformed the no-captions group. The researchers argue that students would benefit from a cycle of repeated viewing, progressing from L1 captions to L2 captions and finally to no captions, particularly when using challenging video material.

The effect of pictorial support and written annotations on comprehension of aural texts in multimedia environments was investigated by Jones and Plass (2002) with beginning-level French classes. Final comprehension measures showed that students acquired more vocabulary and recalled the passage better with the help of both pictorial and written annotations instead of pictures only or written annotations only. Delayed posttests revealed that the pictorial annotations had a stronger and longer-lasting effect than written annotations, both for vocabulary retention and for listening comprehension.

The differences between pictorially assisted or captions-assisted listening and authentic listening raises questions about the transferability of skills from a learning context to a real-life context, an area for further research. While the listening supports provided in the above studies may be helpful for developing word recognition skills and learning vocabulary, they do not foster the development of compensatory strategies where listeners take advantage of real-life contextual information and limited word recognition skills to fill gaps in comprehension.

Research in Teaching Bottom-Up Skills

Segalowitz and Segalowitz (1993) maintain that automatization of word recognition skills, i.e., fluent bottom-up processing, is critical for successful listening comprehension. Motivated by this theoretical premise, Poelmans

(2003) investigated the effects of training in top-down comprehension skills ("traditional listening") over against bottom-up recognition training. Contrary to expectations, she found no significant differences between the two groups in the final comprehension measure. Poelmans attributes this finding to a discrepancy between the contents and exercises of the training and testing conditions, as well as insufficient training. The decontextualized nature of the stimulus materials may also explain the finding. Training in word recognition skills that acknowledges the contextual nature of listening is another area for further research.

However, Osada (2001) attributes lack of success in listening to an overemphasis on bottom-up skills. Based on his analysis of answers to questions and idea unit analysis, he found that low-proficiency Japanese students of English tended to adopt a mental translation approach to listening. He argues for more emphasis on a top-down approach because, given the constraints of working memory, beginner-level listeners cannot construct meaning when they process connected speech on a word-by-word basis only.

The computer can be used to slow down speech to allow listeners some control over linguistic input for purposes of word recognition. Zhao (1997) investigated the effects of modifying speech rate using four different conditions: (1) no repetition of the passage or adjustment of speech rate; (2) no repetition, with the option of adjusting speech rate; (3) option of both speech rate adjustment and repetition of any part of the passage; and (4) no adjustment of the speech rate with the option of repetition. Comprehension was overwhelmingly higher when students were permitted to adjust the speech rate. In general, listeners slowed down the speech rate; however, individual variations were noted in the degree to which each listener slowed the rate. While this technique is helpful for recognizing words not initially distinguishable in connected speech, listeners may choose to listen at a speech rate slower than necessary. This will not help them develop strategies to cope with speech in real time.

Efficient and effective use of bottom-up skills in comprehension appears to be related to the degree to which word recognition skills are automatized. Meccarty (2000) found that both L2 grammatical knowledge and vocabulary were significantly correlated with listening comprehension, although only vocabulary knowledge could explain the variance. The variance for listening, however, is less than for reading. Mecartty concludes that, although comprehension processes in listening and reading share similar characteristics, vocabulary knowledge was less important for listening. Determining the remaining factors accounting for the variance in listening performance, some likely related to the acoustic trait, is another area for future research.

Research in Raising Metacognitive Awareness of Listening

The literature base in listening strategy instruction has grown very little in recent years. However, studies on the differences between more skilled and less skilled listeners by Goh (2000, 2002a), Hasan (2000), Mareschal (2002), Peters (1999), and Vandergrift (2003b) have produced some useful insights. Grounding their research in earlier work by O'Malley and Chamot (1990), the findings of Goh, Mareschal, Peters, and Vandergrift highlight the importance of the effective use of metacognitive strategies for successful listening comprehension. In a study of adolescent learners of French, Vandergrift (2003b) found significant quantitative differences for four strategies: (1) total metacognitive strategy use, (2) comprehension monitoring, (3) questioning elaboration (flexibility in considering various possibilities before deciding on a framework for interpretation), and (4) online translation (by the less skilled listener). A qualitative analysis of think-aloud protocols reinforced these differences and, in addition, found that the successful listener used an effective combination of metacognitive and cognitive strategies, a finding also reported by Goh (2002a) and Mareschal (2002).

Given the importance of metacognitive awareness in successful listening, Vandergrift investigated the effect of a strategies-based approach on student awareness of the process of listening. Students completed listening tasks where they also engaged in prediction, monitoring, problem solving, and evaluation (the major groups of metacognitive strategies). These tasks helped students learn or bring to consciousness metacognitive knowledge for self-regulation in listening. Both elementary school students (Vandergrift, 2002) and university students of French (Vandergrift, 2003a) found it motivating to learn to understand rapid, authentic texts and responded overwhelmingly in favor of this approach. Students commented on the power of predictions for successful listening, the importance of collaboration with a partner for monitoring, and the confidence-building role of this approach for enhancing their ability to comprehend oral texts.

The use of metacognitive strategies is not unique to successful L2 listening. Although L1 listeners have automatized word recognition skills, they also use metacognitive strategies for self-regulation of listening when they need to redirect attention to bolster waning interest or to critically evaluate what they hear. Imhof (2001) reports on a study of university students enrolled in a communications class who were taught three strategies and asked to apply them in a number of situations: attention management, asking pre-questions, and elaboration. After some adaptation of the strategies to personal needs over time, students reported improved listening habits: more sustained attention, more comprehensive understanding, deeper level of processing, and more reflective assessment.

These qualitative studies point to the promise of a strategies-based approach to teaching L2 listening. However, the long-term effects of this approach on listening achievement need to be examined in carefully designed classroom studies.

Instructional Observations

The results of the studies just described lead to the following observations concerning instruction in listening:

1. Limitations of working memory dictate that supports provided to the listener should relate directly to the text and the listening task. Advance organizers that distract from the main focus of the text use up precious attention space and limit the amount of working memory available to attend to text and task.
2. Captions, annotations, and computer programs to slow down speech may be useful for developing word recognition skills and learning vocabulary; however, their value in teaching students how to listen is questionable. Given that written support is usually not available in authentic, real-time listening, students need to learn to rely only on the acoustic signal and relevant contextual factors to develop listening strategies. The use of captions, other written support, and reduced speech rate may encourage word-by-word decoding rather than foster the development of compensatory strategies that can help students cope with the demands of real-time listening. In fact, it may short-circuit the development of productive strategies.

3. Visual supports that are natural to the listening situation can provide important contextual information to help the listener. These map meaning automatically into long-term memory, freeing attentional capacity to concentrate on other details. However, picture "pop-ups" in multimedia environments are not helpful for learning to listen in real time. While they may be helpful for learning vocabulary, they may also short-circuit the development of listening strategies.
4. As noted earlier in this chapter, context is important to listening. Listeners use any relevant information at their disposal to interpret what they hear. Decontextualized word automatization activities, such as those carried out by Poelmans (2003) under laboratory conditions, deprive listeners of contextual clues available in real-life listening.
5. A strategies-based approach to listening instruction with beginner-level listeners builds confidence, raises awareness of the process of listening, and helps listeners learn to use effective combinations of metacognitive and cognitive strategies to understand texts in real time.

Teaching Students How to Listen

Instruction in the Process of Listening

Instruction in listening has too often been associated with testing, focusing on the product of listening (Sheerin, 1987). A focus on the right answer only, when the listener is incapable of keeping up with the speech rate, often creates a high level of anxiety, which, in turn, affects attention capacity (Arnold, 2000). While a focus on product allows the teacher to verify comprehension, the answer (correct or incorrect) reveals nothing about the process; i.e., how students arrived at comprehension. To help listeners develop strategies to compensate for gaps in understanding, teachers need to understand how listeners arrived at answers, particularly incorrect answers (Field, 2003). This information can then be used for diagnostic purposes, particularly in helping the less skilled listener to discover and try out more efficient strategies.

Recent literature on listening instruction indicates a greater interest in raising student awareness of the process of listening (Berne, 1998; Mendelsohn, 2001). A process approach can help students learn *how* to listen, guiding them through the stages that seem to characterize real-life listening (Field, 2001; Goh, 2002b; Mendelsohn, 2001; Vandergrift, 2003a). Using this approach, teachers can help beginning-level students learn how to comprehend short, authentic texts on topics related to student level and interest (e.g., announcements and advertisements). The metacognitive strategies underlying this approach help listeners become more aware of how they can use what they already know to fill gaps in their understanding. The steps in this cycle and the metacognitive strategies underlying each step are presented in Figure 1.

Figure 1. Listening Instruction Stages and Related Metacognitive Strategies

Stage of listening Instruction	Related Metacognitive Strategies
Planning/predicting stage	
1. Once students know topic and text type, they predict types of information and possible words they may hear.	1. Planning and directed attention
First verification stage	
2. Students verify initial hypotheses, correct as required, and note additional information understood.	2. Monitoring
3. Students compare what they have written with peers, modify as required, establish what needs resolution and decide on details that still need special attention.	3. Monitoring, planning, and selective attention
Second verification stage	
4. Students verify points of disagreement, make corrections, and write down additional details understood.	4. Monitoring and problem solving
5. Class discussion in which all contribute to reconstruction of the text's main points and most pertinent details, interspersed with	5. Monitoring and evaluation

reflections on how students arrived at the meaning of certain words or parts of the text.

Final verification stage

6. Students listen for information that they could not decipher earlier in the class discussion.

6. Selective attention and monitoring

Reflection stage

7. Based on discussion of strategies used to compensate for what was not understood, students write goals for next listening activity.

7. Evaluation

This cycle, based on Field (2001) and Vandergrift (2003a), has been used successfully with beginning-level language learners at different ages, as noted in the previous section. This approach can also be used with profit by more advanced-level listeners faced with a difficult text or an unfamiliar variant of the target language. Field argues that this approach can help "risk takers" (listeners who do not verify hypotheses) to carefully evaluate their hypotheses in the light of contradictory evidence, and "risk avoiders" (listeners who are afraid to make hypotheses in case of failure) to make plausible predictions and accept that a potential discrepancy between predictions and outcome is not a mark of failure (Stanovich, 1980). Vandergrift argues that this approach helps listeners develop metacognitive knowledge, critical to the development of self-regulated listening (Chamot, Barnhardt, El-Dinary, & Robbins, 1999; Flavell, 1979; Wenden, 1998). Field and Vandergrift would agree that students need systematic practice in using listening strategies that will be useful outside of the classroom; this pedagogical cycle models real-life listening.

The value of a strategic, process approach to listening instruction is increasingly recognized. However, research evidence for the long-term impact of individual listening strategy instruction remains inconclusive (Chamot, 1995). Field (2001) suggests that a focus on individual strategies may help listeners learn to use one or two strategies successfully but not improve overall as listeners. Research on skilled listeners has described their approach to the listening task as "orchestrating strategies in a continuous metacognitive cycle" (Vandergrift, 2003b, p. 487) or "coupling strategies together like links in a fence" (Murphy, 1985, p. 38). The apparent interconnectedness of strategy use may explain why individual strategies instruction has not been as successful as hoped.

The recent literature on the L2 listening instruction suggests that students can benefit from an approach where strategies are taught in an integrated fashion. Guiding listeners through the process as a whole (the metacognitive cycle described above) as part of regular listening activities can help learners to improve overall as listeners (Field, 1998, 2001; Goh, 2002b; Holden, 2002; Vandergrift, 2002, 2003a). Students need repeated and systematic exposure to the same sequence of metacognitive strategies used by skilled listeners. This can be done through a variety of tasks, some more comprehension practice-oriented (as described above) and some more communicative in orientation (see White, 1998). However, all tasks should be grounded in the same metacognitive cycle. While the teacher will initially play a greater role, scaffolding should be gradually removed so that students do the work themselves, and the process can eventually become automatic. This methodology appears promising and has theoretical support. Moreover, Buck, who maintains that listening ability can only be achieved by listening to a lot of realistic texts for communicative purposes, suggests that listening instruction "can be greatly facilitated if teachers understand the nature of listening comprehension and can sensitize student to important issues and provide the optimum listening practice" (1995, p. 128). The potential of a process approach to L2 listening instruction, in essence "optimum listening practice," is presently only supported by anecdotal evidence and qualitative studies, which show positive student attitudes and growing metacognitive awareness of the process of listening (e.g., Goh, 2002a; Vandergrift, 2002, 2003a). Nevertheless, the relative effects of this approach on actual student achievement in listening, particularly with beginning-level listeners, need to be empirically investigated in carefully designed, controlled classroom studies.[1]

Computer applications of a similar approach have been proposed by Hoven (1999) in a theoretical model for computer-enhanced language learning that raises awareness of strategic processes for listening. The proposed software is learner-centered; it helps listeners set goals and gives them informed control over task, topic, text content, and pace of learning. Although this theoretical model has potential for using Web-based media and computers for listening instruction, the necessary software must still be designed and then empirically tested.

Instruction in Lexical Segmentation

As noted above, a process approach to listening instruction can enable beginning-level learners to achieve some success in using strategies to comprehend authentic texts. While students express appreciation for how this approach teaches them to use what they do know and to infer what they do not understand, students also express frustration at not being able to segment all the words out of the stream of sound. Top-down processing strategies may help in recognition of some words, but listeners are not always able to recognize even the words that they do know (Field, 2001). Listeners also need judicious practice in perception skills that will help them overcome the word segmentation skills of their native language and learn to identify words in L2 connected speech (Goh, 2002b; Rost, 2002). In fact, Hulstijn (2001) suggests that the development of a top-down, strategy-based approach for listening (and reading) is inadequate for linguistic input to become intake for L2 learning. He argues that bottom-up skills must also be developed so that all the components of the acoustic signal become meaningful units for the listener.

Attention to prosodic features such as stress and intonation are important for word segmentation in listening comprehension. Given that prosodic features influence how listeners chunk and interpret connected speech, attention to these features of text will be helpful for word recognition (Lynch, 1998). In her examination of prosodic cues in processing for comprehension, Harley (2000) concluded that English comprehension may be facilitated if students, regardless of age or language origin, pay attention to pause-bounded units rather than syntactic cues. In addition, research by Field (2003) suggests that listeners use a "strong-syllable" strategy with a high degree of success for word recognition and comprehension by placing word boundaries before stressed syllables. While this strategy may be helpful in recognizing individual words, segmenting of reduced forms such as contractions is even more complicated.

Hulstijn (2003) maintains that a strong second language program must include tasks that help listeners automatize bottom-up processing skills for word recognition. He describes a six-step procedure by which listeners can practice word acquisition skills: (1) listen to the recording, (2) ask themselves whether they have understood what they heard, (3) replay the recording as often as necessary, (4) consult the written text to read what they have just heard, (5) recognize what they should have understood, and (6) replay the recording as often as necessary to understand all of the oral text without written support. Hulstijn and colleagues have developed a multimedia software program (123LISTEN) that allows the teacher to segment digitized video or audio texts into short chunks, each segment accompanied by a written transcript of the text. Listeners can choose three modes of listening: (1) nonstop listening without text, (2) listening by segment with delayed text display, and (3) listening by segment with simultaneous text display. Grounded in cognitive theories of connectionism and symbolism, the approach of 123LISTEN is intended to "help learners build associative networks allowing for fast, parallel processing of linguistic information" (Hulstijn 2003, p. 12).

Hulstijn argues that the real value of this software is the second mode where students listen first and then try to interpret what they are hearing. Only after attempting to understand what they have heard (using prediction and monitoring strategies) should students verify their understanding, using text display to read the words in the segment.[2] However, listeners might benefit even more from this approach if they first listened to the text as a whole, using the process approach described above. This would allow listeners to use prediction and monitoring strategies to greater advantage for deeper cognitive processing of the text before written segments are actually displayed for verification or visual representation of the acoustic signal.

Training in perception can take many forms. Goh (2002b) recommends analysis of parts of the text transcript (using the overhead projector) during the discussion phase of a process approach. Field (2003) recommends dictation as well as other remedial exercises to deal with special problems in concatenated speech such as reduced forms, assimilation, elision, resyllabification, and cliticization. Hulstijn (2001) recommends listening practice at an "*i* minus one" level, to develop automaticity in word recognition, e.g., listening to texts in which students can recognize most words and finding the differences between the aural form of the text and a written form that deviates slightly. While training activities such as these may lack the motivational dimension of a top-down, strategies-based approach, Hulstijn (2001) further suggests that the computer, "the ideal slave," combined with human imagination, has the potential of making bottom-up training more appealing.

Summary

To summarize, listening comprehension involves two types of processes that interact freely with each other to help listeners construct a meaningful interpretation of what they hear. Teaching listeners how to use these processes in efficient and effective ways will need to balance a top-down, strategies-based approach with remedial, bottom-up training. While a top-down approach will help listeners develop real-life listening skills, it is not adequate for developing word recognition skills. At the same time, a more remedial bottom-up skills approach will help learners develop word recognition skills, but it must be used judiciously at early levels of language learning so that learners do not develop an inefficient online translation approach to listening (Eastman, 1991; Vandergrift, 2003b).

Is it possible to combine these two approaches into one integrated model of L2 listening instruction? The reflection stage of the process approach to listening (macro-analysis of the text) described earlier could be expanded to include a more micro-analysis of the text. This would allow listeners to consult a written form of the text after completing the verification stages. If this is carried out with the class as a whole, some of this analysis could take place during the second verification stage where the text is reconstructed by the class. However, given the individual and unique ways in which listeners sometimes arrive at comprehension, the micro-analysis might be more beneficial and efficient if it were done in the language laboratory where listeners can work at their own pace on individual comprehension difficulties. Further elaboration and empirical testing of an integrated model incorporating both approaches to teaching listening would be an important avenue for future research.

Research on Different Types of Listening

Academic Listening

The scope of research on academic listening reported in Flowerdew (1994) continues to be the most comprehensive treatment of this dimension of listening to date. However, an interesting study by Littlemore (2001) on the widespread use of metaphor in university lectures adds important information to this research base. Metaphorical language often leads to *misunderstandings* by L2 listeners, resulting in misinterpretation of the lecture. Littlemore suggests that misinterpretations are much more serious than *nonunderstanding*, in which listeners are aware of a gap in understanding and can use clarification strategies to remedy comprehension. She recommends strategies for both lecturers and students to alleviate this problem.

Recognizing that academic listening involves more than lectures and note-taking, Feak and Salehzadeh (2001) report on the development and face validation of a listening placement test using video. Students were presented with multiple speaker interactions, where the visual element complemented the spoken element. Results of the pilot test indicated overwhelming agreement by both students and instructors that the video was a valid test of language use in diverse academic environments, not just the lecture hall.

Bidirectional Listening

The research on bidirectional or collaborative listening suggests that, compared to unidirectional listening, the cognitive demands made on the listener are much heavier (Lynch, 2002; Rost, 2002). To participate in a conversation, the listener must process the input in real time, clarify understanding when comprehension is uncertain, critically evaluate what is understood, and then respond. This dimension of listening does not receive enough research attention (e.g., Lynch, 2002) considering that bidirectional listening is what listeners engage in most often. In fact, some would argue that this is the only dimension of listening worth teaching; see the debate between Ridgway (2000a; 2000b) and Field (2000) in *ELT Journal, 54* (2).

Teaching listeners when and how to use efficient clarification strategies remains an important objective for research into this dimension of listening. Lam and Wong (2000) trained students in strategies such as self-clarification, seeking clarification, and verifying interventions of other members of a discussion group. However, students became bogged down in linguistic problems, especially when group members did not support each other in clarification efforts. Obviously, training in interaction strategies requires linguistic support (appropriate formula statements in L2) as students seek clarification due to comprehension problems.

Although listeners may use clarification strategies to signal a comprehension problem, they can also use receipt tokens to signal understanding and contribute to the construction of spoken discourse. Gardner (1998) investigated the use and meaning of receipt tokens such as "mm hm," "yeah," and "mm" in interaction, and their characteristics in terms of placement in conversation and prosodic shape. He provides evidence for the multiple meanings conveyed by these tokens and concludes that listeners, as conversationalists, need to be made aware of the utility and impact of these tokens and then provided with opportunities for practice and feedback.

Building on the already sizable literature on the impact of interaction on comprehension, Cabrera and Martinez (2001) confirm the importance of different types of interactional modification, i.e., repetitions, comprehension checks and gestures, in helping young children to listen. When the Spanish-speaking children listened to English stories with both interactional and linguistic adjustments (as opposed to linguistic adjustments only) the level of comprehension was significantly higher. This classroom study confirms earlier work by Pica (1994) and others on the listening interface in negotiation of meaning and its contribution to comprehension and language learning.

Narrow Listening

"Narrow listening" (Krashen, 1996) advocates providing listeners with large amounts of comprehensible input for language acquisition (see Krashen, 1987). Students listen repeatedly to oral texts on topics of their choosing, at their own pace, without the threat of evaluation. Dupuy (1999) investigated the effects of this approach on the language development of university students of French at different course levels. Analysis of self-assessment questionnaires showed that students at all levels found Narrow listening helpful in improving comprehension, fluency, and vocabulary. Students at all levels made significant self-reported gains in comprehension, with beginning students reporting greater gains than intermediate students.

Listening to Train the Ear

The Tomatis approach, which has received more attention in Europe than in North America, is based on the premise that the ear is the key organ to language learning. The Tomatis approach uses special headsets to enhance sound perception, allowing the listener to perceive sounds through bone as well as air. Tomatis's unique theory of language acquisition assumes that there is a close link between speech perception and speech production and that the ear can be trained or reeducated to perceive and analyze sounds through an auditory selection process. In a controlled experiment, Joiner (2000) found that the Tomatis group slightly outperformed the control group in comprehension, and many participants reported salutary effects on pronunciation skills and singing on key. Although technology requirements presently preclude widespread classroom use of the Tomatis approach, research in Europe continues (Kaunzuer, 2001).

Sociolinguistic Dimensions of Listening Instruction

Arguing that research on L2 listening has focused largely on psycholinguistic aspects, Carrier (1999) discusses how the social context of listening also influences comprehension. She points out how status relationships between interlocutors affect language behavior and the amount of negotiation in face-to-face interactions. This can help or hinder comprehension. Teachers need to help students understand this dynamic and provide strategies that are helpful to negotiate meaning, in spite of the unequal status of the interlocutors.

Harris (2003) affirms the importance of understanding nonverbal elements and nonverbal paralinguistic elements in communication to the listener, even though these components are not part of the acoustic signal. Illustrative gestures, when they correspond with the L2 word (s), can facilitate word recognition and provide important clues for interpreting other parts of the text. However, when these gestures are culturally bound or amplify the meaning of the corresponding word(s), listeners at all proficiency levels need to attend to these gestures ("listen with their eyes") to understand their meaning within the text and/or cultural context.

Related to the sociolinguistic dimension of listening is the question of the variety of language used as linguistic model in listening instruction. Fox (2002) explores questions such as which variety to use in the beginning stages of language learning and when to introduce other varieties. Building on the concept of "pedagogical norm" (Valdman, 2000), Fox formulates the following comprehension norms: (1) students will listen to language heard by native speakers in authentic contexts; (2) students will speak with one accent but learn to understand many others (based on native speakers' idealized view of their own linguistic behavior); (3) students will understand careful speech of educated native speakers (based on native speakers' expectations on what is appropriate for language learners); and (4) processing and learning factors need to be considered in introducing different accents (a psycholinguistic rather than sociolinguistic norm) (Fox, 2002, p. 215). These norms, she argues, provide a model for eventual introduction of a number of varieties of language, and the social and situational variants within each variety.

Directions for Future Research

This review has attempted to reflect the range of research during the past five years relating to listening instruction. Listening is the least explicit of all the language skills. Oral texts exist in real time and need to be processed quickly; when the text is over, only a mental representation remains. Since these processes are covert, listening is a difficult skill to research. This may explain the limited number of studies, particularly in listening instruction. Regardless, instruction that facilitates cognitive processing in listening comprehension needs more rigorous research, given the overall importance of listening for language learning.

First of all, if we wish to teach students how to listen (i.e., learn to listen), we need to investigate pedagogic approaches that do not short-circuit the strategic dimension of L2 listening. When students are provided with visual or written supports that are not authentic to the listening context, they are learning to listen. While this is a valid objective for language acquisition, students will not learn how to listen and rely on all the contextual clues available for comprehension in authentic, real-time listening contexts if this is the only focus of L2 listening.

Second, we need to continue to investigate the relative contribution of top-down and bottom-up processing at different proficiency levels for different tasks. A clearer understanding of the interaction among processing, proficiency level, and task will help listening teachers know what to emphasize at different language levels for different tasks. Furthermore, integrated models of listening instruction, such as the one proposed in this chapter, must be tested for their relative effectiveness in teaching students how to listen and how to develop word recognition skills.

Third, future research should investigate the conditions that are needed for technology-enhanced language learning to exert a beneficial influence on the learners' listening comprehension strategy development. In her comprehensive review of the literature, Joiner (1997) recommended more research on the effective use of technology in listening instruction. The benefits for teaching word recognition skills have been demonstrated. However, use of multimedia environments will only improve listening performance if the methodological innovations are grounded in theories of L2 listening and L2 acquisition (Rogers, 2002; Tschirner, 2001).

Fourth, bidirectional listening is the predominant type of listening, yet it is rarely researched. We need further research on teaching listeners in classroom settings how to negotiate meaning, clarify misunderstandings, and contribute to the conversation with a more proficient speaker.

Fifth, research into the components of L2 listening (i.e., the factors that explain variance in L2 listening) will help teachers better understand what needs to be emphasized in listening instruction.

To conclude, Rost maintains that two overlapping processes, "learning to listen in the L2 and learning the L2 through listening," are involved in L2 listening development (2002, p. 91). This review of recent research in listening instruction has attempted to clarify what learning to listen means and how teachers can help students "learn to listen," so that their students, in turn, can better "listen to learn."

Acknowledgments

I would like to thank Catherine Mareschal for her help in locating source materials for this chapter and drafting summaries of the studies related to technology-enhanced listening instruction.

Notes

1. An empirical, longitudinal investigation of the relative effectiveness of a process approach compared to a comprehension-only approach with beginner-level learners of French, English, and Italian will be conducted at the University of

Ottawa during the 2004–2005 academic year.

2. An empirical study of relative effectiveness of this mode of 123LISTEN is presently being conducted at the University of Amsterdam.

ANNOTATED BIBLIOGRAPHY

Buck, G. (2001). *Assessing listening*. Cambridge: Cambridge University Press.

The emphasis of this volume is on the assessment of listening comprehension, but it also includes useful information for classroom instruction and research. The overview of listening theory in the first two chapters is both comprehensive and accessible. In addition, the chapters on creating listening tasks (Chapter 5) and providing suitable texts (Chapter 6) are of particular interest to the listening teacher.

Field, J. (2001). Finding one's way in the fog: Listening strategies and second-language learners. *Modern English Teacher*, *9* (1), 29–34.

Field presents a task-based approach to listening instruction that leads students through the stages of real-life listening. He argues that this kind of listening practice helps students realize that partial understanding and formation of hypotheses are part of the process of L2 listening. This article demonstrates how this approach can help L2 listeners access authentic texts and experience success in real-life listening.

Flowerdew, J., & Miller, L. (2004). *Second language listening: Theory and practice*. New York: Cambridge University Press.

This volume, designed to be used with both preservice and in-service teachers, combines up-to-date listening theory with case studies of actual pedagogical practice. The authors describe current models of listening theory, exemplifying each with a textbook task. They address the role of technology in teaching listening, questioning techniques, and developing effective listening tests.

Goh, C. (2002b). *Teaching listening in the language classroom*. Singapore: SEAMEO Regional Language Centre.

This is a practitioner's handbook. After a brief introduction to some of the theoretical principles underlying the process of listening, Goh describes how to (1) design listening comprehension tasks, (2) develop lessons from listening tasks,

(3) raise students' metacognitive awareness of the listening process, and (4) select and exploit authentic texts in the classroom. The value of this little volume lies in the concrete suggestions for teaching L2 listening skills and strategies, grounded in psycholinguistic theory about listening processes. The chapter on increasing metacognitive awareness underscores the importance of teaching students how to listen.

Rost, M. (2002). *Teaching and researching listening.* London: Longman.

This comprehensive volume presents a conceptual background of listening, some principles of listening instruction, and some potential areas for research in listening. Section I offers readers an overview of some of the processes involved in listening, primarily L1 listening. Section II outlines some principles of instructional design, as well as methods of teaching and assessing listening. Section III introduces research methods and action research frameworks, offering some concrete topics for teachers to try with their classes. Section IV provides information on a range of resources to help the teacher-researcher. This volume outlines many important issues relating to listening in L1 and L2. Practicing teachers may find the section on teaching not concrete enough to inform classroom practice; however, the teacher-researcher, interested in issues and a range of research methodologies, will find the section on research very informative.

Vandergrift, L. (2003a). From prediction through reflection: Guiding students through the process of L2 listening. *Canadian Modern Language Review, 59* (3), 425–440.

The effects of a task-based, process approach to listening instruction are examined in this article. Students responded positively, calling attention to the value of predictions, the usefulness of discussion with a partner, and the motivational effect of learning to understand authentic texts. This study illustrates the potential for developing metacognitive processes and metacognitive knowledge for successful L2 listening strategies in early stages of language learning.

White, G. (1998). *Listening.* Oxford: Oxford University Press.

This is primarily a resource book of listening activities and practical guidance for the listening teacher. After analyzing the shortcomings of traditional approaches to teaching listening, White presents her skills-based approach. The chapters of particular interest include (1) activities to help students understand what it means to become a good listener, (2) activities on real-life listening, and (3) making listening materials. Although light on theory, this volume has concrete ideas for teaching listening at different proficiency levels.

OTHER REFERENCES

Arnold, J. (2000). Seeing through listening comprehension exam anxiety. *TESOL Quarterly*, *34*, 777–786.

Berne, J. E. (1998). Examining the relationship between L2 listening research, pedagogical theory and practice. *Foreign Language Annals*, *31*, 169–190.

Buck, G. (1995). How to become a good listening teacher. In D. Mendelsohn & J. Rubin (Eds.), *A guide for the teaching of second language listening* (pp. 113–128). San Diego, CA: Dominie Press.

Cabrera, M. & Martinez, P. (2001). The effects of repetition, comprehension checks, and gestures, on primary school children in an EFL situation. *ELT Journal*, *55* (3), 281–288.

Carrier, K. (1999). The social environment of second language listening: Does status play a role in comprehension? *Modern Language Journal*, *83*, 65–79.

Chamot, A. U. (1995). Learning strategies and listening comprehension. In D. Mendelsohn & J. Rubin (Eds.), *A guide for the teaching of second language listening* (pp. 13–30). San Diego: Dominie Press.

Chamot, A. U., Barnhardt, S., El-Dinary, P. B., & Robbins, J. (1999). *The learning stratigies handbook*. White Plains, NJ: Longman.

Dupuy, B. C. (1999). Narrow listening: An alternative way to develop and enhance listening comprehension in students of French as a foreign language. *System*, *27*, 351–361.

Eastman, J. K. (1991). Learning to listen and comprehend: The beginning stages. *System*, *19*, 179–188.

Feak, C. B., & Salehzadeh, J. (2001). Challenges and issues in developing an EAP video listening placement assessment: A view from one program. *English for Specific Purposes*, *20*, 477–493.

Field, J. (1998). Skills and strategies: Towards a new methodology for listening. *ELT Journal*, *52*, 110–118.

Field, J. (2000). "Not waving but drowning" : A reply to Tony Ridgway. *ELT Journal*, *54*, 186–195.

Field, J. (2002). The changing face of listening. In J. Richards & W. Renandya (Eds.), *Methodology in language teaching: An anthology of current practice* (pp. 242–247).

Cambridge: Cambridge University Press.

Field, J. (2003). Promoting perception: Lexical segmentation in second language listening. *ELT Journal, 57*, 325–334.

Flavell, J. (1979). Metacognition and cognitive monitoring: A new area of cognitive development enquiry. *American Psychologist, 34*, 906–911.

Flowerdew, J. (1994). *Academic listening: Research perspectives.* Cambridge: Cambridge University Press.

Fox, C. (2002). Incorporating variation in the French classroom: A pedagogical norm for listening comprehension. In S. M. Gass, K. Bardovi-Harlig, S. M. Magnan, and J. Walz (Eds.) *Pedagogical norms for second and foreign language learning and teaching: Studies in honour of Albert Valdman* (pp. 201–219). Amsterdam: Benjamins.

Gardner, R. (1998). Between speaking and listening: The vocalisation of understandings. *Applied Linguistics, 19*, 204–224.

Ginther, A. (2002). Context and content visuals and performance on listening comprehension stimuli. *Language Testing, 19*, 133–167.

Goh, C. (2000). A cognitive perspective on language learners' listening comprehension problems. *System, 28*, 55–75.

Goh, C. (2002a). Exploring listening comprehension tactics and their interaction patterns. *System, 30*, 185–206.

Harley, B. (2000). Listening strategies in ESL: Do age and L1 make a difference? *TESOL Quarterly, 34*, 769–776.

Harris, T. (2003). Listening with your eyes: The importance of speech-related gestures in the language classroom. *Foreign Language Annals, 36*, 180–187.

Hasan, A. (2000). Learners' perceptions of listening comprehension problems. *Language, Culture and Curriculum, 13*, 137–153.

Herron, C., Cole, S., York, H., & Linden, P. (1998). A comparison study of student retention of foreign language video: Declarative versus interrogative advance organizers. *Modern Language Journal, 82*, 237–247.

Holden, W. (2002). Listen and learn. *English Teaching Professional, 23*, 18–20.

Hoven, D. (1999). A model for listening and viewing comprehension in multimedia environments. *Language Learning and Technology, 3*, 88–103.

Hulstijn, J. H. (2001). Intentional and incidental second language vocabulary learning: A reappraisal of elaboration, rehearsal and automaticity. In P. Robinson (Ed.), *Cognition and second language instruction* (pp. 258–286). Cambridge: Cambridge University Press.

Hulstijn, J. H. (2003, in press). Connectionist models of language processing and the training of listening skills with the aid of multimedia software. *Computer Assisted Language Learning*.

Imhof, M. (2001). How to listen more effectively: Self-monitoring strategies in L1.

International Journal of Listening, 14, 2–19.

Joiner, E. (1997). Teaching listening: How technology can help. In M. Bush, & R. Terry (Eds.), *Technology-enhanced language learning* (pp. 77–121). Lincolnwood, IL: NTC Publishing Group.

Joiner, E. (2000). Listening training for language learners: The Tomatis approach to second language acquisition. *Dimension, 2000*, 13–27.

Jones, L. & Plass, J. (2002). Supporting listening comprehension and vocabulary acquisition in French with multimedia annotations. *The Modern Language Journal*, 86, 546–561.

Kaunzner, U. (2001). *Das Ohr als Schlüssel zur Fremdsprachenkompetenz* [The ear as the key to foreign language competence]. Tübingen: Stauffenburg/Groos.

Kim, J. (2002). Affective reactions to foreign language listening retrospective interviews with Korean EFL students. *Language Research*, 38, 117–151.

Krashen, S. (1987). *Principles and practice in second language acquisition*. Englewood Cliffs, NJ: Prentice Hall.

Krashen, S. (1996). The case for Narrow Listening. *System*, 24, 97–100.

Lam, W., & Wong, J. (2000). The effects of strategy training on developing discussion skills in an ESL classroom. *ELT Journal*, 54, 245–255.

Littlemore, J. (2001). The use of metaphor in university lectures and the problems that it causes for overseas students. *Teaching in Higher Education*, 6, 333–349.

Long, D. R. (1990). What you don't know can't help you. *Studies in Second Language Acquisition*, 12, 65–80.

Lynch, T. (1998). Theoretical perspectives on listening. *Annual Review of Applied Linguistics*, 18, 3–19.

Lynch, T. (2002). Listening: Questions of level. In R. B. Kaplan, (Ed.), *Oxford handbook of applied linguistics* (pp. 39–48). Oxford: Oxford University Press.

Mareschal, C. (2002). *A cognitive perspective on the listening comprehension strategies of second language learners in the intermediate grades*. Unpublished MA thesis, University of Ottawa.

Markham, P., Peter, L., & McCarthy, T. (2001). The effects of native language vs. target language captions on foreign language students' DVD video comprehension. *Foreign Language Annals*, 34, 439–445.

Mecartty, F. (2000). Lexical and grammatical knowledge in reading and listening comprehension by foreign language learners of Spanish. *Applied Language Learning*, 11, 323–348.

Mendelsohn, D. (1998). Teaching listening. *Annual Review of Applied Linguistics*, 18, 81–101.

Mendelsohn, D. (2001). Listening comprehension: We've come a long way, but.... *Contact*, 27, 33–40.

Morley, J. (1999). Current perspectives on improving aural comprehension. Retrieved from http://www.eslmag.com/MorleyAuralStory.htm.

Murphy, J. M. (1985). *An investigation into the listening strategies of ESL college students.* (ERIC Document Reproduction Service No. ED278275).

O'Malley, M., & Chamot, A. U. (1990). *Learning strategies in second language acquisition.* Cambridge: Cambridge University Press.

Osada, N. (2001). What strategy do less proficient learners employ in listening comprehension?: A reappraisal of bottom-up and top-down processing. *Journal of the Pan-Pacific Association of Applied Linguistics, 5,* 73–90.

Oxford, R. (1993). Research update on teaching L2 listening. *System, 21* (2), 205–211.

Peters, M. (1999). *Les stratégies de compréhension auditive chez des élèves du Bain Linguistique en français langue seconde* [The listening comprensión strategies of students in a French immersion program]. Unpublished Ph.D. dissertation. University of Ottawa.

Pica, T. (1994). Research on negotiation: What does it reveal about second language learning conditions, processes and outcomes. *Language Learning, 44,* 493–527.

Poelmans, P. (2003). *Developing second-language listening comprehension: Effects of training lower-order skills versus higher-order strategy.* Unpublished Ph.D. dissertation, University of Amsterdam.

Ridgway, T. (2000a). Listening strategies—I beg your pardon? *ELT Journal, 54,* 179–185.

Ridgway, T. (2000b). Hang on a minute! A reply to John Field. *ELT Journal, 54,* 196–197.

Rogers, C. V. (2002). Tradition and technology in language teaching. *Dimension,* 2002, 17–32.

Rubin, J. (1994). A review of second language listening comprehension research. *Modern Language Journal, 78,* 199–221.

Segalowitz, N., & Segalowitz, S. (1993). Skilled performance practice and the differentiation of speed-up of automatization effects: Evidence from second language word recognition. *Applied Psycholinguistics, 19,* 53–67.

Sheerin, J. (1987). Listening comprehension: Teaching or testing? *ELT Journal, 4,* 126–131.

Stanovich, K. E. (1980). Toward an interactive-compensatory model of individual differences in the development of reading fluency. *Reading Research Quarterly, 16,* 32–71.

Swaffar, J. K., & Bacon, S. M. (1993). Reading and listening comprehension: Perspectives on research and implications for practice. In A. H. Omaggio (Ed.), *Research in language learning: Principles, processes, and prospects* (pp.124–155). Lincolnwood, IL: National Textbook.

Tschirner, E. (2001). Language acquisition in the classroom: The role of digital video. *Computer Assisted Language Learning, 14,* 305–319.

Tsui, A., & Fullilove, J. (1998). Bottom-up or top-down processing as a discriminator of L2 listening performance. *Applied Linguistics, 19,* 432–451.

Tyler, M. (2001). Resource consumption as a function of topic knowledge in nonnative and native comprehension. *Language Learning, 51,* 257–280.

Valdman, A. (2000). Comment gérer la variation dans l'enseignement du français langue étrangère aux États-Unis [How to manage language variation in the teaching of French as a foreign language in the United States]. *French Review, 73,* 648–666.

Vandergrift, L. (2002). "It was nice to see that our predictions were right:" Developing metacognition in L2 listening comprehension. *Canadian Modern Language Review, 58,* 555–575.

Vandergrift, L. (2003b). Orchestrating strategy use: Toward a model of the skilled second language listener. *Language Learning, 53,* 463–496.

Wenden, A. (1998). Metacognitive knowledge and language learning. *Applied Linguistics, 19,* 515–537.

Zhao, Y. (1997). The effects of listeners' control of speech rate on second language comprehension. *Applied Linguistics, 18,* 49–68.

2. RESEARCH IN THE TEACHING OF SPEAKING

Michael McCarthy and Anne O'Keeffe

This chapter reviews research and practice in six main areas relevant to the teaching of speaking: (1) the growing influence of spoken corpora, (2) the debates concerning native speaker (NS) and nonnative speaker (NNS) models for spoken pedagogy, (3) the issue of authenticity in spoken materials, (4) approaches to understanding speaking in the classroom, (5) the selection of texts and aspects of spoken language for the teaching of speaking, and (6) developments in materials and methods for the teaching of speaking. Spoken corpora, whether NS corpora collected in "old" or "new" variety locations or NNS corpora based on learner data or expert/successful user data, have generated vigorous debate as to how spoken language should be modeled for teaching, and their influence is being seen in shifts in methodology toward language-awareness-based approaches as well as new materials based on lexicogrammatical and discoursal corpus evidence. Various approaches to understanding classroom speaking are also reviewed, including discourse analysis, conversation analysis, cognitive approaches, and the Vygotskian perspective. Applications of insights from these approaches are reviewed, especially how the approaches affect the selection of texts and language features to be taught. Finally, practical discussion on the teaching of specific spoken genres is reviewed and probable future directions are discussed.

The Growth of Spoken Corpora

In the five years since Anne Burns summarized the then current research in the teaching of speaking (Burns, 1998), it is probably fair to say that there has been no paradigm shift in methods and practices, and much of the landscape so accurately described by Burns remains unchanged. However, our knowledge concerning spoken language has indeed changed, mainly through developments in spoken corpus linguistics. Burns's survey devoted subheadings to the influence of discourse analysis and conversation analysis; it had no section devoted to spoken corpora, nor did Bygate's survey of theoretical perspectives on speaking in the same volume of *ARAL* (Bygate, 1998). It is hard to imagine this present survey article, five years on, without an account of spoken corpora and their growing influence on the pedagogy of speaking. New understandings have prompted new debates about the *what* and the *how* of the teaching of speaking, and the debate is seeing its fruits in a number of applications.

In recent years advances have been achieved in spoken corpus size, in the number of languages that now boast spoken corpora, and in applications that have taken corpus linguistics beyond its roots in stylistics and lexicography into the realms of spoken lexicogrammar, discourse and conversation analysis, and pragmatics.

For English, spoken corpora which have been or are being exploited for the teaching of speaking include the spoken components of the British National Corpus (BNC) (Aston & Burnard, 1998) and of the Bank of English (see Moon, 1997), the British/Irish CANCODE spoken corpus (Carter, 1998; McCarthy, 1998), the Michigan Corpus of Academic Spoken English (MICASE) (Simpson, Lucka, & Ovens, 2000) and the Longman Spoken American Corpus (Stern, 1997). The spoken component of the American National Corpus will undoubtedly also contribute to spoken pedagogy research when it is released (scheduled for mid-2003) (Ide & Macleod, 2001; Ide, Reppen, & Suderman, 2002).

The expansion of spoken corpora to embrace a wider range of language varieties is also raising new issues for pedagogical modeling. In the case of English, the ICE (International Corpus of English) project makes available spoken data for the Englishes of Hong Kong (Bolton, Gisborne, Hung, & Nelson, 2003), New Zealand (Holmes, 1996), Singapore (Ooi, 1997), Great Britain (Nelson, Wallis, & Aarts, 2002), Ireland (Kallen & Kirk, 2001), Nigeria (Banjo, 1996), and the Caribbean (Nero, 2000), with others under development. Spoken Irish English is also attested in the Limerick Corpus of Irish English (L-CIE) (Farr, Murphy, & O'Keeffe, in press). Other new English spoken corpus investigations include the work of Cheng and Warren (1999, 2000) for Hong Kong. Corpora are also currently influencing the teaching of spoken French, with similar debates about the modeling of spoken language for pedagogy as those underway with regard to English (Beeching, 1997; Di Vito, 1998; Kinginger, 1999; Lawson, 2001).[1]

Native Speaker (NS) and Nonnative Speaker (NNS) Models for the Teaching of Speaking

A number of recent publications debate the issue of NS versus learner and NNS corpora (Flowerdew, 2000; Nero, 2000; Prodromou, 2003; Seidlhofer, 2001, this volume; Warschauer, 2000). Prodromou (1997), whose work is based on a mixed NS/NNS spoken English corpus, had already raised issues concerning the undermining effect of spoken corpora for NNS faced with varieties and cultures that they can "never master, never own" (p. 5). Reacting to similar concerns, Seidlhofer proposes a spoken corpus of English as a lingua franca (ELF), which will help to profile ELF as robust and independent of English as a native language and may establish "something like an index of communicative redundancy" with pedagogical applications (Seidlhofer, 2001, p. 147). The shift away from the NS as the sole model for spoken pedagogy is further underlined by the introduction into the debate of terms aimed at leveling the playing field between NS and NNS as potential models. Building on earlier work by Leung, Harris, and Rumpton (1997) such terms include "expert users" (McCarthy, 2001, pp. 139–142) and "successful users of English" (SUEs) (Prodromou, 2003), with a focus on the modeling of successful language users (whether NS or NNS) in nonpedagogical contexts. Meanwhile the *The Louvain International Database of Spoken English Interlanguage* (LINDSEI), set up in 1995 (see De Cock, 1998, 2000), provides spoken data for the analysis of learner language (see also Granger, Hung, & Petch-Tyson, 2002).

From "Spoken Language" to "Speaking:" Relevant Data for Input

Bygate (1998) observed that second language speaking (except for pronunciation) had been something of a Cinderella compared with listening, reading, and writing, but recent research is redressing that imbalance (see also Bygate, 2001). Current debates include whether speaking materials do or should truly reflect naturally occurring spoken language, what teachers' and learners' perceptions are of the importance of using real speech samples (Hughes, 2002; Timmis, 2002), and whether learner output reflects authentic spoken patterns. However, there is by no means universal agreement on the relationship between descriptions of spoken language and methods, materials, and activities.

Naturally occurring data have not been the only source for the pedagogic modeling of speech. Debate continues as to how elicited speech data compare with naturally occurring speech, especially data generated by discourse completion tasks (DCTs), which aim to describe what constitutes spoken pragmatic competence based on informants' intuitive reactions to situational prompts. Golato (2003) looks at differences between naturally occurring data analyzed using conversation analysis (CA), and DCTs constructed on the basis of naturally occurring conversations. Golato notes that while CA clearly enables the study of language organization in natural settings, CA analyses cannot necessarily be extrapolated to other situations. DCTs, however, may be construed as a condensation of the informant's prior experience with language. Golato also evaluates other data collection procedures (questionnaires, recall protocols, role play, etc.) and discusses the problems and prospects for generalizing from different kinds of data. Billmyer and Varghese (2000) argue that, in practice, DCTs will continue to be an important resource for spoken pragmatic pedagogy. Their study examines systematic modifications (adding information on social and contextual variables) to DCT situational prompts and responses from NS and NNS. Modified prompts produced longer, more elaborated responses from both NS and NNS informants. Yuan (2001) further finds that orally produced DCTs generate more natural speech features than written DCTs. Such findings suggest that carefully constructed DCTs are not without positive value in speaking pedagogy.

McCarthy (2001) and McCarthy and Carter (2001) have continued to argue for a description of spoken grammar and vocabulary that is independent, based on the evidence of spoken corpora, and not presented merely as a list of deviations from written norms, as a means of providing systematic linguistic input for pedagogies of speaking (see also Hughes, 2002; Carter, Hughes, & McCarthy, 2000). However, not least of the problems of using spoken data in pedagogy is the question of what the basic unit of spoken grammar might consist of. In the absence of well-formed sentences (which are famously rare in casual, NS conversation), clause- and phrase-based units seem to be more appropriate (Burns, 2001; Foster, Tonkyn, & Wigglesworth, 2000). On the other hand, corpus analysts and other linguists alike have in recent years stressed the central role of fixed "chunks" of various kinds in everyday, fluent speech. Wray (2000, 2002), investigating formulaic sequences (which include idioms, collocations, and institutionalized sentence frames), stresses that such sequences circumvent the analytical processes associated with the interpretation of open syntactic frames in terms of both reception and production. Attempts to encourage the analysis of formulaic sequences in second language pedagogy are criticized as "pursuing native-like linguistic usage by promoting entirely unnative-like processing behaviour" (Wray, 2000, p. 463). Wray's work attempts to move away from a static, behaviorist account of formulaic sequences, emphasizing their nature as "a dynamic response to the demands of language use," which "will manifest differently as those demands vary from moment to moment and speaker to speaker" (Wray, 2002, p. 5). Hunston (2002), discussing lexicogrammatical patterns as evidenced in the Bank of English corpus, suggests that sequences such as verb complementation patterns, if learned and stored as holistic units, can contribute greatly to spoken fluency, producing, when chained together in connected, meaningful strings, "pattern flow." Hunston advocates a task-based approach to this aspect of fluency, rejecting presentational approaches as inappropriate to the need to raise awareness of features of speaking as a whole, as opposed to learning individual patterns.

Authenticity and Spoken Materials

Despite advances in recording technology and available descriptions of naturally occurring conversations, dialogues produced for classroom use are for the most part scripted. While there are often sound pedagogical reasons for using scripted dialogues, their status as a vehicle for enhancing conversation skills has been challenged in recent years (Burns, 2001; Burns, Joyce & Gollin, 2001; Carter, 1998). Burns (2001) notes that scripted dialogues rarely reflect the unpredictability and dynamism of conversation, or the features and structures of natural spoken discourse, and that students who encounter only scripted spoken language have less opportunity to extend their linguistic repertoires in ways that prepare them for unforeseeable interactions outside of the classroom.

Carter (1998) compared real data from the CANCODE spoken corpus with dialogues from textbooks and found that the textbook dialogues lacked core spoken language features such as discourse markers, vague language, ellipses, and hedges (see also Burns, 2001). Burns (2001) and Carter (1997) both refer to the lack of three-part exchanges in question and answer sequences in textbooks. They point out that the two-part question–answer sequences often appearing in textbook dialogues are not the norm in real conversations; replies to questions are usually followed up by some fixed or routinized phrase such as *really*, *I thought so* (however, see the later discussion of exchange structure).

Modeling Speaking in the Classroom

Discourse Analysis: Exchange Structure and Classroom Speaking

Kasper begins by considering the widely held view that "the IRF routine is an unproductive interactional format for the learning of pragmatics and discourse" (2001, p. 518). Exchanges consisting of the familiar classroom pattern of initiation (I), response (R), and follow-up (F), often referred to as IRF exchanges, fail to give opportunities for tackling the complex demands of everyday conversation, especially since teachers usually exercise the follow-up role, while learners often remain in passive, respondent roles. However, Kasper goes on to argue that the negative reputation enjoyed by the IRF exchange may not be the whole story and that what really matters is the kind of interactional status assigned by the teacher to individual learners: where students are seen as primary interactants in speaking activities, teachers offer them more participation rights in the conversation. Kasper refers to evidence that suggests that teachers can help their learners to become actively involved in interaction, even within the typical IRF patterning found in teacher-fronted classroom dialogue.

McCarthy (2002, 2003) argues that responding and follow-up moves play a key role in "listenership," the manifestation of engagement in the discourse even when one is not in the role of main speaker, a situation NNSs often find themselves in. For McCarthy, listenership is not the same as "listening" in the conventional four skills paradigm, and is an important component of the speaking skill. However,

Ohta (2001) finds that the overwhelming majority of classroom follow-up moves are spoken by the teacher; learners get few opportunities to use typical listener follow-ups and only experience the teacher's moves as peripheral participants. Ohta argues for peer-to-peer interaction as providing the best opportunities for learners to produce appropriate listener behavior. Notwithstanding, exposure to the teacher's use of follow-up moves along with explicit guidance on the use of responsive moves can help students gradually move toward more productive use in peer-to-peer speaking activities. S. Walsh (2002) distinguishes different modes of teacher talk and illustrates how these may hinder or optimize learner contributions. More generally, Hall and M. Walsh (2002) give a relevant and wide-ranging survey of current research into teacher–student interaction and language learning (see also Morita, 2000).

Conversation Analysis and Speaking Tasks

Advocacy of conversation analysis (CA) as a means of understanding and improving speaking in pedagogical contexts has continued to grow in recent years. Wong (2000) notes that CA illuminates how local choices unfold in interaction and can home in on aspects of talk which are relevant for the participants themselves. Ducharme and Bernard (2001) argue along the same lines in their study of learners of French, using micro-analyses of videotaped interactions and retrospective interviews to gain insights into the perspectives of participants. Mori (2002) uses CA to analyze a speaking activity in a class of NNS learners of Japanese, where students exchanged experiences and opinions with Japanese NSs invited to the class. The resulting interaction resembled an interview, with a succession of questions by the students and answers from the NS guests. Interestingly, more natural discussion came about when students made spontaneous utterances and when they seemed to be attending more to the moment-by-moment unfolding of the talk. Mori ponders how the talk revealed the speakers' orientation toward the institutionalized nature of the task. Overall, the CA argument is that factors of task design and execution can influence the resultant talk in ways that CA can make plain, with clear implications for the improvement of the design and implementation of speaking tasks. However, Rampton, Roberts, Leung, and Harris (2002) warn of the lack of a "learning" dimension in CA studies of this kind. Because CA is a very local kind of analysis, it lends itself less easily to providing evidence of actual development of speaking ability over time.

Cognitive Approaches to Speaking Tasks

Other recent work examines the design and implementation of speaking tasks from the point of view of fluency, complexity and accuracy of production (see Bygate, 2001 for an overview of the evolution of research in this area). Robinson (2001) claims that increasing the cognitive complexity of speaking tasks affects production, with greater lexical variation manifested in more complex versions and greater fluency evidenced in simpler versions of the task. Yuan and Ellis (2003) assert that pretask planning positively aids learners' spoken production, especially with regard to fluency and complexity, albeit accuracy may not benefit so obviously. Yuan and Ellis also examine online planning, where learners are given unlimited time to formulate and monitor their speech while performing, and claim that online planning positively influences accuracy and grammatical complexity. Repetition and recycling and their contribution to the increasing integration over time of fluency, complexity, and accuracy of oral production is also receiving attention (Bygate, 2001; Lynch & Maclean, 2001). Additionally, the role of the teacher vis-à-vis the design and execution of tasks and the teacher's role of providing scaffolding (see the section on Vygotsky, below) to help learners develop their oral competence has come under the spotlight (Samuda, 2001).

The Vygotskian Perspective on Speaking

Since the publication of Lantolf and Appel's (1998) and Lantolf's (2000) influential works on Vygotsky, interest has grown in how such a perspective feeds into speaking pedagogy. Of central importance are the notions of scaffolding and the zone of proximal development (ZPD). Scaffolding is the cognitive support provided by an adult or other guiding person to aid a child or learner, and is realized in dialogue so that the child/learner can come to make sense of difficult tasks. The ZPD is the distance between where the child/learner is developmentally and what s/he can potentially achieve in interaction with adults or more capable peers (Vygotsky, 1978). In the Vygotskian paradigm, instructors and pupils (or peers) interactively coconstruct the arena for development; it is not predetermined and has no lockstep limits or ceiling. Meaning is created in dialogue (including dialogue with the self, often manifested in "private speech") during goal-directed activities. Attempts to see how these notions operate in reality in classrooms include Machado (2000), who demonstrates how peer-to-peer scaffolding in the preparatory phases of spoken classroom tasks (mutual help with the interpretation of the tasks and the wording of meanings) is reflected in evidence of internalization of such help in the performance phases of the same tasks. Machado suggests that peer-to-peer scaffolding may be just as important as expert–novice scaffolding, a theme reiterated by Ko, Schallert, and Walters (2003), who examine what marks out higher quality from lower quality negotiation-of-meaning interactions during a storytelling task (see also Kasper, 2001). As well as through teachers' contributions, improved storytelling was assisted by peer contributions in a negotiation phase between the first and second telling of a story, which, the researchers suggest, shows learners playing a central role in scaffolding (see also Shumin, 2002).

However, Kinginger (2002) warns against the incorporation of Vygotskian notions such as scaffolding and the ZPD into existing practices in oral pedagogy in ways that the notions simply become a justification for current practices (e.g., the input–output hypotheses, all and any types of pair- and group-work tasks, teacher feedback moves, etc.) rather than a genuine reexamination of the role of social interaction in language development. In this respect, Kinginger highlights the work of Merrill Swain and her associates (Swain, 2000; Nassaji & Swain, 2000; Swain & Lapkin, 2000), who see the ZPD more as an open-ended opportunity for unanticipated development and unpredictability rather than some fixed territory circumscribed by input and output or the closed cycles of teacher–learner exchanges.

Descriptive Frameworks and the Teaching of Speaking

Hughes (2002) takes the view that, in general, insights from disciplines such as discourse analysis and CA have been slow to filter through to the teaching of speaking. However, increasingly, applied linguists are addressing the applicability of such insights. Slade (1997) rejects the notion that casual conversation cannot be taught explicitly because it is unstructured. Explicit features that can be taught, she argues, include generic descriptions at the macro-level and moves and speech functions at the micro-level (however, see Lee, 2001, on the as-yet inadequate generic modeling of speech; see also Hughes, 2002, p.

36). Shumin (2002) also supports the view that speaking needs to be taught explicitly, and a number of authors point to the active promotion of language awareness as a way forward (Carter, 1997; Clennell, 1999; O'Keeffe & Farr, 2003; van Lier, 1998). Hughes (2002) notes that awareness-raising approaches should not be judged by the amount of speech learners produce but more in terms of depth of understanding of speaking and of why speakers make the choices they do.

Burns (2001) surveys the potential contribution to the pedagogy of speaking of systemic functional linguistics (SFL), exchange structure (IRF) analysis, CA, critical discourse analysis (CDA), and speech act theory and pragmatics. She sees these as relevant "tools" that can "underpin communicative language teaching" (2001, p. 125) and that the teacher can draw on depending on student needs and the types of discourse features to be foregrounded.

SFL, according to Burns, can provide a framework for analyzing samples of spoken discourse to highlight key aspects of a text, for example, its genre, as well as the relationship between the Hallidayan notions of *field*, *tenor*, and *mode* and lexicogrammatical choice. Burns sees IRF analysis as a useful complement to SFL because it focuses on the moment-by-moment process of interaction in context. She suggests that it can help students to increase their linguistic repertoire (e.g., an awareness of follow-up moves) as well as equipping them with skills to renegotiate their positions in encounters outside of the classroom. Within a CA framework, Burns suggests, language tasks can be developed to explore features of conversation such as turn-taking organization and sequencing (e.g., discussing speaker roles, rights to turns, etc.) and turn types (e.g., observing the nature of preferred and dispreferred responses, and developing strategies such as repair and reformulation). Burns also sees potential for pedagogical applications from CDA (see Coffin, 2001), which offers opportunities for classroom focus on aspects of power and gatekeeping roles within spoken interactions. Speech act theory and pragmatics, like CA, according to Burns, focus on the microstructures of conversation and can offer teachers the opportunity to highlight for students the appropriateness of utterances, how speakers negotiate certain situations (e.g., accepting/rejecting invitations) as well as providing a framework for the performance of speech acts, for example, through role plays and simulations (see also Burns, Joyce, & Gollin, 2001).

Spoken Language Materials in the Classroom

Selecting Spoken Texts for Classroom Use

Burns, Gollin, and Joyce (1997) suggest that if learners are involved in spoken text analysis, it should be directly applicable to the speaking task. They suggest as an example that learners could be presented with a partially transcribed text and be given the task of listening to the tape recording so as to fill in features such as backchannel responses raise awareness of such conversational features. They also suggest that learners transcribe small amounts of their own conversation and compare particular features such as length of turn and overlaps with NS transcripts. For a teacher wishing to use spoken data in the classroom, they suggest the following analytical framework: (1) transcribe the recording, (2) give the background information to the text, (3) analyze the text using an analytical approach (e.g. SFL, IRF, etc.; see the review of Burns, 2001, above), and (4) identify the significant teaching points which arise from the analysis. This approach, as in Burns (2001), argues for teachers to be well versed in methods of analysis of spoken language and aligns with the general move toward the exploitation of attested spoken data.

Selecting Aspects of Spoken Language to Focus on in Teaching

Burns, Joyce, and Gollin (2001) offer a practical handbook for teaching spoken discourse that provides guidelines for collecting, transcribing, and using authentic language, as well as tasks and case studies. Riggenbach (1999) provides numerous template activities to practice macro- (e.g., turn-taking) and micro- (e.g., pronunciation) speaking skills. In what still remains one of the few papers to give practical direction as to syllabus design for teaching conversation, Dörnyei and Thurrell (1994) noted that teachers are often unsure about which topic areas they should focus on in teaching conversation. Based on a synthesis of research from fields such as discourse analysis, CA, and the study of communicative competence, they suggest teaching points under four headings: conversational rules and structure (e.g., openings, topic shifting and closing), conversational strategies (e.g., paraphrase, asking for repetition and clarification), functions and meaning in conversation (e.g., illocutionary functions), and social and cultural contexts (e.g., social norms of appropriateness). Boyer's (2003) textbook integrates traditional speaking domains such as pronunciation, stress patterns, intonation and language functions (e.g., making suggestions), with lexicogrammar in spoken language (e.g., question tags, pronouns), conversational strategies (changing the topic), discourse-level features (e.g., ellipsis, small talk) and situational contexts (e.g., stages in a medical consultation). Other recent textbooks on teaching conversation include Zelman and Moran (1996) and Measday (1998).

Teaching Distinct Genres of Spoken Interaction

Small Talk

Shumin (2002) stresses the need for learners to be able to engage in small talk in the target language (i.e., inconsequential talk about the weather, traffic, and so on). Such interactional talk functions to create a sense of social communion. Shumin therefore suggests that from the outset adult learners should develop skill in short, interactional exchanges in which they are required to make only one or two utterances at a time (e.g., *I hate rush-hour traffic — me too*).

Cunningham Florez (1999) suggests that speaking lessons can follow a classic pattern of preparation, presentation, practice, evaluation, and extension, and gives the example of teaching small talk. In the preparation phase, learners are shown visuals of people in informal settings and brainstorm on what they might be saying. The presentation phase then has video clips of people doing small talk, during which students focus on the topics of talk and the language involved. The practice phase maintains the dual focus on topics and language with simple dialogues generated by the learners based on the material of the earlier stages. In the evaluation phase, learners compare their dialogues with a teacher-prepared dialogue, and discuss similarities and differences. Finally, the extension phase sends the learners out into the community (where this is feasible) to observe small talk in real settings and then report back to their class. A combination of traditional pedagogic structuring and the learner-as-researcher is at the center of this kind of activity, especially in relation to a conversational genre difficult to recreate naturally in an institutional setting.

Discussions

Green, Christopher, and Lam (2002) note that discussion skills are much neglected in the EFL/ESL classroom, and are critical of overly structured discussion activities. However, Shumin (2002) notes that the totally unstructured alternative of simply assigning a topic to students for discussion is not enough to ensure that speaking skills will be developed. In this respect, Green et al. (2002) suggest a three-stage format for the implementation of successful classroom discussions that are not overly controlled: (1) prediscussion (discussion groups are formed, with four per group as the optimum, possible topics are chosen; responsibility for researching the topic are divided within the groups); (2) discussion (the groups discuss the topic while partner groups observe and monitor); and (3) postdiscussion (peer-feedback from the observer-evaluators, plus teacher feedback, and finally groups decide on ways to extend the topic or choose a new topic). Lam and Wong (2000) identify key strategies that students need in order to play an effective part in discussion: seeking clarification, clarifying oneself, and checking that other people have understood one's message. While Lam and Wong's study underscores the value of strategy training, they raise two issues: (1) the necessity to support strategy training with linguistic scaffolding and (2) the importance of peer help and cooperation in facilitating strategy use. A number of recent classroom resource books on discussions are now widely available, for example, Barnard (1997), Folse and Ivone (2002a, 2002b), Kehe (1998), and Wallwork (1997a, 1997b).

Narratives

Slade (1997), in her research into workplace talk, found that social conversations were dominated by narrative genres, but noted that such genres are rarely represented in language teaching materials. She identifies four types of stories common in casual talk (narratives, anecdotes, exempla, and recounts) and argues strongly that the generic structure of narratives can be taught explicitly and that those aspects of storytelling that are culturally specific can be discussed (for further description of everyday storytelling see Norrick, 2000). Jones (2002) proposes a strategy for teaching the narrative pattern of "the reminiscence story." Based on Deacon (2000), Jones looks at the technique of the "split story," which involves telling students a story, but stopping at a crucial point and inviting students to provide their own imaginative ending (see also Jones, 2001). According to Wajnryb (2003), stories are a familiar and reassuring way of acquiring language and therefore can be easily applied to the language classroom. Wajnryb's (2003) textbook aims to promote the exploration of storytelling as discourse in the language classroom and provides examples of meaningful activities which can be used in a range of teaching situations (see also Paran and Watts, 2003, for a collection of stories and related classroom activtities).

Future Directions

Hughes (2002) repeatedly stresses the need for proper social and cultural contextualization of speaking activities, and there certainly seems to be a growing awareness that speaking activities, however cleverly designed, should not take place in a void, separated from the social and cultural life of the learner; undoubtedly this will be an important direction for future research in the teaching of speaking. Alongside this, new definitions of "literacy" are emerging that are no longer singularly focused on writing, but see literacy as encompassing an awareness of the nature of written and spoken texts and the development of literacy as intimately bound up with communicative activity in the classroom (Kern, 2000; Warschauer & Whittaker, 2001).

Technology and the blurring of the traditional speech–writing division as new modes of communication emerge are also at the center of discussions of how to enhance speaking pedagogy. Payne and Whitney (2002), for example, already claim that synchronous computer-mediated communication (CMC) can indirectly improve L2 speaking proficiency by fostering the same cognitive mechanisms that underlie spontaneous conversational speech. Their study shows that an experimental group for whom two of four contact hours per week took place in an internet chatroom environment performed better in speaking than a control group. One important implication of the use of technological support, Payne and Whitney claim, is that learning environments can, by design, reduce the cognitive burden and thereby have a facilitating effect for oral production. Simpson (2002), also investigating synchronous CMC, suggests that the communication, although written, is "conversation-like" and asserts that CMC generates communicative strategies that are medium-appropriate, borrowing from conversation, but taking on a special identity of their own. Although in its early days, such research points to fresh possibilities for enhancing the teaching of speaking.

When the time comes for the next *ARAL* review of teaching speaking, we can expect further progress in the application of spoken corpus research. Published classroom materials are likely to increasingly reflect the growing body of research into spoken discourse, and useful insights may be available as to the global use of spoken English with implications for teaching it in an international context.

Note

1. English dominates the present discussion, though it is apparent that similar problems exist in the establishment of pedagogical models for speaking of multinational languages such as French and Spanish. North American universities often insist on the spoken model of metropolitan France rather than that of nearby French Canada, and publishers routinely sanction language teaching materials for use in Latin America in terms of their faithfulness to European (Castilian) Spanish norms.

ANNOTATED BIBLIOGRAPHY

Burns, A. (2001). Analysing spoken discourse: Implications for TESOL. In A. Burns & C. Coffin (Eds.), *Analysing English in a global context: A reader* (pp. 123–148). London: Routledge.

A wide-ranging survey of the potential contribution to language teaching of a number of approaches to the analysis of discourse, including systemic functional linguistics, exchange structure analysis, conversation analysis, critical discourse analysis, and speech act theory and pragmatics. The essence of each approach is summarized; from each approach, Burns extrapolates relevant analytical tools that can be applied to conversational data for the purposes of language teaching.

Burns, A., Joyce, H., & Gollin, S. (2001). *"I see what you mean:" using spoken discourse in the classroom.* Sydney: National Centre for English Language Teaching and Research.

This is designed as a teachers' handbook for introducing naturally occurring discourse into the classroom. It provides background information on socially based theoretical approaches to the analysis of discourse and a workable framework for syllabus design and classroom implementation. It also gives practical guidance about transcribing spoken language, as well as principles for assessment.

Bygate, M. (2001). Speaking. In R. Carter & D. Nunan (Eds.), *The Cambridge guide to teaching English to speakers of other languages* (pp. 14–20). Cambridge: Cambridge University Press.

Bygate's chapter provides an historical perspective for the teaching of oral language (or lack thereof) over the years across different approaches and methodologies. It also surveys the characteristics of speech and stresses how it is distinct from writing both as a process and a product. Contrasting perspectives and research on speaking tasks in language learning are cogently summarized and the need for more longitudinal classroom-based research in this area is highlighted.

Hughes, R. (2002). *Teaching and researching speaking*. London: Pearson.

Hughes's book gives a great deal of historical and contextual background for the research and teaching of speaking and is a good source of information on current paradigms and issues. In dealing with the question of teaching materials, Hughes discusses the issues surrounding the role of "real" speech in the classroom. The book also includes suggestions for action research for both classroom practitioners and students and is a useful source of information on available resources for researching and teaching speaking, both in print and new media (CD-ROM and the Internet).

OTHER REFERENCES

Aston, G., & Burnard, L. (1998). *The BNC handbook: Exploring the British National Corpus with SARA*. Edinburgh: Edinburgh University Press.

Banjo, A. (1996). The sociolinguistics of English in Nigeria and the ICE project. In S. Greenbaum (Ed.), *Comparing English world-wide: The International Corpus of English* (pp. 239–248). Oxford: Oxford University Press.

Barnard, R. (1997). *Good news, bad news: News stories for listening and discussion: Student book*. Oxford: Oxford University Press.

Beeching, K. (1997). French for specific purposes: The case for spoken corpora. *Applied Linguistics*, *18*, 374–394.

Billmyer, K., & Varghese, M. (2000). Investigating instrument-based pragmatic variability:

Effects of enhancing discourse completion tests. *Applied Linguistics, 21*, 517–552.

Bolton, K., Gisborne, N., Hung, J., & Nelson, G. (2003). *The International Corpus of English project in Hong Kong.* Amsterdam: Benjamins.

Boyer, S. (2003). *Understanding spoken English: A focus on everyday language in context.* Glenbrook, NSW: Boyer Educational Resources.

Burns, A. (1998). Teaching speaking. *Annual Review of Applied Linguistics, 18*, 102–123.

Burns, A., Gollin, S., & Joyce, H. (1997). Authentic spoken texts in the language classroom. *Prospect, 12*, 72–86.

Bygate, M. (1998). Theoretical perspectives on speaking. *Annual Review of Applied Linguistics, 18*, 20–42.

Carter, R. (1997). Speaking Englishes, speaking cultures, using CANCODE. *Prospect, 12*, 4–11.

Carter, R. (1998). Orders of reality: CANCODE, communication and culture. *ELT Journal, 52*, 43–56.

Carter, R., Hughes, R., & McCarthy, M. J. (2000). *Exploring grammar in context.* Cambridge: Cambridge University Press.

Cheng, W., & Warren, M. (1999). Facilitating a description of intercultural conversations: The Hong Kong Corpus of conversational English. *ICAME Journal, 23*, 5–20.

Cheng, W., & Warren, M. (2000). The Hong Kong Corpus of Spoken English: Language learning through language description. In L. Burnard & T. McEnery, *Rethinking language pedagogy from a corpus perspective* (pp. 133–144). Frankfurt am Main: Lang.

Clennell, C. (1999). Promoting pragmatic awareness and spoken discourse skills within EAP classes. *ELT Journal, 53*, 83–91.

Coffin, C. (2001). Theoretical approaches to written language—a TESOL perspective. In A. Burns & C. Coffin (Eds.), *Analysing English in a global context: A reader* (pp. 93–122). London: Routledge.

Cunningham Florez, M. (1999). Improving adult English language learners' speaking skills. *ERIC Digest, June 1999.* (ED425304). National Center for ESL Literacy Education. Retrieved September, 2003, from http://www.cal.org/ncle/digests/Speak.htm.

Deacon, B. (2000). Sp-Stories-lit. *The Language Teacher, 24*, 32–33.

De Cock, S. (1998). A recurrent word combination approach to the study of formulae in the speech of native and non-native speakers of English. *International Journal of Corpus Linguistics, 3*, 59–80.

De Cock, S. (2000). Repetitive phrasal chunkiness and advanced EFL speech and writing. In C. Mair & M. Hundt (Eds.), *Corpus linguistics and linguistic theory. Papers from the Twentieth International Conference on English Language Research on Computerized corpora (ICAME 20), Freiburg im Breisgau 1999* (pp. 51–68). Amsterdam: Rodopi.

Di Vito, N. (1998). *Patterns across spoken and written French. Empirical research on the interaction among forms, functions and genres*. Boston: Houghton Mifflin.

Dörnyei, Z., & Thurrell, S. (1994). Teaching conversational skills intensively: Course content and rationale. *ELT Journal, 48*, 40–49.

Ducharme, D., & Bernard, R. (2001). Communication breakdowns: An exploration of contextualization in native and non-native speakers of French. *Journal of Pragmatics, 33*, 825–847.

Farr, F., Murphy, B., & O'Keeffe, A. (In press). The Limerick Corpus of Irish English: Design, description and application. *Teanga, 21*.

Flowerdew, J. (2000). Globalization discourse: A view from the East. *Discourse and Society, 13*, 209–225.

Folse, K.S., & Ivone, J. A. (2002a). I. Ann Arbor: University of Michigan Press.

Folse, K. S., & Ivone, J. A. (2002b). *More discussion starters: Activities for building speaking fluency*. Ann Arbor: University of Michigan Press.

Foster, P., Tonkyn, A., & Wigglesworth, G. (2000). Measuring spoken language: A unit for all reasons. *Applied Linguistics, 21*, 354–375.

Golato, A. (2003). Studying compliment responses: A comparison of DCTs and recordings of naturally occurring talk. *Applied Linguistics, 23*, 90–121.

Granger, S., Hung, J., & Petch-Tyson, S. (Eds.). (2002). *Computer learner corpora, second language acquisition and foreign language teaching*. Amsterdam: Benjamins.

Green, C. F., Christopher E. R., & Lam J. (2002). Developing discussion skills in the ESL classroom. In J. C. Richards & W. A. Renandya (Eds.), *Methodology in language teaching: An anthology of current practices* (pp. 225–233). Cambridge: Cambridge University Press.

Hall, J. K., & Walsh, M. (2002). Teacher–student interaction and language learning. *Annual Review of Applied Linguistics, 22*, 186–203.

Holmes, J. (1996). The New Zealand spoken component of ICE: Some methodological challenges. In S. Greenbaum (Ed.), *Comparing English World-Wide: The International Corpus of English* (pp. 163–178). Oxford: Oxford University Press.

Hunston, S. (2002). Pattern grammar, language teaching and linguistic variation. In R. Reppen, S. Fitzmaurice, & D. Biber (Eds.), *Using corpora to explore linguistic variation* (pp. 167–183). Amsterdam: Benjamins.

Ide, N., & Macleod, C. (2001). The American National Corpus: A standardized resource of American English. *Proceedings of Corpus Linguistics 2001*, Lancaster, UK: University of Lancaster. Retrieved September, 2003, from http://americannationalcorpus.org/pubs.html.

Ide, N., Reppen, R., & Suderman, K. (2002). The American National Corpus: More than the web can provide. In *Proceedings of the Third Language Resources and Evaluation Conference* (LREC) (pp. 839–44). Las Palmas, Canary Islands, Spain. Retrieved September

2003 from http://americannationalcorpus.org/pubs.html.

Jones, R. E. (2001). A consciousness-raising approach to the teaching of conversational story telling skills. *ELT Journal, 55*, 155–163.

Jones, R. E. (2002). We used to do this and we'd also do that: A discourse pattern for teaching the reminiscence story. *The Language Teacher 26* (2). Retrieved September, 2003, from http://langue.hyper.chubu.ac.jp/jalt/pub/tlt/02/feb/ jones.html.

Kallen, J. L., & Kirk, J. M. (2001). Convergence and divergence in the verb phrase in Irish standard English: A corpus-based approach. In J. M. Kirk & D. P. Ó Baoill (Eds.), *Language links: The languages of Scotland and Ireland* (pp. 59–79). Belfast: Cló Ollscoil na Banríona.

Kasper, G. (2001). Four perspectives on L2 pragmatic development. *Applied Linguistics, 22*, 502–530.

Kehe, D. (1998). *Discussion strategies*. Brattleboro, VT: Pro Lingua Associates.

Kern, R. (2000). *Literacy and language teaching*. Oxford: Oxford University Press.

Kinginger, C. (1999). Videoconferencing as access to spoken French. *Canadian Modern Language Review, 55*, 468–489.

Kinginger, C. (2002). Defining the zone of proximal development in US foreign language education. *Applied Linguistics, 23*, 240–261.

Ko. J., Schallert D. L., & Walters, K. (2003). Rethinking scaffolding: Examining negotiation of meaning in an ESL storytelling task. *TESOL Quarterly, 37*, 303–324.

Lam, W., & Wong, J. (2000). The effects of strategy training on developing discussion skills in an ESL classroom. *ELT Journal, 54*, 245–255.

Lantolf, J. P. (2000). *Sociocultural theory and second language learning*. Oxford: Oxford University Press.

Lantolf, J. P., & Appel, G. (Eds). (1998). *Vygotskyan approaches to second language research*. Norwood, NJ: Ablex.

Lawson, A. (2001). Rethinking French grammar for pedagogy: The contribution of spoken corpora. In R. C. Simpson & J. M. Swales (Eds.), *Corpus linguistics in North America: Selections from the 1999 Symposium* (pp. 179–194). Ann Arbor: University of Michigan Press.

Lee, D. (2001). Genres, registers, text types, domains, and styles: Clarifying the concepts and navigating a path through the BNC jungle. *Language Learning & Technology, 5*, 37–72.

Leung, C., Harris, R., & Rampton, B. (1997). The idealised native speaker, reified ethnicities, and classroom realities. *TESOL Quarterly, 31*, 543–558.

Lynch, T., & Maclean, J. (2001). 'A case of exercising': Effects of immediate task repetition on learners' performance. In M. Bygate, P. Skehan, & M. Swain (Eds.), *Researching pedagogic tasks: Second language learning, teaching and testing* (pp. 141–162). Harlow, UK: Pearson.

Machado, A. (2000). A Vygotskian approach to evaluation in foreign language learning contexts. *ELT Journal, 54*, 335–345.

McCarthy, M. J. (1998). *Spoken language and applied linguistics*. Cambridge: Cambridge University Press.

McCarthy, M. J. (2001). *Issues in applied linguistics*. Cambridge: Cambridge University Press.

McCarthy, M. J. (2002). Good listenership made plain: British and American non-minimal response tokens in everyday conversation. In R. Reppen, S. Fitzmaurice & D. Biber (Eds.), *Using corpora to explore linguistic variation* (pp. 49–71). Amsterdam: Benjamins.

McCarthy, M. J. (2003). Talking back: 'Small' interactional response tokens in everyday conversation. *Research on Language in Social Interaction, 36*, 33–63.

McCarthy, M. J., & Carter, R. A. (2001). Ten criteria for a spoken grammar. In E. Hinkel & S. Fotos (Eds.), *New perspectives on grammar teaching in second language classrooms* (pp. 51–75). Mahwah, NJ: Lawrence Erlbaum.

Measday, E. (1998). *Speak out!: Authentic communication activities for the intermediate and advanced ESL student*. Dubuque, IA: Kendall/Hunt.

Moon, R. (1997). Vocabulary connections: Multi-word items in English. In N. Schmitt & M. J. McCarthy (Eds.), *Second language vocabulary: Description, acquisition and pedagogy* (pp. 40–63). Cambridge: Cambridge University Press.

Mori, J. (2002). Task design, plan, and development of talk-in-interaction: An analysis of a small group activity in a Japanese language classroom. *Applied Linguistics, 23*, 323–347.

Morita, N. (2000). Discourse socialization through oral classroom activities in a TESL graduate program. *TESOL Quarterly, 34*, 279–310.

Nassaji, H., & Swain, M. (2000). A Vygotskian perspective on corrective feedback in L2: The effect of random versus negotiated help on the learning of English articles. *Language Awareness, 9*, 34–51.

Nelson, G., Wallis, S., & Aarts, B. (2002). *Exploring natural language: Working with the British component of the International Corpus of English*. Amsterdam: Benjamins.

Nero, S. J. (2000). The changing faces of English: A Caribbean perspective. *TESOL Quarterly, 34*, 483–510.

Norrick, N. R. (2000). *Conversational narrative: Storytelling in everyday talk*. Amsterdam: Benjamins.

Ohta, A. S. (2001). *Second language acquisition processes in the classroom: Learning Japanese*. Mahwah, NJ: Erlbaum.

O'Keeffe, A. & Farr, F. (2003). Using language corpora in language teacher education: Pedagogic, linguistic and cultural insights. *TESOL Quarterly, 37*, 389–418.

Ooi, V. (1997). Analysing the Singapore ICE corpus for lexicographic evidence. In M. Ljung (Ed.), *Corpus-based studies in English* (pp. 245–260). Amsterdam: Rodopi.

Paran, A., & Watts, E. (Eds.) (2003). *Storytelling in ELT*. Whitstable, UK: International

Association of Teachers of English as a Foreign Language (IATEFL).

Payne, J. S., & Whitney, P. J. (2002). Developing L2 oral proficiency through synchronous CMC: Output, working memory, and interlanguage development. *CALICO Journal, 20*, 7–32.

Prodromou, L. (1997). Global English and its struggle against the octopus. *IATEFL Newsletter, 135*, 12–14.

Prodromou, L. (2003). In search of the successful user of English. *Modern English Teacher, 12*, 5–14.

Rampton, B., Roberts, C., Leung, C., & Harris, R. (2002). Methodology in the analysis of classroom discourse. *Applied Linguistics, 23*, 373–392.

Riggenbach, H. (1999). *Discourse analysis in the language classroom, Vol. 1: The spoken language.* Ann Arbor: University of Michigan Press.

Robinson, P. (2001). Task complexity, task difficulty, and task production: Exploring interactions in a componential framework. *Applied Linguistics, 22*, 27–57.

Samuda, V. (2001). Guiding relationships between form and meaning during task performance: The role of the teacher. In M. Bygate, P. Skehan, & M. Swain (Eds.), *Researching pedagogic tasks: Second language learning, teaching and testing* (pp. 119–140). Harlow, UK: Pearson.

Seidlhofer, B. (2001). Closing a conceptual gap: The case for a description of English as a Lingua Franca. *International Journal of Applied Linguistics, 11*, 133–158.

Seidlhofer, B. (this volume). Research perspectives on teaching English as a lingua franca.

Shumin, K. (2002). Factors to consider: Developing adult EFL students' speaking abilities. In J. C. Richards & W. A. Renandya (Eds.), *Methodology in language teaching: An anthology of current practices* (pp. 201–211). Cambridge: Cambridge University Press.

Simpson, J. (2002). Discourse and synchronous computer-mediated communication: Uniting speaking and writing? In K. Spelman Miller & P. Thompson (Eds.), *Unity and diversity in language use* (pp. 57–71). London: Continuum.

Simpson, R. C., Lucka, B., & Ovens, J. (2000). Methodological challenges of planning a spoken corpus with pedagogical outcomes. In L. Burnard & T. McEnery (Eds.), *Rethinking language pedagogy from a corpus perspective: Papers from the Third International Conference on Teaching and Language Corpora* (TALC) (pp. 43–49). Frankfurt: Lang.

Slade, D. (1997). Stories and gossip in English: The macro-structure of casual talk. *Prospect, 12*, 72–86.

Stern, K. (1997). The Longman Spoken American Corpus: Providing an in-depth analysis of everyday English. *Longman Language Review, 3*, 14–17.

Swain, M. (2000). The output hypothesis and beyond: Mediating acquisition through collaborative dialogue. In J. P. Lantolf (Ed.), *Sociocultural theory and second language acquisition* (pp. 97–114). New York: Oxford University Press.

Swain, M., & Lapkin, S. (2000). Task based second language learning: The uses of the first language. *Language Teaching Research, 4,* 253–276.

Timmis, I. (2002). Native-speaker norms and International English: A classroom view. *ELT Journal, 56,* 240–249.

van Lier, L. (1998). The relationship between consciousness, interaction and language learning. *Language Awareness, 7,* 128–145.

Vygotsky, L. S. (1978). *Mind and society: The development of higher mental processes.* Cambridge, MA: Harvard University Press.

Wajnryb, R. (2003). *Stories: Narrative activities for the language classroom.* Cambridge: Cambridge University Press.

Wallwork, A. (1997a). *Discussions A-Z.* Cambridge: Cambridge University Press.

Wallwork, A. (1997b). *Discussions A-Z advanced teacher's book: A resource book of speaking activities.* Cambridge: Cambridge University Press.

Walsh, S. (2002). Construction of obstruction: Teacher talk and learner involvement in the EFL classroom. *Language Teaching Research, 6,* 3–23.

Warschauer, M. (2000). The changing global economy and the future of English teaching. *TESOL Quarterly, 34,* 511–535.

Warschauer, M., & Whittaker, P. F. (2001). The Internet for English language teaching: Guidelines for teachers. J. C. Richards & W. A. Renandya (Eds.), *Methodology in language teaching: An anthology of current practices* (pp. 368–373). Cambridge: Cambridge University Press.

Wong, J. (2000). Delayed next turn repair initiation native/non-native speaker English conversation. *Applied Linguistics, 21,* 244–267.

Wray, A. (2000). Formulaic sequences in second language teaching: Principle and practice. *Applied Linguistics, 21,* 463–489.

Wray, A. (2002). *Formulaic language and the lexicon.* Cambridge: Cambridge University Press.

Yuan, Y. (2001). An enquiry into empirical pragmatics data-gathering methods: Written DCTs, oral DCTs, field notes, and natural conversations. *Journal of Pragmatics, 33,* 271–292.

Yuan, F., & Ellis, R. (2003). The effects of pre-task planning and on-line planning on fluency, complexity and accuracy in L2 monologic oral production. *Applied Linguistics, 24,* 1–27.

Zelman, N. E., & Moran, P. R. (1996). *Conversation inspirations* (2nd. ed.). Brattleboro, VT: Pro Lingua.

3. RESEARCH ON TEACHING READING

William Grabe

This chapter builds on prior reviews of reading theory, research, and assessment published in the *Annual Review of Applied Linguistics* and uses them and additional current research to develop a set of 10 instructional implications for second language reading. The review draws upon both L1 and L2 research to demonstrate support for instructional approaches that (1) ensure fluency in word recognition; (2) emphasize the learning of vocabulary; (3) activate background knowledge; (4) ensure acquisition of linguistic knowledge and general comprehension; (5) teach recognition of text structures and discourse organization; (6) promote development of strategic readers rather than mechanical application of strategy checklists; (7) build reading fluency and rate; (8) promote extensive reading; (9) develop intrinsic motivation for reading; and (10) contribute to a coherent curriculum for student learning. There is empirical support for each of these implications, although at the same time, additional research related to many is needed to further identify aspects of effective L2 reading instruction in particular settings. While further research alone does not guarantee improved reading pedagogy, it provides one means of identifying specific aspects of reading abilities and testing alternative instructional practices and is thus a crucial component in the search for more effective outcomes.

This review of research on teaching reading has two primary purposes. It will extend the three reviews of second language reading that appeared in Volume 18 of *ARAL* on reading theory (Hudson, 1998), reading assessment (Perkins, 1998), and reading instruction (with an emphasis on extensive reading) (Bamford & Day, 1998). It will also focus specifically on research that supports instructional practices to improve second language (L2) reading comprehension and highlights areas where further research is needed.[1]

Much as with any language skill, the teaching of reading is a complex matter. Obvious variables such as student proficiency, age, L1/L2 relations, motivation, cognitive processing factors, teacher factors, curriculum and materials resources, instructional setting, and institutional factors all impact the degree of success of reading instruction. One could easily come to the conclusion that reading is too complex a process for straightforward connections between research and instructional practices. Nevertheless, there are good reasons for optimism in writing an overview of research on teaching reading.

One reason for optimism is that research on English L1 reading has made remarkable advances in the past 15 years, and it is possible to synthesize this research in ways that generate major implications for reading instruction. Second, research on reading instruction in L2 settings has provided additional insights that often converge with the L1 reading research literature. Third, the real distinctions between L1 reading and L2 reading (e.g., Bernhardt, 2003; Grabe & Stoller, 2002; Koda, 2004) do not prevent researchers and practitioners from drawing major implications from L1 research findings in general, and especially from research on instructional issues. At the same time, it is essential to recognize that instruction will need to vary in important ways for L2 learners depending on context, learner needs, and language proficiency levels.

In this overview, several issues will not be covered. First, it is not possible to consider every variation of L2 (or L1) student type in relation to reading instruction. To maintain a reasonable focus on the key issues of reading instruction for applied linguists, this overview will focus on students who need to develop academic reading abilities in school settings. Separate reviews would be required for adult literacy training for nonacademic purposes (e.g., see Comings, Garner, & Smith, 2000–2002; Curtis & Longo, 1999; Davidson & Strucker, 2002; Wagner & Venezky, 1999), for reading disability instruction (Shaywitz, 2003; Torgesen, 2002; Torgeson et al., 2001; Wolf, 2001), and for elementary literacy skills, particularly issues surrounding phonological awareness, sound–letter correspondences, print readiness, and the emergence of reading abilities (Carver, 2000; Geva & Siegal, 2000; Muter & Diethelm, 2001; National Reading Panel, 2000; Snow, Burns, & Griffin,1998; Verhoeven, 2000).

Second, to maintain the focus on reading instruction, this review also will not directly address research for purposes of theory building. There will be no overview of theoretical perspectives on L1 or L2 reading (but see Alderson, 2000; Bernhardt, 2000; Geva & Siegal, 2000; Geva & Verhoeven, 2000; Geva & Wang, 2001; Grabe & Stoller, 2002; Kamil, Mosenthal, Pearson, & Barr, 2000; Koda, 2004; National Reading Panel, 2000; Noordman & Vonk, 1999; Perfetti, 1999, 2003; Perfetti, Van Dyke, & Hart, 2001; Pressley, 2002c; Stanovich, 2000). The research reviewed below will focus specifically on the extent to which implications for instruction are supportable and strong enough to be persuasive even if the research does not provide direct experimental tests of specific teaching practices, very difficult to do in any case (see Shanahan, 2002).

Third, this review will not cover theoretical issues that have specific relevance to L2 reading contexts. For example, it will not discuss the impact of transfer effects from the L1 to the L2, issues of linguistic distance between L1 and L2, or the orthographic depth hypothesis (cf. Koda, 2004). Nor will it review recent studies relevant to the linguistic threshold hypothesis (cf. Bernhardt, 2000; Pichette, Segalowitz, & Connors, 2003) or research specifically on working memory, automaticity, or attention and awareness (cf. Robinson, 2001; Segalowitz, 2000, 2003; Segalowitz & Hulstijn, in press).

As a way to organize the potentially overwhelming available information, I will state a set of implications for reading instruction that are empirically supportable and then review recent evidence in turn for each implication. This review will not separate L1 research from L2 research with regard to reading instruction, though it will refer specifically to L2 research whenever recent L2 studies apply to instructional practices. For many of the subsections to follow, the review focuses on instructional research in L1 settings because there is so much more empirical research to draw on.

Implications for Reading Instruction from Reading Research

Over the past 10 years, a set of implications for L2 reading instruction has emerged from overviews of the research literature (Grabe, 2000; Grabe & Stoller, 2002). This review uses a version of these implications as a way to examine how research supports effective reading-instruction practices, and how teaching, materials development, and curriculum design could be adapted to become more effective.

Based on extensive and still accumulating research, the following implications for academic reading instruction and curriculum design are reasonably well supported. Although stated as instructional implications, all but the last of these goals can also be viewed as component abilities of learners that need to be developed for effective reading comprehension.

1. Ensure word recognition fluency.
2. Emphasize vocabulary learning and create a vocabulary-rich environment.
3. Activate background knowledge in appropriate ways.
4. Ensure effective language knowledge and general comprehension skills.
5. Teach text structures and discourse organization.
6. Promote the strategic reader rather than teach individual strategies.
7. Build reading fluency and rate.
8. Promote extensive reading.
9. Develop intrinsic motivation for reading.
10. Plan a coherent curriculum for student learning.

It should be noted that a long list of important implications does not, in and of itself, amount to any sort of universal curriculum for reading instruction, and such a claim is not being made here. In fact, any instructional setting and any group of curriculum developers must determine priorities based on student needs, institutional expectations, and resource constraints. Therefore, the goal of the sections below is only to show that these implications are all potentially important components of an extended reading curriculum. Many of these implications should be considered, in one form or another, in any effective reading curriculum. However, the choices of which factors finally to emphasize rest with local contexts and goals, and with the relevance and persuasiveness of supporting research.

Each subsection below will be divided into two parts. The first part will briefly note L1 and L2 research that supports the instructional implication identified. The second part will consider evidence for teaching the ability and the impact of such instruction on reading comprehension development.

Research on Reading Instruction

Ensure Word Recognition Fluency

Word recognition fluency has been widely recognized in L1 reading research as an important factor in explaining reading comprehension abilities, particularly at earlier stages of reading development (Perfetti, 1985; Stanovich, 2000). Word recognition fluency has not been a major focus of L2 research (cf. Koda, 1996), though in the early 1990s, research by Segalowitz (1991) demonstrated that word recognition automaticity was an important factor in distinguishing proficiency levels of very advanced L2 readers (in terms of overall reading fluency). There are a number of more recent studies that are also suggestive in this regard. For example, Segalowitz, Segalowitz, and Wood (1998) demonstrated that L2 university students who were more fluent readers overall had better word recognition automaticity skills. In addition, they showed that less fluent students improved their L2 word recognition automaticity through L2 instruction over the course of an academic year. Their results argue that increased word recognition automaticity results from incidental exposure to vocabulary through instruction over extended periods of time.

Kroll, Michael, Tokowicz, and Dufour (2002) report on a study in which greater L2 word recognition fluency is associated with higher proficiency levels among university students. L2 students with five years of target-language learning experience were significantly faster on an L2 word naming task than students with less L2 learning experience. The study does not indicate whether increased fluency leads to increased language proficiency, or the reverse, or some reciprocal causality. In a large-scale longitudinal study, Droop and Verhoeven (2003) used a decoding fluency measure and found only moderate to small relations ($r = .39$ to .46) between decoding fluency and reading comprehension for third- and fourth-grade L2 students. They also used structural equation modeling and found only a small relation between decoding fluency at an earlier assessment time and reading comprehension at a later time. In a recent training study, Fukkink, Hulstijn, and Simis (2003) report fluency gains through word recognition training for eighth-grade EFL students in Holland. Students showed significant gains in word reading fluency with just two training sessions.

The second issue for word recognition fluency is whether or not fluency can be taught in normal instructional settings, and whether or not fluency instruction would also improve reading comprehension. The results of Segalowitz et al. (1998) show that academic L2 instruction in general can lead to greater automatization of high frequency words at the same time that students gain in language proficiency. Further research tracking the effects of ongoing word recognition fluency instruction is needed in L2 contexts. It is generally assumed that repeated exposures to high-frequency words through extended print exposure (e.g., extensive reading of level-appropriate texts) would contribute to automatic word recognition and comprehension gains. However, no causal connection between word recognition improvement and reading improvement in L2 settings has yet been demonstrated.

In L1 reading research, such a connection was explored by Tan and Nicholson (1997; Nicholson & Tan, 1999). In their study, they trained below-average grade 3–5 students to develop word recognition automaticity through flash card practice. Results showed that experimental students outperformed a control group not only in fluency but also in passage comprehension. In another study, Levy, Abello, and Kysynchuk (1997) carried out training studies with fourth-grade students and demonstrated that both word recognition training and repeated readings of texts had a positive impact on comprehension of texts that included all the words used in the fluency training. In a second language context, Fukkink et al. (2003) explored speed of processing training and its impact on comprehension with eighth-grade EFL students with 2½ years of English coursework, but they were not able to demonstrate a significant relation between the two. Like Levy et al., they also used comprehension measures that involved words used in the fluency training sessions, and training sessions appeared to be of similar intensity.

Research on the effects of word recognition fluency training on comprehension development is a relatively new area and multiple studies are needed. It will take time for the real impact of fluency on comprehension to be sorted out (a) for different groups of L2 (and L1) students, (b) in different settings, (c) with different amounts of training, (d) with different training tasks, (e) with different assessment measures, and (f) with differing amounts of overall exposure to the L2. Based on the conflicting results to date, it may be the case that word recognition fluency is an enabling skill for comprehension rather than a required skill (cf. discussions in Fukkink et al., 2003; Levy et al., 1997). For example, a lack of word recognition fluency may impede comprehension, but above a certain fluency threshold, the differing rates of word recognition fluency may not have a major impact on comprehension, particularly if comprehension is measured with tests that do not impose time pressure on performance. Further L2 research on the role of word recognition fluency on comprehension is an area that deserves more attention and additional research studies.

A final issue involves how best to teach word recognition fluency effectively as part of a reading curriculum (e.g., through timed word recognition practice, greater phonological awareness, morphological awareness training, extended reading practice, assisted reading activities). Instructional recommendations have been made along this line by Anderson (1999), Hulstijn, (2001), Nation (2001), and Segalowitz (2000). Research that demonstrates the effectiveness of specific instructional practices for greater fluency in word recognition is needed.

Emphasize Vocabulary Learning and Create a Vocabulary-Rich Environment

The relation between vocabulary knowledge and reading comprehension has been powerfully demonstrated in both L1 and L2 contexts (also see Halstijn, 1997; Nation, 2002; Read, this volume). In L1 reading research, there have been many studies that demonstrate the strong relationship between vocabulary and reading. In an early large-scale study, Thorndike (1973) surveyed reading in 15 countries (with over 100,000 students) and reported median correlations across countries and age groups of between $r = .66$ and $r = .75$ for reading and vocabulary. Stanovich (2000) reported on research that supports this relationship, noting strong correlations between vocabulary and reading for third- through seventh-grade L1 students ($r = .64$ to .76). In a set of unusual research studies, Carver (2003) has argued that the relationship between reading comprehension and vocabulary knowledge is so strong that research can produce perfect correlations. When reliable vocabulary tests are converted to grade-level equivalent scores, and when reliable reading comprehension measures are also converted to grade-level equivalent scores, Carver predicts that the corrected correlations between the two measures will be almost perfect. While the argument is almost startling in its assertion, Carver presents extensive evidence from multiple sources of assessment data to support his position. For purposes of this review, it is safe to claim that there is a strong and reliable relationship between L1 vocabulary knowledge and reading comprehension.

In L2 settings, Droop and Verhoeven (2003) demonstrate a powerful relation between vocabulary knowledge and later reading ability with third- and fourth-grade language minority children in Holland. Similarly, Schoonen, Hulstijn, and Bossers (1998) reported that L2 vocabulary knowledge was a very strong predictor of L2 reading ability for eighth-grade EFL students in Holland ($r^2 = .71$). In research on L2 language assessment, there are many reports of strong relationships between vocabulary and reading comprehension. Pike (1979) reported corrected correlations between vocabulary and reading on a TOEFL administration on the order of .84 to .95. Laufer (1997) cited several assessment studies with strong correlations between reading and vocabulary knowledge (.50 to .75). Qian (2002) found strong correlations, from .68 to .82, between TOEFL reading subsection scores and three vocabulary measures.

The related question is whether or not instruction in vocabulary will improve reading comprehension abilities in any direct and immediate way.[2] This relationship has been an important issue in L1 research, and it has been difficult to demonstrate. In the 1980s, Beck and her colleagues showed that intense vocabulary instruction led to improved reading comprehension for fourth-grade elementary L1 students (Beck, Perfetti, & McKeown, 1982; McKeown, Beck, Omanson, & Pople, 1985). There has been little research in this area since then, in both L1 and L2 contexts, to support the instructional connection between vocabulary knowledge and comprehension.

Activate Background Knowledge in Appropriate Ways

Almost all reading researchers agree that background knowledge plays an important role in reading comprehension. It is well documented that readers comprehend texts better when texts are culturally familiar or when they relate to well-developed disciplinary knowledge of a reader. More generally, background knowledge is essential for all manner of inferences and text model construction during comprehension. It is also important for disambiguating lexical meanings and syntactic ambiguities. The complications appear to arise with texts that present relatively new information or information from fields for which readers have no special expertise. In many cases, these are informational texts requiring the learning of new information by students. The limited role of background knowledge for comprehending new topics was clearly documented by Bernhardt (1991), and additional studies reviewed in Alderson (2000) present conflicting evidence on the role of background knowledge on reading assessment. Nonetheless, background knowledge appears to provide strong support for comprehension in many contexts.

From an instructional perspective, the issue becomes whether or not there are specific benefits for promoting appropriate background knowledge for students encountering new information in instructional texts. Will the activation of background knowledge lead to better comprehension? Chen and Graves (1995) conducted one of the few L2 studies to pursue this issue directly. They demonstrated that the use of text previewing led to significantly better comprehension in comparison with both a control group and a group that activated general background knowledge. The finding can be interpreted straightforwardly as support for the activation of specific information that is relevant to the text as opposed to activating more general background knowledge. Additional studies of this type would help clarify more precisely the role of background knowledge for text comprehension in learning contexts.

Ensure Effective Language Knowledge and General Comprehension Skills

Text comprehension requires both (a) language knowledge and (b) recognition of key ideas and their relationships (through various comprehension strategies). The role of both of these factors in comprehension is reviewed here. Language knowledge, for purposes of this review, primarily involves vocabulary knowledge (see above) and grammar knowledge. There is a range of research that argues for a strong relation between grammar knowledge and reading. Furthermore, research on syntactic processing, or word integration processes (integrating lexical and syntactic information into clause-level meaning units), also suggests significant relations between syntactic parsing abilities and comprehension abilities (Fender, 2001, 2003).

While relatively few research studies of reading development include grammar measures, a recent L2 study by van Gelderen, et al. (2002) examined the relations between linguistic knowledge, metacognitive knowledge (what we know about how we use language and how we read), and word processing speed, on the one hand, and reading comprehension on the other. The students, both Dutch and Turkish, were tested in their L1 (Dutch native speakers), L2 (Dutch EFL students, Turkish speakers of L2 Dutch), and L3 (Turkish EFL students in Holland). Van Gelderen et al. (2002) report a very strong correlation ($r = .73$) between Dutch L1 and EFL L2 grammar knowledge and reading abilities and an even stronger correlation ($r = .78$) between Dutch L2 and EFL L3 (Turkish students in Holland) grammar knowledge and reading.

L2 assessment research on the relationship between grammar and reading has also demonstrated surprisingly strong relations. Alderson (1993), discussing research for the development of IELTS, reported correlations between reading and grammar of .80. Similarly strong correlations have been reported for the TOEFL on a regular basis (comparing the reading and grammar subsections). Pike (1979) reported corrected correlations among subsections of a TOEFL test of (.80 to .85). Recently, Enright, et al. (2002), presenting on TOEFL research involving the development of the New TOEFL, reported a very strong relationship between the structure and reading subsections of the current TOEFL ($r = .91$) and a strong relationship between the structure section of the current TOEFL and the piloted reading section of the New TOEFL ($r = .83$). Similarly very strong correlations have been reported recently in research with Dutch, Turkish, and Moroccan students in Holland (Droop & Verhoeven, 2003).

The strong relationship between grammar and reading has not led to a call for extended grammar instruction as a direct support for L2 reading comprehension. Instead, grammar is better seen as an indirect support system that is developed through comprehension instruction and strategy training (e.g., establishing the main idea, summarizing information, recognizing discourse structure, and monitoring comprehension). Some of the strategies that are important for comprehension involve grammatical knowledge while others focus on processing skills and background knowledge.

A number of individual comprehension strategies have been shown to have a significant impact on reading comprehension abilities. In L1 settings, the report of the National Reading Panel (2000) and the follow-up overview by Trabasso and Bouchard (2002) have identified the following individual reading strategies as having a significant influence on reading comprehension:

- Prior knowledge activation
- Mental imagery
- Graphic organizers
- Text structure awareness
- Comprehension monitoring
- Question answering
- Question generating
- Mnemonic support practice
- Summarization

Similar discussions of effective instructional strategies in L1 settings are reviewed by Duke and Pearson (2002) and Vacca (2002). There is little equivalent recent L2 research demonstrating the effectiveness of specific comprehension strategies or synthesizing prior research, although earlier work by Carrell (e.g., 1984; Carrell, Pharis, & Liberto, 1989) has demonstrated the importance of text structure awareness, semantic mapping, and prior knowledge activation in L2 studies.

Teach Text Structures and Discourse Organization

In L1 settings, multiple studies demonstrated the importance of text structure awareness in the 1980s, focusing primarily on comprehension and learning from expository texts (see Goldman & Rakestraw, 2000; Trabasso & Bouchard, 2002). In many L2 settings, when considering older students and more advanced L2 students, a similar emphasis is typically placed on expository prose processing for learning purposes. These students need to understand the more abstract patterns of text structuring in expository prose that support readers' efforts at comprehension. While advanced learning texts are typically denser and present more complex information than more general texts, they are, nevertheless, assumed to be understandable with relatively little ambiguity when assigned in school settings. (This assumption is often mistaken, however.)

Texts have numerous signaling systems that help a reader to interpret the information being presented (e.g., pronominal systems, other antecedent referencing, given before new information, thematic signaling, transition words and structures, and syntactic mechanisms for foregrounding and backgrounding).

Most important, texts incorporate discourse structures, sometimes understood as knowledge structures or basic rhetorical patterns in texts (see Grabe, 1997; Meyer & Poon, 2001; Mohan, 1986). Discourse structures have functional purposes and these purposes are recognized by good readers and writers, if only implicitly in some cases. These functional purposes are supported by well-recognized conventions and systems that lead a reader to preferred interpretations (see Grabe, 2003; Tang, 1992). Moreover, these discourse mechanisms extend to the level of genre and larger frames of discourse that organize textual information for the reader. In a recent study, Chu, Swaffar, and Charney (2002) demonstrated the importance of larger frames of discourse in a study of text recall based on text organization differences. They tested 120 Taiwanese university students on four English passages using Chinese rhetorical patterns and four English passages using English rhetorical patterns. The students recalled more information from the passages following Chinese rhetorical patterns.

A major issue concerning the influence of text structure is the extent to which such knowledge can be directly taught to students so that it will lead to improved comprehension. There are three major lines of research (mostly L1) on the effect of text structure instruction. One line of research involves the impact of direct instruction that explicitly raises student awareness of specific text structuring. This research emphasizes the uses of transition words; explanations for rhetorical patterns in texts, topic sentences, sentence-initial phrases, anaphoric linkages, and definite reference to prior text ideas; and awareness of the role of various grammatical structures to build coherence in text interpretation (Duke & Pearson, 2002; Goldman & Rakestraw, 2000). A recent study by Meyer and Poon (2001) demonstrated that structure strategy training significantly improved recall from texts for both younger adults and older adults. Experimental subjects were trained over six sessions (90 minutes each) to read texts and recognize various structural patterns in texts (e.g., comparison and contrast, problem/solution, cause and effect). The experimental group recalled significantly more information in recalls after each training period than did a control group.

A second line of research develops student awareness of text structure through graphic organizers, semantic maps, outline grids, tree diagrams, and hierarchical summaries (e.g., Dymock, 1999; Tang, 1992; Trabasso & Bouchard, 2002). This research demonstrates that students comprehend texts better when they are shown visually how text information is organized (along with the linguistic clues that signal this organization). A third line of instructional training follows from instruction in reading strategies. Because a number of reading strategy training approaches include attention to structure, main idea identification, and text study skills, this line of instructional research is also a source of studies supporting text structure instruction. Thus, strategy training which includes summarizing, semantic mapping, predicting, forming questions from headings and subheadings, and using adjunct questions appears to improve awareness of text structure and text comprehension (Duke & Pearson, 2002; Trabasso & Bouchard, 2002).

Overall, however, there is relatively little recent L2 research on this area of text structure and comprehension. Much more research is needed in L2 contexts to determine the extent to which different types of text structure knowledge support comprehension and in which contexts, and what types of instruction will be most effective.

Promote the Strategic Reader Rather Than Teach Individual Strategies

In L1 settings, reading comprehension instruction today is equated with strategic reading development. There is now considerable research to show that reading comprehension is strongly influenced by reading instruction that emphasizes the coordinated use of multiple strategies while students actively seek to comprehend texts (Block & Pressley, 2002; National Reading Panel, 2000; Pearson & Duke, 2002; Pressley, 2002b, 2002c; Trabasso & Bouchard, 2002). Such instruction combines direct teaching of several strategies while students are reading and comprehending a text. The teacher and students engage in discussions about the text while also learning to use key strategies in effective combinations. Students learn to engage with texts strategically through a process of teacher modeling, teacher scaffolding and support, and gradual independent use of strategies to comprehend the text better. There is general agreement among L1 researchers that instruction that focuses on student learning repertoires of strategies is more effective than individual strategy instruction (Baker, 2002; Brown, 2002; Duke & Pearson, 2002; Pressley, 2002a, 2002b).

Many approaches involving multiple strategies tend to focus on four to eight major strategies, though other approaches may incorporate up to 20 to 30 distinct strategies over a longer period of time. The following 10 approaches are commonly referenced as effective combined-strategies instruction that improves reading comprehension:

1. KWL: Know, Want to know, Learned
2. ETR: Experience – Text – Relate
3. QAR: Question – Answer – Response
4. DR-TA: Directed Reading and Thinking Activities
5. Reciprocal Teaching
6. Collaborative Strategic Reading (CSR)
7. Direct Explanation
8. Questioning the Author
9. Transactional Strategies Instruction (TSI)
10. Concept-Oriented Reading Instruction (CORI)

The first four instructional approaches—KWL, ETR, QAR, DR-TA—have in common a narrow focus based on a well-specified instructional technique or template. These approaches generally have not been supported directly by empirical research. Instead, they draw their support from research on effective strategies that are incorporated into the approach (such as those listed above in the section on comprehension instruction; e.g., questioning, comprehension monitoring, summarizing) (see Trabasso & Bouchard, 2002).

The second set of instructional approaches—Reciprocal Teaching, Collaborative Strategic Reading, Direct Explanation, Questioning the Author—presents a more open framework for instruction in which multiple types of tasks and activities are included. In these approaches, there is a shift from a specific technique to a more complex set of tasks that interact in potentially unpredictable and unscripted ways, depending on how a given lesson proceeds. In these four approaches, there is an equal emphasis on comprehension and on learning from the text while developing strategic reading abilities. Reciprocal Teaching has been validated in numerous studies and in three different meta-analyses (see Trabasso & Bouchard, 2002). The other approaches have support that draws primarily on related research (e.g., Collaborative Strategic Reading draws on the Reciprocal Teaching research) as well as a few studies specific to each approach.

The last two comprehension-strategies approaches—Transactional Strategies Instruction (TSI) and Concept-Oriented Reading Instruction (CORI)—provide yet larger curricular frameworks for strategic comprehension instruction, but they also incorporate comprehension instruction activities that go beyond strategy development (e.g., vocabulary development, fluency practice, extensive reading). Both have been validated through multiple studies and both represent approaches that fully engage students in all aspects of strategic reading instruction (El-Dinary, 2002; Guthrie & Ozgungor, 2002; Guthrie and collaborators, 1996, 1998, 1999, 2000; Pressley, 2002c).

L2 reading research has not been developed extensively in the direction of strategic engagement with texts. Janzen (1996, 2001; Janzen & Stoller, 1998) reports results of L2 adaptations of Transactional Strategies Instruction and provides instructional descriptions. Klingner and Vaughn (2000) report on Collaborative Strategies Instruction specifically in an L2 context. Kern (2000) reports on applications of DR-TA to university foreign language instruction. Anderson (1999) and Cohen (1998) both discuss the effectiveness of direct teacher modeling of strategies for reading. Two L2 strategy-instruction approaches, Cognitive Academic Language Learning Approach, (CALLA; Chamot & O'Malley, 1994), and Strategy-Based Instruction (SBI; Cohen, 1998), could be adapted more specifically to an extended academic reading curriculum. Most of the L2 efforts to develop strategic engagement with texts have yet to be researched carefully for their effectiveness in promoting reading comprehension skills.

To summarize the current research on strategic reading instruction, most contemporary discussions among L1 researchers center on the use of and training in multiple strategies to achieve comprehension (commonly including summarizing, clarifying, predicting, imaging, forming questions, using prior knowledge, monitoring, and evaluating). As the multiple strategies research suggests, most researchers now see the real value in teaching strategies as combined-strategies instruction rather than as independent processes or as processes taught independently of basic comprehension with instructional texts (Baker, 2002; Duke & Pearson, 2002; Guthrie & Ozgungor, 2002; Pearson & Duke, 2002; Pressley 2000, 2002a, 2002b).

Build Reading Fluency and Rate

The importance of reading fluency has taken on much greater prominence in the past few years, particularly in L1 settings. Because reading fluency, as opposed to automatic word recognition, is not a commonly discussed factor in reading development, it is useful to provide a careful definition. Reading fluency involves both word recognition accuracy and automaticity; it requires a rapid speed of processing across extended text (i.e., reading efficiency); it makes appropriate use of prosodic and syntactic structures; it can be carried out for extended periods of time; and it takes a long time to develop (following Kuhn & Stahl, 2003; National Reading Panel, 2000; Segalowitz 2000).

The National Reading Panel (2000) devoted a major section of its report to research on fluency development and fluency instruction. Its meta-analysis demonstrates that fluency can be taught and that it has a positive impact on reading comprehension abilities. Kuhn and Stahl (2003), reporting on a more inclusive meta-analysis, come to similar conclusions. Almost any kind of independent or assisted repeated reading program, done carefully and appropriately, will have a direct positive effect on reading fluency and an indirect positive effect on comprehension improvement. There are many ways to develop re-reading instruction for fluency purposes, and they are well reviewed in Kuhn and Stahl (2003), National Reading Panel (2000), and Samuels (2002). Fluency instruction is also sometimes combined with other effective instructional practices. Stahl, Henbach, and Cramond (1996) reported on a combined curriculum of reading fluency, comprehension instruction, and extensive reading that demonstrated powerful positive effects for 14 second-grade L1 classrooms with low-proficiency readers (cf. Elley, 2000, below).

A further line of fluency research involves efforts to have students read under some amount of time pressure. Breznitz (1997; Breznitz & Share, 1992) has shown that with low-level grade 1 students, reading under mild time pressure increased reading efficiency and led to better text comprehension. Similar enhanced comprehension performance has been demonstrated by Walczyk, Kelly, Meche, and Braud (1999) with university freshmen students reading under mild time pressure. In this latter research, Walzcyk demonstrated both that fluency processes show a stronger relation to reading abilities when students read under time pressure and that their reading comprehension scores improved (cf. Meyer, Talbot, and Florencio,1999, for potentially contradictory findings).

There is little L2 reading research on reading fluency training, though this issue has recently emerged as a goal for instructional practices in L2 settings (Anderson, 1999; Hulstijn, 2001; Nation, 2001). L2 reading research should explore the best conditions and the best instructional practices that would support reading fluency development and at least provide indirect support for reading comprehension improvement.

Promote Extensive Reading

The true experimental research on extensive reading is seemingly contradictory, but the preponderance of nonexperimental research is overwhelmingly in favor of extensive reading as a support for both reading comprehension development and reading fluency (as well as incidental learning of a large recognition vocabulary and word recognition fluency). The L1 research reviewed by the National Reading Panel (2000) did not find a single experimental study (i.e., pre-and postmeasures for an experimental and control group) that demonstrated significantly better reading comprehension abilities for an extensive reading group. However, Kuhn and Stahl (2003), among others, have pointed out that the limited range of studies reviewed by the National Reading Panel ruled out much persuasive research. In fact, it is difficult to create experimental conditions in real educational settings that would control enough other variables for a sufficiently long period of time to ascertain the true independent influence of extensive reading on comprehension abilities.

Kuhn and Stahl point out that there is good evidence for a strong relationship between reading comprehension abilities and extensive reading over a long period of time. This view is strongly supported by two specific research programs. Over a decade from 1990 to 2000, Stanovich (see Stanovich, 2000) and his colleagues have demonstrated in multiple studies that the amount of people's overall exposure to print has a direct relation to vocabulary knowledge and comprehension abilities. Strong arguments have also been made by Guthrie, et al. (1999). In an important study, they demonstrated that, for students from grades 3 to 10 (grades 3, 5, 8, and 10), amount of reading significantly predicted text comprehension.

In L2 settings, Elley (2000) provides the strongest ongoing evidence for the effect of extensive reading (and fluency training), although he reviews book flood approaches that also include a range of additional instructional practices, and not just the effect of extensive reading. Reporting on a series of large-scale curricular research studies, he has demonstrated that modified book floods—along with careful attention to training teachers to use the books effectively in class— lead consistently to significant results in comprehension development (reporting on major studies in Niue, Fiji, Singapore, Sri Lanka, South Africa, and Solomon Islands, 1977–1998). There are a number of additional brief reports and small-scale studies on the effectiveness of extensive reading, but there are no other major research studies that provide strong evidence for the influence of extensive reading on reading comprehension abilities (see Day & Bamford, 1998). Further research in this area would be welcome.

Develop Intrinsic Motivation for Reading

In L1 settings, the strongest evidence of the direct impact of positive motivation on reading comes from Guthrie and his colleagues. In two studies, they demonstrated the impact of reading engagement on both reading amount (reading extensively) and reading comprehension. First, Wigfield and Guthrie (1997) demonstrated that motivation and engagement with reading were significantly related to amount of reading. More highly motivated fourth- and fifth-grade students engaged in significantly more reading. In a further study, Guthrie et al. (1999) demonstrated that higher motivation among third- and fifth-grade students significantly increased their amount of reading and their text comprehension. In examining related questions of whether or not motivation (defined as reading engagement) could be taught directly through classroom instruction, Guthrie and colleagues (1996, 1998) have demonstrated that Concept-Oriented Reading Instruction (CORI) developed significantly higher levels of student motivation than control classes among third- and fifth-grade students.

Schiefele (1999), focusing more specifically on the concept of reader interest, demonstrated that personal interest (long-term intrinsic interest), as opposed to situation interest (temporary curiosity), is a significant predictor of comprehension and learning from texts. In a review of 22 studies, she demonstrates a moderate but consistent influence of personal interest on text learning. She relates her work to motivation as a more general construct and argues persuasively that motivation is a major independent factor influencing reading abilities.

In L2 settings, there is little research specifically on the relation between motivational variables and reading comprehension. Most L2 motivation research focuses more generally on language abilities. Dörnyei (2001) provides an excellent overview of motivational factors and their influences on L2 learning. In addition to covering L2 motivation research for the past decade, he devotes serious attention to motivation instruction and teacher motivation (see also Guthrie & McCann, 1997; Ruddell & Unrau, 1997, for L1 views on teaching for reading motivation).

Plan a Coherent Curriculum for Student Learning

In both L1 and L2 settings, there are many discussions of how to develop a coherent effective curriculum for improving reading comprehension. However, there are few research studies carried out to support the stronger claims of various instructional approaches. This mismatch is not surprising. It is very difficult to control enough of the possible confounding variables in quasi-experimental studies of sufficient duration to assess curricular effectiveness. In L1 settings, many researchers have been stressing the importance of coherent integrated curricula that combine content and comprehension instruction (Block & Pressley, 2002; Guthrie, 2003; Pressley, 2002c).

In L1 settings, there are two general curricular approaches that have demonstrated significant improvement in reading comprehension in comparison to control groups. Transactional Strategies Instruction (TSI), noted earlier, provides a general curricular approach to content and reading learning (for grades 1–6), emphasizing strategic engagement with text for improved comprehension. A carefully designed study (Brown, Pressley, Van Meter, & Schuder, 1996) provides direct support for this approach. The extensive research on CORI (Content-Oriented Reading Instruction) successes (in grades 3–6) represents the most powerful case for the effectiveness of a coherent integrated curriculum that teaches content and reading comprehension in major thematic units throughout the school year (e.g., Guthrie, 2003).

In L2 settings, there are not yet any comparable large-scale studies that demonstrate empirically the effectiveness of content and reading curricula. The limited research on effective integrated content and language curricula to date is reviewed in Stoller (this volume). Despite the limited evidence for a coherent integrated reading curriculum, the logic of the evidence reviewed in this chapter makes a compelling case for the development of coherent L2 curricula. How else can a student efficiently develop all the appropriate skills, strategies, metacognitive awareness, and knowledge integration that will lead to major gains in reading comprehension abilities?

From Research to Instruction

In reviewing the research that supports instructional practices for reading comprehension, three issues deserve mention. First, L1 and L2 reading abilities are similar enough in terms of cognitive processing skills that L2 researchers and practitioners can draw on—but not accept wholesale—L1 instructional research when it seems appropriate to do so. At the same time, there are enough specific differences between L1 and L2 reading for this linkage to be a debatable issue (cf. Bernhardt, 2003; Koda, 2004). Differences in L2 language proficiency, orthographic systems, fluency, and processing abilities, as well as L1 transfer and interference factors, all suggest that L2 reading can be a distinct cognitive activity (particularly for older L2 students and EFL students). However, there is also sufficient evidence to suggest that many, if not most, of the effective instructional practices in L1 settings will also be effective in L2 settings (with reasonable adaptations). Whether L1 and L2 readers are actually engaging in cognitive processing in the same ways, or with the same combinations of component-skills strengths, while reading is an issue that requires its own review article (see Akamatsu, 2002, 2003; Bernhardt, 2000; Chiappe, Siegal, & Wade-Woolley, 2002; Droop & Verhoeven, 2003; Geva & Wang, 2001; Koda, 2004; Segalowitz, 2003; Verhoeven, 2000; Wade-Woolley, 1999).

A second issue that arises when research suggests the influence of specific skills and abilities on reading is whether these specific abilities develop first or overall good reading comprehension develops first. There are enough true experimental studies that involve training to reach a general conclusion that being a good reader often follows after early component abilities develop. However, it is also highly likely that overall reading abilities and specific component abilities have reciprocally causal relationships (e.g., vocabulary, phonological awareness, reading fluency). The key for establishing causal importance for component abilities is that specific instructional practices can then be supported in a reading curriculum. In several cases, the causal evidence is available from training studies; in other cases, such as vocabulary knowledge, the lack of direct causal evidence does not diminish the obvious reciprocal causality between comprehension and vocabulary development.

A final issue for a review of instructional practices is the need to establish that important specific components of reading comprehension can be taught in effective ways as part of a coherent curriculum. There is more to the art of teaching and curriculum development than a useful list of objectives for a curriculum. How one progresses from a list of goals and objectives to an effective curriculum requires a different review entirely, though the research on CORI points out one strong path for reading instruction in an academic English environment (see also Stoller, this volume).

Conclusions

It is often the case that teachers, teacher trainers, and materials writers do not refer to research studies to support practices that they have seen "work for them" informally. As a result, there is a significant amount of practitioner knowledge built up in programs and classrooms around the world in support of specific instructional approaches. In many cases, this knowledge works well and supports students' reading development. In fact, many teachers and teacher trainers might say that they already know many of the points made in this review from their own classroom experiences and expertise in teaching reading. There is certainly a need to recognize practitioner knowledge, good teaching ideas, and positive instructional outcomes. Teachers cannot wait for "the definitive research study"; it will never happen in any case. At the same time, the informal notion of "doing what works," by itself, can limit progress with, and dissemination of, effective reading instruction. Practitioner knowledge is typically not open to comparisons and competition from new ideas (except fashions and bandwagons), and it is easily abused when teaching practices become fossilized or politicized.

The reasons to look for reliable evidence in support of instructional practices are to minimize some of the negative consequences of informal practitioner lore and be more effective in helping students develop as readers. Research studies do not guarantee such benefits, but they represent important ways to test instructional practices and search for more effective outcomes. The ideal for effective reading instruction, then, is a merging of practitioner knowledge and persuasive research support: Both are needed for effective instruction. It is an obvious cliché to say that more research on reading instruction is needed at this point. However, I have tried to highlight the fact that there is not enough research being done, particularly in L2 contexts, on the effectiveness of instructional practices and the direct effects of specific abilities on reading comprehension development.

Notes

1. I would like to thank Bill Crawford for reading over this manuscript and providing thoughtful comments.

2. The further question of what methods are most effective for vocabulary learning belongs in a review of vocabulary development and instruction (see Read, this volume).

ANNOTATED BIBLIOGRAPHY

Alderson, J. (2000). *Assessing reading*. New York: Cambridge University Press.

Bernhardt, E. B. (2000). Second language reading as a case study of reading scholarship in the 20th century. In M. Kamil, P. Mosenthal, P. D. Pearson & R. Barr (Eds.), *Handbook of reading research, Volume III* (pp. 791–811). Mahwah, NJ: Erlbaum.

These two overviews of L2 reading provide a strong foundation for current research agendas in L2 reading and strong insights into the nature of L2 reading development. They also provide interesting complementary perspectives on L2 reading theory.

Block, C., & Pressley, M. (Eds.). (2002). *Comprehension instruction: Research-based best practices*. New York: Guilford Press.

This is a very important edited volume on reading strategies and reading strategy instruction with articles by many of the leading people in L1 reading-education research. Strong arguments for effective reading strategies and combined strategy instruction are presented across multiple chapters. Almost all of the strategies and combined strategy practices mentioned in the present review are discussed in this volume.

Elley, W. (2000). The potential of book flooding for raising literacy levels. *International Review of Education*, 46, 233–255.

This article presents one of the more remarkable reviews of a quarter century of pioneering research. Elley's work on the strong positive effects of book floods and extensive reading on L2 reading and language skills development is documented through major curriculum research projects in the Pacific Islands, Sri Lanka, South Africa, and Singapore. This article provides the strongest evidence to date of the powerful effects of extensive reading for L2 students.

Guthrie, J. (2003). Concept-Oriented Reading Instruction. In A. Sweet & C. Snow (Eds.), *Rethinking reading comprehension* (pp. 115–140). New York: Guilford Press.

This chapter provides a review of almost a decade of work on Concept-Oriented Reading Instruction. In the very areas that it is typically so hard to document improvement empirically—motivation, extensive reading, curriculum innovation—the author has carried out persuasive research studies that should be read and considered carefully by anyone teaching reading or in charge of reading curriculum revisions.

Kuhn, M., & Stahl, S. (2003). Fluency: A review of development and remedial practices. *Journal of Educational Psychology*, 95, 3–21.

This review of research on reading fluency brings together much of the reliable research on fluency instruction and its impact on comprehension. The authors make persuasive arguments that both repeated reading practices and extensive reading are beneficial for reading comprehension development in L1 settings.

National Reading Panel. (2000). *Teaching children to read: An evidence based assessment of the scientific research literature on reading and its implications for reading instruction* (National Institute of Health Pub. No. 00-4769). Washington, DC: National Institute of Child Health and Human Development.

This review volume covers seven major areas of reading research and their impact on reading comprehension and reading instruction. Reviews cover research and instructional practices related to phonological awareness, phonics instruction, fluency, vocabulary, comprehension strategies, teacher education for reading teachers, and the use of computer technologies. The report has been the source of many subsequent discussions and it raises many important issues for future research, especially for L2 learners. It is also free by ordering on the web through the National Institute of Child Health and Human Development (NICHHD), at least in the United States.

Perfetti, C. (2003). The universal grammar of reading. *Scientific Studies of Reading*, 7, 3–24.

This article succinctly outlines a number of key findings and conclusions on the nature of reading, drawing on his research over the past decade. He presents a compelling argument that reading across all orthographies depends on certain universal processing mechanisms and resources. In particular, he emphasizes the idea that reading in every language involves learning how the writing system corresponds to the spoken language. The ways in which readers in each language employ these universal principles and resources may be a cause of processing differences cross-linguistically (and for L2 readers), but the resources themselves that are available for reading development do not seem to vary in dramatic ways.

OTHER REFERENCES

Akamatsu, N. (2002). A similarity in word-recognition procedures among second language readers with different first language backgrounds. *Applied Psycholinguistics*, 23, 117–133.

Akamatsu, N. (2003). The effects of first language orthographic features on second language reading in texts. *Language Learning*, 53, 207–231.

Alderson, C. (1993). The relationship between grammar and reading in an English for academic purposes test battery. In D. Douglas & C. Chapelle (Eds.), *A new decade of language testing research: Selected papers from the 1990 Language Testing Research Colloquium* (pp. 203–219). Alexandria, VA: TESOL.

Anderson, N. (1999). *Exploring second language reading*. Boston: Heinle & Heinle.

Baker, L. (2002). Metacognition in comprehension instruction. In C. Block & M. Pressley (Eds.), *Comprehension instruction: Research-based best practices* (pp. 77–95). New York: Guilford Press.

Bamford, J., & Day, R. (1998). Teaching reading. *Annual Review of Applied Linguistics*, 18, 124–141.

Beck, I., Perfetti, C., & McKeown, M. (1982). The effects of long-term vocabulary instruction on lexical access and reading comprehension. *Journal of Educational Psychology*, *74*, 506–521.

Bernhardt, E. B. (1991). *Reading development in a second language.* Norwood, NJ: Ablex.

Bernhardt, E. B. (2003). Challenges to reading research from a multilingual world. *Reading Research Quarterly*, *38*, 112–117.

Breznitz, Z. (1997). Enhancing the reading of dyslexic children by reading acceleration and auditory masking. *Journal of Educational Psychology*, *89*, 103–113.

Breznitz, Z., & Share, D. (1992). Effects of accelerated reading rate on memory for text. *Journal of Educational Psychology*, *84*, 193–199.

Brown, R. (2002). Straddling two worlds: Self-directed comprehension instruction for middle schoolers. In C. Block & M. Pressley (Eds.), *Comprehension instruction: Research-based best practices* (pp. 337–350). New York: Guilford Press.

Brown, R., Pressley, M., Van Meter, P., & Schuder, T. (1996). A quasi-experimental validation of transactional strategy instruction with low-achieving second-grade readers. *Journal of Educational Psychology*, *88*, 18–37.

Carrell, P. (1984). The effects of rhetorical organization on ESL readers. *TESOL Quarterly*, *18*, 441–469.

Carrell, P., Pharis, B., & Liberto, J. (1989). Metacognitive strategy training for ESL reading. *TESOL Quarterly*, *23*, 647–678.

Carver, R. (2000). *The causes of high and low reading achievement.* Mahwah, NJ: Erlbaum.

Carver, R. (2003). The highly lawful relationships among pseudoword decoding, word identification, spelling, listening, and reading. *Scientific Studies of Reading*, *7*, 127–154.

Chamot, A., & O'Malley, M. (1994). *The CALLA handbook.* Reading, MA: Addison-Wesley.

Chiappe, P., Siegal, L., & Wade-Woolley, L. (2002). Linguistic diversity and the development of reading skills: A longitudinal study. *Scientific Studies of Reading*, *6*, 369–400.

Chen, H-C., & Graves, M. (1995). Effects of previewing and providing background knowledge on Taiwanese college students' comprehension of American short stories. *TESOL Quarterly*, *29*, 663–686.

Chu, H. J., Swaffar, J., & Charney, D. (2002). Cultural representations of rhetorical conventions: The effects on reading recall. *TESOL Quarterly*, *36*, 511–541.

Cohen, A. D. (1998). *Strategies in learning and using a second language.* New York: Longman.

Comings, J., Garner, B., & Smith, C. (Eds.). (2000–2002). *Annual Review of Adult Learning & Literacy* [3 vols]. San Francisco: Jossey-Bass.

Curtis, M., & Longo, A. (1999). *When adolescents can't read: Methods and materials that work.* Cambridge, MA: Brookline Books.

Davidson, R., & Strucker, J. (2002). Patterns of word recognition errors among adult basic education native and non-native speakers of English. *Scientific Studies of Reading*, *6*, 299–

316.

Day, R., & Bamford, J. (1998). *Extensive reading in the second language.* New York: Cambridge University Press.

Dörnyei, Z. (2001). *Teaching and researching motivation.* New York: Longman.

Droop, M., & Verhoeven, L. (2003). Language proficiency and reading ability in first and second language learners. *Reading Research Quarterly, 38,* 78–103.

Duke, N., & Pearson, P.D. (2002). Effective practices for developing reading comprehension. In A. Farstrup & S. Samuels (Eds.), *What research has to say about reading instruction* (3rd ed.) (pp. 205–242). Newark, DE: International Reading Association.

Dymock, S. (1999). Learning about text structure. In G. B. Thompson & T. Nicholson (Eds.), *Learning to read: Beyond phonics and whole language* (pp. 174–192). New York: Teachers College Press.

El-Dinary, P. B. (2002). Challenges of implementing transactional strategies instruction for reading comprehension. In C. Block & M. Pressley (Eds.), *Comprehension instruction: Research-based best practices* (pp. 201–215). New York: Guilford Press.

Elley, W. (2001). Literacy in the present world: Realities and possibilities. In. L. Verhoeven & C. Snow (Eds.), *Literacy and motivation* (pp. 225–242). Mahwah, NJ: Erlbaum.

Enright, M., Bridgeman, B., Cline, M., Eignor, D., Lee, Y. W., & Powers, D. (2002, April). Evaluating measures of communicative language abilities. Paper presented at annual TESOL Convention. Salt Lake City, UT.

Fender, M. (2001). A review of L1 and L2/ESL word integration skills and the nature of L2/ESL word integration development involved in lower-level text processing. *Language Learning, 51,* 319–396.

Fender, M. (2003). English word recognition and word integration skills of native Arabic- and Japanese-speaking learners of English as a second language. *Applied Psycholinguistics, 24,* 289–315.

Fukkink, R., Hulstijn, J., & Simis, A. (2003). *Does training of second-language word recognition skills affect reading comprehension? An experimental study.* Submitted manuscript.

Geva, E., & Siegal, L. (2000). Orthographic and cognitive factors in the concurrent development of basic reading skills in two languages. *Reading and Writing: An Interdisciplinary Journal, 12,* 1–30.

Geva, E., & Verhoeven, L. (2000). Introduction: The development of second language reading in primary children—Research issues and trends. *Scientific Studies in Reading, 4,* 261–266.

Geva, E., & Wang, M. (2001). The development of basic reading skills in children: A cross-language perspective. *Annual Review of Applied Linguistics, 21,* 182–204.

Goldman, S., & Rakestraw, J. (2000). Structural aspects of constructing meaning from text.

In M. Kamil, P. Mosenthal, P. D. Pearson & R. Barr (Eds.), *Handbook of reading research. Volume III* (pp. 311–335). Mahwah, NJ: Erlbaum.

Grabe, W. (1997). Discourse analysis and reading instruction. In T. Miller (Ed.), *Functional approaches to written texts: Classroom applications* (pp. 2–15). Washington, DC: USIA.

Grabe, W. (2000). Reading research and its implications for reading assessment. In A. Kunnan (Ed.), *Fairness and validation in language assessment* (Studies in Language Testing 9, pp. 226–262). Cambridge: Cambridge University Press.

Grabe, W. (2003). Using discourse patterns to improve reading comprehension. In K. Hill (Ed.), *Proceeding of the 2002 JALT Conference* (pp. 9–16). Tokyo: JALT Publications.

Grabe, W., & Stoller, F. (2002). *Teaching and researching reading*. New York: Longman.

Guthrie, J., & McCann, A. (1997). Characteristics of classrooms that promote motivations and strategies for learning. In J. Guthrie & A. Wigfield (Eds.), *Reading engagement: Motivating readers through integrated instruction* (pp. 128–148). Newark, DE: International Reading Association.

Guthrie, J., & Ozgungor, S. (2002). Instructional contexts for reading engagement. In C. Block & M. Pressley (Eds.), *Comprehension instruction: Research-based best practices* (pp. 275–288). New York: Guilford Press.

Guthrie, J., Van Meter, P., Hancock, G., McCann, A., Anderson, E., & Alao, S. (1998). Does Concept-Oriented Reading Instruction increase strategy use and conceptual learning from text? *Journal of Educational Psychology, 90*, 261–278.

Guthrie, J., Van Meter, P., McCann, A., Wigfield, A., Bennett, L., Poundstone, C., Rice, M., Faibisch, F., Hunt, B., & Mitchell, A. (1996). Growth in literacy engagement: Changes in motivations and strategies during Concept-Oriented Reading Instruction. *Reading Research Quarterly, 31*, 306–332.

Guthrie, J., Wigfield, A., Metsala, J., & Cox, K. (1999). Motivational and cognitive predictors of text comprehension and reading amount. *Scientific Studies of Reading, 3*, 231–256.

Guthrie, J., Wigfield, A., & Von Secker, C. (2000). Effects of integrated instruction on motivation and strategy use in reading. *Journal of Educational Psychology, 92*, 331–341.

Hudson, T. (1998). Theoretical perspectives on reading. *Annual Review of Applied Linguistics, 18*, 43–60.

Hulstijn, J. (1997). Mnemonic methods in foreign language vocabulary learning. In J. Coady & T. Huckin (Eds.), *Second language vocabulary acquisition* (pp. 203–224). New York: Cambridge University Press.

Hulstijn, J. (2001). Intentional and incidental second language vocabulary learning: A reappraisal of elaboration, rehearsal and automaticity. In P. Robinson (Ed.), *Cognition and second language instruction* (pp. 258–286). New York: Cambridge University Press.

Janzen, J. (1996). Teaching strategic reading. *TESOL Journal, 6* (1), 6–9.

Janzen, J. (2001). Strategic reading on a sustained content theme. In J. Murphy & P. Byrd (Eds.), *Understanding the courses we teach: Local perspectives on English language teaching* (pp. 369–389). Ann Arbor: The University of Michigan Press.

Janzen, J., & Stoller, F. (1998). Integrating strategic reading into L2 instruction. *Reading in a Foreign Language, 12* (1), 251–269.

Kamil, M., Mosenthal, P., Pearson, P. D., & Barr, R. (Eds.). (2000). *Handbook of reading research, Volume III*. Mahwah, NJ: Erlbaum.

Kern, R. (2000). *Literacy and language teaching*. New York: Oxford University Press.

Klingner, J., & Vaughn, S. (2000). The helping behaviors of fifth graders while using collaborative strategic reading during ESL content classes. *TESOL Quarterly, 34*, 69–98.

Koda, K. (1996). L2 word recognition research: A critical review. *Modern Language Journal, 80*, 450–460.

Koda, K. (2004). *Insights into second language reading*. New York: Cambridge University Press.

Kroll, J., Michael, E., Tokowicz, N., & Dufour, R. (2002). The development of lexical fluency in a second language. *Second Language Research, 18*, 137–171.

Laufer, B. (1997). The lexical plight in second language reading: Words you don't know, words you think you know, and words you can't guess. In J. Coady & T. Huckin (Eds.), *Second language vocabulary acquisition* (pp. 20–34). New York: Cambridge University Press.

Levy, B., Abello, B., & Kysynchuk, L. (1997). Transfer from word training to reading in context: Gains in reading fluency and comprehension. *Learning Disability Quarterly, 20*, 173–188.

McKeown, M., Beck, I., Omanson, R., & Pople, M. (1985). Some effects of the nature and frequency of vocabulary instruction on the knowledge and use of words. *Reading Research Quarterly, 20*, 522–535.

Meyer, B., Talbot, A., & Florencio, D. (1999). Reading rate and prose retrieval. *Scientific Studies of Reading, 3*, 303–329.

Meyer, B., & Poon, L. (2001). Effects of structure strategy training and signaling on recall of texts. *Journal of Educational Psychology, 93*, 141–159.

Mohan, B. (1986). *Language and content*. Reading, MA: Addison-Wesley.

Muter, V., & Diethelm, K. (2001). The contribution of phonological skills and letter knowledge to early reading development in a multilingual population. *Language Learning, 51*, 187–219.

Nation, I. S. P. (2001). *Learning vocabulary in another language*. New York: Cambridge University Press.

Nation, I. S. P. (2002). Vocabulary. In D. Nunan (Ed.), *Practical English language education* (pp. 129–152). New York: McGraw-Hill.

Nicholson, T., & Tan, A. (1999). Proficient word identification for comprehension. In G.

Thompson & T. Nicholson (Eds.), *Learning to read: Beyond phonics and whole language* (pp. 150–173). New York: Teachers College Press.

Noordman, L., & Vonk, W. (1999). Discourse comprehension. In A. Friederici (Ed.), *Language comprehension: A biological perspective* (pp. 229–263). New York: Springer.

Pearson, P. D., & Duke, N. (2002). Comprehension instruction in the primary grades. In C. Block & M. Pressley (Eds.), *Comprehension instruction: Research-based best practices* (pp. 247–258). New York: Guilford Press.

Perfetti, C. (1985). Reading ability. New York: Oxford University Press. Perfetti, C. (1999). Comprehending written language: A blueprint for the reader. In C. Brown & P. Hagoort (Eds.), *Neurocognition of language* (pp. 167–208). Oxford: Oxford University Press.

Perfetti, C., Van Dyke, J., & Hart, L. (2001). The psycholinguistics of basic literacy. *Annual Review of Applied Linguistics, 21*, 127–149.

Perkins, K. (1998). Assessing reading. *Annual Review of Applied Linguistics, 18*, 208–218.

Pichette, F., Segalowitz, N., & Connors, K. (2003). Impact of maintaining L1 reading skills on L2 reading skill development in adults: Evidence from speakers of Serbo-Croatian learning French. *Modern Language Journal, 87*, 391–403.

Pike, L. (1979). *An evaluation of alternative item formats for testing English as a foreign language.* TOEFL Research Reports, No. 2. Princeton, NJ: Educational Testing Service.

Pressley, M. (2000). What should comprehension instruction be the instruction of? In M. Kamil, P. Mosenthal, P. D. Pearson, & R. Barr (Eds.), *Handbook of reading research* (Vol. 3, pp. 545–561). Mahwah, NJ: Erlbaum.

Pressley, M. (2002a). Comprehension strategy instruction: A turn-of-the-century status report. In C. Block & M. Pressley (Eds.), *Comprehension instruction: Research-based best practices* (pp. 11–27). New York: Guilford Press.

Pressley, M. (2002b). Metacognition and self-regulated instruction. In A. Farstrup & S. Samuels (Eds.), *What research has to say about reading instruction* (3rd ed.) (pp. 291–309). Newark, DE: International Reading Association.

Pressley, M. (2002c). *Reading instruction that works* (2nd ed.). New York: Guilford Press.

Qian, D. (2002). Investigating the relationship between vocabulary knowledge and academic reading performance: An assessment perspective. *Language Learning, 52*, 513–536.

Read, J. (this volume). Research in teaching vocabulary.

Robinson, P. (Ed.). (2001). *Cognition and second language instruction.* New York: Cambridge University Press.

Ruddell, R., & Unrau, N. (1997). The role of responsive teaching in focusing reader intention and developing reading motivation. In J. Guthrie & A. Wigfield (Eds.), *Reading engagement: Motivating readers through integrated instruction* (pp. 102–125). Newark, DE: International Reading Association.

Samuels, S. (2002). Reading fluency: Its development and assessment. In A. Farstrup & S. Samuels (Eds.), *What research has to say about reading instruction* (3rd ed.), (pp. 166–183). Newark, DE: International Reading Association.

Schiefele, U. (1999). Interest and learning from text. *Scientific Studies of Reading, 3*, 257–279.

Schoonen, R., Hulstijn, J., Bossers, B. (1998). Metacognitive and language-specific knowledge in native and foreign language reading comprehension: An empirical study among Dutch students in grades 6, 8 and 10. *Language Learning, 48*, 71–106.

Segalowitz, N. (1991). Does advanced skill in a second language reduce automaticity in the first language. *Language Learning*, 41, 59–83.

Segalowitz, N. (2000). Automaticity and attentional skill in fluent performance. In H. Riggenbach (Ed.), *Perspectives on fluency* (pp. 200–219). Ann Arbor: University of Michigan Press.

Segalowitz, N. (2003). Automaticity and second language development. In C. Doughty & M. Long (Eds.), *The handbook of second language acquisition* (pp. 382–408). Oxford: Blackwell.

Segalowitz, N., & Hulstijn, J. (In press). Automaticity in bilingualism and second language learning. In J. F. Kroll & A. M. B. De Groot (Eds.), *Handbook of bilingualism: Psycholinguistic approaches*.

Segalowitz, S., Segalowitz, N., & Wood, A. (1998). Assessing the development of automaticity in second language word recognition. *Applied Psycholinguistics, 19*, 53–67.

Shanahan, T. (2002). What reading research says: The promises and limitations of applying research to reading education. In S. Samuels & A. Farstrup (Eds.), *What research has to say about reading instruction* (2nd ed.), (pp. 8–24). Newark, DE: International Reading Association.

Shaywitz, S. (2003). *Overcoming dyslexia*. New York: Knopf.

Snow, C., Burns, S., & Griffin, P. (1998). *Preventing reading difficulties in young children*. Washington, DC: National Academy Press.

Stahl, S., Heubach, K., & Cramond, P. (1997). *Fluency-oriented reading instruction* (Reading Research Report No. 79). Athens, GA: National Reading Research Center.

Stanovich, K. (2000). *Progress in understanding reading: Scientific foundations and new frontiers*. New York: Guilford Press.

Stoller, F. (this volume). Content-based instruction: Perspectives on curriculum. planning.

Tan, A., & Nicholson, T. (1997). Flashcards revisited: Training poor readers to read words faster improves their comprehension of texts. *Journal of Educational Psychology, 89*, 276–288.

Tang, G. (1992). The effect of graphic representation of knowledge structures on ESL reading comprehension. *Studies in Second Language Acquisition, 14*, 177–195.

Thorndike, R. L. (1973). *Reading comprehension education in 15 countries*. Stockholm:

Almquist & Wiksell.

Torgesen, J. (2002). The prevention of reading difficulties. *Journal of School Psychology, 40*, 7–26.

Torgesen, J., Alexander, A., Wagner, R., Rashotte, C., Voeller, K., Conway, T., et al. (2001). Intensive remedial instruction for children with severe reading disabilities. *Journal of Learning Disabilities, 34*, 33–58.

Trabasso, T., & Bouchard, E. (2002). Teaching readers how to comprehend text strategically. In C. Collins & M. Pressley (Eds.), *Comprehension instruction: Research-based best practices* (pp. 176–200). New York: Guilford Press.

Vacca, R. (2002). Making a difference in adolescent school lives: Visible and invisible aspects of content area reading. In A. Farstrup & S. J. Samuels (Eds.), *What research has to say about reading instruction* (3rd ed.), (pp. 124–139). Newark, DE: International Reading Association.

van Gelderen, A., Schoonen, R., Hulstijn, J., Snellings, P., Simis, A., & Stevenson, M. (2002). *Roles of linguistic knowledge, metacognitive knowledge and processing speed in L3, L2 and L1 reading comprehension.* Submitted manuscript.

Verhoeven, L. (2000). Components of early second language reading and spelling. *Scientific Studies of Reading, 4*, 313–330.

Wade-Woolley, L. (1999). First language influences on second language word reading: All roads lead to Rome. *Language Learning, 49*, 447–471.

Wagner, D., & Venezky, R. (1999). Adult literacy: The next generation. *Educational Researcher, 28* (1), 1–9.

Walczyk, J., Kelly, K., Meche, S., & Braud, H. (1999). Time limitations enhance reading comprehension. *Contemporary Educational Psychology, 24*, 156–165.

Wigfield, A., & Guthrie, J. (1997). Relations of children's motivations for reading to the amount and breadth of their reading. *Journal of Educational Psychology, 89*, 420–432.

Wolf, M. (Ed.). (2001). *Time, fluency and dyslexia.* Parkton, MD: York.

4. RESEARCH IN TEACHING WRITING

Tony Silva and Colleen Brice

On the basis of our examination of L2 writing scholarship published between 2000 and the present, we describe and reflect on developments relating to the teaching of L2 writing. While our primary focus is applied research, we have also addressed basic research that has clear implications for pedagogy. The paper includes an overview of relevant basic research (i.e., research on the phenomenon of second language writing), a discussion of relevant applied research (i.e., research on second language writing instructional principles and practices), an examination of some general issues and concerns that have important implications for second language writing instruction, and an assessment of the current status of the field along with our thoughts on where it might go in the future.

It is an exciting time to be working in the area of second language writing. Due partly to globalization and the subsequent need to communicate via computer, second language writing has become an important if not dominant focus of work in second language studies. Additionally, second language writing scholarship, in responding to the current situation, has increased its breadth and depth and has begun to break free from the constraints imposed on it by its parent disciplines, applied linguistics and composition studies, vis-à-vis theory, research, and instruction. In short, the study of second language writing has become a legitimate area of inquiry in its own right. We have come to these conclusions partly as a result of the review of current research on the teaching of second language writing that was done in preparation for writing this chapter.

In this chapter, we review and reflect on developments in second language writing instruction over the last three to four years—though we sometimes address earlier work to provide contextual information for current studies. The scholarship we report on here focuses primarily on applied research, but we have also included basic research which has clear implications for pedagogy—as any principled discussion of teaching must take into account research and theory. To make our task manageable, we have limited ourselves to looking at published work—specifically, refereed journal articles, book chapters, and books; we have not addressed here scholarship in the form of dissertations, ERIC documents, or in-house publications. We have attempted to be comprehensive, but inevitably things get left out: We apologize in advance for any omissions.[1] We will (1) briefly address relevant basic research (i.e., research on the phenomenon of second language writing); (2) discuss applied research (i.e., research on second language writing instructional principles and practices); (3) examine some general issues and concerns that have important implications for second language writing instruction, but that do not fit in the first two categories; and (4) conclude with an assessment of the current status of the field and our thoughts on where it might go in the future.[2]

Review of Research

Basic Research

Composing processes. Work on composing has intensified and taken on greater depth and breadth. While general composing processes (Fukao & Fujii, 2001; Lally, 2000a; Sasaki, 2002; Zhu, 2001b) and comparisons of first and second language composing (Chenoweth & Hayes, 2001; Lally, 2000b; Roca de Larios & Murphy, 2001; Thorson, 2000) are still issues of interest, work on subprocesses has increased and become more sophisticated. These subprocesses include revising (Kobayashi & Rinnert, 2001; Miller, 2000; Sengupta, 2000; Sze, 2002), formulating (Roca de Larios, Marín, & Murphy, 2001; Zimmerman, 2000), pausing (Miller, 2000; Sasaki, 2000), reviewing and annotation of text (Cresswell, 2000), backtracking (Manchón, Roca de Larios, & Murphy, 2000a), text generation (Armengol-Castells, 2001; Chenoweth & Hayes, 2001), idea generation (Lally, 2000a), task representation (Ruiz-Funes, 2001), noticing (Qi & Lapkin, 2001), and summarizing (Yang & Shi, 2003).

Variables seen to affect composing have also received more attention. These include the use of the L1 in L2 writing (Aidman, 2002; Brooks-Carson & Cohen, 2000; Lally, 2000a; Wang & Wen, 2002; Woodall, 2002); L2 proficiency (Kobayashi & Rinnert, 2001; Manchón, Roca de Larios, & Murphy, 2000b; Wang & Wen, 2002; Woodall, 2002); writing fluency (Chenoweth & Hayes, 2001; Hatasa & Soeda, 2000; Miller, 2000; Sasaki, 2000); the use of learning and writing strategies (Ching, 2002; Khaldieh, 2000; Olivares-Cuhat, 2002; Sasaki, 2000); textual quality and complexity (Sasaki, 2000); text pattern knowledge (Schindler, 2000); linguistic experience (Chenoweth & Hayes, 2001); writing experience (Kobayashi & Rinnert, 2001); writing tasks (Wang & Wen, 2002); task difficulty (Woodall, 2002); writing skill level (e.g., expert vs. novice); (Sasaki, 2000); medium of composing (Y.-J. Lee, 2002); writing anxiety (Cheng, 2002); writer goals (Cumming, Bush, & Zho, 2002); linguistic knowledge, metacognitive knowledge, and retrieval speed (Schoonen et al., 2002); and age of exposure to an L2 (Arrecco & Ransdell, 2002).

Perhaps the most interesting and important trend in work on composing relates to the contexts in which it is done. Work in FL (as opposed to SL) contexts is now clearly dominant. This includes EFL writing in Spain (Armengol-Castells, 2001; Manchón, Roca de Larios, & Murphy, 2000a, 2000b; Roca de Larios, Marín, & Murphy, 2001), Japan (Fukao & Fujii, 2001; Kobayashi & Rinnert, 2001; Sasaki, 2000, 2002), Hong Kong (Sengupta, 2000), Germany (Zimmerman, 2000), China (Wang & Wen, 2002), Italy (Cresswell, 2000), Bulgaria (Rainville, 2000), and Malaysia (Ching, 2002). It also includes FL writing in French (Chenoweth & Hayes, 2001; Lally, 2000, 2000b), Spanish (Ruiz-Funes, 2001), German (Chenoweth & Hayes, 2001; Thorson, 2000), and Arabic (Khaldieh, 2000) in North America; Japanese as foreign language in Australia (Hatasa & Soeda, 2000); and French as a foreign language in Germany (Schindler, 2000). In addition, an extensive bibliography (Silva, Brice, Kapper, Matsuda, & Reichelt, 2001) and literature reviews (Manchón, 2001b; Roca de Larios, Marin, & Murphy, 2001) on L2 composing processes and an analysis of the socially mediated nature of L2 comparing processes (Roca de Larios & Murphy, 2001) have been produced.

Written texts. While work on text is still dominant in the literature, within textual studies there is a trend toward greater variety with regard to foci, context, genre, and level. Local foci include cohesive devices (Biesenbach-Lucas, Meloni, & Weasenforth, 2000; Hinkel, 2001, 2002a; Liu, 2000; Zhang, 2000), coherence-creating devices (Lee, 2002a, 2002b), error analysis (Coates, Sturgeon, Bohannan, & Pasini, 2002; Feng, Ogata, & Yano, 2000; Khuwaileh & Shoumali, 2000), syntactic features (Gallagher & McCabe, 2001; Grant & Ginther, 2000; Hinkel, 2002a, 2003; Huie & Yahya, 2003; K. Hyland, 2000a, 2000b, 2002a, 2002b, 2002d, 2002f), and lexical features (Jarvis, 2002; Okamura & Shaw, 2000; Reynolds, 2002). Global foci include obliqueness—reflecting a failure to address the writing task (Chandrasegaran, 2000), communication strategies (Chimbganda, 2000), organizational patterns (L. Flowerdew, 2000b; Hirose, 2003), genre awareness (Ramanathan & Kaplan, 2000), topical structure (Simpson, 2000), textual features related to individualism and collectivism (Wu & Rubin, 2000), the pragmatics of letter writing (Al-Khatib, 2001), genre-based instruction (Cargill, Cadman, & McGowan, 2001; K. Hyland, 2002c, 2003; Weber, 2001), rhetorical strategies (Garcia, 2001), and written discourse analysis (Kaplan & Grabe, 2002).

The contexts for textual work reflect a move from SL to FL and from North America to outside North America. Even though most of the scholarship addresses texts written in English (EFL), this scholarship is being done in a wide variety of places, e.g., Australia (Cargill et al., 2001), Botswana (Chimbganda, 2000), China (Zhang, 2000), Ecuador (Thatcher, 2000), England (Thompson & Tribble, 2001), Finland (Jarvis, 2002), Hong Kong (Bruce, 2002; Candlin, Bhatia, & Jensen, 2002; L. Flowerdew, 2000b; K. Hyland, 2000a, 2000b, 2002a; Lee, 2002a, 2002b), Iran (Kiany & Khezri Nejad, 2001), Japan (Feng et al. 2000; Gallagher & McCabe, 2001; Hirose, 2003), Jordan (Al-Khatib, 2001; Khuwaileh & Shoumali, 2000), Korea (Kim, 2001), Luxembourg, (Weber, 2001), Mexico (Garcia, 2001), Singapore (Chandrasegaran, 2000), Spain (Gallagher & McCabe, 2001), and Taiwan (Wu & Rubin, 2000).

The genres examined in this work also vary greatly and reflect a move from the "general essay" to more particular genres and from school-sponsored writing to that done in "real-world" contexts. While the general essay continues to be focused on in classroom, laboratory, and testing situations, more frequently other genres are being used. These include e-mail (Biesenbach-Lucas et al., 2000); nursing notes (Parks, 2000) and care plans (Parks, 2001); personal letters (invitations) (Al-Khatib, 2001) and business letters (cover letters for manuscript submissions) (Okamura & Shaw, 2000); research proposals (Cargill et al., 2001); business manuals and auditing reports (Thatcher, 2000); formal legal essays (Weber, 2001) and legal problem answers (Bruce, 2002); theses, both undergraduate (Hyland, 2002a) and doctoral (Thomson & Tribble, 2001); medical research articles (Coates et al., 2002); narratives (Tickoo, 2000); autobiographies/personal narratives (Dyer & Friederich, 2002); project reports (L. Flowerdew, 2000b); published research articles (K. Hyland, 2002b, 2002e); textbooks (K. Hyland, 2002b, 2002e); and summaries (Kim, 2001; Rivard, 2001).

Assessment. Research on assessment in second language writing has expanded in scope over the past several years, going beyond a focus on results to consider a broad array of methodological, political, and ethical questions related to various stakeholders (testers, test takers, test users, and interpreters) and their roles in the assessment process. The relationships among raters' target language status (native versus nonnative), the ratings they assign, and their reasons for those ratings continue to be issues of interest, particularly in foreign language learning contexts—EFL in Japan (Cornwell & McKay, 2000; Rinnert & Kobayashi, 2001), Germany (Reichelt, 2003), and China (Shi, 2001); and foreign languages in the United States (Breiner-Sanders, Sender, & Terry, 2002), including German (Reichelt, 2003), French (Robinson, 2000), and Japanese (Kondo-Brown, 2002). A cross-cultural study (Reichelt, 2003) compared the rating criteria employed by teachers of German in two contexts: Germany and the United States. Similarly, research investigating the relationship between ratings assigned and different assessment modes and task types continues to grow. Modes examined include direct versus indirect assessment (Crusan, 2002), computerized text analysis versus human rating (Li, 2000a), portfolio-based assessment versus direct assessment (Brauer, 2000b; Song & August, 2002), and analytic versus holistic scoring (Bacha, 2001).

However, inquiry on L2 writing assessment has branched out to identify variables other than rater TL status and assessment mode that play salient roles in the assessment process. These variables include raters' prior experiences teaching and rating writing (Cumming, Kantor, & Powers, 2002; Erdosy, 2001; Hamp-Lyons, 2003; Turner & Upshur, 2002), the nature of the writing samples to be rated (Boldt, Valsecchi, & Weigle, 2001; Turner, 2000; Turner & Upshur, 2002; Weigle, Boldt, & Valsecchi, 2003), raters' biases toward particular types of writers and criteria (Kondo-Brown, 2002), topic familiarity (Stapleton, 2001), and even the purposes for L2 writing and L2writing instruction (e.g., general or specific) (Cumming, 2001b). To gain insight into the influence of these variables, researchers have shifted their attention from characteristics of the raters themselves to their rating processes, examining the thinking processes and behaviors they engage in while they actually rate student writing (Cumming, Kantor, & Powers, 2002; Erdosy, 2001) and collaborate with other raters to develop assessment scales for particular contexts (Turner, 2000).

Research in this area has also acknowledged the need for assessment to take into account the specific characteristics of the language learning and educational contexts. Two studies have described the development of assessment schemes for use with learners in specific contexts—Japanese students in EFL classes (Stewart, Rehorick, & Perry, 2001) and international students in intensive English for Academic Purposes courses in the United States (Wilhelm & Rivers, 2001). Cornwell and McKay (2000) describe the development and validation of a Daly Miller Writing Apprehension Test for EFL students in Japan. Another study (Escamilla & Coady, 2001) has argued for the need to develop context-sensitive writing assessment in bilingual Spanish–English courses.

Assessment for the purposes of placing students into and allowing students out of writing courses has also grown as a focus of inquiry. Researchers have studied the extent to which students' ability to perform in courses is predicted by different types or modes of assessment, including direct versus indirect placement testing (Crusan, 2002), direct exit tests (Braine, 2001b; Song & August, 2002), indirect proficiency tests (Kiany & Khezri Nejad, 2001), and portfolio-based exit assessment (Song & August, 2002). The results of these studies indicate that timed, direct essay tests seriously underpredict ESL students' abilities to write under natural conditions, holding them back, in some cases repeatedly. Such findings highlight the inherently political nature of writing assessment and raise important ethical questions for ESL teachers and testers (for additional perspectives on the political nature of assessment and implications for teachers, see Cumming, 2002; Currie, 2001; and Hamp-Lyons, 2001, 2002).

The students' perspective has also surfaced as an area of interest in assessment scholarship. Bacha (2002) and Basturkmen and Lewis (2002) have compared students' perceptions of their own achievement with their teachers' perceptions. Rating scales derived from student samples have been discussed (Turner & Upshur, 2002). In addition, two historical accounts of L2 writing assessment have been published (Hamp-Lyons, 2001, 2002) as well as an essay on the difficulties facing L2 writing assessment vis-à-vis the notion of standards (Cumming, 2001a).

Applied Research

Content-based writing instruction. The development and implementation of content based writing instruction programs has continued and flourished in recent years. Foci for such programs and courses include health—physical, emotional, and mental (Bailey, 2000); intellectual commentary (Bernard, 2000); psychology (Carson, 2000); applied linguistics literature (Casanave, 2003); critical thinking skills in engineering (L. Flowerdew, 2000a), academic and professional work (Pally, 2001); topics from students' fields (Hansen, 2000); material from a variety of disciplines—e.g., linguistics, environmental science, computer science (Kasper, 2000b); art history and film (Kirshner & Wexler, 2002); authentic science writing (Lang & Albertini, 2001); American history (Nelson & Burns, 2000); film and society (Pally, 2000a); and mystery novels (Heyden, 2001). In addition, Katznelson, Perpignan, and Rubin (2001) and Pally, Katznelson, Perpignan, and Rubin (2002) look at what they call by-products (changes students undergo as they develop writing skills in an academic course) of content based writing approaches. For more details on content-based writing instruction in L2 writing programs cited above, see Pally (2000b).

Voice and identity. Recent years have seen a revival of interest in matters of L2 writer voice and identity. A large part of this revival is a special issue of the *Journal of Second Language Writing* on voice in L2 writing edited by Belcher and Hirvela (2001c). In this issue, Ivanic and Camps (2001) argue that L2 student writers can use lexical, syntactic, organizational, and material aspects of writing to construct identity or voice. Matsuda (2001b) suggests that the notion of voice is not exclusively tied to individualism and shows different ways in which voice is constructed in Japanese and English. Prior (2001) argues for a view in which voice is simultaneously personal and social—this follows from his view of discourse as fundamentally historical, situated, and indexical. Hirvela and Belcher (2001) address a tendency in L2 writing instruction and research to overlook the voices and identities already possessed by L2 writers, especially at the graduate level. The special issue closes with Atkinson's (2001) response to the foregoing papers.

However, this special issue is not the only source of new work on voice and identity. K. Hyland (2002a, 2002d) examines the presence of authorial identity in academic writing via an analysis of L2 writers' personal pronoun use. Kells (2002) looks at ethnolinguistic identities and language attitudes of Mexican-American bilingual college writers. Russell and Yoo (2001) address subjectivity underlying students' investment in L2 writing. Stapleton (2002) critiques the notions of voice, authorial identity, and authorial presence and argues against their use as tools in L2 writing pedagogy. Vollmer (2002) argues for understanding L2 writing as active participation in the construction of discourse identity. Leki (2001b) talks about hearing voices—i.e., those of students enrolled in L2 writing courses.

Reading and writing. The connection between reading and writing also continues to be explored. Matsuda (2001a) chronicles the genesis of reading and writing in L2 studies. Grabe overviews the links between theory and practice (2001) and research and practice (2003) of the reading–writing relationship. Carson (2001) analyzes the tasks involved in reading and writing in undergraduate and graduate courses, and Leki (2001c) examines different approaches to linking reading and writing instruction. Abu Rass (2001) describes the design of an integrated reading and writing course; Chen (2001) calls for continued inclusion of models in L2 writing instruction; and Dobson and Feak (2001) offer a cognitive modeling approach to teaching L2 writers to critique nonliterary text. For more detail on some of the aforementioned texts, see Belcher and Hirvela (2001a, 2001b).

Computers and technology. The use of computers and technology is rapidly expanding in second and foreign language writing pedagogy, and correspondingly, research in this area has seen dramatic growth. In the past four years, more than two dozen publications have addressed issues related to the use of technology in L2 composition, and these studies have focused on a wide variety of contexts, including EFL situations—in Sweden (Sullivan & Lindgren, 2002), Hong Kong (Braine, 2001a; Li, 2000b), Korea (Suh, 2002), Taiwan (Liaw & Johnson, 2001), Japan (Fedderholdt, 2001; Feng et al., 2000; Greene, 2000; Stapleton, 2003), and Singapore (Yuan, 2003); ESL situations—in Canada (Li & Cumming, 2001) and in the United States (Biesenbach-Lucas et al., 2000; Bloch, 2002; Kasper, 2002; Lam, 2000)—as well as Spanish (González-Bueno & Pérez, 2000) and German (Abrams, 2001; Thorson, 2000) FL contexts in the United States. In addition, self-initiated writing involving technology has been studied outside the classroom (Lam, 2000).

Computer software has been developed to identify and correct typical collocational errors (Shei & Pain, 2000) and morphological errors (Feng et al., 2000) in L2 writing. In addition, software that is able to tag linguistic features at the discourse, sentence, and word levels has been employed to analyze differences in writing at different proficiency levels (Grant & Ginther, 2000), and software that traces writers' keystrokes has been used to study writers' composing and revision processes (Sullivan & Lindgren, 2002; Thorson, 2000; Warden, 2000). The major focus in the research, however, is the examination of the effects of various technologies on the quality, quantity, and processes of L2 writing. This work has compared the effects of word-processed and e-mail–generated texts on language use (Biesenbach-Lucas et al., 2000); traditional and LAN (local area network) classrooms on writing improvement (Braine, 2001a); different types of e-mail tasks on language complexity and accuracy (Li, 2000b); e-mail journaling on accuracy and fluency (González-Bueno & Pérez, 2000); computer-mediated and traditional pen-and-paper writing on the social roles adopted by writers during group journaling (Abrams, 2001), and on writing improvement and revision behaviors (Li & Cumming, 2001). Noncomparative research addresses the impact of computers on L2 writing (Pennington, 2003), L2 acquisition (Kramsch, A'Ness, & Lam, 2000), student awareness of limitations of Web-based sources (Stapleton, 2003), and student reactions to computer-mediated writing instruction (Suh, 2002).

Several articles describe technology-related assignments and curricula, such as cross-cultural e-mail correspondence units (Fedderholdt, 2001; Liaw & Johnson, 2001); a design model for computer-mediated writing (Greene, 2000); technology-enhanced research writing units (Kasper, 2000b; Moulton & Holmes, 2000); online correction of e-mail assignments (Melby-Mauer, 2003); integration of online communication into academic writing courses (Warschauer, 2002); the implementation of CommonSpace in the composition classroom (Bloch & Brutt-Griffler, 2001); the use of concordances to learn features of genre (Weber, 2001); the use of chat rooms (Yuan, 2003); and the use of computer recordings of one's own composing and revision activities to promote self-assessment (Sullivan & Lindgren, 2002).

Grammar and vocabulary. Research in this category encompasses work that focuses on linguistic accuracy in L2 student writing—a term that is used rather broadly in the literature to refer to sentence level issues and below (grammar, vocabulary, convention use)—and the relationship between accuracy in these areas and pedagogical techniques (also referred to as "error feedback" or "error treatment"). Such inquiry has a long history in L2 studies that continues to the present. Since 2000, one book and several articles on error treatment have been published. The book (Ferris, 2002) is aimed at L2 writing instructors and provides them with a concise review of research on error in L2 writing and guidelines for providing instruction and feedback on grammatical error in student writing. Frodesen and Holten (2003) present an overview of the role of grammar in L2 writing.

In the research, the relationship between different error treatments and students' written accuracy continues to be a central concern. Feedback treatments that have been examined vary in terms of focus of attention (on error versus higher order concerns) (Fazio, 2001) and explicitness (error type labeled versus error location identified versus no feedback) (Ferris & Roberts, 2001). Inquiry has broadened, however, to examine the effects of different error treatments on students' editing processes as well as their products, trying to determine whether specific types of markings influence students' attention to error during editing (Fazio, 2001; Ferris & Roberts, 2001; F. Hyland, 2003; Kubota, 2001) or their awareness of correct forms in TL writing/input (Tsang, 2000). Other work advocates increased attention to grammar in the composition classroom (Muncie, 2002a; Myles, 2002).

Innovative approaches to helping students edit for grammatical error have also been presented. Hinkel (2002b) advocates the contextualized teaching of grammar (employing analysis of authentic texts) to heighten learners' awareness of TL use. Yates and Kenkel (2002) advocate and illustrate error feedback practices that are informed by current SLA theory and cognizant of the inherently interrelated nature of discourse types and sentence level grammar choices. In addition, Jabbour (2001) discusses the use of collocation and corpus linguistics to teach grammar and vocabulary.

Finally, work in the area of vocabulary has examined the role of task type (timed writing versus multiple drafting) on the accuracy, range, and sophistication of students' vocabulary use (Muncie, 2002b) and discussed the use of dictionaries to teach vocabulary (Odlin, 2001).

Peer interaction. A handful of publications in the past four years have addressed issues related to peer interaction. They are about evenly divided in focus between second and foreign language contexts and address a range of academic levels, including secondary EFL in Hong Kong (Tsui & Ng, 2000), university EFL in Israel (Levine, Oded, Connor, & Asons, 2002), precollege ESL in the United States (Di Giovanni & Nagaswami, 2001), and university composition, both ESL (de Guerrero & Villamil, 2000; Porto, 2001) and mixed NES/ESL (Zhu, 2001a). Interest has moved from the comparison of students' uses of and attitudes toward peer versus teacher response (F. Hyland, 2000; Muncie, 2000; Tsui & Ng, 2000) to the examination of a number of other variables seen to influence students' uses of peer feedback and the quality and quantity of interaction among peers in writing groups. These include the language status (ESL vs. NES) of the participants (Zhu, 2001a), the language learning and cultural context (SL vs. FL) (Levine et al., 2002), the mode of interaction (online versus face-to-face) (Di Giovanni & Nagaswami, 2001), the status of peer participants relative to one another (de Guerrero & Villamil, 2000), written versus oral peer response (Bartels, 2003), comparative effects of working alone or with a peer (Franken & Haslett, 2002), and comparative effects of peer review in electronic and traditional modes (Liu & Sadler, 2003). In addition to these articles, a book on peer response (Liu & Hansen, 2002) provides an overview of the research in the area and guidelines for the integration and implementation of a variety of peer response activities. Ferris (2003b) offers a briefer overview of issues in peer feedback.

Plagiarism. Research continues to delve into the complex issues related to plagiarism in L2 writing. Inquiry remains focused on school-sponsored writing, but several school contexts have been examined, including undergraduate (Bloch, 2001; F. Hyland, 2001; Mounsey, 2001; Pecorari, 2001; Prochaska, 2001); graduate (Barks & Watts, 2001); ESL in the United States (Barks & Watts, 2001; Bloch, 2001; Pecorari, 2001; Prochaska, 2001); ESL in New Zealand (F. Hyland, 2001); ESL/EFL in Mexico (Mounsey, 2001); and EFL in Japan (LoCastro & Masuko, 2002; Yamada, 2000) and China (Sapp, 2002). Studies have examined the processes involved in writing from source material (Barks & Watts, 2001); the role of print versus electronic media (Bloch, 2001); teachers' feedback on plagiarism (F. Hyland, 2001); students' understanding of plagiarism (F. Hyland, 2001; Mounsey, 2001); individual and institutional policies on plagiarism (Pecorari, 2001, Sapp, 2002); the practical and political implications of the lack of a clear definition of the construct (Prochaska, 2001); possible causes of plagiarism (LoCastro & Masuko, 2002; Sapp, 2002); the role of attitudes, cultural expectations, and educational context (Sapp, 2002); how students can be helped to avoid plagiarism (Yamada, 2003); and how teachers can modify their conceptions of and responses to plagiarism (Sapp, 2002).

Teacher response. Perceived as one of the most important and time-consuming aspects of teaching writing, response has been the subject of only a handful of studies over the past several years. This research, however, has made some significant methodological and conceptual advances in understanding this complex, multidimensional activity. Several studies have investigated both what students do with teacher feedback and how this feedback appears to affect the quality of their writing (Ashwell, 2000; DiPuma & Maslekoff, 2001; F. Hyland, 2000; Kasanga, 2001; Storch & Tapper, 2002; Warden, 2000). Ashwell (2000) examined whether the feedback sequence currently recommended in multiple draft writing (providing feedback on content in earlier drafts and form in later drafts) is more effective than other patterns in effecting improvement in students' writing and inspiring revision and editing.

Attention has also been given to authentic (as opposed to manipulated) teacher feedback and its effectiveness in communicating with students. F. Hyland (2000) examined the ways in which students' concerns and revision ideas are overridden by their teachers' feedback. Hyland and Hyland (2001) analyzed teacher feedback according to its functions (praise, criticism, suggestions) and forms. Sanson-Moorey (2001) discusses student–teacher conferences. In addition, reviews of the research on teacher response have appeared (Ferris, 2003a, 2003b; Goldstein, 2001).

Literature and film. The role of literature in L2 composition pedagogy has been a long-standing topic of debate in the field; however, it has been the focus of only a handful of articles published in the past several years (Belcher & Hirvela, 2000; Hirvela, 2001; Newell, Garriga, & Peterson, 2001; Vandrick, 2003). Belcher and Hirvela (2000) present a comprehensive review of the interrelated but separate histories of the literature–composition debate in L1 and L2 writing. This article also lays out the pros and cons of using literature in the L2 writing classroom. Hirvela (2001) talks about the place of literature in the L2 writing curriculum; and Newell, Garriga, and Peterson (2001) discuss reading to write on literature, in the form of critical responses to literary texts. Recent work has also advocated the use of film in L2 writing instruction as a means of promoting language acquisition (verbal, written, and visual) and motivating students (Fluitt-Dupuy, 2001; Kasper, 2000a; Kasper & Singer, 2001).

General Issues and Concerns

<u>Foreign language writing</u>. Research focusing on foreign (as opposed to second) language contexts has proliferated, evidence both of the growth of L2 writing as a discipline and the changing role of writing in the 21st century. The focus of this research has expanded, both geographically and conceptually. Studies have reported on EFL writing instruction in Bulgaria (Rainville, 2000), Japan (Hirose, 2001; Hirose & Sasaki, 2000), Tunisia (Ghrib-Maamouri, 2001), and the Ukraine (Tarnopolsky, 2000); and on writing instruction in various FLs taught in U.S. university settings, including Spanish (Roebuck, 2001; Ruiz-Funes, 2001), German (Reichelt & Waltner, 2001), and French (Calvez, 2000; Kelley, 2001). In addition, two collections focusing on FL contexts appeared: a special volume of *MEXTESOL Journal* on L2 writing (Hayward, 2001) and an edited collection discussing FL instruction in Switzerland, Italy, Denmark, Germany, and the United States (Brauer, 2000d). The latter collection presents an historical account of foreign language pedagogy research over the past 50 years (Homstad & Thorson, 2000b).

Descriptive work in this area has presented the curriculum of specific writing courses and the theoretical motivation for them (Hirose, 2001; Kelley, 2001; Reichelt & Waltner, 2001; Roebuck, 2001); detailed the changing role of writing in a given context and the authors' experiences as teachers of writing in these contexts (Rainville, 2000; Tarnopolsky, 2000); described the use of particular techniques in the FL classroom, including intensive and extensive writing (Homstad & Thorson, 2000a), portfolios (Brauer, 2000b), brainstorming (Hornung, 2000; M. Schrader, 2000), creative writing (R. Schrader, 2000), workshopping (Svendsen, 2000), the computer (Nelson, 2000), and the Internet (Blatt, 2000); and outlined curricular modifications teachers have made to better respond to students' interests and proficiency levels (Reichelt & Waltner, 2001; Tarnopolsky, 2000). An approximately equal number of FL studies have investigated various aspects of the FL writing process, including the effects of different instructional treatments on writing quality (Hirose & Sasaki, 2000); the effects on linguistic accuracy of different task types (Calvez, 2000) and different task representations (Ruiz-Funes, 2001); and the major writing difficulties experienced by FL students (Ghrib-Maamouri, 2001).

In addition, fundamental questions that have previously been neglected or considered irrelevant have come to the fore of FL writing research. One such question has been raised by Reichelt (1999, 2001) and Leki (2001e)—namely, what is (are) the purpose (s) of FL writing? In a review of research on the effects of instruction and task type on U.S. students' FL writing, Reichelt (2001) found no unified sense of purpose for writing in the FL curriculum, which, she argues, is the precursor to a coherent research agenda and informed pedagogical decision making. Similarly, Leki (2001e) argues that the greatest ideological challenge facing English teachers working in non-English dominant (FL) contexts is the question of the purpose of FL writing instruction, yet she notes that this question is rarely addressed. Finally Brauer (2000a) argues for the expansion of the function of writing in FL classrooms.

Approach, technique, and curriculum design. Much research published in the past several years describes and/or investigates particular approaches, curricula, and teaching techniques for L2 composition. The curricula that are presented vary widely in terms of foci, reflecting a local, needs-based approach to curriculum development. These foci include the investigation of writing in one's own academic discipline (Lax & Reichelt, 2001; Vann & Myers, 2001); the analysis of language use in media (Hunter & Morgan, 2001); writing for university exams (Weigle & Nelson, 2001); basic writing tasks required in undergraduate (Carson, 2001) and postgraduate study (Cargill, Cadman, & McGowan, 2001; Carson, 2001); writing based on learners' interests (Hall, 2001); a problem posing critical literacy approach (Quintero, 2002); a self-access approach (Nakayama, 2002); a cognitive modeling approach to critique writing (Dobson & Feak, 2001); evaluation in academic writing (Bloch, 2003); and genre approaches to L2 writing instruction (Johns, 2003). In addition, discussions of the issues teachers may need to consider when designing literacy courses (Leki, 2001c; Lunsford, 2001) and advanced EAP curricula were published (Reid, 2001), and an article on the development of models of adult L2 writing instruction appeared (Cumming & Riazi, 2000).

Instructional techniques described in the literature address a wide variety of issues as well, including coherence (Lee, 2002a, 2002b); heuristic devices (Beck, 2002); narrative crisis conventions (Tickoo, 2001); strategy and self-regulation (Ching, 2002); Grice's Maxims (White, 2001); one-on-one tutoring (Shin, 2002); argumentation (Livie, 2000); genre (Badger & White, 2000); dialogue journaling (Hansen-Thomas, 2003; Myers, 2001; Sanders, 2000); scaffolding (Cotterall &

Cohen, 2003); working memory strategies (Ransdell, Lavelle, & Levy 2002); explicit linguistic preparation (Ruan, 2001); using the resources of the writing center (Thonus, 2002, 2003; Williams, 2002); oral versus literate strategies of communication (Atari & Triki, 2000) and text patterns (Yamada, 2000). The effects of instruction in particular aspects of writing on student improvement in those aspects of writing has also been examined (Archibald, 2001; Olivares-Cuhat, 2002).

L2 writing programs. Recent years have also seen acceleration in the development of innovative programs and courses for L2 academic writing worldwide. These developments include a writing center at Hong Kong Polytechnic (Xiao, 2001); a Spanish writing center at the University of Minnesota (Strong & Fruth, 2001); an ESP writing program at Sultan Kaboos University in Oman (J. Flowerdew, 2001); an introduction to academic writing course at Aichi Prefectural University in Japan (Hirose, 2001); an ESL academic-social learning community program at Kingsborough Community College in New York (Babbit, 2001); an interdisciplinary, interinstitutional learning communities program at San Diego State University (Johns, 2001); cooperative learning, learner-centered, learning and cross-cultural exchange program at Iowa State University (Vann & Myers, 2001); a language-based academic induction program focused on genre used in the university at Adelaide University in Australia (Cargill, Cadman, & MacGowan, 2001); an advanced university course on language and public life at Ryerson Polytechnic University in Canada (Hunter & Morgan, 2001); a task-based composition course for resident ESL writers at the University of Illinois at Chicago (Williams, 2001); a course in advanced writing for university examinations at Georgia State University (Weigle & Nelson, 2001); a course linking ESL writing and the study of Greek and Latin roots in English at Hunter College in New York (Smoke, Green, & Isenstead, 2001); and an EAP professional development course at Macquarie University in Australia. For more details on these programs see Leki (2001a), from which all the foregoing chapters come, and the editor's introduction to the collection (2001d). In addition, Matsuda and Jablonski (2000) discuss the relationship between ESL writing and Writing Across the Curriculum programs.

Ideology. Current explicit commentary on ideological matters has its roots in a cluster of papers in the early- to mid-1990s. Santos (1992) claimed that L1 writing tended toward the ideological; and L2 writing, the pragmatic. Johns (1992), largely in agreement with Santos, warned against the uncritical acceptance of L1 writing ideology. Benesch (1993) responded to Santos, suggesting that all forms of ESL instruction are ideological, that neutrality is a myth, and that Santos's pragmatic position supports the status quo. Severino (1993) also responded to Santos, arguing that L2 writing pedagogy is just as ideologically charged as L1 writing pedagogy, though not as openly articulated and discussed. Allison (1994), in response to Benesch (1993), denied any necessary connection between pragmatism and an accommodationist ideology and challenges what he sees as Benesch's "ideologist" discourse. Benesch (1994) challenged Allison's claim that English for academic purposes has sufficiently addressed ideological issues. In 2001, Benesch and Santos reviewed and refined their earlier discussion. Benesch focused on critical theory and pedagogy and its opponents and argued for a "critical pragmatism." Santos laid out her views on critical theory and pedagogy and offered critiques of critical approaches to EAP and L2 writing.

A smaller cluster of work at the end of the century looked at ideology from a cultural perspective. Ramanathan and Atkinson (1999) claimed that L1 composition's principles and practices reflect an individualist ideology and that applying them to students whose culture may not share this ideology is problematic. Elbow (1999) agrees with what he calls Ramanathan and Atkinson's root claim about cross cultural differences, but argues that the notions of voice, peer review, critical thinking, and textual ownership (the four areas addressed by Ramanathan and Atkinson) are not inherently individualistic. Atkinson (2000a) claims that Elbow's outsider status (outside of L2 writing) causes some misunderstandings with regard to the L2 writing context but also generates insights and synergies vis-à-vis L2 writing. Other examples of papers addressing ideological concerns include Valdés (2000), who addresses language bigotry in mainstream composition classes against speakers of nonprestige varieties of English; Currie (2001), who explores the role of power in the evaluation of L2 students' writing; Belcher (2001), who looks at L2 writing theory in terms of research methodology, discourse style, and gender sensitivity; Ramanathan (2003), who investigates the politics of textual production and consumption; Canagarajah (2002), who explains how pedagogical approaches can help L2 writers position themselves in vernacular and academic communities; Smoke (2001), who discusses strategies to advocate for ESL student support services;

and Leki (2003a), who wonders if writing has been overrated.

History and development. The L2 writing area of interest that has seen, perhaps, the most dramatic growth is the history and development of the field. The new millennium brought a discussion of the future of L2 writing that specifically looked at the question of whether increased interest in and importance of L2 writing was matched by increased production of L2 writing specialists (Santos, Atkinson, Erickson, Matsuda, & Silva, 2000). The views expressed in this piece range from pessimistic (Atkinson) to optimistic (Silva) with mixed views from Santos, Erickson, and Matsuda. In a response to this discussion, Kaplan (2000) suggested that the focus of the discussion was limited to the current situation in North America but that L2 writing was neither restricted to North America, nor was it solely a contemporary issue and offered illustrations. There were two published responses to Kaplan's critique. Santos (2000) accepted Kaplan's critique, whereas Atkinson (2000b) took issue with it, suggesting that L2 writing is not, as Kaplan purports, a relatively well-established international research field with a critical mass of committed scholars.

A number of historical overviews were produced. Leki (2000) and Silva and Matsuda (2002) examined developments in L2 writing in the context of applied linguistics. Matsuda (2003) provided an historical review of L2 writing in the 20th century from an interdisciplinary perspective—looking at the influence of composition studies and second language studies. Kroll (2001) addressed developments in L2 writing via a personal reflection of her work in the field, as did several L2 scholars in Blanton and Kroll (2002a). Reichelt (2001) presented an overview of pedagogical issues and approaches in FL writing. Connor (2003) overviewed work in contrastive rhetoric over the past 30 years. Kapper (2002) reviewed the first 10 years of research published in the *Journal of Second Language Writing*. Silva and Matsuda (2001b) traced the evolution of L2 writing over the previous 40 years. Kaplan and Grabe (2002) presented a 50-year history of written discourse analysis; Cumming (2001c) surveyed two decades of research on L2 writing acquisition; and Brauer (2000c) traced the history of L2 writing over the past 30 years.

Atkinson (2003a) edited a special issue of the *Journal of Second Language Writing* reviewing contemporary work in L2 writing—post process. In this issue, foci include basic issues (Atkinson, 2003a), genre (K. Hyland, 2003), gender/class/race (R. Kubota, 2003), culture (Atkinson, 2003b), a sociopolitical orientation to research (Casanave, 2003a), and a push for giving more attention to interdisciplinarity, postmodernism, and globalization (Leki, 2003b). In another group effort, Matsuda, Canagarajah, Harklau, K. Hyland, and Warschauer (2003) focused on important currents that have shaped inquiry in L2 writing during the previous decade: generation 1.5 students (Harklau), multiliteracies (Canagarajah), technology (Warschauer), discourse analysis (K. Hyland), and multidisciplinary inquiry (Matsuda, 2003a). Finally, *CCC* (*College Composition and Communication*) acknowledged the growing importance of L2 writing by publishing a (long overdue) position paper on second language writing and writers (2001), describing the L2 writer population and addressing such issues as placement, assessment, class size, credit, and teacher preparation and support.

Early L2 Writing

Research on L2 composition has historically focused on higher education contexts, and as is evident from this review, this is still true today. The dominance of higher education contexts in L2 writing scholarship is the result of a combination of factors related to access, resources, and disciplinarity (see Matsuda & DePew, 2002b, for a discussion of these factors). However, recent years have seen substantial growth in the amount of work focusing on early L2 literacy issues, a response, in large part, to the rapidly growing population of ESL users in pre-K–12 contexts in the United States and abroad. This shift toward nonuniversity contexts was marked by a special edition of the *Journal of Second Language Writing*, edited by Matsuda and DePew (2002a), which presented four research articles on early literacy. In the past four years, a total of about two dozen or so studies have addressed early L2 literacy issues, and these studies have addressed a wide variety of issues (as is evident in the sections above) and been conducted in a wide variety of contexts, including Casablanca, Morocco (Blanton, 2002); Catalonia, Spain (Torras & Celaya, 2001); Montreal (Fazio, 2001; Maguire & Graves, 2001); Bulgaria (Rainville, 2000); the Ukraine (Tarnopolsky, 2000); Japan (Kobayashi & Rinnert, 2002); Hong Kong (Sengupta, 2000; Tsui & Ng, 2000); and the United States (Buckwalter & Lo, 2002; Harklau, 2001; Huie & Yahya, 2003; Jarvis, 2002; Lang & Albertini, 2001; Malloy, 2001; Reynolds, 2002).

This scholarship has also varied in terms of participants, examining a variety of levels within the pre-K–12 spectrum, including preschool (Buckwalter & Lo, 2002), primary school (Blanton, 2002; Huie & Yahya, 2003; Maguire & Graves, 2001), middle school (Fazio, 2001; Jarvis (2002), Lang & Albertini, 2001; Malloy, 2001; Reynolds, 2002; Torras & Celaya, 2001), secondary school (Harklau, 2001; Kobayashi & Rinnert, 2002; Lang & Albertini, 2001; Rainville, 2000; Sengupta, 2000; Tsui & Ng, 2000), and pre-university (Tarnopolsky, 2000). In addition to these studies, a resource book for K–12 teachers was published (Peregoy & Boyle, 2001), and a call for more scholarship on writing in classroom-based research (both on how students learn to write in L2 and on how they learn an L2 through writing) was made (Harklau, 2002).

Conclusion

On the basis of the foregoing, we feel that, with regard to second language writing instruction, "the times they are a-changin" (Dylan, 1964), and that this change is welcome and salutary for the field. We see a transition in process, a transition from the view that second language writing teachers should play the role of passive consumers of imported instructional approaches and methods and their accompanying research programs (e.g., controlled composition, current–traditional rhetoric, process approaches, and English for academic purposes/genre approaches—see Blanton (1995), Raimes (1991), Reid (1993), and Silva (1990) for overviews of approaches to second language writing instruction). This transition resists one-size-fits-all, off-the-shelf approaches promulgated and promoted by self-proclaimed pundits who imply that a particular orientation to writing instruction will prove successful at all times, in all places, and for all students.

We see a transition toward a view of second language writing teachers as experienced and seasoned professionals with an understanding of the nature of the phenomenon of second language writing and a familiarity with relevant theory and research from within and without the field, who, in an informed and principled way, develop curricula and materials that make sense for their students; their teaching styles; and their political, institutional, and classroom contexts; and who are unencumbered by the limitations of L2 writing's parent disciplines (e.g., the applied linguistics belief in the primacy of speech and composition studies' neglect of second language issues).

As for the research related to second language writing instruction, we also see positive developments. We see an increasing amount of published research addressing a greater variety of issues, with more breadth, depth, and sophistication—research that is more innovative and more global in its origin and that maintains a better balance of basic and applied issues, fosters more model and theory building, and encourages a greater recognition of the role of politics and ideology in inquiry. For all these reasons, we feel, as we said earlier, that it is indeed an exciting time to be working in the area of second language writing.

Notes

1. We examined the following sources to locate relevant research: indexes (Current Index to Journals in Education, Education Index, ERIC, Linguistics and Language Behavior Abstracts, Research in Education, World Cat); published bibliographies (selected annotated bibliography of scholarship in L2 writing in the *Journal of Second Language Writing, 9* (1) *–12* (3) (2000–present); and periodicals (*Academic Writing; ADE Bulletin; ADFL Bulletin; Annual Review of Applied Linguistics; Applied Language Learning; Applied Linguistics; Assessing Writing; Australian Review of Applied Linguistics; Babel; The Canadian Modern Language Review; Cardiovascular Research; College Composition and Communication; College ESL; Composition Studies; Computers & Composition; Computer Assisted Language Learning; ELT Journal; English for Specific Purposes; English Teaching Forum; Foreign Languages and Their Teachers; Foreign Language Annals; The French Review; Glottodidactica; Hermes: Journal of Linguistics; International Journal of English Studies; International Review of Applied Linguistics; Issues in Writing; ITL: Review of Applied Linguistics; JALT Journal; Journal of Adult Migrant Education; Journal of Basic Writing; Journal of Deaf Studies and Deaf Education; Journal of English for Academic Purposes; Journal of Language for International Business; Journal of Literacy Research; Journal of Pragmatics; Journal of Second Language Writing; Journal of Teaching Writing; Language Awareness; Language, Culture, and Curriculum; Language Learning; Language Learning & Technology; Language Research Bulletin; Language Teaching Research; Language Testing; Learning and Instruction; MEXTESOL Journal; The*

Modern Language Journal; RELC Journal; Research in the Teaching of English; System; Teaching English in the Two-Year College; Technical Communication Quarterly; TESL Canada Journal; TESL-EJ; TESL Reporter; TESOL HEIS News: ESL in Higher Education Newsletter; TESOL Journal; TESOL Quarterly; World Englishes; Writing Instructor; Writing on the Edge; and Written Communication.

2. In an attempt to make this review of research coherent and useful, we have developed a categorization system, recognizing that this system reflects our biases and that others might organize this material in very different ways.

ANNOTATED BIBLIOGRAPHY

Belcher, D., & Connor, U. (Eds.). (2001). *Reflections on multiliterate lives.* Buffalo, NY: Multilingual Matters.

This book is a collection of personal accounts of the literacy experiences of successful academics from a variety of countries and disciplines. These accounts, presented in narratives and interviews, illustrate the contributors' struggles and achievements involved in becoming multiliterate.

Belcher, D., & Hirvela, A. (2001a). *Linking literacies: Perspectives on L2 reading–writing connections.* Ann Arbor: University of Michigan Press.

This collection provides a theoretical overview of the connection between reading and writing in a second language. It looks at how L1 composition studies has influenced L2 reading–writing theory and pedagogy as well as how L2 reading–writing scholarship has created an identity of its own.

Blanton, L. L., & Kroll, B. (Eds.). (2002). *ESL composition tales: Reflections on teaching.* Ann Arbor: University of Michigan Press.

In this collection, several veteran L2 writing scholars write openly and honestly about their careers, thus creating, in effect, a collective history of the development of contemporary thinking about L2 writing and writing instruction.

Brauer, G. (Ed.). (2000d). *Writing across languages.* Stamford, CT: Ablex.

The intention of this volume is to question why so little attention is paid to writing in language education. It considers perspectives from Switzerland, Italy, Denmark, Germany, and the United States at all levels of instruction.

Casanave, C. P. (2002). *Writing games: Multicultural case studies of academic literacy practices in higher education.* Mahwah, NJ: Erlbaum.

This monograph uses the metaphor of "games" to explore how writers from different cultural backgrounds write in academic settings and the ways in which their writing affects their developing identities as students and professionals.

Ferris, D. R. (2002). *Treatment of error in second language writing.* Ann Arbor: University of Michigan Press.

This book overviews the theory and research on error feedback in L2 writing and provides guidelines and suggestions for teaching editing and responding to error in student writing.

Ferris, D. (2003b). *Response to student writing: Implications for second language students.* Mahwah, NJ: Erlbaum.

Aimed at teachers of ESL writers and L2 teacher educators, this book provides an overview of the research on response to first and second language writing and offers practical guidelines for responding to ESL writers' texts.

Hinkel, E. (2002a). *Second language writers' text: Linguistic and rhetorical features.* Mahwah, NJ: Erlbaum.

This book, based on the results of a large-scale empirical study, provides a comprehensive and detailed analysis of L2 writers' texts and how these texts differ from those of L1 writers.

Kroll, B. (Ed.). (2003). *Exploring the dynamics of second language writing.* Cambridge: Cambridge University Press.

This collection's 13 original articles provide a series of discussions of basic issues in and multiple aspects of L2 writing that are important to new and experienced teachers at the postsecondary level.

Leki, I. (Ed.). (2001a). *Academic writing programs.* Alexandria, VA: TESOL.

This volume in the Case studies in TESOL practice series focuses on novel L2 writing courses and programs in a range of academic settings. Each chapter establishes the context of the course and describes its unique features.

Liu, J., & Hansen, J. G. (2002). *Peer response in second language writing classrooms*. Ann Arbor: University of Michigan Press.

This book presents an overview of the research on peer response in second and foreign language writing and offers practical guidelines for implementing peer response in different contexts.

Manchón, R. M. (2001a). *Writing in the L2 classroom: Issues in research and pedagogy*. Murcia, Spain: Universidad de Murcia.

This collection, comprised of 10 original articles, offers theoretical perspectives on L2 writing, research on L2 writers and their texts, a look at issues in L2 pedagogy, and an extensive bibliography of scholarship on L2 composing.

Ransdell, S., & Barbier, M-L. (Eds). (2002). *New directions for research in L2 writing*. Boston: Kluwer.

This 12-chapter volume provides an entrée to current psycholinguistic research on L2 writing in the experimental tradition in the international context and is aimed at describing, predicting, and, ultimately, explaining L2 writing.

Silva, T., & Matsuda, P. K. (Eds.). (2001a). *Landmark essays on ESL writing*. Mahwah, NJ: Erlbaum.

This collection of 15 original articles on L2 writing systematically delineates and explores central issues in field with regard to theory, research, instruction, assessment, politics, articulation with other disciplines, and standards.

Silva, T., & Matsuda, P. K. (Eds.). (2001b). *On second language writing*. Mahwah, NJ: Erlbaum.

This 16-article reprint collection represents the development of the field of ESL writing from a historical perspective with the aim of providing ready access to primary works that have shaped the field and placing them in their historical contexts.

OTHER REFERENCES

Abrams, Z. I. (2001). Computer-mediated communication and group journals: Expanding the repertoire of participant roles. *System, 29*, 489–503.

Abu Rass, R. (2001). Integrating reading and writing for effective language teaching. *English Teaching Forum, 39* (1), 30–33.

Aidman, M. (2002). Early bilingual writing: Some influences of the mother tongue on written genre learning in the majority language. *Australian Review of Applied Linguistics, 25* (1), 1–18.

Al-Khatib, M. A. (2001). The pragmatics of letter-writing. *World Englishes, 20* (2), 179–200.

Allison, D. (1994). Comments on Sarah Benesch's "ESL ideology, and the politics of pragmatism." A reader reacts...*TESOL Quarterly, 28* (3), 618–623.

Archibald, A. (2001). Targeting L2 writing proficiencies: Instruction and area of change in students'writing over time. *International Journal of English Studies, 1* (2), 153–174.

Armengol-Castells, L. (2001). Text-generating strategies of three multilingual writers: A protocol-based study. *Language Awareness, 10* (2/3), 91–106.

Arrecco, M. R., & Ransdell, S. (2002). Early exposure to an L2 predicts good L1 as well as good L2 writing. In S. Ransdell & M.-L. Barbier (Eds.), *New directions for research in L2 writing* (pp. 123–131). Dordrecht, The Netherlands: Kluwer.

Ashwell, T. (2000). Pattern of teacher response to student writing in a multiple draft composition classroom: Is content feedback followed by form feedback the best method? *Journal of Second Language Writing, 9* (3), 227–57.

Atari, O. F., & Triki, M. A. (2000). The formal features of oral and literate strategies of communication: Their implications for EFL writing revision. *International Review of Applied Linguistics, 38* (2), 95–107.

Atkinson, D. (2000a). On Peter Elbow's response to "Individualism, academic writing, and ESL writers," by Vai Ramanathan and Dwight Atkinson. *Journal of Second Language Writing, 9* (1), 71–76.

Atkinson, D. (2000b). On Robert B. Kaplan's response to Terry Santos et al.'s "On the future of second language writing." *Journal of Second Language Writing, 9* (3), 317–320.

Atkinson, D. (2001). Reflections and refractions on the JSLW special issue on voice. *Journal of Second Language Writing, 10* (1/2), 107–124.

Atkinson, D. (2003a). L2 writing in the post-process era: Introduction. *Journal of Second Language Writing, 12* (1), 3–15.

Atkinson, D. (2003b). Writing and culture in the post-process era. *Journal of Second Language Writing, 12* (1), 49–63.

Babbit, M. (2001). Making writing count in an ESL learning community. In I. Leki (Ed.), *Academic writing programs* (pp. 49–60). Alexandria, VA: TESOL.

Bacha, N. (2001). Writing evaluation: What can analytic versus holistic essay scoring tell us? *System, 29* (3), 371–383.

Bacha, N. (2002). Testing writing in the EFL classroom: Student expectations. *English Teaching*

Forum, 40 (2), 14-19, 27.

Badger, R., & White. G. (2000). A process genre approach to teaching writing. *ELT Journal, 54* (2), 153-60.

Bailey, N. (2000). *E. pluribus unum:* Health as content for a community of learners. In M. Pally (Ed.), *Sustained content teaching in academic ESL/EFL* (pp. 179-199). Boston: Houghton Mifflin.

Barks, D., & Watts, P. (2001). Textual borrowing strategies for graduate-level ESL writers. In D. Belcher & A. Hirvela (Eds.), *Linking literacies: Perspectives on L2 reading-writing connections* (pp. 209-228). Ann Arbor: University of Michigan Press.

Bartels, N. (2003). Written peer response in L2 writing. *English Teaching Forum, 41* (1), 34-37.

Basturkmen, H., & Lewis, M. (2002). Learner perspectives of success in an EAP writing course. *Assessing Writing, 8* (1), 31-46.

Beck, A. (2002). Writing strategies worksheet. *TESOL Journal, 11* (1), 34-35.

Belcher, D. (2001). Does second language writing have gender? In T. Silva & P. K. Matsuda (Eds.), *On second language writing* (pp. 59-71). Mahwah, NJ: Erlbaum.

Belcher, D., & Hirvela, A. (2000). Literature and L2 composition: Revisiting the debate. *Journal of Second Language Writing, 9* (1), 21-39.

Belcher, D., & Hirvela, A. (Eds.). (2001b). Introduction. *Linking literacies: Perspectives on L2 reading-writing connections* (pp. 1-14). Ann Arbor: University of Michigan Press.

Belcher, D., & Hirvela, A. (Eds.). (2001c). *Journal of Second Language Writing, 10* (1/2) [Special issue on voice in L2 writing].

Benesch, S. (1993). ESL, ideology, and the politics of pragmatism. *TESOL Quarterly, 27* (4), 705-717.

Benesch, S. (1994). The author responds...*TESOL Quarterly, 28* (3), 623-624.

Benesch, S. (2001). Critical pragmatism: A politics of L2 composition. In T. Silva & P. K. Matsuda (Eds.), *On second language writing* (pp. 161-172). Mahwah, NJ: Erlbaum.

Bernard, R. W. (2000). Reflecting on commentary: Mind, intellect, and a use of language. In M. Pally (Ed.), *Sustained content teaching in academic ESL/EFL* (pp. 200-215). New York, NY: Houghton Mifflin.

Biesenbach-Lucas, S., Meloni, C., & Weasenforth, D. (2000). Use of cohesive features in ESL students' e-mail and word-processed texts: A comparative study. *Computer Assisted Language Learning, 13* (3), 221-237.

Biesenbach-Lucas, S., & Weasenforth, D. (2001). E-mail and word processing in the ESL classroom: How the medium affects the message. *Language Learning & Technology, 5* (1), 135-165.

Blanton, L. (1995). Elephants and paradigms: Conversations about teaching L2 writing. *College*

ESL, 5 (1), 1–21.

Blanton, L. (2002). Seeing the invisible: Situating L2 literacy acquisition in child-teacher interaction. *Journal of Second Language Writing, 11* (4), 295–310.

Blatt, I. (2000). Internet writing and language learning. In G. Brauer (Ed.), *Writing across languages* (pp. 89–98). Stamford, CT: Ablex.

Bloch, J. (2001). Plagarism and the ESL student: From printed to electronic texts. In D. Belcher & A. Hirvela (Eds.), *Linking literacies: Perspectives on L2 reading-writing connections* (pp. 209–228). Ann Arbor: University of Michigan Press.

Bloch, J. (2002). Student/teacher interaction via email: The social context of Internet discourse. *Journal of Second Language Writing, 11* (2), 117–134.

Bloch, J. (2003). Creating materials for teaching evaluation in academic writing: Using letters to the editor in L2 composition courses. *English for Specific Purposes, 22* (4), 347–364.

Bloch, J., & Brutt-Griffler, J. (2001). Implementing CommonSpace in the ESL composition classroom. In D. Belcher & A. Hirvela (Eds.), *Linking literacies: Perspectives on L2 reading-writing connections* (pp. 309–334). Ann Arbor: University of Michigan Press.

Boldt, H., Valsecchi, M. I., & Weigle, S. C. (2001). Evaluation of ESL student writing on text-responsible and non-text responsible writing tasks. *MEXTESOL Journal, 24* (3), 13–33.

Braine, G. (2001a). A study of English as a foreign language (EFL) writers on a local-area network (LAN) and in traditional classes. *Computers and Composition, 18*, 275–292.

Braine, G. (2001b). When an exit test fails. *System, 29* (2), 221–234.

Brauer, G. (2000a). Afterword: Expanding the function of writing in foreign and second language education. In G. Brauer (Ed.), *Writing across languages* (pp. 181–184). Stamford, CT: Ablex.

Brauer, G. (2000b). Portfolio learning. *Writing across languages.* In G. Brauer (Ed.), *Writing across languages* (pp. 167–179). Stamford, CT: Ablex.

Brauer, G. (2000c). Product, process, and the writer within: History of a paradigm shift. In G. Brauer (Ed.), *Writing across languages* (pp. 15–22). Stamford, CT: Ablex.

Breiner-Sanders, K. E., Sender, E., & Terry, R. M. (2002). Preliminary proficiency guidelines—writing (revised 2001). *Foreign Language Annals, 35* (1), 9–15.

Brooks-Carson, A. W., & Cohen, A. D. (2000). Direct vs. translated writing: Strategies for bilingual writers. In B. Swierzbin, B. Morris, M. E. Anderson, C. A. Klee, & E. Tarone (Eds.), *Social and cognitive factors in second language acquisition* (pp. 397–423). Somerville, MA: Cascadilla.

Bruce, N. (2002). Dovetailing language and content: Teaching balanced argument in legal problem answer writing. *English for Specific Purposes, 21*, 321–345.

Buckwalter, J. K., & Lo, Y. G. (2002). Emergent biliteracy in Chinese and English. *Journal of Second Language Writing, 11* (4), 269–293.

CCCC Committee on Second Language Writing. (2001). Statement on second language writing and writers. *College Composition and Communication, 52* (4), 669–674.

Calvez, D. J. (2000). Advanced undergraduate French composition: Problems and solutions. *Foreign Language Annals, 33* (1), 93–102.

Canagarajah, S. (2002). Multilingual writers and the academic community: Towards a critical relationship. *Journal of English for Academic Purposes, 1* (1), 29–44.

Candlin, C. N., Bhatia, V. K., & Jensen, C. H. (2002). Developing legal writing materials for English second language learners: Problems and perspectives. *English for Specific Purposes, 21* (4), 299–320.

Cargill, M., Cadman, K., & McGowan, U. (2001). Postgraduate writing: Using intersecting genres in a collaborative content-based program. In I. Leki (Ed.), *Academic writing programs* (pp. 85–96). Alexandria, VA: TESOL.

Carson, J. (2000). Reading and writing for academic purposes. In M. Pally (Ed.), *Sustained content teaching in academic ESL/EFL* (pp. 19–34). Boston: Houghton Mifflin.

Carson, J. (2001). A task analysis of reading and writing in academic contexts. In D. Belcher & A. Hirvela (Eds.), *Linking literacies: Perspectives on L2 reading–writing connections* (pp. 48–83). Ann Arbor: University of Michigan Press.

Casanave, C. P. (2003). Multiple uses of applied linguistics literature in a multidisciplinary graduate EAP class. *ELT Journal, 57* (1), 43–50.

Chandrasegaran, A. (2000). An analysis of obliqueness in student writing. *RELC Journal, 31* (1), 23–44.

Chen, L. (2001). On the function of models in English composition. *Foreign Languages and Their Teaching, 4* (144), 28–29, 38.

Cheng, Y. (2002). Factors associated with foreign language writing anxiety. *Foreign Language Annals, 35* (5), 647–656.

Chenoweth, N. A., & Hayes, J. R. (2001). Fluency in writing: Generating text in L1 and L2. *Written Communication, 18* (1), 80–98.

Chimbganda, A. B. (2000). Communication strategies used in the writing of answers in biology by ESL first year science students of the University of Botswana. *English for Specific Purposes, 19*, 305–329.

Ching, L. C. (2002). Strategy and self-regulation instruction as contributors to improving students' cognitive model in an ESL program. *English for Specific Purposes, 21*, 261–289.

Coates, R., Sturgeon, B., Bohannan, J., & Pasini, E. (2002). Language and publication in *Cardiovascular Research* articles. *Cardiovascular Research, 53*, 279–285.

Connor, U. (2003). Changing currents in contrastive rhetoric: Implications for teaching and research. In B. Kroll (Ed.), *Exploring the dynamics of second language writing* (pp. 218–241). New York: Cambridge University Press.

Cornwell, S., & McKay, T. (2000). Establishing a valid, reliable measure of writing apprehension for Japanese students. *JALT Journal, 22* (1), 114–139.

Cotterall, S., & Cohen, R. (2003). Scaffolding for second language writers: Producing an academic essay. *ELT Journal, 57* (2), 158–166.

Cresswell, A. (2000). Self-monitoring in student writing: Developing learner responsibility. *ELT Journal, 54* (3), 235–244.

Crusan, D. (2002). An assessment of ESL writing placement assessment. *Assessing Writing, 8* (1), 17–30.

Cumming, A. (2001a). The difficulty of standards, for example in L2 writing. In T. Silva & P. K. Matsuda (Eds.), *On second language writing* (pp. 209–229) Mahwah, NJ: Erlbaum.

Cumming, A. (2001b). ESL/EFL instructors' practices for writing assessment: Specific purposes or general purposes? *Language Testing, 18* (2), 207–224.

Cumming, A. (2001c). Learning to write in a second language: Two decades of research. *International Journal of English Studies, 1* (2), 1–24.

Cumming, A. (2002). Assessing L2 writing: Alternative constructs and ethical dilemmas. *Assessing Writing, 8* (2), 73–83.

Cumming, A., Bush, M., & Zho, A. (2002). Investigating learners' goals in the context of adult second-language writing. In S. Ransdell, & M.-L. Barbier (Eds.), *New directions in for research in L2 writing* (pp. 189–208). Dordrecht, The Netherlands: Kluwer.

Cumming, A., Kantor, R., & Powers, D. E. (2002). Decision making while rating ESL/EFL writing tasks: A descriptive framework. *The Modern Language Journal, 86* (1), 67–96.

Cumming, A., & Riazi, G. (2000). Building models of adult second-language instruction. *Learning and Instruction, 10* (1), 55–71.

Currie, P. (2001). On the question of power and control. In T. Silva & P. K. Matsuda (Eds.), *On second language writing* (pp. 29–38). Mahwah, NJ: Erlbaum.

de Guerrero, M. C. M., & Villamil, O. S. (2000). Activating the ZPD: Mutual scaffolding in L2 peer revision. *The Modern Language Journal, 84* (1), 51–68.

Di Giovanni, E., & Nagaswami, G. (2001). Online peer review: An alternative to face-to-face? *ELT Journal, 55* (3), 263–272.

Di Puma, L., & Maslekoff, D. (2001). Students' attention to in-text teacher feedback & their rationale for revisions. *MEXTESOL Journal, 24* (3), 53–70.

Dobson, B., & Feak, C. (2001). A cognitive modeling approach to teaching critique to nonnative speakers. In D. Belcher & A. Hirvela (Eds.), *Linking literacies: Perspectives on L2 reading–writing connections* (pp. 186–200). Ann Arbor: University of Michigan Press.

Dyer, B., & Friederich, L. (2002). The personal narrative as cultural artifact: Teaching autobiography in Japan. *Written Communication, 19* (2), 265–296.

Dylan, B. (1964). "The times, they are a changin."

Elbow, P. (1999). Individualism and the teaching of writing: Response to Vai Ramanathan and Dwight Atkinson. *Journal of Second Language Writing, 8* (3), 327–338.

Erdosy, M. U. (2001). The influence of prior experience on the construction of scoring criteria for ESL composition: A case study. *International Journal of English Studies, 1* (2), 175–196.

Escamilla, K., & Coady, M. (2001). Assessing the writing of Spanish-speaking students: Issues and suggestions. In S. R. Hurley & J. V. Tinajero (Eds.), *Literacy assessment of second language learners* (pp. 43–63). Boston: Allyn & Bacon.

Fazio, L. L. (2001). The effect of corrections and commentaries on the journal writing accuracy of minority- and majority-language students. *Journal of Second Language Writing, 10* (4), 235–249.

Fedderholdt, K. (2001). An email exchange project between non-native speakers of English. *ELT Journal, 55* (3), 273–280.

Feng, C., Ogata, H., & Yano, Y. (2000). Mark-up-based writing error analysis model in an on-line classroom. *Computer Assisted Language Learning, 13* (1), 79–97.

Ferris, D. (2003a). Responding to writing. In B. Kroll (Ed.), *Exploring the dynamics of second language writing* (pp. 119–140). New York: Cambridge University Press.

Ferris, D., & Roberts, B. (2001). Error feedback in L2 writing classes: How explicit does it need to be? *Journal of Second Language Writing, 10* (3), 161–184.

Flowerdew, J. (2001). Toward authentic, scientific-purpose writing at the lower levels of proficiency. In I. Leki (Ed.), *Academic writing programs* (pp. 21–33). Alexandria, VA: TESOL.

Flowerdew, L. (2000a). Critical thinking development and academic writing for engineering students. In M. Pally (Ed.), *Sustained content teaching in academic ESL/EFL* (pp. 96–116). Boston: Houghton Mifflin.

Flowerdew, L. (2000b). Using a genre-based framework to teach organizational structure in academic writing. *ELT Journal, 54* (3), 369–378.

Fluitt-Dupuy, J. (2001). Teaching argumentative writing through film. *TESOL Journal, 10* (4), 10–15.

Franken, M., & Haslett, S. (2002). When and why talking can make writing harder. In S. Ransdell, & M.-L.Barbier (Eds.), *New directions for research in L2 writing* (pp. 209–229). Dordrecht, The Netherlands: Kluwer Academic.

Frodesen, J., & Holten, C. (2003). Grammar and the ESL writing class. In B. Kroll (Ed.), *Exploring the dynamics of second language writing* (pp. 141–161). New York: Cambridge University Press.

Fukao, A., & Fujii, T. (2001). Investigating difficulties in the academic writing process: Interview as a research tool. *Language Research Bulletin, 16*, 29–40.

Gallagher, C., & McCabe, A. (2001). Academic register and the nominal group. *Language*

Research Bulletin, *16*, 53–67.

Garcia, S. S. (2001). Diferencias en las convenciones retóricas del Inglés y del Español y su escritura en Inglés como idioma extrajero por Hispanohablantes Mexicanos [Differences in the rhetorical conventions of English and Spanish and the writing in English as a foreign language of Spanish speaking Mexicans]. *MEXTESOL Journal*, *24* (3), 35–51.

Ghrib-Maamouri, E. (2001). Thinking and writing in EFL: Cutting off Medusa's head. *ITL Review of Applied Linguistics*, *133/134*, 243–269.

Goldstein, L. (2001). For Kyla: What does the research say about responding to ESL writers? In T. Silva & P. K. Matsuda (Eds.), *On second language writing* (pp. 73–89). Mahwah, NJ: Erlbaum.

González-Bueno, M., & Pérez, L. C. (2000). Electronic mail in foreign language writing: A study of grammatical and lexical accuracy, and quantity of language. *Foreign Language Annals*, *33* (2), 189–198.

Grabe, W. (2001). Reading-writing relations: Theoretical perspectives and instructional practices. In D. Belcher & A. Hirvela (Eds.), *Linking literacies: Perspectives on L2 reading-writing connections* (pp. 15–47). Ann Arbor: University of Michigan Press.

Grabe, W. (2003). Reading and writing relations: Second language perspectives on research and practice. In B. Kroll (Ed.), *Exploring the dynamics of second language writing* (pp. 242–262). New York: Cambridge University Press.

Grant, L., & Ginther, A. (2000). Using computer-tagged linguistic features to describe L2 writing differences. *Journal of Second Language Writing*, *9* (2), 123–145.

Greene, D. (2000). A design model for beginner-level computer-mediated EFL writing. *Computer Assisted Language Learning*, *13* (3), 239–252.

Hall, D. (2001). Relinquishing teacher control: Learners as generators of course content. In I. Leki (Ed.), *Academic writing programs* (pp. 147–157). Alexandria, VA: TESOL.

Hamp-Lyons, L. (2001). Fourth generation writing assessment. In T. Silva & P. K. Matsuda (Eds.), *On second language writing* (pp. 117–127). Mahwah, NJ: Erlbaum.

Hamp-Lyons, L. (2002). The scope of writing assessment. *Assessing Writing*, *8*, 5–16.

Hamp-Lyons, L. (2003). Writing teachers as assessors of writing. In B. Kroll (Ed.), *Exploring the dynamics of second language writing* (pp. 162–189). New York: Cambridge University Press.

Hansen, J. G. (2000). Interactional conflicts among audience, purpose, and content knowledge in the acquisition of academic literacy in an EAP course. *Written Communication*, *17* (1), 27–52.

Hansen-Thomas, H. (2003). A case study of reflective journals in a university-level EFL writing course in Hungary. *English Teaching Forum*, *41* (1), 22–28.

Harklau, L. (2001). From high school to college: Student perspectives on literacy practices.

Journal of Literacy Research, 33 (1), 33–70.

Harklau, L. (2002). The role of writing in classroom second language acquisition. *Journal of Second Language Writing, 11* (4), 329–350.

Hatasa, Y. A., & Soeda, E. (2000). Writing strategies revisited: A case of non-cognate L2 writers. In B. Swierzbin, B. Morris, M. E. Anderson, C. A. Klee, & E. Tarone (Eds.), *Social and cognitive factors in second language acquisition* (pp. 375–396). Somerville, MA: Cascadilla.

Hayward, N. (Ed.). (2001). *MEXTESOL Journal: Special Issue, Topics in ESL/EFL Writing, 24* (3).

Heyden, T. (2001). Using sustained content-based learning to promote advanced ESL writing. *TESOL Journal 10* (4), 16–20.

Hinkel, E. (2001). Matters of cohesion in L2 academic texts. *Applied Language Learning, 12* (2), 111–132.

Hinkel, E. (2002b). Teaching grammar in writing classes: Tenses and cohesion. In E. Hinkel & S. Fotos (Eds.), *New perspectives on grammar teaching in second language classrooms* (pp. 181–198). Mahwah, NJ: Erlbaum.

Hinkel, E. (2003). Simplicity without elegance: Features of sentences in L1 and L2 academic texts. *TESOL Quarterly, 37* (2), 275–301.

Hirose, K. (2001). Realizing a giant first step toward improved English writing: A case in a Japanese University. In I. Leki (Ed.), *Academic writing programs* (pp. 35–46). Alexandria, VA: TESOL.

Hirose, K. (2003). Comparing L1 and L2 organizational patterns in the argumentative writing of Japanese EFL students. *Journal of Second Language Writing, 12* (2), 181–209.

Hirose, K., & Sasaki, M. (2000). Effects of teaching metaknowledge and journal writing on Japanese university students' EFL writing. *JALT Journal, 22* (1), 94–113.

Hirvela, A. (2001). Connecting reading and writing through literature. In D. Belcher & A. Hirvela (Eds.), *Linking literacies: Perspectives on L2 reading–writing connections* (pp. 109–134). Ann Arbor: University of Michigan Press.

Hirvela, A., & Belcher, D. (2001). Coming back to voice: The multiple voices and identities of mature multilingual writers. *Journal of Second Language Writing, 10* (1/2), 83–106.

Homstad, T., & Thorson, H. (2000a). Quantity vs. quality: Using intensive and extensive reading in the FL classroom. In G. Brauer (Ed.), *Writing across languages* (pp. 141–152). Stamford, CT: Ablex.

Homstad, T., & Thorson, H. (2000b). Writing and foreign language pedagogy: Theories and implications. In G. Brauer (Ed.), *Writing across languages* (pp. 3–14). Stamford, CT: Ablex.

Hornung, A. (2000). Method awareness and the teaching of writing. In G. Brauer (Ed.), *Writing across languages* (pp. 131–140). Stamford, CT: Ablex.

Huie, K., & Yahya, N. (2003). Learning to write in the primary grades: Experiences of English language learners and mainstream students. *TESOL Journal, 12* (1), 25–38.

Hunter, J., & Morgan, B. (2001). Language and public life: Teaching multiliteracies in ESL. In I. Leki (Ed.), *Academic writing programs* (pp. 99–109). Alexandria, VA: TESOL.

Hyland, F. (2000). ESL writers and feedback: Giving more autonomy to students. *Language Teaching Research, 4* (1), 33–54.

Hyland, F. (2001). Dealing with plagiarism when giving feedback. *ELT Journal, 55* (4), 375–381.

Hyland, F. (2003). Focusing on form: Student engagement with teacher feedback. *System, 31* (2), 217–230.

Hyland, F., & Hyland, K. (2001). Sugaring the pill: Praise and criticism in written feedback. *Journal of Second Language Writing, 10* (3), 185–212.

Hyland, K. (2000a). Hedges, boosters and lexical invisibility: Noticing modifiers in academic texts. *Language Awareness, 9* (4), 179–197.

Hyland, K. (2000b). "It might be suggested that..." : Academic hedging and student writing. *Australian Review of Applied Linguistics, 16*, 83–97.

Hyland, K. (2002a). Authority and invisibility: Authorial identity in academic writing. *Journal of Pragmatics, 34* (8), 1091–1112.

Hyland, K. (2002b). Directives: Argument and engagement in academic writing. *Applied Linguistics, 23* (2), 215–239.

Hyland, K. (2002c). Genre: Language, context, and literacy. *Annual Review of Applied Linguistics, 22*, 113–135.

Hyland, K. (2002d). Options of identity in academic writing. *ELT Journal, 56* (4), 351–358.

Hyland, K. (2002e). What do they mean? Questions in academic writing. *Text, 22* (4), 529–557.

Hyland, K. (2003). Genre-based pedagogies: A social response to process. *Journal of Second Language Writing, 12* (1), 17–29.

Ivanic, R., & Camps, D. (2001). I am how I sound: Voice as self-representation in L2 writing. *Journal of Second Language Writing, 10* (1/2), 3–33.

Jabbour, G. (2001). Lexis and grammar in second language reading and writing. In D. Belcher & A. Hirvela (Eds.), *Linking literacies: Perspectives on L2 reading-writing connections* (pp. 291–308). Ann Arbor: University of Michigan Press.

Jarvis, S. (2002). Short texts, best-fitting curves and new measures of lexical diversity. *Language Testing, 19* (1), 57–84.

Johns, A. (1992). Too much on our plates: A response to Terry Santos' "Ideology in composition: L1 and ESL." *Journal of Second Language Writing, 2* (1), 83–88.

Johns, A. (2001). An interdisciplinary, interinstitutional, learning communities program: Student involvement and student success. In I. Leki (Ed.), *Academic writing programs* (pp. 61–72). Alexandria, VA: TESOL.

Johns, A. (2003). Genre and ESL/EFL composition instruction. In B. Kroll (Ed.), *Exploring the dynamics of second language writing* (pp. 195–217). New York: Cambridge University Press.

Kaplan, R. (2000). Response to "On the future of second language writing." Terry Santos, et al. *Journal of Second Language Writing, 9* (3), 311–314.

Kaplan, R. B., & Grabe, W. (2002). A modern history of written discourse analysis. *Journal of Second Language Writing, 11* (3), 191–223.

Kapper, J. L. (2002). The first 10 years of the *Journal of Second Language Writing:* An updated retrospective. *Journal of Second Language Writing, 11* (2), 87–89.

Kasanga, L. A. (2001). Responding to feedback in revision in multiple-draft writing. *TESL Reporter, 34* (2), 1–14.

Kasper, L. F. (2000a). The imagery of rhetoric: Film and academic writing in the discipline-based ESL course. *Teaching English in the Two-Year College, 28* (1), 52–59.

Kasper, L. F. (2000b). Sustained content study and the Internet: Developing functional and academic literacies. In M. Pally (Ed.), *Sustained content teaching in academic ESL/EFL* (pp. 54–73). Boston: Houghton Mifflin.

Kasper, L. F. (2002). Technology as a tool for literacy in the age of information: Implications for the ESL classroom. *Teaching English in the Two-Year College, 30* (2), 129–144.

Kasper, L. F., & Singer, R. (2001). Unspoken content: Silent film in the ESL classroom. *Teaching English in the Two-Year College, 29* (1), 16–33.

Katznelson, H., Perpignan, H., & Rubin, B. (2001). What develops along *with* the developments of second language writing? Exploring the "by-products." *Journal of Second Language Writing, 10* (3), 141–159.

Kelley, A. K. (2001). Some suggestions for teaching intermediate composition. *French Review, 75* (1), 128–140.

Kells, M. H. (2002). Linguistic contact zones in the college writing classroom: An examination of ethnolinguistic identity and language attitudes. *Written Communication, 19* (1), 5–43.

Khaldieh, S. D. (2000). Learning strategies and writing processes of proficient versus less proficient learners of Arabic. *Foreign Language Annals, 33* (5), 522–534.

Khuwaileh, A. A., & Shoumali, A. A. (2000). Writing errors: A study of the writing ability of Arab learners of academic English and Arabic at university. *Language, Culture, and Curriculum, 13* (2), 174–183.

Kiany, G. R., & Khezri Nejad, M. (2001). On the relationship between English proficiency, writing ability, and the use of conjunctions in Iranian EFL learners' compositions. *ITL Review of Applied Linguistics, 133/134,* 227–241.

Kim, S.-A. (2001). Characteristics of EFL readers' summary writing: A study with Korean university students. *Foreign Language Annals, 34* (6), 569–581.

Kirschner, M., & Wexler, C. (2002). Caravaggio: A design for an interdisciplinary content-based EAP/ESP unit. *Journal of English for Academic Purposes, 1* (2), 163–183.

Kobayashi, H., & Rinnert, C. (2001). Factors relating to EFL writers' discourse level revision skills. *International Journal of English Studies, 1* (2), 71–101.

Kobayashi, H., & Rinnert, C. (2002). High school student perceptions of first language literacy instruction: Implications for second language writing. *Journal of Second Language Writing, 11* (2), 91–116.

Kondo-Brown, K. (2002). A FACETS analysis of rater bias in measuring Japanese second language writing performance. *Language Testing, 19* (1), 3–31.

Kramsch, C., A'Ness, F., & Lam, W.S.E. (2000). Authenticity and authorship in the computer-mediated acquisition of L2 literacy. *Language Learning and Technology, 4* (2), 78–104.

Kroll, B. (2001). The composition of a life in composition. In T. Silva, & P. Matsuda (Eds.), *On second language writing* (pp.1–16). Mahwah, NJ: Erlbaum.

Kubota, M. (2001). Error correction strategies used by learners of Japanese when revising a writing task. *System, 29,* 467–480.

Kubota, R. (2003). New approaches to gender, class, and race in second language writing. *Journal of Second Language Writing, 12* (1), 31–47.

Lally, C. G. (2000a). First language influences in second language composition: The effect of pre-writing. *Foreign Language Annals, 33* (4), 428–432.

Lally, C. G. (2000b). Writing across English and French: An examination of strategy use. *The French Review, 73* (3), 525–538.

Lam, S. E. L. (2000). L2 literacy and the design of the self: A case study of a teenager writing on the Internet. *TESOL Quarterly, 34* (3), 457–482.

Lang, H. G., & Albertini, J. A. (2001). Construction of meaning in the authentic science writing of deaf students. *Journal of Deaf Studies and Deaf Education, 6* (4), 258–284.

Lax, J., & Reichelt, M. (2001). Writing about writing: An innovative first-year composition curriculum. *Issues in Writing, 11* (1), 64–82.

Lee, I. (2002a). Helping students develop coherence in writing. *English Teaching Forum, 40* (3), 32–39.

Lee, I. (2002b). Teaching coherence to ESL students: A classroom inquiry. *Journal of Second Language Writing, 11* (2), 135–159.

Lee, Y.-J. (2002). A comparison of composing processes and written products in timed-essay tests across paper-and-pencil and computer modes. *Assessing Writing, 8* (2), 135–157.

Leki, I. (2000). Writing, literacy, and applied linguistics. *Annual Review of Applied Linguistics, 20,* 99–115.

Leki, I. (2001b). Hearing voices: L2 students' experiences in L2 writing courses. In T. Silva & P. K. Matsuda (Eds.), *On second language writing* (pp. 17–28). Mahwah, NJ: Erlbaum.

Leki, I. (2001c). Interlude: Developing meaningful literacy courses. In D. Belcher & A. Hirvela (Eds.), *Linking literacies: Perspectives on L2 reading–writing connections* (pp. 201–208). Ann Arbor: University of Michigan Press.

Leki, I. (2001d). Introduction: Accessing communities and disciplines through L2 writing programs. In I. Leki (Ed.), *Academic writing programs* (pp. 1–4). Alexandria, VA: TESOL.

Leki, I. (2001e). Material, educational, and ideological challenges of teaching EFL writing at the turn of the century. *International Journal of English Studies*, *1* (2), 197–209.

Leki, I. (2003a). A challenge to second language writing professionals: Is writing overrated? In B. Kroll (Ed.), *Exploring the dynamics of second language writing* (pp. 315–331). New York: Cambridge University Press.

Leki, I. (2003b). Coda: Pushing L2 writing research. *Journal of Second Language Writing*, *12* (1), 103–105.

Levine, A., Oded, B., Connor, U., & Asons, I. (2002). Variation in EFL-ESL peer response. *TESL-EJ*, *6* (3), A-1.

Li, Y. (2000a). Assessing second language writing: The relationship between computerized analysis and rater evaluation. *ITL Review of Applied Linguistics*, *127/128*, 37–51.

Li, Y. (2000b). Linguistic characteristics of ESL writing in task-based e-mail activities. *System*, *28*, 229–245.

Li, J., & Cumming, A. (2001). Word processing and second language writing: A longitudinal case study. *International Journal of English Studies*, *1* (2), 127–152.

Liaw, M.-L., & Johnson, R. J. (2001). E-mail writing as a cross-cultural learning experience. *System*, *29* (2), 235–251.

Liu, D. (2000). Writing cohesion: Using content lexical ties in ESOL. *English Teaching Forum*, *38* (1), 28–33.

Liu, J., & Sadler, R. W. (2003). The effect and affect of peer review in electronic versus traditional modes of L2 writing. *Journal of English for Academic Purposes*, *2* (3), 193–227.

Livie, K. (2000). Teaching argumentative writing strategies with popular culture. *TESOL HEIS News: ESL in Higher Education Newsletter*, *19* (2), 11.

LoCastro, V., & Masuko, M. (2002). Plagiarism and academic writing of learners of English. *Hermes, Journal of Linguistics*, *28*, 11–38.

Lunsford, A. A. (2001). Afterword: Lessons on linking literacies for L1 teachers. In D. Belcher & A. Hirvela (Eds.), *Linking literacies: Perspectives on L2 reading-writing connections* (pp. 335–338). Ann Arbor: University of Michigan Press.

Maguire, M. H., & Graves, B. (2001). Speaking personalities in primary school children's L2 writing. *TESOL Quarterly*, *35* (4), 561–593.

Malloy, M. E. (2001). The foreign language literacy classroom "translating event" as reading and composing: Eighth graders read cross-cultural children's literature. In D. Belcher &

A. Hirvela (Eds.), *Linking literacies: Perspectives on L2 reading-writing connections* (pp. 135–163). Ann Arbor: University of Michigan Press.

Manchón, R. M. (2001b). Trends in the conceptualization of second language composing strategies: A critical analysis. *International Journal of English Studies, 1* (2), 47–70.

Manchón, R. M., Roca de Larios, J., & Murphy, L. (2000a). An approximation to the study of backtracking in L2 writing. *Learning and Instruction, 10* (1), 13–35.

Manchón, R. M., Roca de Larios, J., & Murphy, L. (2000b). La influencia de la variable "grado de domino de la L2" en los procesos de composición en lengua extranjera: Hallazgos recientes de la investigación [The influence of L2 proficiency on composing processes in a foreign language: Insights from recent research]. In C. Munoz (Ed.), *Segundas lenguas: Adquisición en el aula* (pp. 277–297). Barcelona, Spain: Editorial Ariel.

Matsuda, P. K. (2001a). Reexamining audiolingualism: On the genesis of reading and writing in L2 Studies. In D. Belcher & A. Hirvela (Eds.), *Linking literacies: Perspectives on L2 reading-writing connections* (pp. 84–108). Ann Arbor: University of Michigan Press.

Matsuda, P. K. (2001b). Voice in Japanese written discourse: Implications for second language writing. *Journal of Second Language Writing, 10* (1/2), 35–53.

Matsuda, P. K. (2003). Second language writing in the twentieth century: A situated historical perspective. In B. Kroll (Ed.), *Exploring the dynamics of second language writing* (pp. 15–34). New York: Cambridge University Press.

Matsuda, P. K., Canagarajah, S., Harklau, L., Hyland, K., & Warschauer, M. (2003). Changing currents in second language writing research: A colloquium. *Journal of Second Language Writing, 12* (2), 151–179.

Matsuda, P. K., & DePew, K. E. (Guest Eds.) (2002a). Special Issue: Early second language writing. *Journal of Second Language Writing, 11* (4).

Matsuda, P. K., & DePew, K. E. (2002b). Early second language writing: An introduction. *Journal of Second Language Writing, 11* (4), 261–268.

Matsuda, P. K., & Jablonski, J. (2000). Beyond the L2 metaphor: Towards a mutually transformative model of ESL/WAC collaboration. *Academic Writing, 1*. Retrieved July, 2003, from http://aw.colostate.edu/aw/articles/ matsuda_jablonski2000.htm.

Melby-Mauer, J. (2003). Using e-mail assignments and online correction in ESL instruction. *TESOL Journal, 12* (2), 37–38.

Miller, K. S. (2000). Academic writers on-line: Investigating pausing in the production of text. *Language Teaching Research, 4* (2), 123–148.

Moulton, M. R., & Holmes, V. A. (2000). An ESL capstone course: Integrating research tools, techniques, and technology. *TESOL Journal, 9* (2), 23–29.

Mounsey, J. M. (2001). Our students have the right to know: Teaching about plagiarism in the ESL/EFL classroom. *MEXTESOL Journal, 24* (3), 95–102.

Muncie, J. (2000). Using written teacher feedback in EFL composition classes. *ELT Journal, 54* (1), 47–53.

Muncie, J. (2002a). Finding a place for grammar in EFL composition classes. *ELT Journal, 56* (2), 180–186.

Muncie, J. (2002b). Process writing and vocabulary development: Comparing lexical frequency profiles across drafts. *System, 30,* 225–235.

Myers, J. L. (2001). Self-evaluations of the "stream of thought" in journal writing. *System, 29,* 481–488.

Myles, J. (2002). Second language writing and research: The writing process and error analysis in student texts. *TESL-EJ, 6* (2), A1.

Nakayama, T. (2002). Learning to write in Japanese: Writing contexts, student performance, and instructional approach. *Babel, 37* (1), 27–36, 38.

Nelson, G., & Burns, J. (2000). Managing information for writing university exams in American history. In M. Pally (Ed.), *Sustained content teaching in academic ESL/EFL* (pp. 132–157). Boston: Houghton Mifflin.

Nelson, T. (2000). Using computers to teach writing in the FL classroom. In G. Brauer (Ed.), *Writing across languages* (pp. 99–115). Stamford, CT: Ablex.

Newell, G., Garriga, M. C., & Peterson, S. S. (2001). Learning to assume the role of author: A study of reading to write one's own ideas in an undergraduate ESL composition course. In D. Belcher & A. Hirvela (Eds.), *Linking literacies: Perspectives on L2 reading–writing connections* (pp. 164–185). Ann Arbor: University of Michigan Press.

Odlin, T. (2001). With the dictionary and beyond. In D. Belcher & A. Hirvela (Eds.), *Linking literacies: Perspectives on L2 reading-writing connections* (pp. 271–290). Ann Arbor: University of Michigan Press.

Okamura, A., & Shaw, P. (2000). Lexical phrases, culture, and subculture in transactional letter writing. *English for Specific Purposes, 19,* 1–15.

Olivares-Cuhat, G. (2002). Learning strategies and achievement in the Spanish writing classroom: A case study. *Foreign Language Annals, 35* (5), 561–570.

Pally, M. (2000a). Film and society: A course for analyzing readings, writings, and critical thinking. In M. Pally (Ed.), *Sustained content teaching in academic ESL/EFL* (pp. 158–178). Boston: Houghton Mifflin.

Pally, M. (Ed.). (2000b). *Sustained content teaching in academic ESL/EFL.* Boston: Houghton Mifflin.

Pally, M. (2001). Skills development in "sustained" content-based curricula: Case studies in analytic/critical thinking and academic writing. *Language and Education, 15* (4), 279–305.

Pally, M., Katznelson, H., Perpignan, H., & Rubin, B. (2002). What is learned in sustained-content writing classes along with writing? *Journal of Basic Writing, 21* (1), 90–115.

Parks, S. (2000). Professional writing and the role of incidental collaboration: Evidence from a medical setting. *Journal of Second Language Writing, 9* (2), 101–122.

Parks, S. (2001). Moving from school to the workplace: Disciplinary innovation, border crossing, and the reshaping of a written genre. *Applied Linguistics, 22* (4), 405–438.

Pecorari, D. (2001). Plagiarism and international students: How the English-speaking university responds. In D. Belcher & A. Hirvela (Eds.), *Linking literacies: Perspectives on L2 reading-writing connections* (pp. 229–245). Ann Arbor: University of Michigan Press.

Pennington, M. C. (2003). The impact of the computer in second language writing. In B. Kroll (Ed.), *Exploring the dynamics of second language writing* (pp. 287–310). New York: Cambridge University Press.

Peregoy, S. F., & Boyle, O. F. (2001). *Reading, writing, & learning in ESL: A resource book for K–12 teachers* (3rd ed.). New York: Longman.

Porto, M. (2001). Cooperative writing response groups and self-evaluation. *ELT Journal, 55* (1), 38–46.

Prior, P. (2001). Voices in text, mind, and society: Sociohistoric accounts of discourse acquisition and use. *Journal of Second Language Writing, 10* (1/2), 55–81.

Prochaska, E. (2001). Western rhetoric and plagiarism: Gatekeeping for an English-only international academia. *Writing on the Edge, 12* (2), 65–79.

Qi, D. S., & Lapkin, S. (2001). Exploring the role of noticing in a three-stage second language writing task. *Journal of Second Language Writing, 10* (4), 277–303.

Quintero, E. (2002). A problem-posing approach to using native language writing in English literacy instruction. In S. Ransdell, & M.-L. Barbier (Eds.), *New directions for research in L2 writing* (pp. 231–244). Dordrecht, The Netherlands: Kluwer.

Raimes, A. (1991). Out of the woods: Emerging traditions in the teaching of writing. *TESOL Quarterly, 25* (3), 407–430.

Rainville, A. (2000). EFL and the writing process in Bulgaria. *TESOL Matters, 10* (1), 10.

Ramanathan, V. (2003). Written textual production and consumption (WTPC) in vernacular and English-medium settings in Gujarat, India. *Journal of Second Language Writing, 12* (2), 125–150.

Ramanathan, V., & Atkinson, D. (1999). Individualism, academic writing, and ESL writers. *Journal of Second Language Writing, 8* (1), 45–75.

Ramanathan, V., & Kaplan, R. B. (2000). Genres, authors, discourse communities: Theory and application for (L1 and) L2 writing instructors. *Journal of Second Language Writing, 9* (2), 171–191.

Ransdell, S., Lavelle, B., & Levy, C.M. (2002). The effects of training a good working memory strategy on L1 and L2 writing. In S. Ransdell & M.-L. Barbier (Eds.). *New directions in for research in L2 writing* (pp. 133–144). Dordrecht, The Netherlands: Kluwer.

Reichelt, M. (1999). Toward a more comprehensive view of L2 writing: Foreign language writing in the U.S. *Journal of Second Language Writing, 8* (2), 181–204.

Reichelt, M. (2001). A critical review of foreign language writing research on pedagogical approaches. *The Modern Language Journal, 85,* 578–598.

Reichelt, M. (2003). Defining "Good writing" : A cross-cultural perspective. *Composition Studies, 31* (1), 99–126.

Reichelt, M., & Waltner, K. B. (2001). Writing in a second-year German class. *Foreign Language Annals, 34* (2), 235–245.

Reid, J. (1993). *Teaching ESL writing.* Englewood Cliffs, NJ: Prentice Hall.

Reid, J. (2001). Advanced EAP writing and curriculum design: What do we need to know? In T. Silva & P. K. Matsuda (Eds.), *On second language writing* (pp. 143–160). Mahwah, NJ: Erlbaum.

Reynolds, D. W. (2002). Learning to make things happen in different ways: Causality in the writing of middle-grade English language learners. *Journal of Second Language Writing, 11* (4), 311–328.

Rinnert, C, & Kobayashi, H. (2001). Differing perceptions of EFL writing among readers in Japan. *The Modern Language Journal, 85* (2), 189–209.

Rivard, L. P. (2001). Summary writing: A multi-grade study of French-immersion and Francophone secondary students. *Language, Culture and Curriculum, 14* (2), 171–186.

Robinson, D. W. (2000). Building consensus on the scoring of students' writing: A comparison of teacher scores versus native informants' scores. *The French Review, 73* (4), 667–688.

Roca de Larios, J., Marín, J., & Murphy, L. (2001). A temporal analysis of formulation processes in L1 and L2 writing. *Language Learning, 51* (3), 497–538.

Roca de Larios, J., & Murphy, L. (2001). Some steps toward a socio-cognitive interpretation of second language composition processes. *International Journal of English Studies, 1* (2), 25–45.

Roebuck, R. F. (2001). Teaching composition in the college level foreign language class: Insights and activities from sociocultural theory. *Foreign Language Annals, 34* (3), 206–213.

Ruan, Z. (2001). The effects of linguistic preparation on an EFL writing task. *Foreign Languages and Their Teaching, 4,* 24–27.

Ruiz-Funes, M. (2001). Task representation in foreign language reading-to-write. *Foreign Language Annals, 34* (2), 226–234.

Russell, P. D., & Yoo, J. (2001). Learner investment in second language writing. In X. Bonch-Bruevich, W. J. Crawford, J. Hellermann, C. Higgins, & H. Nguyen (Eds.), *The past, present, and future of second language research: Selected proceedings of the 2000 Second Language Research Forum* (pp. 181–196). Somerville, MA: Cascadilla.

Sanders, K. (2000). Dialogue journals in the adult ESL classroom. In G. Brauer (Ed.), *Writing across languages* (pp. 41–52). Stamford, CT: Ablex.

Sanson-Moorey, B. (2001). Reading and writing in an advanced ESP class: Student conferences and teacher observations. *MEXTESOL Journal, 24* (3), 71–94.

Santos, T. (1992). Ideology in composition: L1 and ESL. *Journal of Second Language Writing, 1* (1), 1–15.

Santos, T. (2000). Response to Kaplan. *Journal of Second Language Writing, 9* (3), 315.

Santos, T. (2001). The place of politics in second language writing. In T. Silva & P. K. Matsuda (Eds.), *On second language writing* (pp. 173–90). Mahwah, NJ: Erlbaum.

Santos, T., Atkinson, D., Erickson, M., Matsuda, P. K., & Silva, T. (2000). On the future of second language writing. *Journal of Second Language Writing, 9* (1), 1–20.

Sapp, D. A. (2002). Towards an international and intercultural understanding of plagiarism and academic dishonesty in composition: Reflections from the People's Republic of China. *Issues in Writing, 13* (1), 58–79.

Sasaki, M. (2000). Toward an empirical model of EFL writing processes: An exploratory study. *Journal of Second Language Writing, 9* (3), 259–291.

Sasaki, M. (2002). Building an empirically-based model of EFL learners' writing processes. In S. Ransdell, & M.-L. Barbier (Eds.), *New directions for research in L2 writing* (pp. 49–80). Dordrecht, The Netherlands: Kluwer.

Schindler, K. (2000). Gemeinsames Schreiben in der Fremdsprache: Muster, kreativität und das Glück des Autors. [General writing in a foreign language: Pattern, creativity, and author's luck.]. *Glottodidactica, 28*, 161–184.

Schoonen, R., van Gelderen, A., de Glopper, K., Hulstijn, J., Snellings, P., Simis, A., & Stevenson, M. (2002). In S. Ransdell, & M.-L. Barbier (Eds.), *New directions for research in L2 writing* (pp. 101–122). Dordrecht, The Netherlands: Kluwer.

Schrader, M. (2000). Automatic writing in the preparation of immigrants for work that is indeed beautiful. In G. Brauer (Ed.), *Writing across languages* (pp. 53–67). Stamford, CT: Ablex.

Schrader, R. (2000). Creative writing with young immigrants. In G. Brauer (Ed.), *Writing across languages* (pp. 25–40). Stamford, CT: Ablex.

Sengupta, S. (2000). An investigation into the effects of revision strategy instruction on L2 secondary school learners. *System, 28* (1), 97–113.

Severino, C. (1993). The sociopolitical implications of response to second language and second dialect writing. *Journal of Second Language Writing, 2* (3), 181–201.

Shei, C. C., & Pain, H. (2000). An ESL writer's collocational aid. *Computer Assisted Language Learning 13* (2), 167–182.

Shi, L. (2001). Native- and nonnative-speaking EFL teachers' evaluation of Chinese students' English writing. *Language Testing, 18* (3), 303–325.

Shin, S. J. (2002). Ten techniques for successful writing tutorials. *TESOL Journal, 11* (1), 25–31.

Silva, T. (1990). Second language composition instruction: Developments, issues, and directions in ESL. In B. Kroll (Ed.), *Second language writing research: Insights for the classroom* (pp. 11–23). New York: Cambridge University Press.

Silva, T., Brice, C., Kapper, J., Matsuda, P. K., & Reichelt, M. (2001). Twenty-five years of scholarship on second language composing processes: 1976–2000. *International Journal of English Studies. 1* (2), 211–240.

Silva, T., & Matsuda, P. K. (2002). Writing. In N. Schmitt (Ed.), *An introduction to applied linguistics* (pp. 251–266). London: Arnold.

Simpson, J. (2000). Topical structure analysis of academic paragraphs in English and Spanish. *Journal of Second Language Writing, 9* (3), 293–309.

Smoke, T. (2001). Instructional strategies for making ESL students integral to the university. In T. Silva & P. K. Matsuda (Eds.), *On second language writing* (pp. 129–441). Mahwah, NJ: Erlbaum.

Smoke, T., Green, T. M., & Isenstead, E. (2001). "This course is giving me cephalgia...:" Linking ESL writing and the Greek and Latin roots of English. In I. Leki (Ed.), *Academic writing programs* (pp. 137–149). Alexandria, VA: TESOL.

Song, B., & August, B. (2002). Using portfolios to assess the writing of ESL students: A powerful alternative? *Journal of Second Language Writing, 11* (1), 49–72.

Stapleton, P. (2001). Assessing critical thinking in the writing of Japanese university students: Insights about assumptions and content familiarity. *Written Communication, 18* (4), 506–548.

Stapleton, P. (2002). Critiquing voice as a viable pedagogical tool in L2 writing: Returning the spotlight to ideas. *Journal of Second Language Writing, 11* (3), 177–190.

Stapleton, P. (2003). Assessing the quality and bias of Web-based sources: Implications for academic writing. *Journal of English for Academic Purposes, 2* (3), 229–245.

Stewart, T., Rehorick, S., & Perry, B. (2001). Adapting the Canadian language benchmarks for writing assessment. *TESL Canada Journal, 18* (2), 48–64.

Storch, N., & Tapper, J. (2002). A useful kind of interaction? Evaluations by university students of feedback on written assignments. *Australian Review of Applied Linguistics, 25* (1), 147–167.

Strong, R. M., & Fruth, J. K. (2001). The Spanish writing center at the University of Minnesota. *ADFL Bulletin, 32* (2), 33–36.

Suh, J.-S. (2002). Effectiveness of CALL writing instruction: The voices of Korean EFL learners. *Foreign Language Annals, 35* (6), 669–679.

Sullivan, K., & Lindgren, E. (2002). Self-assessment in autonomous computer-aided second language writing. *ELT Journal, 56* (3), 258–266.

Svendsen, L. P. (2000). The use of workshops and seminars in the ESL classroom. In G. Brauer

(Ed.), *Writing across languages* (pp. 153–165). Stamford, CT: Ablex.

Sze, C. (2002). A case study of the revision process of a reluctant ESL student writer. *TESL Canada Journal, 19* (2), 21–36.

Tarnopolsky, O. (2000). Writing English as a foreign language: A report from Ukraine. *Journal of Second Language Writing, 9* (3), 209–226.

Thatcher, B. L. (2000). L2 professional writing in a US and South American context. *Journal of Second Language Writing, 9* (1), 41–69.

Thompson, P., & Tribble, C. (2001). Looking at citations: Using corpora in English for academic purposes. *Language Learning & Technology, 5* (3), 91–105.

Thonus, T. (2002). Tutor and student assessments of academic writing tutorials: What is "success"? *Assessing Writing, 8* (2), 110–134.

Thonus, T. (2003). Serving generation 1.5 learners in the university writing center. *TESOL Journal, 12* (1), 17–24.

Thorson, H. (2000). Using the computer to compare foreign and native language writing process: A statistical and case study approach. *The Modern Language Journal, 84,* 155–169.

Tickoo, A. (2000). How to create a crisis: A study of ESL narrative prose. *ITL: Review of Applied Linguistics, 129/130,* 169–190.

Tickoo, A. (2001). How to create a crisis: Empowering the ESL writer with lessons from narrative art. *International Journal of Applied Linguistics, 11* (1), 21–36.

Torras, M. R., & Celaya, M. L. (2001). Age-related differences in the development of written production: An empirical study of EFL school learners. *International Journal of English Studies, 1* (2), 103–126.

Tsang, W. K. (2000). Giving grammar the place it deserves in process writing. *Journal of the Adult Migrant Education Program, 15* (1), 34–45.

Tsui, A. B. M., & Ng, M. (2000). Do secondary L2 writers benefit from peer comments? *Journal of Second Language Writing, 9* (2), 147–170.

Turner, C. E. (2000). Listening to the voices of rating scale developers: Identifying salient features for second language performance assessment. *The Canadian Modern Language Review, 56* (4), 555–584.

Turner, C. E., & Upshur, J. A. (2002). Rating scales derived from student samples: Effects of the scale maker and the student sample on scale content and student scores. *TESOL Quarterly, 36* (1), 49–70.

Valdés, G. (2000). Nonnative English speakers: Language bigotry in English mainstream classrooms. *ADE Bulletin, 124,* 12–17.

Vandrick, S. (2003). Literature in the teaching of second language composition. In B. Kroll (Ed.), *Exploring the dynamics of second language writing* (pp. 263–283). New York: Cambridge University Press.

Vann, R. J., & Myers, C. (2001). Capitalizing on contacts, collaboration, and disciplinary communities: Academic ESL options in a large research university. In I. Leki (Ed.), *Academic writing programs* (pp. 73–84). Alexandria, VA: TESOL.

Vollmer, G. (2002). Sociocultural perspectives on second language writing. *ERIC/CLL News Bulletin, 25* (2), 1–2.

Wang, W., & Wen, Q. (2002). L1 use in the L2 composing process: An exploratory study of 16 Chinese EFL writers. *Journal of Second Language Writing, 11* (3), 225–246.

Warden, C. A. (2000). EFL business writing behaviors in differing feedback environments. *Language Learning, 50* (4), 573–616.

Warschauer, M. (2002). Networking into academic discourse. *Journal of English for Academic Purposes, 1* (1), 45–58.

Weber, J. J. (2001). A concordance- and genre-informed approach to ESP essay writing. *ELT Journal, 55* (1), 14–20.

Weigle, S. C., Boldt, H., & Valsecchi, M. I. (2003). Effects of task and rater background on the evaluation of ESL student writing: A pilot study. *TESOL Quarterly, 37* (2), 345–354.

Weigle, S. C., & Nelson, G. (2001). Academic writing for university examinations. In I. Leki (Ed.), *Academic writing programs* (pp. 121–135). Alexandria, VA: TESOL.

White, R. (2001). Adapting Grice's maxims in the teaching of writing. *ELT Journal, 55* (1), 62–69.

Wilhelm, K. H., & Rivers, M. (2001). An audience approach to EAP writing assessment: Learners, teachers, outsiders. *Applied Language Learning, 12* (2), 177–190.

Williams, J. (2001). A task-based composition course for resident L2 writers. In I. Leki (Ed.), *Academic writing programs* (pp. 111–120). Alexandria, VA: TESOL.

Williams, J. (2002). Undergraduate second language writers in the writing center. *Journal of Basic Writing, 21* (2), 73–91.

Woodall, B. R. (2002). Language-switching: Using the first language while writing in a second language. *Journal of Second Language Writing, 11* (1), 7–28.

Wu, S.-Y., & Rubin, D. L. (2000). Evaluating the impact of collectivism and individualism on argumentative writing by Chinese and North American college students. *Research in the Teaching of English, 35* (2), 148–178.

Xiao, M. K. (2001). The writing assistance programme: A writing center with Hong Kong characteristics. In I. Leki (Ed.), *Academic writing programs* (pp. 7–19). Alexandria, VA: TESOL.

Yamada, K. (2000). Helping novice EFL/ESL academic writers appreciate English textual patterns through summary writing. *JALT Journal, 22* (1), 196–208.

Yamada, K. (2003). What prevents ESL/EFL writers from avoiding plagiarism?: Analyses of 10 North-American college Web sitessites. *System, 31* (2), 247–258.

Yang, L., & Shi, L. (2003). Exploring six MBA students' summary writing by introspection. *Journal of English for Academic Purposes, 2* (3), 165–192.

Yates, R., & Kenkel, J. (2002). Responding to sentence-level errors in writing. *Journal of Second Language Writing, 11* (1), 29–47.

Yuan, Y. (2003). The use of chat rooms in an ESL setting. *Computers and Composition, 20* (2), 194–206.

Zhang, M. (2000). Cohesive features in the expository writing of undergraduates in two Chinese universities. *RELC Journal, 31* (1), 61–95.

Zhu, W. (2001a). Interaction and feedback in mixed peer response groups. *Journal of Second Language Writing, 10* (4), 251–276.

Zhu, W. (2001b). Performing argumentative writing in English: Difficulties, processes, and strategies. *TESL Canada Journal, 19* (1), 34–50.

Zimmerman, R. (2000). L2 writing: Subprocesses, a model of formulating, and empirical findings. *Learning and Instruction 10* (1), 73–99.

RESEARCH IN TEACHING LANGUAGE SYSTEMS

5. RESEARCH IN TEACHING PRONUNCIATION AND INTONATION

Jennifer Jenkins

For several decades of the 20th century, the main interest of pronunciation teaching research was in applying contrastive analysis techniques to the sound segments of the L1 and L2 to identify differences between them and so, it was assumed, to highlight areas where L1 transfer errors were likely to occur. Later in the century, pronunciation teaching research began to move on both by embracing more sophisticated approaches to interlanguage phonology, taking universal, developmental, and other processes into account as well as transfer (see, e.g., the range of research interests documented in Ioup & Weinberger, 1987), and by focusing increasingly on suprasegmental features along with segmental. Still more recently and radically, a number of researchers have ceased treating pronunciation as a somewhat isolated, self-contained linguistic and pedagogic phenomenon, but are forging links with research into other aspects of language and language teaching and also maximizing the opportunities offered by technological advances. This chapter will outline these latest developments in pronunciation research and explore the extent of their influence on pedagogy.

Depending on the second language in question, pronunciation teaching typically covers any or all of the following: consonant and vowel sounds, changes to these sounds in the stream of connected speech, word stress patterns, rhythm, and intonation—what might be described as the nuts and bolts of pronunciation. Some published pronunciation courses and teachers' handbooks still focus exclusively on some or all of these items, often in this order. Others such as Celce-Murcia, Brinton, and Goodwin (1996), Dalton and Seidlhofer (1994), and Morley (1994)—

all books intended for pronunciation teacher education—have taken recent research into consideration and aim, in addition, to promote an awareness of the larger roles pronunciation plays in communication: its influence on speakers' success (or otherwise) in conveying their meaning in specific contexts, its links with their sense of identity, its signaling of their group memberships, the pronunciation choices available to learners, and the like. Of the recent findings of pronunciation research, the most influential in terms of pedagogic developments fall into two main groupings: those concerned with issues of context and those that relate to technological advances. The first group comprises both discourse and sociolinguistic context (the latter including related sociopsychological factors), and the second comprises both new pedagogic possibilities and the potential to challenge earlier claims that had not been supported by empirical evidence. The rest of this chapter is accordingly organized into the following thematic sections:

- The role of pronunciation, and particularly intonation, in discourse
- The relevance to pronunciation teaching of the future social context (s) of L2 use, including sociopsychological factors (identity, attitude, motivation)
- New uses for technology in teaching pronunciation and challenging previous research claims

While some of the research findings have had more influence on pedagogy than others, they have all impinged at least to some extent on the consciousness of pronunciation teachers and materials writers, particularly in the teaching of English. Research into certain other aspects of pronunciation such as Optimality Theory (Prince & Smolensky, 1993), however, has not filtered through to teaching materials or methodology, and so is not discussed in this chapter.

Discourse Approaches

Research into intonation from a discourse perspective (mainly in relation to English, but see, e.g., Moyer, 1999, regarding L2 German) has been ongoing since the pioneering work of David Brazil at Birmingham University from the 1970s until his death in 1995. Brazil's own research into discourse intonation, developed from the work of Halliday and the Prague School (see Halliday, 1970), culminated in the posthumous publication of his 1997 book, which had been published several years earlier in 1985 as a Birmingham University monograph after being rejected by external publishers. At that time, the publishing houses had not considered Brazil's work to contribute usefully to the debate on the relationship between grammar and intonation on the one hand, and intonation and the expression of attitudinal meaning on the other (Hewings & Cauldwell, Foreword to Brazil, 1997, p. vi). Opinions, it seems, are rather less flexible and pedagogy rather slower to adapt with respect to innovations relating to pronunciation than those relating to other linguistic levels, something that will again become evident in the discussion of pronunciation and sociolinguistic context below. More recently, and helped by other research in phonology such as the finding that questions do not have set intonation structure (see the section on technology below), in psycholinguistics (e.g., work on prosodic bootstrapping), and the availability of acoustic analysis techniques for both pedagogy and research (also discussed in the section on technology below), there has been a major reevaluation of discourse intonation. As Pickering (personal communication, June, 2003) puts it: "Essentially, the field seems to have caught up, and with pedagogy just a little bit behind, calls for a discourse approach to intonation seem to be resonating more loudly."

Discourse intonation is, in essence, a model that prioritizes the communicative function of intonation over traditional models based on ascribing attitudinal and grammatical functions to pitch movement (although discourse intonation could be said to embrace these latter functions). It involves both conversational control (turn-taking, introducing and ending topics, etc.), and the establishing of social meanings and roles, by means of the assigning of prominence, key, and tone choice: proclaiming tone (fall) for unshared information and referring tone (fall–rise) for information that the speaker considers part of the shared common ground. As such, it provides both teachers and researchers with "a manageable tool for analysing and interpreting the intonation choices made by speakers in naturally occurring speech" (Hewings & Cauldwell, 1997, p. vi.). A discourse intonation approach is able, for example, to account for the use of HRT (high rising terminal, or *upspeak*) whereby a rising tone is used in places where a falling tone would be expected. This phenomenon has become increasingly prevalent over the past decade, especially but not exclusively in the United Kingdom. A discourse-based interpretation explains it both as "a bonding technique which upspeakers use to promote a sense of solidarity between themselves and their interlocutors" (Bradford, 1996, p. 23) and as serving a participatory function by encouraging the hearer's continued involvement in the exchange.

The few earlier language teaching materials which took account of discourse intonation, such as Brazil, Coulthard, and Johns (1980) and Bradford (1988), applied the model wholesale for productive use. Although learners seemed to benefit from the opportunity to analyze communicative contextualized intonation patterns after the event, it proved difficult to teach some aspects of discourse intonation for production. Particularly problematic, because of the subconscious level of the operation, was the assessment of new or given status and corresponding assignment of tone. Some more recent classroom activities and teacher education materials (e.g., Bowler & Cunningham, 1999; Gilbert, 2001; Hancock, 1995, 2003; Levis, 2001) have therefore tended to focus for production more on prominence, where the "rules" can be applied at a conscious level, and to treat the subtleties of discourse-based tone assignment in interpretation and analyzing activities, or to restrict them mainly to matters of conversation management (turn-taking, etc.) where, again, it is easier to articulate "rules." Pickering and Levis (in press), in addition to these latter phenomena, focus on the use of pitch concord to indicate agreement between interlocutors. This, again, is a feature that may prove to be easier to bring to conscious attention for productive use.

Wennerstrom (2003) employs authentic data as a tool to enable learners to become discourse analysts working on native and (their own) nonnative data as a prelude to developing their productive skills. In those cases where the teaching of discourse tone choice for productive use is advocated, discourse intonation experts have recently been demonstrating how the process may be facilitated by an emphasis on the use of native and nonnative speaker authentic data (see Wennerstrom, 2001), and a concentration on specific contexts of use, often academic. Clennell (1997), for example, focuses on the teaching of discourse-based intonation features in EAP (English for academic purposes) courses to equip international students to communicate effectively in native-English-speaking universities. In a similar vein, Pickering (2001) investigates the extent to which tone choice by international teaching assistants (ITAs) promotes or obstructs their meaning in university classrooms. Pickering (in press) reports further research on the teaching of discourse intonation and includes a section on application to ITA program instruction that is relevant to any ESL situation where nonnative speakers are involved in the academy, recommending a focus on discourse level contexts in order to work with the notion of paragraphing and to improve pitch range.

As is generally the rule in L2 pronunciation, nevertheless, production will follow perception at a later stage (if at all) only when there is sufficient exposure to the feature in question (cf. Celce-Murcia et al., 1996, p. 36, who provide a hierarchical framework moving from analysis and consciousness raising to listening discrimination, and finally to production). In the case of discourse tone choice, the amount of exposure is likely to be rather more than that required for the acquisition of "easier" aspects of pronunciation such as consonant sounds. However, technological approaches to the problem of teaching discourse tone choice productively, such as that of Cauldwell (2002a, 2002b, 2002c), may offer a solution. The pioneering use of CD-ROMs, eminently suitable for self-access, enables large amounts of contextualized native-speaker data to be provided for learners, along with the facility to listen to short extracts and repeat specific features over and over. Although it is too early to make definitive claims, it is possible that the more direct and learner-oriented character of technological approaches may accelerate the process of tone acquisition both by providing a greater amount of exposure to tone in context with the opportunity to mimic repeatedly, and by their appeal to the subconscious as well as the cognitive level.

One final area that merits discussion in relation to discourse intonation is that of the link between tone units and lexical phrases. The lexical approach was first enumerated in detail by Nattinger and DeCarrico (1992) following research such as that of Pawley and Syder (1983), and swiftly popularized by Lewis (1993). It has subsequently become a regular feature in English language teaching, often known as "*chunking.*" Its links with intonation contours were discussed in detail by Seidlhofer and Dalton-Puffer (1995). Since then, a number of intonation teaching materials have taken up the idea of teaching lexical phrases along with their intonation patterns and/or introducing the concept of the tone unit by means of the lexical phrase, along with the idea of teaching "intonational idioms" (Dalton & Seidlhofer, 1994; Wennerstrom, 2001).

The Role of Context of Use

In terms of context of use, we need at once to make a distinction between that second language learning that is undertaken in order to facilitate communication with native speakers of a language, and that undertaken to facilitate international communication (see Widdowson, 2003, Chap. 5). In the first case—the learning of a *foreign* language—the context of use is most likely to be the L2 country and the learner's goal to be the lingua-culture of its native speakers. Although, for various reasons including that of a "critical period" (see Scovel, 1998), adult learners are unlikely to acquire accents identical to those of native speakers (NSs), they may wish to attempt to do so, and some will achieve a fair degree of success. These learners will—or will wish to—acquire not only the phonemic distinctions of the L2 but also near-nativelike realizations of individual phonemes according to the phonetic environment, along with many of the suprasegmental features of the foreign language.

Second and Foreign Language Contexts of Use

Recent research has continued to add to the body of work already existing on the pronunciation needs of L2 speakers to prepare them for interaction with L1 speakers of the language (i.e., for native/nonnative communication). The most recent studies have refined and extended the area of inquiry, moving away from an emphasis on nativelike goals to one that gives greater priority to the listener perspective (both the native's and the nonnative's), with a focus on issues such as the factors involved in the intelligibility or comprehensibility of nonnative speech to native listeners, nonnative listeners' preferred speech rates, and the like (cf. Derwing & Munro, 2001; Derwing, Rossiter, & Munro, 2002). Other recent research in this domain has been investigating the effects of different approaches to pronunciation teaching on learners' accents, including learners' own perspectives, rather than taking the beneficial effects of all pronunciation teaching as a given (cf. Derwing & Rossiter, 2002a, 2002b). Both of these general research directions are already having an effect on second/foreign language pronunciation teaching. Listening activities are becoming more prominent in pronunciation materials, particularly those that help learners deal with the problems of connected speech (in which regard Shockey, 2003, is an important contribution to teacher education). Production activities are moving away from mimicking toward the greater prioritizing of specific pronunciation features, with more priority generally being accorded to suprasegmental than to segmental aspects of the language for this type of communication context.

Meanwhile, contrastive analysis-based research continues in part at least because of the current emphasis in L2 pedagogy on individual learner needs. It would, in any case, have been a serious mistake to throw out the modern contrastive analysis baby with the old contrastive analysis bathwater. Teachers have always continued to believe in the important influence of the mother tongue on L2 pronunciation acquisition, even during periods when researchers were emphatically arguing that L1 transfer was trivial (most notably during the 1970s and 1980s in the United States). Furthermore, the interest in contrastive analytical research itself has never disappeared entirely, even though it is nowadays complemented by an equally robust interest in other approaches to interlanguage phonology, as is evidenced by the range of research papers in Major (1998) and Leather (1999).

Within the current contrastive analysis tradition, there is a growing body of research-based publications for teachers of students from L1s that earlier research had tended to overlook and/or treat superficially, by ignoring, where relevant, the role of local L1-L2 contact. Brown, Deterding, and Low (2000), for example, examine a range of differences between Singaporean and British English, including discourse intonation, pitch range, and lexical stress. Hung (2000, 2002a) uses a contrastive methodology in determining his phonology of Hong Kong English. Deterding and Poedjosoedarmo (1998) is a research-based reference work for teachers, providing both details of the segmental and suprasegmental features of a wide range of different Southeast Asian languages and English, along with practice activities for teachers to use in the classroom. Taking further the current move away from nativelike accents as the goal of pronunciation teaching, the authors question whether learners in countries where the L2 is an official second language should be taught an accent other than their own, a point also raised by Hung (2002b). Further evidence of the continuing pedagogic influence of this type of research is the second edition of Swan and Smith (2002), providing contrastive information for teachers of English of students from a large number L1s, Brown (1997), a book of pronunciation teaching materials for the Singaporean classroom, and Weinberger's (2002) Web site (http://classweb.gmu.edu/accent/), which provides an English passage read by L2 speakers from a comprehensive range of L1 backgrounds.

International Contexts of Use

However, some languages are learned primarily for use in international contexts. In this second case, much of the interaction typically takes place between nonnative speakers (NNSs) from different first language backgrounds, often with no native speakers involved at all. Here, then, we are speaking of an *international* language, of which English in the expanding circle (Kachru, 1992) is currently the example par *excellence*, although other languages such as Spanish may, too, be learned for this purpose. Because of the acknowledged position of English at present as the world's principal international language, or *lingua franca*, the discussion that follows will focus exclusively on the role of international context in the teaching of pronunciation for English as an International Language (EIL). The principles and issues discussed nevertheless apply to the acquisition of the pronunciation of any international language and involve, possibly, the most radical changes of all to L2 pronunciation pedagogy (see also Seidlhofer, this volume).

Essentially research into EIL has demonstrated the importance in EIL communication of pronunciation in general, and of certain pronunciation features in particular. Pronunciation had been marginalized by communicative approaches to language teaching in vogue since the 1980s, in the belief that it was peripheral to successful communication. The EIL research found, on the contrary, both that in interaction between L2 speakers from different L1s, pronunciation plays a critical role in preventing communication breakdowns and that—in line with the distinction between foreign and international languages—the phonological and phonetic factors involved are not necessarily the same as those involved in communication between a native and nonnative speaker of the language.

The main focus of EIL research to date has been the role of pronunciation in promoting intelligibility in NNS–NNS communication, including the part played by accommodation skills. Jenkins (2000, 2002) builds on earlier research in which listeners rated the intelligibility of the pronunciation of speakers from different L1s, such as Smith and Rafiqzad (1979), Smith and Bisazza (1982), Smith and Nelson (1985), and Smith (1992). Her Lingua Franca Core targets those features found in her research to be crucial in promoting intelligible pronunciation for an interlocutor from a different L1: most consonant sounds, vowel quantity, initial and medial consonant clusters, and tonic stress (see Seidlhofer, this volume, for details). Drawing also on Speech/Communication Accommodation Theory (cf. Beebe & Giles, 1984; Giles, Coupland, & Coupland, 1991), Jenkins's research also demonstrates that intelligible pronunciation between speakers from different L1s is not a monolithic phenomenon, but one that requires negotiation and adjustment in accordance with the specific context of the discourse and, above all, in relation to addressor/addressee factors (see Jenkins, 2003, for further discussion and examples of accommodation in EIL communication).

Also on the research agenda, though less extensively explored hitherto, is the link between accent and identity in EIL speech contexts. The prevailing concept of "accent reduction," with its tendency to regard learners as subjects for speech pathology and to exhort them to lose all traces of their L1 accent in their L2 has been questioned by those working from an EIL perspective. Instead, the concept of "accent addition" is being promoted in accordance with the goals of additive bilingualism and in tune with the current emphasis on learner choice (see, in particular, Pakir, 1999). Based on research into pronunciation attitudes, both that of other scholars (see below on sociopsychological issues) and her own EIL research, Jenkins (2000, pp. 209–210) proposes five stages of pronunciation learning:

- Addition of core [i.e., Lingua Franca Core] items to the learner's productive and receptive repertoire
- Addition of a range of L2 English accents to the learner's receptive repertoire
- Addition of accommodation skills
- Addition of non-core items to the learner's receptive repertoire
- Addition of a range of L1 English accents to the learner's receptive repertoire

Learners who have elected to acquire an accent that enables them both to preserve their L1 identity in their L2 English and to be (pronunciation-wise) intelligible to other NNSs will probably aim for the first three stages. However, they may also wish to be able to understand the pronunciation of NSs, certain features of whose speech can, without prior familiarizing, present particular difficulties for NNS listeners (Bent & Bradlow, 2003). In this case, they will probably aim for all five stages. The critical point, though, is that there is no suggestion of losing their

L1 repertoire and, by definition, their L1 identity. This change in emphasis has already filtered through to pronunciation materials, which are tending to incorporate a greater degree of learner choice of target than hitherto, and to move away from nativelike targets for learners whose goal is international intelligibility.

Pronunciation materials are responding to the EIL research in other ways. The most noticeable phenomenon is the large increase in the number of NNSs used in listening activities, thus providing exposure to a range of L2 English accents. Things are moving rather less slowly in relation to production, though the first courses to offer learners the choice of an NS or a local (but internationally intelligible) NNS model are appearing (e.g., Cunningham & Moor, 2003; Sato, Kanechiku, Matsumoto, & Miyata, 2003). Otherwise, it is still a case of adapting existing published pronunciation materials. Jenkins (2003), for example, provides suggestions for adapting minimal pair activities from Brown (1997) and Hancock (1995) to promote production of respectively core sounds and tonic stress, and from Gilbert (2001) to develop EIL accommodation skills.

However, at this stage, the emphasis is more on raising awareness of EIL contextual factors in manuals and materials for teacher education than on providing classroom pronunciation courses. Pennington (1996), though described as "an international approach," largely restricts the NNS element to description while providing production activities that promote NS norms. McKay's (2002) handbook for teachers, on the other hand, raises awareness of the possibility of teaching productive pronunciation for EIL by focusing on the Lingua Franca Core items, although she concludes, in line with Dalton and Seidlhofer (1994), that it may still be valuable to maintain an NS accent as a point of reference in the classroom, thus "preventing speakers of English from moving too far apart in their pronunciation" (p.72). Dalton and Seidlhofer (1994) is itself a handbook for teachers and an early example of a teacher education book taking EIL into consideration in its concern with identity and intelligibility. More recently, Walker (2001) is the first attempt to provide teachers within a specific L2 context, in this case Spain, with a taxonomy of core features that their learners should focus on for EIL purposes. And still more recently, Hung (2002b) has addressed the issue of dictionary transcripts, arguing that these should reflect local (in his case Hong Kong) pronunciations of English rather than elite British or American accents. Although this shift has begun to take place with respect to the indigenized varieties of English of the outer circle, however, more data will be needed before the same approach can be applied systematically to expanding circle Englishes. Finally, Keys and Walker (2002) address the inevitable concern of teachers that a move away from exonormative British or American accent norms and models will be accompanied by a decline in pronunciation standards.

However, there are also sociopsychological factors to be taken into account, particularly those relating to language attitudes, motivation, and identity. Dörnyei and Csizér argue on the basis of empirical evidence that traditional orientations to motivation are being challenged by current developments: "World English is turning into an increasingly international language and it is therefore rapidly losing its national cultural base while becoming associated with a global culture," which, they contend, "undermines the traditional definition of integrativeness as it is not clear any more who the 'L2 speakers' or the members of the 'L2 community' are" (2002, p. 453). In this respect, the sociopsychological situation is not only unclear, but is also sending out contradictory signals. Bamgbose (1998) describes L2 attitudes to English accents as "a love–hate relationship" and goes on to claim that in the outer circle "one does not wish to sound like a native speaker, but still finds the accent fascinating" (p. 7), but his claim would receive a very ambivalent response in the expanding circle. For, as the research of Dalton, Kaltenboeck, and Smit (1997), Grau (in press), Smit and Dalton-Puffer (2000), Timmis (2002) and others demonstrates, despite recent EIL developments, many teachers and learners still prefer to aim for an approximation of a nativelike rather than a local or internationally acceptable accent. This seems, paradoxically, to be the case even when, as Grau finds in her study, they simultaneously believe that the objective should be international intelligibility and that an L2 accent is acceptable.

Meanwhile, Smit (2002) finds that orientation to the target accent and L1 speaker group as well as self-efficacy and anxiety (that is, "how (in)adequate they feel in their pronunciation," p. 95) play important roles in the acquisition (or not) of a near-native accent. She concludes that her study "supports the so often invoked character of pronunciation as being that aspect of a language which is closest to its speakers' feelings of identity" (p. 102). Her findings resonate in some respects with Lippi-Green's (1997) account of L2 accents in an inner circle context, the United States. Accent is seen both to arouse in L2 speakers feelings of linguistic insecurity, and to relate in critical ways to social identity and the construction of self and *other*. This takes us back to the problem highlighted by Dörnyei and Csizér: the difficulty of establishing the social identity of the L2 community in an international context and the implications for EIL pronunciation. While teachers and learners are becoming aware to some extent of the complex sociopsychological issues involved, there has as yet been no attempt to address them at the wider level through pronunciation teaching methodologies and materials, although more enlightened teacher education courses are beginning to grapple with them.

This is, nevertheless, still early in the day for EIL phonology, and it is likely to be some time before large numbers of teachers elect to offer their students a selection of context-based pronunciation goals—or for students to wish to take advantage of the offer. The EIL perspective is also beset by misinterpretations and misconceptions, particularly by those from regions where there is a strong tradition of educational investment in and attachment to the RP accent, such as Central Europe. For a typical example, see Sobkowiak (2003), who fails to grasp the essential difference between EIL and EFL and the implications for pronunciation norms and goals. The best, then, that may be said about pronunciation in EIL contexts at present is that those who support an EIL approach to pronunciation teaching alongside an ESL/EFL approach can be cautiously optimistic. Some learners are at least beginning to be offered a small element of choice in their pronunciation goals, and with further researching into and refining of the Lingua Franca Core and greater publicizing of the sociolinguistic, sociopsychological, and intelligibility imperatives, the process is likely to gather momentum in pronunciation as in the other linguistic levels (Seidlhofer, 2001; Seidlhofer, this volume).

Computer Technology in Pronunciation Teaching and Research

Earlier uses of computers in pronunciation teaching focused entirely on the identification (often referred to as "speech/voice recognition") and production of individual phonemes. Segmental approaches continue to be developed. For example, the SPECO Project, a new system using advanced speech technology in the clinical remediation of children's speech pathology, is being investigated for its potential in L2 pronunciation teaching (see Roach, 2002). Boersma and Weenink have developed the PRAAT Programme to teach vowel and diphthong production by means of formant plotting; it is available free of charge on www.praat.org

(see Brett, 2002). However, Derwing, Munro, and Carbonaro (2000) find in their research into popular automatic software recognition (ASR) packages for ESL speech that these sorts of packages are still not able to perform as well as human listeners listening to nonnative speech. They conclude that possibilities for using ASR software in the L2 classroom are "intriguing," but that it must be carefully evaluated to ensure that it recognizes nonnative speech and reasonable accuracy levels (to avoid unnecessary correction and frustration) as well as humans do.

Most recently there has been a surge of interest in harnessing computers for teaching the suprasegmentals. Kaltenboeck, for example, has developed a CD-ROM for the teaching of intonation (see Kaltenboeck, 2002). Protea Textware (2001) has published two CD-ROMs, one focusing on connected speech in American English, the other in British English. Cauldwell (2002a, 2002b) has published a CD-ROM, *Streaming Speech*, which deals with a range of aspects of British English pronunciation. In each case, the material on the CD-ROM is underpinned by extensive research, either Cauldwell's own or that of colleagues. For example, the section that deals with connected speech processes is informed by Shockey (2003), the section dealing with units of speech is based on the research of Brazil (1997) and Halliday (1994), and that on the functions of level tone again links with Brazil (1997). One further point about these suprasegmental materials is that they have been designed with an emphasis on promoting learner autonomy, a phenomenon that—as Kaltenboeck (2002) points out—is particularly relevant to the acquisition of pronunciation. In fact, they have probably been able to achieve this goal more successfully than the segmental speech recognition packages because of the shortcomings of the latter identified by Derwing et al. (2002). The suprasegmental materials, though still in their infancy, point to an important teaching tool for the future, one that complements rather than supersedes written materials and classroom teachers by, for example, enabling learners to pin down fleeting and subconsciously processed features such as pitch movement.

One further use of technology in pronunciation teaching is in the field of dictionaries. Many of the major publishers have recently begun issuing CD-ROMs with their dictionaries. Like the other technological advances outlined above, these, too, promote learner autonomy in the acquisition of pronunciation. For example, they offer learners a range of features such as the opportunity to hear words in isolation and, in some cases, in connected speech, and the possibility of recording and listening to themselves to compare their own pronunciation with the dictionary version. Even more useful in terms of self-access pronunciation is the latest edition of Daniel Jones's *English Pronouncing Dictionary* (Roach, Hartman, & Setter, 2003) with CD-ROM, which also provides copious details of both North American and British English pronunciation.

The other way in which technology is proving useful in pronunciation teaching is by enabling researchers to collect corpora with which they can test out and, if necessary, debunk earlier claims that had been based on intuition rather than empirical evidence. So far the challenge to the status quo has involved two main phenomena: final pitch and stress timing. Both Levis (1999a, 1999b), for American English, and Cauldwell (1999), for British English, have arrived at similar conclusions about final pitch. Following in the footsteps of Fries (1964)—probably the first corpus-based study of question intonation (Roach, personal communication, June, 2001)—both collected empirical data from native speakers of the respective varieties of English (as opposed to the invented examples favored by earlier pronunciation researchers) and analyzed them for final pitch direction in yes/no questions. In neither case did the long-held belief that the pitch has a rising tone (strictly speaking, a fall–rise) rather than a falling tone stand up to examination, though as yet few teachers or materials writers have responded to the finding.

Cauldwell also investigated so-called stress-and syllable-timed rhythm; extending the earlier discoveries of Dauer (1983) and Roach (1982), he found that the theory fell down when tested empirically. Cauldwell (1996) is an early version of his resulting article, published in a Hungarian journal. He subsequently tried in vain to place a revised version with an international journal. (The problem, it would seem, was the potential damage it might have inflicted on the publications of certain established authors.) Eventually, he published a second revision of his article on the Web (Cauldwell, 2002a). Here he concludes that

> the continued presence of the refuted hypothesis, that has become hard-wired into our thinking, is an obstacle to progress in understanding the nature of spontaneous speech: long-refuted, it should be now discarded. Life without the stress- and syllable-timing hypothesis will be more difficult, but it should make possible real advances in the understanding of spontaneous speech.

(See also list of Cauldwell's publications, Cauldwell, 2003.) Although most pronunciation teachers and materials still retain at least a vestige of the belief in stress timing, the influence of the research is growing, so that many teachers and especially teacher educators now qualify the claim by referring to stress timing as only a tendency and as occurring mainly in more formal speech. Marks (1999) argues, meanwhile, that the use of rhymes in the classroom is valid in so far as it "provides a convenient framework for the perception and production of a number of characteristic features of English pronunciation which are often found to be problematic for learners: stress/unstress (and therefore the basis for intonation), vowel length, vowel reduction, elision, compression, pause (between adjacent stresses)" (p. 198). This is a sensible recommendation that is likely to continue finding favor with teachers long after they have abandoned any belief in the existence of stress timing.

Conclusion: Current Progress—Future Trends

The research agendas discussed in this chapter have undoubtedly led to a renewed interest in pronunciation as an important skill in second language teaching and learning. Pronunciation, it seems, has regained much of the standing it held in the days of the Reform Movement early in the last century. The research has enabled it to reemerge, though, as a more flexible and more relevant language phenomenon, able to adapt to its context of use and to relate in both teaching and research to other linguistic areas, most notably (but not exclusively) discourse and sociolinguistics. The fact that two pronunciation works were shortlisted for the prestigious BAAL (British Association of Applied Linguistics) Book Prize in the past three years, and that *TESOL Quarterly* will soon publish an issue dedicated to pronunciation, is evidence, if such was needed, that pronunciation has come of age and is unlikely to remain on the margins of language teaching in the 21st century as it did for much of the final part of the twentieth.

ANNOTATED BIBLIOGRAPHY
Celce-Murcia, M., Brinton, D., & Goodwin, J. (1996). *Teaching pronunciation.*
 Cambridge: Cambridge University Press.

A particularly comprehensive reference work for the teaching of American English pronunciation, which draws heavily on second language acquisition research findings, discusses methodological issues, and offers specific guidance for both classroom practice and pronunciation diagnosis and testing. It takes a more modern and inclusive approach than many of its predecessors in the detailed attention it gives to suprasegmentals.

Dalton, C., & Seidlhofer, B. (1994). *Pronunciation* [volume in the Scheme for Teacher Education]. Oxford: Oxford University Press.

In some respects the British-English counterpart of Celce-Murcia et al. (1996), this book also draws extensively on research as well as being ahead of its time in focusing on issues such as identity and intelligibility, which have come to the fore since its publication. A classic in its task-based approach to presenting the research-based issues and evaluating of pronunciation teaching materials, it has subsequently been widely imitated.

Jenkins, J. (2000). *The phonology of English as an international language.* Oxford: Oxford University Press.

The first volume to investigate the implications for pronunciation teaching and use with regard to developments in EIL. Based on empirical research, it proposes a completely new alternative goal for pronunciation teaching in the expanding circle: intelligibility between nonnative speakers instead of the approximation of native-speaker accents.

Lippi-Green, R. (1997). *English with an accent.* London: Routledge.

To my knowledge, this is the only volume dealing specifically with the links between accent and identity, and the role played by accent attitudes on both sides of the "accent bar." Although not specifically concerned with research into the teaching of pronunciation, it provides important insights into issues such as linguistic insecurity, which are of immense relevance to pronunciation pedagogy.

OTHER REFERENCES

Bamgbose, A. (1998). Torn between the norms: Innovations in world Englishes. *World Englishes, 17* (1), 1–14.

Beebe, L. & Giles, H. (1984). Speech-accommodation theories: A discussion in terms of second-language acquisition. *International Journal of the Sociology of Language, 46,* 5–32.

Bent, T., & Bradlow, A. (2003). The interlanguage speech intelligibility benefit. *Journal of the Acoustical Society of America, 114,* 1600–1610.

Bowler, B., & Cunningham, S. (1999). *Headway pronunciation course.* Oxford: Oxford University Press.

Bradford, B. (1988). *Intonation in context.* Cambridge: Cambridge University Press.

Bradford, B. (1996, Summer). Upspeak. *Speak Out! Newsletter of the IATEFL Pronunciation Special Interest Group, 18,* 22–24.

Brazil, D. (1997). *The communicative value of intonation in English.* Cambridge: Cambridge University Press.

Brazil, D., Coulthard, M., & Johns, C. (1980). *Discourse intonation and language teaching.* London: Longman.

Brett, D. (2002). Improved vowel production with the PRAAT programme. In D. Teeler (Ed.), *Talking computers* (pp. 7–10). Whitstable, UK: International Association of Teachers of English as a Foreign Language (IATEFL).

Brown, A. (1997). *Use of English in teaching.* Singapore: Prentice Hall.

Brown, A., Deterding, D., & Low, E. L. (2000). *The English language in Singapore: Research on pronunciation.* Singapore: Singapore Association of Applied Linguistics.

Cauldwell, R. (1996). Stress-timing: Observations, beliefs, and evidence. *Eger Journal of English Studies, 1,* 33–48.

Cauldwell, R. (1999). Judgements of attitudinal meanings in isolation and in context [Brief research report]. Retrieved November 26, 2003, from http://www.phon.ucl.ac.uk/home/johnm/cauld.htm.

Cauldwell, R. (2002a). The functional irrythmicality of spontaneous speech: A discourse view of speech rhythms. Retrieved November 17, 2003, from http://www.solki.jyu.fi/apples.

Cauldwell, R. (2002b). *Streaming speech.* Birmingham, UK: Speechinaction.

Cauldwell, R. (2002c). Streaming speech: Listening and pronunciation for advanced learners of English. In D. Teeler (Ed.), *Talking computers* (pp. 18–22). Whitstable, UK: IATEFL.

Cauldwell, R. (2003). List of publication and teaching materials related to discourse intonation. Retrieved December 1, 2003, from http://www.speechinaction.com/CDIS_Cauldwell_hub.htm.

Chun, D. (2002). *Discourse intonation in L2.* Amsterdam: Benjamins.

Clennell, C. (1997). Raising the pedagogic status of discourse intonation teaching. *Language Teaching Journal, 51* (2), 117–134.

Cunningham, S., & Moor, P. (2003). *Cutting edge advanced.* London: Pearson.

Dalton-Puffer, C., Kaltenboeck, G., & Smit, U. (1997). Learner attitudes and L2 pronunciation in Austria. *World Englishes, 16* (1), 115–128.

Dauer, R. (1983). Stress-timing and syllable-timing re-analyzed. *Journal of Phonetics, 11*, 51–62.

Derwing, T., & Munro, M. (2001). What speaking rates do nonnative listeners prefer? *Applied Linguistics, 22* (3), 324–337.

Derwing, T., & Rossiter, M. (2002a). ESL learners' perceptions of their pronunciation needs and strategies. *System, 30*, 155–166.

Derwing, T., & Rossiter M. (2002b). The effects of pronunciation instruction on the accuracy, fluency and complexity of L2 accented speech. *Applied Language Learning, 13* (1–2), 1–17.

Derwing, T., Munro, M., & Carbonaro, M. (2000). Does popular speech recognition software work with ESL speech? *TESOL Quarterly, 34* (4), 592–603.

Derwing, T., Rossiter, M., & Munro, M. (2002). Teaching native speakers to listen to foreign-accented speech. *Journal of Multilingual and Multicultural Development 23* (4), 245–259.

Deterding, D., & Poedjosoedarmo, G. (1998). *The sounds of English*. Singapore: Prentice Hall.

Dörnyei, Z., & Csizér, K. (2002). Some dynamics of language attitudes and motivation: Results of a longitudinal nationwide survey. *Applied Linguistics, 23* (4), 421–462.

Fries, C. (1964). On the intonation of 'yes-no' questions in English. In D. Abercrombie (Ed.), *In honour of Daniel Jones* (pp. 242–254). London: Longman.

Gilbert, J. (2001). *Clear speech from the start*. Cambridge: Cambridge University Press.

Giles, H., Coupland, N., & Coupland, J. (Eds.). (1991). *Contexts of accommodation: Developments in applied sociolinguistics*. Cambridge: Cambridge University Press.

Grau, M. (in press). English as an international language—What do future teachers have to say? In C. Gnutzmann (Ed.), *The globalisation of English and the English language classroom*. Clevedon: Multilingual Matters.

Halliday, M. (1970). *A course in spoken English: Intonation*. Oxford: Oxford University Press.

Halliday, M. (1994). *An introduction to functional grammar* (2nd ed.). London: Edward Arnold.

Hancock, M. (1995). *Pronunciation games*. Cambridge: Cambridge University Press.

Hancock, M. (2003). *English pronunciation in use*. Cambridge: Cambridge University Press.

Hewings, M., & Cauldwell, R. (1997). Foreword. In D. Brazil, *The communicative value of intonation in English* (pp. v–vii). Cambridge: Cambridge University Press.

Hung, T. (2000). Towards a phonology of Hong Kong English. *World Englishes, 19* (3), 337–356.

Hung, T. (2002a). Languages in contact: Hong Kong English phonology and the influence of Cantonese. In A. Kirkpatrick (Ed.), *Englishes in Asia* (pp. 191–200). Melbourne: Language Australia Ltd.

Hung, T. (2002b). 'New' English words in international English dictionaries. *English Today, 18* (4), 29–34.

Ioup, G., & Weinberger, S. (Eds.). (1987). *Interlanguage phonology*. Cambridge, MA: Newbury House.

Jenkins, J. (2002). A sociolinguistically-based, empirically-researched pronunciation syllabus for English as an International Language. *Applied Linguistics, 23* (1), 83–103.

Jenkins, J. (2003). Intelligibility in lingua franca discourse. In J. Burton & C. Clennell (Eds.), *Interaction and language learning* (pp. 85–97). Alexandria, VA: TESOL.

Kachru, B. (1992). Teaching World Englishes. In B. Kachru (Ed.), *The other tongue. English across cultures* (2nd ed.) (pp. 355–365). Urbana, IL: University of Illinois Press.

Kaltenboeck, G. (2002). Computer-based intonation teaching: Problems and potential. In D. Teeler (Ed.), *Talking computers* (pp. 11–17). Whitstable, UK: IATEFL.

Keys K., & R. Walker (2002). Ten questions on the phonology of English as an International Language. *English Language Teaching Journal, 56* (3), 298–302.

Leather, J. (Ed.). (1999). *Phonological issues in language learning*. Malden, MA: Blackwell.

Levis, J. (1999a). Intonation in theory and practice revisited. *TESOL Quarterly, 33* (1), 37–63.

Levis, J. (1999b). The intonation and meaning of normal yes/no questions. *World Englishes, 18* (3), 373–380.

Levis, J. (2001). Teaching focus for conversational use. *English Language Teaching Journal, 55* (1), 47–54.

Lewis M. (1993). *The lexical approach*. Hove, UK: Language Teaching Publications.

Major, R. (Ed.). (1998). *Studies in Second Language Acquisition, 20* (2) [special issue on interlanguage phonology and phonetics].

Marks, J. (1999). Is stress-timing real? *English Language Teaching Journal, 53* (3), 191–199.

McKay, S. (2002). *Teaching English as an international language*. Oxford: Oxford University Press.

Morley, J. (Ed.). (1994). *Pronunciation pedagogy and theory: New views, new directions*. Alexandria, VA: TESOL.

Moyer, A. (1999). Ultimate attainment in L2 phonology. *Studies in Second Language Acquisition, 21,* 81 108.

Nattinger, J., & DeCarrico, J. (1992). *Lexical phrases and language teaching*. Oxford: Oxford University Press.

Pakir, A. (1999). Connecting with English in the context of internationalization. *TESOL Quarterly, 33* (1), 103–114.

Pawley, A., & Syder, F. (1983). Two puzzles for linguistic theory: Nativelike selection and nativelike fluency. In J. Richards, & R. Schmidt (Eds.), *Language and communication* (pp. 191–226). London: Longman.

Pennington, M. (1996). *Phonology in English language teaching: An international approach*. London: Longman.

Pickering, L. (2001). The role of tone choice in improving ITA communication in the classroom. *TESOL Quarterly, 35* (2), 233–255.

Pickering, L. (in press). Structure and function of intonational paragraphs in native and nonnative speakers' instrumental discourse. *Journal of English for Specific Purposes.*

Pickering, L., & Levis, J. (in press). Assessing intonation patterns of English language learners. *Language Learning.*

Prince, A., & Smolensky, P. (1993). *Optimality Theory: Constraint interaction in generative grammar.* Piscataway, NJ: Rutgers University, Cognitive Sciences Center.

Protea Textware Pty Ltd (2001). PO Box 49, Hurstbridge, Victoria 3099, Australia.

Roach, P. (1982). On the distinction between "stress-timed" and "syllable-timed" languages. In D. Crystal (Ed.), *Linguistic controversies* (pp.73–79). London: Edward Arnold.

Roach, P. (2002). SPECO: Computer-based phonetic training for children. In D. Teeler (ed.), *Talking computers* (pp. 25–27). Whitstable, UK: IATEFL.

Roach, P., Hartman, J., & Setter, J. (2003). (Eds.). *English pronouncing dictionary* (16th ed.). Cambridge: Cambridge University Press.

Sato, K., Kanechiku, K., Matsumoto, H., & Miyata, S. (2003). *Life watch: Ready to talk about Japan* [coursebook and video]. Tokyo: Asahi Press.

Scovel, T. (1998). *Psycholinguistics.* Oxford: Oxford University Press.

Seidlhofer, B. (2001). Closing a conceptual gap: The case for a description of English as lingua franca. *International Journal of Applied Linguistics, 11* (2), 133–158.

Seidlhofer, B. (this volume). Research perspectives on teaching English as a lingua franca.

Seidlhofer, B., & Dalton-Puffer, C. (1995). Appropriate units in pronunciation teaching: Some programmatic pointers. *International Journal of Applied Linguistics, 5* (1), 135–146.

Shockey, L. (2003). *Sound patterns of spoken English.* Oxford: Blackwell.

Smit, U. (2002). The interaction of motivation and achievement in advanced EFL pronunciation learners. *International Review of Applied Linguistics, 40,* 89–116.

Smit, U., & Dalton, C. (2000). Motivation in advanced EFL pronunciation learners. *International Review of Applied Linguistics, 38* (3/4), 229–246.

Smith, L. (1992). Spread of English and issues of intelligibility. In B. Kachru (Ed.), *The other tongue: English across cultures,* 2nd ed. (pp. 75–90). Urbana, IL: University of Illinois Press.

Smith, L., & Bisazza, J. (1982). The comprehensibility of three varieties of English for college students in seven countries. *Language Learning, 32,* 259–270.

Smith, L., & Nelson, C. (1985). International intelligibility of English: Directions and resources. *World Englishes, 4* (3), 333–342.

Smith, L., & Rafiqzad, K. (1979). English for cross-cultural communication: The question of intelligibility. *TESOL Quarterly, 13* (3), 371–380.

Sobkowiak, W. (2003). Why not LFC? *Zeszyty Naukowe Panstwowej Wyzszej Szkoly Zawodowej w Koninie* [Scientific Journal of the Public Vocational School in Konin], *1* (2), 114–124.

Swan, M., & Smith, B. (Eds.). (2002). *Learner English* (2nd ed.). Cambridge: Cambridge University Press.

Timmis, I. (2002). Native-speaker norms and International English. *English Language Teaching Journal, 56* (3), 240–249.

Walker, R. (2001). Pronunciation priorities, the Lingua Franca Core, and monolingual groups. *Speak Out! Newsletter of the IATEFL Pronunciation Special Interest Group, 28*, 4–9.

Weinberger, S. (2002). Speech action archive Webpage. Retrieved March, 2002, from http://classweb.gmu.edu/accent/.

Wennerstrom, A. (2001). *The music of everyday speech: Prosody and discourse analysis*. Oxford: Oxford University Press.

Wennerstrom, A. (2003). Students as discourse analysts in the conversation class. In J. Burton & C. Clennell (Eds.), *Interaction and language teaching* (pp. 161–175). Alexandria, VA: TESOL.

Widdowson, H. (2003). *Defining issues in English language teaching*. Oxford: Oxford University Press.

6. CURRENT DEVELOPMENTS IN RESEARCH ON THE TEACHING OF GRAMMAR

Hossein Nassaji and Sandra Fotos

With the rise of communicative methodology in the late 1970s, the role of grammar instruction in second language learning was downplayed, and it was even suggested that teaching grammar was not only unhelpful but might actually be detrimental. However, recent research has demonstrated the need for formal instruction for learners to attain high levels of accuracy. This has led to a resurgence of grammar teaching, and its role in second language acquisition has become the focus of much current investigation. In this chapter we briefly review the major developments in the research on the teaching of grammar over the past few decades. This review addresses two main issues: (1) whether grammar teaching makes any difference to language learning; and (2) what kinds of grammar teaching have been suggested to facilitate second language learning. To this end, the chapter examines research on the different ways in which formal instruction can be integrated with communicative activities.

Continuing in the tradition of more than 2000 years of debate regarding whether grammar should be a primary focus of language instruction, should be eliminated entirely, or should be subordinated to meaning-focused use of the target language (for historical reviews see Howatt, 1984; Kelly, 1969), the need for grammar instruction is once again attracting the attention of second language acquisition (SLA) researchers and teachers. We briefly review arguments against and in support of grammar teaching before examining the approaches to grammatical instruction investigated in current research.[1]

Arguments Against Grammar Teaching

Much grammar research over the past few decades has concentrated on determining whether grammar should be taught at all. This focus has been motivated in part by debates in the field of cognitive psychology over the role of explicit versus implicit language learning and whether such learning occurs through conscious manipulation of information or primarily through unconscious processes when people are exposed to language input (Bialystok, 1990, 1994; N. Ellis, 1994; Reber, 1967, 1989, 1993). Theoretically, the debate was represented by Krashen's (1981) distinction between conscious learning and unconscious acquisition of language. It was claimed that language should be acquired through natural exposure, not learned through formal instruction. It was therefore believed that formal grammar lessons would develop only declarative knowledge of grammar structures, not the procedural ability to use forms correctly, and that there was no interface between these two types of knowledge since they existed as different systems in the brain (see reviews in DeKeyser, 1998, 2001; R. Ellis, 2001, 2002a; Skehan, 1998).

This position was supported by evidence from studies on the acquisition of English morphology, particularly the findings that speakers of different first languages (L1s) learn English morphemes in a similar order (Bailey, Madden, & Krashen, 1974; Dulay & Burt, 1974). These results led to the claim that similar processes underlie both first and second language (L2) learning and that, if L1 learners do not require formal instruction to learn languages, neither should L2 learners (Krashen, 1981; Schwartz, 1993; Zobl, 1995). Schwartz (1993), for example, claimed that "only positive data can effect the construction of an *interlanguage grammar* [italics are the author's] that is comparable to the knowledge system that characterizes the result of first language acquisition" (p. 147).

Similar claims were also made in the context of Universal Grammar (UG) and its application to SLA. Researchers argued that if UG is accessible to L2 learners, then L2 learning, like L1 learning, occurs mainly through the interaction of UG principles with input (Cook, 1991; Dulay, Burt, & Krashen, 1982; Schwartz, 1993; also see Goldschneider & DeKeyser, 2001). Again, formal instruction was seen to be unnecessary.

Research Supporting Grammar Teaching

Current research in SLA, however, has led to a reconsideration of the role of grammar in the L2 classroom. There are at least four reasons for the reevaluation of grammar as a necessary component of language instruction.

First, the 1980s hypothesis that language can be learned without some degree of consciousness has been found theoretically problematic. Schmidt (1990, 1993, 2001) suggests that conscious attention to form, or what he calls "noticing," is a necessary condition for language learning (see also Leow, 1998, 2001, 2002; Rutherford, 1987, 1988; Tomlin & Villa, 1994). He emphasizes the role of attention:

> The concept of attention is necessary in order to understand virtually every aspect of second language acquisition (SLA), including the development of interlanguages (ILs) over time, variation within IL at particular points in time, the development of L2 fluency, the role of individual differences such as motivation, aptitude and learning strategies in L2 learning, and the ways interaction, negotiation for meaning, and all forms of instruction contribute to language learning. (Schmidt, 2001, p. 3)

Although some researchers have questioned Schmidt's noticing hypothesis (e.g., Truscott, 1998), most SLA investigators agree that noticing or awareness of target forms plays an important role in L2 learning (e.g., Bialystok, 1994; Bygate, Skehan, & Swain, 2001; DeKeyser, 1998, Doughty, 2001; R. Ellis, 2001, 2002a; Ellis, Basturkmen, & Loewen, 2001a, 2001b; Fotos, 1993, 1994, 1998; Nassaji, 1999, 2000, 2002; Nassaji & Swain, 2000; Robinson, 1995, 2001; Skehan, 1998; Swain & Lapkin, 2001). In addition, investigators such as Skehan (1998) and Tomasello (1998) have presented findings indicating that language learners cannot process target language input for both meaning and form at the same time. Thus, it is necessary for learners to notice target forms in input; otherwise they process input for meaning only and do not attend to specific forms, and consequently fail to process and acquire them.

A second reason for the renewed interest in L2 grammar instruction is evidence that L2 learners pass through developmental sequences. Based on empirical evidence from German learners of English, Pienemann (1984, 1988,

1999) developed what has been known as the *teachability hypothesis*, which suggests that while certain developmental sequences are fixed and cannot be altered by grammar teaching, other structures can benefit from instruction any time they are taught. Based on this hypothesis, it is possible to influence sequences of development favorably through instruction if grammar teaching coincides with the learner's readiness to move to the next developmental stage of linguistic proficiency (Lightbown, 2000). Recent suggestions on the place of grammar in the second language curriculum, particularly in classrooms with a communicative focus (e.g., R. Ellis, 2002b), take these considerations into account.

A third reason for renewed interest in grammar instruction is a large body of research pointing to the inadequacies of teaching approaches where the focus is primarily on meaning-focused communication, and grammar is not addressed. Extensive research on learning outcomes in French immersion programs by Swain and her colleagues showed that, despite substantial long-term exposure to meaningful input, the learners did not achieve accuracy in certain grammatical forms (Harley & Swain, 1984; Lapkin, Hart, & Swain, 1991; Swain, 1985; Swain & Lapkin, 1989). This research suggested that some type of focus on grammatical forms was necessary if learners were to develop high levels of accuracy in the target language. Thus, communicative language teaching by itself was found to be inadequate (also see Celce-Murcia, Dörnyei, & Thurrell, 1997; R. Ellis, 1997, 2002b; Mitchell, 2000).

A fourth reason for the reconsideration of grammar teaching in the L2 classroom is evidence for the positive effects of grammar instruction. This evidence comes from a large number of laboratory and classroom-based studies as well as extensive reviews of studies on the effects of instruction over the past 20 years (R. Ellis, 1985, 1990, 1994, 2001, 2002a; Larsen-Freeman & Long, 1991; Long, 1983, 1988, 1991). For example, studies of the effects of instruction on the development of specific target language forms (e.g., Cadierno, 1995; Doughty, 1991; Lightbown, 1992; Lightbown & Spada, 1990) as well as corrective feedback on learner errors (Carroll & Swain, 1993; Nassaji & Swain, 2000) indicate that grammatical instruction has a significant effect on the attainment of accuracy. In an early review, Long (1983) concluded that grammar instruction contributes importantly to language learning. In later reviews, R. Ellis (1990, 1994, 1997, 2001, 2002a), N. Ellis (1995), and Larsen-Freeman and Long (1991) suggest that, while instructed language learning may not have major effects on sequences of acquisition, it has facilitative effects on both the rate and the ultimate level of L2 acquisition. Similarly, a recent meta-analysis of 49 studies on the effectiveness of L2 instruction (Norris & Ortega, 2000) concludes that explicit instruction (presenting the structure, describing and exemplifying it, and giving rules for its use) results in substantial gains in the learning of target structures in comparison to implicit instruction (usually consisting of communicative exposure to the target form) alone, and that these gains are durable over time.

How Much and What Type of Grammar Teaching?

Despite such empirical support for grammar instruction, however, there is still controversy over the relative importance of explicit grammar teaching. This is due to the complex relationship between teaching and learning, and the fact that how something is taught is not directly related to how it is learned. At one extreme are those who have persistently denied the importance of any explicit instruction in language acquisition. Krashen (1993), for example, describes the effects of grammar instruction as "peripheral and fragile" (p. 725), arguing that explicit grammatical knowledge about structures and rules for their use may never turn into implicit knowledge underlying unconscious language comprehension and production. He suggests that studies showing an effect for formal instruction present only "modest increases in consciously-learned competence consistent with the claims of the Monitor hypothesis" (Krashen, 1999, p. 245). Truscott (1996, 1998) also rejects the value of explicit grammar instruction on similar grounds, arguing that its effects are short-lived and superficial and that grammar instruction alone may not promote what he called "genuine knowledge of language" (p.120). Truscott suggests that if studies have shown benefits for form focused instruction, such results have been obtained from tests that measure only explicit metalinguistic knowledge, not the learner's ability to use the target language in spontaneous communication.

Other researchers have taken a more cautious approach, not questioning the need for explicit instruction but rather objecting to traditional grammar teaching pedagogy which treats language as an object of learning and has consisted of grammar lessons in which grammatical structures are explicitly presented by the teacher in a decontextualized manner. The traditional assumption has been that through such conscious presentation and manipulation of forms through drills and practice, learners will develop the kind of knowledge they need for communicative language use. However, Skehan (1996) suggests that this traditional presentation-practice model is not supported by current research. He maintains that "the belief that a precise focus on a particular form leads to learning and automatization...no longer carries much credibility in linguistics or psychology" (p. 18).

Even those researchers who support explicit grammar instruction have suggested that it may not directly lead to implicit knowledge or to immediate changes in the learner's interlanguage (Batstone, 1994; R. Ellis, 2002a, 2000b, 2003; R. Ellis, Basturkmen, & Locwen, 2002; Lightbown, 2000). For example, Ellis et al. point out

> while there is substantial evidence that focus-on-forms instruction results in learning as measured by discrete-point language tests (e.g., the grammar test in the TOEFL), there is much less evidence to show that it leads to the kind of learning that enables learners to perform the targeted form in free oral production (e.g., in a communicative task). (2002, p. 421)

While not denying a role for explicit instruction, N. Ellis (2002) suggests that language learning is ultimately implicit in nature, "the slow acquisition of form-function mappings and the regularities therein. This skill, like others, takes tens of thousands of hours of practice, practice that can not be substituted for by provision of a few declarative rules" (p. 175). Ellis's consideration is supported by other researchers, particularly those involved in research on cognitive processing (for example, see DeKeyser, 2001; Doughty, 2001; Robinson, 1995, 1996, 2001).

However, this does not mean that grammar instruction is not useful. Rather, what is suggested is that learners must also have opportunities to encounter, process, and use instructed forms in their various form-meaning relationships so that the forms can become part of their intelanguage behavior (see Larsen-Freeman, 2003). Reviewing research on the effects of grammar instruction on SLA, Spada (1997) notes that when learners receive communicative exposure to grammar points introduced through formal instruction, their awareness of the forms becomes longer-lasting and their accuracy of use improves. Reviewing recent studies on formal instruction, R. Ellis (2002a) suggests that when grammar instruction is extensive and is sustained over a long period of time (several days or weeks), such instruction contributes to the development of implicit knowledge as measured by performance on free production tasks. Instruction also promotes accuracy in the use of difficult forms such as English articles. He therefore notes (2001, 2002b, 2003) that current research strongly supports the need for provision of communicative opportunities containing instructed grammar forms, and he recommends a combination of form focused instruction and meaningful communication, suggesting possible intervention points for instruction in a task-based communicative curriculum (2002b).

Thus, current research indicates that learners need opportunities to both encounter and produce structures which have been introduced either explicitly, through a grammar lesson, or implicitly, through frequent exposure (also see reviews in Gass, Mackey, & Pica, 1998; N. Ellis, R. Ellis, 2001, 2002a, 2000b, 2003; Lightbown, 2000, 1995, 2002), a consideration raised several decades ago by Swain in her work on learner output (1985, 1995).

Current Approaches to Grammar Teaching

Because of problems presented by traditional structure-based grammar teaching, Long, (1991) proposed an approach that he termed "focus on FORM," distinguishing it from a "focus on FORMS" approach to teaching grammar (see the discussion in Long & Robinson, 1998). Whereas focus on FORMS involves discrete grammatical forms selected and presented in an isolated manner, focus on FORM involves the teacher's attempts to draw the student's attention to grammatical forms in the context of communication (also see DeKeyser, 1998; Doughty & Varela, 1998; Long, 2000). Using a psycholinguistic perspective, Doughty (2001) has recently described the cognitive processes that take place when learners become aware of forms in input. However, Long (2000) takes a more pedagogic view, suggesting that this approach is effective for teaching grammar since it is learner-centered and tuned to the learner's internal syllabus.

Although no research has directly compared the effectiveness of a focus on form and a focus on forms approach, and the difference between them is suggested to be difficult to operationalize (R. Ellis, 2002b), the idea of focus of form has been widely advocated in the literature. Pedagogically focus on form can be achieved in many different ways. For example, Nassaji (1999, 2000) proposed that focus on form can be achieved through *process* or through *design*. Focus on form through *process* occurs in the context of natural communication when both the teacher and the learner's primary focus is on meaning. Focus on form through *design* is deliberate and is achieved through designing tasks which have deliberate explicit focus. Focus on form can also be achieved *reactively* through providing reactional feedback on learners' errors or *preemptively* through discussing grammatical forms irrespective of whether an error has occurred or not (Ellis et al., 2001a, 2001b; Long & Robinson, 1998).

A number of researchers have argued (e.g., Doughty & Varela, 1998; R. Ellis 1994, 2002a, 2002b, 2003; Robinson, 2001) that if the goal of second language learning is the development of communicative competence, enabling learners to use language for communicative purposes, then grammar and communication must be integrated. However, the challenge is to identify the best ways of doing so in L2 classrooms (Nassaji, 1999; Nassaji & Cumming, 2000) and to maximize the opportunity for a focus on grammar without sacrificing the focus on meaning and communication. Several proposals have been made during the last 10 years on ways to combine some form of grammar instruction with the provision of opportunities for communicative input and output, and a number of studies have researched their effectiveness.

In the next section, we briefly review research on alternative ways of treating grammar, including studies on processing instruction, interactional feedback, textual enhancement, focused grammar tasks, collaborative output tasks, and discourse-based grammar teaching in L2 classrooms.

Processing Instruction

VanPatten (1993, 1996, 2002) suggests that one way to teach grammar communicatively is through processing input or what he called *processing instruction*. In this approach an initial exposure to explicit instruction is combined with a series of input processing activities, consisting mainly of tasks that encourage the comprehension of the target structure rather than its production (see also R. Ellis, 1995, 2003). These activities have been suggested to help learners to create form-meaning connections in input and hence process grammar for meaning (Lee

& VanPatten, 1995). Due to the explicit focus on form component of this approach, some researchers have equated it with Long's focus on forms (e.g., Sheen, 2002). VanPatten (2002), however, argues that since the aim of this approach is "to assist the learner in making form–meaning connections during IP [input processing]; it is more appropriate to view it as a type of focus on form" (p. 764).

A number of studies have been conducted by VanPatten and his colleagues to investigate the effectiveness of processing instruction for the learning of grammar (Cadierno, 1995; VanPatten & Cadierno, 1993; VanPatten & Oikennon, 1996) and the results indicate a favorable effect. Additional studies have been carried out involving a range of grammatical structures and target languages. While some have produced evidence supporting the advantage of input processing instruction over traditional grammar instruction, others have failed to produce such evidence (Allen, 2000; Benati, 2001). DeKeyser and Sokalski (2001) suggest that the effectiveness of processing instruction depends on the morphosyntactic complexity of the target structure as well as the length of the testing time, suggesting that input processing is more effective for promoting comprehension skills, whereas production-based instruction is more effective for promoting production skills. Thus, the effectiveness of this type of instruction may depend on the nature of grammatical form as well as the type of skill involved. More research is required to explore the exact effect of input processing and the ways in which it may influence different language skills.

Interactional Feedback

Interactional feedback refers to various negotiation and modification strategies such as repetitions, clarification requests, confirmation checks, and the like, which are made by learners or directed to them to facilitate understanding. Such interactions draw the learners' attention implicitly or explicitly to aspects of the target language such as grammatical forms (Lyster & Ranta, 1997; Nassaji & Swain, 2000; Van den Branden, 1997). This approach is based on the theory that such interactional strategies highlight linguistic or pragmatic problems, pushing learners to intentionally modify their output in order to produce more accurate and comprehensible utterances (see R. Ellis, 1997, 2003, for a discussion of the Interaction Hypothesis; also see Gass et al., 1998). Researchers have also made a distinction between two types of negotiation, negotiation of meaning and negotiation of form (R. Ellis, 2002b; Lyster & Ranta, 1997; van Lier, 1988).

Negotiation of meaning refers to conversational strategies used to signal or repair problems in communication. These strategies are typical of ordinary conversation or teacher–students interaction in L1 subject-matter classrooms (see Nassaji & Wells, 2000). Negotiation of form, for example, recasts, refers to interactional strategies used mainly to respond to erroneously used forms (Lyster & Ranta, 1997).

A growing body of research has explored the effectiveness of interactional feedback for SLA. Some of these studies have investigated the effects of these interactions on the development of L2 grammar forms (Doughty & Varela, 1998; Iwashita, 2003; Long, Inagaki, & Ortega, 1998; Nassaji, 1999; Nassaji & Swain, 2000; also see the review in Gass, Mackey, & Pica, 1998). For example, a series of studies conducted by Mackey and her colleagues (Mackey, 1999; Mackey & Oliver, 2002; Mackey & Philp, 1998, McDonough & Mackey, 2000) examined the effect of interactional feedback on the development of English questions and found that compared with control groups, the feedback groups progressed further in terms of their ability to form questions. Doughty and Varela (1998) investigated recasts on the learning of past and conditional sentences, finding that learners who received corrective recasts in response to their errors made more progress in use of past tense forms than those who did not. Lyster (2001) investigated the role of interactional feedback with respect to error types and its effects on immediate learner repair. He found that, while negotiation of form was more effective than recasts and explicit corrections in relation to lexical and grammatical errors and the unsolicited use of learner's first language, recasts were more effective in relation to phonological errors.

Ohta (2000, 2001) used a sociocultural framework to examine the role of private speech in adult foreign language learners of Japanese, finding that learners favorably responded to recasts. Within the same framework, Aljaafreh and Lantolf (1994) investigated the effects of interactional feedback in the context of adult ESL writing, and found that feedback negotiated between the learner and the teacher and within the learner's zone of proximal development played an important role in second language learning (see also Nassaji & Cumming, 2000). Nassaji and Swain (2000) conducted a similar study comparing negotiated feedback with random feedback. These researchers also found that negotiated feedback was more effective than feedback provided randomly and nonnegotiatively, though the effects of the two were strongly mediated by the explicit nature of the feedback.

Thus, the results of studies on interactional strategies suggest the effectiveness of these strategies in promoting SLA. However, as Nicholas, Lightbown and Spada (2001) have pointed out, no firm conclusions can yet be drawn, particularly about the role of recasts. For example, Lyster and Ranta (1997) found that, although recasts were the most frequently used interactional strategy by teachers in French Immersion classrooms, elicitation was more effective in encouraging learners to reformulate their erroneous utterances. However, a study by Ellis, Basturkmen, and Loewen (2001a) found that recasts were not only the most frequently used type of strategy, but that they also led to a high degree of uptake of the target forms. Such results indicate that more research is needed to examine the effects of interactional strategies not only in response to different types of grammar features but also in different classroom contexts.

Textual Enhancement

There are a number of studies that have investigated the effects of textual enhancement on drawing the learner's attention to grammar, and the method has been described as the least explicit and the least intrusive method of focus on form (Doughty & Varela, 1998). It involves highlighting certain features of input that might go unnoticed under normal circumstances by typographically manipulating them through boldfacing, italicizing, underlining, or capitalizing. The assumption is that such manipulations enhance the perceptual saliency of the target structures, and this, hence, increases their chance of being noticed. A related technique is the provision of numerous instances of target linguistic forms in the input, called an *input flood* (Trahey & White, 1993). Again, the assumption is that frequent exposure to target items enhances their saliency and hence results in noticing the forms (Schmidt, 1990; Sharwood Smith, 1993). Whereas studies by Doughty (1991) and Fotos (1994) reported positive results in terms of awareness of target structures and proficiency gains resulting from textually enhanced structures, a study by White (1998) did not show that learners who received textually enhanced input differed significantly in their ability to use the target structure compared with those who did not. White concluded that the method of enhancement may not have been sufficiently explicit to draw the learners' attention to the type of linguistic features that involved L1–L2 contrasts. Similarly, Leow (2001) investigated the effects of textual enhancement on learning Spanish formal imperatives and found no advantage for enhanced text over unenhanced text. Finally, Izumi (2002) compared two types of focus on form strategies, output and visual input enhancement, on the learning of English relativization by adult ESL learners, finding that those who produced output developed more than those merely received input. However, the visual enhancement did not result in gains in accuracy using the target form.

Thus, the results of the studies on textual enhancement suggest that, while this strategy may promote noticing of grammatical forms (Fotos, 1994, 1998), it may not be sufficient for their acquisition. Thus, while noticing may be a necessary condition for acquisition, it is not the only condition. As Batstone notes, if learners want to learn grammar effectively, they have to "act on it, building it into their working hypothesis about how grammar is structured" (1994, p. 59). This may not happen unless the learners are exposed to continued and sustained noticing activities as well as ample opportunities for producing the target form.

Task-Based Instruction

Focused tasks. The use of communicative tasks has been widely advocated in second language classrooms, but usually these tasks have been interpreted as having a primary focus on meaning. Thus, Nunan (1989) defined communicative tasks as "a piece of classroom work which involves learners in comprehending, manipulating, producing, or interacting in the target language while their attention is principally focused on meaning rather than on form" (p. 10). However, three types of structure-based tasks have been proposed recently to promote learner awareness and practice of target forms. Although the tasks are aimed at making grammar forms salient to the learner, this is achieved through communicative activities. Such tasks promote awareness, since the learners' attention is drawn to the nature of the target structure; yet they are also communicative, since the learners are engaged in meaning-focused interaction. Rod Ellis (2003; Nobuyoshi & Ellis, 1993) has described such tasks as "focused" compared with unfocused tasks that are designed purely for communication. He describes these tasks (2003, p. 151) as (1) structure-based production tasks, (2) comprehension tasks, and (3) consciousness-raising tasks.

For structure-based production tasks, use of the target form is required to complete purely communicative activities (R. Ellis, 1995; Loschky & Bley-Vroman, 1993; Mackey, 1999; Nobuyoshi & Ellis, 1993). Thus, the task material is not grammatical in nature, although the learners must produce the target structure to complete the task. Comprehension tasks are designed so that learners must attend to and comprehend target forms in carefully structured input (R. Ellis, 1995; VanPatten, 1996), and they usually consist of a stimulus requiring the learner to make a response (R. Ellis, 2003). Whereas the previous two task types introduce grammar structures implicitly in communicative contexts, consciousness-raising tasks (Fotos, 1993, 1998, 2002; Fotos & Ellis, 1991; Leow, 2001; Sheen, 1992) require learners to communicate with each other about target grammar structures; thus the grammar forms are the task content. Such tasks present examples of the target structure and require learners to manipulate the structure, often generating rules for its use (Ellis, 2003).

Research on the use of such tasks suggests that grammar points with a few easily taught rules are more amenable to form-focused instruction through task performance than structures that are governed by a great many rules (see DeKeyser, 1998; R. Ellis, 1995, 2003; Robinson, 1996). However, it has also been found (R. Ellis, 2003; Loschky & Bley-Vroman, 1993; Robinson, 1996) that meaning-focused activities such as tasks containing communicative instances of target forms are useful for developing learner awareness of grammar structures that are too complex to be understood through formal instruction alone. Additional research (Robinson, 2001) indicates that complex tasks result in greater attention to input as well as increased awareness of output compared with simple tasks. Thus, tasks with grammar structures as implicit or explicit content, even cognitively demanding tasks, appear to be effective in promoting awareness of the target grammar structure, but, again, further research is indicated.

<u>Collaborative output tasks</u>. As mentioned, research by Swain and her colleagues has shown that despite many years of exposure to meaningful input, French immersion students often lacked high levels of accuracy in certain grammatical forms. Swain (1985, 2000, 2001) suggests that this is because the learners were not pushed beyond their current level of interlanguage. She therefore argues that output of the L2 plays an important role in SLA (1985, 1995, 2000, 2001, in press). Thus, when learners attempt to produce the L2, they notice that they are not able to say what they want to say (Robinson, 2001; Swain, 2000, 2001), and this "pushes" them to achieve greater accuracy. Pushed output also provides opportunities for formulating and testing hypothesis. When learners produce the target language, such production allows for deeper syntactic processing because

they have to "move from the semantic, open-ended, strategic processing prevalent in comprehension to the complete grammatical processing needed for accurate production" (Swain, 2000, p. 99). In a recent article, Swain (in press) describes the output hypothesis, the research context in which it was formulated, and the research evidence that supports its various functions. She also argues for the importance of output as a process, not just a product of language learning.

One way of promoting pushed output is through focused communicative tasks where learners are pushed to reproduce language forms accurately (R. Ellis, 1997, 2003; Nobuyoshi & Ellis, 1993). Another way of achieving this is through the use of collaborative output tasks that require learners to cooperatively produce language (Swain, 2001). For example, the *dictogloss* (Wajnryb, 1990) has been effectively used for such collaborative output tasks. Here the teacher reads a short L2 text twice and asks the learners to work in groups or pairs to reproduce the text as accurately as possible. The effectiveness of dictogloss has been investigated in studies by Swain and her colleagues (Kowal & Swain, 1994; Swain, 2000; Swain & Lapkin, 1998, 2001). These researchers suggest that dictogloss tasks not only promote meaningful interaction in the L2 but also lead to improvement in accuracy in the use of target forms. Kowal and Swain (1994) also found that when learners produced the target language during such tasks, they noticed gaps in their linguistic knowledge which then triggered a cooperative search for the solution. Comparing the effect of a dictogloss task with a jigsaw task in which pairs of students worked together to create a story based on a series of pictures, Swain and Lapkin (2001) note that the dictogloss task led to more accurate reproduction of the target forms than the jigsaw task but both "generated a similar and substantial proportion of language related episodes" (p. 111). Thus, the various task-based approaches to grammar instruction appear to be successful in promoting awareness of target forms and promoting accuracy gains but, again, further comparative research is necessary.

Discourse-Based Approaches

Discourse-based grammar teaching is an important component of other recent approaches to grammar teaching reviewed in this discussion. Here instruction of target forms is supported by extensive use of authentic or simplified discourse, including corpus analysis, to supply learners with abundant examples of contextualized usages of the target structure to promote the establishment of form-meaning relationships (Batstone, 1994; Carter, Hughes, & McCarthy, 2000; Celce-Murcia, 2002, Celce-Murcia, Dörnyei, & Thurrell, 1997; Hinkel, 1999, 2002a, 2002b 2002c; Hughes & McCarthy, 1998). Research by Carter, Hughes, and McCarthy (2000) and Hughes and McCarthy (1998) emphasizes the difference between spoken and written English grammars and recommends the use of corpus analysis to provide learners with authentic examples of spoken L2 forms. Celce-Murcia and Olshtain (2000) call for the end of a primarily sentence-based approach to grammar instruction, noting that grammar instruction requires both a top-down and bottom-up approach (Nassaji, 2002). The first relates target structures to the macrostructure of the text as a whole, a discourse-analytic approach, whereas the second specifies the function of target structures, a microanalytic approach.

In her studies of ESL learners' writing Hinkel (1999, 2002a, 2002b, 2002c) finds that even highly educated learners tend to be influenced by their cultural rhetorical and discourse traditions when writing in the L2, and require extensive and persistent instruction in L2 grammar and the complex feature of L2 texts. Noting that grammar teaching is usually treated separately from the teaching of writing, she recommends that instruction in L2 writing include explicit instruction on grammar, lexical forms and rhetorical patterns as exemplified by authentic text and discourse (2002a). She also presents research findings (2002b, 2002c) indicating that, although difficult forms, such as the English tenses and passive need to be instructed, such forms "cannot be studied in isolation from their syntactic functions and pragmatic uses" (2002b, p. 235). Thus, recent approaches to grammar emphasize the need for provision of extensive exposure to, as well as focus on, the target forms to promote their acquisition.

Conclusion

Current research clearly indicates that grammar feedback is necessary in order for language learners to attain high levels of proficiency in the target language. However, traditional structure-based grammar teaching approaches have been replaced by treatments which may or may not include an explicit discussion of target forms and the rules for their use, but present the forms in numerous communicative contexts designed to promote learner awareness of meaning–form relationships and to permit processing of the form to occur over time.

Although the exact nature of this kind of instruction and the various forms it can take in second language classrooms are still far from clear, it is now suggested that among the essential conditions for acquisition of grammatical forms are (1) learner noticing and continued awareness of target forms, (2) repeated meaning-focused exposure to input containing them, and (3) opportunities for output and practice. It is also recognized that, because the acquisition of grammar is affected by internal processing constraints, spontaneous and accurate production cannot be instantaneous but will naturally require time as learners move toward mastery.

Note

1. The authors would like to thank Rod Ellis, Eli Hinkel, and Merrill Swain for their helpful comments on a draft of this chapter.

REFERENCES

Aljaafreh, A., & Lantolf, J. (1994). Negative feedback as regulation and second language learning in the zone of proximal development. *Modern Language Journal, 78,* 465–483.

Allen, Q. (2000). Form-meaning connections and the French causative. *Studies in Second Language Acquisition, 22,* 69–84.

Bailey, N., Madden, C., & Krashen, S. (1974). Is there a "natural sequence" in adult second language learning? *Language Learning, 24,* 235–243.

Batstone, R. (1994). *Grammar.* Oxford: Oxford University Press.

Benati, A. (2001). A comparative study of the effects of processing instruction and output-based instruction on the acquisition of the Italian future tense. *Language Teaching Research, 5,* 95–127.

Bialystock, E. (1990). The competence of processing: Classifying theories of second language acquisition. *TESOL Quarterly, 24,* 635–648.

Bialystok, E. (1994). Representation and ways of knowing: Three issues in second language acquisition. In N. Ellis (Ed.), *Explicit and implicit learning of languages* (pp. 549–569). London: Academic Press.

Bygate, M., Skehan, P., & Swain, M. (Eds.). (2001). *Researching pedagogic tasks: Second language learning, teaching and testing.* New York: Longman.

Cadierno, T. (1995). Formal instruction from a processing perspective: An investigation into the Spanish past tense. *Modern Language Journal, 79,* 179–193.

Carroll, S., & Swain, M. (1993). Explicit and implicit negative feedback: An empirical study of the learning of linguistic generalizations. *Studies in Second Language Acquisition, 15,* 357–386.

Carter, R., Hughes, R., & McCarthy, M. (2000). *Exploring grammar in context.* Cambridge: Cambridge University Press.

Celce-Murcia, M. (2002). Why it makes sense to teach grammar in context and through discourse. In E. Hinkel & S. Fotos (Eds.), *New perspectives on grammar teaching in second language classrooms* (pp. 119–134). Mahwah, NJ: Erlbaum.

Celce-Murcia, M., Dörnyei, Z., & Thurrell, S. (1997). Direct approaches in L2 instruction: A turning point in communicative language teaching? *TESOL Quarterly, 31,* 141–152.

Celce-Murcia, M., & Olshtain, E. (2000). *Discourse and context in language teaching: A guide for teachers.* Cambridge: Cambridge University Press.

Cook, V. (1991). *Second language learning and language teaching.* London: Edward Arnold.

DeKeyser, R. (1998). Beyond focus on form: Cognitive perspectives on learning and practicing second language grammar. In C. Doughty & J. Williams (Eds.), *Focus on form in classroom second language acquisition* (pp. 42–63). New York: Cambridge University Press.

DeKeyser, R. (2001). Automaticity and automatization. In P. Robinson (Ed.). *Cognition and second language instruction* (pp. 125–151). Cambridge: Cambridge University Press.

DeKeyser, R., & Sokalski, K. (2001). The differential role of comprehension and production practice. *Language Learning, 51,* 81–112.

Doughty, C. (1991). Second language instruction does make a difference: Evidence from an empirical study of SL relativization. *Studies in Second Language Acquisition, 13,* 431–496.

Doughty, C. (2001). Cognitive underpinnings of focus on form. In P. Robinson (Ed.), *Cognition and second language instruction* (pp. 206–257). Cambridge: Cambridge University Press.

Doughty, C., & Varela, E. (1998). Communicative focus on form. In C. Doughty & J. Williams (Eds.), *Focus on form in classroom second language acquisition* (pp. 114–138). Cambridge: Cambridge University Press.

Dulay, H., & Burt, M. (1974). Natural sequences in child second language acquisition. *Language Learning, 24,* 37–53.

Dulay, H., Burt, M., & Krashen, S. (1982). *Language two.* New York: Oxford University Press.

Ellis, N. (1994). Implicit and explicit processes in language acquisition: An introduction. In N. Ellis (Ed.), *Implicit and explicit learning of languages* (pp. 1–32). San Diego, CA: Academic Press.

Ellis, N. (1995). Consciousness in second language acquisition: A review of field studies and laboratory experiments. *Language Awareness, 4,* 121–146.

Ellis, N. (2002). Frequency effects in language processing: A review with implications for theories of implicit and explicit language acquisition. *Studies in Second Language Acquisition, 24,* 143–188.

Ellis, R. (1985). *Understanding second language acquisition.* Oxford: Oxford University Press.

Ellis, R. (1990). *Instructed second language acquisition: Learning in the classroom.* Oxford, UK: Blackwell.

Ellis, R. (1994). *The study of second language acquisition.* Oxford: Oxford University Press.

Ellis, R. (1995). Interpretation tasks for grammar teaching. *TESOL Quarterly, 29,* 87–106.

Ellis, R. (1997). *SLA research and language teaching.* Oxford: Oxford University Press.

Ellis, R. (2001). Introduction: Investigating form-focused instruction. *Language Learning, 51* Supplement, 1–46.

Ellis, R. (2002a). Does form-focused instruction affect the acquisition of implicit knowledge? *Studies in Second Language Acquisition, 24,* 223–236.

Ellis, R. (2002b). The place of grammar instruction in the second/foreign curriculum. In E. Hinkel & S. Fotos (Eds.), *New perspectives on grammar teaching in second language classrooms* (pp. 17–34). Mahwah, NJ: Erlbaum.

Ellis, R. (2003). *Task-based language learning and teaching.* Oxford: Oxford University Press.

Ellis, R., Basturkmen, H., & Loewen, S. (2001a). Learner uptake in communicative ESL lessons. *Language Learning, 51,* 281–318.

Ellis, R., Basturkmen, H., & Loewen, S. (2001b). Preemptive focus on form in the ESL classroom. *TESOL Quarterly, 35,* 407–432.

Ellis, R., Basturkmen, H., & Loewen, S. (2002). Doing focus-on-form. *System, 30,* 419–432.

Fotos, S. (1993). Consciousness-raising and noticing through focus on form: Grammar task performance versus formal instruction. *Applied Linguistics, 14,* 385–407.

Fotos, S. (1994). Integrating grammar instruction and communicative language use through grammar consciousness-raising tasks. *TESOL Quarterly, 28* (2), 323–351.

Fotos, S. (1998). Shifting the focus from forms to form in the EFL classroom. *ELT Journal, 52,* 301–307.

Fotos, S. (2002). Structure-based interactive tasks for the EFL grammar learner. In E. Hinkel & S. Fotos (Eds.), *New perspectives on grammar teaching in second language classrooms* (pp. 135–155). Mahwah, NJ: Erlbaum.

Fotos, S., & Ellis, R. (1991). Communicating about grammar: A task-based approach. *TESOL Quarterly, 25,* 605–628.

Gass, S., Mackey, A., & Pica, T. (1998). The role of input and interaction in second language acquisition. *The Modern Language Journal 82* (3), 229–305.

Goldschneider, J. M., & DeKeyser, R. M. (2001). Explaining the "natural order of L2 morpheme acquisition" in English: A meta-analysis of multiple determinants. *Language Learning, 51,* 1–50.

Harley, B., & Swain, M. (1984). The interlanguage of immersion students and its implications for second language teaching. In A. Davies, C. Criper, & A. P. R. Howatt (Eds.),

Interlanguage (pp. 291–311). Edinburgh, Scotland: Edinburgh University Press.

Hinkel, E. (1999). Objectivity and credibility in L1 and L2 writing. In E. Hinkel (Ed.), *Culture in second language teaching and learning* (pp. 90–108). Cambridge: Cambridge University Press.

Hinkel, E. (2002a). Grammar teaching in writing classes: Tenses and cohesion. In E. Hinkel & S. Fotos (Eds.), *New perspectives on grammar teaching in second language classrooms* (pp.181–198). Mahwah, NJ: Erlbaum.

Hinkel, E. (2002b). Why English passive is difficult to teach (and learn). In E. Hinkel & S. Fotos (Eds.) *New perspectives on grammar teaching in second language classrooms* (pp. 233–260). Mahwah, NJ: Erlbaum.

Hinkel, E. (2002c). *Second language writers' text: Linguistic and rhetorical features*. Mahwah, NJ: Erlbaum.

Howatt, A. (1984). *A history of English language teaching*. Oxford: Oxford University Press.

Hughes, R., & McCarthy, M. (1998). From sentence to discourse: Discourse grammar and English language teaching. *TESOL Quarterly, 32*, 263–287.

Iwashita, N. (2003). Negative feedback and positive evidence in task-based interaction: Differential effects on L2 development. *Studies in Second Language Acquisition, 25*, 1–36.

Izumi, S. (2002). Output, input enhancement and the noticing hypothesis: An experimental study on ESL relativization. *Studies in Second Language Acquisition, 24*, 541–577.

Kelly, L. (1969). *25 centuries of language teaching*. Rowley, MA: Newbury House.

Kowal, M., & Swain, M. (1994). Using collaborative language production tasks to promote students' language awareness. *Language Awareness, 3*, 73–93.

Krashen, S. (1981). *Second language acquisition and second language learning*. Oxford: Oxford University Press.

Krashen, S. (1993). The effect of formal grammar teaching: Still peripheral. *TESOL Quarterly, 27*, 722–725.

Krashen, S. D. (1999). Seeking a role for grammar: A review of some recent studies. *Foreign Language Annals, 32*, 245–257.

Lapkin, S., Hart, D., & Swain, M. (1991). Early and Middle French immersion programs: French language outcomes. *Canadian Modern Language Review, 48*, 11–40.

Larsen-Freeman, D., & Long, M. (1991). *An introduction to second language acquisition research*. London: Longman.

Larsen-Freeman, D. (2003). *Teaching language: From grammar to grammaring*. Boston: Heinle & Heinle.

Lee, J., & VanPatten, B. (1995). *Making communicative language teaching happen*. San Francisco: McGraw-Hill.

Leow, R. (1998). Toward operationalizing the process of attention in SLA: Evidence for Tomlin and Villa's (1994) fine-grained analysis of attention. *Applied Psycholinguistics, 19*, 133–159.

Leow, R. (2001). Attention, awareness, and foreign language behavior. *Language Learning, 51*, 113–155.

Leow, R. (2002). Models, attention, and awareness in SLA: A response to Simard and Wong's "Alertness, orientation, and detection: The conceptualization of attention functions in SLA." *Studies in Second Language Acquisition, 24*, 113–119.

Lightbown, P. (1992). What have we here? Some observations on the influence of instruction on L2 learning. In R. Philipson, E. Kellerman, L. Selinker, M. Sharwood Smith, & M. Swain (Eds.), *Foreign language pedagogy research: A commemorative volume for Claus Faerch* (pp. 197–212). Clevedon, UK: Multilingual Matters.

Lightbown, P. (2000). Anniversary article: Classroom SLA research and second language teaching. *Applied Linguistics, 21*, 431–462.

Lightbown, P., & N. Spada. (1990). Focus on form and corrective feedback in communicative language teaching: Effects on second language learning. *Studies in Second Language Acquisition, 12*, 429–448.

Long, M. (1983). Does second language instruction make a difference? A review of the research. *TESOL Quarterly, 17*, 359–382.

Long, M. (1988). Instructed interlanguage development. In L. Beebe (Ed.), *Issues in second language acquisition: Multiple perspectives* (pp. 115–141). Rowley, MA: Newbury House.

Long, M. (1991). Focus on form: A design feature in language teaching methodology. In K. DeBot, R. Ginsberg, & C. Kramsch (Eds.), *Foreign language research in cross-cultural perspective* (pp. 39–52). Amsterdam: Benjamins.

Long, M. (2000). Focus on form in task-based language teaching. In R. D. Lambert & E. Shohamy (Eds.), *Language policy and pedagogy: Essays in honor of A. Ronald Walton* (pp. 179–192). Philadelphia: Benjamins.

Long, M., Inagaki, S., & Ortega, L. (1998). The role of implicit negative feedback in SLA: Models and recasts in Japanese and Spanish. *Modern Language Journal, 82* (3), 357–371.

Long, M., & Robinson, P. (1998). Focus on form: Theory, research and practice. In C. Doughty & J. Williams (Eds.), *Focus on form in classroom language acquisition* (pp. 15–41). Cambridge: Cambridge University Press.

Loschky, L., & Bley-Vroman, R. (1993). Grammar and task-based methodology. In G. Crookes & S. Gass (Eds.), *Tasks and language learning* (pp. 123–163). Clevedon, UK: Multilingual Matters.

Lyster, R. (2001). Negotiation of form, recasts, and explicit correction in relation to error types and learner repair in immersion classrooms. *Language Learning, 51 Supplement*, 265–301.

Lyster, R., & Ranta, L. (1997). Corrective feedback and learner uptake: Negotiation of form in communicative classrooms. *Studies in Second Language Acquisition, 19*, 37–66.

Mackey, A. (1999). Input, interaction and second language development: An empirical study of question formation. *Studies in Second Language Acquisition, 21*, 557–587.

Mackey, A., & Oliver, R. (2002). Interactional feedback and children's L2 development. *System, 30* (4), 459–477.

Mackey, A., & Philp, J. (1998). Conversational interaction and second language development: Recasts, responses, and red herrings? *Modern Language Journal, 82* (3), 338–356.

McDonough, K., & Mackey, A. (2000). Communicative tasks, conversational interaction and linguistic form: An empirical study of Thai. *Foreign Language Annals, 33* (1), 82–92.

Mitchell, R. (2000). Applied linguistics and evidence-based classroom practice: The case of foreign language grammar pedagogy. *Applied Linguistics, 21*, 281–303.

Nassaji, H. (1999). Towards integrating form-focused instruction and communicative interaction in the second language classroom: Some pedagogical possibilities. *The Canadian Modern Language Review, 55*, 385–402.

Nassaji, H. (2000). A reply to Sheen. *The Canadian Modern Language Review, 56*, 507–513.

Nassaji, H. (2002). Schema theory and knowledge-based processes in second language reading comprehension: A need for alternative perspectives. *Language Learning, 52*, 439–481.

Nassaji, H., & Cumming, A. (2000). What is in the ZPD: A case study of a young ESL student and teacher interacting through dialogue journals. *Language Teaching Research, 4*, 95–121.

Nassaji, H., & Swain, M. (2000). A Vygotskian perspective on corrective feedback: The effect of random versus negotiated help on the learning of English articles. *Language Awareness, 9*, 34–51.

Nassaji, H., & Wells, G. (2000). What's the use of 'triadic dialogue'?: An investigation of teacher-student interaction. *Applied Linguistics, 21*, 376–406.

Nicholas, H. Lightbown, P., & Spada, N. (2001). Recasts as feedback to language learners. Language Learning, *51*, 719–758.

Nobuyoshi, J., & Ellis, R. (1993). Focused communication tasks and second language acquisition. *ELT Journal, 47*, 113–128.

Norris, J., & Ortega, L. (2000). Effectiveness of L2 Instruction: A research synthesis and quantitative meta-analysis. *Language Learning, 50*, 417–428.

Nunan, D. (1989). *Designing tasks for the communicative classroom.* Cambridge: Cambridge University Press.

Ohta, A. (2000). Rethinking recasts: A learner-centered examination of corrective feedback in the Japanese classroom. In J. Hall & L. Verplaeste (Eds.), *The construction of second and foreign language learning through classroom interaction* (pp. 47–71). Mahwah, NJ: Erlbaum.

Ohta, A. (2001). *Second language acquisition processes in the classroom: Learning Japanese.*

Mahwah, NJ: Erlbaum.

Pienemann, M. (1984). Psychological constraints on the teachability of languages. *Studies in Second Language Acquisition, 6,* 186–214.

Pienemann, M. (1988). Determining the influence of instruction on L2 speech processing. *AILA Review, 5,* 40–72.

Pienemann, M. (1999). *Language, processing and second language development: Processability theory.* Amsterdam: Benjamins.

Reber, A. (1967). Implicit learning of artificial grammars. *Journal of Verbal Learning and Verbal Behavior, 6,* 855–863.

Reber, A. (1989). Implicit learning and tacit knowledge. *Journal of Experimental Psychology-General, 118,* 219–235.

Reber, A. (1993). *Implicit learning and tacit knowledge: An essay on the cognitive unconscious.* Oxford: Clarendon Press.

Robinson, P. (1995). Attention, memory, and the noticing hypothesis. *Language Learning, 45* (2), 283–331.

Robinson, P. (1996). Learning simple and complex second language rules under implicit, incidental, rule-search and instructed conditions. *Studies in Second Language Acquisition 18,* 27–68.

Robinson, P. (2001). Task complexity, cognitive resources and syllabus design: A triadic framework for examining task influence on SLA. In P. Robinson (Ed.), *Cognition and second language instruction* (pp. 287–318). Cambridge: Cambridge University Press.

Rutherford, W. (1987). *Second language grammar learning and teaching.* New York: Longman.

Rutherford, W. (1988). Grammatical consciousness raising in brief historical perspective. In W. Rutherford & M. Sharwood Smith (Eds), *Grammar and second language teaching* (pp. 15–19). New York: Newbury House.

Schmidt, R. W. (1990). The role of consciousness in second language learning. *Applied Linguistics, 11* (2), 129–158.

Schmidt, R. W. (1993). Awareness and second language acquisition. *Annual Review of Applied Linguistics, 13,* 206–226.

Schmidt, R. W. (2001). Attention. In P. Robinson (Ed.), *Cognition and second language instruction* (pp. 3–32). Cambridge: Cambridge University Press.

Schwartz, B. (1993). On explicit and negative data effecting and affecting competence and linguistic behavior. *Studies in Second Language Acquisition, 15,* 147–163.

Sharwood Smith, M. (1993). Input enhancement in instructed SLA: Theoretical bases. *Studies in Second Language Acquisition, 15,* 165–179.

Sheen, R. (1992). Problem solving brought to task. *RELC Journal, 23,* 44–59.

Sheen, R. (2002). 'Focus on form' and 'focus on forms.' *ELT Journal, 56,* 303–304.

Skehan, P. (1996). Second language acquisition research and task-based instruction. In J. Willis & D. Willis (Eds.), *Challenge and change in language teaching* (pp. 17–30). Oxford: Heinemann.

Skehan, P. (1998). *A cognitive approach to language learning.* Oxford: Oxford University Press.

Spada, N. (1997). Form-focused instruction and second language acquisition: A review of classroom and laboratory research. *Language teaching, 29,* 1–15.

Swain, M. (1985). Communicative competence: Some rules of comprehensible input and comprehensible output in its development. In S. Gass & C. Madden (Eds.), *Input in second language acquisition* (pp. 235–253). Rowley, MA: Newbury House.

Swain, M. (1995). Three functions of output in second language learning. In G. Cook & B. Seidlhofer (Eds.), *Principle and practice in applied linguistics: Studies in honour of H. G. Widdowson* (pp. 125–144). Oxford: Oxford University Press.

Swain, M. (2000). The output hypothesis and beyond: Mediating acquisition through collaborative dialogue. In J. P. Lantolf (Ed.), *Sociocultural theory and second language learning* (pp. 97–114). Oxford: Oxford University Press.

Swain, M. (2001). Integrating language and content teaching through collaborative tasks. *Canadian Modern Language Review, 58,* 44–63.

Swain, M. (In press). The output hypothesis: Theory and research. In E. Hinkel (Ed.), *Handbook on research in second language teaching and learning.* Mahwah, NJ: Erlbaum.

Swain, M., & Lapkin, S. (1989). Canadian immersion and adult second language teaching—What's the connection. *Modern Language Journal, 73,* 150–159.

Swain, M., & Lapkin, S. (1998). Interaction and second language learning: Two adolescent French immersion students working together. *Modern Language Journal, 82,* 320–337.

Swain, M., & Lapkin, S. (2001). Focus on form through collaborative dialogue: Exploring task effects. In M. Bygate, P. Skehan & M. Swain (Eds.), *Researching pedagogic tasks: Second language learning, teaching and testing* (pp. 99–118). Harlow, UK: Pearson Education.

Tomlin, R. S., & Villa, V. (1994). Attention in cognitive science and second language acquisition. *Studies in Second Language Acquisition, 16,* 183–202.

Tomasello, M. (1998). Introduction: A cognitive-functional perspective on language structure. In M. Tomasello (Ed.), *The new psychology of language: Cognitive and functional approaches to language structure* (pp. vii–xxiii). Mahwah, NJ: Erlbaum.

Trahey, M., & White, L. (1993). Positive evidence and preemption in the second language classroom. *Studies in Second Language Acquisition, 15,* 181–204.

Truscott, J. (1996). The case against grammar correction in L2 writing classes. *Language Learning, 46,* 327–369.

Truscott, J. (1998). Noticing in second language acquisition: A critical review. *Second

Language Research, *14*, 103–135.

Van den Branden, K. (1997). Effects of negotiation on language learners' output. *Language Learning, 47,* 589–636.

van Lier, L. (1988). *The classroom and the language learner.* London: Longman

VanPatten, B. (1993). Grammar teaching for the acquisition-rich classroom. *Foreign Language Annals, 26,* 435–450.

VanPatten, B. (1996). *Input processing and grammar instruction in second language acquisition.* Norwood, NJ: Ablex.

VanPatten, B. (2002). Processing instruction: An update. *Language Learning, 52,* 755–803.

VanPatten, B., & Cadierno, T. (1993). Explicit instruction and input processing. *Studies in Second Language Acquisition, 15,* 225–244.

VanPatten, B., & Oikennon, S. (1996). Explanation vs. structured input in processing instruction. *Studies in Second Language Acquisition, 18,* 495–510.

Wajnryb, R. (1990). *Grammar dictation.* Oxford: Oxford University Press.

White, J. (1998). Getting the learners' attention: A typographical input enhancement study. In C. Doughty & J. Williams (Eds.), *Focus on form in classroom second language acquisition* (pp. 85–113). Cambridge: Cambridge University Press.

Zobl, H. (1995). Converging evidence for the "acquisition–learning" distinction. *Applied Linguistics, 16,* 35–56.

7. RESEARCH IN TEACHING VOCABULARY

John Read

This review surveys research on second language vocabulary teaching and learning since 1999. It first considers the distinction between incidental and intentional vocabulary learning. Although learners certainly acquire word knowledge incidentally while engaged in various language learning activities, more direct and systematic study of vocabulary is also required. There is a discussion of how word frequency counts and information on word meaning from computer corpora can inform the selection of words to be studied, with a particular focus on spoken vocabulary. This leads to a consideration of learner dictionaries and some research evidence on how effectively students can use them to understand the meanings of words. Then classroom research on teaching vocabulary is discussed. Another significant topic is the design of computer-based language learning programs to enhance opportunities for learners to expand their vocabulary knowledge. Finally, a summary of recent work on vocabulary testing is presented.

Second language learners are typically conscious of the extent to which limitations in their vocabulary knowledge hamper their ability to communicate effectively in the target language, since lexical items carry the basic information load of the meanings they wish to comprehend and express. This gives vocabulary study a salience for learners that may be lacking in the acquisition of other features of the language system. However, language teachers are often unsure about how best to incorporate vocabulary learning into their teaching. Traditional techniques of presenting new words in class or requiring students to memorize lists of vocabulary items seem old-fashioned in the context of current task-based language programs.

The debate in SLA about the need to focus on form in classroom communication activities (see Doughty & Williams, 1998) has centered almost entirely on the acquisition of grammar, but there are similar issues involved in finding a place for the systematic study of vocabulary in the language curriculum.

There was a boom in second language vocabulary studies in the 1990s and early 2000s, reflected in the number of books published in the last seven years, particularly by Cambridge University Press, which almost seemed to corner the market for such publications. Thus, the four volumes in the annotated bibliography at the end of this chapter, along with others such as Coady and Huckin (1997) and Singleton (1999), give comprehensive coverage of theory, research, and practice related to second language vocabulary teaching and learning up to the end of the decade. This review, then, will concentrate somewhat selectively on work that has appeared since 1999, with particular attention to interesting new developments.[1]

Incidental and Intentional Learning

One distinction that has been influential in vocabulary studies is that between incidental and intentional learning. The basic issue is the extent to which learners can acquire word knowledge incidentally, in the sense of being a by-product of their main learning activity inside or outside the classroom, rather than through activity that is primarily intended to enhance their vocabulary knowledge. Thus, as applied in the literature, the distinction involves both where the learner's attention is concentrated and the pedagogical context in which the opportunity for learning is available. There is no doubt that incidental learning occurs, particularly through extensive reading in input-rich environments, albeit at a rather slow rate. In the heyday of the communicative approach to language teaching, the concept of incidental learning offered the seductive prospect that, provided the learners had access to sufficient comprehensible input, L2 vocabulary acquisition would largely take care of itself, without the need for any substantial pedagogical intervention. However, the research makes it clear that this strong position is no longer tenable.

A significant collection of papers edited by Wesche and Paribakht (1999) gives a good overview of the research findings and issues, including a representative set of research reports on incidental learning of words in a second language from both written and spoken input. More recent studies involving reading tasks include those by Swanborn and de Glopper (2002), who showed that incidental learning of words was influenced by the readers' purpose and level of reading ability, and by Pulido (2003), who also found a significant effect for reader ability, as well as for topic familiarity and passive sight vocabulary. In the case of spoken input, Vidal (2003) showed that university students in Spain retained knowledge of a small but significant number of words one month after listening to videotaped lectures in English. The words more likely to be retained included technical terms that were central to comprehending the lecture topic and words that were explicitly elaborated by the lecturer by means of naming, definition, or description.

In an important discussion of incidental and intentional vocabulary learning from a psycholinguistic perspective, Hulstijn (2001) points out that, whereas the distinction can be maintained operationally in research studies by directing the participants' attention toward or away from vocabulary, it has little theoretical significance in influencing whether words that learners encounter will be retained in long-term memory. Instead, it "is the quality and frequency of the information processing activities (i.e., elaboration on aspects of a word's form and meaning, plus rehearsal) that determine retention of new information" (Hulstijn, 2001, p. 275). He argues that, in the classroom context, incidental and intentional learning should be seen as complementary activities. This leads to two crucial implications for teaching:

1. If learners are to have the automatic access to a rich L2 lexicon that is the foundation of fluent communicative ability, psycholinguistic research indicates that it is necessary to re-visit such unfashionable procedures as regular rehearsal of words, rote learning, and training in automatic word recognition as one component of vocabulary learning, particularly for beginning and intermediate-level learners (Hulstijn, 2001, pp. 275–285). Any gains from incidental learning will be modest for them, when compared with what can be achieved with more "intentional" or direct forms of vocabulary study.
2. Where vocabulary learning is more incidental to classroom activity, Laufer and Hulstijn (2001) argue that learning tasks can be graded according to the level of vocabulary processing that they generate. The authors propose that there are three factors in "task-induced involvement" : the learners'

need to achieve, a requirement that they *search* for information on the meaning or form of the word, and *evaluation* of how the information obtained applied to the particular use of the word in question. From an analysis of previous research, they found that tasks incorporating two or three of the factors led to better retention of the target vocabulary than those with only one factor. Then they obtained confirming evidence from parallel experiments with adult learners in the Netherlands and Israel (Hulstijn & Laufer, 2001). As they predicted, learners who wrote compositions using a set of target words remembered them better than those who encountered the words in a reading comprehension task and, in the Israeli experiment, the learners who wrote the missing words in gaps in the reading text retained more of the words than those who just read marginal glosses.

Vocabulary Selection and Coverage

High-Frequency Words

The first priority in direct vocabulary teaching is to focus on which words are to be studied. A fundamental feature of the lexicon, which governs many decisions about teaching and learning, is the fact that a small proportion of the total number of the words in the language are highly frequent, and vice versa. There is an obvious payoff for learners of English in concentrating initially on the 2000 most frequent words, since they have been repeatedly shown to account for at least 80 percent of the running words in any written or spoken text. As a pedagogical reference work on the most frequent words, West's classic (1953) *General Service List* is yet to be superseded. Although the list can be faulted for being dated in some respects, frequency counts derived from much larger contemporary computer corpora confirm that most of the words would still be included were it to be compiled afresh today.

The pedagogical value of the *General Service List* lay in the semantic basis of its selection and presentation. First, words were included not purely on the criterion of frequency but also to achieve efficient coverage of the meanings that learners were most likely to need to express. In addition, the vocabulary was listed in word families, comprising stem words together with their inflected and derived forms (see Bauer & Nation, 1993, for a more formal method of determining word families), and the relative frequency of different meanings of the word forms were recorded.

The most comprehensive and usable word frequency lists based on a modern computer corpus are those derived from the British National Corpus (BNC) by Leech, Rayson, and Wilson (2001). The lists, which are available both in book form and on the Lancaster University Web site, cover the whole corpus as well as separate counts for the written and spoken components. There are also frequency counts for the different word classes. In several of the lists, the words are clustered into lemmas (consisting of a base word and its inflected forms), but there is no semantic classification that would allow for identification of the relative frequency of different meanings. For such information the teacher or the more advanced learner can turn to the Web site of the BNC or one of the other sites offering public access to corpus examples of words in context (see Conrad, 2002, pp. 89–90 for annotated addresses). Alternatively, it is necessary to rely on the indirect guidance provided by the entries for polysemous words in one of the major learner dictionaries (see below), which present the meanings as determined by lexicographic analysis of a large corpus.

The Vocabulary of Speech

Reliable data on the occurrence of words in speech remains relatively limited. Although spoken vocabulary is now better represented in corpora and word lists, it still only accounts for 10 percent of the texts in the BNC and correspondingly, specialized spoken corpora tend to be much smaller than those based on written texts. An important spoken corpus is the five-million-word Cambridge and Nottingham Corpus of Discourse in English (CANCODE) (McCarthy, 1998). Not surprisingly, a comparison by McCarthy and Carter (1997) of the most frequent words in CANCODE with those in a comparable corpus of written English revealed noticeable differences in the relative frequency of many words, reflecting among other things the distinctive discourse markers of spoken language.

One commonsense assumption is that the amount of vocabulary learners need for everyday speech is rather less than that for dealing with the written language. A target of 2000 word families has been widely accepted, based in part on the results of a study of Australian workers in the 1950s, which showed that 2000 words covered 99 percent of the vocabulary in their speech. In addition, McCarthy and Carter (2003, p. 5) show in graphic form how the frequency of words in a large sample of the spoken BNC drops quite sharply after about the first 2000. However, a recent analysis of CANCODE data by Adolphs and Schmitt (2003) indicated that a vocabulary of this size gives barely 95 percent coverage of conversational discourse. Although the 95 percent figure may seem a minor shortfall in percentage terms, it represents a substantial number of unknown words for a learner with a 2000-word vocabulary, leading Adolphs and Schmitt to suggest that knowledge of 3000 words is a more realistic goal for learners to be able to cope with the lexical demands of everyday conversation.

It should be emphasized that these figures of 2000 and 3000 actually refer to word families rather than individual words. A study by Schmitt and Zimmerman (2002) provided clear evidence that college ESL students have at best partial knowledge of the derived forms of stem words (e.g., *persistent*, *persistently*, and *persistence* from *persist*). This means that, to some extent, learners are familiar with the other members of a word family, given knowledge of the stem word, but it cannot be assumed. As a result, the 2000- and 3000-word figures considerably understate the actual number of words that need to be learned in some sense.

There has been very little research on the actual ability of learners to cope with listening or speaking tasks, given knowledge of a specific proportion of the vocabulary required. One study of Japanese learners' listening comprehension by Bonk (2000) showed that, although some learners could achieve adequate understanding of short expository texts by knowing as little as 80 percent of the vocabulary, most needed more than 95 percent coverage, and quite a few students could not really understand the texts even though they apparently had some knowledge of all the words. These results are comparable to those obtained by Hu and Nation (2000) in a similarly designed study of the relationship between vocabulary coverage and reading comprehension of fiction texts. Hu and Nation also found that knowledge of 80 percent of the words was the minimum threshold but that most learners needed to know around 98 percent in order to read independently. Thus, while further investigation is necessary, it appears that the vocabulary learning goals for minimum levels of both listening and reading comprehension need to be set somewhat higher than the 95 percent coverage that has been widely recommended until now.

Specific Purpose Vocabulary

When we move beyond the high-frequency vocabulary represented by the first 2000 word families, it is necessary to take into account of the needs and interests of specific groups of learners in selecting words for study. Given the demand for teaching English for academic purposes (EAP) in universities worldwide, particular attention has been paid to academic vocabulary, which can be approached in two ways. One is to focus on subtechnical words occurring frequently across a range of academic texts, and the other is to identify the technical terms associated with particular disciplines.

A major contribution to the former approach is Coxhead's (2000) Academic Word List, a compilation of 570 word families based on a careful analysis of a 3.5 million word corpus of written academic texts assembled specifically for this purpose. There were 28 subject areas represented in the texts, and the words were selected based not only on frequency but also range: they had to occur a minimum number of times in more than half of the subject areas. Coxhead's analysis showed that the word list covered 10 percent of the running words in the corpus beyond the 76 percent coverage achieved by the General Service List. The list is of particular value for students in EAP programs preparing for undergraduate study and provides the basis for the development of teaching resources in that context. Like the BNC lists (Leech et al., 2001) discussed above, it does not contain any information about the meanings of the words in academic texts, and here again teachers are reliant on learner dictionaries and concordancing of available corpora, as well as their own judgment, to identify the specific meanings to focus on.

The other approach to academic vocabulary is to identify terms that are specific to a particular discipline. Ward (1999) created a corpus of engineering texts for EAP students in that discipline and found that the 2000 most frequent word families in the corpus achieved 95 percent coverage of the texts, which was a substantially better result than could be obtained from a combination of the General Service List and a general academic word list. At a more conceptual level, Chung and Nation (2003) developed a four-step semantically based procedure for identifying technical terms in academic textbooks. Their analysis showed that one-third of the words in an anatomy textbook and one-fifth of those in an applied linguistics text were technical in nature, in that these words were closely or exclusively related to their respective field of study. The figures were much higher than previously suggested, as in Nation's (2001, p. 12) estimate of 5 percent, and highlight the additional challenge that EAP learners face in learning vocabulary beyond the high-frequency and subtechnical categories.

Ward's (1999) creation of a relatively small corpus of discipline-specific texts is part of a trend in the teaching of language for specific purposes whereby advanced learners are encouraged to access locally compiled corpora to investigate both word frequency and the meanings and uses of particular lexical items in their field of study. Based on her experience with a small corpus of medical research articles, Gavioli (2002) endorses the pedagogical value of such explorations but also advises caution in allowing students to make generalizations about word usage without reference to confirming evidence from a much larger and more general corpus.

Learner Dictionaries

Apart from word lists, the basic reference source for teachers and learners alike is the dictionary, which is now available in a variety of forms. Nesi (1999) noted the increasing use of electronic dictionaries on the Web, on CD-ROMs, in small hand-held units—and most recently in the guise of scanner pens. Small handheld dictionaries are particularly favored by learners in Hong Kong, Taiwan, and Japan for their convenience and relatively low cost. Nevertheless, hard copy versions in book form still hold their own for both classroom and individual use throughout the world.

Huge resources are devoted to the development, production, and marketing of learner dictionaries, particularly by the five major British publishers that dominate the market, but there is comparatively little evaluation of their effectiveness for vocabulary teaching. As Chan and Taylor (2001) found in their analysis of dictionary reviews published since 1987, the language teachers and applied linguists who review the dictionaries tend to write short descriptive accounts, often without even specifying any criteria for evaluation. A recent example of a review of this general type is Tribble's (2003) comparison of the CD-ROM versions of the five leading advanced learners' dictionaries. From the reviewer's perspective, the electronic editions certainly appeared to have attractive features, such as audible pronunciation of words and hyperlinks both to entries for related words and to a range of reference notes, corpus examples, and practice exercises.

However, as Nesi (2000) points out, the amount of research on *learners'* preferences and their actual use of the dictionaries is remarkably limited. One methodological problem in undertaking such studies in the past has been the difficulty of monitoring dictionary use unobtrusively and obtaining accurate records on which entries were accessed or how much time was spent reading each one. This issue can now be addressed by setting computer-based tasks, although of course it is an open question whether learners access a dictionary electronically in the same way that they consult one manually.

Nesi (2000) conducted a series of studies in which students accessed dictionary entries as they performed either reading comprehension or sentence writing tasks. The results showed that the comprehension scores were not affected by whether the participants looked up words or not. With regard to the relative merits of different dictionary features, Nesi found that neither the particular defining style used by a dictionary nor the inclusion of examples in a dictionary entry had a measurable effect on learners' ability to produce acceptable sentences incorporating the target word. However, nationality was a significant variable in successful dictionary use, in that learners in Portugal performed much better than a comparable group in Malaysia. Nesi attributed the differences to the fact that the Portuguese learners had studied English as a foreign language and thus more experience of using dictionaries, whereas the Malaysians had acquired their much more extensive knowledge of English vocabulary through informal exposure in a second language environment. Another possible factor was the relative linguistic distance of Portuguese and Bahasa Malaysia from English.

In a subsequent study, Nesi and Haill (2002) analyzed how successfully international students at a British university were able to identify the correct meaning of unfamiliar words in a self-selected reading text when they looked them up in a dictionary. The researchers found that more than half of the students failed in the task at least once, most commonly because they chose the wrong dictionary entry or the wrong meaning of a polysemous word. This suggests that there are definite limits on the ability of learners to make full use of the information about words in a dictionary if they consult it independently, without the guidance of a teacher.

Vocabulary in the Classroom

There is comparatively little research to report on methods of presenting and practicing vocabulary in the classroom. The basic principles of direct vocabulary teaching are well established, and good accounts can be found in Sökmen (1997) and Nation (2001, Chap. 3). As for classroom practice, Burns and de Silva Joyce (2001a) directed an action research project on teaching vocabulary in the Adult Migrant English Program throughout Australia, and have edited a collection of reports by the participating teacher-researchers on the wide range of practical studies that they conducted (Burns & de Silva Joyce, 2001b).

One common task that teachers set for more advanced learners is to select and record their own words to study, based on individual needs or interests. The vocabulary notebook is a useful tool for this purpose (Fowle, 2002). However, Moir and Nation (2002) present a cautionary tale from their research in an intensive ESL class at a New Zealand university, where the students were required to study 30 self-selected words every week. The researchers found that, with one notable exception, the learners tended to choose unsuitable words, which they learned by cramming the night before the weekly test each Friday and then promptly forgot. In this case, negative washback from the test was, among other factors, working against the longer-term vocabulary building goals of the program.

Apart from investigating particular classroom activities, some researchers have focused on the opportunities for vocabulary acquisition offered by classroom talk in general. Lightbown, Meara, and Halter (1998) analyzed transcripts of teacher-centered activities in classes following both the audiolingual and communicative approaches to language teaching. They found that, although the communicative teachers used a wider range of words, the oral input in both types of classroom contained relatively few new words that might contribute to a growth in the learners' vocabulary knowledge. The lexical value of the teacher talk, particularly by the audiolingual teachers, was in providing repeated exposure to the high-frequency vocabulary of English.

In a similar study, Tang and Nesi (2003) compared transcripts from secondary school English classrooms in Hong Kong and Guangzhou. Their results showed the influence of the rather different types of language syllabus and teaching methods in the two administrative divisions of China where these cities are located. The teacher in Hong Kong adopted a more flexible approach, incorporating a range of activities, materials, and topics, which produced more lexical variation and lower-frequency words. In Guangzhou, the treatment of vocabulary was much more systematic, within a strictly controlled lesson plan that left little opportunity for spontaneous interaction between the teacher and students. Although both teachers engaged in explicit teaching of preselected words, using a variety of techniques, the Hong Kong classroom offered more interactionally modified input and opportunities for incidental learning. In that sense, it could be seen as a lexically richer environment for vocabulary acquisition.

Computer Applications

With the increasing use of computers to deliver language learning programs, there are new opportunities to enhance vocabulary acquisition, either directly through vocabulary learning activities or more incidentally in the context of reading tasks.

As an example of the direct approach, Groot (2000) describes a program called CAVOCA (Computer Assisted Vocabulary Acquisition), which was designed to promote longer-term retention of useful words by presenting each one in numerous carefully selected sentences and short texts. The learners are thus encouraged to induce the meaning (s) of each word and to pay attention to its various properties. In a series of small experiments with Dutch university students learning English, Groot and his associates found evidence of a better retention rate by this method than by paired associate learning, but he concludes that the most efficient approach would be a combination of the two.

In the case of reading tasks undertaken on a computer, learners can readily have access to an electronic dictionary or to hyperlinks providing glosses and other useful information about particular words in the text which they are unlikely to know. Research in this area over the last 10 years has demonstrated that the provision of glosses can assist vocabulary learning from texts, without interfering with the reading process. Recent studies have sought to establish more specifically how best to present the glosses. For instance, in her study of Belgian university students who were advanced learners of French, De Ridder (2002) found that marking glossed words with underlining and a blue font induced more clicking on the link, but it did not improve the learners' retention of the word meaning, as compared to a text in which the links were not visible on the screen.

A second line of investigation has been the relative effectiveness of different forms of multimedia glossing. In a series of studies, Chun, Plass, and their associates found that students who selected both pictorial and written annotations of words, whether it be in reading (Plass, Chun, Mayer, & Leutner, 1998) or listening (Jones & Plass, 2002) tasks on computer, retained more of the vocabulary than students who accessed only one type of gloss or none at all. The researchers argue that the two types of lexical information led to richer mental representations of the words, making them easier to retrieve from memory. Al-Seghayer (2001) looked more specifically at two forms of visual glossing—still pictures and video clips with sound—and found that the video condition led to significantly more vocabulary learning. This contrasted with the results of an earlier study by Chun and Plass (1996), who concluded that still pictures provided a more stable image that facilitated the remembering of the word.

Other researchers have looked at offering various forms of information about the target words. Laufer and Hill (2000) highlighted 12 words in a short L2 text and provided separate buttons for the L2 meaning, the L1 translation, the pronunciation, and additional information on each one. Israeli students mostly chose the Hebrew translation, but there was no significant relationship between their choice of button and retention of the words. However, students in Hong Kong, who took the task more seriously overall, tended to access more of the information about each word; for them, poorer retention was associated with looking up the Chinese translation.

A different kind of computer application to vocabulary learning through reading is represented by TextLadder, a program developed by Ghadirian (2002) to select and order a series of texts to allow for multiple exposures to a set of target words in contexts with mostly familiar vocabulary. Given a reasonably large number of simplified texts that are suitable for the learners' interests and needs, the program selects those with a high proportion of the target words overall and a minimum of five repetitions of individual words; it also orders them according to the percentage of high-frequency vocabulary which they contain. There is not yet published evidence as to whether the reading of a series of texts from a program like TextLadder does, in fact, promote efficient learning of the target words. However, it can be seen as potentially an alternative means of achieving what specially written graded readers have traditionally been designed to do. (For investigations of the vocabulary learning potential in graded readers, see Nation & Wang, 1999 and Waring & Takaki, 2003).

Assessing Vocabulary Knowledge

In vocabulary testing, it has become conventional to distinguish between breadth and depth of vocabulary knowledge. Breadth refers to a general estimate of how many words the learner knows, usually by reference to samples of words from specified frequency levels in a vocabulary list. The best-known instrument for this purpose is Nation's Vocabulary Levels Test, which covers the 10,000 most frequent words in English in five bands and involves a simple task of matching words and definitions. Originally developed 20 years ago as a simple diagnostic tool for classroom use, it is now widely used for placement purposes in language teaching programs and as a measure in vocabulary research. For instance, Cameron (2002) reports on the use of the test to identify gaps in the receptive vocabulary knowledge of students from ethnic minority or refugee backgrounds in a secondary school in the United Kingdom. Two studies by Beglar and Hunt (1999) and Schmitt, Schmitt, and Clapham (2001) have produced revised and validated forms of the test.

Depth of knowledge focuses on the idea that for useful higher-frequency words learners need to have more than just a superficial understanding of the meaning; they should develop a rich and specific meaning representation as well as knowledge of the word's formal features, syntactic functioning, collocational possibilities, register characteristics, and so on. One practical measure of depth is Read's (1998) word associates format, which requires learners to identify words that are semantically associated with a given target word. Dutch researchers (Bogaards, 2000; Greidanus & Nienhuis, 2001) have found modified versions of the procedure to be a probing test of the vocabulary knowledge of more advanced foreign language learners. In Canada, Qian (1999, 2002) used the word associates test in his investigation of the relationship between L2 vocabulary knowledge and reading comprehension ability. He showed that this depth measure accounted for a significant amount of the variance in the reading scores beyond what was predicted by a vocabulary breadth test.

Conclusion

It is clear from this review that the vigorous research activity in L2 vocabulary teaching and learning during the 1990s is continuing in the present decade. There has been a noticeable increase in articles on vocabulary being published in several of the journals in applied linguistics in recent years. The focus here has been on research with relatively direct applications to the language classroom, but there is a great deal more work that is advancing our understanding of vocabulary acquisition processes and of the nature of vocabulary itself.

Obviously the computer has had a substantial impact on vocabulary studies. Because orthographic words are such readily identifiable and countable units, computerized corpus analysis has revolutionized the study of word frequency, word meanings in context, and the collocational patterns of words. The results of these analyses are being incorporated in course books, dictionaries, and reference works, but in addition, learners can have direct access to corpus evidence themselves through what Johns (2002) has called "data-driven learning." Increasingly, the computer is also an access medium to the second language through local and Web-based electronic resources; here we have described several applications with the potential to enhance vocabulary learning in that environment.

It is important to make one final observation: Virtually all of the literature in the present review has treated vocabulary in terms of individual words. This is not the result of any conscious selection criterion on my part, and it appears to reflect the current state of play. However, I should point out that one impact of corpus analysis on vocabulary study is to highlight the significance of multiword lexical units and indeed to challenge the validity of the traditional division between vocabulary and grammar. Although teachers and learners are certainly aware of the learning difficulties posed by idioms and collocations (see, e.g., Nesselhauf, 2003), the role of multiword units goes much further than that. It is beyond the scope of this review to explore the implications of these fresh insights for vocabulary learning and for language teaching in general, but the work of applied linguists such as Wray (2000, 2002) on formulaic language may yet transform our understanding of vocabulary and the way it is taught.

Note

1. I am grateful to Norbert Schmitt for useful comments on an earlier version of this chapter.

ANNOTATED BIBLIOGRAPHY

Nation, I. S. P. (2001). *Learning vocabulary in another language.* Cambridge: Cambridge University Press.

The most comprehensive and authoritative volume on second language vocabulary learning that is currently available. It covers an impressive range of both previous and contemporary research, including the numerous contributions of the author and his students, as the basis for a wealth of practical advice on promoting effective vocabulary acquisition in second language teaching programs.

Read, J. (2000). *Assessing vocabulary.* Cambridge: Cambridge University Press.

An analysis of various types of vocabulary tests within a broader framework of second language vocabulary assessment. It includes a review of research in both language testing and SLA as well as an analytical approach to the design of vocabulary measures for teaching and research purposes.

Schmitt, N. (2000). *Vocabulary in language teaching.* Cambridge: Cambridge University Press.

This book written for classroom teachers covers a similar range of topics to those in Nation's book, but they are treated at a more introductory level. In each chapter, there are practical exercises and a discussion of the implications for teaching.

Schmitt, N., & McCarthy, M. (Eds.). (1997). *Vocabulary: Description, acquisition and pedagogy.* Cambridge: Cambridge University Press.

A major anthology of 15 state-of-the-art papers contributed by many leading figures in vocabulary studies. The section on pedagogy includes chapters on vocabulary teaching methods, vocabulary in syllabus design, vocabulary reference works, and vocabulary testing.

WEB SITES

www.swan.ac.uk/cals/calsres/varga – Vocabulary Acquisition Research Group Archive (VARGA)

The archive, which is maintained by Paul Meara, is a bibliographic record of publications on vocabulary teaching and learning, with separate alphabetically ordered pages for each year since 1984.

www.vuw.ac.nz/lals/staff/paul_nation/index.html – Paul Nation's home page

This page has a link to Nation's wide-ranging bibliography on vocabulary, built up over many years of scholarship in the field. Items are listed alphabetically by author, as well as being individually coded by topic according to a classification system presented at the top of the list. Another link goes to a downloadable Zip file containing software that can be used to analyze the vocabulary content of texts in terms of the General Service List (most frequent 2000 words) and the Academic Word List.

www.lextutor.ca – The Compleat Lexical Tutor

This Web site established by Tom Cobb has a range of resources of great value to learners, teachers, and researchers for both English and French vocabulary. It includes vocabulary levels tests, information about high-frequency words (audible pronunciation, definitions, corpus examples), lexical analysis of input texts (frequency lists, concordances, statistics), and a program to create cloze passages.

www.vuw.ac.nz/lals/div1/awl/index.html – The Academic Word List online

The complete list, together with background information on its creation and use, has been made available on this page by Averil Coxhead. Numerous texts based on the list, together with gap-fill exercises, are available on Andy Gillett's EAP site at www.uefap.co.uk/vocab/vocfram.htm . Another site developed by Sandra Haywood (www.nottingham.ac.uk/%7Ealzsh3/ acvocab/index.htm) includes two useful tools for teachers: AWL Highlighter, which highlights the AWL words in any input text, and AWL Gapmaker, which creates gap-fill exercises by replacing AWL words in a text with blanks to be completed by the learners.

OTHER REFERENCES

Adolphs, S., & Schmitt, N. (2003). Lexical coverage of spoken discourse. *Applied Linguistics*, 24, 425–438.

Al-Seghayer, K. (2001). The effect of multimedia annotation modes on L2 vocabulary acquisition: A comparative study. *Language Learning and Technology*, 5, 202–232.

Bauer, L., & Nation, I. S. P. (1993). Word families. *International Journal of Lexicography*, 6, 253–279.

Beglar, A., & Hunt, A. (1999). Revising and validating the 2000 word level and the university word level vocabulary tests. *Language Testing*, 16, 131–162.

Bogaards, P. (2000). Testing L2 vocabulary at a high level: The case of the Euralex French tests. *Applied Linguistics*, 21, 490–516.

Bonk, W. J. (2000). Second language lexical knowledge and listening comprehension. *International Journal of Listening*, 14, 14–31.

Burns, A., & de Silva Joyce, H. (2001a). Researching and teaching vocabulary in the AMEP. *Prospect*, 16, 20–34.

Burns, A., & de Silva Joyce, H. (Eds.). (2001b). *Teachers' voices 7: Teaching vocabulary.* Sydney: National Centre for English Language Teaching and Research, Macquarie University.

Cameron, L. (2002). Measuring vocabulary size in English as an additional language. *Language Teaching Research*, 6, 145–173.

Coady, J., & Huckin, T. (Eds.). (1997). *Second language vocabulary acquisition: A rationale for pedagogy.* Cambridge: Cambridge University Press.

Conrad, S. (2002). Corpus linguistic approaches for discourse analysis. *Annual Review of Applied Linguistics* 22, 75–95.

Coxhead, A. (2000). A new academic word list. *TESOL Quarterly*, 34, 213–238.

Chan, A. Y. W., & Taylor, A. (2001). Evaluating learner dictionaries: What the reviews say. *International Journal of Lexicography*, 14, 163–180.

Chun, D. M., & Plass, J. L. (1996). Effects of multimedia annotations on vocabulary acquisition. *Modern Language Journal*, 80, 183–198.

Chung, T. M., & Nation, P. (2003). Technical vocabulary in specialised texts. *Reading in a Foreign Language*, 15, 103–116.

de Ridder, I. (2002). Visible or invisible links: Does the highlighting of hyperlinks affect incidental vocabulary learning, text comprehension, and the reading process? *Language Learning and Technology*, 6, 123–146.

Doughty, C., & Williams, J. (Eds.). (1998). *Focus on form in classroom second language acquisition.* Cambridge: Cambridge University Press.

Fowle, C. (2002). Vocabulary notebooks: Implementation and outcomes. *ELT Journal, 56*, 380–388.

Gavioli, L. (2002). Some thoughts on the problem of representing ESP through small corpora. In B. Kettemann & G. Marko (Eds.), *Teaching and learning by doing corpus analysis* (pp. 293–303). Amsterdam: Rodopi.

Ghadirian, S. (2002). Providing controlled exposure to target vocabulary through the screening and arranging of texts. *Language Learning and Technology, 6*, 147–164.

Greidanus, T., & Nienhuis, L. (2001). Testing the quality of word knowledge in L2 by means of word associations: Types of distractors and types of associations. *Modern Language Journal, 85*, 567–577.

Groot, P. J. M. (2000). Computer assisted second language vocabulary acquisition. *Language Learning and Technology, 4*, 60–81.

Hu, M. H-C., & Nation, P. (2000). Unknown vocabulary density and reading comprehension. *Reading in a Foreign Language, 13* (1), 403–430.

Hulstijn, J. H. (2001). Intentional and incidental second language vocabulary learning: A reappraisal of elaboration, rehearsal and automaticity. In P. Robinson (Ed.), *Cognition and second language instruction* (pp. 258–286). Cambridge: Cambridge University Press.

Hulstijn, J. H., & Laufer, B. (2001). Some empirical evidence for the involvement load hypothesis in vocabulary acquisition. *Language Learning, 51*, 539–558.

Johns, T. (2002). Data-driven learning: The perpetual challenge. In B. Kettemann & G. Marko (Eds.), *Teaching and learning by doing corpus analysis* (pp. 107–117). Amsterdam: Rodopi.

Jones, L. C., & Plass, J. L. (2002). Supporting listening comprehension and vocabulary acquisition in French with multimedia annotations. *Modern Language Journal, 86*, 546–561.

Laufer, B., & Hill, M. (2000). What lexical information do L2 learners select in a CALL dictionary and how does it affect word retention? *Language Learning and Technology, 3*, 58–76.

Laufer, B., & Hulstijn, J. (2001). Incidental vocabulary acquisition in a second language: The construct of task-induced involvement. *Applied Linguistics, 22*, 1–26.

Leech, G., Rayson, P., & Wilson, A. (2001). *Word frequencies in spoken and written English.* London: Longman. [The accompanying Web site is at www.comp.lancs.ac.uk/ucrel/bncfreq/flists.html]

Lightbown, P. M., Meara, P., & Halter, R. H. (1998). Contrasting patterns in classroom lexical environments. In D. Albrechtsen, B. Henriksen, I. M. Mees, & E. Poulsen (Eds.), *Perspectives on foreign and second language pedagogy* (pp. 221–238). Odense: Odense University Press.

McCarthy, M. (1998). *Spoken language and applied linguistics.* Cambridge: Cambridge University Press.

McCarthy, M., & Carter, R. (1997). Written and spoken vocabulary. In N. Schmitt & M. McCarthy (Eds.), *Vocabulary: Description, acquisition and pedagogy* (pp. 20–39). Cambridge: Cambridge University Press.

McCarthy, M. & Carter, R. (2003). What constitutes a basic spoken vocabulary? *Research Notes, 13*: 5–7 [Cambridge: University of Cambridge ESOL Examinations].

Moir, J., & Nation, P. (2002). Learners' use of strategies for effective vocabulary learning. *Prospect, 16,* 18–32.

Nation, P., & Wang, K. (1999). Graded readers and vocabulary. *Reading in a Foreign Language, 12,* 355–380.

Nesi, H. (1999). A user's guide to electronic dictionaries for language learners. *International Journal of Lexicography, 12,* 55–66.

Nesi, H. (2000). *The use and abuse of EFL dictionaries.* Tübingen: Niemeyer.

Nesi, H., & Haill, R. (2002). A study of dictionary use by international students at a British university. *International Journal of Lexicography, 15,* 277–305.

Nesselhauf, N. (2003). The use of collocations by advanced learners of English and some implications for teaching. *Applied Linguistics, 24,* 223–242.

Plass, J. L., Chun, D. M., Mayer, R. E., & Leutner, D. (1998). Supporting visual and verbal learning preferences in a second language multimedia learning environment. *Journal of Educational Psychology, 90,* 25–36.

Pulido, D. (2003). Modeling the role of second language proficiency and topic familiarity in second language incidental vocabulary acquisition through reading. *Language Learning, 53,* 233–284.

Qian, D. D. (1999). Assessing the roles of depth and breadth of vocabulary knowledge. *Canadian Modern Language Review, 56,* 282–307.

Qian, D. D. (2002). Investigating the relationship between vocabulary knowledge and academic reading performance: An assessment perspective. *Language Learning, 52,* 513–536.

Read, J. (1998). Validating a test to measure depth of vocabulary knowledge. In A. Kunnan (Ed.), *Validation in language assessment* (pp. 41–60). Mahwah, NJ: Erlbaum.

Schmitt, N., Schmitt, D., & Clapham, C. (2001). Developing and exploring the behaviour of two new versions of the Vocabulary Levels Test. *Language Testing, 18,* 55–88.

Schmitt, N., & Zimmerman, C.B. (2002). Derivative word forms: What do learners know? *TESOL Quarterly, 36,* 145–171.

Singleton, D. (1999). *Exploring the second language mental lexicon.* Cambridge: Cambridge University Press.

Sökmen, A. (1997). Current trends in teaching second language vocabulary. In N. Schmitt & M. McCarthy (Eds.), *Vocabulary: Description, acquisition and pedagogy* (pp. 237–257). Cambridge: Cambridge University Press.

Swanborn, M. S. L., & de Glopper, K. (2002). Impact of reading purpose on incidental word learning from context. *Language Learning, 52,* 95–117.

Tang, E., & Nesi, H. (2003). Teaching vocabulary in two Chinese classrooms: Schoolchildren's exposure to English words in Hong Kong and Guangzhou. *Language Teaching Research, 7,* 65–97.

Tribble, C. (2003). Five electronic learners'dictionaries. *ELT Journal 57,* 182–197.

Vidal, K. (2003). Academic listening: A source of vocabulary acquisition? *Applied Linguistics, 24,* 56–89.

Ward, J. (1999). How large a vocabulary do EAP engineering students need? *Reading in a Foreign Language, 12,* 309–323.

Waring, R., & Takaki, M. (2003). At what rate do learners learn and retain new vocabulary from reading a graded reader? *Reading in a Foreign Language, 15,* 130–163.

Wesche, M., & Paribakht, S. (Eds.). (1999). *Incidental L2 vocabulary acquisition: Theory, current research, and instructional implications* [Special issue]. *Studies in Second Language Acquisition, 21* (2).

West, M. (1953). *A general service list of English words.* London: Longman.

Wray, A. (2000). Formulaic sequences in second language teaching: Principle and practice. *Applied Linguistics, 21,* 463–489.

Wray, A. (2002). *Formulaic language and the lexicon.* Cambridge: Cambridge University Press.

TEACHING LANGUAGE IN
SPECIFIC SETTINGS

8. TRENDS IN TEACHING ENGLISH FOR SPECIFIC PURPOSES

Diane D. Belcher

This review of trends in the teaching of English for specific purposes (ESP) presents recent developments in ESP praxis from three different but not mutually exclusive points of reference: the sociodiscoursal, sociocultural, and sociopolitical. In addition to a selection of exemplar practices, theoretical analogues are considered for each of these three socially oriented perspectives on ESP. For the sociodiscoursal approach to ESP, genre theory and genre-informed pedagogy are highlighted; for the sociocultural, theories of situated learning and their practical corollaries are focused on; for the sociopolitical, theories and applications of critical pedagogy are emphasized. Possible research directions for all three social turns of ESP are also suggested.

New York: An English as a Second Language textbook focuses predominantly on food-preparation vocabulary, night-school student Eduardo Reyes reported Monday. "I must admit, I would like to learn how to say more than, 'I have diced the onions,' and 'Did he want scrambled or over-easy?'" said a disconsolate Reyes, speaking through a translator, following his first lesson. "I had hoped to learn words for the different parts of the body so I can pursue my dream of becoming a doctor. I have instead learned much about the grilling of chickens" (Siegel, 2002, p. 206).

Although the preceding quotation is actually a parody of a report on a New York City adult literacy class taken from the satirical publication *The Onion*, it may capture for many critics of English for specific purposes (hereafter ESP[1]) what they feel is the essence of the shortcomings of the ESP approach to English language teaching: that it teaches learners enough English to survive in certain narrowly defined venues but not enough to thrive in the world at large. A common litany of complaints includes the observation that texts used in ESP pedagogy are too far removed from the real-life contexts that learners aim for (see Adam and Artemeva, 2002, on "textoids," and Auerbach, 2002, on learner vs. language expert goals). Another common complaint is that many ESP instructors could not (or would not) engage in the type of specialized language use that they attempt to induct learners into, e.g., humanities majors teaching the language of science and technology (Spack, 1988; for a recent response to Spack, see Bruce, 2002). Hand in hand with the latter criticism comes the view that ESP has a strong bent toward accommodationism, or "vulgar pragmatism" (Pennycook, 1997), because it seeks to help learners fit into, rather than contest, existing socioeconomic and political structures no matter how inequitable their power distribution may be.

Those familiar with ESP as it is often practiced today, or as many would like to see it practiced, would likely deny that the *Onion* scenario and much of the criticism of ESP's narrow window on the world have much to do with current ESP best practices. Ideally, ESP pedagogy is driven by learner-centeredness (Johns & Price-Machado, 2001; but see also Hutchinson & Waters, 1987, for a critique of ESP's learner focus). In fact, ESP was, arguably, learner-centered long before the term became popular in ELT, as the four-decades-old approach called ESP (see Swales, 2000) is by definition one that attempts to give learners access to the language they want and need to accomplish their own academic or occupational goals. Whether or not ESP is always as sensitive to learners' needs and successful at meeting them as it should be is another matter. Unlike other pedagogical approaches, which may be less specific-needs-based and more theory-driven, ESP pedagogy places heavy demands on its practitioners to collect empirical needs-assessment data, to create or adapt materials to meet the specific needs identified, and to cope with often unfamiliar subject matter and even language use; moreover, they must do all of the above without allowing the aims of a funding agency, an employer, an *au courant* educational theory, or an instructor's own idiosyncratic sense of what's best for language learners to affect attempts to address specific learners' current and future needs.

Perhaps because of its very pragmatism—its eagerness to be responsive to learners' target academic and occupational needs—and its lack of a well-developed, identifiable theoretical base, which Hyland (in press) finds unsurprising given its "pragmatic diversity," ESP appears, at least in its current incarnation, receptive to criticism and input from a number of philosophical and theoretical fronts (Hyland, 2003; Johns, 2002b; Swales, 2000). As a result of this ideological permeability, ESP pedagogy can be viewed at present as developing in three overlapping directions: the sociodiscoursal, sociocultural, and sociopolitical. Although it would be more than unfair to countless ESP practitioners over the past decades to say that they have totally ignored social context (or their social consciences!), it may well be fair to say that never before has ESP emphasized social situatedness as much as it does today. In what follows, I will look at the three aforementioned social turns that ESP has taken, focusing first on their theoretical impetus and then on actual praxis.

The Sociodiscoursal Approach: Situated Genre Analysis

Theory

In many respects, the means and ends of ESP and genre studies are so similar that it is difficult to disentangle the two: both investigate the discourse of specific speech communities, with attention to the types of written and oral texts, or "structured communicative events" (Hyland, 2003), used and valued in those contexts. The fact that such influential and productive scholars as Swales (1990), Johns (2002b) and Hyland (in press) straddle both domains no doubt contributes to some of the blurring of boundaries. Many in ESP would argue that genre analysis is a tool of ESP, an engine for discovery and analysis of target text-types (see Paltridge, 2002, on the text-type/genre distinction) and for generation of genre-oriented teaching materials. Others, such as Hyon (1996) and Hyland (2002), have looked at ESP as a subcategory of genre studies, with North American New Rhetoric, a product of postmodernist theory and L1 composition research (see Hyland, in press), and the Australian Sydney School, derived from Systemic-Functional Linguistics (SFL), as the other two branches. Taking ESP as one's major vantage point on genre, however, it is easy to view ESP as having subsumed the other non-ESP genre studies offshoots, or put another way, as having co-opted them, and becoming the richer for having done so (Hyland, 2003).

Both New Rhetoric (NR) and the Sydney School have provided ESP with previously missing perspectives on genre. As recently as the mid-1990s, Prior observed that ESP, or more specifically, EAP (English for academic purposes), ran the risk of treating students as " 'academic dopes' endlessly re-encoding the abstract rules and conventions of monologic discourses" (1995, p. 78). New Rhetoricians such as Prior deserve credit for bringing a more nuanced view of meaning and text to ESP by calling attention to the seemingly endless variation, dynamism, and situatedness of genre (but see Russell, 1997, on "reinscribed structuralist views," or "neostructuralism"). Influenced by the work of Bakhtin, (1981), Volosinov, Kristeva, and others, New Rhetoricians such as Adam and Artemeva (2002), Bazerman (2002), and, of course, Prior (1998) offer a perspective on discourse as always utterance, i.e., dialogic, or contributing to dialogue, and characterized by addressivity, or anticipation of response; and by heteroglossia, or multivocality, also known as intertextuality, i.e., filled with the voices (prior texts) of others. Russell remarks of Bakhtinian "dialogism's" contribution to our understanding of discourse that it "allow[s] a more dynamic and interactive or ecological approach," going "further than social constructionism toward solving the problems of the relations among language, the individual and the social" (1997, p. 2).

The Sydney School, which Hyland (2003) points to as the most fully theorized of the three genre branches thanks to its SFL basis, is somewhat analogous to NR, insofar as both see text as context, an essential tenet of neo-Firthian, Hallidayan linguistics, yet the Australians have shown more interest in textual than in situational analysis (as well as more interest than either ESP or NR in the education of very young learners). For the Sydney School, however, like the New Rhetoricians, genre is more than the sum of its macro and micro parts. Discourse is seen through the lens of field (ideational content), tenor (interpersonal context), and mode (textuality). The Sydney School's conceptualization of genre is not so complex, however, as to make it virtually unteachable. While for many New Rhetoricians (e.g., Dias, Freedman, Medway, & Pare, 1999), the ability to "genre" (Adam & Artemeva, 2002) is seen as most often learned through immersion in a particular setting;[2] for many in the Sydney School, who view genre knowledge as a source of power in society, explicit genre instruction is, in effect, a moral imperative (Cope & Kalantzis, 1999). Aspects of both stances on the teachability of genre can be found in ESP pedagogy today (e.g., Pang, 2002), as we shall soon see.

New Rhetoric and the Sydney School are not, however, the only influences on ESP's re-envisioning of genre. The relatively new technology-fueled field of corpus linguistics is also further extending our range of view on genre through the collection and analysis of immense computer-compiled corpora of written and oral texts, (e.g., the Collins COBUILD "Bank of English," http://titania.cobuild.collins.co.uk/, retrieved November 20, 2003, which is now at 450 million words and still growing). Corpus linguists are amassing a greater wealth of information on textual variation (Grabe, 2002) for both "authentic" and "classroom" genres (Johns, 1995) than ever before possible (for examples of classroom genres, see the MICASE corpus, http://www.lsa.umich.edu/eli/micase/ATTRIB.html, retrieved November 20, 2003). Hyland's (2000) computer concordance-informed analysis of hedges and boosters in disciplinary texts is but one example among many, in Hyland's own prolific corpus-oriented research and that of others, of how corpus linguistics is expanding the genre knowledge base available to ESP practitioners (see, e.g., Flowerdew, 2003, on professional and learner corpora; Jabbour, 2001, on corpus-derived EAP materials development).

Praxis

The logical next question one might ask following my brief discussion of genre is, How are these theoretical insights and high-tech databanks and analyses reflected in ESP classroom practice? I use the verb "reflected" cautiously in posing this question in order to soften any suggestion of direct causal relationship between recent developments in genre studies and particular ESP pedagogical practices, which would be difficult to demonstrate except in the cases where the materials developers/lesson designers themselves have acknowledged such an influence (or were both genre theorist/researchers and classroom implementers themselves, e.g., Swales). It may be more realistic and accurate to view the theoretical and pedagogical developments as parallel phenomena (but not distantly parallel universes) influenced by ongoing researcher and practitioner conversations about genre. In the following section, I describe recent genre-related practices in both EAP and EOP. These are by no means the only such pedagogical developments of note, but they are particularly salient ones (for additional genre-inspired ESP-related activities/materials see Paltridge, 2001).

English for Academic Purposes (EAP)

Some of the arguments that Swales (1996) has advanced for teaching advanced EAP clearly resonate with those that Sydney School adherents (e.g., Cope

& Kalantzis, 1999) have voiced for beginning EAP for Aboriginal and immigrant child and adult learners: namely, that the genres second language (or dialect) learners need to "do" things in society (see Miller, 1984, on genre as social action) may be hidden or seldom or poorly taught. Swales, through his own ESL teaching and textbook writing with Feak (Swales & Feak, 1994, 2000), has sought to provide graduate-level nonnative English-speaking students (NNESs) with access to some of these "occluded" and semi-occluded genres—e.g., conference abstracts, correspondence with editors, and academic job applications—genres often assumed to be tacitly acquired via the normal progression of academic acculturation, or "generic escalation" (Swales & Luebs, 2002, p. 137).

What is especially noteworthy about Swales and his colleagues' approach to teaching such genres is their avoidance of the "cookie-cutter" approach complained of by New Rhetoricians (e.g., Freedman & Adam, 2000). For example, in the literature review "jigsaw" task that Swales uses in his dissertation classes as a sociorhetorical consciousness-raising activity (Swales & Lindemann, 2002), there is no single right answer, no one organizational strategy suitable for all occasions. Instead, students are asked to arrive at their own rhetorically motivated, discipline-informed arrangements of the citation puzzle pieces. Avoidance of simplistic genre formulas is, in fact, evident throughout Swales and Feak's recent sequel to *Academic Writing for Graduate Students* (1994), which was also notable for its nonprescriptiveness and respect for "students-as-ethnographers" (see Johns, 1995). Swales and Feak note that in *English in Today's Research World* (2000) they "go [even] further" than previously in inviting readers to "conduct mini-analyses of the language and discourse of their fields" and are " 'up front' about areas of uncertainty, ignorance, or conflicting findings" (p. vi) in the research on academic discourse, in other words, about the limitations of any guidance it can provide. Learner autonomy for those already immersed in their disciplines but perhaps still struggling to stay afloat is clearly one of the goals of the Swales and Feak approach to EAP.

Other EAP specialists are also notable for attempting to steer learners clear of formulaic approaches to academic discourse. Reflecting on his own teaching of the notoriously amorphous genre (or genre set) we know as the "academic essay," Dudley-Evans (2002) observes that it makes little sense, given the huge range of rhetorical options, to attempt to present a "pattern of moves" for the essay. Instead,

Dudley-Evans focuses on "issues related to stance or positioning" (p. 235), which is as much of a "genre approach," he argues, as any based on traditional moves analysis. Similarly, Johns (2002a), who often works with at-risk "Generation 1.5" undergraduates, argues for the need to "destabilize" their notions of the "research paper," another highly variable school genre that tempts students to pour content into a familiar five-paragraph essay mold or some other well-rehearsed model template. In Johns's content-based, subject-area-linked EAP classes, students become "genre theorists," reflecting in their writing portfolios on the various stages of their own research writing process—e.g., interviewing, gathering sources, note-taking—and growing in awareness of the complex negotiation of texts and authorial position taking that we call a "research paper."

Academic English for Occupational Purposes (EA/OP)

In EA/OP (academic-for-occupational-purposes English), approaching text as context is an increasingly attainable goal in the classroom as practitioner/researchers discover the advantages of new technologies, e.g., video cameras and networked computers, and resulting access to virtually real-world settings. Technology facilitates not just the recording, collecting, and analyzing of real interactional data but also the generation of teaching materials from those actual occupational situations—doctor/nurse/patient, lawyer/client, businessperson/customer, or air traffic controller/pilot interactions. Traditional presessional needs analyses involving solitary English instructor interpretation of target settings and genres via document analysis, surveys, and interviews—indirect windows on context—are increasingly viewed as inadequate input for a pedagogy seeking to foster facility with genres that "work" in occupational settings.

Video cameras are proving especially invaluable for the study of text in context in EMP (English for medical purposes) curricula. For a course developed for medical students in Hong Kong, Shi, Corcos, and Storey (2001) videotaped ward teaching sessions over the course of three months at two hospitals in order to assess the challenges faced by the students when engaged in the discourse of diagnostic hypothesis making. The tapes not only informed the design of Shi et al.'s EMP course but served as teaching materials, with which the students could hone their critical analysis skills and metalinguistic awareness (see also Eggly, 2002). A still more "virtual" approach to EMP was taken by Muangsamai (2003), who required her premedical students in Thailand to construct Web pages on medical topics utilizing online sources. Forced to make their way through what one student described as an "ocean" of information on the Internet, Muangsamai's students became eager but critical consumers of popular, professional, and pseudoprofessional online health-issue discussions, increasingly aware of scientific, humanitarian, and commercial authorial motivations. Thus, through cyberspace, the students were able to enter into a real world of discourse, albeit both fascinating and disturbing, that traditional print teaching materials might only have offered a pale reflection of.

The Sociocultural Approach: Situated Immersion

Theory

New Rhetoric has done more than help complicate and problematize ESP specialists' perception of text. It has also raised questions, as noted earlier, about the teachability of the "strategic, functional relationship between...[form] and rhetorical situation" (Coe, 2002, p. 203), more commonly referred to as "genre." This NR problem posing cuts to the heart of ESP, calling into question the entire ESP agenda. What would ESP be without the ability to teach the speech genres (broadly defined to include written text) of specific discourse communities? Echoing Vygotsky, Leont'ev, and more recent activity theorists (see Russell, 1997), who stress the fundamental roles of situated learning and scaffolding, or "legitimate peripheral participation" (Lave & Wenger, 1991), New Rhetoricians mount strong arguments for the necessity of immersion in the target situation. Most ESP theorists and practitioners, in fact, would not disagree that immersion is helpful, even essential to target discourse expertise—that on-site learning is the enabler, for many learners, of expertise in academic and workplace genres. For learners faced with linguistic and literacy barriers, however, ESP proponents contend that immersion is not enough. Colleagues or faculty may be eager to take such newcomers underwing but may be ill-equipped to provide the scaffolded cognitive apprenticeships the novices may need (Belcher, 1994, 1998). For those at a linguistic disadvantage, ESP specialists argue, as do Sydney School adherents (e.g., Christie, 1998), that much more explicit, guided "immersion" is called for than normally available *in situ*.

Praxis

ESP practitioners have responded to the context challenge in a number of ways, ranging from attempting to provide a refuge for the new community members to immersing themselves in the community in search of suitable support for language learners.

Academic English for Occupational Purposes (EA/OP)

Some ESP instructors are so much in agreement with New Rhetoricians regarding the limitations of outsiders that rather than attempting to replicate target situation activities in their classrooms, they concentrate on capitalizing on their own strengths as language specialists. These instructors' classes become a type of "safe house" (Canagarajah, 1997), where newcomers can feel comfortable enough to practice the language and literacy skills needed for a relatively self-confident transition into their new discourse community. Miller's (2001) course for engineering undergraduates with little faith in their ability to survive at an English-medium Hong Kong university exemplifies this incremental, emotionally supportive approach. Rather than borrowing from engineering texts for his course, Miller takes a more English for general purposes (EGP) approach, mining material from popular engineering periodicals. "By using more accessible topics and materials," Miller notes, "I maintain my own and my students' confidence in my ability as their language teacher to handle the material well." Miller is far from alone in his EGP approach to EAP (see Adam & Artemeva, 2002, on the use of more generic academic topics; and Belcher & Hirvela, 2001, on the use of literature in EAP). One of the goals of approaches such as Miller's is to arm language learners with the compensatory strategies they need—not all of which directly pertain to language—to function more autonomously during their academic immersion. Commenting on such "strategic" competencies, Casanave has remarked of her own work with graduate students, "I should be paying as much attention to helping both first and second language graduate students...develop skills for dealing with the wide range of social and political interpersonal relationships that interact with locally situated writing activities as I do to helping them learn the language and style of formal academic papers" (2002, p. 215).

Other EA/OP classes do take a more immersion-like, simulation approach but with much scaffolding for both the instructors and the students. While classes team-taught by ESP and subject-area specialists (Dudley-Evans, 1995) or linked with subject-area classes (Johns, 1995) are nothing new, there are other types of expertise infusion now in evidence in ESP pedagogy. One of these is instruction provided increasingly more often by dual-specialist professionals, such as Susan Reinhart (see Feak & Reinhart, 2002), an attorney and EALP (English for academic legal purposes) specialist; Natasha Artemeva (Artemeva & Logie, 2002), a trained engineer and technical writing teacher/researcher; and ENP (English for nursing purposes) specialist Sally Candlin (Candlin, 2002), who has degrees in both nursing and linguistics. Sometimes, however, the most significant subject-area resources in an ESP class are the class members themselves. One EBP (English for business purposes) program in New York City (Boyd, 2002), deliberately strives for a diverse mix of preprofessional and experienced professional business English learners to provide both a more realistic mixed-expertise environment and a more collaboratively informed one. In ESP classes where neither the instructor nor the students have subject-area expertise, experts can be brought in by proxy. In one ENP class (Hussin, 2002), for instance, nursing students are shown videos of experienced nurses performing and talking their way through tasks. In another EMP program (Eggly, 2002) for international medical residents already immersed in their target situation, interactional expertise is brought in via professional actors hired to play patients and help the residents learn to negotiate a variety of doctor–patient interactions. Clearly such classes as described above are not isomorphic with the actual target context, but in many respects they are reasonably close facsimiles of reality.

Some EA/OP programs have moved closer to target contexts by physically taking their students to various field-related environments. In one EALP program (Feak & Reinhart, 2002), students obtain a first-hand, participant–observer perspective on target-area interactions and discourse by sitting in on University of Michigan Law School classes, attending courtroom proceedings and meeting with the judges, as well as touring prisons and talking with inmates. Similarly, in the New York City business English program referred to above (Boyd, 2002), the EBP classes are not only physically located in Columbia University's School of Business, but the students visit Wall Street to meet with an executive to discuss international business issues. In the EMP class for medical residents mentioned above (Eggly, 2002), the students are taken on a tour of Detroit to see for themselves the neighborhoods where their mainly African American patients live—an experience that appears to help the residents feel more comfortable engaging in the personal-topic conversations essential for doctors and their patients. ESP specialists, such as Eggly (2002), who utilize such "field-trip" strategies report that the activities' impact on learner motivation and progress is far greater than the limited "immersion" would suggest.

English for Occupational Purposes (EOP)

Offering classes on-site, in the workplace settings where language learners are already functioning is a long respected and practiced ESP pedagogical intervention. The advantages of teaching on-site are almost too numerous to cite: Learners and their interlocutors well aware of the learners' needs, teachers able to personally observe situated interactions, and workplace realia readily available for classroom simulations. Those who teach on-site are also very much aware of the disadvantages: learners tired after a day's work, erratic attendance and hence unpredictable class size and difficulty sequencing instruction, and often widely varying proficiency levels. Yet, experienced ESP practitioners have developed numerous coping strategies (see Garcia, 2002) and often argue that no off-site venue would allow them to accomplish as much as they do when teaching in their students' target (and current) settings.

With the help of technology, constructivist/collaborative approaches to teaching/learning, and an expanded notion of the language teacher's role, EOP course designers and instructors are finding a number of new ways to maximize the advantages of teaching on-site. Technology has offered teachers the means to overcome the spatial and temporal bounds of their classes by enabling them to audio-or videotape their students on the job during and after their EOP course for ongoing and follow-up needs assessment (e.g., Eggly's, 2002, account of medical residents periodically videotaped in their interactions with real patients in an outpatient clinic). Gu's (2002) report on efforts to compile a corpus of spoken workplace Chinese suggests what can be done for ESP as well: equipping workers with a digital microphone and minidisk digital voice recorder to tape their workplace talk over the course of a normal workweek. Digitalized recordings, video or audio, of course, can be archived for later computer-assisted analysis and, via audio or video streaming, made accessible to anyone with an Internet connection.

In addition to technological enhancements of EOP endeavors, constructivist/ collaborative approaches are being extended beyond more predictable expertise sharing, as with ESP instructors and graduate students, to include factory workers, brewers, home-cleaning-service workers, and others (e.g, Noden, 2002). Rose (2003) has commented recently on the tendency to underestimate the cognitive complexity of the many activities involving literacy, numeracy, use of graphics and spatial thinking in seemingly less-literacy-demanding types of expertise. Many ESP specialists, however, have already arrived at an appreciation of the cognitive demands of such occupations. Orsi and Orsi (2002), for example, describe their reliance on their Argentinian students' knowledge of brewing to continuously inform a course aimed at making the brewers bilingual in "beer talk." EOP instructors have also realized how much more successful at motivating language learning on-site workers can be than the teachers themselves, as Garcia (2002) has noted in her account of EOP classes in Chicago factories.

Perhaps because of their heightened awareness of the array of social, material and affective factors that can motivate and facilitate language learning, and of what language learning can accomplish beyond smoother workplace interactions, some number of on-site EOP specialists now see their role as widening to include more than language teaching. Some of the roles contemporary EOP specialists see themselves playing include builders of self-esteem, facilitators of upward mobility, contributors to improved worker–worker and worker–management relations (even serving as catalysts for unionization, as in Garcia, 2002), improved patient care, and improved treatment of immigrant workers (e.g., through assertiveness training for immigrant nursing students in Bosher & Smalkoski, 2002), and even as life-savers (as Storer, 1999, suggests EOP interventions in the Thai bar scene can accomplish by enabling bar workers to negotiate safe sex with foreign customers). EOP specialists have no doubt long been more than language teachers (an ambitious undertaking in and of itself), but perhaps only recently have they begun to publicly articulate their additional roles, and to view the roles not as fortuitous by-products of language teaching but as deliberate simultaneous goals of it.

The Sociopolitical Approach: Overcoming the "Limit–Situation"

Theory

Critical pedagogists would probably applaud the extra-linguistic accomplishments of many on- and off-site ESP practitioners, yet they, as have some leading ESP specialists, might also point out that such consciously broader-context aims and social awareness are rather late in coming to ESP. Swales observed in his farewell as editor of the "flagship" ESP journal, *English for Specific Purposes*, that its articles had been "strikingly unengaged by issues...of ideology [and] learners' rights" (1994, p. 201). Of his own and other ESP teacher-researchers' classroom practice, Dudley-Evans has remarked that in their efforts to be responsive to "the immediate problems that students faced at a specific time," they were probably unresponsive to "the opportunity to look critically...and to help students develop solutions" (2001, p. xi). Master was among the first in ESP to call for a "critical ESP" that would be more self-reflexive in its role in the global spread of English and its readiness to meet learners' needs as defined by "what the institution or workplace needed of them" (1998, p. 724).

That the field of ESP is looking more often and more self-consciously at the broader implications of its classroom efforts and hearing critical pedagogists' calls for rethinking of ELT's goals is apparent not only in accounts of ESP practice but also in the willingness to bring the voices of critical pedagogy to ESP audiences. Critical pedagogist Benesch's (1999) discussion of "rights analysis" first appeared in *English for Specific Purposes*. Likewise, Pennycook's (1997) argument for "critical" rather than unreflective "vulgar" pragmatism was published by the same journal as well as chosen by its editorial board members as the best article of the year. At first sight, ESP and critical pedagogy would seem to be naturally at odds with each other– the former focused on efficiently and cost-effectively (Johns & Price-Machado, 2001) producing linguistically competent workers and students, and the latter interrogating the established social system's needs and proposing other needs that are not socially reproductive. In other words, critical pedagogy asks *whose* needs are being addressed and *why*. In the minds of a number of critical pedagogists and increasingly more ESP practitioners, however, the aims of these seemingly disparate approaches to ELT can be productively melded.

Critical pedagogy has served as a major port of entry into ESP for a number of critical educational, social, and linguistic theories. Even a short list of those whose theories have informed the work of critical pedagogists, and now through them, ESP, reads like a Who's Who of 20th-century thought: liberatory literacy theorist Freire (1994), whose conceptualizations of "hope" (or struggling against, not accepting, injustices), of "limit-situations" (glossed by Benesch, 2001b, as "personal and social obstacles," p. 164), and of the transmission or "banking" model of education, which Freire has cogently opposed, are now widely known; postmodern philosopher and social critic Foucault (1980), for whom power is "always already there" (p. 141; see also Benesch, 2001a); feminists such as Luke and Gore (1992) and other postmodernists who deconstruct "grand theory" and promote awareness of race, class, and gender; and critical discourse analysts such as Fairclough (1995), who see discourse as never neutral or disinterested. The list could easily continue with Bourdieu, Derrida, Gramsci, and others. Inspired by such thinkers, critical pedagogists argue not that academic and occupational survival be disregarded (see Pennycook, 1997), but that language learners need more than communicative competence and functional literacy: They need voices that will speak for them well enough to make a difference in their own and others' lives. Critical pedagogists have, in fact, adopted many of ESP's techniques, (see Benesch, 2001a, on linked classes) but have, with their raised ideological consciousnesses, retooled them in ways that some ESP practitioners may not recognize but others may already be emulating (see Johns, 1997).

Praxis

Critical pedagogy has entered the EAP classroom by several different means: by critically redefining traditional needs analysis as "rights analysis," moving beyond collaborative learning to collectivist action, and revisioning text as not just situated in a context but the hybrid product of multiple contexts, i.e., as a site for negotiation of personal and social identities, of home and academic or professional values.

Benesch (2001a) challenges EAP practitioners to look beyond the obvious academic literacy demands that often define student "needs" toward the rights of students. By "rights," Benesch means not entitlements but "a framework for understanding and responding to power relations" (2001a, p. 108), or opportunities for participation and resistance, for the education students go to college for. In her subject-area linked EAP classes, Benesch thus sees herself as serving more than students' immediate needs. She does provide support for their efforts to meet institutional literacy expectations, but Benesch also encourages her students to put their developing L2 proficiencies to work in articulating their own academic expectations: their rights to comprehensible lectures, clearly defined assignments, time for class discussion—rights that faculty should be but are not always mindful of. What rights analysis can motivate, Benesch notes of her own teaching, is an EAP instructor's decision to facilitate emotionally supportive collectivist action by, for example, as unrevolutionary but effective an act as suggesting that students sit together for moral support in an intimidating class. Or, rights analysis can lead to a decision to intervene more preemptively, for instance, by bringing readings on women's issues, e.g., anorexia, into the linked EAP classroom, as Benesch (2001a) has, to compensate for lopsided gender representation in a subject-area syllabus (see Santos, 2001, for an alternate reading of such pedagogical decision making). Classes such as Benesch's own are clear and compelling examples of how EAP can, as Pennycook (1997) notes, play a "significant role in the pluralisation of our students' future knowledge" and become a "pedagogy of cultural alternatives" (p. 264).

Another right of EAP students that critical pedagogists have championed is that of control over their own textual identities. Canagarajah, as an Anglo-educated Tamil speaker well aware of the challenges of "shuttling between communities and literacies" (Canagarajah, 2001b, p. 23), has eloquently described, as well as exemplified in his own writing, how a hybrid textual persona enriched by more than one culture or academic community can be successfully negotiated (Canagarajah, 2001a, 2002). One such account Canagarajah (2001a) presents is of a Sri Lankan graduate student who managed "to reconcile" her own religious and required academic discourses, "find[ing] space [in her texts] for her own subjectivity," in this case a strong personal commitment to her faith, without neglecting academic requirements for "objectivity" (p. 128). Such success stories as Canagarajah tells do more than argue against a deficit model of learners; they suggest what students can accomplish and EAP could nurture with a view of membership in a marginalized discourse community as "not always a 'problem'" but "a resource for critical expression and creative negotiation" (Canagarajah, 2001a, p. 130).

Inclusion of the community partnership (CP) approach to L2 literacy may well be objected to as too far removed from either EAP or EOP to be considered even distantly related. In some respects, CP does bear little resemblance to ESP. Yet CP's goals are, in many ways, not unlike those of ESP to prepare learners to succeed in specific discourse communities. And CP's means are often those associated with ESP—providing learners with the specific vocabulary and structures and the enhanced linguistic modalities they want and need to succeed.

The differences, however, between traditional ESP and CP are also striking (see Auerbach, 2002). Rather than assessing the needs or even rights of a particular group of already identified learners, CP advocates may work proactively to identify the learners in need of some intervention, such as unschooled Somali refugee woman reluctant to attend classes or interact in English-speaking environments (Fridland & Dalle, 2002). CP adherents also take a very community-oriented approach to determining a course of action, working hard to solicit community input and build consensus in order to motivate commitment and support for improvement. In their classes, CP instructors strive to sustain motivation among learners by maintaining curricular flexibility, changing a syllabus midstream if new group needs arise, e.g., the need to learn the language of doctor visits (Fridland & Dalle, 2002). Also characteristic of CP are its indirect approaches, such as finding childcare for parents who otherwise could not attend classes (Fridland & Dalle, 2002) or starting a school-community vegetable garden to feed students distracted by hunger (Schofield, 2002). Like Benesch and other critical pedagogists, CP advocates teach the advantages of collectivist action, or community approaches to problems. CP classes, for example, might teach learners the question posing skills needed to participate in community meetings, as Huerta-Macías (2002) did with Hispanic immigrants in Texas faced with forced relocation by a housing authority. Or, CP proponents might facilitate intergenerational community action, as Crockatt and Smythe (2002) note of their work in remote Nunavut, Canada, where community construction of a library reading tent promoted Inuit biliteracy through family literacy events. The CP approach is obviously less individualistically oriented than learner-centered approaches usually are. It can certainly be argued (e.g., Huerta-Macías, 2002), however, that in meeting community needs, individual learner needs are met as well through CP, which might also be titled ECSP, or English for community-specific purposes.

Research Directions for ESP Pedagogy

Despite the research efforts—including both action research and more formal published research—of several generations of ESP specialists, probably few in this field, as is the case throughout ELT, are satisfied with the current state of knowledge. Those interested in genre analysis, for example, have called attention to how many genres remain under- or uninvestigated. It seems that we are just beginning to understand part-genres, blended genres, genre sets, and genre systems (Bazerman, 2002; Bhatia, 2002; Swales, 2002). With the advent of computer-mediated communication have come a host of entirely new genres, situated somewhere between oracy and literacy yet also extending beyond those realms in their inclusion of visual and auditory "literacies" as well—via color, sound, graphics, and video (Kress, 1998). Few literate occupations or academic sites, in the developed or developing world, will likely escape the impact of these emerging cybergenres. One of the resulting challenges for ESP researchers will be to find ways to facilitate practitioners' conceptualization and operationalization of a more broadly inclusive multiliteracies approach to fostering and assessing genre competence—a "big tent" approach, to borrow Merrifield's (1998, p. 3) term. Such an approach would encompass a multitude of purposes (as seen from learner, teacher, client, community, and others' vantage points) and the growing variety of communicative practices that can lead to their realization.

For those more interested in context than its texts, there remain many underresearched discourse settings. ESP practitioners who work with learners in areas such as home cleaning or factory work or even nursing (see Bosher & Smalkoski, 2002), which has a longer history as an ESP domain, complain of the paucity of published research and materials. Bhatia (2002) has pointed out that even in other areas that have been studied more in depth, we still know little about the nature of expertise—what makes someone a communicatively competent doctor, lawyer, engineer, or businessperson. Research-based definitions of community-specific expertise could guide and buttress the types of evidence-based arguments for prior or continuing support that ESP practitioners are often expected to make. Ideally, such definitions of expertise would be based on data gathered from *both* top-down and bottom-up perspectives (Merrifield, 1998): not limited to the expectations of managers, administrators, and other powerful policymakers but including the view from the assembly line or the outpatient clinic or even the ESP classroom.

With regard to critical approaches, we appear to be only on the cusp of understanding how to help people accomplish change through language. Martin (2002a) has noted of critical inquiry that more is needed than critique of power: "we need to know how people commune in ways that rework its [power's] circulation...personally, locally, nationally, and globally" (p. 187). We can begin the type of inquiry Martin calls for, he suggests, by analyzing the peace and reconciliation discourses of "peoples [such as European and indigenous South Africans] learning to live together in their 'new' worlds" (2002a, p. 187). Traditional ESP practitioners might argue that I have again wandered far afield of the usual SP in ESP, yet others would contend that peace-making and other far-reaching community goals are purposes that can be served well by ESP practices (see Master, 1998). Researchers could help ESP achieve more of a community-oriented outlook by assisting in the development of improved means of promoting dialogue, consensus building, and values clarification among diverse, unequally empowered stakeholders. Perhaps the most salutary outcome of such developments would be, ideally, a view of accountability as more mutual (Merrifield, 1998)— a shared responsibility of teachers, students, employees, and other community members as well as of those in positions of greater power and in control of funding. Speaking more specifically of adult literacy education, Demetrion (2000) has argued for a "more expansive notion of the public good" that would move us beyond the popular "cost-benefit utilitarian model" (which currently drives much ESP program assessment; see, for example, Friedenberg, Kennedy, Lomperis, Martin, & Westerfield, 2003, on the "cost-benefit analysis/return on investment model" of workplace program evaluation). The curricula of numerous ESP practitioners, from Chicago to Soweto, clearly already exemplify an expansive notion of public good, but persuasive means of assessing ESP's present and potential contributions to the advancement of individuals and communities are still at a relatively early stage of development (see Weinstein, 2001, on the limitations of "alternative assessments").

In attempting to characterize all the research goals on my wish list above, I would describe them as aimed at deeper knowledge of texts and contexts, and broader knowledge of more, and more varied, school, workplace, and other community settings. In addition, however, I would characterize the goals as aimed at a multidimensional knowledge (cf. Bhatia, 2002) of where discourses and their communities, as well as the ESP professionals committed to understanding and teaching them, are situated in the world at large.

Notes

1. The term *language (s) for specific purposes* (LSP), is preferred of late by many (see the journal *LSP and Professional Communication*, retrieved November 20, 2003, from: http://www.dsff-lsp.dk/centres/dsff/LSPVol1No12001/, as well as Swales, 2000). The term "LSP" highlights the universality of the "specific" approach to linguistic inquiry and teaching, which is actually used in the study and teaching of the specific varieties and registers of many languages other than English. This article, however, will limit its scope to SP as it relates to English language teaching (ELT), hence ESP. Under the ESP umbrella, I will include both EAP, English for academic purposes, and EOP, English for occupational purposes—a not infrequently problematic distinction, in that the categories often overlap. English classes for medical students, for example, could be considered both EAP and EOP instruction.

2. That not all New Rhetoric proponents question the value of explicit genre instruction is evident in the composition textbooks produced by American New Rhetoricians Charles Bazerman (1995, 1997) and Thomas Huckin (Huckin & Olsen, 1991) (J. Bloch, personal communication, January 2003). There appears to be a Canadian–American divide in New Rhetoric, which may reflect the routine teaching of first-year composition classes in U.S. colleges as opposed to the more specialized, individualized writing-center approach (often affiliated with specific "faculties") more common in Canada. Martin (2002b) too has noted "family differences" and "fuzzy borders" among his colleagues in what is known "across the Pacific" (but not necessarily in Australia) as the "Sydney School" (p. 278).

ANNOTATED BIBLIOGRAPHY

Benesch, S. (2001a). *Critical English for academic purposes: Theory, politics, and practice.* Mahwah, NJ: Erlbaum.

For those interested in how a critical approach to pedagogy can be realized in the EAP classroom, Benesch provides clearly reasoned, well illustrated accounts of her own classroom practice. The author is especially adept at articulating in practitioner-friendly terms her own critical stance and that of the critical theorists who have influenced her. Benesch's book helps readers redefine EAP, especially the subject-area linked EAP class, as much more than a "service" to the rest of the academic community.

Candlin, C. (Ed.). (2002). *Research and practice in professional discourse.* Hong Kong: City University of Hong Kong Press.

Candlin's edited volume is impressive in the scope of its coverage of what Bhatia refers to (in this same volume) as "professional discourse analysis." The 26 chapters report and reflect on discourse practices in a broad range of areas, including health and social care, business communication, the academy, and the media. Although the methods focused on, such as ethnography, genre analysis, corpus linguistics, and conversational analysis, primarily relate to research rather than to pedagogy, ESP practitioners, who are, by necessity and choice, discourse analysts, should find much of interest in this volume.

Hewings, M. (Ed.) (2001). *Academic writing in context: Implications and applications: Papers in honour of Tony Dudley-Evans.* Birmingham, UK: University of Birmingham Press.

This collection of 15 original essays is an unusually stimulating and engaging Festschrift, quite appropriate as a tribute to one of the most significant contributors to the popularity and development of ESP over the course of three decades. The chapters cover a wide array of EAP topics, ranging from issues relevant to the socialization of novice academic readers and writers, to the specific rhetorical and linguistic features of genres within and across various disciplines.

Johns, A. (Ed.). (2002). *Genre in the classroom: Multiple perspectives.* Mahwah, NJ: Erlbaum.

Johns has assembled, in this 17-chapter volume, representatives of all three major schools of thought in genre studies: the Sydney School, New Rhetoric, and ESP. The contributors consider what a genre approach can (or cannot) offer classroom practitioners. This volume succeeds as few others have in showcasing the multiplicity of views on genre as a concept and as a facilitator of literacy and language learning.

Orr, T. (Ed.). (2002). *English for specific purposes.* Alexandria, VA: TESOL.
Like other volumes in the TESOL Case Studies Series, this book was written by and for practitioners. Readers should find especially helpful the concise and straightforward accounts of the curricular decision-making processes of each of the ESP contributors. The 12 chapters address classroom-practice issues in both academic and workplace settings, many of which are familiar ESP domains, such as English for legal purposes, for medical purposes, and for business. Much less familiar sites of ESP practice, however, are also represented, including English for shipbuilding, for tourism, and for the horse-racing business.

OTHER REFERENCES

Adam, C., & Artemeva, N. (2002). Writing instruction in English for academic purposes (EAP) classes: Introducing second language learners to the academic community. In A. Johns (Ed.), *Genre in the classroom: Multiple perspectives* (pp. 179–196). Mahwah, NJ: Erlbaum.

Artemeva, N., & Logie, S. (2002). Introducing engineering students to intellectual teamwork: The teaching and practice of peer feedback in the professional communication classroom. *Language and Learning across the Disciplines, 6* (1), 62–85.

Auerbach, E. (2002). Shifting roles, shifting goals: Integrating language, culture, and community. In E. Auerbach (Ed.), *Community partnerships* (pp. 1–12). Alexandria, VA: TESOL.

Bakhtin, M. (1981). *The dialogic imagination.* Austin: University of Texas Press.

Bazerman, C. (1995). *The informed writer.* Boston, MA: Houghton Mifflin.

Bazerman, C. (1997). *Involved: Writing for college, writing for your self.* Boston: Houghton Mifflin.

Bazerman, C. (2002). Rhetorical research for reflective practice: A multi-layered narrative. In C. Candlin (Ed.), *Research and practice in professional discourse* (pp. 79–93). Hong Kong: City University of Hong Kong Press.

Belcher, D. (1994). The apprenticeship approach to advanced academic literacy: Graduate students and their mentors. *English for Specific Purposes, 13,* 23–34.

Belcher, D. (1998). Nonnative writing in a corporate setting. In R. Brown (Ed.), *Inhouse training in technical communication* (pp. 143–154). Arlington, VA: Society for Technical Communication.

Belcher, D., & Hirvela, A. (2001). Literature and L2 composition: Revisiting the debate. *Journal of Second Language Writing, 9,* 21–39.

Benesch, S. (1999). Rights analysis: Studying power relations in an academic setting. *English for Specific Purposes, 18,* 313–327.

Benesch, S. (2001b). Critical pragmatism: A politics of L2 composition. In T. Silva & P. Matsuda (Eds.), *On second language writing* (pp. 161–172). Mahwah, NJ: Erlbaum.

Bhatia, V. K. (2002). Professional discourse: Towards a multi-dimensional approach and shared practice. In C. Candlin (Ed.), *Research and practice in professional discourse* (pp. 39–60). Hong Kong: City University of Hong Kong Press.

Bosher, S., & Smalkoski, K. (2002). From needs analysis to curriculum development: Designing a course in health-care communication for immigrant students in the USA. *English for Specific Purposes, 21,* 59–80.

Boyd, F. (2002). An ESP program for students of business. In T. Orr (Ed.), *English for specific purposes* (pp. 41–56). Alexandria, VA: TESOL.

Bruce, N. (2002). Dovetailing language and content: Teaching balanced argument in legal problem answer writing. *English for Specific Purposes, 21,* 321–346.

Canagarajah, S. (1997). Safe houses in the contact zone: Coping strategies of African American students in the academy. *College Composition and Communication, 48,* 173–196.

Canagarajah, S. (2001a). Addressing issues of power and difference in ESL academic writing. In J. Flowerdew & M. Peacock (Eds.), *Research perspectives on English for academic purposes* (pp. 117–131). Cambridge: Cambridge University Press.

Canagarajah, S. (2001b). The fortunate traveler: Shuttling between communities and literacies by economy class. In D. Belcher & U. Connor (Eds.), *Reflections on multiliterate lives* (pp. 23–37). Clevedon, UK: Multilingual Matters.

Canagarajah, S. (2002). *Critical academic writing and multilingual students.* Ann Arbor: University of Michigan Press.

Candlin, S. (2002). A triple jeopardy: What can discourse analysts offer health professionals? In C. Candlin (Ed.), *Research and practice in professional discourse* (pp. 293–308). Hong Kong: City University of Hong Kong Press.

Casanave, C. (2002). *Writing games: Multicultural case studies of academic literacy practices in higher education.* Mahwah, NJ: Erlbaum.

Christie, F. (1998). *Pedagogy and the shaping of consciousness: Linguistic and social processes.* London: Cassell.

Coe, R. (2002). The new rhetoric of genre: Writing political briefs. In A. Johns (Ed.), *Genre in the classroom: Multiple perspectives* (pp. 197–207). Mahwah, NJ: Erlbaum.

Collins-COBUILD. The Bank of English. Retrieved November 20, 2003, from http://titania.cobuild.collins.co.uk/.

Cope, B., & Kalantzis, M. (1999). *Multiliteracies and the design of social futures.* London: Routledge.

Crockatt, K., & Smythe, S. (2002). Building culture and community: Family and community literacy partnerships in Canada's North. In E. Auerbach (Ed.), *Community partnerships* (pp.

91–105). Alexandria, VA: TESOL.

Demetrion, G. (2000). Reflecting on culture wars in adult literacy education: Exploring critical issues in "Contested ground." Retrieved November 6, 2003, from http://www.nald.ca/fulltext/cultrwar/page1.htm.

Dias, P., Freedman, A., Medway, P., & Pare, A. (1999). *Worlds apart: Acting and writing in academic and workplace contexts.* Mahwah, NJ: Erlbaum.

Dudley-Evans, T. (1995). Common-core and specific approaches to the teaching of academic writing. In D. Belcher & G. Braine (Eds.), *Academic writing in a second language* (pp. 293–312). Norwood, NJ: Ablex.

Dudley-Evans, T. (2001). Foreword. In S. Benesch, *Critical English for academic purposes: Theory, politics, and practice* (pp. ix–xiii). Mahwah, NJ: Erlbaum.

Dudley-Evans, T. (2002). The teaching of the academic essay: Is a genre approach possible? In A. Johns (Ed.), *Genre in the classroom: Multiple perspectives* (pp. 225–235). Mahwah, NJ: Erlbaum.

Eggly, S. (2002). An ESP program for international medical graduates in residency. In T. Orr (Ed.), *English for specific purposes* (pp. 105–115). Alexandria, VA: TESOL.

Fairclough, N. (1995). *Critical discourse analysis.* London: Longman.

Feak, C., & Reinhart, S. (2002). An ESP program for students of law. In T. Orr (Ed.), *English for specific purposes* (pp. 7–23). Alexandria, VA: TESOL.

Flowerdew, L. (2003). A combined corpus and systemic-functional analysis of the problem-solution pattern in a student and professional corpus of technical writing. *TESOL Quarterly, 37,* 489–511.

Foucault, M. (1980). Power and strategies. In C. Gordon (Ed.), *Power/knowledge: Selected interviews and other writings, 1972–1977* (pp. 134–145). New York: Pantheon.

Freedman, A., & Adam, C. (2000). Write where you are: Situating learning to write in university and workplace settings. In P. Dias & A. Pare (Eds.), *Transitions: Writing in academic and workplace settings* (pp. 31–60). Creskill, NJ: Hampton Press.

Freire, P. (1994). *Pedagogy of hope: Reliving pedagogy of the oppressed.* New York: Continuum.

Fridland, G., & Dalle, T. (2002). "Start with what they know, build with what they have:" Survival skills for refugee women. In E. Auerbach (Ed.), *Community partnerships* (pp. 27–39). Alexandria, VA: TESOL.

Friedenberg, J., Kennedy, D., Lomperis, A., Martin, W., & Westerfield, K. (2003). *Effective practices in workplace language training: Guidelines for providers of workplace English language training services.* Alexandria, VA: TESOL.

Garcia, P. (2002). An ESP program for union members in 25 factories. In T. Orr (Ed.), *English for specific purposes* (pp. 161–173). Alexandria, VA: TESOL.

Grabe, W. (2002). Narrative and expository macro-genres. In A. Johns (Ed.), *Genre in the classroom: Multiple perspectives* (pp. 249–267). Mahwah, NJ: Erlbaum.

Gu, Y. (2002). Towards an understanding of workplace discourse: A pilot study for compiling a spoken Chinese corpus of situated discourse. In C. Candlin (Ed.), *Research and practice in professional discourse* (pp. 137–185). Hong Kong: City University of Hong Kong Press.

Huerta-Macías, A. (2002). Getting an even start: Family literacy through participation and collaboration. In E. Auerbach (Ed.), *Community partnerships* (pp. 121–131). Alexandria, VA: TESOL.

Huckin, T., & Olsen, L. (1991). *Technical writing and professional communication for nonnative speakers of English*, (2nd ed.). New York: McGraw-Hill.

Hussin, V. (2002). An ESP program for students of nursing. In T. Orr (Ed.), *English for specific purposes* (pp. 25–39). Alexandria, VA: TESOL.

Hutchinson, T., & Waters, A. (1987). *English for specific purposes.* Cambridge: Cambridge University Press.

Hyland, K. (2000). *Disciplinary discourses: Social interactions in academic writing.* London: Longman.

Hyland, K. (2002). *Teaching and researching writing.* London: Longman.

Hyland, K. (2003). Genre-based pedagogies: A social response to process. *Journal of Second Language Writing, 12,* 17–29.

Hyland, K. (in press). *Genre and second language writing.* Ann Arbor: University of Michigan Press.

Hyon, S. (1996). Genres in three traditions: Implications for ESL. *TESOL Quarterly, 30,* 693–722.

Jabbour, G. (2001). Lexis and grammar in second language reading and writing. In D. Belcher & A. Hirvela (Eds.), *Linking literacies: Perspectives on L2 reading-writing connections* (pp. 291–308). Ann Arbor: University of Michigan Press.

Johns, A. (1995). Teaching classroom and authentic genres: Initiating students into academic cultures and discourses. In D. Belcher & G. Braine (Eds.), *Academic writing in a second language* (pp. 277–292). Norwood, NJ: Ablex.

Johns, A. (1997). *Text, role, and context: Developing academic literacies.* Cambridge: Cambridge University Press.

Johns, A. (2002a). Destabilizing and enriching novice students' genre theories. In A. Johns (Ed.), *Genre in the classroom: Multiple perspectives* (pp. 237–246). Mahwah, NJ: Erlbaum.

Johns, A. (2002b). Introduction. In A. Johns (Ed.), *Genre in the classroom: Multiple perspectives* (pp. 3–13). Mahwah, NJ: Erlbaum.

Johns, A., & Price-Machado, D. (2001). English for specific purposes (ESP): Tailoring courses to student needs—and to the outside world. In M. Celce-Murcia (Ed.), *Teaching English as* a second or foreign language (pp. 43–54). Boston: Heinle & Heinle.

Kress, G. (1998). Visual and verbal modes of representation in electronically mediated communication: The potentials of new forms of text. In I. Snyder (Ed.), *Page to screen: Taking literacy into the electronic era* (pp. 53–79). London: Routledge.

Lave, J., & Wenger, E. (1991). *Situated learning: Legitimate peripheral participation.* Cambridge: Cambridge University Press.

Luke, C., & Gore, J. (1992). *Feminisms and critical pedagogy.* New York: Routledge.

Martin, J. R. (2002a). Blessed are the peacemakers: Reconciliation and evaluation. In C. Candlin (Ed.), *Research and practice in professional discourse* (pp. 187–227). Hong Kong: City University of Hong Kong Press.

Martin, J. R. (2002b). A universe of meaning—How many practices? In A. Johns (Ed.), *Genre in the classroom: Multiple perspectives* (pp. 269–278). Mahwah, NJ: Erlbaum.

Master, P. (1998). Positive and negative aspects of the dominance of English. *TESOL Quarterly, 32,* 716–725.

Merrifield, J. (1998). Contested ground: Performance accountability in adult basic education. NCSALL Briefs—Report #1. Retrieved November 6, 2003, from http://ncsall.gse.harvard.edu/research/report1.htm.

MICASE (Michigan Corpus of Academic Spoken English). Retrieved November 20, 2003, from http://www.lsa.umich.edu/eli/micase/ATTRIB.html.

Miller, C. R. (1984). Genre as social action. *Quarterly Journal of Speech, 70,* 151–167.

Miller, L. (2001). English for engineers in Hong Kong. In J. Murphy & P. Byrd (Eds.), *Understanding the courses we teach* (pp. 236–255). Ann Arbor: University of Michigan Press.

Muangsamai, P. (2003). EFL learning/writing development in the Internet environment: A case-study from pre-medical students' perspectives. Unpublished dissertation, Ohio State University.

Noden, P. (2002). An ESP program for a home-cleaning service. In T. Orr (Ed.), *English for specific purposes* (pp. 189–204). Alexandria, VA: TESOL.

Orsi, L., & Orsi, P. (2002). An ESP program for brewers. In T. Orr (Ed.), *English for specific purposes* (pp. 175–188). Alexandria, VA: TESOL.

Paltridge, B. (2001). *Genre and the language learning classroom.* Ann Arbor: University of Michigan Press.

Paltridge, B. (2002). Genre, text type, and the English for academic purposes (EAP) classroom. In A. Johns (Ed.), *Genre in the classroom: Multiple perspectives* (pp. 73–90). Mahwah, NJ: Erlbaum.

Pang, T. (2002). Textual analysis and contextual awareness building: A comparison of two approaches to teaching genre. In A. Johns (Ed.), *Genre in the classroom: Multiple*

perspectives (pp. 145–161). Mahwah, NJ: Erlbaum.
Pennycook, A. (1997). Vulgar pragmatism, critical pragmatism, and EAP. *English for Specific Purposes, 16*, 253–269.
Prior, P. (1995). Redefining the task: An ethnographic examination of writing and response in graduate seminars. In D. Belcher & G. Braine (Eds.), *Academic writing in a second language* (pp. 47–82). Norwood, NJ: Ablex.
Prior, P. (1998). *Writing/disciplinarity: A sociohistoric account of literate activity in the academy.* Mahwah, NJ: Erlbaum.
Rose, M. (2003). At last: Words in action: Rethinking workplace literacy. *Research in the Teaching of English, 38*, 125–128.
Russell, D. (1997). Rethinking genre in school and society: An activity theory analysis. *Written Communication, 14*, 504–554.
Santos, T. (2001). The place of politics in second language writing. In T. Silva & P. Matsuda (Eds.), *On second language writing* (pp. 173–190). Mahwah, NJ: Erlbaum.
Schofield, A. (2002). Wild power: School-community partnerships in a South African school district. In E. Auerbach (Ed.), *Community partnerships* (pp. 159–169). Alexandria, VA: TESOL.
Shi, L., Corcos, R., & Storey, A. (2001). Using student performance data to develop an English course for clinical training. *English for Specific Purposes, 20*, 267–291.
Siegel, R. (Ed.). (2002). *The onion ad nauseam: Complete news archives, 13.* New York: Three Rivers.
Spack, R. (1988). Initiating ESL students into the academic discourse community: How far should we go? *TESOL Quarterly, 22*, 29–51.
Storer, G. (1999). Working the bars. *English for Specific Purposes, 18*, 367–374.
Swales, J. (1990). *Genre analysis: English in academic and research settings.* New York: Cambridge University Press.
Swales, J. (1994). From John M. Swales. *English for Specific Purposes, 13*, 200–203.
Swales, J. (1996). Occluded genres in the academy: The case of the submission letter. In E. Ventola & A. Mauranen (Eds.), *Academic writing: Intercultural and textual issues* (pp. 45–58). Amsterdam: Benjamins.
Swales, J. (2000). Languages for specific purposes. *Annual Review of Applied Linguistics, 20*, 59–76.
Swales, J. (2002). On models in applied discourse analysis. In C. Candlin (Ed.), *Research and practice in professional discourse* (pp. 61–77). Hong Kong: City University of Hong Kong Press.
Swales, J., & Feak, C. (1994). *Academic writing for graduate students.* Ann Arbor: University of Michigan Press.

Swales, J., & Feak, C. (2000). *English in today's research world: A writing guide.* Ann Arbor: University of Michigan Press.

Swales, J., & Lindemann, S. (2002). Teaching the literature review to international graduate students. In A. Johns (Ed.), *Genre in the classroom: Multiple perspectives* (pp. 105–119). Mahwah, NJ: Erlbaum.

Swales, J., & Luebs, M. (2002). Genre analysis and the advanced second language writer. In E. Barton & G. Stygall (Eds.), *Discourse studies in composition* (pp. 135–154). Cresskill, NJ: Hampton Press.

Weinstein, G. (2001). Developing adult literacies. In M. Celce-Murcia (Ed.), *Teaching English as a second or foreign language* (pp. 171–186). Boston: Heinle & Heinle.

9. TRENDS IN TEACHING STANDARD VARIETIES TO CREOLE AND VERNACULAR SPEAKERS

Hazel Simmons-McDonald

This chapter discusses some approaches used to teach a standard variety to creole and vernacular speakers. It focuses attention on issues related to the use of creoles and vernaculars in instruction to help creole speakers develop literacy in a second language. Research has shown that literacy development, academic skills, and learning strategies transfer from the first language to the second and that literacy in the first language is a crucial base for literacy development in the second language. Advocacy for vernacular literacy as a means of facilitating the learning of a standard language differs in situations where creole has the same lexical base as the second (standard) language as opposed to situations in which the creole has a different lexical base than the second language. The policy literature as well as that describing approaches to second language learning by creole and creole-influenced vernacular speakers is discussed primarily with relevance to the Caribbean region. The chapter then surveys the literature describing approaches used in similar contexts elsewhere. Outcomes resulting from the implementation of specific policies and approaches in the contexts presented, to the extent that such outcomes have been documented, are also explored.

Explicit recommendations for incorporating creoles and vernaculars in language education programs for purposes of helping speakers of these varieties learn a second language began to appear around the mid- to late 1960s. Before then, in schools in the Caribbean, the common practice was to prohibit and suppress the use of Creole on school premises. Native speakers of creoles found themselves in 'immersion' situations in which the goal was monolingualism in English but that often lacked much of the scaffolding that immersion contexts usually provide. A result of this was that many learners completed primary schooling without having achieved required levels of proficiency in the official, standard language; many were not functionally literate,[1] and as a consequence, they were denied access to secondary (high) school in territories where access to higher education was determined on the basis of performance in an examination.

The plight of creole speakers within education systems across the region became the subject of discussion in several articles (Carrington 1968, 1969; Carrington, Borely, & Knight, 1972a, 1972b; Craig, 1966, 1976, 1983; Le Page, 1968). At the same time, in the United States, educators and linguists were drawing attention to the problems that speakers of what was then called Black English were experiencing in schools[2] (e.g., Aarons, Gordon, & Stewart, 1969; Abrahams & Gay, 1975; Fasold 1971; Fishman & Leuders-Salmon, 1972; Jacobson, 1971; Kochman, 1969, 1972; Labov, 1967; among several others). In Britain, there was also "disquiet" (Sutcliffe, 1982) about the way in which West Indian children fared in British schools; some articles on that subject focused on the nature of the problem while some also offered solutions (e.g., Dalphinis, 1986; Edwards, 1976, 1979; Feigenbaum, 1975; Sutcliffe, 1982). A special committee (Rampton/Swann)[3] was also set up to investigate the education of children from ethnic minority groups, particularly those students of West Indian origin. Linguists who had contributed to the discussion of standard and nonstandard varieties had made the point that languages are ordered, systematic, and rule governed, and that, linguistically, one language system could not be considered to be superior or inferior or more valid relative to another (e.g., Feigenbaum, 1975). However, in most sociolinguistic contexts in which a Creole or "creole influenced vernacular" (CIV) (Craig, 1999) coexisted with a standard variety, the former was inevitably stigmatized and excluded from the domain of education because of negative attitudes stemming partly from ascription of the Creole to slavery. The unfortunate and most worrisome issue was that in school contexts in which a Creole or creole-influenced vernacular was the dominant variety used by some learners, the latter were underachieving in their learning of the language of the school (e.g., English/French) and in other subjects as compared with their peers who spoke a standard variety.

Awareness of these difficulties resulted in the development and use of instructional programs that were intended to help the creole and CIV speaker to learn and use the standard language variety that was in use for academic purposes. In the Caribbean there were efforts to design and use programs tailored to meet the needs of creole and creole-influenced vernacular speakers. Craig (1999) cited as examples of such programs those emerging from the work of the Language Materials Workshop at the University of the West Indies and the subsequent Caribbean-wide Primary Education Project in the mid 1970s. Around the same time, the UNESCO Language Arts Project was launched in the Eastern Caribbean. This consisted of carefully prepared and graded materials that used the audiolingual approach to teach English as a second language to creole and CIV speakers in primary schools. Unfortunately, no formal research was done to determine whether the latter program had achieved its objectives before it was discarded some three or four years after it had been introduced. Teacher reports indicated that students had become bored with the drills, which they found to be repetitive.

Across the Caribbean in the Francophone territory Haiti, French Creole had been permitted, by decree in 1979, to be used in schools for communication in the classroom and also as a subject of instruction. Valdman reported that in 1982 there was "a fierce verbal war" being waged in the media over the merits of the educational reform strategy being promoted "vigorously" by the then Minister of Education; the reform advocated the use of French Creole as "the main classroom vehicle for the first four years of primary education" (1988, p. 67). The arguments put forward for and against the use of the Creole were similar to those expressed elsewhere in the Caribbean and recently in the United States with regard to "Ebonics."

During the same period, programs were designed in the United Kingdom to address the needs of students who spoke creole or CIV varieties from the Caribbean. An example of one such program overtly contrasted dialect with standard English utterances and required the learner through the use of different types of drills to discriminate or identify the difference between or to translate from one variety to the other (Feigenbaum, 1975). This approach was intended to help students become aware of the differences between the standard and nonstandard without involving them in grammatical explanation. Dalphinis (1985) presented information on other programs in existence in the 1970s.

Progress has been made in some territories regarding the use of creole and CIVs in education. In the Seychelles and the Netherlands Antilles, for example, changes in education policy led to the inclusion of CIV in schools. Most Caribbean territories have been more tentative or perhaps reticent regarding the role of Creole and CIV for education purposes. It is possible that theoretical and social perspectives on what is appropriate in certain contexts may have influenced both policy and practice. Several of the articles included in Tabouret-Keller, LePage, Gardner-Chloros, and Varro (1997) present a global perspective of the political, social, and pedagogical factors affecting vernacular literacy in countries where such programs have been introduced. The next section presents an overview of policy positions on the use of Creole and CIV in education.

Teaching Standard to Creole and CIV Speakers: Policy Issues and Program Models

Historically, education systems and education policy in the Caribbean were patterned on those of the countries that colonized the various territories in the region. In the Anglophone territories, English was the language of instruction, and the approaches used to teach were those normally used for teaching native speakers of English regardless of whether a high percentage of learners were Creole or CIV speakers. The situations in the Francophone territories such as Haiti, Martinique, and Guadeloupe were similar. In the case of the latter two overseas departments of France, legislation was passed to allow the use of CIV in the classroom for specified purposes, but the number of programs incorporating the vernacular was negligible and could not be sustained. Included among the reasons given for the lack of success of these programs were lack of parental enthusiasm and children dropping out (Carrington, 1997). Perhaps the overriding factor in these territories was political; while it may have been fashionable to agitate against the establishment for recognition of the vernacular, as long as these islands remained departments of France, French as the official language would continue to be perceived as the language of success and upward mobility.

In the case of Haiti, the majority of the populace speaks French Creole and a small number (5%) are considered to be balanced bilinguals (Valdman, 1988, p. 67). Among reasons given for the lack of success of the reform initiative to incorporate Creole in instructional programs in schools were, first, that "the privileged classes do not wish to change the order of the society. They prefer to maintain the language filter that restricts entry to their class and access to the control systems of the society" (Carrington, 1997, p. 86), and, second, it would be impossible to achieve bilingualism in a society that is over 90% monolingual in Creole. As DeJean put it "For the economically weakest country in the Americas, already burdened with a rate of illiteracy that is one of the highest in the world, to undertake the project of creating from the whole cloth a bilingual society out of a population that is massively monolingual would be foolish because it can't be achieved" (1993, p. 78). DeJean went on to observe that "Scorn and disdain for Creole [and the] conviction of the inferior and inadequate character of the popular speech would be, in the whole of the population, the basis of a popular resistance to the establishment of the experimental classes and the reform programs" (1993, p. 79). Although in Haiti, as in the other territories in the Caribbean, there has been agitation for the use of Creole and CIV in education as a vehicle for speakers of these varieties to acquire literacy, the point is that without political will and social motivation such reform programs will be difficult to implement with success. As Carrington has pointed out "Neither the political directorate nor the masses who might be empowered by vernacular literacy appear to recognize the point of it" (1997, p. 86).

Calls for the use of Creole and CIV in education have come mainly from linguists, some of whom have delineated conditions to guide policymaking for introducing vernacular literacy in certain contexts while being careful to point out that the business of policymaking was the responsibility of the state (e.g., Craig, 1980; Devonish, 1986a/b). One of the earliest suggestions was made by Midgett who proposed, in the case of St. Lucia, that Patois (i.e., French Creole) be used "interchangeably with less formal more colloquial English" as a means of establishing English "in the minds of students as a functional equivalent of Patois" (1970, p. 167). Carrington (1976) presented six principles that described conditions considered favorable for the use of Creole as a language of instruction. Roberts suggested that an "integrative approach" which allows for the use of Creole in an "integrative, appropriate way in the school system" be used. Such an approach, in his view, would "give confidence to pupils who, as they (got) older, (would) feel secure enough to use the full range of their linguistic competence to full effect in their speech and writing" (1993, pp. 12–14). Devonish referred to two policy papers[4] presented in Grenada to promote the standardization of Grenadian English-lexicon Creole and its "official use in the society at large and, more specifically, in the education system" (1986a, p. 40); Devonish went on to explain that the proposals were not adopted because teachers were divided on the question as to whether the proposals were relevant and whether Grenada had a language problem. However, he reiterated the recommendation that English-lexicon Creoles be standardized and adopted for wide use in society and education with regard to other Anglophone territories such as Jamaica and Guyana (e.g., Devonish, 1986b).

Craig (1980) described a typology of educational models that presented the linguistic, socioeconomic, and cultural factors that should be considered in determining which model would be best in a given context. These were as follows: (1) school monolingualism in the dominant language, which ignores the home language of the child; (2) transitional bilingualism, which allows use of the child's home language only to the extent that the child can learn enough of the school language to use it for academic purposes in school; (3) monoliterate bilingualism, which develops literacy in the language that is dominant in the community but permits development of both languages for oral–aural skills; (4) partial bilingualism, which develops literacy and oral–aural fluency in the child's home language only for "certain types of subject matter that have to do with the immediate society and culture" (1980, p. 248); (5) full bilingualism, which allows development of all skills in both languages in all domains; and (6) monolingualism in the home language in which the objective is to develop literacy in the home language of the child.

The model most widely implemented in the Anglophone territories of the Caribbean was school monolingualism, which promoted literacy in the official language English. In other territories such as the Netherlands Antilles and Haiti, a bilingual model, which promoted the use of Papiamentu and Haitian French Creole respectively, in grades 1 through 6, was implemented for some time. Based on general reports (e.g., DeJean, 1993; Valdman, 1988) on the Haitian situation, it is possible to infer that the success of the vernacular programs has been below expectations, while research reports on the situation in the Netherlands Antilles are rare. Siegel reported on research done on three types of instructional programs, namely, instrumental, accommodation and awareness that incorporate a Creole or CIV. He explained that, in instrumental programs, the "stigmatized variety"[5] is used "as a medium of instruction to teach initial literacy and content and subjects such as mathematics, science and health" while, in accommodation programs,[6] students are allowed and encouraged to use their home language in speaking and sometimes in writing. In awareness programs, the CIV is "an object of study in the context of discussions of language diversity or of literature" (1999a, p. 705). These programs dovetail with some of the typologies articulated earlier by Craig (1980) but exclude others such as the first, monolingualism in the official language, and the last, monolingualism in the home language, for obvious reasons.

Bryan and Burnette reported that in Dominica teachers are using Kwéyòl (French Creole) "to aid understanding among children in the primary and secondary sector" (2003, p. 151) which suggests that an accommodation program may be in use in that territory. Winer reported an increased acceptance of Trinidadian Creole (TC) in schools in Trinidad and Tobago. She observed: "Although few would advocate the use of TC as the primary educational medium, even in primary education, there is a widely recognized need, from teachers and community, for its use in education as complementary, additive, and transitional to standard English" (1990, p. 245). The increased acceptance to which Winer refers is also the experience in most other Anglophone territories in which the Caribbean Secondary Examination Certificate, administered by the Caribbean Examination Council (CXC), is taken by students at the end of secondary school. The examination allows for the use of Creole in creative writing in presenting the dialogue of characters, for example, in situations where use of the Creole variety would be natural and realistic. However, for all other purposes, the examination does stress that responses be written in standard English.

In St. Lucia, the official policy is that English should be used as the language of instruction, but teachers, especially in the rural areas, sometimes use Kwéyòl to new students who are native speakers of that variety to facilitate their understanding of classroom procedures. That many Creole and CIV native speakers have not fared as well as their English-speaking counterparts in examinations like the Common Entrance[7] has been one of the primary reasons for the call to explore other methods such as the use of the mother tongue in education. But this call has not been restricted solely to the Caribbean region.

The children of immigrants to the United Kingdom, Canada, and North America, and students who migrated to these countries, have experienced difficulties learning English, which has led to consultations among linguists and educators regarding the approaches that should be used to facilitate their learning of the standard language. An example would be the International Creole Workshops organized by Florida International University, which sought the input of linguists and educators in the formulation of approaches for instructing French Creole speakers, primarily from Haiti, who had migrated to the United States. Siegel referred to another consultation organized in Toronto to consider "educational inequities faced by the large number of Caribbean immigrants living in Ontario, Canada" (1999b, p. 512). He reported that out of that consultation a committee was formed to produce a resource book for teachers of Caribbean students. Winer, writing about Caribbean immigrants in North America, suggested that "any approach to the teaching of students whose first language is English Creole, recognized or not, must include knowledge about and acceptance of the language and its culture, contrasted specifically with English language and culture varieties" (1993, p. 195). Kephart, considering the fact that many children on Carriacou speak a variety different from metropolitan English, suggested that learning to read Carriacou Creole English (CCE) might "assist" their learning of metropolitan English (2003, p. 238).

An interesting development in the United Kingdom is reflected in the efforts of Morris and Nwenmely to teach Kwéyòl to St. Lucian and Dominican immigrants and their children as a means of developing their literacy skills. The Kwéyòl project emerged as an offshoot of the national literacy campaign launched in the United Kingdom in 1975. The aim of that campaign was to teach English-speaking people who had difficulty reading and writing. Morris and Nwenmely (1993) explained that the organizers were concerned that they were unable to meet the needs of students from the Eastern Caribbean. The Kwéyòl project was launched to help them address those needs:

> The Kwéyòl Project was financed through Tower Hamlets Institute of Adult Education to enable a young St. Lucian medical student...to co-ordinate the launching of the first phase of the (Patwa) Project classes .... This ran parallel with the development of a Black Studies course. It was felt important to develop the two courses in parallel, in order to enhance and encourage an Afrikan educational and cultural perspective which would in turn facilitate understanding of the historical development of the Kwéyòl language in the Caribbean (Morris & Nwenmely, 1993, p. 261).

In this context, instruction in Kwéyòl was seen as a means of preserving the home language and culture of Eastern Caribbean migrants to Britain. Morris and Nwenmely reported: "A great many people see the advantages of being able to read and write the mother tongue as a way of affirming cultural pride, roots and increasing self-worth and confidence" (1993, p. 267). In their view, the study of Kwéyòl also rekindled interest in academic study for adults as well as young people.

Other models have focused not exclusively on Creole speakers but on CIV and speakers of a standard variety who interact as a heterogeneous group in a classroom. Such heterogeneous classrooms are the norm in most schools in St. Lucia and Dominica as well as other territories. Simmons-McDonald (1996) outlined the principles for a model that would tailor instruction to the needs of heterogeneous groups comprising Kwéyòl, CIV, and standard English [8] speakers, and later (2000) developed a formal model for implementation that was accepted by the Ministry of Education for experimental use in a carefully monitored pilot project.

Some attempts were made in the French West Indian island of Guadeloupe to use French Creole in school to help students learn standard French. Durizot (1996) reported that in 1977 two schools [9] in Guadeloupe included a French Creole program to help native speakers of French Creole who had difficulty learning French. That program was later discontinued because parents opposed the use of Creole in school. Later, in 1983, an officially sanctioned program was introduced in one institution, Capesterre College, and emphasized reading and writing in Creole for six hours per week. In other parts of the world, for example, the Seychelles, a policy was taken several years ago to include the French Creole variety Seselwa in education. The Creole, along with English and French, was elevated to the status of an official language in 1979 (Bollée, 1993). Bollée reported that later, in 1981, Creole became "the first national language of the Republic, English, second, and French, third" (1993, p. 87). In that year, a decision was taken to make Creole the "primary medium of instruction in the schools."

Prior to the inclusion of Creole in education, student performance in the acquisition of the standard languages was poor. Bollée reproduced a report from the newspaper which read as follows: "Nearly half of the school leavers could not properly write, read or express themselves in French or English after nine years of primary education" (1993, p. 88). Creole was taught in an instrumental program as part of an integrated curriculum in the first four years of primary school (grades P1 to P4). Over the next three years (grades P5 to P7) it was taught as a subject and up to P9 as "the language medium for political education, creative arts, family life education and extracurricular activities" (Bollée, 1993, p. 89). The results emerging from the reforms in the Seychelles indicate that some success was achieved in terms of student performance. Quoting from a contemporary newspaper, Bollée made the following report:

> Nearly three-quarters of P3 pupils in 1984 "could read and write in Creole anything that can be expected of children of that age and intellectual development." As to the positive effects of the introduction of Creole on other subjects, teachers of mathematics reported "very encouraging results," and the English section, an "excellent overall performance of P3 pupils in English." (*Seychelles Nation* of April 26, 1985, p. 2, quoted in Bollée, 1993)[10]

It is clear from the report that there was some resistance to the introduction of Creole as the primary medium of education and that acceptance of it was slow. However, the political will and the valuation of the language in the society appear to have influenced its successful implementation within the education system. Systematic research on student performance has been rare; however, Siegel (1999b) cited two studies, the first done by Ravel and Thomas (1985) and the second by Bickerton (1988) that reported some measure of success in the performance of the students. For example, Siegel highlighted the finding from the Ravel and Thomas study that showed better performance by Creole-educated students in grade 3 in 1984 than that of their predecessors in 1983 who had been instructed in English. Reports such as these, as well as research findings that show positive effects of mother tongue instruction, have encouraged continued interest in the implementation of Creole and CIV as varieties for instruction in the Caribbean and elsewhere. A brief summary of the main findings of this research is presented in the following section.

The Influence of Research

Research on second language learning in certain mainstream contexts has influenced, to some degree, models that advocate the use of creole and CIV in education for the purpose of helping native speakers of these varieties learn a standard variety. Some findings in bilingual, bidialectal contexts have revealed that the acquisition of two or more languages has positive effects on metalinguistic development (Bialystok, 1991). Comparisons of children who had acquired literacy in two languages indicated better performance by these children when they attempted to acquire a third language than by monolingual or bilingual children who had not acquired literacy in their home language (Swain & Lapkin, 1991). Cummins (1991) reviewed studies that showed that "the better developed children's L1 conceptual foundation, the more likely they are to develop similarly high levels of conceptual abilities in their L2" (cited in Cummins, 1994, p. 38). He further reported that the "positive results of programs that continue to promote literacy in L1 throughout elementary school can be attributed to the combined effect of reinforcing students' cultural identity and their conceptual growth" (1994, p. 39). Ovando and Collier made the point that "cognitive and academic development of a student's first language provides especially crucial and academic support for second-language acquisition" (1998, pp. 88–89). They explained further that if cognitive and academic success in L2 is to be assured, both the oral and written aspects of a student's first language system must be "developed to a high cognitive level" through the years of elementary school. Their comment on this particular point is worth noting:

> It is extremely important that cognitive development continue through a child's first language at least through the elementary school years. Extensive research has demonstrated that children who reach full cognitive development in two languages (generally reaching the threshold in L1 by around age 11 to 12) enjoy cognitive advantages over monolinguals. (Ovando & Collier, 1998, p. 90)

Craig examined test results for students in the Anglophone West Indian territories (excluding the Bahamas) and concluded that "the creole-influenced majority student population of the Caribbean experiences a magnitude of difficulty in acquiring English language and literacy which is at least equivalent to that experienced by the African American Vernacular English (AAVE) student population in the USA" (1999, p. 29). The point of Craig's statement is that, regardless of the students' first language (i.e., AAVE or English Creole or French Creole), or the differences in the relationship between the first language and the respective standard, the learning outcomes and the language learning difficulties experienced by Creole and CIV speakers are startlingly similar. Comparisons of West Indian students and student groups in the United Kingdom also led Craig (1999) to conclude that the performance of CIV speakers in the West Indies is significantly lower than the equivalent age cohorts in the United Kingdom. A key issue is that populations of Creole and CIV speakers experience similar problems when they are in a formal language-learning situation in which they are required to learn a standard variety as a second language. A comparison of selected works shows that this is not a trivial coincidence (e.g., Rickford, 1999; Simmons-McDonald, 2001; Winch & Gingell, 1994).

Ovando and Collier (1998) summarized several other studies that had reported cognitive benefits experienced by learners who acquire two languages in early childhood. One such benefit is that the subsequent acquisition of a third language is much easier. Others included "cognitive advantages over monolinguals on measures of cognitive flexibility, linguistic and metalingusitic abilities, concept formation, divergent thinking, and creativity" (Ovando & Collier, 1998, p. 256). Research also showed that literacy skills learned in a first language transfer to a second language (e.g., Cummins, 1993). The evidence provided by these studies also dismissed concerns that learners' first language would interfere with the learning of a second. Winch and Gingell compared the writing of Creole and CIV speakers in primary schools in St. Lucia with that of students in the United Kingdom who had had no Creole influence. They attributed most of the errors to "a misunderstanding of the relationship between speech and writing" rather than to interference (1994, p. 177). Some of the errors they identified indicated the learners' inability to handle the features of formal English, and they were identical to errors made by native speakers of English attending school in the United Kingdom. The error types they listed fell into the following categories: (1) context dependent, (2) topicalization, (3) genre difficulties, (4) repetition, and (5) errors due to ambitious constructions (p. 178).

Other research done with creole and CIV groups also provided evidence that the first language of the learner could help and not hinder the learner in the acquisition of a second language. Siegel (1997) reported on an evaluation undertaken in 1989 of a pre-school program in Papua New Guinea to teach initial literacy using Tok Pisin. He examined the term test results of "ex prep" students who had gone through the prep-school program and those who had not gone through the program. He also used interviews and questionnaires, the results of which showed that community schoolteachers had reported that there were no "special problems of interference" and that the influence of the home language, Tok Pisin, could "only be seen sometimes in spelling and pronunciation" (1997, p. 92). The results of that study also showed that the "ex prep" students learned the second language, English, "more easily" than the "no prep" students, that they did better academically, participated more in class, and had a lower dropout rate. Additional, and perhaps the most important, finding was that the students who had been involved in the prep-school program (the ex-prep) "scored significantly higher, not lower, in term tests than those who had not been involved...the higher achievements were in English, as well as in Maths and General Subjects" (p. 94). Siegel concluded that preliminary formal instruction in a pidgin language was better than none at all and that it was not a hindrance to students' later academic achievement. In the same article, Siegel cited a prior study (Murtagh, 1982) conducted with children whose mother tongue was Kriol and who were learning English as a second language. The students in a bilingual program, using Kriol and English, had "greater English-language proficiency" than the Kriol-speaking students who were in a monolingual English program (1997, p. 98).

In another paper, Siegel (1999a) sought to answer the question of whether or not "there is evidence for the assumption that working with a stigmatized variety in the classroom is detrimental to the acquisition of the standard". He examined available evidence from instrumental, accommodation, and awareness programs and concluded that the studies demonstrated "various positive results of making use of the students' own varieties of language in education (such as) greater participation rates, higher scores on tests measuring reading and writing skills in standard English, and increases in overall academic achievement" (1999a, p. 710). In summary, research done in both mainstream second language-learning situations in which the learners' native language may have been a standard variety and in other situations in which learners' native language was either a Creole or a CIV has provided evidence showing that nurturing and developing a child's first language and teaching literacy in it first did not hamper the learning of a second (standard) language, but was beneficial to the learner in many ways.

Recent Programs, Approaches, and Research

In Caribbean territories with English-lexicon vernaculars, CIV speakers have generally been taught as though English were their native language, and all that was required was for their errors to be corrected. This "correction" approach was widely used and still is today by less experienced teachers in several schools. This approach simply meant that teachers would correct vernacular utterances (or sentences) as being wrong and would reinforce the English equivalent through repetition. Researchers have pointed out that this approach only served to give learners the impression that their language was inferior and that it failed to move learners beyond the vernacular. In the case of St. Lucian speakers of French Creole, Simmons-McDonald (1998) showed that Kwéyòl-speaking children learning English in school first acquired an English-lexicon vernacular, then slowed down in their learning of standard English because the vernacular was widely spoken in their communities and met their communicative needs adequately. They seemed to see no point in acquiring the standard when they could get by with using St. Lucia English-lexicon vernacular (SLEV). She pointed out that approaches that identified the vernacular structures as errors in need of eradication would not be successful, and that the standard had to be considered not as an extension of SLEV, but as a third alternative lect, the acquisition of which would need to be facilitated through the implementation of "a carefully thought-out program of instruction."

The early systematic approaches to teaching a standard variety to Creole and CIV speakers in the Caribbean are those that were referred to earlier in this discussion, namely, the materials and teachers' guides that were produced by the Language Materials Workshop in Jamaica, the UWI/USAID Primary Education Project, which, we are told, had a "specially designed Language Arts component" intended to cater to the needs of Creole-influenced children across the Caribbean (Craig, 1999, p. 33) and the UNESCO Language Arts Project in the Eastern Caribbean that used audiolingual methods to teach English. Now, many of the ideas for teaching Creole and CIV learners are presented in resource manuals for teachers. These vary as regards the inclusion of theory and the scope of coverage of topics.

One resource for Jamaican teachers prepared by Velma Pollard appeared in 1993. The approach advocated in this manual is contrastive. It is organized in four sections that focus on words with similar sounds but different meanings, words that are different but mean the same things, different grammatical structures that convey the same meaning in the two varieties, and idiomatic speech and writing. The text presents teachers with concrete examples on how to teach the differences, including the use of literature selections as stimuli. Teachers are directed to the relevant theory through a list of references in an appendix. The manual is used in Jamaica, but it was not possible to determine whether any systematic research had been done to assess teachers' responses to it or whether it met its objective of helping teachers "help their students move from being able to use only one language JC (Jamaican Creole) to being able to use the two languages...[needed] to operate successfully in the Jamaican situation" (Pollard, 1993, p. v).

Another program developed by Craig (1999) is also designed as a resource for teachers. This program, Teaching English to Speakers of a Related Variety (TESORV), is intended to help teachers teach language and literacy to CIV speakers. It provides a theoretical perspective as well as practical teaching activities and resources. Craig contends that certain prerequisites related to learner needs must be considered before teaching programs are designed. These are: (1) making provision for continuity in the learners' cognitive growth (in the vernacular) and (2) developing language awareness. In TESORV, the teaching and learning experiences that are suggested by the prerequisites require recognition of "the difference between using the vernacular and using English and (keeping) the two separate," using the "life experiences of learners and the vernacular culture and environment in integration with the culture of the wider world," and insistence on "clarity of goals and objectives in the use of the vernacular and of English" (Craig, 1999, pp. 44–45). The teaching approach promotes the development of language awareness, direct procedures that focus on "perception/reception...of the form and meaning of new language elements (in English), on internalization or understanding and re-composing what has been perceived/received and creative utilization of what has been internalized" (1999, p. 45).

TESORV uses an eclectic approach that incorporates selected foreign language methods, and use of the vernacular in carefully designed activities that develop the learners' language awareness and literacy abilities within a language experience framework. A major emphasis is on active student participation in language learning. Craig made the following assertion with regard to TESORV:

It seems clear that the necessary teaching/learning orientation for vernacular speakers synthesizes the accumulated wisdom of the major approaches to language teaching, while at the same time rejecting such practices as ignore the specific needs and characteristics of vernacular speakers and the sociolinguistic factors relevant to both their use of the vernacular and their use of the official language English (Craig, 1999, p. 82).

In some ways, TESORV is not new because it uses approaches and methods in existence for some time. However, in its pulling together of the various methodological strands and in its provision of detailed guidelines for the incorporation of the vernacular, it provides a comprehensive approach to vernacular instruction. The program includes sample activities, procedures to be used, scheme of work and syllabus resources, and a wealth of information about language and differences between vernacular structures and English. In this way, it attempts to fill a gap not usually addressed in most teacher training programs, namely, the linguistic background that is essential to teachers who work in a creole and creole-influenced context.

TESORV is grounded in the findings of research on language acquisition/learning conducted over decades within and outside of the Caribbean region, and it is used by many teachers across the territories. As far as I am aware, its introduction within the Caribbean was not linked to a research program that could provide information on its efficacy in helping creole and CIV speakers learn the standard variety. In fact, precisely because TESORV uses such a range of methods, it would be useful to determine its success as a teaching approach within the context of a well-designed research study. Unfortunately, the research study component of many programs implemented within and outside the Caribbean has been missing and this constitutes a severe lack in the literature on vernacular literacy. This lack has been noted elsewhere in the literature; for example, Siegel observed that "very little research has been done on the use of Creoles and minority dialects in education" (1999b, p. 519). This remains an area of vital importance for applied linguists and educators to address.

Other recent programs, though not excluding contrasts between the Creole/CIV and the standard variety as an activity that can be judiciously employed in the classroom, have not used a contrastive approach as central but have focused instead on the use of literature as a means of developing literacy in the standard variety. These programs vary with regard to their overt use of the vernacular in the classroom. One study by Wilson, Smikle, and Grant (2001) used a literature-based approach to develop early literacy skills in the early primary grades in selected Jamaican schools. The authors did not mention vernacular speakers explicitly in the exposition of the study, but they referred to a Ministry of Education study, which had shown that "more than two-thirds of grade six pupils had scores considered to be below acceptable levels in English language skills" (2001, p. 1). The use of Jamaican Creole (JC) is so widespread in Jamaica that it would be unusual if those students who had low scores did not include a proportion of JC speakers. Similarly, it would be very unlikely that the sample used in this study did not include JC speakers. It is only in one concluding statement that the authors made direct reference to Creole speakers, thus implying that the sample included JC speakers.

Wilson et al. developed and implemented a literature-based program of work and used evidence from emergent literacy studies to justify their choice of this approach. They selected approximately 121 titles from the following categories: informational books, folktales, realistic fiction, nonfiction, traditional literature, and fantasy. Their selections also included multicultural literature. The approach was implemented within the context of a carefully monitored research experiment that sought to answer six questions, including whether the literature-based language approach to reading would affect the learners' reading attitude and reading comprehension. The study was conducted in 14 primary schools with students in grades 1 and 2 and consisted of a sample of 120 in the experimental groups and 109 in the control groups. The researchers used Literature-Based Language Arts Project (LBLAP) assessment instruments to test word recognition, comprehension, reading interest/attitude and orientation to book print. The main approach comprised teachers reading aloud to students and using a set of classroom activities that included story retelling, choral reading, paired reading, and whole class discussion, among others. The data gathering instruments included close observation of lessons and administration of the LBLAP tests. The study found that the experimental groups had higher gain scores than the control groups on all the measures and that the difference was significant. The investigators found that reading attitudes improved with grade level and that the higher attitude scores were found in the experimental group. The researchers concluded that LBLAP "is a means of fostering language acquisition for Creole-speaking children, enabling children who do not come to school speaking English to acquire grammatical patterns of that language" (Wilson et al., 2001, p. 54).

Within the St. Lucian context, Simmons-McDonald (2000) conducted an experiment that explored the effects of an integrated approach in a tripartite model tailored to the needs of children who were native speakers of either St. Lucian French Creole (SLFC/Kwéyòl), a (French) Creole-influenced English-lexicon vernacular (SLEV), or St. Lucian Standard English (SLSE). The model promoted Kwéyòl for its native speakers in initial literacy development, while they acquired English for communicative purposes as well as literacy in English. It also promoted Kwéyòl as a subject for study and for communication purposes by CIV and English speakers for cultural reasons. The principles of the model were summarized as follows:

> The model is developed within the context of an integrated program that incorporates a rich literature selection that promotes the acquisition of literacy through literature. The model allowed for a treatment that would expose learners to one-and-a-half hours of instruction in Kwéyòl and three-and-a-half hours in English on a daily basis. During the time devoted to Kwéyòl instruction learners would be exposed to a programme that in the early grades (K–grade I) would focus on emergent literacy in Kwéyòl. As literacy in Kwéyòl developed and learners acquired communicative skills in English the focus through Grades II to VI would shift increasingly to the development of literacy in English but with continuing literacy development in their native language. An integrated programme of study would provide the framework for the introduction of rich reading selections, including narrative choices in which the characters expressed themselves in vernacular varieties as well as English, thereby providing a natural context for the judicious comparison of varieties. (Simmons-McDonald, in press)

The experiment implemented a modified version of the French Creole model, using a small group of learners in grades 5 and 6 identified by their teachers as having severe reading problems. The experiment was conducted in six intensive sessions each of one week's duration over three terms, and was modified to allow for 45 minutes of instruction in Kwéyòl and one hour of English in each instructional session. A single subject research design (Neuman & McCormick, 1995) was used in the experiment because it allowed for the subjects to be used as their own controls. Included in the experiment were two boys and a girl, all native speakers of Kwéyòl, drawn from a larger group who had been found to be reading two to four grade levels below their required age. By the end of the experiment, two of the children who had been beginning readers were reading at grade 1 level; the oldest boy, Ado, who had been reading at grade 1 level with an accuracy rate of 85.5% in English at the start of the study was reading grade 3 materials fluently and had a 97% accuracy score in the last recorded session, as shown in Figure 1. Results for Kwéyòl literacy were also very encouraging. All the children could read several of the Kwéyòl folk tales included in the reading selection independently.

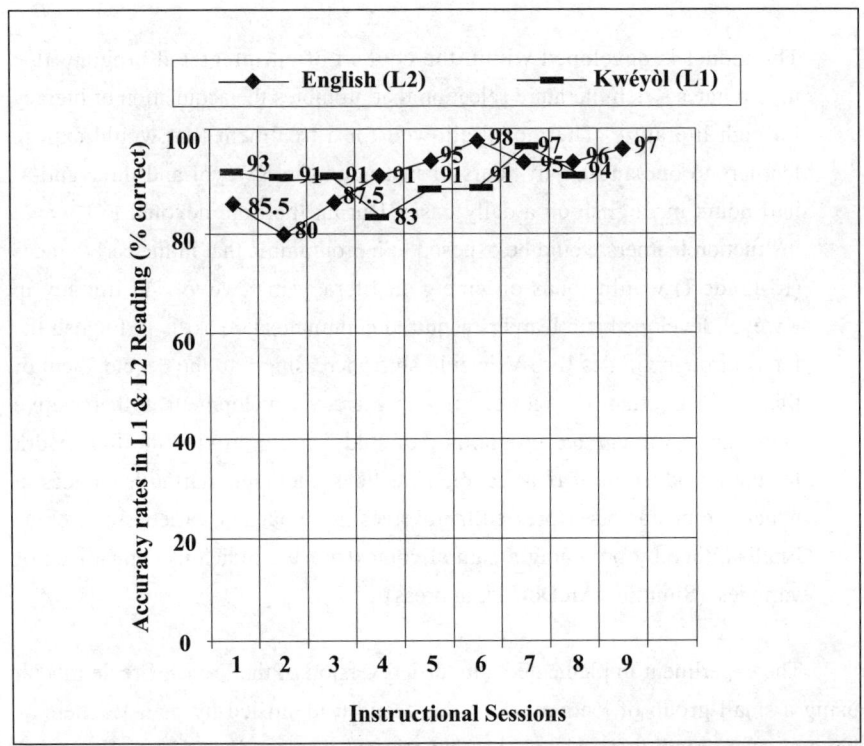

Figure 1. Reading accuracy percentages for Kwéyòl (L1) and English (L2) for Ado (from Simmons-McDonald, in press)

The concluding statement pointed to the fact that, although only a scaled-down version of the French Creole model had been implemented, "all the subjects who had been listed as being at risk at the start of the study and who had only limited word recognition abilities at the kindergarten level developed fluency in reading texts at least one grade level higher than their levels of proficiency at the start of the study. In the case of the oldest child, gains in accuracy in both languages exceeded expectations, as this subject was able to read texts at grade 3 level by the end of the experiment" (Simmons-McDonald, in press). It was clear that the integrated and culturally rich literature base advocated by the model fully engaged the learners and encouraged development across language varieties.

Elsewhere, experiments have used literature-based approaches in vernacular literacy programs. One experiment with African American Vernacular English (AAVE) speaking students and other students from different minority groups who were considered to be at risk was reported by Rickford (1999). Rickford proposed two "essential means" for helping schools succeed in the teaching of reading to African American and other minority populations. These were "increased use of culturally congruent literature...the inclusion of more tests in which students can see characers like themselves portrayed," and modification of the "teaching and testing of reading comprehension...to make it more engaging and challenging" (1999, p. xii). Among other benefits, Rickford reported positive results in the literacy development of the students in her study.

The shift toward other approaches such as those used in the studies discussed in this section is not uncommon. Gerbault reported that such a shift in practice reflected the shift in pedagogical theory "from a focus on teaching to a focus on learning and 'learner-centredness' that had implications for a number of theoretical positions regarding the pedagogy of literacy" (1997, p. 147). She pointed out that this pedagogy "borrowed principles from a variety of pedagogical theories," and that it "also developed its own principles to cope with specific challenges in the practice of teaching vernacular literacy" (1997, p. 144). Some of these principles include the use of approaches that focus more on learners and on their active participation in lessons; on the integration of reading, writing, and numeracy skills; and on teaching initial literacy in the language that the learner can speak. Gerbault noted that these approaches have also been used in adult programs as well.

The selection of articles included in Tabouret-Keller et al. (1997) gave indications of some similar developments in adult programs in global contexts; Siegel (1999b) provided a listing of comparable programs that have been reported on in formal and nonformal education. As noted earlier, Siegel commented on the scant research available and observed that most of the studies done, including some discussed in the foregoing sections, have been done on instrumental programs that used Creole as the medium of instruction. The absence of research data on some programs and approaches as well as scant descriptions of the procedures used in some programs make it difficult to compare the effects of these programs on different groups of Creole and CIV speakers and also make replication of the studies in different contexts impossible. Further, the lack of published evidence showing the benefits of selected pedagogical approaches on speakers of Creoles and CIV makes the task of promoting the inclusion of Creole and CIV in formal education systems more difficult when it is precisely in that context—in which the majority of Creole-speaking children are enrolled—that such programs are likely to have a positive and lifelong impact. Governments in the Caribbean and possibly elsewhere remain skeptical about the efficacy of vernacular literacy or vernacular education programs. It is only by providing evidence about program efficacy based on experiments using different approaches to literacy instruction, describing these approaches carefully, and collecting data on their relative benefits to creole and CIV groups, that informed decisions will be made. Applied linguists have much to contribute to these ongoing efforts.

Notes

1. Defined in the sense of having fundamental skills as described by Williams and Snipper, for example, "Now *functional literacy* is often used to denote the ability to read and write well enough to understand signs, read newspaper headlines, fill out job applications, make shopping lists, and write checks" (1990, p. 4).

2. The terms used to refer to the vernacular spoken by African Americans in the United States of America have changed over time. In the 1960s and 70s, Black English Vernacular (BEV) was widely used. This was replaced by the term African American Vernacular English (AAVE) which is now used variably with the controversial term "Ebonics." In this chapter, the term AAVE will be used.

3. Cited in Sutcliffe, 1982, p. 73.

4. Papers presented by Devonish "The question of what medium of instruction should be used in education" and Kephart "Some background for language planning in Grenada" to the National Seminar on Education held in Grenada in July, 1979.

5. Siegel uses the term "stigmatized variety" to refer to the nonstandard variety. Here the terms "Creole" and "Creole-Influenced Vernacular" are used to refer to the same entities.

6. He acknowledged Wiley, 1996, for "accommodation programs."

7. Also referred to as the 11+ Examination, this is given to children at the end of primary school and determines selection for secondary (high) school.

8. In St. Lucia, Kwéyòl, an English-lexicon vernacular, St. Lucian English vernacular (SLEV), and standard English are widely spoken. Classrooms, particularly in rural areas, would consist of a mix of students who speak either or a combination of these varieties as (a) first language (s). (Also see Aceto and Williams, 2003, for descriptions of other contact situations.)

9. In 1957 the "Association Guadeloupéenne de l'éducation populaire," was formed by a primary school teacher, Gérard Louriette. It was his initiative that promoted the use of French Creole in the two schools. He prepared materials for the program and also wrote books promoting literacy in French Creole and its use in teaching French.

10. The article from the *Seychelles Today* of April 26, 1985, was reporting on the situation before the reforms were introduced. Bollée (1993, p. 88) commented that prior to the 1981 reform "a large percentage of illiterates continued to be produced."

ANNOTATED BIBLIOGRAPHY

Craig, D. (1999). *Teaching language and literacy: Policies and procedures for vernacular situations*. Georgetown, Guyana: Education and Development Services Inc.

This book is a rich resource for teachers of students who speak Creole and CIV as a native language and who are learning a standard language in school. Craig carefully presents issues related to the development of vernacular education in the Caribbean and elsewhere, and he does a close analysis of the results of regional examinations to show that Creole and CIV speakers within the region are at a disadvantage. One of the strengths of the text is its careful explication of the theoretical positions on which the TESORV model is based. Each of the teaching and learning principles that are discussed in the earlier section of the book is elaborated and exemplified in the second part in the syllabus resources. The text also presents and explains procedures for primary, post-primary, and secondary education levels. It presents an eclectic approach that embraces, explicates, and provides suggestions for using contrastive approaches to show morphological and syntactic differences between internationally accepted English (IAE) and CIVs. It presents word formation principles with a wealth of examples; explains and provides examples and teaching points on syntax. A very useful syllabus resource is one titled "The Vernacular in our Lives," that provides help on how to include the vernacular in the classroom for purposes of maintaining the home language and culture of the children and for strengthening their language awareness. This much-needed text fills a large gap in the teacher training repertoire in the Caribbean by presenting valuable background on linguistics and the practice of teaching language that student teachers need to help them cater to the needs of Creole and CIV speakers.

Rickford, A. (1999). *I can fly*. Lanham, MD: University Press of America.

This text exemplifies one approach that uses culturally relevant literature to motivate adolescent AAVE-speaking students and students from other minority groups to read, discuss literature and engage in critical thinking at a high level. Written as a dissertation, the book in all its aspects presents the kind of careful exposition and analysis that allows authorities to evaluate the principles and procedures of an approach and make informed decisions about it. The first part presents the conceptual framework and a description of the situational contexts and sample for the study. The second part focuses on the analysis of the narratives that were used. The results, presenting both qualitative and quantitative analyses, provide interesting insights into the responses of the students to the experiment itself. This text is included because it presents a practical approach to dealing with the problems of AAVE speakers and other minority students within the school system and the positive results provide the hope and certitude that inequalities in education can be addressed and can produce positive outcomes for speakers of minority dialects.

Tabouret-Keller, A., Le Page, R., Gardner-Chloros, P., & Varro, G. (Eds.). (1997). *Vernacular literacy: A re-evaluation.* Oxford: Clarendon Press.

This text provides a global perspective of the issues related to vernacular literacy and a review of some programs that have been undertaken in several countries. The contributions in the first part of the text focus on broad issues related to vernacular literacy, including political, social, economic and pedagogical concerns in different contexts. The case studies in the second section provide a basis for comparison of different programs that have been done in different nations. The comprehensive coverage of theoretical and practical issues makes this text an important reference for researchers and practitioners in the field of vernacular literacy.

OTHER REFERENCES

Aarons, A., Gordon, B. & Stewart, W. (Eds.). (1969, Spring/Summer). Linguistic Cultural Differences in American Education: Special Anthology Issue. *Florida Foreign Language Reporter.*

Abrahams, R. D. & Gay, G. (1975). Talking black in the classroom. In P. Stroller (Ed.), *Black American English: Its background and its usage* (pp. 158–167). New York: Dell.

Aceto, M. & Williams, J. (Eds.). (2003). *Contact Englishes of the Eastern Caribbean.* Amsterdam: Benjamins.

Bialystok, E. (Ed.). (1991). *Language processing in bilingual children.* Cambridge: Cambridge University Press.

Bollée, A. (1993). Language policy in the Seychelles and its consequences. *International Journal of the Sociology of Language, 102,* 85–99.

Bryan, B. & Burnette, R. (2003). Language variation and language use among teachers in Dominica. In M. Aceto & J. Williams (Eds.), *Contact Englishes of the eastern Caribbean* (pp. 141–153). Amsterdam: Benjamins.

Carrington, L. (1968). English language learning problems in the Caribbean. *Trinidad & Tobago Modern Language Review,* No. 1.

Carrington, L. (1969). Deviations from standard English in the speech of primary school children in St. Lucia and Dominica. *IRAL, 7* (3), 165–184.

Carrington, L. (1976). Determining language education policy in Caribbean sociolinguistic complexes. *International Journal of the Sociology of Education, 8,* 127–143.

Carrington, L. (1997). Social contexts conducive to the vernacularization of literacy. In A. Tabouret-Keller, R. LePage, P. Gardner-Chloros, & G. Varro (Eds.), *Vernacular literacy: A re-evaluation* (pp. 82–92). Oxford: Clarendon Press.

Carrington, L., Borely, C., & Knight, H. (1972a). 'Away Robin run': A critical description of the teaching of the Language Arts in the primary schools of Trinidad and Tobago. St. Augustine, Trinidad: University of the West Indies Institute of Education.

Carrington, L., Borely, C., & Knight, H. (1972b). The linguistic exposure of Trinidad children. St. Augustine, Trinidad: University of the West Indies Institute of Education.

Craig, D. (1966). Teaching English to Jamaican Creole speakers: A model of a multi-dialect situation. Language Learning, 16 (1 & 2), 49–61.

Craig, D. (1976). Bidialectal education: Creole and standard in the West Indies. International Journal of the Sociology of Language, 8, 93–134.

Craig, D. (1980). Models for educational policy in creole-speaking communities. In A. Valdman & A. Highfield (Eds.), Theoretical orientations in creole studies (pp. 245–266). New York: Academic Press.

Craig, D. (1983). Teaching standard English to nonstandard speakers: Some methodological issues. Journal of Negro Education, 52 (1), 65–74.

Cummins, J. (1993). Bilingualism and second language learning. Annual Review of Applied Linguistics, 13, 51–70.

Cummins, J. (1994). Knowledge, power and identity in teaching English as a second language. In F. Genessee (Ed.), Educating second language children (pp. 33–58). Cambridge: Cambridge University Press.

Dalphinis, M. (1985). Caribbean and African languages. London: Karia Press.

Dalphinis, M. (1986). Language and communication: Problems and resolutions of the Creole question within the British educational system. In A. Saakana & A Pearse (Eds.), Toward the decolonization of the British educational system (pp. 79–94). London: Frontline Journal/ Karhak House.

DeJean, Y. (1993). An overview of the language situation in Haiti. International Journal of the Sociology of Language, 102, 73–83.

Devonish, H. (1986a). The decay of neo-colonial official language policies. The case of the English-lexicon Creoles. In M. Görlach & J. Holm (Eds.), Focus on the Caribbean (pp. 23–51). Amsterdam: Benjamins.

Devonish, H. (1986b). Language and liberation: Creole language and politics in the Caribbean. London: Karia Press.

Durizot, P. (1996). La question du Créole à l'école en Guadeloupe. Paris: L'Harmattan.

Edwards, V. (1976). Effects of dialect on the comprehension of West Indian children. Educational Research, 18 (2), 83–95.

Edwards, V. (1979). The West Indian language issue in British schools. London: Routledge & Kegan Paul.

Fasold, R. W. (1971). What can an English teacher do about nonstandard dialect? In R.

Jacobson (Ed.), *Studies in English to speakers of other languages and standard English to speakers of a non-standard dialect* (pp. 82–91). New York State English Council.

Feigenbaum, I. (1975). The use of nonstandard English in teaching standard: Contrast and comparison. In P. Stroller (Ed.), *Black American English, its background and its usage* (pp. 143–167). New York: Dell.

Fishman, J., & Leuders-Salmon, E. (1972). What has the sociology of language to say to the teacher? On teaching the standard variety to speakers of dialectal or sociolectal varieties. In J. Cazden & D. Hymes (Eds.), *Functions of language in the classroom* (pp. 67–83). New York: Teachers College Press.

Gerbault, J. (1997) Pedagogical aspects of vernacular literacy. In A. Tabouret-Keller, R. Le Page, P. Gardner-Chloros, & G. Varro (Eds.), *Vernacular literacy: A re-evaluation* (pp. 142–185). Oxford: Clarendon Press.

Jacobson, R. (Ed.) (1971). *Studies in English to speakers of other languages and standard English to speakers of a non-standard dialect.* New York State English Council.

Kephart, R. (2003). Creole English on Carriacou: A sketch and some implications. In M. Aceto & J. Williams (Eds.), *Contact Englishes of the Eastern Caribbean* (pp. 227–239). Amsterdam: Benjamins.

Kochman, T. (1969, Spring/Summer). Social factors in the consideration of teaching Standard English. In A. Aarons, B. Gordon, & W. Stewart (Eds.), Linguistic and cultural differences in American education: Special anthology issue. *Florida Foreign Language Reporter*, pp. 87–92.

Kochman, T. (1972). Black American speech events, and a language program for the classroom. In C. Cazden, V. John, & D. Hymes (Eds.), *Functions of language in the classroom* (pp. 211–261). New York: Teachers College Press.

Labov, W. (1967). Some sources of reading problems for speakers of the Black English vernacular. In A. Frazier (Ed.), *New directions in elementary English* (pp. 140–167). Champaign, IL: National Council of Teachers of English.

Le Page, R. B. (1968). Problems to be faced in the use of English as the medium of instruction in four West Indian territories. In J. Fishman (Ed.), *Language problems of developing nations* (pp. 431–443). New York: Wiley.

Midgett, D. (1970). Bilingualism and linguistic change in St. Lucia. *Anthropological Linguistics, 12*, 158–170.

Morris, C., & Nwenmely, H. (1993). The Kwéyòl language and literacy project. *Language and Education, 7* (4), 259–270.

Neuman, S., & McCormick, S. (Eds.). (1995). *Single-subject experimental research: Applications for literacy.* Newark, DE: International Reading Association.

Ovando, C., & Collier, P. (1998). *Bilingual and ESL classrooms: Teaching in multicultural contexts*. Boston: McGraw-Hill.

Pollard, V. (1993). *From Jamaican Creole to standard English: A handbook for teachers*. New York: Caribbean Research Center, Medgar Evers College.

Roberts, P. (1993). Affective factors in the use of creole in the classroom: The resolution of a paradox. Paper presented at Society of Pidgin and Creole Linguistics conference. Amsterdam.

Siegel, J. (1997). Using a pidgin language in formal education: Help or hinderance? *Applied Linguistics*, *18* (1), 86–100.

Siegel, J. (1999a). Stigmatized and standardized varieties in the classroom: Interference or separation? *TESOL Quarterly*, *33* (4), 701–728.

Siegel, J. (1999b). Creoles and minority dialects in education: An overview. *Journal of Multilingual and Multicultural Development*, *20* (6), 508–531.

Simmons-McDonald, H. (1996). Language education policy: The case for Creole in formal education in St. Lucia. In P. Christie (Ed.), *Caribbean language issues old and new* (pp. 120–142). Barbados: University of West Indies Press.

Simmons-McDonald, H. (1998). Developmental patterns in the acquisition of English negation by speakers of St. Lucian French Creole. In P. Christie, B.

Lalla, V. Pollard, & L. Carrington (Eds.), *Studies in Caribbean language II* (pp. 75–99). Trinidad and Tobago: Society for Caribbean Linguistics.

Simmons-McDonald, H. (2000, August). Language education and the vernacular speaker: A model for multilingual competence. Paper presented at the 13th Biennial conference of the Society for Caribbean Linguistics, Mona, Jamaica. Forthcoming.

Simmons-McDonald, H. (2001, February). *Vernacular literacy: Influencing policy through pedagogical experimentation*. Paper presented at the annual conference of the American Association for Applied Linguistics Conference, St. Louis, MO.

Simmons-McDonald, H. (in press). The effects of vernacular instruction on the development of bi-literacy abilities of native speakers of French Creole. In I. Robertson & H. Simmons-McDonald (Eds.), *Exploring the boundaries of Caribbean creole languages*. Barbados, Jamaica, Trinidad & Tobago: University of West Indies Press.

Stroller, P. (1975). *Black American English, its background and its usage*. New York: Dell.

Sutcliffe, D. (1982). *British Black English*. Oxford: Basil Blackwell.

Swain, M., & Lapkin, S. (1991). Heritage language children in an English-French bilingual program. *Canadian Modern Language Review*, *47* (4), 635–641.

Valdman, A. (1988). Diglossia and language conflict in Haiti. *International Journal of the Sociology of Language*, *71*, 67–80.

Wiley, T. (1996). *Literacy and language diversity in the United States*. McHenry, IL: Center for Applied Linguistics/Delta Systems.

Williams, J., & Snipper, G. (1990). *Literacy and bilingualism.* New York: Longman.

Wilson, D., Smikle, J., & Grant, N. (2001). *Using children's literature to improve literacy skills in early primary grades: A study of the literature-based language arts project 1998–2000.* Kingston, Jamaica: University of the West Indies.

Winch, C., & Gingell, J. (1994). Dialect interference and difficulties with writing: An investigation in St. Lucian primary schools. *Language and Education, 8* (3), 157–182.

Winer, L. (1990). Orthographic standardization for Trinidad and Tobago: Linguistic and sociopolitical considerations. *Language Problems and Language Planning, 14* (3), 237–268.

Winer, L. (1993). Teaching speakers of Caribbean English Creoles in North American classrooms. In W. A. Glowka & C. D. Lance (Eds.), *Language variation in North American English: Research and teaching* (pp. 191–198). New York: Modern Language Association of America.

10. RESEARCH PERSPECTIVES ON TEACHING ENGLISH AS A LINGUA FRANCA

Barbara Seidlhofer

This chapter shows just how deeply affected English has already been through its unprecedented spread, and the unique function it has as *the* world language. It argues, however, that it would be premature to launch into a discussion of the teaching of this lingua franca before certain prerequisites have been met. The most important of these are a conceptualization of speakers of lingua franca English as language users in their own right, and the acknowledgment of the legitimacy of, and indeed the need for, a description of salient features of English as a lingua franca (ELF), alongside English as a native language (ENL). The presentation summarizes the empirical research into the lingua franca use of English, which has recently gathered considerable momentum. It sets this research in relation to other relevant work in descriptive linguistics, sociolinguistics, and applied linguistics for language pedagogy. Finally, it discusses the implications of this historically unique situation for potential developments in the pedagogy of English teaching and outlines some research questions that must be addressed if advances in the teaching of English as a lingua franca are to have a secure theoretical and descriptive base.

In the early 21st century, English in the world is in a state of delicate balance, or what physicists call "unstable equilibrium:" while the majority of the world's English users are now to be found in countries where it is a foreign language, control over the norms of the language still rests with speakers for whom it is the first language. Beneke (1991) estimates that about 80 percent of verbal exchanges in which English is used as a second or foreign language do not involve any native speakers of English (also see Gnutzmann, 2000); thus Graddol concludes that "Native speakers may feel the language 'belongs' to them, but it will be those who speak English as a second or foreign language who will determine its world future" (1997, p. 10). This is, therefore, an interesting time for considering the increasing use of English in what Kachru (1992) has termed the Expanding Circle,[1] and to reflect on the consequences that the global spread of English is likely to have on the conceptualization, development, and teaching of English.

Defining Terms

English as an International Language

Wherever English is referred to as the preferred option for communication among people from different first language backgrounds, the denomination *English* tends to get modified by the addition "as a (n) x" : "English as an international language" (EIL) (e.g., Jenkins, 2000; McKay, 2002), "English as a lingua franca" (ELF) (e.g., Gnutzmann, 2000; Seidlhofer, 2001), "English as a global language" (e.g., Crystal, 1997; Gnutzmann, 1999a), "English as a world language" (e.g., Mair, 2003), "English as a medium of intercultural communication" (e.g., Meierkord, 1996). The term *International English* is sometimes used as a shorthand for EIL, but is misleading in that it suggests that there is one clearly distinguishable, codified, and unitary variety called *International English*, which is certainly not the case.

In fact, the term 'International English' is sometimes employed for the English used in territories where it is a majority first language or an official additional language, as in Todd and Hancock (1986) and Trudgill and Hannah (2002). The same approach is also taken by the International Corpus of English, or ICE; see, for example, Greenbaum's explanation "Excluded from ICE is the English used in countries where it is not a medium for communication between natives of the country" (1996, p.4). This definition of International English, limiting itself as it does to contexts with an *institutionalized intranational* role for English, (i.e., Kachru's Inner and Outer Circles) is thus not only different but actually in complementary distribution with the lingua franca perspective of the Expanding Circle, which is the focus of this paper.

It is important to note that the term *International English* is thus used in reference to two quite different linguacultural situations: on the one hand, there are Kachru's Outer Circle countries, where English can be said to be localized to meet domestic, intranational purposes. On the other hand, there is English as a globalized means for international communication, which, of course, transcends all national boundaries. The difference between localized and globalized forms of EIL naturally cuts across the Outer/Expanding Circle distinction, since communities that use English intranationally in the Outer Circle also participate in the global uses of English as do, of course, Inner Circle speakers. English has expanded in its use across all of the regions that Kachru has so clearly distinguished.

Whatever terms are chosen, then, it is obvious that the uses of English internationally are not only to be associated with the Expanding Circle but also include speakers of English as a native language in all its dialects (i.e., Kachru's Inner Circle), as well as speakers of New Englishes, or indigenized/nativized varieties (i.e., Kachru's Outer Circle). All these contribute to the phenomenon captured by the term *World Englishes* (for comprehensive overviews of which, see Jenkins, 1998, 2002, 2003; McArthur, 1998; and Melchers & Shaw, 2003).

English as a Lingua Franca

The term *lingua franca* is usually taken to mean "any lingual medium of communication between people of different mother tongues, for whom it is a second language" (Samarin, 1987, p. 371). In this definition, then, a lingua franca has no native speakers, and this notion is carried over into definitions of English as a lingua franca (henceforth ELF), as in the following two examples:

[ELF is] a "contact language" between persons who share neither a common native tongue nor a common (national) culture, and for whom English is the chosen foreign language of communication (Firth, 1996, p. 240).

ELF interactions are defined as interactions between members of two or more different linguacultures in English, for none of whom English is the mother tongue (House, 1999, p. 74).

While these definitions could be said to capture ELF in its purest form, it has to be remembered that ELF interactions often also include interlocutors from the Inner and Outer Circles, and can indeed take place in these contexts, such as at academic conferences in Madras or meetings of the United Nations in New York. Whatever the setting, ELF interactions often occur in influential networks, (i.e., global business, politics, science, technology and media discourse), "[so] it seems vital to pay more attention to the nature of ELF interactions, and ask whether and how they are different from both interactions between native speakers, and interactions between native speakers and nonnative speakers. An answer to this question would bring us closer to finding out whether and in what ways ELF interactions are actually *sui generis*" (House, 1999, p. 74).

What House identifies here is crucial for appreciating the current unprecedented linguistic situation. For the first time in history, a language has reached truly global dimensions, and as a consequence, is being shaped, in its international uses, at least as much by its nonnative speakers as its native speakers. This process has been accelerated by the dramatic expansion of electronic communication through the Internet, which has so far enhanced the social prestige attributed to typical global users of English—global players, indeed—although there are already signs that English may not always enjoy the status of the primary Internet language. For the moment, however, the situation seems to be as Brumfit describes it:

> The members of the expanding circle who do use English are an increasingly significant group who operate in an increasingly global economy which has an impact on the economy in all countries...[and] the Internet, mobile phones and other technology increasingly establish the potential for use of English which is quite independent of the controls offered by traditional educational systems, publishing outlets and radio/television (Brumfit, 2002, p. 5).

Another factor accelerating language change is that the overall changes in the environments in which English is used mean that the language is used more and more for practical purposes by people with very varied norms and scopes of proficiency. Many interactions in English are between participants who do not control standard grammar and whose lexis and pronunciation do not conform to any recognized norm. We could describe this as a process of internationalisation and destandardization. Nonstandard, unedited English is becoming more and more visible (Melchers & Shaw, 2003, p. 195).

In short, then, ELF has taken on a life of its own, independent to a considerable degree of the norms established by its native users, and that warrants recognition. It is for this reason that ELF would appear to be the preferred term for this phenomenon —not because most lingua franca definitions restrict it to communication among nonnative users as such, but because it best signals that it is those nonnative users that provide the strongest momentum for the development of the language in its global uses as "agents of language change" (Brutt-Griffler, 1998, p. 387).

Conceptualizing ELF

The global spread of English, its causes, and its consequences have long been a focus of critical discussion, but this discussion has not on the whole linked up with a consideration of what has been, and is, happening to the forms of the language as such. In other words, the realization of the global role of English has not so far led to any radical reconceptualization of this English. Instead, what we see is what has been referred to as a "conceptual gap" (Seidlhofer, 2001) in the place where ELF should, by now, be firmly established in people's minds, alongside the notions of English as a native language (ENL).

One main reason for this state of affairs is perhaps that the notion of a language is so closely and automatically tied up with its native speakers that it is very difficult to open up conceptual space for ELF. The problematic and crucial role of the nativeness criterion is also reflected in Outer Circle Englishes. The terms generally employed to refer to Indian English or Nigerian English are nativized or indigenized varieties, although they are also called *nonnative* varieties, even by Kachru himself. What this nomenclature would seem to indicate is just how deeply ingrained the notion of nativeness is in any considerations of language theorizing, description, and therefore teaching, and hence how urgent, and how difficult, it is to shed the conceptual straightjacket of English as a native language when tackling the task of working out appropriate frameworks for ELF (see Brutt-Griffler, 2002; Seidlhofer, 2002b; Seidlhofer & Jenkins, 2003, for discussions of the relationship of Outer and Expanding Circle theorizing and description). As a prominent Outer Circle scholar puts it, in spite of the consensus on the viability of non-native Englishes, there are issues that still remain unsettled. These include the status of innovations in the nativization process, the continued use of native norms as a point of reference, the ambivalence between recognition and acceptance of non-native norms, the adequacy of pedagogical models, and the overriding need for codification. Underlying these issues is the constant pull between native and non-native English norms. Innovations in non-native Englishes are often judged not for what they are or their function within the varieties in which they occur, but rather according to how they stand in relation to the norms of native Englishes (Bamgbose, 1998, p. 1).

Bamgbose is talking about the Outer Circle here, but the same point applies to ELF more generally. Due to the conceptual gap noted above, then, there is virtually no awareness that English as a lingua franca might be what House (1999) calls *sui generis*, a linguistic phenomenon in its own right. Instead, rather than a difference perspective with an acknowledgement of plurality, a tenacious deficit view of ELF in which variation is perceived as deviation from ENL norms and described in terms of errors or fossilization is still pervasive. This view has, of course, been successfully questioned for the Outer Circle, but hardly any recognition has so far been given to the fact that many of the same processes are taking place in the Expanding Circle, which is therefore still expected to conform to the Inner Circle.

The nonrecognition of ELF may also explain why, despite certain dissenting voices (e.g., Cook, 1999; Firth & Wagner, 1997; Kasper, 1998; Sridhar & Sridhar, 1986) virtually all SLA research operates with a native-speaker model and tends to construct nonnative speakers as defective communicators. It is also one reason why learner corpus research (see e.g., Granger, 1998) has so far been geared towards highlighting the difficulties specific L1 groups have with native English to make it easier for those learners to conform to ENL, and why dictionaries and grammars based on the large native-speaker corpora can lay claim to a monopoly of "real English."

The current situation is thus characterized by an inverse relationship between perceived significance and relevance of English in the world at large and linguistic description focusing on the core native-speaker countries—one embracing pluralism, the other ignoring it. It may well be, however, that the balance of power in this unstable equilibrium is about to change. An important factor in this will be the availability of descriptions of ELF.

A quarter of a century after the groundbreaking work on Outer Circle English entered the mainstream, the same kind of conceptual appraisal is now occurring for Expanding Circle English. An important contribution in this respect comes from Brutt-Griffler's *World English* (2002). Although there have certainly been discussions of the status and role of EIL from a sociopolitical perspective (notably Pennycook, 1994; Phillipson, 1992), Brutt-Griffler's account provides a more detailed theoretical framework for the global spread of English, with more explanatory power than has hitherto been available. Brutt-Griffler identifies four central features of the development of global language:

1. Econocultural functions of the language (i.e., World English is the product of the development of a world market and global developments in the fields of science, technology, culture, and the media.)
2. The transcendence of the role of an elite lingua franca; (i.e., World English is learned by people at various levels of society, not just by the socioeconomic elite.)
3. The stabilization of bilingualism through the coexistence of world language with other languages in bilingual/multilingual contexts; (i.e., World English tends to establish itself alongside local languages rather than replacing them, and so contributes to multilingualism rather than jeopardizes it) and
4. Language change via the processes of world language convergence and world language divergence (i.e., World English spreads due to the fact that many people learn it rather than by speakers of English migrating to other areas; thus two processes happen concurrently: new varieties are created and unity in the world language is maintained.)

It is beyond the scope of the present chapter to elaborate on the significant ways in which Brutt-Griffler's perspective challenges accounts of "linguistic imperialism" and "linguistic genocide." In a nutshell, she demonstrates that English owes its global spread as much to the struggle *against* imperialism as to imperialism itself (2002, Ch. 4). The point to be emphasized in the present context, however, is that in Brutt-Griffler's account, bi- or multilingualism is an intrinsic design feature of World English. She provides a carefully researched and well-argued basis for acknowledging the active role of ELF users as *agents* in the spread and development of English: they are not just at the receiving end, but contribute to the shaping of the language and the functions it fulfils and so, as speech communities, take possession of the language. Clearly, this is a perspective with very considerable implications for the conceptualization of English as a lingua franca.

A reconceptualization of ELF, then, would appear to illuminate the following factors:

- Questioning of the deference to hegemonic native-speaker norms in all contexts
- Emphasizing the legitimacy of variation in different communities of use
- Highlighting the need to pursue the attitudinal and linguistic implications of the global spread of English
- Acknowledging the need for description and codification

Describing ELF

But it is clearly not enough simply to recognize the need for a reconceptualization and change of attitude. If we are to think differently about English, we need to know more about what forms it takes in different contexts of use, including lingua franca settings. In other words, changes on the conceptual and attitudinal levels have to be substantiated by descriptive work.

A lesson to be learned from work on Outer Circle varieties of English is that a conceptualization of ELF as discussed in the preceding section, even if its desirability is acknowledged in principle, is unlikely to happen as long as no comprehensive and reliable descriptions of salient features of ELF are available. Description is also important because establishing a linguistic reality, named and captured in reference works alongside ENL and Outer Circle Englishes, is a precondition for acceptance. At present, the idea that some time in the future there may be a descriptive basis for an eventual codification of ELF may sound controversial and utopian, but in fact empirical work on various levels of linguistic description has been under way for several years now. The objective of such research varies from study to study, but taken together, this gradually accumulating body of work will lead to a better understanding of the nature of ELF as such, and this fact alone is likely to have a positive effect on how it is regarded and to lend support to its recognition.

For two main reasons, this research is being undertaken preliminarily on *spoken* data: first, the language is at one remove from the stabilizing and standardizing influence of writing, and second, spoken interactions are overtly reciprocal, allowing studies to capture the online negotiation of meaning in the production and reception of utterances, thus facilitating observations regarding mutual intelligibility among interlocutors.

To make their scope manageable, scholars tend to limit their research primarily in terms of (a) level of language, (b) linguacultural background of interlocutors or (c) domain. These studies, as I have indicated, relate to spoken data, but ELF also manifests itself in the written mode, and this I discuss in the section on Modes of Use.[2]

Descriptions at Specific Levels of Language

In recent years, ELF descriptions have focused on two levels of language: phonology and pragmatics. In what follows, an overview will be given of the most important findings in these areas. An account will also be given of work on ELF lexicogrammar, which is only at its beginnings.

Phonology is a comparatively closed system, and virtually all ELF users speak the language with some trace (more or less pronounced, so to speak) of their L1 accent. It is therefore not surprising that the first comprehensive study of characteristics of ELF interaction should be available in this area, namely, Jenkins's *The Phonology of English as an International Language* (2000). Here Jenkins gives an additional reason for focusing attention on phonological features; it is that, in her data, pronunciation was by far the most frequent cause of intelligibility problems in ELF interactions. Jenkins's work (see also Jenkins, 1998; 2002; in press; this volume), culminating in what she has termed the phonological "Lingua Franca Core," thus takes as its starting point the need for empirical data drawn from interactions between L2 speakers of English to assess which phonological features are—and which are *not*—essential for intelligible pronunciation when English is spoken in lingua franca contexts.

The data on which the phonological Lingua Franca Core (LFC) is based was collected from speakers with a wide range of L1s over several years and by a number of different means: field observation, in which the focus was on instances of miscommunication and communication breakdown in mixed-L1 classrooms and social settings; recordings of different L1 pairs and groups of students engaged in communication tasks such as information gap activities; and an investigation into the production and reception of nuclear (tonic) stress of a group of different L1 users of English. The analysis of the data was carried out to identify which pronunciation "errors" led to intelligibility problems for a different L1 interlocutor and which did not. Those that caused such problems were then incorporated into the LFC, while those that did not were considered, as far as ELF is concerned, to be non-core—different from NS production, but not for that reason "wrong." The core areas thus identified are as follows:

1. The consonant inventory with the exception of the dental fricatives / θ / and / ð /, and of dark 'l' [ɫ], none of which caused any intelligibility problems in the lingua franca data.
2. Additional phonetic requirements: aspiration of word-initial voiceless stops /p/, /t/, and /k/, which were otherwise frequently heard as their lenis counterparts /b/, /d/, and /g/; and shortening of vowel sounds before fortis consonants, and the maintenance of length before lenis consonants, e.g., the shorter / æ / in the word s<u>a</u>t as contrasted with the phonetically longer / æ / in the word s<u>a</u>d.
3. Consonant clusters: no omission of sounds in word-initial clusters, e.g. in p<u>r</u>oper and <u>str</u>ap; omission of sounds in word-medial and word-final clusters only permissible according to L1 English rules of syllable structure so that, for example, the word *friendship* can become /frendʃɪp/ but not /frenʃɪp/ or /fredʃɪp/.
4. Vowel sounds: maintenance of the contrast between long and short vowels, such as the / ɪ / and / iː / in the words *live* and *leave*; L2 regional vowel qualities otherwise intelligible provided they are used consistently, with the exception of the substitution of the sound / ɜː / especially with / ɑː /.
5. Production and placement of nuclear (tonic) stress, especially when used contrastively (e.g., He came by TRAIN vs. He CAME by train).

Worth emphasizing in the present context is that Jenkins's LFC does not include, for instance, some sounds which are regarded, and taught, as "particularly English" ones (and also as particularly difficult) in countless classrooms, such as the th-sounds / θ / and / ð / and the dark l allophone, [ɫ]. In the conversations analyzed by Jenkins, mastery of these sounds proved not to be crucial for mutual intelligibility, and so various substitutions, such as /f, v/ or /s, z/ or /t, d/ for / θ, ð / are permissible, and indeed are also found in some native-speaker varieties. The sounds / θ /, / ð/ and [ɫ] are therefore designated non-core. The same is true of the following features:

- Vowel quality
- Weak forms
- Other features of connected speech such as assimilation
- Pitch direction to signal attitude or grammatical meaning
- Word stress placement
- Stress-timing

Jenkins has repeatedly pointed out that her LFC may need to be modified in the light of more data, maybe from additional L1s, but to date no studies that investigated her findings from the perspective of such additional languages have falsified her results. Whether or not modifications become necessary with more research, Jenkins's work is groundbreaking in that in the genuine difference (rather than deficit) perspective she takes, divergences from native speaker realizations in the non-core areas are regarded as perfectly acceptable instances of L2 sociolinguistic variation.[3]

As mentioned above, the availability of a substantial treatment of ELF phonology is primarily due to two factors, namely the importance of pronunciation for intelligibility and the relative manageability of its features. The interest in ELF pragmatics seems to be attributable to somewhat different reasons. With phonological matters, one is dealing with fairly specific features of the language itself; however, one is necessarily on less solid ground with pragmatics, which does not comprise a closed set of features for study. Pragmatics is thus less constrained and thus less manageable in research; furthermore, unlike the case for pronunciation features, violations of ENL pragmatic norms rarely lead to loss of intelligibility (in so far as this becomes manifest in interactions). Nevertheless, a range of studies has been undertaken in this area. This may be due to the perceptual salience of some pragmatic features (such as long pauses, overlapping speech, or abrupt topic changes), as well as to a tradition of taking account of pragmatics in studies of intercultural communication (see e.g., Blommaert & Verschueren, 1991; Bremer, Roberts, Vasseur, Simonot, & Broeder, 1996; Spencer-Oatey, 2000). It is worth emphasizing, however, that while distinctive features of pronunciation can be observed even in short stretches of speech, and it is therefore possible to arrive at generalizable findings on the basis of a relatively small corpus, analogous pragmatic features are likely to occur much more sporadically, and therefore studies in the area of pragmatics would require much larger databases. Probably mainly for this reason, the existing individual studies of the (intercultural) pragmatics of nonnative–nonnative communication in English are not as easy to summarize. However, some fairly clear insights are emerging.

Most research in this area is being conducted by scholars in a number of Expanding Circle countries. Thus Firth (1996), Meierkord (1996, 2002), House (1999, 2002), Lesznyák (2002, 2003, 2004), and Wagner and Firth (1997) analyze data from a wide range of first language backgrounds. Their findings obviously vary with the research questions posed and the contexts in which the data were captured (e.g., dinner conversations, group discussions, simulated conferences, and business telephone calls). Nevertheless, some generalizations about the pragmatics of ELF can be made, all interrelated but listed separately here:

- Misunderstandings are not frequent in ELF interactions; when they do occur, they tend to be resolved either by topic change or, less often, by overt negotiation using communication strategies such as rephrasing and repetition.
- Interference from L1 interactional norms is very rare—a kind of suspension of expectations regarding norms seems to be in operation.
- As long as a certain threshold of understanding is obtained, interlocutors seem to adopt what Firth (1996) has termed the "let-it-pass principle," which gives the impression of ELF talk being overtly consensus-oriented, cooperative and mutually supportive, and thus fairly robust.

While the finding of a high level of cooperation and mutual support is a general one across studies, House (1999, 2002) does sound a more skeptical note, pointing to the danger that superficial consensus may well hide sources of trouble at a deeper level, a caveat that needs to be taken seriously and investigated further. Other features of ELF pragmatics that House has pointed to are the tendency of interlocutors to behave in a fairly "self-centered" way and to pursue their own agendas and, in certain groups, to engage in series of "parallel monologues" rather than dialogues.

It will not come as a surprise that interlocutors' cultural background and shared knowledge (or lack thereof) have been found to be important factors in ELF conversations. On the basis of her empirical study of small talk conversations, Meierkord concludes that lingua franca communication is "both a linguistic masala and a language 'stripped bare' of its cultural roots" (Meierkord, 2002, p. 128f.); while Pölzl demonstrates that speakers' cultural identity "can be asserted, negotiated or expanded in lingua franca contact situations" (Pölzl, 2003).

It will be apparent that some of the findings summarized here actually seem to contradict each other. The explanation for this may be that work on ELF pragmatics is still very much in its initial phase, and the findings available to date result from research on a fairly limited database. It is therefore conceivable that further research might show some of the present findings to be a function of the type and purpose of the interactions investigated. Indeed, the differences in the analyses available to date would seem to underline the need for a far larger corpus and ideally, a thick description (Geertz, 1973) of the same data from various angles, so that shared, generalizable features, and processes can be brought to light.

Lexicogrammar, the remaining level of language to be discussed here, constitutes the area in which, apart from a few initial observations summarized below, the smallest amount of description has been undertaken to date. This may be rather surprising because lexicogrammatical features are probably the most noticeable, intuitively accessible ones in ELF speech. Again, the reason for the current dearth of findings may well be that in order to arrive at reliable results, a very large corpus would be a prerequisite.

It is hoped that it will be possible to meet this need through a new research initiative which aims at the compilation of a sizeable and feasible corpus dedicated to capturing the use of ELF by speakers from a variety of first language backgrounds and in a range of settings and domains. The compilation of this corpus, the Vienna-Oxford International Corpus of English (VOICE), is now in progress at the University of Vienna under Seidelhofer's direction (see Seidlhofer, 2002a; 2002b).[4]

10. RESEARCH PERSPECTIVES ON TEACHING ENGLISH AS A LINGUA FRANCA

Like the other data referred to so far, what is captured in VOICE is spoken ELF. More specifically, it is unscripted, largely face-to-face interaction among fairly fluent speakers from a wide range of first language backgrounds whose primary and secondary socialization (i.e., upbringing and education) did not take place through English. The recorded and transcribed speech events range over a variety of settings (professional, informal, educational), functions (exchanging information, enacting social relationships) and participants' roles and relationships (e.g., acquainted/ unacquainted, symmetrical/asymmetrical). They are realized as private and public dialogues, private and public group discussions and casual conversations, and one-to-one interviews.

While the primary aim of VOICE is to provide a basis for whatever type of research scholars wish to conduct, it is envisaged that a useful first research focus might be to complement the work already done on ELF phonology and the initial findings on ELF pragmatics summarized above by concentrating on lexicogrammar, an aspect that tends to be regarded as particularly central to language pedagogy. It is hoped that this general corpus will make it possible to take stock of how the speakers providing the data actually communicate through ELF, and to attempt a characterization of how they use, or rather co-construct, English to do so. The overall objective will be to find out what salient common features of ELF use (if any, notwithstanding all the diversity) emerge, irrespective of speakers' first languages and levels of L2 proficiency.

At this stage, no reliable findings based on quantitative investigations can yet be reported. But many theses and seminar projects conducted on VOICE data at the University of Vienna (e.g., Hollander, 2002; Kordon, 2003; Seidlhofer, 2003) have brought to light certain regularities that at least point to some hypotheses, which in turn are proving useful for formulating more focused research questions. In particular, typical "errors" that most English teachers would consider in urgent need of correction and remediation, and that consequently often get allotted a great deal of time and effort in English lessons, appear to be generally unproblematic and no obstacle to communicative success. These include

- Dropping the third person present tense *–s*
- Confusing the relative pronouns *who* and *which*

- Omitting definite and indefinite articles where they are obligatory in ENL, and inserting them where the do not occur in ENL
- Failing to use correct forms in tag questions (e.g., *isn't it?* or *no?* instead of *shouldn't they?*)
- Inserting redundant prepositions, as in *We have to study about...*)
- Overusing certain verbs of high semantic generality, such as *do, have, make, put, take*
- Replacing infinitive-constructions with *that-clauses*, as in *I want that*
- Overdoing explicitness (e.g. *black color* rather than just *black*)

However, there are recurrent events in these interactions that do cause communication problems and misunderstandings. Unsurprisingly, not being familiar with certain vocabulary items can give rise to problems, particularly when speakers lack paraphrasing skills. Most interesting, perhaps, are cases of "unilateral idiomaticity" (Seidlhofer, 2002b), where particularly idiomatic speech by one participant can be problematic when the expressions used are not known to the interlocutor (s). Characteristics of such unilateral idiomaticity are, for example, e.g., metaphorical language use, idioms, phrasal verbs, and fixed ENL expressions such as *this drink is on the house* or *can we give you a hand*. Other ongoing work in this area (Dewey, 2003, on lexicogrammar, and Prodromou, 2003, on phraseology, particularly idiomaticity) seems to corroborate these initial findings.

Descriptions of ELF Used by Interlocutors from Particular Linguacultural Backgrounds

While most published descriptive ELF studies either try to include speakers from as wide a range of L1s as possible or leave that variable to chance, there are others who prefer to clearly delimit which subset of speakers they want to investigate, concentrating on ELF in specific regions. For example, as the contributions to Kirkpatrick (2002) make clear, English in East and Southeast Asia is increasingly being used by nonnative speakers for communication with other nonnative speakers in the region (see also Okudaira, 1999). Thus English has become the de facto official language of the Association of South East Asian Nations (ASEAN), and empirical work is underway to describe how this ELF is used (see in particular the journal *Asian Englishes*, published by ALC Press,

Tokyo). Chinese is often mentioned, alongside Spanish, as the most likely rival of English for global lingua franca status after 2050 (see Graddol, 1997), but current statistics demonstrate the remarkable spread of English in the Peoples' Republic of China, and recent estimates put the numbers of English speakers in China at "over 200 million and rising" (Bolton, 2002, p. 182). Accordingly, there are now descriptions of "China English," and already the question is arising as to whether it can be regarded as a nativized variety of English (Kirkpatrick & Zhichang, 2002).

Another region where ELF is of very topical concern is Europe, particularly in the expanding European Union (see Berns, de Bot, & Hasebrink, in press; Cenoz & Jessner, 2000; Deneire & Goethals, 1997; Dörnyei & Csizér, 2002; Graddol, 2001; Hartmann, 1996; Preisler, 1999; van Els, 2000). While the fear that English might take over the entire EU has given rise to a strong policy of supporting societal multilingualism and individual plurilingualism (Beacco & Byram, 2003; Phillipson, 2003; but see also House, 2003), there are, at the same time, efforts under way by linguists to establish whether there may be a distinct regional ELF developing in Europe. Penz (in press) discusses instances of successful intercultural communication among speakers from a variety of European languages. Jenkins, Modiano, and Seidlhofer (2001) mention recurrent features that they have observed in this "Euro-English", but also point out that empirical work in this area is only in its initial stages. A geographically more focused project is a corpus of English as a lingua franca in the Alpine-Adriatic region, currently in its pilot phase (James, 2000). This project aims to capture the English used in casual conversations among young people whose first languages are German, Italian, Slovene, and Friulian. James sets out hypotheses as to what findings the future analysis of this use of English might yield and links these up with current work in such areas as bi/multilingualism, (native English) casual conversation, and pidgin and creole linguistics. Outside the European Union, in officially quadrilingual Switzerland there is now a lively debate about English as a lingua franca for Switzerland, referred to as "Pan Swiss English" (Dröschel, Durham, & Rosenberger, in press; Watts & Murray, 2001; see also Murray, 2003).

Descriptions of ELF Used in Particular Domains

International business has long had to face up to the realities of ELF, but generally there has not been a great deal of interaction and cross-fertilization between what happens in multinational companies and what is investigated in descriptive linguistics. However, Firth (1996), Gramkow Andersen (1993), Hollqvist (1984), Louhiala-Salminen (2002), and Meeuwis (1994) illustrate the potential that empirical research holds for a better understanding of how ELF functions in international business settings. In a recent study, Haegeman (2002) investigates ELF business telephone calls made by employees of companies in Flanders, Belgium, and in particular highlights the structural adjustments that the interlocutors make to orient themselves toward are another's perceived variable competence in the language.

Academic communication is another domain in which ELF is prominent. Again, the study of spoken ELF in this area (as opposed to investigations of the written language, see next section) is in its infancy. At the English department of Tampere University, Finland, a corpus of English as a Lingua Franca in Academic settings (ELFA) is now being compiled. This seeks to capture spoken interactions among speakers of different, mostly European, L1s in international degree programs and other university activities regularly carried out in English. Preliminary findings reveal both similarities and differences compared to NS academic speaking. One such similarity is that metadiscourse seems connected to hedges (as in *perhaps we could eh look an extract now*), while a difference that seems to be emerging is a particularly high occurrence of self-repairs (Mauranen, 2003, in press). These examples show how pragmatic functions are expressed in this domain of ELF talk, but they also raise the interesting question of how these are realized at the other levels of language. Thus such hedging may be realized lexicogrammatically in different ways in different domains and by speakers from different first languages. Equally, there may be similarities across domains and first language backgrounds in the formal realizations of these functions. It is precisely these empirical issues that call for further descriptive work.[5] Another domain in which English has long been used as a lingua franca is international air and sea travel, and proposals have been made for designing an effective mode of communication for these purposes (see Weeks, Glover, Johnson, & Strevens, 1988). But it is surprising how little research has been undertaken to date in describing this lingua franca as it actually occurs (but see Intemann, 2003, and Sampson & Zhao, 2003).

As will be evident from the examples briefly reviewed here, the bulk of the descriptive work still needs to be done. However, what is clear is that this is a very active field of research that will be able to benefit from recent advances in computer-aided description and draw on a wealth of relevant sociolinguistic work on language variation and change, bi- and multilingualism, and language contact. Obviously, ELF is a natural language and can thus be expected to undergo the same processes that affect other natural languages, especially in contact situations—for instance, regularization is evident in most of the data analyzed so far. Another important insight from the study of intercultural ELF interactions is that proficiency in the language code only accounts for part of the success or failure of communication; at least as important is a more general communicative capability, such as sensitivity to the limits of shared systemic and schematic knowledge, as well as accommodation skills (the significance of the latter is particularly clearly demonstrated in Jenkins, 2000). Also of great interest is that this work will put to the test some of the concepts and analytic tools that have emerged from analyses of native-speaker language use but have, at least implicitly, been assumed to be universally applicable. As Meierkord puts it, "a lot of the existing definitions and categories are ethnocentric constructs that do not stand a test with intercultural data and need a re-definition." Analyzing ELF will thus be a challenging exercise seeking to combine continuity and change.

ELF and Modes of Use

The research reported above has been conducted on spoken ELF, for it is in the immediacy of interaction and the co-construction of spoken discourse that variation from the familiar standard norms becomes most apparent. But English has, of course, become internationalized across modes of written discourse as well, particularly as these have developed to serve specific academic and other institutional purposes, and a good deal of descriptive work has been done on identifying their typical generic features (e.g., Bhatia, 1993; Swales, 1990; and numerous papers in the journal *English for Specific Purposes*). Although lexically and generically distinctive, these modes of written ELF have, so far at least, conformed to the norms of standard grammar. It stands to reason that in written language use, where there is no possibility of the overt reciprocal negotiation of meaning typical of spoken interaction, there is more reliance on established norms, and these are naturally maintained by a process of self-regulation whereby these norms are followed in the interests of maintaining global mutual intelligibility

(Widdowson, 1997a). Even here, however, questions have arisen about the legitimacy of these norms, and the extent to which written English (in articles in learned journals, for example) should be subjected to correction to conform to native speaker conventions of use, thus allowing ENL journals to exert a gatekeeping function based not on academic expertise but purely on linguistic criteria whose relevance for international intelligibility has not actually been demonstrated (Ammon, 2000, 2001). As these written modes become increasingly used and appropriated by nonnative users, one might speculate—in line with what we know about language variation and change in general and Brutt-Griffler's notion of macro-acquisition in particular—that, in time, self regulation might involve a detachment from a dependence on native norms, so that these written modes also take on the kind of distinctive features that are evident in spoken ELF.

Whatever the focus of the descriptive work on ELF now being undertaken, it will be able to build on scholarship in the areas of native language variation and change (e.g., Chambers, Trudgill, & Schilling-Estes, 2001), indigenized varieties (e.g., Kachru, 1992; Schneider, 2003), and language contact (Goebl, Nelde, Stary, & Wölck, 1996), as well as studies of simplification in language use and language pedagogy (e.g., Tickoo, 1993), plus older conceptual and empirical work on English as an international language (e.g., Basic English; see Seidlhofer, 2002c). Two research projects that may prove to be of particular relevance for formulating research questions and hypotheses concerning the description of ELF are the International Corpus of English (ICE) and the International Corpus of Learner English (ICLE) already mentioned. ICE, which captures 1 million words of spoken and written texts each in over a dozen varieties is described as "the first large-scale effort to study the development of English as a world language" (ICE Web site: http://www.ucl.ac.uk/english-usage/ice/index.htm, accessed November 19, 2003). ICE components available at present are those of East Africa, Great Britain, India, New Zealand, Philippines (written only) and Singapore. But it needs to be pointed out that this world language is defined in terms of speakers for whom English is "either a majority first language...or an official additional language" (Greenbaum, 1996, p. 3). So although the corpus is indeed international and captures Englishes across the globe, it is important to realize that it actually excludes the use of English by the worldwide majority of English speakers, namely those for whom it mainly functions as an international lingua franca, most of whom are nonnative speakers of English. However, discussions such as those found in the contributions to, e.g., Greenbaum and Nelson (1996), Mair and Hundt (2000), and Renouf (1998) can serve as excellent sensitizing devices for processes of language variation and change that are likely to be at work in ELF as well.

There is also one large-scale project focusing on the English of learners from a great variety of first language backgrounds: the International Corpus of Learner English (ICLE) at the Centre for English Corpus Linguistics in Louvain, Belgium (see de Haan, 1998; the contributions to Granger, 1998; Granger, Hung, & Petch-Tyson, 2002; and more extensive studies based on this corpus, e.g., Lorenz, 1999). However, the main thrust of this research enterprise is not a description of ELF use as conceived of in the present chapter. Rather, ICLE intends, as indeed its name indicates, to identify characteristics of written *learner* English from different L1 backgrounds, with the objective to facilitate comparisons between these foreign-language productions and those of native speakers, and so to highlight the difficulties specific L1 groups have with native English in order to make it easier for learners to conform to ENL if they so wish. In this respect, investigations of ICLE data could serve as empirical tests of the points made in Swan and Smith (2001). The compilation of a spoken companion corpus, LINDSEI, is now under way (see http://www.fltr.ucl.ac.be/fltr/germ/etan/cecl/Cecl-Projects/Lindsei/lindsei.htm, retrieved November 19, 2003). The main difference between ICLE/LINDSEI and VOICE thus lies in the researchers' orientation towards the data and the purposes they intend the corpora to serve. However, it is possible that some of the findings emerging from learner corpora could also contribute to a better understanding of English as a lingua franca. For instance, what is frequently reported as overuse or underuse of certain expressions in learner language as compared to ENL (e.g., Chen, 1998; Lorenz, 1998) may turn out to be features characterizing successful ELF use. In other words, some so-called deviations from ENL norms reported in learner corpora research could serve as pointers in the process of profiling ELF.

Teaching ELF?

It seems, then, that the growing awareness of the unique global role of English and its cultural, ecological, sociopolitical and psychological implications is gradually leading to the realization that these momentous developments also have linguistic consequences that are waiting to be noticed and described. Although this descriptive work is only in its early stages, the fact that it is being undertaken does raise the question as to what implications the eventual availability of ELF descriptions may have for the teaching of English (see Gnutzmann & Intemann, in press). Obviously, if a language is perceived to be changing in its forms and its uses, it is reasonable to expect that something in the teaching of it will also change. However, this is not to say that descriptive facts can, or should, determine what is taught. This caveat is an important theme in Widdowson (2003), a book that combines considerations of the global role of English with a critical evaluation of the pedagogic relevance of linguistic description. As Widdowson puts it, "linguistic descriptions cannot automatically meet pedagogic requirement," and it would therefore be wrong to assume that "findings should directly and uniquely inform what is included in language courses" (Widdowson, 2003, p. 106). Language pedagogy should thus refer to, but not defer to, linguistic descriptions.

In the case of ELF, then, the crucial recent innovation is that linguistic descriptions that teaching professionals can refer to if they so wish *are* becoming available. So far, the absence of sufficient descriptive work as a necessary precondition for ELF-focused curricula has been an obstacle to the adoption of ELF for teaching, even where this is perceived as appropriate. This has made it difficult for resistance to ENL norms in pedagogy (e.g., Canagarajah, 1999; Pennycook, 1999) to move from programmatic statements to realizations in teaching practice. This lack is gradually being remedied by the linguistic research described here, now being carried out with increasing intensity, and in a favorable climate of opinion which is critical of the hegemony of traditional norms of language use. Thus research on ELF is consistent with work undertaken on indigenized varieties of English in postcolonial contexts (for example, in the journals *English World-Wide* and *World Englishes*), in the book series *Varieties of English Around the World* (published by Benjamins), and with positions taken on linguistic imperialism (e.g., Phillipson, 1992), critical discourse analysis (Fairclough & Wodak, 1997), and the sociopolitics of language teaching (e.g., Hall & Eggington, 2000; Ricento, 2000; Singh, Kell, & Pandian, 2002). These intellectual developments are of course responses to both the current rate of globalization in general, and to the spread of English as the epiphenomenon accompanying it. Both have speeded up in recent years, particularly due to the pervasive influence of the Internet, which is "going to change the way we think about language in a fundamental way" (Crystal, 2001, p. 238). As Melchers and Shaw put it, "wide use of English is a natural consequence of the way the world is now" (2003, p. 196).

So it would seem that a critical mass has been gathering that will make possible an eventual reconceptualization of the subject "English" in terms of ELF where this is deemed desirable. Thus McKay argues for the development of "a comprehensive theory of teaching and learning English as an international language" (2002, p. 125). This theory needs to take into account the crosscultural nature of the use of English in multilingual communities, the questioning of native-speaker models, and the recognition of the equality of the varieties of English that have resulted from the global spread of the language. As for actual teaching goals and approaches, McKay (pp. 127 ff.) identifies the following priorities:

Goals:
- Ensuring intelligibility rather than insisting on correctness
- Helping learners develop interaction strategies that will promote comity (friendly relations)
- Fostering textual competence (reading and writing skills for learner-selected purposes)

Approaches:
- Sensitivity in the choice of cultural content in materials
- Reflexivity in pedagogical procedures
- Respect for the local culture of learning

McKay's proposals for "rethinking goals and approaches" (her subtitle) usefully present the state of the art of approaching EIL pedagogy. An important next step will be to take into account new developments in the conceptualization and description of ELF because, after all, it is the language itself that constitutes the essential content of language teaching. The most radical changes in English teaching are likely to happen once rethinking in pedagogy and reconceptualization in language description find expression in new curricula and materials (see Smit, 2003; and also Whittaker & Whittaker, 2002, for an example of a textbook explicitly aiming at ELF rather than ENL).

It will thus be apparent that it would be premature to make detailed pedagogical suggestions at this stage. However, it is worth attempting a broad outline of likely consequences of an orientation towards teaching ELF. Some of these would simply result from the recognition of excellent proposals and practices already available in the public domain, so far not taken up in mainstream English teaching but likely to be found supremely relevant to EFL contexts. For one thing, a reorientation of English away from the fascination with ENL and toward the cross-cultural role of ELF will make it easier to take on board findings from research into the related areas of *intercultural communication* (e.g., Bremer et al., 1996; Buttjes & Byram, 1990; Byram & Fleming, 1998; Byram & Grundy, 2003; Gumperz & Roberts, 1991) and language awareness (e.g., Bolitho, Carter, Hughes, Ivanic, Masuhara, & Tomlinson, 2003; Doughty, Pearce, & Thornton, 1971; Hawkins, 1991; James & Garrett, 1991; van Lier, 1995; and Widdowson, 1997b).

Abandoning unrealistic notions of achieving perfect communication through 'native-like' proficiency in English would free up resources for focusing on capabilities that are likely to be crucial in ELF talk. These are discussed in work on communication strategies (e.g., Kasper & Kellerman, 1997) and accommodation skills (e.g., Giles & Coupland, 1991; Jenkins, 2000, Ch. 7). They include the following: drawing on extralinguistic cues, identifying and building on shared knowledge, gauging and adjusting to interlocutors' linguistic repertoires, supportive listening, signaling noncomprehension in a face-saving way, asking for repetition, paraphrasing, and the like. Needless to say, exposure to a wide range of varieties of English and a multilingual, comparative approach (in the spirit of the Language Awareness/*Eveil aux Langues* project of the Council of Europe; see, e.g., Candelier & Macaire, 2000; Masats, n.d.), are likely to facilitate the acquisition of these communicative abilities. Such synergies achieved through the meeting of languages in classrooms would also make overlong instruction in English (conceptualized as ENL) superfluous. Indeed, it would no longer be self-evident that a subject called English needs to remain in all language teaching curricula—for some contexts, it might be worth considering whether so-called English courses in secondary school that often range over up to nine years or more could be replaced by a subject designated *language awareness* which would include instruction in ELF awareness as one element. The focus here would be on teaching *language* rather than *languages* (see Edmondson, 1999). The assumption underlying this admittedly bold idea is that the demand for English will be self-sustaining, both societally and throughout individuals' lives, and need not—and indeed cannot—be met within the confines of a school subject. What can be done in teaching is to provide a basis that students can learn and can subsequently use for fine-tuning (usually after leaving school) to any native or nonnative varieties and registers that turn out to be relevant for their individual requirements (see Widdowson, 2003). Such a basis for subsequent learning could indeed be formulated with reference to the core features of ELF that current descriptive research aims to establish.

Obviously, changes in teaching also bring with them changes in assessment. In her book on the phonology of English as an international language, Jenkins comes to the conclusion that "an overhaul of pronunciation testing" (2000, p. 212) will be necessary. She argues that instead of assessing learners' approximation to a NS accent, greater account will have to be taken of "the ways in which [candidates] adapt their pronunciation to facilitate one another's understanding, and the extent to which they successfully achieve mutually intelligible pronunciation" (p. 213). Focusing on lexicogrammar, Lowenberg (2002) presents a strong argument for reviewing testing practices once nativized forms are found to be developing in the Expanding Circle. He concludes with the observation that "the existence of [such] norms casts serious doubt on the hitherto assumed validity in the Expanding Circle of certain item types in English proficiency tests that are based solely on Inner Circle norms" (Lowenberg, 2002, p. 434). In this process of attitude change, the recognition of Expanding Circle language rights is likely to benefit from the pioneering work for the codification and acceptance of indigenized Outer Circle varieties (e.g., Bamgbose, 1998).

All these developments are bound to affect teacher education in a major way. Teachers of English need to understand the implications of the unprecedented spread of the language and the complex decisions they will be required to take. While in a traditional foreign language teaching framework it has been possible to rely on fairly clear and stable norms and goals, these certainties have been called into question by the recognition of the global lingua franca role English has to serve. As a result, the teaching of English is going through a truly postmodern phase in which old forms and assumptions are being rejected while no new orthodoxy can be offered in their place. This state of affairs makes the familiar distinction between education and training more relevant than ever: Rather than just being trained in a restricted set of pre-formulated techniques for specific teaching contexts, teachers will need a more comprehensive education which enables them to judge the implications of the ELF phenomenon for their own teaching contexts and to adapt their teaching to the particular requirements of their learners. Such teacher education would foster an understanding of the processes of language variation and change, the relationship between language and identity, the importance of social-psychological factors in intercultural communication and the suspect nature of any supposedly universal solutions to pedagogic problems.

As an illustration of the kinds of issues teachers will have to take an informed stand on, two very different opinions about the spread of nonnative forms of English are juxtaposed below. The first one comes from a chapter entitled "Global English (?)" in Görlach's (2002) book *Still More Englishes*. The second quotation, which seems to be on its way to the status of a classic, is from Jenkins's *The Phonology of English as an International Language:*

The demand for English will continue and possibly increase, which means that more and more people will acquire broken, deficient forms of English which are adequate to the extent that they permit the communicational functions they were learnt for.... However, the incomplete acquisition reflected in such instances will never become the basis for a linguistic norm, which is, and has always been, based on the consent of the learned and guided by the accepted written norm, which has remained surprisingly homogeneous around the globe.... There is no danger of such deviant uses "polluting" the standards of native speakers even if they become a minority in the global anglophone community. Int[ernational] E[nglish] will not be corrupted by such uses.... (Görlach, 2002, p. 12–13)

There is really no justification for doggedly persisting in referring to an item as 'an error' if the vast majority of the world's L2 English speakers produce and understand it. Instead, it is for L1 speakers to move their own receptive goal posts and adjust their own expectations as far as international (but not intranational) uses of English are concerned.... The perhaps unpalatable truth for NSs is that if they wish to participate in international communication in the 21st Century, they too will have to learn EIL. (Jenkins, 2000, pp. 160, 227).

It will be evident from this chapter that a great deal of work remains to be done before ELF can become a well-founded reality in language pedagogy. In addition to the open descriptive questions, several areas of pedagogic research need investigating. Thus Jenkins (2000, Ch. 7 & 8) identifies several issues that have to be addressed for a successful implementation of her Lingua Franca Core, such as the problem that the very tendency toward accommodation so helpful for phonological convergence in multilingual settings will probably prove to be counterproductive in monolingual classes, in which it is likely to reinforce learners' L1 identities and thus their L1 accents. Another problematic question posed by a focus on intelligibility rather than correctness is how to find a way to measure communicative success defined as the degree to which candidates understand each others' pronunciation (as well as lexicogrammar) and find it acceptable (see also Walker, 2001). A promising way forward in this respect is close observation and detailed analysis of ELF classrooms, ideally stretching over fairly long periods of time, such as the project conducted by Smit (2003). Apart from such pedagogic research questions, the important issue of attitudes towards ELF, by researchers, teachers, learners and the public at large, has only begun to be addressed. In this respect, Rubdy and Saraceni (in press), which includes contributions on ELF by Jenkins, Kirkpatrick, McKay, Prodromou, and Seidlhofer, promises to be an example of constructive debate.

In conclusion, it may be worth emphasizing some important social and psychological advantages that a proper conceptualization of ELF is bound to have for the actual speakers involved. For ENL, and ENL speakers, the option of distinguishing ELF from ENL is likely to be beneficial in that it leaves varieties of native English intact for all the functions that only a first language can perform and as a target for learning in circumstances where ENL is deemed appropriate, as well as providing the option of code-switching between ENL and ELF. This takes pressure off a monolithic concept of English pulled in different directions by divergent demands and unrealistic expectations, a state of affairs frustrating for speakers of both ENL and ELF.

Finally, if ELF is conceptualized and accepted as a distinct manifestation of English not tied to its native speakers, this perspective opens up entirely new options for the way the world's majority of English teachers can perceive and define themselves: instead of being nonnative speakers and perennial, error-prone learners of ENL, they can be competent and authoritative users of ELF. The language teaching profession has too long been obsessed with the native speaker teacher–nonnative speaker teacher dichotomy. The work on ELF described here offers the prospect of abolishing this counterproductive and divisive terminology which hinges on a negative particle, and which has had correspondingly negative effects on English language pedagogy.

Notes:

1. The term *Expanding Circle* can be understood as referring to the actual physical spread of English to various regions of the world. But it is worth noting that English is expanding across a range of different domains of use in which the Inner and Outer Circle speakers are also implicated, so in that sense they are also, of course, part of the expansion.

2. Distinguishing ELF in relation to domain and linguacultural background of speakers would seem to correspond to the distinction between register and dialect varieties, i.e., what Halliday, McIntosh, and Strevens (1964) refer to as variety according to user (dialect) and variety according to use (register). It is important to stress, therefore, that although domain and linguacultural background will clearly influence the forms ELF takes since it is after all a naturally occurring and therefore adaptive means of communication, since it has no native speakers, ELF functions as a register—albeit an unusual one—and not as a dialect as this is usually defined (cf. also James, 2000; Widdowson, 1997a).

3. For a broader contextualisation and discussion of this work, see Jenkins, this volume; for full details of both core and non-core features, see Jenkins, 2000, Ch. 6.

4. See www.univie.ac.at/Anglistik/VOICE. This project is being supported by Oxford University Press, hence the *Oxford* element in its name.

5. This also raises the question as to whether it is justified to refer to ELF as an emerging variety in its own right. Some people think it can ultimately be so described (e.g., Meierkord & Knapp, 2002), and Chambers (2000, p. 285) predicts "a supranational standard" for Global English in less than a century from now. Others are more skeptical (e.g., Gnutzmann, 1999b; Görlach, 1999, 2002). Everything, of course, hinges on the definition of the term *variety* and, importantly, on what emerges from the empirical work described in this chapter

ANNOTATED BIBLIOGRAPHY

Brutt-Griffler, J. (2002). *World English: A study of its development.* Clevedon: Multilingual Matters.

This is a thorough and dispassionate enquiry into the underlying issues. It argues that English owes its existence as a world language not to imperialism alone but also to the struggle against imperialism. Brutt-Griffler's notion of "macroacquisition," the insistence on the significance of societal (rather than individual) SLA, contributes to theories of language spread and language change in that it emphasizes the proactive and not simply the reactive role of users of English in these processes.

Gnutzmann, C. (Ed.). (1999a). *Teaching and learning English as a global language. Native and non-native perspectives.* Tübingen: Stauffenburg.

This collection of papers, which approaches the theme from a wide variety of perspectives, has to be given credit as one of the earliest concerted efforts to gauge the impact of the unprecedented global spread of English on pedagogy. In this sense, the volume offers a kind of snapshot of this new area of enquiry finding its feet and so promotes awareness of a range of possible responses to new challenges and opportunities. However, the book predates the recognition of the crucial role of substantial descriptive work on ELF, which this chapter has argued is a prerequisite for a genuine reconceptualization of ELT.

Jenkins, J. (2000). *The phonology of English as an international language: New models, new norms, new goals.* Oxford: Oxford University Press.

This book is a trailblazer for the teaching of ELF. It unequivocally follows the implications of the international role of English through in both description and suggestions for teaching. It argues that for international uses of English, what counts is mutual intelligibility among ELF users rather than approximation to native-speaker models. The focus may be on phonology, but the in-depth discussion of relevant sociolinguistic and sociopsychological research and its clear delineation of implications for EIL teaching make this book an essential contribution to the theme of this chapter in general.

McKay, S. (2002). *Teaching English as an international language: Rethinking goals and approaches.* Oxford: Oxford University Press.

This handbook for teachers offers a comprehensive but accessible account of a range of issues that need to be considered for developing a thoughtful and culturally sensitive approach to the teaching of English as an international language. It brings readers up to date with current thinking in this area and offers an even-handed appraisal of different proposals which encourages teachers to draw their own conclusions based on their local expertise.

Seidlhofer, B. (2001). Closing a conceptual gap: The case for a description of English as a lingua franca. *International Journal of Applied Linguistics, 11*, 133–158.

In view of the global role of English the orientation to nativespeaker norms is now largely recognized as inappropriate and counterproductive for ELF contexts. But it persists because discussions about 'global English' on the meta-level have not been accompanied by substantial empirical work on the most extensive contemporary use of English worldwide, namely, English as a lingua franca, largely among nonnative speakers. The paper seeks to demonstrate that this is due to a failure to conceptualize speakers of lingua franca English as language users in their own right, and to acknowledge the need for a description of lingua franca English alongside English as a native language. The paper proposes a research agenda to remedy this situation and concludes with a consideration of the potentially very significant impact that an understanding of salient features of ELF would have for pedagogy and teacher education.

Widdowson, H. G. (2003). *Defining issues in English language teaching.* Oxford: Oxford University Press.

This book is true to its title in that it puts its finger on the issues that need thinking through carefully in view of the global spread of English. It makes clear that the changing role and nature of the language requires a reconsideration of some common assumptions about English as a subject for teaching. This reconsideration involves a critical reappraisal of criteria for goals for learning, the relevance of corpus descriptions for the specification of course content and methodology, and the significance of the learner's first language in the learning process.

OTHER REFERENCES

Ammon, U. (2000). Towards more fairness in international English: Linguistic rights of non-native speakers? In R. Phillipson (Ed.), *Rights to language: Equity, power, and education. Celebrating the 60th birthday of Tove Skutnabb-Kangas* (pp. 111–116). Mahwah, NJ: Erlbaum.

Ammon, U. (Ed.). (2001). *The dominance of English as a language of science: Effects on other languages and language communities.* Berlin: Mouton de Gruyter.

Bamgbose, A. (1998). Torn between the norms: innovations in world Englishes. *World Englishes, 17,* 1–14.

Beacco, J.-C., & Byram, M. (2003). *Guide for the development of language education policies in Europe: From linguistic diversity to plurilingual education.* Strasbourg: Language Policy Division, Council of Europe.

Beneke, J. (1991). Englisch als lingua franca oder als Medium interkultureller Kommunikation [English as lingua franca or as medium of intercultural communication]. In R. Grebing (Ed.), *Grenzenloses Sprachenlernen* (pp. 54–66). Berlin: Cornelsen.

Berns, M., de Bot, K., & Hasebrink, U. (Eds.). (in press). *In the presence of English: Media and European youth.* Amsterdam: Benjamins.

Bhatia, V. K. (1993). *Analysing genre: Language use in professional settings.* London: Longman.

Blommaert, J., & Verschueren, J. (Eds.). (1991). *The pragmatics of international and intercultural communication.* Amsterdam: Benjamins.

Bolitho, R., Carter, R., Hughes, R., Ivanic, R., Masuhara, H., & Tomlinson, B. (2003). Ten questions about language awareness. *ELT Journal, 57,* 251–259.

Bolton, K. (2002). Chinese Englishes: From Canton jargon to global English. *World Englishes, 21,* 181–199.

Bremer, K., Roberts, C., Vasseur, M.-T., Simonot, M., & Broeder, P. (Eds.). (1996). *Achieving understanding: Discourse in intercultural encounters.* London: Longman.

Brumfit, C. J. (2002). *Global English and language teaching in the twenty-first century.* Centre for Language in Education Occasional Papers No. 59, University of Southampton.

Brutt-Griffler, J. (1998). Conceptual questions in English as a world language. *World Englishes, 17,* 381–392.

Buttjes, D., & Byram, M. (Eds.). (1990). *Mediating languages and cultures: Towards an intercultural theory of foreign language education.* Clevedon: Multilingual Matters.

Byram, M., & Fleming, M. (Eds.). (1998). *Language learning in intercultural perspective.* Cambridge: Cambridge University Press.

Byram, M., & Grundy, P. (Eds.). (2003). *Context and cultures in language teaching and learning.* Clevedon: Multilingual Matters.

Canagarajah, S. (1999). *Resisting linguistic imperialism in English teaching*. Oxford: Oxford University Press.

Candelier, M., & Macaire, D. (2000). L'éveil aux langues a l'école primaire et la construction de compétences—pour mieux apprendre les langues et vivre dans une société multilingue et multiculturelle [Language awareness in primary school and the development of competencies—for better language learning and for living in a multilingual, multicutural society]. Actes de colloque de Louvain *Didactique des langues romanes: Le développement des compétences chez l'apprenant*. Bruxelles: De Boek.

Cenoz, J., & Jessner, U. (Eds.). (2000). *English in Europe: The acquisition of a third language*. Clevedon: Multilingual Matters.

Chambers, J. K. (2000). World enough and time: Global enclaves of the near future. *American Speech, 75*, 285–287.

Chambers, J K., Trudgill, P., & Schilling-Estes, N. (Eds.). (2001). *The handbook of language variation and change*. Oxford: Blackwell.

Chen, H. (1998). Underuse, overuse, and misuse in a Taiwanese EFL learner corpus. In S. Granger & J. Hung (Eds.), *Proceedings of the First International Symposium on Computer Learner Corpora, Second Language Acquisition and Foreign Language Teaching* (pp. 25–28). Hong Kong: The Chinese University.

Cook, V. (1999). Going beyond the native speaker in language teaching. *TESOL Quarterly, 33*, 185–209.

Crystal, D. (1997). *English as a global language*. Cambridge: Cambridge University Press.

Crystal, D. (2001). *Language and the Internet*. Cambridge: Cambridge University Press.

de Haan, P. (1998). How native-like are advanced learners of English? In A. Renouf (Ed.), *Explorations in corpus linguistics* (pp. 55–65). Amsterdam: Rodopi.

Deneire, M., & Goethals, M. (Guest Eds.). (1997). Special issue on English in Europe. *World Englishes, 16/*1.

Dewey, M. (2003, April). Codifying lingua franca English. Paper presented at IATEFL Conference, Brighton.

Dörnyei, Z., & Csizér, K. (2002). Some dynamics of language attitudes and motivation: Results of a nationwide survey. *Applied Linguistics, 23*, 421–462.

Doughty, P., Pearce, J., & Thornton, G. (1971). *Language in use*. London: Edward Arnold.

Dröschel, Y., Durham, M., & Rosenberger, L. (in press). Swiss English or simply non-native English? A discussion of two possible features. In D. J. Allerton, C. Tschichold, & J. Wieser (Eds.), *Linguistics, language learning and language teaching*. Basel: Schwabe.

Edmondson, W. (1999) Die fremdsprachliche Ausbildung kann nicht den Schulen überlassen werden! [Foreign language training connot be left to the schools]. *Praxis, 46*, 115–123.

Fairclough, N. L., & Wodak, R. (1997). Critical discourse analysis. In T. A. van Dijk (Ed.),

Discourse studies: A multidisciplinary introduction, Vol. 2: Discourse as social interaction (pp. 258–284). London: Sage.

Firth, A., (1996). The discursive accomplishment of normality. On 'lingua franca' English and conversation analysis. *Journal of Pragmatics, 26*, 237–259.

Firth, A. & Wagner, J. (1997). On discourse, communication, and (some) fundamental concepts in SLA research. *Modern Language Journal, 81*, 285–300.

Geertz, C. (1973). *The interpretation of cultures.* New York: Basic Books.

Giles, H., & Coupland, N. (1991). *Language: Contexts and consequences.* Milton Keynes: Open University Press.

Gnutzmann, C. (1999b). English as a global language: Perspectives for English language teaching and for teacher education in Germany. In C. Gnutzmann (Ed.), *Teaching and learning English as a global language: Native and non-native perspectives* (pp. 157–169). Tübingen: Stauffenburg.

Gnutzmann, C. (2000). Lingua franca. In M. Byram (Ed.), *The Routledge encyclopedia of language teaching and learning* (pp. 356–359). London: Routledge.

Gnutzmann, C., & Intemann, F. (Eds.). (in press). *The globalisation of English and the English language classroom.* Clevedon: Multilingual Matters.

Goebl, H., Nelde, P., Stary, Z., & Wölck, W. (Eds.). (1996). *Kontaktlinguistik. Contact linguistics. Linguistique de contact.* Vol. 1. Berlin: De Gruyter.

Görlach, M. (1999). Varieties of English and language teaching. In C. Gnutzmann (Ed.), *Teaching and learning English as a global language: Native and non-native perspectives* (pp. 3–21). Tübingen: Stauffenburg.

Görlach, M. (2002). *Still more Englishes.* Amsterdam: John Benjamins.

Graddol, D. (1997). *The future of English?* London: British Council.

Graddol, D. (2001). The future of English as a European language. *The European English Messenger, 10*, 47–55.

Gramkow Andersen, K. (1993). *Lingua franca discourse: An investigation of the use of English in an international business context.* Unpublished MA thesis, Aalborg University, Denmark.

Granger, S. (Ed.). (1998). *Learner English on computer.* London: Longman.

Granger, S., Hung, J., & Petch-Tyson, S. (Eds.). (2002). *Computer learner corpora, second language acquisition and foreign language teaching.* Amsterdam: Benjamins.

Greenbaum, S. (Ed.). (1996). *Comparing English worldwide: The international corpus of English.* Oxford: Clarendon.

Greenbaum, S., & Nelson, G. (Guest Eds.) (1996). Special issue on studies on International Corpus of English (ICE). *World Englishes*, 15/1.

Gumperz, J., & Roberts, C. (1991). Understanding in intercultural encounters. In J. Blommaert & J. Verschueren (Eds.), *The pragmatics of international and intercultural communication* (pp. 51–90). Amsterdam: Benjamins.

Haegeman, P. (2002). Foreigner talk in lingua franca business telephone calls. In K. Knapp & C. Meierkord (Eds.), *Lingua franca communication* (pp. 135–162). Frankfurt a.M.: Lang.

Hall, J. K., & Eggington, E. (Eds). (2000). *The sociopolitics of English language teaching.* Clevedon: Multilingual Matters.

Halliday, M. A. K., McIntosh, A., & Strevens, P. (1964). *The linguistic sciences and language teaching.* London: Longman.

Hartmann, R. R. K. (Ed.). (1996). *The English language in Europe.* Oxford: Intellect.

Hawkins, E. (1991). *Awareness of language: An introduction* (Rev. ed.). Cambridge: Cambridge University Press.

Hollander, E. (2002). *Is ELF a pidgin? A corpus-based study of the grammar of English as a lingua franca.* Unpublished MA thesis, University of Vienna.

Hollqvist, H. (1984). The use of English in three large Swedish companies. *Studia Anglistica Upsaliensia, 55.*

House, J. (1999). Misunderstanding in intercultural communication: Interactions in English as a lingua franca and the myth of mutual intelligibility. In C. Gnutzmann (Ed.), *Teaching and learning English as a global language* (pp. 73–89). Tübingen: Stauffenburg.

House, J. (2002). Pragmatic competence in lingua franca English. In K. Knapp & C. Meierkord (Eds.), *Lingua franca communication* (pp. 245–267). Frankfurt: Lang.

House, J. (2003). English as a lingua franca: A threat to multilingualism. *Journal of Sociolinguistics, 7* (4), 624–630.

Intemann, F. (2003, June). Taipei ground, confirm the last transmission was in English? Some comments on aviation English as a world language. Paper delivered at conference on The Globalisation of English and the English Language Classroom. Technische Universität, Braunschweig.

James, A. (2000). English as a European lingua franca: Current realities and existing dichotomies. In J. Cenoz & U. Jessner (Eds.), *English in Europe: The acquisition of a third language* (pp. 22–38). Clevedon: Multilingual Matters.

James, C., & Garrett, P. (Eds.). (1991). *Language awareness in the classroom.* London: Longman.

Jenkins, J. (1998). Which pronunciation norms and models for English as an International Language? *ELT Journal, 52,* 119–126.

Jenkins, J. (2002). A sociolinguistically based, empirically researched pronunciation syllabus for English as an International Language. *Applied Linguistics, 23,* 83–103.

Jenkins, J. (2003). *World Englishes.* London: Routledge.

Jenkins, J. (in press). Global intelligibility and local diversity: Possibility or paradox? In R. Rubdy & M. Saraceni (Eds.), *English in the world: Global rules, global roles.* Bangkok:

IELE Press at Assumption University.
Jenkins, J., Modiano, M., & Seidlhofer, B. (2001). "Euro-English." *English Today, 17*, 13–19.
Kachru, B. (Ed.). (1992). *The other tongue* (2nd ed.) Urbana: University of Illinois Press.
Kasper, G. (1998). A bilingual perspective on interlanguage pragmatics. In J. H. O'Mealy & L. E. Lyons (Eds.), *Language, linguistics and leadership* (pp. 89–108). Honolulu: University of Hawai'i Press.
Kasper, G., & Kellerman, E. (Eds.). (1997). *Communication strategies: Psycholinguistic and sociolinguistic perspectives.* London: Longman.
Kirkpatrick, A. (Ed.). (2002). *Englishes in Asia: Communication, identity, power and education.* Melbourne: Language Australia. Ltd.
Kirkpatrick, A. (in press). Which model of English: Native speaker, nativised or lingua franca? In R. Rubdy & M.Saraceni (Eds.), *English in the world: Global rules, global roles.* Bangkok: IELE Press at Assumption University.
Kirkpatrick, A., & Zhichang, X. (2002). Chinese pragmatic norms and "China English." *World Englishes, 21,* 269–279.
Kordon, K. (2003). *Phatic communion in English as a lingua franca.* Unpublished MA thesis, University of Vienna.
Lesznyák, A. (2002). From chaos to the smallest common denominator. Topic management in English lingua franca communication. In K. Knapp & C. Meierkord (Eds.), *Lingua franca communication* (pp. 163–193). Frankfurt a.M.: Lang.
Lesznyák, A. (2003). *Dynamism versus stability. Nonnative speaker discourse in a lingua franca and a foreign language context.* Unpublished Ph.D. dissertation, University of Hamburg.
Lesznyák, A. (2004) *Communication in English as an international lingua franca: An exploratory case study.* Norderstedt, Germany: Books on Demand.
Lorenz, G. (1998). Overstatement in advanced learners' writing: stylistic aspects of adjective intensification. In S. Granger (Ed.), *Learner English on computer* (pp. 53–66). London: Longman.
Lorenz, G. (1999). *Adjective intensification — learners versus native speakers: A corpus study of argumentative writing.* Amsterdam: Rodopi.
Louhiala-Salminen, L. (2002). The fly's perspective: Discourse in the daily routine of a business manager. *English for Specific Purposes, 21,* 211–231.
Lowenberg, P. (2002). Assessing English proficiency in the Expanding Circle. *World Englishes, 21,* 431–435.
Mair, C. (Ed.). (2003). *The politics of English as a world language: New horizons in postcolonial cultural studies.* Amsterdam: Rodopi.
Mair, C., & Hundt, M. (Eds.) (2000). *Corpus linguistics and linguistic theory.* Amsterdam: Rodopi.

Masats, D. (n.d.). Language awareness: An international project. Retrieved November 19, 2003, from http://jaling.ecml.at/english/welcome_page.htm.

Mauranen, A. (2003). Academic English as lingua franca— a corpus approach. *TESOL Quarterly*, *37*, 513–527.

Mauranen, A. (in press). "They're a little bit different". Variation in hedging in academic speech. In K. Aijmer & A-B. Stenström (Eds.), *Discourse patterns in spoken and written corpora*. Amsterdam: John Benjamins.

McArthur, T. (1998). *The English languages*. Cambridge: Cambridge University Press.

McKay, S. L. (in press). EIL curriculum development. In R. Rubdy & M. Saraceni (Eds.), *English in the world: Global rules, global roles*. Bangkok: IELE Press at Assumption University.

Meeuwis, M. (1994). Nonnative-nonnative intercultural communication: An analysis of instruction sessions for foreign engineers in a Belgian company. *Multilingua*, *13*, 59–82.

Meierkord, C. (1996). *Englisch als Medium der interkulturellen Kommunikation. Untersuchungen zum non-native-/non-native speaker Diskurs*. Frankfurt a.M.: Lang.

Meierkord, C. (2000). Interpreting successful lingua franca interaction. An analysis of nonnative / non-native small talk conversations in English. Linguistik online 5. Retrieved November 19, 2003, from http://www.linguistik-online.de/1_00/MEIERKOR.HTM.

Meierkord, C. (2002). "Language stripped bare" or "linguistic masala"? Culture in lingua franca communication. In K. Knapp & C. Meierkord, (Eds.), *Lingua franca communication* (pp. 109–133). Frankfurt a.M.: Lang.

Meierkord, C., &. Knapp, K. (2002). Approaching lingua franca communication. In K. Knapp & C. Meierkord, (Eds.), *Lingua franca communication* (pp. 9–28). Frankfurt a.M.: Lang.

Melchers, G., & Shaw, P. (2003). *World Englishes*. London: Arnold.

Murray, H. (2003). Swiss English teachers and Euro-English: Attitudes to a non-native variety. In H. Murray (Ed.), *Anglais, English, inglese, Englais...English! Bulletin Vals-asla*, *77*, 147–165.

Okudaira, A. (1999). A study of international communication in regional organisations: The use of English as the official language of ASEAN. *Asian Englishes*, *2*, 91–107.

Pennycook, A. (1994). *The cultural politics of English as an international language*. London: Longman.

Pennycook, A. (1999). Pedagogical implications of different frameworks for understanding the global spread of English. In C. Gnutzmann (Ed.), *Teaching and learning English as a global language: Native and non-native perspectives* (pp. 147–155). Tübingen: Stauffenburg.

Penz, H. (in press). Successful intercultural communication. In B. Kettemann & G. Marko (Eds.), *Expanding circles, transcending disciplines, and multimodal texts*. Tübingen: Narr.

Phillipson, R. (1992). *Linguistic imperialism*. Oxford: Oxford University Press.

Phillipson, R. (2003). *English-only Europe? Challenging language policy.* London: Routledge.
Pölzl, U. (2003). Signalling cultural identity in a global language. The use of L1/Ln in ELF. *Vienna English Working Papers, 12* (2), 3–23 (Available: http://www.univie.ac.at/Anglistik/views/current.htm).
Preisler, B. (1999). Functions and forms of English in an EFL country. In T. Bex & R. J. Watts (Eds.), *Standard English: The widening debate* (pp. 239–268). London: Routledge.
Prodromou, L. (2003). In search of the successful user of English. *Modern English Teacher, 12,* 5–14.
Prodromou, L. (in press). Defining the "successful bilingual speaker" of English. In R. Rubdy & M. Saraceni (Eds.), *English in the world: Global rules, global roles.* Bangkok: IELE Press at Assumption University.
Renouf, A. (Ed.). (1998). *Explorations in corpus linguistics.* Amsterdam: Rodopi.
Ricento, T. (Ed.). (2000). *Ideology, politics and language policies: Focus on English.* Amsterdam: Benjamins.
Rubdy, R., & Saraceni, M. (Eds.). (in press). *English in the world: Global rules, global roles.* Bangkok: IELE Press at Assumption University.
Samarin, W. (1987). Lingua franca. In U. Ammon, N. Dittmar, & K. Mattheier (Eds.), *Sociolinguistics: An international handbook of the science of language and society* (pp. 371–374). Berlin: Walter de Gruyter.
Sampson, H., & Zhao, M. (2003). Multilingual crews: Communication and the operation of ships. *World Englishes, 22,* 31–43.
Schneider, E. (2003). The dynamics of New Englishes: From identity construction to dialect birth. *Language, 79,* 233–281.
Seidlhofer, B. (2002a). The case for a corpus of English as a lingua franca. In G. Aston & L. Burnard (Eds.), *The roles of corpora of contemporary English in language description and language pedagogy* (pp. 70–85). Bologna: Cooperativa Libraria Universitaria Editrice Bologna.
Seidlhofer, B. (2002b). *Habeas corpus* and divide et impera: 'Global English' and applied linguistics. In K. Spelman Miller & P. Thompson (Eds.), *Unity and diversity in language use* (pp. 198–217). London: Continuum.
Seidlhofer, B. (2002c). The shape of things to come? Some basic questions. In K. Knapp & C. Meierkord (Eds.), *Lingua franca communication* (pp. 269–302). Frankfurt a.M.: Lang.
Seidlhofer, B. (2003, September). Lexicogrammar in ELF: Some findings from VOICE. Paper presented at the colloquium *Research into English as a lingua franca: The state of the art.* British Association of Applied Linguistics Conference, Leeds.
Seidlhofer, B. (in press). English as a lingua franca in the expanding circle: What it isn't. In R. Rubdy & M. Saraceni (Eds.), *English in the world: Global rules, global roles.* Bangkok:

IELE Press at Assumption University.

Seidlhofer, B., & Jenkins, J. (2003). English as a lingua franca and the politics of property. In C. Mair (Ed.), *The politics of English as a world language: New horizons in postcolonial cultural studies* (pp. 139–154). Amsterdam: Rodopi.

Singh, M., Kell, P., & Pandian, A. (2002). *Appropriating English: Innovation in the global business of English language teaching.* New York: Peter Lang.

Smit, U. (2003). *English as a lingua franca (ELF) as medium of learning in a hotel management educational program: An applied linguistic approach. Vienna English Working Papers, 12* (2), 40–75 (Available: http://www.univie.ac.at/ Anglistik/views/current.htm).

Spencer-Oatey, H. (Ed.). (2000). *Culturally speaking.* London: Continuum.

Swales, J. (1990). *Genre analysis.* Cambridge: Cambridge University Press.

Swan, M., & Smith, B. (2001). *Learner English. A teacher's guide to interference and other problems* (2nd ed.). Cambridge: Cambridge University Press.

Sridhar, K., & Sridhar, S. N. (1986). Bridging the paradigm gap: Second language acquisition theory and indigenised varieties of English. *World Englishes, 5,* 3–14.

Tickoo, M. L. (Ed.). (1993). *Simplification: Theory and application.* Singapore: SEAMEO Regional Language Centre.

Todd, L., & Hancock, I. (1986). *International English usage.* London: Croom Helm.

Trudgill, P., & Hannah, J. (2002). *International English: A guide to varieties of standard English* (4th ed.). London: Arnold.

van Els, T. (2000, Sept. 22). *The European Union, its institutions and its languages.* Public lecture given at the University of Nijmegen, the Netherlands.

van Lier, L. (1995). *Introducing language awareness.* Harmondsworth: Penguin.

Wagner, J., & Firth, A. (1997). Communication strategies at work. In G. Kasper & E. Kellerman (Eds.), *Communication strategies: Psycholinguistic and sociolinguistic perspectives* (pp. 323–344). London: Longman.

Walker, R. (2001). International intelligibility. *English Teaching Professional, 21,* 10–13.

Watts, R., & Murray, H. (Eds.). (2001). *Die fünfte Landessprache? Englisch in der Schweiz* [The fifth official language? English in Switzerland]. Akademische Kommission der Universität Bern.

Weeks, F., Glover, A., Johnson, E., & Strevens, P. (1988). *Seaspeak training manual: Essential English for international maritime use.* Oxford: Pergamon.

Whittaker, P., & Whittaker, J. (2002). *English for Europe.* Olomouc, Czech Republic: InSTEP.

Widdowson, H. G. (1997a). EIL, ESL, EFL: Global issues and local interests. *World Englishes, 16,* 135–146.

Widdowson, H. G. (1997b). The pedagogic relevance of language awareness. *Fremdsprachen Lehren und Lernen, 26,* 33–43.

CURRICULUM, PEDAGOGY, AND TEACHER PREPARATION

11. CROSSING FRONTIERS: NEW DIRECTIONS IN ONLINE PEDAGOGY AND RESEARCH

Richard Kern, Paige Ware, and Mark Warschauer

Research on networked language learning is now entering its second decade. While earlier research tended to focus on the linguistic and affective characteristics of computer-assisted discussion in single classrooms, more recent research has increasingly focused on long-distance collaboration. This type of learning environment is challenging to arrange, because it involves diverse learners who operate with different cultural backgrounds, communicative expectations, and rhetorical frameworks. These features, as well as the fact that the communication takes place both inside and outside of class and on students' own schedules, also pose special research challenges. This chapter summarizes what knowledge has been gained about learning and instruction in long-distance online exchanges, focusing on three key themes: (a) linguistic interaction and development, (b) intercultural awareness and learning, and (c) development of new multiliteracies and their relations to identity. In each area, research has indicated that there is no single *effect* of using online communication, but rather that processes and results vary widely depending on a range of logistical, pedagogical, and social factors.

Research on online language learning is now entering its second decade. Early studies on networked computer use for language learning tended to focus on the most quantifiable and easily measured aspects of online communication. For example, a number of studies (e.g., Kern, 1995; Sullivan & Pratt, 1996; Warschauer, 1996a) compared amount of participation in face-to-face and computer-assisted discussion. Other studies attempted to quantify the linguistic features, language functions, and learning resources used in online communication (Chun, 1994; Herring, 1996; Kern, 1995; Ortega, 1997; Warschauer, 1996a). Still others focused on affect and motivational patterns (Beauvois, 1992; Kelm, 1992; Meunier, 1998).

Beginning several years ago, a second wave of online language learning research pushed for greater attention to particular practices of use, described and evaluated in terms of their specific social contexts, what Kern and Warschauer (2000) refer to as a *sociocognitive* turn in research on network-based language teaching. The studies collected in Warschauer and Kern (2000) attempted to expand the body of online pedagogical research into the areas of *context, interaction*, and *multimedia networking*. The focus went beyond the texts of online interaction to the broader contextual dynamics that shaped (and were shaped by) those texts. This required a shift from primarily quantitative research methods to principally qualitative methods that attempted to account for classroom cultures as well as language use.

More recently, this second wave of online language learning has been deepened by a shift in focus from single classrooms to long-distance collaboration projects. This shift accomplishes three things. First, it expands the focus beyond language learning to an emphasis on *culture* (i.e., intercultural competence, cultural learning, cultural literacy). Second, it expands the notion of context beyond the local (often institutional) setting to include broad social discourses. Third, it problematizes the notions of its own inquiry, namely, communication and intercultural competence.

This chapter summarizes the most important studies in this second wave of online language learning research, with a focus on three key themes: (1) linguistic interaction, (2) intercultural learning, and (3) literacy and identity. In each of these three areas, research has indicated that there is no single automatic "effect" of using online communication, but rather that processes and results vary widely depending on a range of logistical, pedagogical, and social factors.

Linguistic Interaction

The nature of interaction and how it impacts linguistic development has been one of the most important areas of research in second language learning (for a review, see Pica, 1994). It has been suggested that computer-mediated communication (CMC) provides an ideal medium for students to benefit from interaction, since the written nature of the discussion allows greater opportunity to attend to and reflect on the form and content of the communication. Yet most of the early research on the linguistic nature of CMC focused on counting or categorizing individual students' comments rather than qualitatively analyzing how and in what ways students actually negotiated meaning with each other. Recent studies have begun to explore the nature of online student interaction by investigating empirically the relationships among particular language outcomes, the online tools used, and the purposes informing those uses.

Negotiation of Meaning

Drawing on interactionist theories of language acquisition that view negotiation of meaning as an important process in language development, several studies have addressed the question of how best to promote meaning negotiation online. Synchronous interaction has been the predominant choice for this research. In a significant shift in research design from earlier studies that relied mainly on single classroom contexts, over half of the studies reviewed here (Kitade, 2000; Kötter, 2003; Toyoda & Harrison, 2002; Tudini, 2003) brought native- and target-language speakers together from different geographical locations into real-time chat discussions.

To investigate which kinds of classroom tasks promote meaning negotiation online, Blake (2000) examined the interactions of 50 intermediate L2 Spanish learners using *Remote Technical Assistance*, a synchronous chat program. Pairs of students carried out online jigsaw, information-gap, or decision-making tasks, with the jigsaw tasks ultimately promoting the most negotiations. Although the total number of negotiations comprised only a small fraction of the overall conversational turns, Blake argues that CMC provides a good environment for negotiating meaning. However, Blake found a predominance of *lexical* negotiations and relatively few *syntactic* negotiations, leaving open questions about issues of grammatical development.

In a similar vein, Smith (2003) examined negotiation of meaning among 28 intermediate-level English learners communicating on ChatNet during a series of jigsaw and decision-making tasks "seeded" with new lexical items. Smith found that learners did negotiate for meaning when they encountered new words, and that decision-making tasks supported negotiation more than jigsaw tasks (cf. Blake, 2000). Importantly, Smith extends the commonly referenced face-to-face model of meaning negotiation (Varonis & Gass, 1985) to deal specifically with new constraints in CMC.

Another group of synchronous chat studies looks at meaning negotiation as it relates to linguistic and metalinguistic awareness. Pellettieri (2000) studied the interaction of 10 dyads of English-speaking intermediate adult students of Spanish in *ytalk*, a UNIX software program that supports synchronous network-based communication. She examined task-based real-time computer interaction by analyzing the modifications that learners made in response to negotiation signals as well as to corrective feedback. Using frameworks developed from oral interaction, she showed how computer-mediated interaction provided a useful mechanism for helping learners achieve higher levels of metalinguistic awareness. Kitade (2000) examined how students of Japanese benefited from opportunities to interact with native and nonnative speakers in synchronous communication. She found that learners used strategies such as self-correction and collaboration to exploit the linguistic and interactional features of online chatting.

An advantage of online chatting for promoting linguistic and metalinguistic awareness is the ease with which conversational interactions can be downloaded and studied. In their discourse analysis of chat logs between five students of advanced level Japanese and native speakers, Toyoda and Harrison (2002) made suggestions for how students could examine their chat logs to become attentive to language use. Using the Varonis and Gass (1985) model of meaning negotiation, Toyoda and Harrison categorized 45 triggers of miscommunication into nine categories at the word, sentence, and discourse levels. They found that as students moved from the word level to the discourse level, it was difficult to determine whether successful negotiation had taken place. They argue that studying chat logs can help students learn to analyze difficult grammatical and syntactical features of the target language, develop communication strategies for coping with the short reaction time of synchronous discussion, and reflect on how particular words can trigger cultural misunderstandings.

Two recent studies have extended the above research designs by examining bilingual interactions in a multiple-user domain object-oriented, or MOO, environment (that is, an Internet environment that permits multiple users to participate simultaneously), (Kötter, 2003; Schwienhorst, 2002). Kötter's primary focus was linguistic and metalinguistic awareness and the exploitation of the bilingual format of tandem learning, a model of peer interaction that emphasizes autonomy and reciprocity (see Brammerts, 1996). He examined how 29 German and American students in a Vassar-Münster project using *MOOssiggang* code-switched and negotiated meaning. Compared to research results in face-to-face contexts, Kötter found several differences in students' communicative choices: no repetitions, few recasts, few comprehension checks, and many more requests for clarification, elaboration, or reformulation of their partners' ideas. Examining the use of the MOO environment to promote learner autonomy, Schwienhorst (2002) reported on learners' repair strategies in a tandem project between students in Germany and Ireland. He examined how students used translation and paraphrase to make conversational repairs and became more autonomous in their regulation of native and nonnative discourse in their chatting.

Tudini (2003) reported on a distance learning study involving nine Italian learners at the University of South Australia and 49 online Italian native speakers to ascertain whether negotiation is a feature of unsupervised open-ended "conversational" chats with native speakers. Using the *Ci sei* chat tool, Tudini found that about 9 percent of the distance learners' turns involved negotiation, a figure that confirms, though at a slightly lower percentage, earlier studies of meaning negotiation. Although in this exploratory stage she did not impose the kinds of task-based assignments common to other studies of CMC (e.g., Blake, 2000; Pellettieri, 2000; Smith, 2003), Tudini suggests a need in distance learning for both open-ended as well as more goal-directed tasks.

Together, these studies suggest that CMC has increasingly complexified and problematized current notions of meaning negotiation. The medium changes communication dynamics so that online meaning negotiation does not correspond in all respects with face-to-face negotiation (Smith, 2003). Further, these communication dynamics are likely to be altered even more as the medium itself changes to include aural and visual resources, and as users of the medium shift from monolingual interactions to bilingual discourse (e.g., Kötter, 2003). Finally, the increasing number of online learner interactions that cross geographical, linguistic, cultural, social, and institutional lines strongly calls for more detailed investigation into what Toyoda and Harrison (2002) characterize as the "discourse" level of negotiation of meaning. As Ware (2003) found in her study on asynchronous interactions between German and American students (described later), the occurrence of meaning negotiation itself may well necessitate willingness to maintain prolonged engagement in interaction, even in the wake of cultural misunderstandings that can occur at the discourse level.

Language Outcomes

The above studies leave open the question of how online interaction translates to language use and development in other contexts. Several recent studies attempt to tackle this question head-on, one focusing on oral interaction as the dependent variable (Abrams, 2003), and the others on writing (Davis & Thiede, 2000; Schultz, 2000; Sotillo, 2000).

Abrams (2003) considers both synchronous and asynchronous modes of CMC in her investigation of how characteristics of learners' online language use transfer to their face-to-face oral interaction in a third-semester German course. Students in the synchronous conferencing group produced more language in subsequent face-to-face discussion than did their counterparts in either the asynchronous conferencing group or the control group. However, no statistically significant differences were found across groups in terms of quality of language, as measured by lexical richness, lexical diversity, and syntactic complexity.

Online chatting does not necessarily lead to more complex second language writing either. In her study that ferreted out differences between language use in asynchronous and synchronous modes of interaction, Sotillo (2000) compared the discourse functions and syntactic complexity of 25 ESL students' writing. She found that synchronous discussions elicited conversation that was more similar to face-to-face communication in terms of discourse functions: requests, apologies, complaints, and responses. Asynchronous writing promoted more sustained interactions and greater syntactic complexity.

Other research has attended specifically to the use of asynchronous writing as a pedagogical tool for promoting second language writing development. Schultz (2000) focused on two kinds of linguistic interaction, computer-mediated and oral discussion, as possible modes for peer feedback. Comparing how second language learners made use of peer editing feedback that had been provided in these two forms of discussion, she found a complex interrelationship of students' level, activity, and medium, rather than a simple conclusion of superiority or inferiority for computer-mediated feedback. Davis and Thiede (2000) investigated the nature and degree of language learners' imitation and accommodation of writing styles and found that second language students shifted their style in response to their first language interlocutors.

Researchers examining learning produced through online discourse must grapple with growing concerns about the dynamic between online language use and language use and acquisition in other contexts. There is a need for research that specifically documents how online language use might or might not transfer to other dimensions of language learning, such as oral performance (e.g., Abrams, 2003), syntactic complexity (e.g., Schultz, 2000), and grammatical development. Also, longitudinal studies are needed that investigate the effects of reported short-term gains on long-term acquisition.

In short, researchers must carefully document the relationships among media choice, language usage, and communicative purpose, but they must also attend to the increasingly blurry line separating linguistic interaction and extralinguistic variables. With the trend toward using online communication as a pedagogical tool, language teachers are likely to link native and nonnative speakers in a growing variety of exchange projects. Studies of linguistic interaction will likely need to account for a host of independent variables: the instructor's role as mediator, facilitator, or teacher; cross-cultural differences in communicative purpose and rhetorical structure; institutional convergence or divergence on defining course goals; and the affective responses of students involved in online language learning projects. In the following section we will see how some of these factors have already begun to be researched.

Intercultural Learning

Intercultural projects take as their goal not only the enhancement of learners' language development but also the enrichment of their cultural and intercultural competence. Of particular importance is learners' capacity to view their own culture (s) in dynamic relation to another group's perspective. Early accounts of online collaborative projects (e.g., Cononelos & Oliva, 1993; Cummins & Sayers, 1995; Warschauer, 1995, 1996b) emphasized their potential for supporting intercultural understanding as well as language acquisition. Later accounts (e.g., Fischer, 1998; Kern, 2000; Kinginger, Gourves-Hayward, & Simpson, 1999) demonstrated that cross-cultural understanding did not automatically result from online communication. The projects summarized below can be broken into two categories: descriptive reports that focus on the pedagogical apparatus and discourse-analytic studies that explore linguistic and sociocultural dimensions of online intercultural exchange.

Pedagogy

A number of reports focus on the pedagogical design of intercultural projects, which have grown in sophistication and tend to include multiple components. Meskill and Ranglova (2000) discuss the revamping of the EFL curriculum at the University of Sofia, Bulgaria, using technology to provide students new means of approaching language and culture. Their curriculum is based on contemporary U.S. and British short stories, incorporating the perspectives of TESOL graduate students in the United States who communicated regularly via e-mail with the EFL students. The American students also made tape recordings of selected dialogs and descriptive narratives from the readings, which were used for listening comprehension and to launch discussion in Bulgaria. Questions about language use were researched collaboratively using online concordancing and style-checking programs, leading to a student-generated grammar for future students in the program.

Müller-Hartmann (2000) reported on another literature-based project involving 11th- and 12th-grade high school classes in Germany, the United States and Canada, focusing on how task properties, setting, teacher and learner roles, and the structure of interpersonal exchanges affected students' intercultural learning. He found that the instructional tasks related to the joint reading of literature largely supported students' intercultural competence, positive attitudes, knowledge about one another's cultures, and their interpretive skills and intercultural literacy.

Von der Emde, Schneider, and Kötter (2001) describe a pedagogical experience using a MOO for exchanges between third-semester German students at Vassar and English students at the University of Münster, Germany. They focus on students creating their own cultural spaces and identities on the MOO, which was used as a chat room for discussion of texts as well as for collaborative, interdisciplinary research projects. Significantly, their account touches on issues of play and its importance in broadening the range of language use and in building a sense of community among participants.

Gilberte Furstenberg, celebrated for her work in multimedia computer-assisted language learning (CALL) (e.g., Furstenberg & Levet, 1999; Furstenberg, Murray, Malone, & Farman-Farmaian, 1993) has created a Web-based platform for collaborative cross-cultural exploration named *Cultura* (Furstenberg, 2003; Furstenberg, Levet, English, & Maillet, 2001). Although it has been used primarily in French and English at MIT and the Institut National des Télécommunications in France, *Cultura* is designed to be used for other languages and cultures as well. Furstenberg and her colleagues understand culture not as a static phenomenon but as a dynamic process, and they get students to explore this dynamism by going straight to the biggest problems of human communication: a culture's "essentially elusive, abstract, and invisible" aspects. Students attempt to render these aspects concrete and visible through a pedagogical approach that incorporates questionnaires, observation-based hypotheses, analysis of parallel texts (see also Belz, 2002; Kinginer et al., 1999), and discussion of a broad range of other materials. Through the interactive exchange of viewpoints and perspectives, students using *Cultura* are not "receiving culture" but are involved in a reciprocal construction of one another's cultures. The cultural literacy that *Cultura* aims to develop is therefore not transmitted (as in an E. D. Hirsch "list" variety), but rather created and *problematized* through juxtapositions of materials, interpretations, and responses to interpretations.

This marks a key pedagogical change: The teacher shifts out of the "omniscient informant" role and focuses on structuring, juxtaposing, interpreting, and reflecting on intercultural experiences. Learners' understandings are confirmed, questioned, or contradicted in the light of new materials. Technologically, Furstenberg and her colleagues note two key computer features that support their approach: the ability to juxtapose different types of materials on the same screen and the electronic forum environment, allowing students to exchange their respective viewpoints (which can be archived for further analysis).

Although publications related to this project have to date been primarily descriptive, *Cultura* has the potential to be a key project in the sociocultural strand of second language acquisition studies. The fact that student data have been archived back to 1997 and are now being made available means that researchers will have an extremely valuable corpus to study. Furthermore, bilingual search capabilities and tools allowing researchers to look at contributions across multiple exchanges are now being developed for *Cultura*, making the archived data even more useable.

Analyzing Intercultural Communication

Another group of recent publications analyzes the vicissitudes of intercultural communication. In a series of articles, Belz (2002, 2003; Belz & Müller-Hartmann, 2003) presents findings to date from the German component of the Penn State Telecollaboration Project.[1] The German project involved fourth-semester German students at Penn State and students enrolled in a teacher education proseminar at the Justus-Liebig-Universitat in Giessen, Germany. The project goal was to develop students' foreign language competence and intercultural awareness by discussing their interpretations of parallel German and American films and texts on the general theme of "family issues" via e-mail and synchronous chat. Students then created Web sites to portray their multiple perspectives on cross-cultural themes evoked by the texts discussed.

Belz (2002) found that connectivity does not necessarily translate into learning. Whereas the U.S. students tended to perceive improvement in terms of language and culture knowledge, many of their German counterparts did not. Even the American students attributed their cultural learning less to the teacher's goals in the assigned tasks and more to ancillary communicative events that occurred while completing the tasks. Moreover, the Americans sometimes criticized the level of German students' participation (e.g., when developing their Web pages). At the same time, from the German students' point of view, the U.S. students were too reticent with personal information and seemed more interested in completing the project than in discussing the topics. A key feature of Belz's (2002) analysis is interpreting these findings by linking *structure* (e.g., institutional affordances and constraints) and *agency* (e.g., language learning and use) in students' interactions. For example, Belz attributes the Germans' response partly to their limited access to the Internet, which made it difficult for them to write outside of class time. Additional institutional factors that posed challenges to the exchange were grades, accreditation, and academic calendars.

Belz (2003) takes another angle on the exchange, focusing on the interaction of three students (two German and one American) to explore linguistic dimensions of online intercultural competence. Using appraisal theory and epistemic modality to ground her analysis, Belz examines learners' language choices in their electronic correspondence to assess the development of their attitudes toward both self and other. Belz interprets her data to suggest that German interactional style tends to accentuate the information-conveying function of language and notes more negative evaluation in the two Germans' discourse than in the American's. Belz suggests that learners should retain their "natural" discourse style, but that each side crucially needs to become aware of the existence of culturally dominant patterns and how they may affect their intercultural interactions.

Belz and Müller-Hartmann (2003) provide a third perspective on the project: a candid account of how social, cultural, and institutional affordances and constraints affected their own involvement and communication as teachers. Their account of the tensions involved in collaborating frames differences not as "obstacles to be overcome" but as valuable learning opportunities in intercultural exploration. Their reflections emphasize the need to move beyond reductive accounts of the instructor in online classrooms as a "guide on the side" and stress the importance of the teacher in identifying and explaining culturally contingent patterns of interaction in electronic discourse.

O'Dowd (2003) provides a qualitative analysis of a yearlong e-mail exchange between two classes in Spain and Britain, remarking on the varied success of paired exchanges. Those that did not function well led to a reinforcement of stereotypes and a confirmation of negative attitudes (echoing Belz, 2002). Pairs that worked well tended to invest a lot of time in their messages, and were sure to include some personal, "off-task" messages, to acknowledge their partners' comments, and to respond to their questions. They also tended to take the sociopragmatic rules of each other's language into account and included questions that encouraged feedback and reflection. O'Dowd found that factors cited as influential in previous studies (e.g., motivation, proficiency level, computer access, and interest in the target culture) were not significant in interviews with the Spanish and English students in his study. Success was tied more to the reactions students received when they explained aspects of their culture to their partner (interest encouraged them to write more, to learn more, and to change their attitudes toward the target culture).

Interrogation of Communication and Culture

In showing that intercultural understanding does not necessarily emerge from online interaction, Belz's and O'Dowd's studies point to a number of questions: What *kind* of cultural contact is afforded by the technological medium? If the medium itself changes the ways in which communication takes place, what does it mean to be a competent communicator in a *virtual* world? Along with Belz and O'Dowd, a number of scholars have explored these questions, showing that differences in communicative genres, linguistic styles, academic cultures, and socioinstitutional and cultural characteristics can all affect the degree to which cultural understanding can be negotiated.

Kramsch and Thorne (2002) question the assumption that the type of communication students engage in over global networks (which tends to favor phatic contact and positive presentation of self) naturally supports the development of cross-cultural understanding. Reinterpreting a French–American e-mail exchange (Kern, 2000), they argue that it was not linguistic misunderstandings but a clash in cultural frames and communicative genres that hindered students' ability to develop common ground for cross-cultural understanding. Specifically, what needed to be negotiated "was not only the connotations of words...but the stylistic conventions of the genre (formal/informal, edited/unedited, literate/orate), and more importantly the whole discourse system to which that genre belonged" (p. 98). They argue that demands on communicative competence and negotiation may be quite different on the Internet (Blake, 2000; Kötter, 2003; Pellettieri, 2000 explore some of these differences), and they call for a reassessment of what these terms mean in globalized communication.

Thorne (2003) offers further reinterpretation of this exchange, pointing out that although communicative practices are tightly bound to the materiality of their medium, they are not *determined* by the medium but rather negotiated dynamically through "cultures of use" (norms and attributions that evolve out of everyday use of a medium). Moreover, cultures of use surrounding a given Internet communication tool (e.g., e-mail, chat rooms, instant messaging) may differ across social, generational, institutional, and national groups. For example, Thorne found that some of the students in the Penn State Foreign Language Project felt that e-mail was a much less appropriate medium for personal exchange with peers than instant messaging, and that their personal relationships with keypartners improved after switching to instant messaging.

In their case study of two British and two American learners of French who participated in the electronic discussion forum of the French newspaper *Le Monde*, Hanna and de Nooy (2003) reiterate the crucial role of genre in intercultural communication. They demonstrate that the very ease of entering into electronic discussion with native speakers can be deceptive, obfuscating ways in which a genre such as "discussion" may be shaped differently by the cultural values and generic expectations of its habitual participants. Politeness and linguistic accuracy hold little truck in this online community. A willingness to be socialized into its operative discourse rules gets newcomers much further. Hanna and de Nooy's analysis of native/nonnative interactions shows how genre and culture are used to explain and justify each other, and therefore how essential it is to analyze what would constitute successful participation in any given communication context.

Analyzing a telecollaborative project between university students in Germany and in Texas, Ware (2003) found that in the wake of misunderstandings, students tended to avert joint development of topics and instead to revert to a task-based approach to their assignments (cf. Belz, 2003). Both groups of students participated beyond course expectations in terms of the quantity of writing they produced, but there was a surprising lack of real interpersonal interaction (as marked by response to direct questions, use of second-person pronouns, elaboration, etc.). In a qualitative analysis of student attitudes, she found that time pressures and institutional constraints negatively influenced students' communicative choices, leading to what she calls "missed communication" (i.e., moments of miscommunication, disengagement, or missed opportunities for intercultural learning). The key significance of Ware's findings is that missed communication can be *facilitated* by many forms of computer-mediated communication. For example, the delayed response time and the lack of social consequences for dropping topics in many online contexts allows participants to be less active conversational partners. Expectations about appropriate communication in the online medium may furthermore pose challenges to the development of intercultural competence; the ability to engage in communication at a deep level of intercultural inquiry may be impeded by an online discourse norm that often favors brevity over sustained attention.

Taken together, these studies point to (1) the importance of investigating what *successful participation* means in different contexts (e.g., different CMC contexts, different cross-cultural contexts, different pedagogical contexts); (2) the importance of the *personal* in intercultural projects—that is, learners' sensitivity to one another's cultural identities and communicative styles; and (3) the importance of *teacher involvement* in discerning, explaining, and reflecting upon culturally contingent patterns of interaction with their students.

Literacy and Identity

A third prominent theme in recent research on online L2 learning and interaction is that of literacy development and, in particular, the relationship of literacy to identity. Warschauer (1999; 2000b) explored these topics in his ethnographic multisite case study of four college technology-enhanced language and writing classes. A key finding of his research was how seriously learners took the objective of learning new semiotic skills in online media, rather than, for example, viewing themselves as carrying out computer-assisted language learning (CALL). Warschauer's concept of *electronic literacies* thus arose as an alternative to the concept of CALL when applied to online instruction. Following this line of work, Shetzer and Warschauer (2000; 2001) further developed the concept of electronic literacies and how best to develop them, focusing on issues of communication, construction of knowledge, research, and autonomous learning.

Another key theme of Warschauer's work was that of how identity issues mediate language and literacy practices in online instruction. Drawing on the experiences of multiethnic students in Hawaii (Warschauer, 2000a) and comparing them to online communication practices in Singapore (Warschauer, 2001) and Egypt (Warschauer, El Said, & Zohry, 2002), he demonstrated how the highly flexible, interactive, and multimodal aspects of online communication made it an ideal medium for exploration and expression of identity (Warschauer, 2002).

The theme of literacy and identity has been carried further forward in the ethnographic work of Lam (2000, 2003), who conducted case studies of four Chinese immigrant youth, examining their language use in both school and out-of-school settings. The four immigrants had, to varying degrees, relatively unsuccessful experiences with English at school, experiencing a lack of motivation to engage in English either in the classroom or on the playground. Yet all four gained status as English users online, both through the Web sites they created and through their e-mails or chats with interlocutors, often using new hybrid forms of language that creatively combined media and/or language forms (e.g., drawing on both Cantonese and English). In doing so, they assimilated to neither a national (e.g., American) or racial-ethnic (e.g., Chinese-American) identity, but instead explored their own pluralistic identities based on affiliation with like-minded individuals and groups, for example, fans of Japanese animation who flocked to the *anime* Web site of one of the youths Lam studied.

With colleagues Kramsch and A'Ness, Lam analyzed and theorized the issues involved in online literacies, drawing on her own data as well as a study of college students creating a Spanish-language CD-ROM (Kramsch, A'Ness, & Lam, 2000). Their article illustrates how the very concept of authorship is changing in new media, with students empowered not only to author texts but also to help rewrite the very rules by which texts are created. They conclude that this ability, together with the authenticity of audience in online communication, creates new possibilities of *agency*, that is, the power to take meaningful action and see the results of one's decisions and choices (cf. Murray, 1997).

This body of ethnographic work by Warschauer and Lam has several important implications for language pedagogy and research. First, because language learners do not just speak a language (a standard singularity) but speak from particular social positions (a plurality), teachers and researchers should be less concerned with learners' conformity to standard language norms in their online language use and more concerned with how well learners can use all their available linguistic, cognitive, and social resources to negotiate the linguistic, interactional, and cultural demands of online discourse. Second, what is important about language and literacy development on the Internet is not just the ability to read and write in comprehensible language, but also the ability to negotiate new roles and identities. Socialization and identity construction can have either a facilitating or restrictive effect on language and literacy development, depending in part on whether instructors encourage learners to participate as creative producers of new media and as agents of purposeful communication and action.

Conclusion

Whereas earlier research investigated computer-mediated communication through the lenses of previous forms of spoken or written interaction, more recent research is allowing us to better understand the Internet as an authentic communication medium in its own right. Though we have not seen any single *computer effect* that guarantees certain outcomes in Internet-based learning, we have learned how the affordances of this new medium problematize some of our earlier notions of interaction, culture, identity, and literacy. This research suggests that language educators should use the Internet not so much to teach the same thing in a different way, but rather to help students enter into a new realm of collaborative inquiry and construction of knowledge, viewing their expanding repertoire of identities and communication strategies as resources in the process.

Note

1. The Penn State Telecollaboration Project, funded by a U.S. Department of Education International Research and Studies Program Grant, studies intercultural communication in university-level foreign language classes, focusing on language acquisition, cultural awareness, and beliefs about language learning. One class in each language (French, German, Spanish) uses e-mail, Web-based threaded discussion, and synchronous chat for communication and collaboration with a partner class abroad, while the second class serves as a control group, using the same electronic media for intraclass communication only (Thorne, 2003).

ANNOTATED BIBLIOGRAPHY

Belz, J. A. (2003). Linguistic perspectives on the development of intercultural competence in telecollaboration. *Language Learning and Technology*, *7* (2), 68–117.

This article explores linguistic dimensions of intercultural competence by analyzing the online discourse of two German students and an American student participating in a university-level foreign language telecollaborative project. Using appraisal theory and epistemic modality in her analysis, Belz argues that such linguistically grounded analyses can augment content analyses in studies that examine the development of student attitudes toward self and other in online exchange projects. She suggests that the differences in interactional styles exhibited by the three students in her study are indications that learners need to become aware of the existence of culturally dominant communication patterns and of how those patterns may affect their intercultural interactions.

Furstenberg, G. (2003). Reading between the cultural lines. In P. Patrikis (Ed.), *Reading between the lines: Perspectives on foreign language literacy* (pp. 74–98). New Haven, CT: Yale University Press.

This chapter provides fascinating glimpses into the experiences of students exploring two cultures interactively through language, illustrating the design and principles of *Cultura* (described in Furstenberg, Levet, English, & Maillet, 2001). In this project culture is problematized through juxtapositions of materials, interpretations, and responses to interpretations. Students see that there can be variability in "insider" views, and yet they can also be brought to see coherent patterns, which allow them to explore the contours of cross-cultural differences in concepts, values, and discourses.

Kramsch, C., & Thorne, S. (2002). Foreign language learning as global communicative practice. In D. Block & D. Cameron (Eds.) *Globalization and language teaching* (pp. 83–100). London: Routledge.

This paper calls into question notions of what it means to be a competent communicator in the virtual world. Kramsch and Thorne analyze a French–American e-mail exchange and find that a clash in cultural frames and communicative genres hindered students' ability to develop common ground for cross-cultural understanding. The French students, who were operating out of a discourse of truth, and the American students, operating out of a discourse of trust, found themselves engaged in communicative cross-purposes that extended well beyond linguistic misunderstandings alone. They argue that terms like communicative competence and negotiation must be reassessed in global communicative practices, which are closely bound together with local cultural and situational contexts.

Lam, W. S. E. (2003). *Second language literacy and identity formation on the Internet: The case of Chinese immigrant youth in the United States.* Unpublished doctoral dissertation, University of California, Berkeley.

This recent dissertation presents four case studies of Chinese immigrant youths, showing how they came to occupy new social positions and identities by acquiring and appropriating new discourses in online environments (one of these case studies was published as Lam, 2000). Lam's study considers not only how social contexts shape language use in online environments but also, and most importantly, how online communication shapes social contexts and participants' identity formation. Furthermore, her work draws attention to the ways in which language functions in relation to other forms of online semiosis.

Warschauer, M., & Kern, R. (Eds.). (2000). *Network-based language teaching: Concepts and practice.* New York: Cambridge University Press.

This edited book draws together 10 valuable papers, including theoretical pieces and research studies, on the teaching and learning of second languages using computer networks. Especially valuable to second language researchers and educators will be the introduction by Kern and Warschauer, which introduces a sociocognitive perspective on computer-assisted language learning; the studies by Davis and Thiede, Schultz, and Pelletierri, which analyze L2 computer-mediated interaction and its outcomes; and a chapter by Warschauer, which summarizes his earlier (Warschauer, 1999) ethnographic case study of online language learning.

Warschauer, M. (2002). Languages.com: The Internet and linguistic pluralism. In I. Snyder (Ed.), *Silicon literacies: Communication, innovation, and education in the electronic age* (pp. 62–74). London: Routledge.

This paper draws on data from Hawai'i, Egypt, and Singapore to analyze the relationship of online communication to the exploration and expression of language users' plural and evolving identities. Drawing on theories of globalization, the paper illustrates how the Internet supports both international networks (by facilitating the expansion of global English) and local identities (by allowing diverse forms of grassroots communication and publishing in a variety of local languages and dialects).

OTHER REFERENCES

Abrams, Z. I. (2003). The effect of synchronous and asynchronous CMC on oral performance in German. *Modern Language Journal, 87* (2), 157–167.

Beauvois, M. H. (1992). Computer-assisted classroom discussion in the foreign language classroom: Conversation in slow motion. *Foreign Language Annals, 25* (5), 455–464.

Belz, J. A. (2002). Social dimensions of telecollaborative foreign language study. *Language Learning & Technology, 6* (1), 60–81.

Belz, J. A., & Müller-Hartmann, A. (2003). Teachers as intercultural learners: Negotiating German-American telecollaboration along the institutional fault line. *Modern Language Journal, 87* (1), 71–89.

Blake, R. (2000). Computer mediated communication: A window on L2 Spanish interlanguage. *Language Learning & Technology, 4* (1), 120–136.

Brammerts, H. (1996). Language learning in tandem using the Internet. In M. Warschauer (Ed.), *Telecollaboration in Foreign Language Learning: Proceedings of the Hawaii Symposium* (pp. 121–130). Honolulu: University of Hawaii Second Language Teaching and Curriculum Center.

Chun, D. M. (1994). Using computer networking to facilitate the acquisition of interactive competence. *System, 22* (1), 17–31.

Cononelos, T., & Oliva, M. (1993). Using computer networks to enhance foreign language/culture education. *Foreign Language Annals, 26* (4), 527–534.

Cummins, J., & Sayers, D. (1995). *Brave new schools: Challenging cultural illiteracy through global learning networks.* New York: St. Martin's Press.

Davis, B., & Thiede, R. (2000). Writing into change: Style-shifting in asynchronous electronic discourse. In M. Warschauer & R. Kern (Eds.), *Network-based language teaching: Concepts and practice* (pp. 87–120). Cambridge: Cambridge University Press.

Fischer, G. (1998). *E-mail in foreign language teaching: Toward the creation of virtual classrooms.* Tübingen, Germany: Stauffenburg.

Furstenberg, G., & Levet, S. (1999). *Dans un quartier de Paris.* New Haven, CT: Yale University Press.

Furstenberg, G., Levet, S., English, K., & Maillet, K. (2001). Giving a virtual voice to the silent language of culture: The CULTURA project. *Language Learning & Technology, 5* (1), 55–102.

Furstenberg, G., Murray, J. H., Malone, S., & Farman-Farmaian, A. (1993). *A la rencontre de Philippe.* New Haven, CT: Yale University Press.

Hanna, B. E., & de Nooy, J. (2003). A funny thing happened on the way to the forum: Electronic discussion and foreign language learning. *Language Learning & Technology, 7* (1), 71–85.

Herring, S. C. (Ed.). (1996). *Computer-mediated communication: Linguistic, social and cross-cultural perspectives.* Amsterdam: Benjamins.

Kelm, O. R. (1992). The use of synchronous computer networks in second language instruction:

A preliminary report. *Foreign Language Annals, 25* (5), 441–454.

Kern, R. G. (1995). Restructuring classroom interaction with networked computers: Effects on quantity and quality of language production. *Modern Language Journal, 79* (4), 457–476.

Kern, R. G. (2000). *Literacy and language teaching.* Oxford: Oxford University Press.

Kern, R. G., & Warschauer, M. (2000). Theory and practice of network-based language teaching. In M. Warschauer & R. Kern (Eds.), *Network-based language teaching: Concepts and practice* (pp. 1–19). Cambridge: Cambridge University Press.

Kinginger, C., Gourves-Hayward, A., & Simpson, V. (1999). A tele-collaborative course on French-American intercultural communication. *French Review, 72* (5), 853–866.

Kitade, K. (2000). L2 learners' discourse and SLA theories in CMC: Collaborative interaction in Internet chat. *Computer Assisted Language Learning, 13* (2), 143–166.

Kötter, M. (2003). Negotiation of meaning and codeswitching in online tandems. *Language Learning & Technology, 7* (2), 145–172.

Kramsch, C., A'Ness, F., & Lam, E. (2000). Authenticity and authorship in the computer-mediated acquisition of L2 literacy. *Language Learning & Technology, 4* (2), 78–104.

Lam, W. S. E. (2000). L2 literacy and the design of the self: A case study of a teenager writing on the Internet. *TESOL Quarterly, 34* (3), 457–482.

Meskill, C., & Ranglova, K. (2000). Curriculum innovation in TEFL: A study of technologies supporting socio-collaborative language learning in Bulgaria. In M. Warschauer & R. Kern (Eds.), *Network-based language teaching: Concepts and practice* (pp. 20–40). Cambridge: Cambridge University Press.

Meunier, L. (1998). Personality and motivational factors in electronic networking. In J. Muyskens (Ed.), *New ways of teaching and learning: Focus on technology and foreign language education* (pp. 145–197). Boston: Heinle & Heinle.

Müller-Hartmann, A. (2000). The role of tasks in promoting intercultural learning in electronic learning networks. *Language Learning & Technology, 4* (2), 129–147.

Murray, J. H. (1997). *Hamlet on the holodeck: The future of narrative in cyberspace.* New York: Free Press.

O'Dowd, R. (2003). Understanding the "other side": Intercultural learning in a Spanish-English e-mail exchange. *Language Learning & Technology, 7* (2), 118–144.

Ortega, L. (1997). Processes and outcomes in networked classroom interaction: Defining the research agenda for L2 computer-assisted classroom discussion. *Language Learning & Technology, 1* (1), 82–93.

Pellettieri, J. (2000). Negotiation in cyberspace: The role of *chatting* in the development of grammatical competence. In M. Warschauer & R. Kern (Eds.), *Network-based language teaching: Concepts and practice* (pp. 59–86). Cambridge: Cambridge University Press.

Pica, T. (1994). Research on negotiation: What does it reveal about second-language learning

conditions, processes, and outcomes? *Language Learning, 44* (3), 493–527.
Schultz, J. M. (2000). Computers and collaborative writing in the foreign language curriculum. In M. Warschauer & R. Kern (Eds.), *Network-based language teaching: Concepts and practice* (pp. 121–150). Cambridge: Cambridge University Press.
Schwienhorst, K. (2002). Evaluating tandem language learning in the MOO : Discourse repair strategies in a bilingual Internet project. *Computer-Assisted Language Learning, 15* (2), 135–146.
Shetzer, H., & Warschauer, M. (2000). An electronic literacy approach to network-based language teaching. In M. Warschauer & R. Kern (Eds.), *Network-based language teaching: Concepts and practice* (pp. 171–185). Cambridge: Cambridge University Press.
Shetzer, H., & Warschauer, M. (2001). English through Web page creation. In J. Murphy & P. Byrd, (Eds.), *Understanding the courses we teach: Local perspectives on English language teaching* (pp. 429–455). Ann Arbor: University of Michigan Press.
Smith, B. (2003). Computer-mediated negotiated interaction: An expanded model. *Modern Language Journal, 87* (1), 38–57.
Sotillo, S. (2000). Discourse functions and syntactic complexity in synchronous and asynchronous communication. *Language Learning & Technology, 4* (1), 82–119.
Sullivan, N., & Pratt, E. (1996). A comparative study of two ESL writing environments: A computer-assisted classroom and a traditional oral classroom. *System, 24* (4), 491–501.
Thorne, S. L. (2003). Artifacts and cultures-of-use in intercultural communication. *Language Learning & Technology, 7* (2), 38–67.
Toyoda, E., & Harrison, R. (2002). Categorization of text chat communication between learners and native speakers of Japanese. *Language Learning & Technology, 6* (1), 82–99.
Tudini, V. (2003). Using native speakers in chat. *Language Learning & Technology, 7* (3), 141–159.
Varonis, E. M., & Gass, S. (1985). Non-native/non-native conversations: A model for negotiation of meaning. *Applied Linguistics, 6*, 71–90.
von der Emde, S., Schneider, J., & Kötter, M. (2001). Technically speaking: Transforming language learning through virtual learning environments (MOOs). *Modern Language Journal, 85* (2), 210–225.
Ware, P. D. (2003). *From involvement to engagement in online communication: Promoting intercultural competence in foreign language education.* Unpublished doctoral dissertation, University of California, Berkeley.
Warschauer, M. (Ed.). (1995). *Virtual connections: Online activities and projects for networking language learners.* Honolulu: Second Language Teaching and Curriculum Center, University of Hawai'i.
Warschauer, M. (1996a). Comparing face-to-face and electronic communication in the second

language classroom. *CALICO Journal, 13* (2), 7–26.
Warschauer, M. (Ed.). (1996b). *Telecollaboration in foreign language learning: Proceedings of the Hawai'i Symposium*. Honolulu: University of Hawai'i Second Language Teaching and Curriculum Center.
Warschauer, M. (1999). *Electronic literacies: Language, culture, and power in online education*. Mahwah, NJ: Erlbaum.
Warschauer, M. (2000a). Language, identity, and the Internet. In G. Rodman (Ed.), *Race in cyberspace* (pp. 151–170). New York: Routledge.
Warschauer, M. (2000b). Online learning in second language classrooms: An ethnographic study. In M. Warschauer & R. Kern (Eds.), *Network-based language teaching: Concepts and practice* (pp. 41–58). Cambridge: Cambridge University Press.
Warschauer, M. (2001). Singapore's dilemma: Control vs. autonomy in IT-led development. *The Information Society, 17* (4), 305–311.
Warschauer, M. (2002). Languages.com: The Internet and linguistic pluralism. In I. Snyder (Ed.), *Silicon literacies: Communication, innovation, and education in the electronic age* (pp. 62–74). London: Routledge.
Warschauer, M., El Said, G. R., & Zohry, A. (2002). Language choice online: Globalization and identity in Egypt. *Journal of Computer-Mediated Communication, 7* (4). Retrieved December, 2003, from http://www.ascusc.org/jcmc/vol7/issue4/warschauer.htm.

12. CONTENT-BASED INSTRUCTION: PERSPECTIVES ON CURRICULUM PLANNING

Fredricka L. Stoller

Content-based instruction (CBI), distinguished by its dual commitment to language- and content-learning objectives, has been translated into practice in diverse ways to meet the needs of second and foreign language student populations. This article explores the general characteristics of and challenges associated with content-based curricula by reviewing (1) case studies that document outcomes of CBI programs at elementary, secondary, and higher education levels and (2) curricular models that have been implemented in first and second language contexts. Included in this review of curricular models, because of its implications for second and foreign language contexts, is a brief explanation of Concept-Oriented Reading Instruction (CORI), an approach to content learning and reading development that has been used and extensively researched in first language settings. Empirical studies focusing on CORI, immersion models, and other CBI-related issues (including teacher–student interactions; teachers' oral discourse; and teachers' attention to language, content, and task) are summarized to illustrate the complexities of content-based curricula. The article concludes with a call for further research that can inform the practices of teachers, curriculum and course designers, materials developers, and individuals involved with assessment in content-based settings.

Content-based instruction (CBI), distinguished by its dual commitment to language-and content-learning objectives, is not a new topic of exploration in the *Annual Review of Applied Linguistics* (*ARAL*). In the 10th volume of *ARAL*, Spanos (1990) identified the 1980s as a decade in which applied linguists exhibited substantial interest in "integrated instruction," with five promising book-length publications on instructional approaches that combined language- and content-learning objectives (Brinton, Snow, & Wesche, 1989; Cantoni-Harvey, 1987; Crandall, 1987; Enright & McCloskey, 1988; Mohan, 1986). Despite the interest that was generated by these publications and others in incorporating nonlanguage subject matter into second and foreign language courses, the widespread adoption of content-based instruction, at that time, was met by many challenges, including coordination between language and content instructors, administrative support, materials development, and program evaluation.

In the 13th issue of *ARAL*, Crandall (1993) provided a historical overview of CBI in the United States. As part of her overview, she reported data on the changing demographics of second language (L2) student populations—in K–12, adult, and higher-education settings—that led to an increased concern for students' language *and* content learning needs. To meet those needs, Crandall summarized sound instructional strategies that fit easily into content-based paradigms, including cooperative learning, task-based and experiential learning, whole language strategies, and the use of graphic organizers. (See Schleppegrell & Achugar, 2003; Short, 1999; Smallwood & McCargo, 1999; and Snow, 2001, for more recent discussions of instructional strategies that promote language and content learning.) Added to the challenges introduced by Spanos (1990) earlier was Crandall's call for case studies that explored the difficulties experienced by L2 learners in their content classes and the effectiveness of integrated instruction. The paucity of research in these areas made it difficult for practitioners to identify optimal conditions for integrated instruction, including its timing, the relative effectiveness of different program models, and particularly useful instructional strategies, texts, and assessment measures.

In the 18th issue of *ARAL*, Snow (1998) examined the impact of content-based instruction on (1) instructional practices, (2) assessment, and (3) teacher training, with additional commentary on language and content teachers' efforts at collaboration. Unlike the previous *ARAL* articles, Snow summarized classroom-based research, extending beyond program outcomes, including studies that focused on the characteristics of disciplinary language (Short, 1994, 1997), changes in the pedagogical orientation of content-area university faculty after training seminars (Snow, 1997), and the impact of CBI on English as a second language (ESL) students' academic progress (Kasper, 1997).

Although the focus of these three *ARAL* articles on content-based instruction shifted between 1990 and 1998, what remained constant throughout these explorations of CBI was the rationale for instructional approaches that integrate content- and language-learning objectives. All three authors emphasized that CBI, in its various guises (Snow, 1998), provides a means for students to continue their academic development while also improving their language proficiency. Wesche and Skehan (2002) have supported this claim:

> In successful CBI, learners master both language and content through a reciprocal process as they understand and convey varied concepts through their second language...CBI may be seen as particularly relevant to learners who are preparing for full-time study through their second (or weaker) language, at any level of education. (p. 220–221)

This present *ARAL* article, an extension of earlier discussions, explores content-based instruction, with an emphasis on the following: recent indications of a global interest in CBI; support for CBI and the common curriculum-level challenges that emerge from course outcomes; curricular models, originating from first and second language contexts; and empirical studies with implications for the development of content-based curricula. The article concludes with a call for further research, with the hopes that future *ARAL* articles on CBI will be able to report on larger numbers of empirical studies that can inform the practices of teachers, curriculum and course designers, materials developers, and individuals involved with assessment in the context of content-based classrooms.

Global Interest in Content-Based Instruction

The notion of integrating content- and language-learning objectives has stimulated interest globally among language professionals and some content specialists. Since Snow's ARAL article, numerous book-length publications have appeared with a focus on some aspect of language and content integration (e.g., Crandall & Kaufman, 2002; de Courcy, 2002; Echevarria & Graves, 2003; Echevarria, Vogt, & Short, 2000; Johns, 1997; Johnson & Swain, 1997; Kasper,

2000; Mohan, Leung, & Davison, 2001; Pally, 2000). An entire issue of *The Canadian Modern Language Review/La Revue Canadienne des Langues Vivantes* (Wesche, 2001) was devoted to immersion and content-based language teaching in Canada (see also Wesche, 2000). Similarly, the Summer/Autumn 2001 *TESOL Journal* (Murphy & Stoller, 2001b) explored sustained content language teaching and the ways in which the concept is being translated into practice in various instructional settings. During the same time frame, numerous countries in the European Community formalized Content and Language Integrated Learning (CLIL) and engaged in innovative initiatives integrating language and content as part of its "Plurilingual Education" agenda (Marsh, n.d.; Marsh & Langé, 1999; see also Pufahl, Rhodes, & Christian, 2000).

Other indications of a global interest in integrating content and language teaching include a fall 2003 international conference with the theme of "Integrating content and language: Meeting the challenge of a multilingual higher education," hosted by the University of Maastricht, The Netherlands (see http://www.unimaas.nl/icl/index.htm). European initiatives involving the integration of content and language learning objectives are complemented by interests in other parts of the world where increasing numbers of educational institutions are using a foreign language (often English) as a medium of instruction for lectures, primary and supplementary readings, and class discussions (Crandall & Kaufman, 2002). The University of Maastricht conference followed an earlier one that focused on "Integrating content and language: Providing access to knowledge through language," hosted by Peninsula Technikon, South Africa, in March 2001. Many of the papers presented at the conference in South Africa reveal the challenges faced by university lecturers, including many in South Africa, in the wake of increasingly wide access to universities and technical colleges for previously marginalized student populations whose first language is not the language of instruction (see http://www.pentech.ac.za/pil88/ for specifics about conference papers). In another African setting, 50 educators from more than 11 countries in sub-Saharan Africa enrolled in an online course entitled "Africa online: English language teaching using web resources to develop content-based materials for the classroom" (Opp-Beckman, 2002). Two goals of the online course were to familiarize participants with three content areas (i.e., entrepreneurship, civic education, HIV-AIDS education) and to guide participants in incorporating these content areas into their

English language teaching. In the United States, the Content-Based Language Teaching through Technology (CoBaLTT) initiative, launched in 1999 by the Center for Advanced Research on Language Acquisition (CARLA) at the University of Minnesota, was designed to assist K–16 foreign language teachers in creating content-based curricula and utilizing technology to support content-based language instruction (see http://carla.acad.umn.edu/COBALTT.html). The American Council on Immersion Education (ACIE), by means of its newsletter *The Bridge: From Research to Practice* (see http://carla.acad.umn.edu/acie-bridges.html), regularly highlights issues related to content-based instruction for the immersion context.

Support from CBI Course Outcomes

Over the years, much support for CBI has followed from the outcomes of actual CBI courses (and programs) that have documented successes with combined language and content instruction. Although there have been few controlled empirical studies to support the claims made by individuals associated with those courses, the fact that students are reported to exit the courses with improved language abilities and content-area knowledge attests, at one level, to the perceived successes of CBI. It is through case-studies that we gain a sense of the characteristics of and challenges associated with content-based curricula.

At the elementary school level, there are numerous examples of successful FLES (foreign language in the elementary school) programs. Gilzow and Branaman (2000) showcase seven early-start, long-sequence foreign language programs, identified by two projects funded by the U.S. Department of Education (i.e., the National K–12 Foreign Language Survey Project and the Improving Foreign Language Education in Schools Project). The goal of the two projects was to identify model foreign language programs that would provide interested educators with insights into establishing, implementing, and maintaining similar programs. Among the seven model programs are five content-enriched programs in which concepts from regular school subject matter (e.g., math, science, geography) are taught (and reinforced) in English lessons. The two other model programs—one a partial immersion program and the other a middle-school immersion continuation program—teach school subject matter in the foreign language. Although many factors have contributed to the successes of these model curricula, four factors are identified by Gilzow and Branaman as worthy of special attention. One key to their success is flexibility, demonstrated in the ability of the seven model programs to respond to unanticipated events. Another key to success depends upon teamwork among foreign language teachers, regular classroom teachers, administrators, parents, and community members. In some cases, teamwork with nearby universities added to the success of the programs, "with benefits ranging from professional development opportunities and shared technical expertise to long-range articulation plans and teacher recruitment possibilities" (p. 5). The third key to success is linked to leadership, in the form of one or two individuals with a vision of foreign language teaching who can inspire and organize people and resources to build their programs. The fourth key to success is tied to a shared commitment, among program staff, to the program and the goal of providing foreign language education to young learners. This commitment has been translated into a range of activities including ongoing program building, grant proposals, fund raising, advocacy events, and systematic efforts to motivate students.

At the middle-school level, Bunch, Abram, Lotan, and Valdés (2001) report on a project in which two social studies and two language arts teachers, with the cooperation of university faculty and graduate assistants, are reforming social studies classes to combine an explicit focus on academic language development with Complex Instruction, an approach that emphasizes higher-order thinking, small-group interaction, and writing. One goal of Complex Instruction is to engage students in multiple-ability activities designed to promote more equal participation among English language learners and mainstream students who find themselves in the same classroom. As might be expected, the effort to integrate a specific focus on academic language in the context of a mainstream social studies class has been accompanied by challenges, including social studies and language arts teachers' diverse reactions to interdisciplinary responsibilities and even larger issues like standardized testing. Although data on the impact of this curricular innovation on students' growth in academic language and content mastery are not yet available, the project suggests interesting approaches for meeting the language and content learning needs of a heterogeneous student population.

Langman (2003) reports on a different middle-school mainstreaming effort, set into place after all teachers in the school received ESL training. In a yearlong case study of one seventh-grade science classroom with an ESL-trained science teacher, Langman found that the ESL strategies used by the teacher (e.g., using visuals, writing objectives on the board), although somewhat effective in conveying content, were less than effective in developing students'academic English. Because students received no explicit language instruction, Langman concluded that students were reduced to "incidental language learning opportunities" (p. 14), resulting in little English improvement in one school year. The documented failure of the school's policy, largely motivated by a principal's interest in better test scores, provides "evidence in support of focused language instruction as a necessary part of the curriculum for middle-school second language learners, together with content-based instruction" (p. 24).

At the tertiary level, numerous case studies have reported efforts to integrate content and language learning. Early on, Krueger and Ryan (1993) and Stryker and Leaver (1997) compiled case studies of content-based instruction in postsecondary foreign language classes. More recently, Bueno (2002; see also Dupuy, 2000, and Hoecherl-Alden, 2000) documented efforts to convert a third-year composition and conversation foreign language course into a content-based course. Bueno's experience highlights some of the challenges that teachers face when switching from a skills-based to a content-based curricular orientation including (1) the determination of course content in response to diverse student interests, (2) the selection of content resources and the designation of targeted grammar points for students with varied proficiency levels, and (3) the sequencing of structured input and output activities. In response to the challenges associated with determining content around which a foreign language course is developed, Bragger and Rice (1999) have proposed a developmental model for "content-oriented instruction" that moves students from familiar to less familiar academic and cultural content in a foreign language curriculum. A carefully orchestrated transition from familiar to unfamiliar content has been billed as one way to minimize "the 'sudden jumps'in difficulty" (p. 373) that typically frustrate foreign language students and faculty in curricula defined by language and literature classes.

In a South African higher-education setting, Parkinson (2000) has advocated a theme-based approach as the organizing principle for an English for Specific Purposes course. Parkinson involves students in learning science content to assist them in acquiring the range of literacies associated with science learning. The course uses themes (e.g., wastewater treatment, ozone) in slightly different ways, the differences seen in "the extent to which students are exposed to real data (measurements) and whether they collect the data themselves or not" (p. 376).

Added to this set of case studies are efforts to integrate language and content learning in tertiary-level ESL classes. Pally (2000) and Murphy and Byrd (2001), for example, compiled case studies showcasing efforts to integrate *one* subject area into language classes for an extended period of time (up to a full semester), thus the designations "sustained content-based instruction" (Pally, 2000) and "sustained-content language teaching" (Murphy & Stoller, 2001a). What distinguishes these case studies from others is their commitment to an exploration of one content area, or carrier topic, that simulates the demands of mainstream university-level courses, with the addition of explicit instruction in language and academic skills. Examples of sustained-content language teaching, like those mentioned below, illustrate its versatility (in terms of content selection, source of content, skills foci, syllabus design, and task orientation), usefulness for integrating language- and content-learning objectives, and ability to provide students with opportunities for deep engagement with content. Brinton (2001), as an example, uses sustained content (centered on the city of Los Angeles) while structuring her class around a genre-based syllabus; Carson (2000) uses sustained content (focusing on psychology) to complement an integrated-skills task-based English for Academic Purposes (EAP) curriculum; Janzen (2001) combines sustained content (on special effects in movies) with a discrete-skill focus, emphasizing reading skill and strategy development; and Weissberg and Lipoufski (2002) exploit local issues (in the community, county, and state) to restructure a reading and vocabulary course. Mendelsohn (2001) combines sustained content (on Canadian language and culture) with a strategy-based approach, exposing students to content and language learning strategies that will assist them in handling EAP tasks. The content in Mendelsohn's course, like many of the other examples, "is not only treated as a vehicle for language learning but is given major prominence" (p. 309). Despite the growing interest in a sustained-content orientation, and the many ways in which the concept has been translated into practice in second and foreign language curricula, as illustrated by these examples, some in the field see limitations in crafting a curriculum around a single content area. Davison and Williams (2001), for instance, have noted that restricting a curriculum to a single subject area limits language coverage, thereby disadvantaging the very students meant to be served by such curricula.

Crandall and Kaufman (2002) compiled a more eclectic set of case studies on CBI in second and foreign language higher-education settings. The case studies in their edited volume showcase the "commonality of purpose" (p. 1) among distinct approaches to integrating content and language objectives; these studies bring attention to approaches to CBI that go well beyond the models popularized by Brinton, Snow, and Wesche (1989) and those referred to by Crandall (1993), Snow (1998), and Spanos (1990) (e.g., adjunct, integrated, language sensitive, sheltered, theme based). For example, Stewart, Sagliano, and Sagliano (2002) demonstrate the evolution of a modified adjunct course to a *collaborative interdisciplinary team-teaching* approach in an EFL setting. Brinton and Jensen (2002) describe a *simulated adjunct* ESL course in which authentic content and tasks are imported from a subject-area course into a language course. Iancu (2002) describes a *bridge* program that links a general education course with four language-skill courses. Snow and Kamhi-Stein (2002) describe a *modified adjunct* model characterized by the pairing of a general education class with study group sections that are team taught by an ESL instructor and peer study group leader. (See also Ronesi, 2001, for a description of a university CBI program with adjunct study sessions supported by undergraduate students trained to assist ESL classmates.)

While illustrating diverse ways of combining content- and language-learning objectives and encouraging collaboration between language and content faculty, this representative set of case studies highlights a common set of challenges faced by teachers and program administrators. With implications for curriculum development efforts in other settings, these challenges include the following:

- The identification and development of appropriate content
- The selection and sequencing of language items dictated by content sources rather than a predetermined language syllabus
- The alignment of content with structures and functions that emerge from the subject matter (Short, 1999)
- The choice of appropriate materials and the decision to use (or not to use) textbooks
- Faculty development that assists language instructors in handling unfamiliar subject matter and content-area instructors in handling language issues
- Language- and content-faculty collaboration

- The institutionalization of CBI in light of available resources and the needs of faculty and students
- Systematic assessment to demonstrate (1) students' language and content learning and (2) program effectiveness

Curricular Models

The case studies just mentioned reveal many of the ways in which content-based instruction can be structured to meet the needs of diverse student populations. In reviewing curricular approaches to content-based instruction, Met (1998; see also Snow, 2001) demonstrates how different models of content-based instruction constitute a continuum, showcasing the shifting emphasis on content and language, most often a response to the exigencies of the instructional settings in which they are implemented. At one end of the continuum are "content-driven" approaches with strong commitments to content-learning objectives (immersion, partial immersion, sheltered subject-area courses); at the other end of the continuum are "language-driven" approaches with strong commitments to language learning objectives, using content mainly as a springboard for language practice. Language courses built around themes, for example, vary in their commitment to content-learning objectives, depending on the weighting of different curricular elements (Davison & Williams, 2001).

Wesche and Skehan (2002) visualize a continuum with different end points. They have depicted content-based instruction, and its many variations, on a continuum with "strong" forms of CBI at one end of the continuum and "weak" forms of CBI at the other end. The so-called strong forms place the greatest emphasis on the mastery of nonlinguistic subject matter (parallel to Met's content-driven approaches) and the weak forms of CBI focus on language learning (parallel to Met's language-driven approaches).

On either continuum, there are approaches to content-based instruction that fall somewhere between the end points, demonstrating more balanced commitments to the language and content learning needs of target student populations. Subject-area courses, paired with language support courses, the latter often labeled adjunct or linked courses (see Johns, 1997), fall somewhere in the middle of the continuum. Stoller (2002) has proposed ways in which to modify theme-based courses (often placed at the language or weak end of the continuum) so that students are better prepared for the demands of future subject-area courses where they will be expected to develop some degree of content-area expertise and to display their grasp of knowledge on formal assessment measures. Although some CBI models, like Stoller's modified theme-based model, aim at addressing students' language and content learning needs (thus falling toward the middle of the continuum), Davison and Williams (2001) have claimed that few, if any, comprehensive models or teaching materials are appropriately placed at the center of the language and content continuum.

Besides the CBI models that are traditionally placed on these content-to-language emphasis continua, there are other curricular models to consider. One commonly referred to curricular model, the Cognitive Academic Language Learning Approach, or CALLA, was developed by Chamot and O'Malley (1987, 1994). CALLA is noted for its three-way commitment to content, language, and strategy training. More recently, Short (2002) introduced the Language-Content-Task (LCT) framework (see Figure 1), which is structured around three components associated with academic literacy: knowledge of the target language (L), knowledge of the content area (C), and knowledge of how tasks (T) are to be completed to succeed in academic settings. These three components, and their interactions, represent the core of the LCT curricular framework, applied by Short to sheltered social studies classes at the middle-school level, but widely applicable to other disciplines. Although sheltered instruction has been implemented in a variety of ways (e.g., Echevarria & Graves, 2003; Short, 1999), in this framework, teachers are encouraged to structure their lessons so that language, content, and tasks are dealt with individually and in interaction with one another. The language domain helps students master semantic, syntactic, and pragmatic aspects of the language, in addition to the traditional four skills (reading, writing, speaking, and listening). The content domain focuses on school curriculum objectives and the content introduced in the textbook and other instructional materials. This domain emphasizes the importance of addressing the learning strategies that students need to access, process, and remember content. The third domain consists of common academic tasks (and training in accomplishing the tasks) that engage students in the use of strategies to improve their academic performance and the application of content knowledge, thereby allowing teachers to evaluate students' understanding and recall of information. The intersection of the three domains of the LCT framework provides "the glue for students to pull together their knowledge of language, content, and task so that they can participate actively in the academic classroom" (Short, 2002, p. 20).

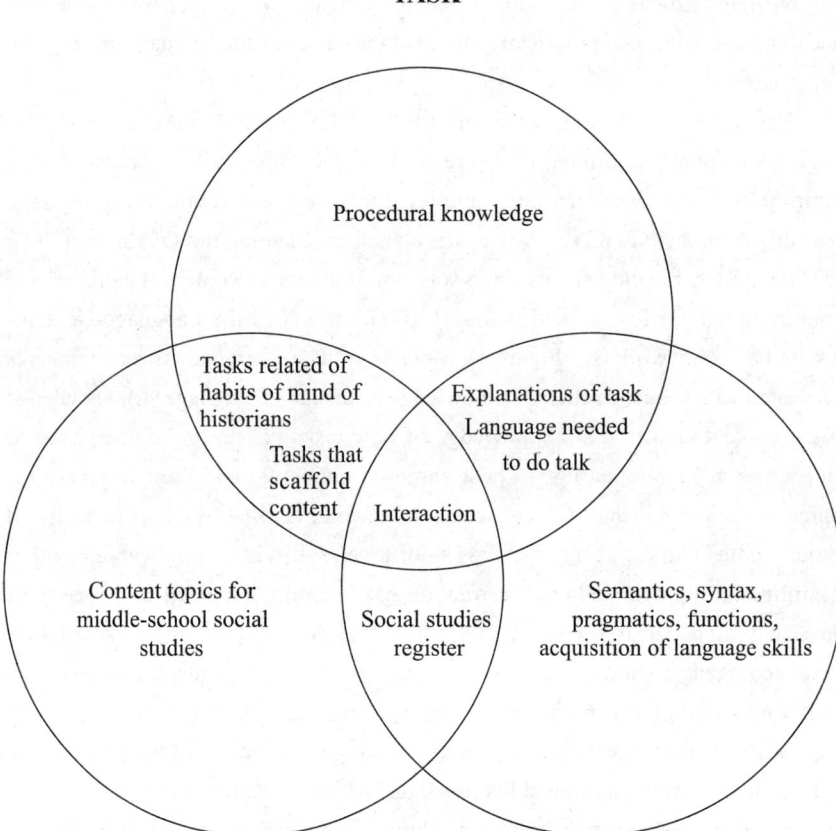

Figure 1. Language-Content-Task Framework, as applied to a sheltered social studies context. (Copyright © 2000 by D. J. Short. Used with permission.)

One curricular framework rarely referred to in second and foreign language discussions of content-based instruction is Concept-Oriented Reading Instruction (CORI), an approach to content learning and reading development used (and extensively researched) in first language settings (e.g., Guthrie et al., 1998; Guthrie, Schafer, Von Secker, & Alban, 2000; Guthrie & Ozgungor, 2002; Guthrie, Wigfield, & Von Seker, 2000). CORI, which has major implications for second and foreign language content-based curricula, began with instructional principles for stimulating interest and motivation to read. It has evolved into a more elaborate, yet flexible approach organized around four stages: (1) immersion into a main theme through students' personal engagement with the topic, (2) wide reading and information gathering on the theme across multiple information sources, (3) reading strategy instruction to assist with comprehension, and (4) project work leading to a product that demonstrates what students have learned. A significant component of CORI is strategies instruction to support the extensive and varied input from text material required for thematic instruction; yet it also incorporates comprehension instruction activities that go beyond strategy training (e.g., vocabulary development, fluency practice, extensive reading). In the development of the four stages of CORI, students engage in content discussions and activities that require the purposeful use of multiple strategies such as forming questions, noting text structure and text characteristics, activating background knowledge, answering questions, taking notes, determining main ideas, synthesizing information, paraphrasing, summarizing, monitoring and repairing comprehension, integrating information through graphic organizers, and carrying out a range of project tasks. These strategies are developed as part of explicit instruction while students are reading interesting texts to find information related to their projects; they are accompanied by consistent teacher modeling, teacher scaffolding, and extensive practice.

A number of larger goals are associated with CORI. With an emphasis on student motivation to read and to learn, the approach involves discussions that center around content, reading goals, strategies, and learning while students are engaged with multiple informational texts. As Guthrie and Ozgungor (2002) note, "CORI begins with knowledge goals and situates the critically important reading comprehension strategies within a rich subject-matter domain" (p. 281).

Another important aspect of CORI is its commitment to curricular coherence

(Guthrie, Cox, et al., 2000), often lacking in many content-based approaches (Stoller & Grabe, 1997; see also Davison & Williams, 2001). In CORI, coherence is operationalized by nurturing sustained student engagement with content material, by assisting students with making connections across texts and across subject areas, by helping students see the transferability of the strategies that they are mastering, and by guiding students in building upon prior knowledge and interests. (See Swan, 2003, for more detailed discussions of the differences between coherent and fragmented curricula in the context of CORI.)

Collaborative Strategic Reading (CSR), designed for English language learners, is an instructional framework that is rarely mentioned in discussions of CBI even though it combines cooperative learning principles and reading comprehension strategy instruction to promote content learning, language mastery, and reading comprehension (Klingner & Vaughn, 2000). During CSR, students work collaboratively to comprehend content-area texts, the belief being that cognitive development is stimulated by social interaction (the result of cooperative learning activities). While working in groups, students apply four strategies to their content reading: They preview (i.e., predict what the passage might be about), "click and clunk" (i.e., identify difficult words and concepts and use fix-up strategies to make sense of difficult texts), get the gist (i.e., restate the most important ideas in portions of the text), and wrap up (i.e., summarize what has been learned). CSR teachers, like CORI teachers, introduce the four strategies (and the approach) through modeling, role playing, thinking aloud, and discussing why, when, and how to use the strategies.

Quite different from the curricular orientations just described is Foreign Languages Across the Curriculum (FLAC), sometimes referred to as Languages Across the Curriculum (LAC), which broadens the scope of CBI curricular models by giving students the opportunity to build upon, and thereby supplement, formal language education through the use of foreign languages in courses outside of foreign language and literature departments (Klee, 2000; see also Krueger & Ryan, 1993; Straight, 1994; Stryker & Leaver, 1997). In FLAC programs, foreign languages are used for instructional purposes (i.e., in lecturing, in recitation sections, and/or for reading of authentic materials) in courses that focus on subject matter such as history, social sciences, and business. FLAC programs are often adopted as part of an institutional effort to internationalize the curriculum.

Empirical Studies

Although much of the professional literature advocating content-based approaches relies on nonempirical support, numerous empirical studies have implications for CBI curriculum development. CORI, mentioned earlier, is an example of a first language approach to language (mainly reading) and content learning that has been the subject of extensive research. Results from CORI studies have shown that students at multiple grade levels outperform control groups in text comprehension, uses of strategies for learning, and motivation for learning (e.g., Guthrie & Ozgungor, 2002; Guthrie, Wigfield, & Von Seker, 2000; Guthrie et al., 1998). The main elements of CORI—including extended reading on and sustained engagement with a theme; strategy training and the purposeful use of strategies; classroom discussions of content, strategies, and learning; information gathering; project work; and student motivation—could easily be adapted to, and investigated in, second and foreign language settings.

Collaborative Strategic Reading (CSR), introduced in the previous section, has also been the subject of empirical research. Klingner and Vaughn (2000) investigated the frequency and means by which 37 bilingual and limited English proficient students in a fifth-grade elementary school classroom helped each other while implementing CSR with science textbook reading. Results revealed that students spent about half of their time identifying and clarifying "clunks" (i.e., difficult words and concepts), with the remainder of their time divided among the other three strategies. Students took the responsibility for learning content, and helping others to do the same seriously. Results of pre- and post-English vocabulary measures indicated gains in vocabulary learning as well.

Continuing a long-standing tradition, numerous Canadian studies focus on immersion-program curricula. Turnbull, Lapkin, and Hart (2001) and Bournot-Trites and Reeder (2001), for example, explore the effects of different immersion models, the proportion of instructional time in English, and the language of testing. Turnbull, Lapkin, and Hart compared French immersion and nonimmersion students' performances on tests of English reading and writing and mathematics. The researchers concluded that immersion does not have a negative impact on students' literacy and mathematical skills in English even though their results, confirming earlier studies, demonstrated a lag in early total immersion students' literacy skills at grade 3. Yet, immersion students who were exposed to some instruction in English language arts (even if only in grade 3) performed as well as nonimmersion students. At grade 6, immersion students' literacy scores were better than their peers' in English-only programs. At both grades 3 and 6, immersion students' math scores were almost identical to nonimmersion peers. (See Thomas & Collier, 2002, for a study of the effectiveness of U.S.-based bilingual, immersion, and mainstream programs for long-term academic achievement.)

Other indications of the strong research tradition in Canada are seen in the work of Burger and Chrétien (2001), who studied the oral language development of students enrolled in a university psychology course and adjunct language course. Results revealed that students can make measurable gains in oral language skills, in terms of both fluency and accuracy, as a result of the paired classes. Their results build upon earlier studies that show the effectiveness of linking a content course and a language support course. Duff (2001a) conducted an ethnographic study of a secondary social studies class and determined that students not only needed to be able to succeed in a variety of speaking, reading, and writing tasks, but they also "needed a current knowledge of popular North American culture, mass media, and newsworthy events; an ability to express a range of critical perspectives on social issues and to enter quick-paced interactions, and a great deal of confidence" (p. 103).

Other studies with implications for content-based curricula have examined the role of discourse—including teachers' oral discourse and teacher–student interactions—in content-based settings. For example, Short (2002) conducted a study to examine teachers' oral discourse to determine whether and how teachers (two certified social studies instructors and two trained ESL teachers) addressed language, content, and task learning (the three major components of the LCT framework mentioned earlier) in U.S. middle-school sheltered social studies classrooms. Data culled from audiotaped classroom observations and a review of lesson plans and classroom practices revealed that teachers placed more emphasis on content and tasks than on language. Only 20 percent of teachers' utterances focused on language development; 95 percent of those language-related utterances was devoted to issues related to pronunciation and vocabulary comprehension. In contrast, 35 percent of oral interactions addressed content, and 44 percent addressed tasks. The lack of attention to language was also evident in the review of lesson plans and instructional practices. Short points out that efforts to address content and tasks are not uncommon in sheltered curricula because of external pressures to cover the standard curriculum and prepare students for state and local testing. Contributing to the lack of attention to language is the fact that, on the one hand, ESL teachers in such settings are struggling with content for which they have not been trained, and the social studies teachers, on the other hand, do not believe that teaching language should be part of their responsibilities. Because of the teachers' uneven attention to language, content, and tasks, neither the lessons of teachers with social studies training nor those with ESL training complement the LCT model proposed by Short (2002). To remedy this problem and move teachers toward addressing students' multifaceted needs, as characterized by the LCT model, Echevarria, Vogt, and Short (2000; see also Short & Echevarria, 1999) have generated guidelines for training and supervising teachers so that they can improve their sheltered content teaching.

Gibbons (2003) investigated how teacher–student interactions in an Australian content-based science classroom (focusing on magnetism) contribute to 9-and 10-year-old ESL students' language development. Drawing on constructs from systemic functional linguistics and sociocultural theory (see also Huang & Morgan, 2003; Mohan & Beckett, 2001), Gibbons examined how teachers mediate between students' current language abilities and understanding of science, on the one hand, and the educational discourse and specialist understanding of science, on the other. Gibbons' data, drawn from 14 hours of classroom discourse, revealed that teachers mediate language and learning by recasting, signaling for reformulations, and modeling alternative ways of reconstructing knowledge for the benefit of others. The interaction between these forms of teacher mediation and ESL students' active participation in the discourse of the classroom resulted in the gradual transformation of student language so that it more closely approximated the specialist discourse of the school curriculum, that is, the targeted academic register.

Creese (2002) examined the discursive practices of 14 content and 12 language specialists working in partnerships in three mainstream classroom settings in London, England, to understand "the ways these teachers' discourses underpin and are unpinned by different sets of knowledge hierarchies within the classroom"

(p. 598). Data drawn from a one-year ethnography revealed that language teachers' knowledge and skills are perceived to have lower status than the subject area teachers.' In these settings, pedagogical approaches perceived as highly effective in many ESL/EFL settings (e.g., scaffolding, making form-function links, noticing gaps in input, providing opportunities for negotiation) were perceived as less important than the content teachers' pedagogical practices. The undermining of the language teachers' contributions to the partnership marginalizes not only the teacher but also the students who are supposed to benefit from the language teachers' presence. (See Leung, 2001, and Leung & Franson, 2001a and 2001b, for other discussions of mainstreaming in England.)

Pica (2002) explored the extent to which learners and teachers modify their interactions, during classroom discussions, about subject-matter content through negotiation of meaning, form-focused intervention, and form-focused instruction. She wanted to determine the extent to which modified interactions, if they occurred, led to input, feedback, and production of modified output that could draw students' attention to form and meaning relationships. Pica conducted her research in a university-based English language institute with two content-based classes. Findings revealed that classroom discussions, the most frequently employed interactional activity in these classrooms, included little negotiation of meaning and negligible amounts of form-focused intervention or instruction, resulting in a "paucity of the kinds of interaction considered helpful to learners' input, feedback and production needs" (p. 10). To better meet students' language-learning needs, Pica has recommended that content-based teachers modify their responses to students' contributions to classroom discussions in ways that would generate more input, feedback, and modified student output. Pica's recommendations reinforce similar suggestions made by Doughty and Varela (1998), whose research indicates ways in which teachers recast students' responses to further students' development of verb form and meaning in content-based science and math classes for ESL students. Pica has also suggested that teachers follow up classroom discussions with interactive, form-focusing tasks to draw students' attention to developmentally difficult form-meaning relationships. (See also Swain, 1998, 2001, for results of studies on the role of output in prompting metalinguistic reflection and the role of collaborative tasks, focusing on content, in drawing learners' attention to language.)

A Call for Further Research

Additional empirical research on content-based instruction is needed. In the Winter 2001 *TESOL Quarterly*, 10 specialists in the field were asked to identify research priorities for the near future. Three of the specialists identified research areas that are directly pertinent to content-based instruction. Christian (2001), for example, identified the need to understand (1) the relationship between school-based language instruction and students' needs to master content through L2 literacy, (2) the acquisition of literacy competence and subject-matter learning as critical factors in academic success, and (3) the processes involved in, and interactions among, acquiring literacy competence, subject matter learning, and L2 learning. Duff (2001b) pinpointed the need to understand the impact of participation in language programs on students' L2 abilities, content knowledge, and career outcomes as particularly relevant. Freeman (2001) called for a better understanding of the role of teachers' subject matter knowledge on classroom instruction. The focus of Freeman's suggested research agenda is linked most strongly to teachers' knowledge of applied linguistics subject matter and the English language, but such research could easily be extended to other subject-matter knowledge.

Elsewhere, Short (1999) and Gottlieb (1999) have pointed out the need for systematic research on assessment in the context of content-based instruction. Because it is difficult to separate language learning issues from content learning issues in the assessment process, we need to find a way to determine if students are unable to demonstrate knowledge because of a language barrier or because of a lack of understanding of content material. Short (1999) has called for "a new paradigm for assessment" (p. 131), one that moves beyond standardized tests and toward assessment that monitors students' academic progress, language learning, and content learning. Leung (2001) has called for an assessment of educational and public policy and its influence on the content and language learning of L2 students who are placed into mainstream curricula.

The challenges intimated by the case studies reviewed here suggest the need for research in additional areas related to content-based curricula. Wesche and Skehan (2002) have identified the interface of language and content as "the most important pedagogical issue for CBI at all program levels" (p. 225), making it worthy of investigation. Fruitful areas of investigation include the selection, sequencing, and balance of content and language; the relationships among input, output, and feedback; student engagement with the information gathering, processing, and reporting process; strategy training; the contextualization of grammar instruction; the relationship between tasks and texts; and the development of curricular coherence, to name just a few areas that would benefit from further exploration. Studies such as those suggested here are needed to inform the practices of teachers, curriculum and course designers, materials developers, and those involved with assessment. The result could be more effective approaches to content-based instruction which would benefit students who desire stronger content- and language-learning abilities.

ANNOTATED BIBLIOGRAPHY

Crandall, J. A., & Kaufman, D. (Eds.). (2002). *Content-based instruction in higher education settings*. Alexandria, VA: TESOL.

This volume represents the most recent compendium of case studies showcasing the different ways in which content-based instruction has been adapted in ESL and EFL settings.

Echevarria, J., Vogt, M. E., & Short, D. J. (2000). *Making content compre-hensible for English language learners: The SIOP model*. Needham Heights, MA: Allyn & Bacon.

This volume presents a field-tested model of sheltered instruction that specifies features of effective sheltered lessons. The volume provides guidance for teacher supervisors who are in the position to observe and quantify sheltered teaching.

Guthrie, J. T., & Ozgungor, S. (2002). Instructional contexts for reading engagement. In C. Collins Block & M. Pressley (Eds.), *Comprehension instruction: Research-based best practices* (pp. 275–288). New York: Guilford Press.

This chapter provides a thorough description of Concept-Oriented Reading Instruction (CORI) as applied in different grades and different schools. The chapter provides an example of an eight-week CORI unit, which is followed by a discussion of the principles that account for the effectiveness of CORI. Evidence from longitundinal and cross-sectional studies of CORI are presented to illustrate the benefits of CORI for reading comprehension, reading motivation, and knowledge acquisition. Although the authors do not address the use of CORI in L2 contexts, the chapter offers many insights that are pertinent to discussions of content-based instruction in L2 contexts.

Short, D. J. (2002). Language learning in sheltered social studies classes. *TESOL Journal, 11* (1), 18–24.

This article introduces a content-based curricular framework—the Language-Content-Task (LCT) framework—that is structured around three components associated with academic literacy: knowledge of the target language (L), knowledge of the content area (C), and knowledge of how tasks (T) are to be completed to succeed in academic settings. The article showcases how the framework can be used in a sheltered social studies curriculum and how it was applied to classroom-based research.

Swan, E. A. (2003). *Concept-oriented reading instruction: Engaging classrooms, lifelong learners.* New York: Guilford Press.

This book explores Concept-Oriented Reading Instruction (CORI) in very practical terms. The book is replete with concrete examples showcasing the CORI framework in actual use. Like the Guthrie & Ozgungor (2002) chapter cited earlier, this volume is not directed at L2 teachers. Yet the potential for adapting CORI for content-based classrooms in L2 settings makes this a worthwhile volume for practitioners (including those interested in curriculum and course design, and materials development).

Wesche, M. B. (Ed.). (2001). French immersion and content-based language teaching in Canada/Immersion et apprentissage axe sur le contenu au Canada [Special issue]. *The Canadian Modern Language Review/La Revue canadienne des langues vivantes, 58* (1).

The entire volume is dedicated to an exploration of French immersion and content-based instruction in Canada. The eight studies reported address the conditions and processes underlying successful language and content teaching and learning.

OTHER REFERENCES

American Council on Immersion Education (ACIE). *The bridge: From research to practice* [Newsletter]. Retrieved September, 2003, from http://carla.acad.umn.edu/acie-bridges.html.

Bournot-Trites, M., & Reeder, K. (2001). Interdependence revisited: Mathematics achievement in an intensified French immersion program. *The Canadian Modern Language Review/La Revue canadienne des langues vivantes, 58* (1), 27–43.

Bragger, J. D., & Rice, D. B. (1999). The message is in medium: A new paradigm for content-oriented instruction. *Foreign Language Annals, 32* (3), 373–391.

Brinton, D. M. (2001). A theme-based literature course: Focus on the City of Angels. In J. Murphy & P. Byrd (Eds.), *Understanding the courses we teach: Local perspectives on English language teaching* (pp. 281–308). Ann Arbor: University of Michigan Press.

Brinton, D. M., & Jensen, L. (2002). Appropriating the adjunct model: English for academic purposes at the university level. In J. A. Crandall & D. Kaufman (Eds.), *Content-based instruction in higher education settings* (pp. 125–137). Alexandria, VA: TESOL.

Brinton, D., Snow, M. A., & Wesche, M. (1989). *Content-based second language instruction.* New York: Newbury House.

Bueno, K. A. (2002). Creating community and making connections in the third-year Spanish course: A content-based approach. *Foreign Language Annals, 35* (3), 333–341.

Bunch, G. C., Abram, P. L., Lotan, R. A., & Valdés, G. (2001). Beyond sheltered instruction: Rethinking conditions for academic language development. *TESOL Journal, 10* (2/3), 28–33.

Burger, S., & Chrétien, M. (2001). The development of oral production in content-based second language courses at the University of Ottawa. *The Canadian Modern Language Review/La Revue canadienne des langues vivantes, 58* (1), 84–102.

Cantoni-Harvey, G. (1987). *Content-area language instruction: Approaches and strategies.* Reading, MA: Addison-Wesley.

Center for Advanced Research on Language Acquisition (CARLA), University of Minnesota. Content-based language teaching through technology. Retrieved October, 2003, from http://carla.acad.umn.edu/COBALTT.html.

Carson, J. G. (2000). Reading and writing for academic purposes. In M. Pally (Ed.), *Sustained content teaching in academic ESL/EFL: A practical approach* (pp. 19–34). Boston: Houghton Mifflin.

Chamot, A. U., & O'Malley, J. M. (1987). The Cognitive Academic Language Learning Approach: A Bridge to the Mainstream. *TESOL Quarterly, 21* (2), 227–249.

Chamot, A. U., & O'Malley, J. M. (1994). *The CALLA handbook: Implementing the Cognitive Academic Language Learning Approach.* Reading, MA: Addison-Wesley.

Christian, D. (2001). Dual-language education for English language learners. *TESOL Quarterly,*

35 (4), 601–602.

Crandall, J. A. (Ed.). (1987). *ESL through content-area instruction; Mathematics, science, and social studies.* Englewood Cliffs, NJ: Prentice Hall.

Crandall, J. A. (1993). Content-centered learning in the United States. *Annual Review of Applied Linguistics, 13,* 111–126.

Creese, A. (2002). The discursive construction of power in teacher partnerships: Language and subject specialists in mainstream schools. *TESOL Quarterly, 36* (4), 597–616.

Davison, C., & Williams, A. (2001). Integrating language and content: Unresolved issues. In B. Mohan, C. Leung, & C. Davison (Eds.), *English as a second language in the mainstream: Teaching learning and identity* (pp. 51–70). New York: Longman.

de Courcy, M. (2002). *Learners' experiences of immersion education: Case studies of French and Chinese.* Clevedon, UK: Multilingual Matters.

Doughty, C., & Varela, E. (1998). Communicative focus on form. In C. Doughty & J. Williams (Eds.), *Focus on form in second language classrooms* (pp. 114–138). New York: Cambridge University Press.

Duff, P. A. (2001a). Language literacy, content, and (pop) culture: Challenges for ESL students in mainstream courses. *The Canadian Modern Language Review/La Revue canadienne des langues vivantes, 58* (1), 103–132.

Duff, P. A. (2001b). Learning English for academic and occupational purposes. *TESOL Quarterly, 35* (4), 606–607.

Dupuy, B. C. (2000). Content-based instruction: Can it help ease the transition from beginning to advanced foreign language classes? *Foreign Language Annals, 33,* 205–223.

Echevarria, J., & Graves, A. (2003). *Sheltered content instruction: Teaching English-language learners with diverse abilities* (2nd ed.) Boston: Allyn & Bacon.

Enright, D. S., & McCloskey, M. (1988). *Integrating English.* Reading, MA: Addison-Wesley.

Freeman, D. (2001). Teacher learning and student learning in TESOL. *TESOL Quarterly, 35* (4), 608–609.

Gibbons, P. (2003). Mediating language learning: Teacher interactions with ESL students in a content-based classroom. *TESOL Quarterly, 37* (2), 247–273.

Gilzow, D., & Branaman, L. E. (2000). *Lessons learned: Model early foreign language programs.* Washington, DC: Center for Applied Linguistics and McHenry, IL: Delta Systems.

Gottlieb, M. (1999). Assessing ESOL adolescents: Balancing accessibility to learn with accountability for learning. In C. J. Faltis & P. Wolfe (Eds.), *So much to say: Adolescents, bilingualism, & ESL in the secondary school* (pp. 176–201). New York: Teachers College Press.

Guthrie, J. T., Van Meter, P., Hancock, G. R., McCann, A., Anderson, E., & Alao, S. (1998). Does Concept-Oriented Reading Instruction increase strategy use and conceptual learning from text? *Journal of Educational Psychology, 90* (2), 261–278.

Guthrie, J. T., Cox, K. E., Knowles, K. T., Buehl, M., Mazzoni, S., & Fasculo, L. (2000). Building toward coherent instruction. In L. Baker, M. J. Dreher, & J. T. Guthrie (Eds.), *Engaging young readers: Promoting achievement and motivation* (pp. 209–237). New York: Guilford Press.

Guthrie, J. T., Schafer, W. D., Von Secker, C., & Alban, T. (2000). Contributions of integrated reading instruction and text resources to achievement and engagement in a statewide school improvement program. *Journal of Educational Research, 93*, 211–226.

Guthrie, J. T., Wigfield, A., & Von Seker, C. (2000). Effects of integrated instruction on motivation and strategy use in reading. *Journal of Educational Psychology, 92* (2), 331–341.

Hoecherl-Alden, G. (2000). Turning professional: Content-based communication and the evolution of a cross-cultural language curriculum. *Foreign Language Annals, 33*, 614–621.

Huang, J., & Morgan, G. (2003). A functional approach to evaluating content knowledge and language development in ESL students' science classification texts. *International Journal of Applied Linguistics, 13* (2), 234–262.

Iancu, M. A. (2002). To motivate and educate, collaborate and integrate: The adjunct model in a bridge program. In J. A. Crandall & D. Kaufman (Eds.), *Content-based instruction in higher education settings* (pp. 139–153). Alexandria, VA: TESOL.

Janzen, J. (2001). Strategic readings on a sustained content theme. In J. Murphy & P. Byrd (Eds.), *Understanding the courses we teach: Local perspectives on English language teaching* (pp. 369–389). Ann Arbor: University of Michigan Press.

Johns, A. M. (1997). *Text, role, and context: Developing academic literacies*. New York: Cambridge University Press.

Johnson, R. K., & Swain, M. (Eds.). (1997). *Immersion education: International perspectives*. New York: Cambridge University Press.

Kasper, L. F. (1997). The impact of content-based instructional programs on the academic progress of ESL students. *English for Specific Purposes, 16* (4), 309–320.

Kasper, L. F. (Ed.). (2000). *Content-based college ESL instruction*. Mahwah, NJ: Erlbaum.

Klee, C. A. (2000). Foreign language instruction. In J. W. Rosenthal (Ed.), *Handbook of undergraduate second language education* (pp. 49–72). Mahwah, NJ: Erlbaum.

Klingner, J. K., & Vaughn, S. (2000). The helping behaviors of fifth graders while using collaborative strategic reading during ESL content classes. *TESOL Quarterly, 34* (1), 69–98.

Krueger, M., & Ryan, F. (Eds.). (1993). *Language and content: Discipline- and content-based approach to language study*. Lexington, MA: Heath.

Langman, J. (2003). The effects of ESL-trained content-area teachers: Reducing middle-school students to incidental language learners. *Prospect, 18* (1), 14–26.

Leung, C. (2001). Evaluation of content-language learning in the mainstream classroom. In B. Mohan, C. Leung, & C. Davison (Eds.), *English as a second language in the mainstream:*

12. CONTENT-BASED INSTRUCTION: PERSPECTIVES ON CURRICULUM PLANNING 339

Teaching learning and identity (pp. 177–198). New York: Longman.

Leung, C., & Franson, C. (2001a). Curriculum identity and professional development: System-wide questions. In B. Mohan, C. Leung, & C. Davison (Eds.), *English as a second language in the mainstream: Teaching learning and identity* (pp. 199–214). New York: Longman.

Leung, C., & Franson, C. (2001b). Mainstreaming: ESL as a diffused curriculum concern. In B. Mohan, C. Leung, & C. Davison (Eds.), *English as a second language in the mainstream: Teaching learning and identity* (pp. 165–176). New York: Longman.

Marsh, D. (n.d.). Using languages to learn and learning to use languages. Retrieved April 23, 2003, from TIE-CLIL Web site: http://www.tieclil.org/html/ products.

Marsh, D., & Langé, G. (Eds.). (1999). *Implementing content and language integrated learning: A research driver TIE-CLIL foundation course reader.* Jyväskylä, Finland: Continuing Education Centre, University of Jyväskylä.

Mendelsohn, D. J. (2001). Canadian language and culture. A course for nine academic credits. In J. Murphy & P. Byrd (Eds.), *Understanding the courses we teach: Local perspectives on English language teaching* (pp. 309–326). Ann Arbor: University of Michigan Press.

Met, M. (1998). Curriculum decision-making in content-based language teaching. In J. Cenoz & F. Genesee (Eds.), *Beyond bilingualism: Multilingualism and multilingual education* (pp. 35–63). Philadelphia, PA: Multilingual Matters.

Mohan, B. (1986). *Language and content.* Reading, MA: Addison-Wesley.

Mohan, B., & Beckett, G. H. (2001). A functional approach to research on content-based language learning: Recasts in causal explanations. *The Canadian Modern Language Review/ La Revue canadienne des langues vivantes, 58* (1), 133–155.

Mohan, B., Leung, C., & Davison, C. (Eds.). (2001). *English as a second language in the mainstream: Teaching learning and identity.* New York: Longman.

Murphy, J., & Byrd, P. (Eds.). (2001). *Understanding the courses we teach: Local perspectives on English language teaching.* Ann Arbor: University of Michigan Press.

Murphy, J., & Stoller, F. L. (2001a). Sustained-content language teaching: An emerging definition. *TESOL Journal, 10* (2/3), 3–5.

Murphy, J., & Stoller, F. L. (Eds.). (2001b). *TESOL Journal, 10* (2/3) [Special topics issue on sustained content for language teaching].

Opp-Beckman, L. (2002). Africa online: A Web- and content-based English language teaching course. *TESOL Journal, 11* (3), 4–8.

Pally, M. (Ed.). (2000). *Sustained content teaching in academic ESL/EFL: A practical approach.* Boston: Houghton Mifflin.

Parkinson, J. (2000). Acquiring scientific literacy through content and genre: A theme-based language course for science students. *English for Specific Purposes, 19,* 369–387.

Peninsula Technikon. (2001, March). Integrating content and language: Providing access to knowledge through language. Conference proceedings. Retrieved September, 2003, from http://www.pentach.ac.za/pil88/.

Pica, T. (2002). Subject-matter content: How does it assist the interactional and linguistic needs of classroom language learners? *The Modern Language Journal, 81*, 1–19.

Pufahl, I., Rhodes, N. C., & Christian, D. (2000). *Foreign language teaching: What the United States can learn from other countries.* Washington, DC: Center for Applied Linguistics.

Ronesi, L. (2001). Training undergraduates to support ESL classmates: The English Language Fellows Program. *TESOL Journal, 10* (2/3), 23–27.

Schleppegrell, M., & Achugar, M. (2003). Learning language and learning history: A functional linguistics approach. *TESOL Journal, 12* (2), 21–27.

Short, D. J. (1994). Expanding middle school horizons: Integrating language, culture, and social studies. *TESOL Quarterly, 28*, 581–608.

Short, D. J. (1997). Reading and 'riting and...social studies: Research on integrated language and content in second classrooms. In M. A. Snow & D. M. Brinton (Eds.), *The content-based classroom: Perspectives on integrating language and content* (pp. 213–232). New York: Longman.

Short, D. J. (1999). Integrating language and content for effective sheltered instruction programs. In C. J. Faltis & P. Wolfe (Eds.), *So much to say: Adolescents, bilingualism, & ESL in the secondary school* (pp. 105–137). New York: Teachers College Press.

Short, D. J., & Echevarria, J. (1999). *The sheltered instruction observation protocol: A tool for teacher-research collaboration and professional development.* Santa Cruz: Center for Research on Education, Diversity & Excellence, University of California, Santa Cruz.

Smallwood, B. A., & McCargo, C. (Eds.). (1999). *Integrating language and content in secondary school: Instructional strategies and thematic units for English, mathematics, science, and social studies.* Washington, DC: Center for Applied Linguistics.

Snow, M. A. (1997). Teaching academic literacy skills: Discipline faculty take responsibility. In M. A. Snow & D. M. Brinton (Eds.), *The content-based classroom: Perspectives on integrating language and content* (pp. 290–304). New York: Longman.

Snow, M. A. (1998). Trends and issues in content-based instruction. *Annual Review of Applied Linguistics, 18*, 243–267.

Snow, M. A. (2001). Content-based and immersion models for second and foreign language teaching. In M. Celce-Murcia (Ed.), *Teaching English as a second or foreign language* (3rd ed., pp. 303–318). Boston: Heinle & Heinle.

Snow, M. A., & Kamhi-Stein, L. D. (2002). Teaching and learning academic literacy through Project LEAP. In J. A. Crandall & D. Kaufman (Eds.), *Content-based instruction in higher education settings* (pp. 169–181). Alexandria, VA: TESOL.

Spanos, G. (1990). On the integration of language and content instruction. *Annual Review of*

Applied Linguistics, 10, 227–240.

Stewart, T., Sagliano, M., & Sagliano, J. (2002). Merging expertise: Developing partnerships between language and content specialists. In J. A. Crandall & D. Kaufman (Eds.), *Content-based instruction in higher education settings* (pp. 29–44). Alexandria, VA: TESOL.

Stoller, F. L. (2002). Promoting the acquisition of knowledge in a content-based course. In J. A. Crandall & D. Kaufman (Eds.), *Content-based instruction in higher education settings* (pp. 109–123). Alexandria, VA: TESOL.

Stoller, F. L., & Grabe, W. (1997). A six-Ts approach to content-based instruction. In M. A. Snow & D. M. Brinton (Eds.), *The content-based classroom: Perspectives on integrating language and content* (pp. 78–103). New York: Longman.

Straight, H. S. (Ed.). (1994). *Languages across the Curriculum: Translation perspectives VII*. Binghamton, NY: Center for Research in Translation, SUNY at Binghamton.

Stryker, S. B., & Leaver, B. L. (Eds.). (1997). *Content-based instruction in foreign language education: Models and methods*. Washington, DC: Georgetown University Press.

Swain, M. (1998). Focus on form through conscious reflection. In C. Doughty & J. Williams (Eds.), *Focus on form in second language classrooms* (pp. 64–81). New York: Cambridge University Press.

Swain, M. (2001). Integrating language and content teaching through collaborative tasks. *The Canadian Modern Language Review/La Revue canadienne des langues vivantes, 58* (1), 44–63.

Thomas, W. P., & Collier, V. P. (2002). *A national study of school effectiveness for language minority students' long-term academic achievement.* Santa Cruz, CA: Center for Research on Education, Diversity & Excellence, University of California.

Turnbull, M., Lapkin, M., & Hart, D. (2001). Grade 3 immersion students' performances in literacy and mathematics: Province-wide results from Ontario (1998–99). *The Canadian Modern Language Review/La Revue canadienne des langues vivantes, 58* (1), 9–26.

University of Maastricht, Netherlands. (2003, fall). Integrating content and language: Meeting the challenge of a multilingual higher education. Conference program. Retrieved October, 2003, from http://www.unimaas.nl/icl/ index.htm.

Weissberg, R., & Lipoufski, M. (2002). Borders and barriers: A model for a local-issues ESL course. *TESOL Journal, 11* (2), 12–18.

Wesche, M. B. (2000). A Canadian perspective: Second language teaching and learning in the university. In J. W. Rosenthal (Ed.), *Handbook of undergraduate second language education* (pp. 187–208). Mahwah, NJ: Erlbaum.

Wesche, M. B., & Skehan, P. (2002). Communicative, task-based, and content-based language instruction. In R. B. Kaplan (Ed.), *The Oxford handbook of applied linguistics* (pp. 207–228). New York: Oxford University Press.

13. ASPECTS OF COLLABORATION IN PEDAGOGICAL DISCOURSE

Richard Donato

In this review of research, various aspects of collaboration are discussed to understand more completely the phenomenon of jointly constructed activity in pedagogical contexts. This chapter presents the parameter for collaborations, differentiates collaboration from interaction, and reviews studies organized into three themes: collaboration and community, collaboration and language development, and collaboration and identity. Concepts taken from sociocultural theory provide an overarching explanatory framework of learning in the collaborative setting. These concepts include goal-directed activity, human relations, mediation, history, and culture. Consideration for emergent directions for research on collaboration and language learning are presented.

In a volume dedicated to advances in language pedagogy, it should come as no surprise that the topic of collaboration would be addressed. The belief that collaborative activity is consequential to cognitive, social, historical, and affective development has become widely accepted in developmental psychology and educational research. Ironically, although research and theory on interaction is vast in the field of additional language acquisition, relatively few studies specifically take into account the collaborative aspects of learners' jointly constructed activity. This assertion might seem contradictory in view of the ongoing interest in interaction and second language acquisition since the early 1980s.

In this brief review of recent research, I hope to illustrate the various aspects of collaboration that have been described and linked to learner performance and learning outcomes.[1] By reviewing examples of studies that explicitly invoke the concept of collaboration in the analysis, I hope to illustrate how collaborative research differs from other forms of research on interaction and second language acquisition. Additionally, I will argue that sociocultural theory provides an overarching explanatory framework for collaborative learning.

The purpose of this review article is threefold. I first discuss the concept of collaboration and illustrate how it differs from the more general concept of interaction. Against this backdrop, I establish a few overarching themes of collaborative research and review representative research studies that address collaborative activity in classroom settings. Finally, based on the review, I connect research findings to sociocultural theory and outline some critical areas where research is needed on collaboration and language learning in classroom settings.

Collaboration versus Interaction

Although the study of interaction is commonplace in the field of applied linguistics and language learning (Hall & Stoops Verplaetse, 2000), interaction does not categorically mean collaboration. As John-Steiner points out, "in engaging in collaboration in Western societies, partners need to shed some of their cultural heritage, such as the powerful belief in a separate, independent self and in the glory of individual achievement" (2000, p. 204). This observation draws attention to the fact that interaction is defined largely based on the psychological and social orientation of group members and can be easily reduced to little more than individuals working autonomously in the presence of others (Donato, 1994). For an interaction to be called collaborative, several aspects need to be considered. To this end, I examine at three perspectives on collaboration to find common ground. The three perspectives come from contemporary school-based collaborations, affinity groups, and Russian developmental psychology.

Three Converging Perspectives on Collaboration

Fullan (1999), in his discussion of collaborative cultures of change, identifies several features of school-based collaboration and the innovations they produce. According to Fullan, collaborative cultures foster diversity while simultaneously building trust, provoke anxiety and contain it, engage in raising tacit knowledge to explicit knowledge, seek connections to ideas that exist inside and outside of the group, and build coherence. Collaboration is about changing social networks and relations through the meaningful and purposeful joint work these networks carry out in historical and cultural contexts, as in the school and community. The result of collaboration is simultaneously the emergence of new knowledge and growth for the group. Additionally, for change to occur, collaboration needs to enable individuals to engage in continuous collaborative involvement, as opposed to producing solely autonomous knowers removed from social connections.

A good example of a collaborative culture of change can be found in the work of Moll and Greenberg (1990) in creating connections between the cultural funds of knowledge socially shared in households in Mexican communities in Arizona and the academic life of children in classrooms. In this project, learning and development occur in the situated production of culturally and historically meaningful educational activity. Through the collaborative involvement of parents and other adults in the community in the academic life of youngsters, education provides new contexts for learning and becomes a societal activity woven from the systems of knowledge distributed across households. These connections have reciprocal benefits for children and adults. Within the school, children come to understand their social reality better and adults' tacit understandings are the foundation for explicit academic knowledge of their children. Outside the school, children more fully participate in the social life of the community, and adults value and understand more deeply what they do and implicitly know in their daily lives.

Gee (2003) introduces the notion of *affinity groups*, as opposed to the more romanticized and benevolent term *communities of practice* (see also Holland & Lave, 2000 for a discussion of contentious communities of practice). According to Gee, affinity groups are continually immersed in practice and share common features, whether they are found in the workplace, in the community, or on the Internet. Similar to Fullan's ideas, members of affinity groups bond to each other and learn primarily through a jointly constructed endeavor organized around a process that is carried out through members' knowledge located and distributed in a network of relationships. Members of affinity groups are associated with a given semiotic domain and can easily recognize each other as insiders of the group. Gee provides the example of networked computer games where groups of players collaborate, compete, and learn from each other through connecting several game platforms or computers. In this networked collaborative, Gee argues that individuals know each other through the semiotics of the interactions and can identify contributions and strengths that each member brings to the competition.

A third perspective on collaboration is proposed by Petrovsky (1985) in an insightful book entitled the *Individual and the Collective*. Although the book is close to 20 years old, Petrovsky offers a conceptualization of "group" that reflects current understandings while contesting several Western discussions of the topic. Petrovsky addresses the issue that collaboration implies group conformity and neglects the individual. His theory of collective differs in part from contemporary concepts of collaboration in two respects. First, the individual is unique and derivative of the social. Second, the analysis of collaboration entails multiple levels from deeply rooted cooperative efforts toward a central activity to superficial social affinities. For Petrovksy, socially constructed activity mediates all interpersonal relations and is at the core of the collective. Surrounding the activity base is the psychological level of collaboration and includes the attitudes of each member to the aims of the activity and the social and personal significance that each participant assigns to it. The next level reflects interpersonal relations mediated by the activity itself and is constituted by the historical and cultural backgrounds of the members. At this level, affiliations are explained as instantiations of the ideals and values that members of the collective bring to the specific task. Finally, the surface features of the collective are produced by connections that are mainly personal and affective and that can be unrelated to collective aims of the activity.

The usefulness of this multilevel framework is that it is explanatory and moves beyond descriptive global features of affective personal links and externally defined purposes for collaboration (e.g., a task's intended goals). That is, by analyzing the internal structure of collaboration through and across the activity core, the values the participants assign to their collective work, and the relationships that are mediated by and derivative of the activity, collaborative performance can be explained in a coherent way. Additionally, the multilevel analysis provides an insider's view of collaborative activity, accounts for why collaboration may not always appear benign, and underscores why context alone cannot determine the degree of collaboration. Smagorinsky and O'Donnell-Allen (2000) provide an excellent illustration of this model in their investigation of high school students' collaborative work on creating visual and textual interpretations of characters in *Hamlet*.

When taken together, these three conceptualizations reveal common characteristics that set collaborative groups apart from loosely configured individuals. Collaboration involves a meaningful core activity (e.g., playing a networked computer game, creating a visual product, developing curricular innovations) and the social relations that develop as a result of jointly constructed goals for the common endeavor. Additionally, collaboration involves recognition of individuals as parts of a cooperative activity and the acceptance of the contributions of individuals in the service of a larger goal. Finally, collaborative groups build coherence within and among social relations and knowledge located and distributed in its members. In this way, collaboration co-constructs new knowledge that goes beyond any knowledge possessed by a single member in isolation (Donato, 1994). The studies to be reviewed below illustrate these concepts.

Collaboration and Research

Definitions of Collaboration

What is striking is how these three conceptualizations of collaboration differ from how some second language acquisition research typically operationalizes interaction. For example, in many studies of language learning in interactive settings, the relational level of collaborative functioning of participants is ignored. It seems reasonable to assume that outcomes of loosely knit configurations of individuals working together on tasks with preestablished goals and externally defined purposes would be different from collaboratively constructed activity, as defined above (Donato, 1988; 1994). Indeed, in an early study on foreign language learning, Donato (1988) found that students who worked collectively on preparing for a role-play task produced learning outcomes for the group and the individual greater than those of their loosely knit counterparts. Their collective orientation to jointly constructed activity was revealed in the members' extensive use of the pronoun "we," frequent requests for mutual assistance, and a discourse pattern that was synthetic and often indistinguishable from that of a single speaker. Storch (2001) also found that, among four types of relationships in pair work tasks, only those pairs that exhibited a collaborative orientation to their work resulted in co-construction of new knowledge, peer assistance, and the learning of grammatical form and new vocabulary.

Another area that has not received adequate research attention is the importance of time required to establish social relations necessary for collaboration. Few studies of language acquisition in interactive contexts, particularly in the laboratory setting, take into account the temporal requirements for the type of supportive learning relationships, activity-based relations, and goal-directed collaborations outlined in the previous section. One study by Brooks, Donato, and McGlone (1997) found evidence that time was indeed a factor in enabling stable dyads to understand the cooperative and linguistic requirements to complete a jigsaw information-gap task. The study showed that over time (here five such analogous jigsaw information-gap tasks), learners' use of English, metatalk, private speech, and talk about task procedures declined significantly. The conclusion of the study points to three important considerations. First, from a theoretical perspective, collaboration takes time for learners to develop socially and cognitively as supportive learning contexts for each other. Second, from a research perspective, studies of isolated tasks performed in short time frames by individuals not accustomed to working together simply do not capture or depict the realities of how learning is dynamically constructed in collaborative contexts. Finally, from a pedagogical perspective, teachers need to be advised that assessments of student performance cannot be based on a single administration of a task.

Depicting Interactivity

A study of the mathematical problem solving of pairs of 13-year-old children (Kieran, 2003) provides evidence for the need to understand and define clearly how collaboration is carried out during partnered learning activity and how it differs from other forms of group work. In her study, children jointly solved complex algebra problems on flight dealing with the relationships among aircraft, wind speed, time, and headwind or tailwind conditions. Kieran defines a collaboration as educationally productive "if it has an impact on students' future participation in related mathematical problem-solving, whether the future participation involves individual or group work" (2003, p. 195).

Using the interactivity flowchart, Kieran graphically displays paired problem solving on the dimensions of communication (interpersonal and personal) and content (talk to advance mathematical problem solving versus talk to advance the conversation and personal relationships). The interactivity analysis showed differential productivity, both for the dyad and the individual, depending on the patterns of joint work during problem solving. In dyads where interactions were characterized by a high frequency of interpersonal communication and talk to advance the mathematical solution path, individuals were able to draw upon approaches to solving the problem that had been discussed during the pairwise interaction. In dyads where one active member engaged in self-talk while the other reacted to what was overheard, the reactive member of the dyad was not able to draw upon the dyadic problem-solving experience at a later time. Interestingly, in the nonproductive pair, one member of the dyad displayed a high degree of vocalized private speech (e.g., telegraphic, abbreviated, and fragmentary utterances) that did not communicate well to the other partner of the dyad. In this case, only the active member gained new approaches to solving the problem. Kieran rightly points out that it is simply not enough to make available our private mental activity to others (i.e., our inner speech), as argued by Harré and Gillett (1994). Simply externalizing one's inner speech leaves too much unsaid and lacks the necessary elaboration and clarity to be useable by the other member on the dyad.

This study illustrates that not all group work qualifies as collaboration and that different configurations of joint work result in different outcomes. Moreover, research, including research on language learning, must explain the communicative dynamics of interaction and not assume that all forms of communication are created equal or have the same psychological function. One fruitful area which research could explore is to understand how the ubiquitous concept of scaffolding is an epiphenomenon of collaboration and how scaffolding differs from other forms of interactions.

Learning through Collaboration

The goal of collaborative learning is not exclusively to deposit knowledge as unique acquisitions into the minds of the individual. Rather, it involves apprenticing, initiating, and transforming individuals into participating and contributing members of social networks in various communities in which they live (Lave & Wenger, 1991; Sfard, 2003). Learning, in this view, is seen as "improved participation in an interactive system" (Greeno, 1997), an "initiation in a discourse" (Harré & Gillett, 1994), and a "reorganization of an activity" (Cobb, 1998). According to Wenger (1998), learning in the collaborative creates and sustains the relation of mutual accountability with other members of the community. For the language learner, the value of collaboration is not merely the accumulation of language knowledge as an inert, solitary possession (Larsen-Freeman, 2003). Rather, the consequences of collaborative activity are conceptualized as a way to enable the individual to participate in social activities, either as individuals referenced to a social network or directly connected to others, to promote future learning and development through expanding participation, and to create the potential for the individual's reciprocal contribution to the community (Dyson, 2000; Putney, Green, Dixon, Durden, & Yaeger, 2000). In other words, individuals do not leave a collaborative event simply knowing more while remaining isolated from others. Collaboration transforms individuals from marginal members of a community to contributing participants in expanding circles of community practices that they reciprocally help to forge. Thus, collaboration, and the mutuality of learning it brings about, is the *reason* for and the *result* of goal-directed, mediated social relations.

Kinginger's (2000) study on the acquisition of French pronouns of solidarity (*tu vs. vous*) illustrates this point. American students in the United States and French students in France were paired as keypals to discuss parallel texts on remakes of film and children's literature. As an outcome of their collaborative electronic exchanges in and across time, American and French students developed personal relationships, learned appropriate forms of address, and ostensibly gained access into further crosscultural exchanges in their new language. We might imagine how the students' collaboration and new relationships, reflected in relationally appropriate language, resulted in further community participation and learning for both groups beyond the boundaries of the project and of the acquisition of discrete linguistic terms of address. Understanding how participation in collaborative events sets the foundation for future collaborations needs to be a goal of research on collaboration in educational settings. This is particularly true in the case of foreign and second language learning where the expectation is to enable learners to interact in target language communities and cultures other than their own.

In the studies that follow, themes of research on collaboration in foreign and second language contexts are presented. The themes of these studies reveal several aspects of collaboration presented in the previous section. The studies include microgenetic analysis of goal-directed partnered activity (e.g., Platt & Brooks, 2002; and Swain & Lapkin, 2003) and macrogenetic studies of classroom community development (e.g., Boxer & Cortés-Conde, 2000; Duff, 2002; and Verplaetse, 2000). Tasks and activities examined in these studies are largely naturally occurring in classroom contexts and involve, for example, information-gap activities, teacher-directed group discussion, student interviews, text-based conversations, and essay writing and revision. The overarching themes are (1) collaboration and community, (2) collaboration and language development, and (3) collaboration and identity. Based on the brief review of literature below, I identify aspects of collaboration that can contribute to an explanatory theory of collaboration in the language classroom. I conclude by arguing that sociocultural theory provides a framework for describing and explaining the dynamics of collaboration.

Collaboration and Community

Platt and Brooks (2002) examine the dialogic interaction as two high school students of Spanish and two university students of Swahili collaborate on the solution of an information-gap task. Platt and Brooks sought to understand the process of collaboration from the perspective of how learners create engagement in the task rather than mere compliance with task requirements. That is, rather than view the task as only an opportunity to negotiate meaning and encode and decode messages, Platt and Brooks argue that analyses of tasks need to include how learners evolve from loosely knit partnered practice to fully engaged communities of language learning practice. Their analysis of the dyads illustrates how achieving intersubjectivity and subsequent engagement was a tedious process marked by moments of struggle to understand the task at hand. Corroborating the findings of the earlier study of Brooks and Donato (1994), they found that the students' struggle was mediated and resolved by gesture, use of the L1 and L2, and other foreign languages known to the students. What is particularly compelling about this study is that it takes into account the transformation of relations that occurs during student interaction. As students' goals and understanding for activity become more clearly defined and the processes of task completion emerge, variable and random behaviors change to focused procedures exhibiting greater control of the target language and of working with each other as a collaborative community. Thus, learners do not simply comply with the task, but rather they actively construct it.

Verplaetse (2000) reports on the study of a middle-school science teacher during class discussion and the effects of collaborative discussion on mainstreamed

English language learners. Her study provides an example of how the teacher's use of paraphrase and repetition produced an environment where the contributions of all students were accepted, valued, and validated. Moreover, she finds that the teacher modeled the process of scientific inquiry aloud for his students and thereby authorized the right to wonder, pose questions, and engage in exploratory talk on science topics. In addition to the collaborative discussion that modeled scientific inquiry, another important aspect of this study was the consequence of this dialogic collaboration on the participation of English language learners. Verplaetse states that, unlike the other two science classes she observed as part of this study, English language learners volunteered more frequently and participated more actively. She concludes that "given the highly interactive practices of the teacher and students, particularly the nonjudgmental, listening nature of teacher responses, even the English language learners were drawn into the participation" (Verplaetse, 2000, p. 238). This study illustrates how classroom relations and collaboration were forged through the teacher's validation of student contributions. In turn, sanctioning inquiry and authorizing the right to wonder through teacher example enabled students to expand their collaboration involvement and become contributing members of a classroom community.

Collaboration and Grammatical, Pragmatic, and Discourse Development

In this section, four studies are reviewed to illustrate how collaboration involves the development of grammatical, pragmatic, and discourse competence. Three collaborative contexts are reviewed: classroom pair activity, adult–child book reading, and teacher-fronted classroom discussion.

Swain and Lapkin (2003) examined a pair of grade seven French immersion students' collaborative work while (1) completing a jigsaw story task orally and in writing, (2) comparing their written stories to a reformulated version, (3) responding to a stimulated recall task, and (4) revising their stories independently at a later time. The data were coded for all the language-related episodes (LREs), defined as any part of the collaborative dialogues where the learners talk about the language they are using, question an aspect of their language use, or correct themselves or others. LREs involved lexical items, form, and discourse markers, with form receiving the greatest amount of attention during the writing, comparing, and stimulated recall sessions (e.g., reflexive verbs). The analysis of discussions surrounding reformulated texts indicated that approximately two-thirds of reformulations were accepted. At other times, the students' rules for language prevailed over the authority of the edited text. Additionally, they rejected reformulated versions of the text when editing was perceived to change the meaning of the original story. During later independent revisions, both learners were able to revise accurately 78 percent of the post test items indicating the power of collaborative dialogue during the composing, noticing, and recall procedures. A noteworthy feature of the study was researchers' investigation of the learners' perception of their collaborative work, specifically the relational conditions of the task and their investment in the partnered work. In final interviews, the learners were asked to comment on their level of participation compared to their normal work habits. Both learners confirmed that their attention to the task during data collection was similar to how they approached their work outside of the conditions of the study.

Kim and Hall (2002) report on a four-month collaborative book reading project between adults and eight-year-old Korean children using English as the medium of communication. During the book reading, the researcher prompted with questions, elaborated on the children's utterances, and repeated the children's contributions by paraphrasing and shaping what they said into a coherent discourse. After completing all collaborative reading sessions, the children engaged in interactional role-play situations based on school-related events. These interactions were analyzed for quantity of words used, context-specific vocabulary, utterances, and conversational management skill (e.g., initiations, elaborations, conclusions, and self- and other-repair). It was found that the participation of these children in collaborative book reading led to significant changes in their pragmatic ability dealing with a number of words and utterances, and conversational management features. Kim and Hall suggest that in the context of interesting texts and collaborative talk, meaningful opportunities for the development of children's second language competence arise. It is interesting to note that the procedure used by the tutor reflects discourse features similar to the teacher in the Verplaetse study, with similar developmental consequences, i.e., increased language resources, expanded participation in interactions, and the children's growing ability to manage conversation.

In a conversational analytical study of talk-in-interaction, Mori (2002) examines 12 hours of classroom interaction across two instructional contexts in a university upper-level Japanese as a foreign language classroom. In this study, two contexts were analyzed to understand how talk was constructed in collaboration with peers during a planning session for a future discussion of "fathers" with native speaker visitors to the class. It was found that the design of the task (step-by-step requirements for the interview) presented obstacles for the creation of contingent discourse and coherent discussion with the native speaker guests. Instead, during the visits and because of the rigidity of the task requirements, the students' discourse was highly structured, interview-like, and lacked the sequential and contingency-based features of conversation. Ironically, Mori finds that student discourse during the pretask planning was more spontaneous and involved a mutual exchange of ideas. This discourse contrasted sharply with the rigidity of the talk when the students interacted with the native-speaker guests.

Mori's study raises several important pedagogical considerations for understanding discourse development in collaborative discursive contexts in classroom settings. First, tasks may focus too heavily on content and form and thus restrict the collaborative and emergent development of talk necessary for becoming a discursively competent language user. The reason for these constrained pedagogical tasks, as Mori points out, may be the teacher's assumption of the student's linguistic deficiency, an assumption that proved erroneous when examining the discourse of the planning stage of the activity. Second, the structure of the task and its emphasis on information transfer (e.g., "ask the guest what kind of person his/her father is" and "tell the guest about your father") reveals that not all tasks cede control of the content of the talk to the learners. Finally, the native speaker visitors were unaware of the task directions and did not share the same instructional history and goal as the students. Thus, they may have assumed that their role was to respond to questions rather than take conversational initiative to collaborate on developing a more "natural, coherent interaction" (Mori, 2002, p. 341). When juxtaposed with the Kim and Hall study, Mori's study contributes to understanding that collaboration is constituted in particular kinds of contingently organized talk. Moreover, as Platt and Brooks (2002) also argue, the structure of certain tasks inhibits precisely what is needed for collaborative engagement to occur, that is tasks that promote flexible, contingent, and dynamic development of talk in interaction.

The teacher's orchestration of classroom discourse is another type of collaboration examined in the literature. Toth (in press) studies the effects of a teacher's language practice on the verbal responses of second-year university students of Spanish as a foreign language. During two classes, the teacher presented two types of conversational activities to the class based on two different goals for student talk. In the first type of interaction, the teacher structured conversations around Spanish grammatical structures (e.g., present perfect tense, adjective agreement). The second type of interaction was organized around topics and themes that loosely referenced the grammar. That is, in the first case, the topic of conversation was subordinated to the grammar and followed a "meaningful drill" pattern (see Wong & VanPatten, 2003, for a discussion of the limitations of language drill formats). In the second case, the grammar was subordinated to a central topic and followed pragmatic rules of conversation (e.g., conversational implicatures).

Analysis of the discourse of these two interactions revealed two markedly different and contrasting types of responses by the students. During the grammar-focused interactions, students exhibited longer latency gaps and a higher number of remedy sequences where students needed to ask for assistance. Additionally, these remedy sequences were not clarification requests typical of meaning negotiation, but rather expressions of frustration in an attempt to understand the teacher's motivation for the questions posed. This interpretation was corroborated in retrospective interviews with five students who all reported confusion and a lack of awareness of the teacher's conversational moves during the grammatically based meaningful drill interactions. During the topically organized conversations, fewer latency gaps were noted and fewer and shorter remedy sequences emerged during the discussion. Toth concludes that during discussions motivated by the teacher's grammatical agenda, students required more time to respond because they had to focus simultaneously on what they wanted to say and the reason why they needed to say it, i.e., to satisfy the teacher's covert goal for the discussion. In contrast, when conversation was organized in ways that did not violate the students' pragmatic understandings of discourse, time could be used to process the content of an utterance without the additional burden of establishing intersubjectivity at each sentence-level, grammar-focused question.

The conclusions of this study reflect an important concept associated with collaboration. For discursive collaboration to occur, participants need to share conversational goals, perceive these goals for conversation as legitimate, and understand how each participant's actions move the jointly constructed activity forward, as was seen in the work of the students in the Swain and Lapkin study. When this lack of shared goals occurs, collaboration does not take place and the activity dissipates into a confusing exchange of information, meaningful or otherwise. As was also found in the Mori study, not all forms of interaction in the language classroom promote discourse competence; in the case of the Toth study, some forms of classroom interaction may actually contradict what students know intuitively about the pragmatics of conversational collaboration.

Collaboration and Identity

A recent area of research that connects to the issue of collaboration in classroom settings deals with how one's identity is positioned and constructed by self or others during discursive interactions of various kinds. Duff (2002) illustrates how classroom interaction in an ethnically and linguistically diverse grade 10 social studies class attributed identities to students that they may not have wanted to assume. Moreover, her research into classroom language socialization, participation, and identity revealed that, at times, assumptions made about students were based on misinterpretation of students' cultural participation patterns during classroom discussion. Vocal students were positioned, albeit erroneously, as academically superior, whereas quiet students were viewed as academically weaker and less competent.

Duff observes that, despite the teacher's goals of creating an inclusive classroom that valorized the cultural backgrounds and contributions of all students, the interactional behaviors of teachers and students during discursive collaborations on subject matter created conditions that marginalized some students while providing greater social recognition to others. Her study also alerts us to the fact that collaboration has social and personal consequences for participants. She concludes that "large numbers of minority students in schools worldwide are at considerable risk of alienation, isolation, and failure because of the discourse and interactions that surround them on a daily basis" (Duff, 2002, p. 216). This assertion underscores the importance of recognizing that not all communities of practice, such as classroom life, are benign and that collaboration in these communities may create personal affinities or indifferences despite a collective orientation to academic work.

Boxer and Cortés-Conde (2000) examine how relational group identities develop in a university intensive content-based English as a second language class. Relational identity goes beyond biological, individual, and societal identities. Rather, it is established, owned, and transformed by the group as a whole through their goal-directed collaborations with each other. Moreover, Boxer and Cortés-Conde point out the pedagogical importance of relational identities to language development and how both mutually support each other. That is, "as learners become proficient, not only in the language per se but in how to interact with particular individuals, they build a RID (relational identity) that is the foundation for further interaction" (p. 206). Their study explores how a relational identity is fostered or inhibited in a classroom community. Through the analysis of two classes and their discussions of representations of U.S. culture in the media, they find that only one teacher creates the conditions for safely exploring the students' identities in relation to U.S. culture through sharing personal experiences, confronting cultural stereotypes, and airing opinions. In the other class, the teacher created a hierarchical classroom organization by assuming the dominant role of purveyor of cultural information. In this way, he inhibited collaboration and prevented the creation of a relational identity established by the students.

Detailed analysis of the classes revealed that when the teacher took the stance of non-knower and posed questions about students' cultural backgrounds for discussion, students participated actively and collaborated with each other. This discursive collaboration, in turn, led to greater perspectives on U.S. culture and their own while simultaneously creating a classroom community where personal relations, history, and identity mattered. By contrasting the two teachers in this study and comparing this study to others, like the Duff study, it is clear that the outcomes of pedagogical interactions are not always in the best interest of students, despite teachers' best intentions. Moreover, although both classes represent communities of practice, only one class evolved into a fully functioning collaborative where the relational identity of the group fostered a perception of each individual as a valid interlocutor in explorations of U.S. culture and cultural comparisons.

Collaboration and Sociocultural Theory

When reading across the studies, it becomes clear that to describe and explain collaboration, or the lack of it, requires taking into account various aspects of the event. Sociocultural theory provides this conceptual framework for description and explanation of collaboration and the learning and development it simultaneously effects. In what follows, I will outline several important aspects of collaboration that *matter* and need to be considered in any serious investigation of the topic. The aspects of collaboration are not exhaustive and derive from the studies reviewed. Each of the following aspects is relevant to the description and analysis of collaboration in the studies and reflects core concepts of sociocultural theory. Additionally, the aspects are not categorical, but rather act on and interact with each other during the conduct of joint work.

Activity Matters

Sociocultural theory maintains that learning and development emerge and are shaped by the social, cultural, and historical contexts in which individuals engage in meaningful and purposeful joint activity. Moreover, within sociocultural theory, activity is dynamic and not imposed externally on participants. As Newman and Holzman point out, "it is in the *production of activity* that learning and development occur [and]...that the activity of *producing* [is] inseparable from the *product*" (1993, p. 74). Moreover, the production of joint activity creates a zone of proximal development (ZPD) that permits the co-occurrence of learning and development (Newman & Holzman, 1993; Vygotsky, 1986).

Several studies provide evidence for this claim. In the Platt and Brooks study, we observe how a jigsaw information gap task was shaped as students jointly constructed their activity, regulated themselves as participants, and created a ZPD for each other (see also Brooks & Donato, 1994). Swain and Lapkin's study illustrates how two students' collaboration overrode the influence of an authoritative edited version of their written work. In their study, learners' ownership of their own production of words and meanings during essay writing took precedence over accepting an external definition of idealized performance on the essay. These studies illustrate that the collaborative production of educational activity cannot be detached from the product of the activity without the risk of creating an artificial dualism and a discontinuity between the individual and social. From the perspective of sociocultural theory, there is no need to separate collaboration from what is actually learned, where it is learned, and under what conditions it is learned. Thus, when viewed through the lens of sociocultural theory, the dynamics of collaborative production obviate the need to separate language use from language acquisition.

Social Relations Matter

In the studies of identity, it was apparent that socially and culturally constructed collaboration in classrooms often reflected relations of power (e.g., teachers as knowledge brokers) and the associated institutional infrastructure. Individuals are embedded within these figured worlds where they accept or act upon various positionings of whatever powerful discourses they happen to encounter (Holland, Lachicotte, Skinner, & Cain, 2001; Holland & Lave, 2000). From a sociocultural perspective, persons develop through and around the cultural forms by which they are identified and identify themselves, in the context of their affiliations and disaffiliations with those associated with those forms and practices.

In the two studies reviewed, classroom collaborations have been shown to create hierarchies between teacher and students and disaffiliations among student groups. The result of these hierarchical relations can have negative consequences for students such as that in the Duff (2002) study of culturally diverse classrooms and in the Boxer and Cortés-Conde (2000) study of relational identities in adult content-based ESL classes. Conversely, in classes such as that in the Verplaetse (2000) study where individual student contributions were valued and revoiced by the teacher, student ideas became centerpieces for collaborative scientific exploration, including English language learners who were observed to remain in the silent margins of discussion in other classes.

History and Culture Matter

Collaboration can be explained by examining individuals' motives and goals for actions and by situating activity in the social and historical conditions that constitute and shape the actions, and operational composition of these actions, of individuals-in-practice. The results of several studies can be explained through this sociocultural tenet.

In Toth's study (in press), we see how the teacher's covert goals for teacher–student collaboration create obstacles to intersubjectivity and result in interactions that focus on making sense of the teacher's actions and operations rather than co-constructing a meaningful communicative event. It is not hard to explain that the presence of the teacher's grammar goal is the result of the cultural and historical context of language teaching that has emphasized mastery of form (see Dorwick & Glass, 2003 for a similar discussion of foreign language textbooks). In Mori's study, history, or one's past participation in a series of activities, is used to explain why the discourse between the students and the native speaker visitors surfaced as an interrogation rather than a conversation. By examining the history embodied in the students' collaborative planning and the tools that they use, i.e., the task directions, the subsequent interaction with the native speakers is more completely understood and explained.

Mediation Matters

To claim that development of knowledge or self occurs through collaboration requires understanding that the mediation afforded by others or by cultural tools, including language, is instrumental to this process. According to sociocultural theory, mediation, in the form of objects, symbols, or persons, transforms the natural and spontaneous concepts derived through direct contact with experience into higher forms of thinking, referred to as scientific concepts in Vygotskyan theory (Vygotsky, 1986, chap. 6). These higher forms of thinking, derivative of mediated collaborations, may deal with strategic orientations to tasks (e.g., learning strategies, establishing procedures for carrying out an information-gap task), conceptions of self and community (e.g., relational identities), or generalizations of semiotic systems (e.g., problem-solving algorithms or grammar). Since all forms of mediation are developed in a context, they are themselves inherently social, cultural, and historical.

The studies reviewed exemplify the process of mediation and the effects of differing mediation tools on the collaborative activity. In the Mori (2002) study, the task-mediated social relations and produced discourse that was markedly different in two contexts. Platt and Brooks's (2002) analysis of dyads working on information-gap tasks illustrated how talk in L1 and L2 and gesture mediated construction of and subsequent transformation from compliance to engagement in the task. In the Toth (in press) and Verplaetse (2000) studies, we observe how a teacher's goal can serve to mediate the development of classroom discourse and the psychological and affective dispositions of the students participating in the discussion. Mediational tools are, thus, critical, and must be taken into account in any serious examination of the production and product of collaboration.

Emergent Directions in the Study of Pedagogical Collaboration

Several research directions emerge from the review of these studies. First, studies of collaboration need to provide the reader with rich descriptions of the level of collaborative functioning and differentiate collaboration from loosely knit configurations of individuals. To this end, studies of collaboration should include in their research design and descriptions various aspects of collaboration that have proven to be significant and consequential. No study, to my knowledge, considers in the analysis all the aspects of collaboration outlined above and suggested by sociocultural theory.

Many of the studies of collaboration take place in high school or college classrooms or with adults. More research attention to the early language learner, particularly in foreign language classrooms, is needed. In a study conducted by Donato, Tucker, Wudthayagorn, and Igarashi (2000) of an elementary school Japanese foreign language program, it was found that few planned occasions to collaborate were made available to young learners by the teacher. However, it was also found that elementary school students seized opportunities to collaborate spontaneously on utterance construction and to assist actively the spoken performance of each other using learned material (Takahashi, Austin, & Morimoto, 2000). How collaboration takes place in the elementary foreign and second language classroom is a worthwhile line of investigation.

Studies of collaboration need to investigate the role of history in students, teachers, materials, curricular goals, and instruction, and examine how history manifests itself in jointly constructed knowledge. From this perspective, a longitudinal study would focus on learning outcomes over time for individuals and the history within individuals during collaboration work, including identities that are brought to bear on collaborations or constructed in the process.

Another fruitful area concerns the consequences of collaboration at one point in time for providing the foundation for future collaborations and, therefore, expanded zones of proximal development where learning and development may continue. Second and foreign language studies that document this process would contribute to an understanding of the effects of collaboration on initiating and sustaining learner participation in a community of target language speakers. The social participation consequences of collaboration are also not restricted to face-to-face interaction with others. Socially meaningful individual activity, such as learning how to revise one's writing to communicate clearly to an audience, as in the case of the Swain and Lapkin study, is an equally valid social and participatory outcome for collaboration. Additionally, these outcomes contrast with decontextualized measurements of grammatical forms and judgments.

Investigations of scaffolding and co-construction during collaborative activity need to be expanded and elaborated upon to answer such questions as: What evidence is needed to claim that scaffolding occurs? Under what conditions does scaffolding arise and how frequently? How does it differ from other forms of assistance? Is the concept of scaffolding useful and sufficiently robust to explain learning in collaboration; if so, why? Or is scaffolding a discursive manifestation of the overarching construct of activity in the ZPD? Regarding co-construction, we might ask whether collaboration results in co-construction of knowledge or co-opting of knowledge.

Final Comments

The nature of future research into collaboration in language learning pedagogical contexts is an open question. Although this review offers no definitive research plans, a few directions are clearly suggested by the review of literature and theoretical considerations. Based on the review and discussion, three issues warrant attention.

First, research on collaboration needs to *describe* and *explain* the phenomenon comprehensively and adequately. Language acquisition studies from interactionalist perspectives are data-heavy but theory-light. Conversely, research studies from a sociocultural perspective provide rich theoretical concepts to explain what is observed but are often parsimonious with data. Linked to this concern is providing the time required so that collaboration can develop in pedagogical settings and accounting for levels of collaborations when drawing conclusions.

Second, collaborative productivity in language learning needs to be defined better and expanded in all studies, especially within the particular research questions posed. Many studies separate collaborative production from the resulting product creating an artificial language use versus language acquisition dichotomy. The concept of productivity, if more fully explored, might overcome this dualism. Moreover, collaborative productivity needs to be examined for its social and relational consequences, defined in this paper as individual or collective achievements motivated and carried out for a social purpose at the time of collaboration or later. By having a more informed understanding of collaborative productivity, we will avoid providing research answers to superficial questions.

Third, it might be wise to attempt to unite second language learning research with the extensive literature on cooperative learning. There seems to be an intellectual firewall separating the literature on cooperative learning from language learning studies in interactive contexts (McGroarty, personal communication). Cooperative learning has a rich history based on some of the pioneering work of Johnson and Johnson and Slavin (see, e.g., Johnson, Johnson, & Holubec, 1993). Cooperative learning emphasizes the importance of group processing, positive interdependence, and individual accountability as critical elements to productive collaborations in classrooms. Clearly, these concepts come into play in research for differentiating levels of cooperation and for practice in promoting cooperative classrooms.

Collaboration is a powerful concept that moves us beyond reductive input-output models of interaction and acknowledges the importance of goals, the mutuality of learning in activity, and collective human relationships. It is hoped that this brief review has outlined some important issues and has provided direction for integrating language learning research with the everyday human realities of collaboration in pedagogical contexts.

Note

1. Special thanks to David Jelliffe, Jenee Wright, and Javier Coronado Aliegre, University of Pittsburgh, for their valuable contribution to this project. Also thank you to Dan Dewey, University of Pittsburgh, for his reactions to drafts of this paper.

REFERENCES

Boxer, D., & Cortés-Conde, F. (2000). Identity and ideology: Culture and pragmatics in content-based ESL. In J. K. Hall & L. S. Verplaetse (Eds.), *Second and foreign language learning through classroom interaction* (pp. 203–219). Mahwah, NJ: Erlbaum.

Brooks, F., & Donato, R. (1994). Vygotskyan approaches to understanding foreign language learner discourse. *Hispania, 77* (2), 262–274.

Brooks, F., Donato, R., & McGlone, V. (1997). When will they say it right? Understanding learner discourse during collaborative tasks. *Foreign Language Annals, 30* (4), 524–541.

Cobb, P. (1998). Learning from distributed theories of intelligence. *Mind, Culture, and Activity, 5* (3), 187–204.

Donato, R., Tucker, G. R., Wudthayagorn, J., & Igarashi, K. (2000). Attitudes, achievements, and instruction in the later years of FLES. *Foreign Language Annals, 33* (4), 377–393.

Donato, R. (1988). *Beyond group: A psycholinguistic rationale for collective activity in second-language learning.* Unpublished doctoral dissertation, University of Delaware.

Donato, R. (1994). Collective scaffolding in second language learning. In J. P. Lantolf & G. Appel (Eds.), *Vygotskian approaches to second language research* (pp. 33–56). Norwood, NJ: Ablex.

Dorwick, T., & Glass, W. R. (2003). Language education policies: One publisher's perspective. *The Modern Language Journal, 87* (4), 592–594.

Duff, P. A. (2002). The discursive co-construction of knowledge, identity, and difference: An ethnography of communication in the high school mainstream. *Applied Linguistics, 23* (3), 289–322.

Dyson, A. H. (2000). Linking writing and community development through the children's forum. In C. D. Lee & P. Smagorinsky (Eds.), *Vygotskian perspectives on literacy research* (pp. 127–149). Cambridge: Cambridge University Press.

Fullan, M. (1999). *Change forces: The sequel.* London: Falmer Press.

Gee, J. P. (2003). *What video games have to teach us about leaning and literacy.* New York: Palgrave Macmillan.

Greeno, J. G. (1997). On claims that answer the wrong question. *Education Researcher, 26* (1), 5–17.

Hall, J. K., & Verplaetse, L. S. (2000). *Second and foreign language learning through classroom interaction.* Mahwah, NJ: Erlbaum.

Harré, R., & Gillett, G. (1994). *The discursive mind.* Thousand Oaks, CA: Sage.

Holland, D., Lachicotte, W., Skinner, D., & Cain, C. (2001). *Identity and agency in cultural worlds.* Cambridge: Harvard University Press.

Holland, D., & Lave, J. (2000). *History in person: Enduring struggles, contentious practice, intimate identities.* Santa Fe: School of American Research Press.

John-Steiner, V. (2000). *Creative collaboration.* New York: Oxford University Press.
Johnson, D. W., Johnson, R. T., & Holubec, E. J. (1993). *Cooperation in the classroom.* Edina, MN: Interaction Book.
Kieran, C. (2003). The mathematical discourse of 13-year old partnered problem solving and its relation to the mathematics that emerges. In C. Kieran, E. Forman, & A. Sfard (Eds.), *Learning discourse: Discursive approaches to research in mathematics education* (pp. 187–228). Dordrecht: Kluwer.
Kim, D., & Hall, J. K. (2002). The role on an interactive book reading program in the development of second language pragmatic competence. *The Modern Language Journal, 86* (3), 332–348.
Kinginger, C. (2000). Learning the pragmatics of solidarity in the networked foreign language classroom. In J. K. Hall & L. S. Verplaetse (Eds.), *Second and foreign language learning through classroom interaction* (pp. 23–46). Mahwah, NJ: Erlbaum.
Larsen-Freeman, D. (2003). *Teaching language: From grammar to grammaring.* Boston: Thomson Heinle.
Lave, J., & Wenger, E. (1991). *Situated learning: Legitimate peripheral participation.* Cambridge: Cambridge University Press.
Moll, L., & Greenberg, J. (1990). Creating zones of possibilities: Combining social contexts for instruction. In L. Moll (Ed.), *Vygotsky and education* (pp. 319–348). Cambridge: Cambridge University Press.
Mori, J. (2002). Task design, plan, and development of talk-in-interaction: An analysis of a small group activity in a Japanese language classroom. *Applied Linguistics, 23* (3), 323–347.
Newman, F., & Holzman, L. (1993). *Lev Vygotsky, revolutionary scientist.* New York: Routledge.
Petrovsky, A. V. (1985). *The collective and the individual.* Moscow: Progress.
Platt, E., & Brooks, F. B. (2002). Task engagement: A turning point in foreign language development. *Language Learning, 52,* 365–400.
Putney, L. G., Green, J., Dixon, C., Durdin, R., & Yaeger, B. (2000). Consequential progressions: Exploring collective-individual development in a bilingual classroom. In C. D. Lee & P. Smagorinsky (Eds.), *Vygotskian perspectives on literacy research* (pp. 86–126). Cambridge: Cambridge University Press.
Sfard, A. (2003). There is more to discourse than meets the ears: Looking at thinking as communicating to learn more about mathematical learning. In C. Kieran, E. Forman, & A. Sfard (Eds.), *Learning discourse: Discursive approaches to research in mathematics education* (pp. 13–57). Dordrecht: Kluwer.
Smagorinsky, P., & O'Donnell-Allen, C. (2000). Idiocultural diversity in small groups: The role of the relational framework in collaborative learning. In C. D. Lee & P. Smagorinsky

(Eds.), V*ygotskian perspectives on literacy research* (pp. 165–109). Cambridge: Cambridge University Press.

Storch, N. (2001). How collaborative is pair work? ESL tertiary students composing in pairs. *Language Teaching Research, 5,* 29–53.

Swain, M., & Lapkin, S. (2003). Talking it through: Two French immersion learners' response to reformulation. *International Journal of Educational Research, 37,* 285–304.

Takahashi, E., Austin, T., & Morimoto, Y. (2000). Social interaction and language development in a FLES classroom. In J. K. Hall & L. S. Verplaetse (Eds.), *Second and foreign language learning through classroom interaction* (pp. 139–159). Mahwah, NJ: Erlbaum.

Toth, P. (In press). When grammar instruction undermines cohesion in L2 Spanish classroom discourse. *Modern Language Journal, 88* (1).

Verplaetse, L. S. (2000). Mr. Wonder-ful: Portrait of a dialogic teacher. In J. K. Hall & L. S. Verplaetse (Eds.), *Second and foreign language learning through classroom interaction* (pp. 223–241). Mahwah, NJ: Erlbaum.

Vygotsky, L. (1986). *Thought and language.* Cambridge, MA: The MIT Press.

Wenger, E. (1998). Practice. In E. Wenger (Ed.), *Communities of practice: Learning, meaning, community* (pp. 43–102). New York: Cambridge University Press.

Wong, W., & VanPatten, B. (2003). The evidence is IN: Drills are OUT. *Foreign Language Annals, 36* (3), 403–423.

14. CONSTRUCTIVIST ISSUES IN LANGUAGE LEARNING AND TEACHING

Dorit Kaufman

Constructivism has emerged in recent years as a dominant paradigm in education and has had a major intellectual impact on the development of pedagogy, especially in mathematics and science. Rooted in the cognitive developmental theory of Piaget and in the sociocultural theory of Vygotsky, constructivist notions have had an impact on the development and application of technologically enhanced microworlds and on linguistic investigation into literacy and narrative development. To date, constructivism has had little impact on language pedagogy; however, the advent of content-based pedagogical paradigms as an anchor of language education has opened new opportunities for integration of interdisciplinary collaborative approaches for language teaching and learning. Furthermore, the current emphasis on standards-based accreditation and reconceptualization of teacher education programs will likely expand the horizons of language pedagogy, bringing constructivist approaches to the foreground in language teacher education and opening new avenues for linguistic and interdisciplinary classroom-based research.

Overview of Constructivism

Constructivism has been viewed as a philosophy, epistemology, and a theory of communication. In recent decades, it has emerged as a dominant paradigm in education having a major intellectual impact on the development of pedagogy and playing a major role in systemic changes, primarily in the fields of mathematics and science (Brooks, 2002; DeVries & Kohlberg, 1987; Driver, 1983; Forman &

Kuschner, 1977; Gabel, 1994; Kamii, 1981, 1985; Russel, 1993; Sigel, Brozinsky, & Golinkoff, 1981; Tobin, 1993; von Glasersfeld, 1995, 1998; Wang & Walberg, 2001). The emergence of this paradigm has coincided with a shift in pedagogy away from teacher-centered information transmission models toward knowledge-centered and learner-centered approaches that focus on cognitive and social processes in learning. Constructivism as an approach to teaching and learning has evolved from psychology and information processing theories and in recent years has increasingly incorporated ideas from linguistics, anthropology, and sociology (Blumenfeld, Krajcik, Marx, & Soloway, 2001). Constructivism in education is rooted in notions from cognitive and social constructivism. The former is grounded in the work of Piaget (1954, 1955, 1970; Piaget & Inhelder, 1971) and accentuates cognitive development and individual construction of knowledge, and the latter emphasizes social construction of knowledge and is generally attributed to the work of Vygotsky (1962, 1978; but see Smith's [1993] contention that the social construction of knowledge is inherent in Piaget's work). Piaget's developmental theory advocates a holistic approach. Learning is a developmental process that involves change, self-generation, and construction, each building on prior learning experiences. Learning for the child occurs through construction of new understandings through reading, listening, exploration, and experience. This involves three distinct yet interrelated processes of *assimilation, accommodation,* and *equilibrium.* New experiences are *assimilated* and integrated into existing schema or into schema under construction through the process of *accommodation.* The outcome of these processes is *equilibrium*—the achievement of new understandings, coherence, and cognitive stability.

The influence of social and cultural contexts on learning and knowledge construction is underscored in Vygotsky's social constructivist theory (Vygotsky, 1978). In exploring the social origins of thought, Vygotsky advanced the view that children's thinking and meaning-making is socially constructed and emerges out of their social interactions with their environment. Children's learning is facilitated by parents, peers, teachers, and others around them in the community. Vygotsky's zone of proximal development embodies the learners' readiness to learn. It is the distance between the learners' actual developmental level and the level of their potential development. This prospective view of learners' potential for learning guides the design of problem-solving tasks and determines the level and range of scaffolding learners require for accomplishing these tasks. Active engagement, pursuit of diverse paths to discovery, concept acquisition, and external and internal scaffolding are central to the learning process. External scaffolding supports learners' acquisition of knowledge by breaking down tasks into comprehensible components, modeling, coaching, providing feedback, and appropriating responsibility for learning to learners. Internal scaffolding engages the learner in reflection and self-monitoring to enhance acquisition of concepts. Teachers too are learners in this context. They observe and identify students' zone of proximal development (ZPD); design appropriate, authentic, and meaningful learning modules; and provide instructional support and scaffolding to propel students to construction of higher levels of understanding.

Increased attention in recent years to the science of learning, knowing, and developing understandings has brought constructivism, with its emphasis on the combined cognitive and sociocultural impact on learning, to the forefront in education. Constructivism has placed the learner's individual development at the focus of instruction and learning and has acknowledged the critical role in the learning process of endogenous factors and internal schema combined with exogenous social and cultural variables that contribute to the transformation of the learner's internal schema (Cole, 1990). When the combined role of endogenous and exogenous variables is taken into account and constructivism is considered from both Piagetian and Vygotskian perspectives, a common misconception that constructivist learning emerges from learners' knowledge without direct instruction from teachers is refuted. Learners benefit from multiplicity of approaches and learning experiences as they extract salient information in acquiring new knowledge. They also benefit from assistance by teachers who attend to their interpretations and provide relevant guidance and scaffolding to promote meaningful learning. The constructivist experience from both Piagetian and Vygotskian perspectives creates opportunities for learners to engage in hands-on, minds-on manipulation of raw data in quest of identifying new and increasingly complex patterns, acquisition of novel concepts and construction of new understandings. The benefits of constructivist-based educational settings for learners' academic, social, and affective growth have been widely documented (Brooks, 2002; Brooks & Brooks, 1993; Duckworth, 1987; Fosnot, 1993, 1996; Gabel, 1994; Sigel & Cocking, 1977; Tobin, 1993; Tobin, Tippins, & Gallard, 1994; Wheatley, 1991).

Digital Microworlds as Constructivist Learning Environments

Constructivist notions are intrinsic to the journeys of discovery and microworlds of Alice in Lewis Carroll's *Alice in Wonderland*, and *Through the Looking Glass and What Alice Learned There*, and of Milo in Norton Juster's *The Phantom Tollbooth*. On these journeys, Alice and Milo discover concepts in literacy and numeracy through exploration, adventures, and encounters with characters that engage them in creative learning and invite them to experience alternative ways of viewing the world around them. Alice's and Milo's reactions when they emerge from these journeys reflect a burst of innovative ideas, rediscovery of possibilities, quest for new learning, and readiness for outside facilitation and scaffolding. Alice remarks, "Somehow it fills my head with ideas—only I don't know exactly what they are" (Carroll, 2003, book jacket). Milo, upon returning to the real world and readjusting to his ordinary surroundings, discovers that "in the very room in which he sat, there were books that could take you anywhere, and things to invent, and make, and build, and break, and all the puzzle and excitement of everything he didn't know—music to play, songs to sing, and worlds to imagine and then someday to make real. His thoughts darted eagerly about as everything looked new—and worth trying" (Juster, 1961, p. 256).

Imaginary microworlds like *Wonderland, Dictionoplis*, and the *Island of Conclusions* (in *Phantom Tollbooth*), are learning environments that transform learners' preconceptions and engage them through inquiry and discovery in the acquisition of new knowledge about the world. Digital technologies have made Alice's and Milo's microworld explorations possible for all learners within educational contexts. The integration of new technologies across disciplines and educational contexts has grown dramatically in recent years and the impact of constructivism in the development and implementation of virtual environments has intensified with the ever-increasing technological advances that have opened new possibilities. The application of constructivist approaches as instructional modes in these contexts challenges learners' preexisting suppositions and further enhances their construction of knowledge within virtual environments. Learners pursue investigations that lead them to a deeper understanding of literacy, numeracy, and scientific concepts. Computer, video, and wireless technologies have provided optimal media for the application of constructivist principles to learning and teaching, created communities of learners in electronic learning environments, and greatly enhanced student achievement and teacher learning (Beatty, 2003; Bransford, Brown, & Cocking, 2000; Perkins, Schwartz, West, & Wiske, 1995). The new technologies have extended learning environments to nonlinear, multidimensional, and interactive and have greatly expanded the horizons of learners beyond their local communities into a global context.

The potential of technologically enhanced environments for constructivist-based exploratory learning is not a new discovery. Over two decades ago Pappert (1980) used what he called *Piagetian learning* as the organizing principle to develop LOGO, a programming environment for children to explore domains of knowledge that had previously required didactic teaching. Rejecting the notion of digital tools that program the way children learn, Pappert used constructivist principles to create a powerful technological microworld and "a province of Mathland where certain kinds of mathematical thinking could hatch and grow with particular ease. The microworld was an incubator...a growing place for specific species of powerful ideas or intellectual structures" (Pappert, 1980, p. 125). Pappert's LOGO was a revolutionary concept that made computer programming a child's endeavor. By combining Piaget's concept of children as builders of their own intellectual structures with their natural spontaneous learning in interaction with the rich cultural resources that surround them, Pappert had envisioned children programmers acquiring a sense of mastery over a piece of the most modern and powerful technology and establishing "an intimate contact with some of the deepest ideas from science, from mathematics, and from the art of intellectual model building" (p. 5). Pappert's Turtle Graphics had pioneered a new subculture that brought together mathematicians, scholars, scientists, computer scientists, artists, and writers in joint exploration to develop a palette of rich simulated micorworlds and interactive animations as learning environments that can provide stimulating contexts for language elicitation and development of skills and concepts across disciplines.

Digital tools have become extremely powerful as enablers of highly exploratory virtual environments created by interdisciplinary teams. Inquiry-oriented, constructivist-based computer and video-based technologies have become powerful pedagogical tools that extend human capabilities and contexts for social interactions. They scaffold and expand student learning, enhance curriculum development and assessment, and bring real-world problem-solving issues into the classroom for deliberation. They expand professional development opportunities for teachers and build local and global communities within and across disciplines. When the technology is integrated into the curriculum and is used as part of a coherent educational approach, learners develop a deeper understanding of phenomena in the physical and social world. They can work with visualization and modeling software and visit fully immersive 3D interactive reconstructed heritage sites that are no longer in existence or are inaccessible. Such exploratory environments immerse learners in simulated and animated discoveries of an ancient Syngaporian heritage site (Song, Elias, Muller-Witting, & Chan, 2003) and engage them in construction of simulated cities. Technological advances have also increased access to vast resources of data and information and greatly enhanced global connections. The shift from static models drawn on paper to dynamic models in interactive media that provide visualization and analytic tools is profoundly changing the nature of scientific and mathematical inquiry (Bransford et al., 2000; Perkins et al., 1995). When integrated into the curriculum, Internet and online environments and communication create virtual microworlds that expand discourse communities beyond disciplinary boundaries and greatly enhance language development and acquisition of disciplinary concepts.

Constructivist Notions in Linguistic Research

Linguists have increasingly drawn upon Piagetian and Vygotskian perspectives to investigate the role of language in learning contexts and its development at various stages in the acquisition process. Bickerton (1990) distinguished among three types of learning: observational, experiential, and constructional, and discussed the role of language—the system of representation for sorting and manipulating information—as the enabler of constructional learning. Observational and experiential learning that are prevalent in language education contexts depend on the occurrence of external events that are outside the control of the learner, however, constructional learning transcends immediate observational and experiential events and involves knowledge construction that is based on prior observations and experience. Maximization of constructional learning will occur through increased data gathering and that will stimulate internal events in the mind of the learner. It is the learner who controls the selection of relevant raw environmental data to support formulation of inferences and decision making.

A constructivist stance is evident in the investigation of emergent and developing literacy and narration. These cognitive, developmental, socially constructed, and culturally embedded processes are viewed from a child-centered and learner-centered perspective that is compatible with constructivist notions. Research in emergent literacy and narrative development brought together linguists, psychologists, and cognitive scientists who incorporated Piagetian and Vygotskian conceptual frameworks and constructivist notions to underscore the centrality of language and the role of social and cognitive processes in the construction of knowledge and the development of literacy. Early research has targeted primarily alphabetic languages and has focused on the initial stages in children's text production and the centrality of writing to the process of language and literacy development (Dyson, 1989; Ferreiro & Taberosky, 1989; Goodman & Wilde, 1992; Harris & Hatano, 1999; McCabe & Peterson, 1991; Pontecorvo, Orsolini, Burge, & Resnick, 1996; Tolchinsky-Landsmann, 1996). The research included the impact of children's construction of early drawings on literacy development (Levin, Korat, & Amsterdamer, 1996); children's emerging construction of written texts and invented spelling (Read, 1986; Treiman, 1993), and children's construction and emerging concepts about print and reading (Clay, 1991). Piagetian and Vygotskian notions have also influenced research in narrative development. Appleby's (1978) study of the child's developing concept of the story investigated how children assimilate fairy tales into schema formulated through prior experiences with similar tales. Existing schema facilitate developing expectations of characters, patterns of behavior, and appropriate endings in comparable stories. Through accommodation, children construct their representation of the world from encounters embedded within their social contexts and relationships and modify and expand upon their understandings of what constitutes a fairy tale. Appleby studied the conceptual structures and modes of organization of young children's story plots and identified six stages in the development of narrative production that paralleled Vygotsky's stages of concept development.

Research into literacy development has underscored the centrality of language and communication and the role of psychological and social variables in the construction of knowledge (Barton, 1994; Spivey, 1996). Learners conduct operations that include selection, organization, and connection to make meanings and their text construction and decoding are socially motivated. Writers use prior knowledge to conjure an image of their readers as they construct texts and manipulate language to target readers of specific age groups, socioeconomic status, knowledge, beliefs, and values. For readers, meaning-making goes beyond knowing the meanings of words and combining them in grammatical categories. Readers' construction of texts is based on the background knowledge that they bring to the text that is both internally formulated and socially constructed. Recent discussion in the linguistic literature on constructivism has also included application of constructivist scholarship and approaches in applied linguistic research (McGroarty, 1998) and investigation into the role, nature, and quality of exogenous and endogenous scaffolding for language acquisition and narrative development by peers, parents, and teachers (Swain, Brooks, & Tocalli-Beller, 2002), and by the learners themselves (Ko, Schallert, & Walters, 2003).

Pedagogical issues have generally not been central to these linguistic investigations. However, research in emergent literacy and narrative development has generated a rich resource for language educators to draw upon in developing constructivist-based and standards-based learning contexts to engage children in reading and writing and enhance discovery of patterns in spellings and texts as they move from emergent to more conventional spellings and organization in text construction. Mason and Sinha (1993), for example, have drawn upon the research in emergent literacy to develop a Vygotskian model for the early childhood classroom and identified four instructional steps for the acquisition of literacy concepts. These combine home and classroom language, literacy, and play activities and teachers' mediation, support, and close observation of students' changing levels of competence. The first step, *natural involvement*, requires teachers to engage students in real or simulated meaningful literacy activities. In the second step, *mediated learning*, teachers guide students' participation in activities and prepare them through modeling and coaching to become self-directed learners. In the third step, *external activity*, students engage in self-directed and independent learning activities, alone or with peers, with occasional coaching. Finally, in the fourth step, *internal or independent activity*, students proceed unaided through processes of reflection, inquiry, problem solving, and task performance.

Constructivism and Language Pedagogy

Constructivism has hitherto not played a visible role in language pedagogy and teacher education, although notions that are central to constructivism have been integrated into language education through other pedagogical models. In recent years, language pedagogy has integrated a rich palette of instructional approaches that underscore the centrality and diversity of learners and their active engagement in authentic and meaningful pursuits as individuals and within communities of learners. These have been integrated in curriculum design, assessment, and instructional practices and have included cooperative learning (Johnson & Johnson, 1984; Kessler, 1992; Nunan, 1988, 1992) and paradigms that foster learners' autonomy, action research, reflective practices, community partnerships, and alternative assessments that are embedded in their social and cultural environments and educational contexts (Benson, 2001; Brown, 2004; Burns, 1999; Edge, 1996, 2002; Freeman & Richards, 1996; Gebhard & Oprandy, 1999; Graves, 1996; Johnson, 1999; Murphy & Byrd, 2001; Nunan & Lamb, 1996; Richard-Amato, 2003; Shohamy, 2001; van Lier, 1996; Zamel & Spack, 2002). The recent dramatic growth in the ethnic and linguistic diversity in schools has underscored the need for reconceptualizing language teacher education and for placing a greater emphasis on the centrality of sociocultural processes in preparing professionals (Freeman & Johnson, 1998; Hall, 2002; Murrell, 2001; Prabhu, 1996; Johnson, 2000). Increased attention has been given to teachers' own self-image as emerging professionals in both ESL and EFL contexts (Pearson Casanave & Schecter, 1997), and to their developmental discourse about the process of becoming a professional (Bailey & Nunan 1995; Edge, 2002).

Changing demographics have also directed attention to the performance of English language learners (ELL) in schools and research findings on their poor performance in academic areas have underscored the need for a paradigm shift in language pedagogy that led to the advent of Content-Based Language Learning (CBLL) (Brinton, Snow, & Wesche, 1989; Crandall, 1993; Mohan, 1986; Mohan, Leung, & Davison, 2001; Short, 1993; Snow, Met & Genesee, 1989; Stoller, this volume). The approach has increasingly grounded language teaching in academic content across disciplines and has changed the focus of language teaching from teaching language in isolation to its integration in disciplinary content in elementary, secondary, and tertiary contexts in the United States and abroad (Crandall & Kaufman, 2002; Snow & Brinton, 1997). CBLL has provided scaffolding for higher academic success for language learners by grounding language learning in relevant and meaningful content that is aligned with the core curriculum of the school and the specialized academic standards of the respective disciplines. Application of CBLL has also raised awareness of the specialized language of mathematics (Cocking & Mestre, 1988; Crandall, Dale, Rhodes, & Spanos, 1990; Cuevas, 1984) and social studies (Short, 1994) and the challenges involved in integrating the specialized subject matter into language classes. Lack of expertise in the subject matter of the respective disciplines has motivated language educators, to explore collaborative paradigms that have included integrated or linked courses and highly collaborative coteaching or separate and distinct roles for language and content instructors (Crandall & Kaufman, 2002; Snow & Brinton, 1997). Preoccupation with these matters has left the issue of the specialized pedagogy of the disciplines virtually untouched. Integration of the constructivist pedagogy, so prevalent in mathematics and science, has largely been ignored in the language education literature. Consequently little is known about preparing language teacher candidates for embedding constructivist approaches for teaching scientific and mathematical concepts within the framework of language pedagogy.

The effective preparation of language teacher candidates has become even more critical in recent years for a variety of reasons. The changing demographics combined with greater emphasis of language across the curriculum (American Association for the Advancement of Science, 2001) have advanced the impact and visibility of language educators. In addition to providing language-enhanced and content-rich academic preparation for ELL, their role in school settings and in the community has significantly expanded (Clegg, 1996). Language educators increasingly engage in interdisciplinary collaborative activities and curriculum design; as advocates for English language learners, they develop and conduct workshops for colleagues across disciplines to raise cross-cultural awareness and to increase sensitivity to learners' linguistic, academic, social and affective needs. The challenge for teacher education programs has become the design and application of paradigms to prepare teacher candidates for their reconceptualized and greatly expanded professional role in the school and the community as well as the integration of constructivist paradigms that are prevalent in the disciplines within which language instruction is currently embedded. Such a shift in language pedagogy will engage language educators in new patterns of interdisciplinary collaborations and in rethinking of the knowledge base and pedagogical practices in teacher education programs (Kaufman, 1996, 1997, 2000; Kaufman & Grennon Brooks, 1996).

Constructivism and Teacher Change—The Challenge For Teacher Education

Despite research-based developments in pedagogy and the documented benefits of constructivist approaches, the prevalence of traditional teacher-centered classrooms across disciplines has remained a major challenge for advocates of constructivist approaches (Brooks, 2002; Sexton & Griffin, 1997a). The pervasiveness of traditional instructional practices in schools is due to several contributing factors. First, instructional practice hinges upon prior educational experiences that contribute to teachers' beliefs about teaching and learning and shape their teaching behavior in ways that are resistant to change (Cuban, 1993; Johnson, 1992; Pennington, 1995; Richardson, 1990; Shavelson & Stern, 1981). Second, the recent emphasis on accountability, performance-based assessment, and standards-based teaching have often reintroduced lecture and information-transmission instructional modes and have decreased the impetus for innovative and experiential learner-centered pedagogical approaches. Third, the serious shortage of teachers has set in motion alternate routes to obtaining teacher certification. These more intensive but shorter routes to certification have of necessity included little if any exposure to constructivist approaches, fewer opportunities for research and guided clinical practice, and less time and fewer outlets for reflective practice. Since it is these experiential modes that trigger and expedite change in prior suppositions and practice and advance professional growth, reconceptualization of pedagogical practice and adoption of constructivist pedagogy is less likely to occur among alternate route candidates.

For constructivist practices to be more prevalent in schools, they must be more widespread in teacher preparation. Change in teacher candidates is gradual and often imperceptible and is impacted by diverse developmental events that occur during professional preparation. Opportunities for teacher candidates within teacher education programs through coursework, collaborative partnerships, diverse field experiences, and sustained reflection impact the reformulation of their existing notions (Evans, 2002; Goodlad, 1990; Kaufman, 2000; Pennington, 1995). New knowledge and professional practices are individualized constructions that are socially and contextually motivated and co-constructions that occur through reciprocal learning experiences with teacher educators and peers at the university and with students and mentoring teachers in school settings. Collaboration with colleagues across disciplines further enhances accessibility to resources for developing and implementing constructivist, language-enhanced, and content-based learning environments.

Constructivism is open-ended and allows for ambiguity, flexibility, and innovative thinking that is inherent to teacher education programs that continue to evolve in alignment with emerging research. Sexton and Griffin (1997a, 1997b) underscore the open-ended quality of constructivism: "The constructivist paradigm represents a way of thinking that is inherently ambiguous and will require us to be different not just think differently. It is a journey not toward new technique but toward ever expanding epistemological positions" (Sexton & Griffin, 1997b, p. 257). Planning and application of constructivist educational contexts in language teacher education programs are described in Kaufman, (1996, 1997, 2000) and Kaufman and Grennon Brooks (1996). Reconceptualization of teacher education programs will involve teacher candidates' active engagement and autonomy, construction of knowledge through inquiry and reflection as well as involvement in interdisciplinary investigation, collaborative endeavors, fieldwork opportunities for experiential learning, and self-observation and evaluation. In such settings, close observation of teacher candidates allows teacher educators to glean important insights into teacher candidates' assimilation and accommodation of new knowledge, construction of ideas about teaching and learning, and their acquisition and development of the indispensable skills and professional dispositions for embarking on their chosen careers. Language and communication are integral to the creation of constructivist learning environments. Choice of language and modes of interpersonal communication in the classroom can enhance or inhibit the creation of constructivist learning environments. In striving to promote autonomy, creativity, and engagement, teachers' choice of scripts can powerfully motivate or block such endeavors (Stigler & Hiebert, 1999). Linguistic research of classroom discourse would greatly increase awareness of teachers' scripts and their impact on creating constructivist classroom contexts and enhancing student learning.

Constructivism and Standards-Based Teacher Education

The thrust for preparing teacher education programs and institutions for national accreditation by the respective specialized professional associations and accrediting agencies has provided a catalyst for reevaluation and reconceptualization of organizational structures, curricular content, and clinical experiences in teacher education programs (Williams, 2000). Although perceived by many as prescriptive, when approached from a constructivist stance, the accreditation process will likely expand the horizons of teacher preparation through creative and enriching cross-disciplinary endeavors. A critical reflective outlook into current practice, performance-based accountability, a focus on diversity, and partnerships within and beyond the university are an integral part of this process. A constructivist approach to preparing programs and teacher candidates to meet professional, state, and national standards promotes research, partnership, reflection, and a joint formulation of a vision to prepare effective teachers. It permeates emerging institutional conceptual frameworks and engages participants in inquiry and discourse within and across disciplines in the redesign of curriculum and learning experiences, and in alternative assessment approaches for improving learning and teaching.

In recent years there has been a growing consensus that amalgamation of a strong foundational knowledge of the discipline with effective pedagogy is key to preparing qualified teachers and educational reform (Darling-Hammond, 2001; Interstate New Teacher Assessment and Support Consortium [INTASC], 1992, 2002; National Board for Professional Teaching Standards [NBPTS], 1991; National Council for Accreditation of Teacher Education [NCATE], 2001; National Council of Teachers of Mathematics [NCTM], 2000; National Research Council/ National Science Foundation [NRC/NSF], 1996; TESOL, 2002). Language development across the curriculum, interdisciplinary collaboration, and diverse clinical practice opportunities have also been identified as high priority issues for all disciplines in teacher education and have been integrated into the professional standards for teacher candidates and practicing teachers (INTASC, 1992; NBPTS, 2001). The recent reformulation of standards for teacher candidates that were originally developed by the Interstate New Teacher and Support Consortium (INTASC) in 1992 attests to melding of pedagogically focused standards with standards of the respective disciplines. This further underscores the strengthening linkages among foundational theory of the respective disciplines and pedagogical practice achieved though interdisciplinary collaborative processes. Among the first of these redesigned standards, collaborative project of INTASC with the National Science Teacher Association has resulted in new integrated standards for science teacher candidates (INTASC, 2002). Constructivist notions that permeate the document include grounding scientific literacy in real experience, understanding big ideas through inquiry, and applying scientific inquiry to natural events and phenomena within their social context and impact on personal and social lives. Evidence, models, and explanation of unifying concepts and processes of science are an integral part of scientific teaching and learning: "The teacher of science understands that being able to construct explanations is more important than to define the term" (INTASC, 2002, p. 12).

Constructivist notions, while not explicitly underscored, are pervasive in the TESOL standards for teacher education programs (TESOL, 2002). Drawing on linguistic research, the document endorses preparation of candidates who understand the "constructive nature of language" and "how meaning is constructed" and are able to apply this knowledge in educational settings and to use *"linguistic scaffolding"* to enhance student learning (Standard 1.b). The document further underscores the grounding of language in the content area and the melding of a strong linguistic foundation for teacher candidates with a solid grounding in the respective disciplines of the core curriculum. The challenge for language teacher education programs is to reformulate current practices to integrate linguistic research and pedagogy with constructivist notions for the teaching of language through science and mathematics. Integration of cognitive and social constructivist notions into language teacher education will enhance teacher candidates' construction of deeper understandings of mathematical and scientific concepts and will enable them to construct learning environments that will support their own students' cultural identities, language and literacy development, and academic achievement.

Conclusion

The contribution of constructivism to mathematics and science pedagogy, to the development and application of new technologies, and to linguistic research in literacy and narrative development is indisputable. The role of constructivism in language pedagogy has hitherto been minimal but will undoubtedly become more prominent in the coming years and will carve new pathways for teacher candidates' emancipation as professionals. The integrated language and content paradigm as an anchor to language learning and the standards-based program reform and accreditation have created a common goal for educators and interdisciplinary linkages in the preparation of teacher candidates. The process has already engaged many educators across disciplines in joint reformulation of the vision and conceptual framework of teacher education. Integration of constructivism in language pedagogy will further open new avenues for linguistic and interdisciplinary research. Collaborative research among language, mathematics, and science educators and researchers will unravel the symbiosis of emergent literacy and numeracy and the acquisition of language and scientific concepts within a constructivist framework.

REFERENCES

American Association for the Advancement of Science (AAAS). (2001). *Designs for science literacy: Project 2061*. Washington, DC: Author.

Appleby, A. (1978). *The child's concept of story*. Chicago: The University of Chicago Press.

Bailey, K. M., & Nunan, D. (Eds.). (1995). *Voices from the language classroom*. New York: Cambridge University Press.

Barton, D. (1994). *Literacy: An introduction to the ecology of written language*. Malden, MA: Blackwell.

Beatty, K. (2003). *Teaching and researching computer-assisted language learning*. London: Pearson.

Benson, P. (2001). *Autonomy in language learning*. London: Pearson.

Bickerton, D. (1990). *Language and species*. Chicago: The University of Chicago Press.

Blumenfeld, P. C., Krajcik, J. S., Marx, R. W., & Soloway, E. (2001). Promising new instructional practices. In M.C. Wang & H.J. Walberg (Eds.), *Tomorrow's teachers* (pp. 47–78). Richmond, CA: McCutchan.

Bransford, J. D., Brown, A. L., & Cocking, R. R. (2000). *How people learn: Brain, mind, experience, and school.* Washington, DC: National Academy Press.

Brinton, D. M., Snow, M. A., & Wesche, M. B. (1989). *Content-based second language instruction.* New York: Harper and Row.

Brooks, J. G. (2002). *Schooling for life: Reclaiming the essence of learning.* Alexandria, VA: Association for Supervision and Curriculum Development (ASCD).

Brooks, J. G., & Brooks, M. G. (1993). *In Search of understanding: The case for constructivist classrooms.* Alexandria, VA: Association for Supervision and Curriculum Development (ASCD).

Brown, D. (2004). *Language assessment: Principles and classroom practices.* White Plains, NY: Pearson.

Burns, A. (1999). *Collaborative action research for English language teachers.* Cambridge: Cambridge University Press.

Carroll, L. (2003). *Jabberwocky.* Cambridge, MA: Candlewick.

Clay, M. (1991). *Becoming literate: The construction of inner control.* Portsmouth, NH: Heinemann.

Clegg, J. (Ed.). (1996). *Mainstreaming ESL: Case studies in integrating ESL students into the mainstream curriculum.* Clevedon, UK: Multilingual Matters.

Cole, M. (1990). Cognitive development and formal schooling: The evidence from cross-cultural research. In L. Moll (Ed.), *Vygotsky and education: Instructional implications and applications of sociohistorical psychology* (pp. 89–110). New York: Cambridge University Press.

Cocking, R. R., & Mestre, J. P. (Eds.). (1988). *Linguistic and cultural influences on learning mathematics.* Hillsdale, NJ: Erlbaum.

Crandall, J. (1993). Content-centered learning in the United States. *Annual Review of Applied Linguistics, 13,* 111–126.

Crandall, J., Dale, T. C., Rhodes, N. C., & Spanos, G. A. (1990). The language of mathematics: The English barrier. In A. Labarca & L. Bailey (Eds.), *Issues in L2: Theory as practice/ practice as theory* (pp. 129–150). Norwood, NJ: Ablex.

Crandall, J., & Kaufman, D. (2002). *Case studies in content based instruction in higher education.* Alexandria, VA: TESOL.

Cuban, L. (1993). *How teachers taught: Constancy and change in American classrooms* (2nd ed.). New York: Teachers College Press.

Cuevas, G. (1984). Mathematics learning in English as a second language. *Journal of Research in Mathematics Education, 15,* 134–144.

Darling-Hammond, L. (2001). Forward. In L. Darling Hammond (Ed.), *Studies of excellence in teacher education* (pp. v–xi). Washington, DC: American Association of Colleges of Teacher Education (AACTE).

DeVries, R., & Kohlberg, L. (1987). *Programs of early education: The constructivist view.* New York: Longman.

Driver, R. (1983). *The pupil scientist.* Philadelphia: Open University Press.

Duckworth, E. (1987). *The having of wonderful ideas and other essays on teaching and learning.* New York: Teachers College Press.

Dyson, A. (1989). *Multiple worlds of child writers.* New York: Teachers College Press.

Edge, J. (1996). Cross-cultural paradoxes in a profession of values. *TESOL Quarterly, 30,* 9–30.

Edge, J. (2002). *Continuing cooperative development: A discourse framework for individuals as colleagues.* Ann Arbor: The University of Michigan Press.

Evans, L. (2002). What is teacher development. *Oxford Review of Education, 28,* 123–137.

Ferreiro, E., & Taberosky, A. (1989). *Literacy before schooling.* Portsmouth, NH: Heinemann.

Forman, G., & Kuschner, D. (1977). *The child's construction of knowledge.* Belmont, CA: Wadworth.

Fosnot, C. (1993). Rethinking science education: A defense of Piagetian constructivism. *Journal of Research in Science Teaching, 30,* 1189–1201.

Fosnot, C. T. (Ed.). (1996). *Constructivism: Theory, perspectives, and practice.* New York: Teachers College Press.

Freeman, D., & Richards, J. C. (1996). *Teacher learning in language teaching.* New York: Cambridge University Press.

Freeman, D., & Johnson, K. E. (1998). Research and practice in English language teacher education [special issue]. *TESOL Quarterly, 32,* 3.

Gabel D. L. (Ed.). (1994). *A handbook of research on science teaching and learning* [A project of the National Science Teachers Association]. New York: Macmillan.

Gebhard, G., & Oprandy, R. (1999). *Language teaching awareness: A guide to exploring beliefs and practices.* New York: Cambridge University Press.

Goodlad, J. (1990). *Teachers for our nation's schools.* San Francisco: Jossey-Bass.

Goodman, Y. & Wilde, S. (1992). *Literacy events in a community of young writers.* New York: Teachers College Press.

Graves, K. (Ed.). (1996). *Teachers as course developers.* New York: Cambridge University Press.

Hall, J. K. (2002). *Teaching and researching language and culture.* London: Pearson.

Harris, M., & Hatano, G. (Eds.). (1999). *Learning to read and write: A cross-linguistic perspective.* Cambridge: Cambridge University Press.

Interstate New Teacher Assessment and Support Consortium (INTASC). (1992). *Model standards in science for beginning teacher licensing and development: A resource for state dialogue.* Washington, DC: Author.

Interstate New Teacher Assessment and Support Consortium (INTASC). (2002). *Model standards in science for beginning teacher licensing and development: A resource for state dialogue.* Science Standards Drafting Committee, Washington, DC: Author.

Johnson, D. W., & Johnson, R. T. (1984). *Circles of learning: Cooperation in the classroom.* Alexandria, VA: ASCD.

Johnson, K. (1999). *Understanding language teaching: Reason in action.* Boston: Heinle & Heinle.

Johnson, K. E. (1992). The relationship between teachers' beliefs and practices during literacy instruction for non-native speakers of English. *Journal of Reading Behavior, 24,* 83–108.

Johnson, K. E. (Ed.). (2000). Innovations in teacher education: A quiet revolution. *Case Studies in Teacher Education* (pp. 1–7). Alexandria, VA: TESOL.

Juster, N. (1961). *The phantom tollbooth.* New York: Knopf.

Kamii, C. (1981). Application of Piaget's theory to education: The preoperational level. In I. Sigel, D. Brozinsky, & R. Golinkoff (Eds.), *New directions in Piagetian theory and practice* (pp. 231–265). Hillsdale, NJ: Erlbaum.

Kamii, C. (1985). *Young children re-invent arithmetic.* New York: Teachers College Press.

Kaufman, D. (1996). Constructivist-based experiential learning in teacher education. *Action in Teacher Education, 18,* 40–50.

Kaufman, D. (1997). Collaborative approaches in preparing teachers for content-based and language enhanced settings. In M. A Snow & D. M. Brinton (Eds.), *The content-based classroom: Perspectives on integrating language and content* (pp. 175–186). White Plains, NY: Longman.

Kaufman, D. (2000). Developing professionals: Interwoven visions and partnerships. In K. Johnson (Ed.), *Case studies in teacher education* (pp. 51–69). Alexandria, VA: TESOL.

Kaufman, D., & Grennon Brooks, J. (1996). Interdisicplinary collaboration in teacher education: A constructivist approach. *TESOL Quarterly, 30,* 231–251.

Kessler, C. (Ed.). (1992). *Cooperative language learning.* Englewood Cliffs, NJ: Prentice Hall Regents.

Ko, J., Schallert, D. L., & Walters, K. (2003). Rethinking scaffolding: Examining negotiation of meaning in an ESL storytelling task. *TESOL Quarterly, 37,* 303–336.

Levin, I., Korat, O., & Amsterdamer, P. (1996). Emergent writing among Israeli kindergartners: Cross-linguistic commonalties and Hebrew specific issues. In G. Rijlaarsdan, H. van-den Bergh, & M. Couzijn (Eds.), *Theory, models, and methodology: Current trends in research of writing* (pp. 398–419). Amsterdam, Netherlands: Amsterdam University Press.

Mason, J. M., & Sinha, S. (1993). Emerging literacy in the early childhood years: Applying a Vygotskian model of learning and development. In B. Spodek (Ed.), *Handbook of research on the education of young children* (pp. 137–150). New York: Macmillan.

McCabe, A., & Peterson, C. (1991). Getting the story: A longitudinal study of parental styles in eliciting narratives and developing narrative skill. In A. McCabe & C. Peterson (Eds.), *Developing narrative structure* (pp. 217–254). Hillsdale, NJ: Erlbaum.

McGroarty, M. (1998). Constructive and constructivist challenges for applied linguistics. *Language Learning, 48*, 591–622.

Mohan, B.A. (1986). *Language and content.* Reading, MA: Addison-Wesley.

Mohan, B., Leung, C., & Davison, C. (2001). *English as a second language in the mainstream.* Essex, UK: Pearson.

Murphy, J., & Byrd, P. (2001). *Understanding the courses we teach: Local perspectives on English language teaching.* Ann Arbor: University of Michigan Press.

Murrell, P. C. (2001). *The community teacher: A new framework for effective urban teaching.* New York: Teachers College Press.

National Board for Professional Teaching Standards (NBPTS). (1991). *Toward high and rigorous standards for the teaching profession* (3rd ed.). Washington, DC: Author.

National Council for Accreditation of Teacher Education (NCATE). (2001). *Professional standards for the accreditation of schools, colleges, and departments of education.* Washington, DC: Author.

National Council of Teachers of Mathematics (NCTM). (2000). *Principles and standards for school mathematics.* Reston, VA: Author.

National Research Council/National Science Foundation (NRC/NSF). (1996). *From analysis to action: Undergraduate education in science, mathematics, engineering, and technology: Report of a convocation.* Washington, DC: Author.

Nunan, D. (1988). *The learner-centred curriculum.* Cambridge: Cambridge University Press.

Nunan, D. (Ed.). (1992). *Collaborative language learning and teaching.* Cambridge: Cambridge University Press.

Nunan, D., & Lamb, C. (1996). *The self-directed teacher: Managing the learning process.* Cambridge: Cambridge University Press.

Pappert, S. (1980). *Mindstorms: Children, computers, and powerful ideas.* New York: Basic Books.

Pearson Casanave, C., & Schecter, S. R. (Eds.). (1997). *On becoming a language educator: Personal essays on professional development.* Mahwah, NJ: Erlbaum.

Pennington, M. (1995). The teacher change cycle. *TESOL Quarterly, 29*, 705–732.

Perkins, D. N., Schwartz, J. L., West, M. M., & Wiske, M. S. (Eds.). (1995). *Software goes to school: Teaching for understanding with new technologies.* New York: Oxford University Press.

Piaget, J. (1954). *The construction of reality in the child.* New York: Basic Books.

Piaget, J. (1955). *The language and thought of the child.* New York: Meridian.

Piaget, J. (1970). *The science of education and the psychology of the child.* New York: Basic Books.

Piaget, J. & Inhelder, B. (1971). *Psychology of the child.* New York: Basic Books.

Pontecorvo, C., Orsolini, M., Burge, B., & Resnick, L. (1996). *Children's early text construction.* Mahwah, NJ: Erlbaum.

Prabhu, N. S. (1996). Concept and conduct in language pedagogy. In G. Cook & B. Seidlhofer (Eds.), *Principle and practice in applied linguistics: Studies in honour of H.G. Widdowson* (pp. 57–71). Oxford: Oxford University Press.

Read, C. (1986). *Children's creative spelling.* London: Routledge.

Richard-Amato, P. A. (2003). *Making it happen: From interactive to participatory language teaching theory and practice* (3rd ed.). White Plains, NY: Pearson.

Richards, J. (2001). *Curriculum development in language teaching.* Cambridge: Cambridge University Press.

Richardson, V. (1990). Significant and worthwhile change in teaching practice. *Educational Researcher, 19,* 10–18.

Russel, T. (1993). Learning to teach science: Constructivism, reflection, and learning from experience. In K. Tobin (Ed.), *The practice of constructivism in science education* (pp. 247–258). Hillsdale, NJ: Erlbaum.

Sexton, T. L., & Griffin, B. L. (Eds.). (1997a). *Constructivist thinking in counseling practice, research, and training.* New York: Teachers College Press.

Sexton, T. L., & Griffin, B. L. (1997b). The social and political nature of psychological science: The challenges, potential, and future of constructivist thinking. In T. L. Sexton & B. L. Griffin (Eds.), *Constructivist thinking in counseling practice, research, and training* (pp. 249–261). New York: Teachers College Press.

Shavelson, R. J., & Stern, P. (1981). Research on teachers' pedagogical thoughts, judgments, decisions, and behavior. *Review of Educational Research, 51,* 455–498.

Shohamy, E. (2001). *The power of tests: A critical perspective on the uses of language tests.* Essex, UK: Pearson.

Short, D. (1993). Assessing integrated language and content instruction. *TESOL Quarterly, 27,* 627–656.

Short, D. J. (1994). Expanding middle school horizons: Integrating language, culture, and social studies. *TESOL Quarterly, 28* (3), 581–608.

Sigel, I., & Cocking R. R. (1977). *Cognitive development from birth through adolescence: A constructivist perspective.* New York: Holt, Rinehart & Winston.

Sigel, I. E., Brozinsky, D. M., & Golinkoff, R. M. (1981). *New directions in Piagetian theory and practice.* Hillsdale, NJ: Erlbaum.

Smith, L. (1993). *Necessary knowledge.* Hillsdale, NJ: Erlbaum.

Snow, M. A., & Brinton, D. M. (Eds.). (1997). *The content-based classroom: Perspectives on integrating language and content*. White Plains, NY: Longman.

Snow, M. A., Met, M., & Genesee, F. (1989). A conceptual framework for the integration of language and content in second and foreign language instruction. *TESOL Quarterly 23*, 201–217.

Song, M., Elias, T., Muller-Witting, W., & Chan, T. K. Y. (2003). Using virtual reality to bring Syngaporean heritage to life. IEEE *Proceedings Computer Graphics International Conference*, 240–243.

Spivey, N. (1996). *The constructivist metaphor: Reading, writing, and the making of meaning*. San Diego, CA: Academic Press.

Stigler, J. W., & Hiebert, J. (1999). *The teaching gap: Best ideas from the world's teachers for improving education in the classroom*. New York: Free Press.

Stoller, F. (this volume). Content-based instruction: Perspectives on curriculum planning.

Swain, M., Brooks, L., & Tocalli-Beller, A. (2002). Peer-peer dialogue as a means of second language learning. *Annual Review of Applied Linguistics*, *22*, 171–185.

TESOL. (2002). *TESOL/NCATE Standards for accreditation of initial programs in P–12 ESL education*. Alexandria, VA: TESOL.

Tobin, K. (Ed.). (1993). *The practice of constructivism in science education*. Hillsdale, NJ: Erlbaum.

Tobin, K., Tippins, D., & Gallard, A. J. (1994). Research on instructional strategies for teaching science. In D. L. Gabel (Ed.), *A handbook of research on science teaching and learning* (pp. 45–93). [A project of the National Science Teachers Association]. New York: Macmillan.

Tolchinsky-Landsmann, L. (1996). Three accounts of literacy and the role of the environment. In C. Pontecorvo, M. Orsolini, B. Burge, & L. Resnick (Eds.), *Children's early text construction* (pp. 101–126). Mahwah, NJ: Erlbaum.

Treiman, R. (1993). *Beginning to spell*. New York: Oxford University Press.

van Lier, L. (1996). *Interaction in the language curriculum: Awareness, autonomy and authenticity*. New York: Longman.

von Glasersfeld, E. (1995). A constructivist approach to teaching. In L. Steffe & J. Gale (Eds.), *Constructivism in education* (pp. 3–16). Mahwah, NJ: Erlbaum.

von Glasersfeld, E. (1998). Cognition, construction of knowledge and teaching. In M. R. Matthews (Ed.), *Constructivism in science education* (pp. 11–30). London: Kluwer.

Vygotsky, L. (1962). *Thought and language*. Cambridge, MA: MIT Press.

Vygotsky, L. S. (1978). *Mind in society: The development of higher psychological processes*. (M. Cole, V. John-Steiner, S. Scribner, & E. Souberman, Eds. & Trans.). Cambridge, MA: Harvard University Press.

Wang, M. C., & Walberg, H. J. (2001). *Tomorrow's teachers*. Richmond, CA: McCutchan.

Wheatley, G. H. (1991). Constructivist perspectives on science and mathematics learning. *Science Education, 75*, 9–21.

Williams, B. (Ed.). (2000). *Reforming teacher education through accreditation: Telling our story.* Washington, DC: NCATE.

Zamel, V., & Spack, R. (Eds.). (2002). *Enriching ESOL pedagogy: Readings and activities for engagement, reflection, and inquiry.* Mahwah, NJ: Erlbaum.

15. EMERGING RESEARCH AND PRACTICES IN IMMERSION TEACHER EDUCATION

Tony Erben

Due to their unique place and function in society as well as their position on the educational ladder, universities have had a rather belated encounter with immersion education. In fact, it was not until the late 1970s (Day & Shapson, 1993) that universities in Canada were obliged to address a range of pedagogical issues as a direct result of the growth of immersion education in schools, the increasing number of immersion graduates from schools, and the overall educational success of immersion programs. Naturally, these issues are contextually framed and dependent on the historical development of immersion in each country where immersion education occurs. In countries with larger and longer immersion education traditions, the influence on universities has been greater. Three issues are of particular importance here: (1) the linguistic needs of immersion school graduates at university, (2) principles of immersion pedagogy use at the university level, and (3) immersion teacher education. The latter issue is especially pertinent to broader questions of the preparation of second language teachers and will be addressed here.[1]

Research as a Basis for Practice

A decade ago, Richards pointed out that there had been "little systematic study of second language teaching processes that could provide a theoretical basis for deriving practices in second language teacher education" (1990, p. 3). Since then, a substantial amount of research has been undertaken that has broadened our understanding of second language teacher education processes. Similarly, calls for more research into immersion teacher education have been made since the mid-1980s (Allen, Swain, Harley, & Cummins, 1990; Day & Shapson, 1993; Lapkin, Swain with Shapson, 1990, Obadia, 1984; Tardif, 1984). Lapkin and Swain with Shapson (1990) signaled the need for more research into immersion teacher education and called for its inclusion as a major research focus for the 1990s and beyond. They ask several basic questions, including, How do we best study what immersion teachers are doing in their classrooms? Why do teachers do what they do (beliefs)? What are immersion teacher education programs doing (policies, beliefs, practices)?" (Lapkin et al., 1990, p. 668).

These questions are particularly poignant in a context where immersion programs have been implemented, expanded, and exported throughout the world, and where the demand, especially in Canada, for qualified immersion teachers has risen exponentially. Yet, even in this context, universities have only made half-hearted attempts to engage with the philosophical, conceptual, pedagogical and organizational basis of immersion teacher education. As Obadia states: *"Les solutions temporaires semblent avoir revêtu un caractère permanent"* (Temporary solutions have often assumed a permanent character) (1985, p. 416).

Research into immersion teacher education has primarily consisted of (1) reviews geared toward mapping current immersion teacher education models (Erben, 1993; Majhanovich with Gray, 1992; Obadia, 1985; Tardif, 1984; Wilton, Obadia, Roy, Saunders, & Tafler, 1984), (2) descriptive studies that have sought to engage the views of those involved in immersion education (teachers, teacher educators, parents, ministries of education) in order to uncover the essential competencies and prerequisites needed to become an immersion teacher and thereby establish some type of national standard (Bernhardt, 1992; Day & Shapson, 1996a; Frisson-Rickson & Rebuffot, 1986), as well as (3) research investigating immersion teacher education processes itself (Bartlett & Erben, 1995; Bartlett, Erben & Singh, 1996; Erben, 1999; Erben, 2001b; Erben, in press; Erben & Bartlett, 1997). In the past decade, more varied research methodologies, seeking to explicate a broader range of issues/questions while focusing on a wider range of immersion teacher education contexts, have been on the rise.

Reviews and Surveys of Immersion Teacher Education Models

Existing models reflect a conception of immersion teacher education that presents it as resulting from an osmosis among a variety of fields including but not limited to foreign language education, second language acquisition, general education, and curriculum studies. However, as Obadia (1985) notes, there is always a danger that these discipline areas could come to take precedence over the immersion teacher training process itself. This issue explains why, in some programs, the "immersion training part" is operationalized as an add-on to existing foreign language or generalist teacher education programs rather than being conceived of as something distinct. Thus while it may be indispensable for an immersion teacher to be grounded in a knowledge base originating from curriculum content (mathematics, science, history, etc.) and foreign language education (second/foreign language methodology, linguistics, second language acquisition, cultural studies, etc.), Obadia suggests that, in order to refine immersion teacher education, immersion per se needs to be defined in its own right. Consequently, he proposes a *third way*: "It is only after a better insight of what characterizes immersion that we can better understand the training of French immersion teachers and propose...a 'third way' that differs from French second-language and first-language teaching" (Obadia, 1985, p. 415). Obadia's "third way" places immersion at the heart of any immersion teacher education program enabling teacher educators to integrate the various competing theories and practices within a holistic program. Such a program takes account of the sociolinguistic and sociopolitical context into which the immersion teachers are placed when they graduate. Lapkin et al., (1990) and Majhanovich (1990) view immersion teacher education as a continuum, much like the *development-chronology axis* conceptualized by Freeman and Richards (1993). This idea of teacher education as a continuum raises issues such as induction and in-servicing leading to professional development and the development of the profession. For example, a number of "core components" have been flagged for inclusion into preservice programs as the necessary precursors for successfully training of immersion teachers. These include general teacher education units, curriculum units, discipline units, and practicum units. Figure 1 illustrates the educational components around which many preservice immersion teacher education programs have been built (Erben, 2001a; Day & Shapson, 1996a; Majhanovich & Fish, 1988). By the 1990s, a number of experimental models for the training of immersion teachers (Majhanovich with Gray, 1992) were established.

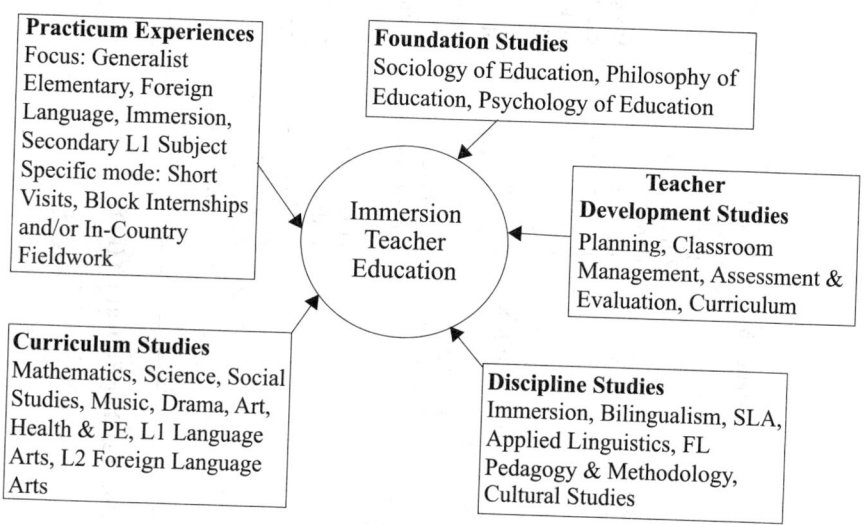

Figure 1. The Educational Components within Immersion Teacher Education

Preservice Models

Existing pre-service immersion teacher education programs differ, depending on a range of contextual factors including: societal and educational objectives of the program, target immersion language, the target student–teacher population, instructional time allocated to the L1 and/or the L2, and the university level at which immersion teacher education commences. Information in Figure 2 is by no means an exhaustive summary, though it serves as a representational cross section of extant immersion teacher education models.

As shown in Figure 2, models for ITE can be fundamentally divided into those that are preservice or initial immersion teacher education programs and those that are in-service or professional development teacher education programs. The former comprises student teachers who have no professional education apart from perhaps secondary school. The latter consists of participants who have

Clientele	Focus	Duration	Delivery Mode	Medium	Intent	Outcomes
Pre-service, full-time or part-time	Undergraduate Graduate	4 years 3 years 2 years 1 year <1 year	•Via L2 immersion (or combined L2 immersion and L1) •Via L2 as native (or combined L2 native and L1) •Via L1	•Face-to-face •Through technology	Core (immersion principles integrated throughout all courses with multiple practicum experiences) Peripheral (immersion is taught as discrete course with no practicum or only with classroom demonstrations)	Any goal-oriented combination of: •L2 proficiency •Content knowledge •Pedagogical knowledge
In-service, full-time or part-time	Upgrading or retraining					

Figure 2. Models of Immersion Teacher Education (ITE)

15. EMERGING RESEARCH AND PRACTICES IN IMMERSION TEACHER EDUCATION   393

already gained some expert knowledge or expertise in a complementary field (for example, generalist primary for L1 children, foreign language education, or even a discipline subject area such as mathematics, science or history. The needs of these individuals will differ from those of preservice student teachers, since they usually only need to gain competence in a set number of additional areas in which they find themselves deficient (usually one or more of L2 proficiency, content knowledge, and pedagogical knowledge). Preservice student teachers need to acquire expert knowledge in the full range of competencies that make up the core skills of an immersion teacher, in addition to proficiency in the immersion language. The differing nature and needs of immersion student-teachers will thus dictate the length of any program of study.

In 1985, Obadia noted that of 47 faculties of education in Canada only 16 offered some type of program, subject or module specifically geared towards immersion teacher training and that of these the majority were simply ad hoc add-on courses *"qui vient s'ajouter à la formation classique de l'enseignant"* (that typically reflect a classic teacher preparation model) (1985, p. 416). By 1993, this number had risen to 23 (Martin, Obadia, & Rodriquez, 1993), and by 2003 the number of faculties of education worldwide offering some type of immersion training rose in excess of 50. However, recently some immersion teacher education programs have also been terminated for lack of student numbers and funding cuts (Karen Johnson, personal communication, November 2003).

Models of ITE may vary in length, clientele, and delivery mode. For example, the ITE model established in the Faculté Saint-Jean at the University of Alberta caters primarily to student teachers who are native Francophone speakers. The Faculté itself is a French-medium department and the program is delivered in native-speaker mode. However, other models, primarily those ITE programs established as add-ons, use the L1 as the medium and mode of delivery, even though these student teachers will graduate and teach immersion through an L2. A third model includes programs that use both the L1 and the L2, where course content is delivered through the medium of both languages in native-speaker mode. An example of this model is the ITE program at Simon Fraser University. Last, there are models that deliver the content of the ITE program through the L2, through immersion mode itself. Examples of such programs primarily exist where the majority of client student teachers only speak the immersion language as their L2, such as the Language and Culture Initial Teacher Education: Primary (LACITEP) model at Central Queensland University, Australia (Erben, Cox, & Phillips, 1993), and the Reciclatge model in Spain[2].

In-Service Models

In-service models of immersion teacher education are primarily framed by the local conditions and needs of immersion teachers, schools, districts, and state authorities. Research in in-service teacher education reveals that, to be effective, in-service models need to be ongoing, relevant, collaborative, building on the prior strengths of participants, allowing participants to reorganize their existing pedagogical schemata, as well as being practical, conceptually based and didactically driven. From early on, a number of successful immersion in-service programs have been documented. One of the earliest (Brine & Shapson, 1989) was an exploratory study of a 12 month model specifically designed for experienced teachers with no immersion background and low L2 proficiency. Results showed that participants' major concerns (linguistic, financial, family, employment, and practica) by the end of the program were significantly reduced and that their effectiveness in L2 oral expression and knowledge of immersion methodology had significantly increased.

More recently, many different types of in-service provision for immersion teachers have been realized. In response to ongoing research into the professional development needs of immersion teachers (see Day & Shapson, 1996a), two organizations in particular merit particular mention. The Canadian Association of Immersion Teachers (http://acpi.scedu.umontreal.ca/) and the Center for Advanced Second Language Research at the University of Minnesota (http://carla.acad. umn .edu/) both host an array of in-service opportunities for immersion teachers. These include but are not limited to regular annual conferences, ongoing short- and long-term workshops/institutes, the publication of newsletters/journals, and the management of listservers and databases as well as the electronic storage of curriculum resources all specifically geared to immersion teachers. Lastly, a recent development in the advancement of professional development opportunities for immersion teachers is the creation of on-line courses for teachers, such as that developed by the Illinois Resource Center (http://www.dualu.org). Whether such in-service provision are effective remain open to investigation.

Descriptive Studies of Immersion Teachers' Competencies and Professional Needs

Met and Lorenz (1998) outline the general characteristics of a good immersion teacher. These include being reflective, interactive, engaging, responsive, flexible, and experiential in teaching approach, as well as knowing group dynamics. More importantly, they also outline practices that immersion teachers do more frequently than nonimmersion teachers, implying that immersion teachers need to be more competent in these skills, including preparing and adapting materials, contextualizing, making the abstract concrete, using more cooperative learning techniques, being aware of literacy development in two languages, teaching social as well as academic language, instructing on the cultures of second language communities, and applying general education trends to language immersion. While Met and Lorenz proposed these practices and characteristics from a recruitment perspective, they very much correspond to the perceived professional development needs flagged as issues in a number of surveys in the past decade. In particular, Day and Shapson (1996a, 1996b) conducted a survey of 2000 immersion teachers. Of all respondents, 67.1 percent indicated that they had not received specialized preparation for teaching immersion, and 30.3 percent received their teacher preparation in their L1. The most common form of professional development available to these teachers were workshops (60.5 percent). In terms of program issues, it was found that 57.1 percent of respondents rated teaching L2 language arts, and 34.9 percent rated immersion pedagogy, as two areas in which they had "great need" and/or "some need" of in-servicing. Other areas which ranked high included the need for in-servicing in developing curriculum and resources, developing L2 cultural and language skills as well as in developing community outreach strategies (see also Koshiyama, 1994).

Empirical Research: Unpacking Immersion Teacher Education Processes

Nowadays there is a general consensus concerning the knowledge bases and competencies required of immersion teachers (Day & Shapson, 1996a). Recent research linked to broader theoretical developments in second language acquisition and teacher education has been carried out in a range of immersion teacher education contexts. Such research has focused on five areas: (1) the effectiveness of immersion teacher education programs, (2) L2 language use and acquisition by student teachers in immersion programs, (3) the nature of acquisition of professional knowledge and competencies through immersion practicum experiences; (4) the implications of using technology and the effects of mediating instruction through technology within immersion programs, and (5) the social dimension of immersion student-teachers' interactions and the professional cultures which develop within immersion teacher education programs.

Effectiveness of Immersion Teacher Education Programs

Nuttall and Langham (1997) carried out an issues-based evaluation of a South African government initiative designed to improve EFL teacher education efforts in that country. The initiative, called the Molteno Project, aimed to establish and infuse English-medium teacher education programs in the principles and practices of learner-centered methodology as well as to develop suitable materials so that teachers are more fully equipped to teach through the medium of English. The study indicates that a cyclical process of classroom research, ongoing EFL professional development after graduation, and teacher-led materials development are important factors in guaranteeing the success of extensive ongoing EFL teacher training. A number of studies, however, have investigated the cognitive and linguistic benefits of such English-medium teacher education programs in various European EFL environments (Finland, Sweden, Ukraine) and found that even when starting from higher EFL proficiency levels, participants continue to achieve significant positive gains (Buchberger, 2000; Tarnopolsky, 1996).

For the most part, studies in Asia are descriptive in nature and focus on issues involving certification (Sadtono, 1995), program implementation (Shiozawa, 1993), and program effectiveness (Guefrachi & Troudi, 2000). Studies that have focused on EFL acquisition through immersion show mixed results. Other studies, however, indicate less success both in terms of the overall level of proficiency realized by student teachers and their ultimate ability to engage in English with their students in their future classrooms. In research conducted in Hong Kong, Johnson (1997) indicates that students' abilities to study effectively through English at the tertiary level remains in doubt. In another study, Lim Swee Eng, Gan, and Sharpe (1997) report that English-medium teacher education programs in Singapore do not necessarily provide future bilingual or English immersion teachers with the necessary communicative competence and confidence to act as suitable language models in the classroom. They suggest that English-medium teacher education programs need to focus on introducing more communicative methods of language teaching to improve the overall English language proficiency of student teachers.

Language Use and Interaction

In a 1998 study of elementary Japanese as a Foreign Language (JFL) learners, Takahashi found patterns of interactional variability arising as a result of goal-directed collaborative group activity. Takahashi discovered that learners' learning and behavior through social interaction in classroom environments were very much influenced by what the teacher did. In contrast, Erben (2001b) reveals that the regulatory behavior and strategic orientation of immersion student teachers in similar classroom-group environments are very much influenced, not by the lecturer or class facilitator, but by the quality of interaction itself, the ability to appropriate mediational means as they are introduced through collective scaffolding, and the willingness of group participants to share in and build a collective pedagogic capital. This suggests that immersion student teachers' level of regulatory contribution to dialogic engagement is not only task-specific but, more important, goal-specific and *dynamic-specific*, that is, indicative of the level of collaborative willingness that participants within a task engage with each other or use mediated tools to help each other.

In 2001, Erben examined immersion student teachers' L2 interactions during microteaching planning and debriefing sessions (see LACITEP model at Central Queensland University, http://handbook.cqu.edu.au/pages/ugprgmcq51.thml). He found that the L2 used by student teachers initially represented a subgoal subordinated to the total activity of microteaching planning and execution. In fact, it was the L1 that in many groups stimulated the collective forming process. The L1 was used as a mediating linguistic tool to establish group roles, construct and confirm referential perspective, edit new information as well as to negotiate rules of participation, moderate the pace of interaction, and manage collaborative input. For an immersion teacher education setting, this is particularly poignant. In many of the first product-oriented immersion studies carried out in Canada during the 1970s, it was observed that children at the initial stages of their L2 immersion experience overwhelmingly used their L1 to negotiate the curriculum. As the children became more proficient, more L2 was used. However, this situation reversed itself somewhat in secondary school immersion settings where students progressively used more L1.

This was not because of low L2 proficiency, but because of adolescent peer pressure and conformity. Like their Canadian early immersion antecedents, the university immersion student teachers in this Australian study initially used more English in the early part of their program, since they did not have the linguistic skills to talk about their microteaching experiences (Erben, 1995). This does not suggest that no L2 was used; on the contrary. What became evident was that the student teachers used the L1 to master the L2, talk about the L2, and construct L2 teacher scripts for their JFL classroom. They used Japanese within discursive events in which their Japanese knowledge sufficed. When it did not, assistance was either given by a more knowledgeable peer, or the novice student-teacher resorted to code switching or to the L1 in its entirety to maintain the momentum of the group's work.

In an ethnographic study within the LACITEP immersion program, Erben and Bartlett (1998) found that, in the context of developing an L2 repertoire to talk about their JFL teaching, student teachers were eventually able to use professional terminology to describe and make sense of their experience. The introduction of a professionally oriented discourse within content-based courses helped student teachers to construct critical and more different ways to understand their actions. In turn, this led student teachers to think and act in different ways, or as Freeman calls it, to "reconstruct practice" (1996, p. 735).

Practicum Experiences

Erben (2001b) carried out a six-month case study using a sociocultural theoretical framework (Tharp & Gallimore, 1988; Wells, 1999). He investigated how immersion student teachers engaged in collective-group curriculum planning during a school-based practicum came to construct L2 pragmatic and sociolinguistic knowledge as well as pedagogic knowledge of immersion teaching. Erben found many complex modes of social interaction among the immersion student teachers. Among others, student-teachers (1) frame their roles in learning, (2) did not recycle their notions of pedagogy and L2 classroom use, but jointly reconstructed new repertoires for engaging in immersion teaching, and (3) became more adept at navigating their regulatory orientations through the ongoing changes in the linguistic complexities of the content of interaction. On the one hand, L2 use was determined by the behavior of the more knowledgeable peer in group microteaching activities, and on the other hand, it was also determined by the receptivity of each individual student teacher to appropriate the use of mediational tools such as the L2. Both factors helped the student teachers to make sense of their engagement with the microteaching context of their learning as well as to understand and control the processes of such engagement itself.

Erben (2001b) outlines a number of possible ways to enhance the collaborative nature of practica such that immersion student teachers have enhanced opportunities to collectively regulate their microgenetic growth, to establish multiple connections of intersubjectivity with peers, and to (re)construct as well as appropriate knowledges different to the ones legitimatized in current practice (see Figure 3). The conception is based on a notion of *continuous strategic engagement*. This is defined as a situation in which a student teacher's engagement with learning is never carried out alone, but is organized around a collective of peers who themselves may be at various levels of

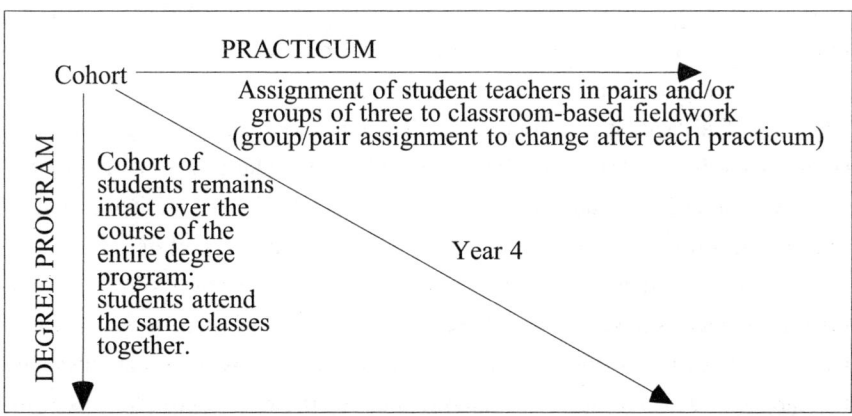

Figure 3. Overcoming the Isolating Student-teacher Practicum (A group-based field experience model of practice teaching)

regulation. Collective engagement may occur at differing levels (for example, in pairs, in groups, in larger groupings or cohorts and in class configurations), with the guiding principle being that a student teacher's learning within a practicum context never takes place in isolation and that every student teacher has the discursive space to collectively construct L2 and pedagogic understandings, to regulate others as well as be regulated by others. To overcome the possible effects of cursory collaborative work routines becoming established within groupings, it is suggested that a more knowledgeable peer or expert, from a higher year level, take on the role of mentor to facilitate and to guide productive collaborations.

Effects of Mediating Instruction through Technology within Immersion Programs

Of the many so-called innovations in the language education industry over the past 30 years, only two innovations have been credited with providing a *unique* contribution to the field. One is immersion pedagogy (Krashen, 1984), and the other is computer-mediated online learning (Warschauer, 1998). However, while the benefits of immersion education and the uses of technology in education have been well documented, research into computer-mediated communication and computer-mediated pedagogy in immersion settings remain at best scant. Erben (1999, 2002) provides a contextualized account of the linguistic and pedagogic changes which occur in a university teacher education immersion classroom (see LACITEP model) when instruction is networked through the medium of one particular online technology, namely audiographics. Audiographic technology is a network-based media tool that facilitates multimedia conferencing, data conferencing, and visual conferencing in the classroom. Providing a two-way audio and two-way virtual–visual computer link, it allows users to learn interactively, and store and/or send images and information (still video images, documents or pictures, CD ROM images, compressed audio or video clips) from separate computers linked over a network. It enables linked sites to share screens in such a way that any information written or typed is immediately seen at all remote sites. Linked sites are thus able to share software tools such as Windows and use these interactively. This work characterizes the linguistic and pedagogic adaptations in the classroom as student teachers develop from other- to self-regulated activity.

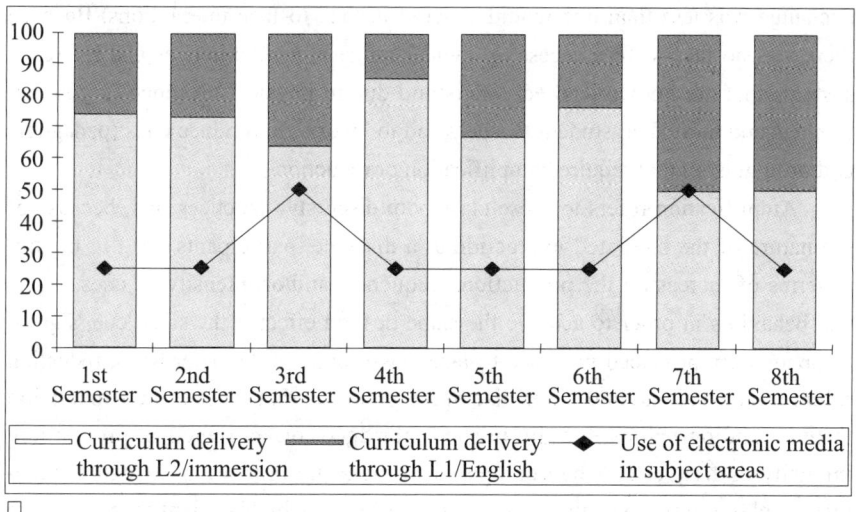

Figure 4. Delivery of Total Curriculum through Immersion and Use of Electronic Media as a Percentage of Subject Contact Time

Figure 4 illustrates the levels of use of a range of electronic media, including e-mail, video conferencing, audiographics, and the like used in the LACITEP degree program. The main component of the study consisted of tracking one third-year LACITEP class over a seven-week period where (1) student teachers were taught a unit (six hours in total divided into 30-minute segments and delivered over a three week period) from the course "Teaching, Learning & Planning" through audiographics with the class being in 'line-of-sight', and where (2) the same student teachers were then taught a subsequent unit from the course "Teaching, Learning & Planning" (eight hours in total divided into thirty minute segments and delivered over a four-week period) where delivery was networked through audiographics and delivered over different sites. Classes were observed and videotaped, and the teacher and student teachers were interviewed at various stages throughout the study. The data were collated in terms of critical incidences of instruction and analyzed for their significance and effects on linguistic and pedagogical processes.

Erben (2001b) noted that there was a narrowing of the range of symbolic cues in mediated interaction. This means that the degree of reciprocity and interpersonal exchange was less than one would observe in face-to-face interactions. Because there was no face-to-face access to a wider range of symbolic cues and reference systems that are known/learned/understood due to physical presence or context; teachers and individual student teachers had to "work" to produce cues (pedagogic and/or linguistic) that required amplification or reduction.

Amplification refers to those classroom discursive practices that, because of the nature of the mediated interaction at a distance, participants need to modify in terms of increasing the production, frequency, and/or intensity of cues, signs, and behaviors in order to achieve the same desired effect if the same cue, sign or behavior were produced in a face-to-face classroom. On the other hand, reduction refers to cues, signs, and other discursive practices that, due to their mediation through audiographics, are diminished, abridged, or shortened in production, intensity or frequency when compared to the same practice in a regular face-to-face classroom. Over the seven-week period in which student teachers were observed, pedagogical and linguistic adjustments did not remain constant. In the beginning, many more instantiations of amplifications and reductions occurred because students and teachers alike attempted to adjust *known* classroom practices and routines to the requirements of engaging in learning and interaction through Japanese immersion that was mediated through audiographics. However, as classroom participants adapted to the use of audiographics, instructional processes came to be increasingly reconstructed in ways that represented a substantive shift away from how these processes occurred in face-to-face immersion classrooms.

Social Dimensions of Student Teachers' Interactions and the Professional Cultures of Immersion Teacher Education Programs

To better understand the various pedagogical attributes of postsecondary immersion endeavors in teacher education, Bartlett and Erben (1995) carried out a 12-month issues-based case study investigation of LACITEP, a four-year bachelor of education degree program through Japanese immersion in Australia (Erben, in press). According to Bartlett and Erben, the interpretation of immersion provided in the literature is largely a linguistic or sociolinguistic one. Far from being merely a linguistic bath, however, their study shows teacher education through immersion to be a multidimensional dialectic phenomenon. In terms of what a preservice immersion teacher is actually immersed in, Bartlett and Erben identify four attributes characterized as *language, culture, context,* and *content knowledge*. By understanding the interplay of these four attributes as a process within different classroom environments, different learning experiences, different group dynamics, different microteaching experiences and subject contexts, Bartlett and Erben framed the outcomes and student achievement levels in the LACITEP immersion program through what might be called an immersion filter, shown in Figure 5.

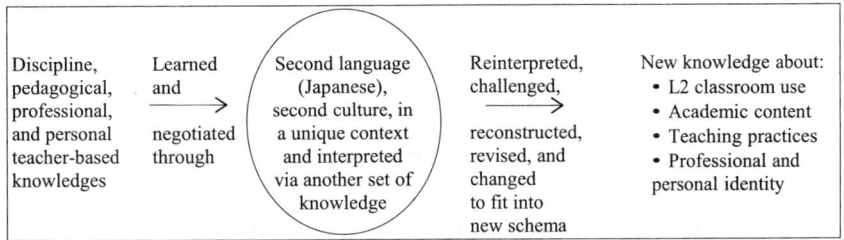

Figure 5. Representation of an Immersion Filter in Teacher Education

Erben (2001a, 2001b) states that an immersion student teacher's cognitive growth is not guaranteed. Within the "situated" process of socialization into a community of JFL immersion practice, cognitive growth is framed by an individual's receptiveness, sensitivity towards and ability to manage those mediational means placed at his/her disposal. This might be by more knowledgeable peers through collective interaction or through interaction with the social setting per se. A more acute receptivity toward appropriating mediational means, a sensitivity toward identifying the quality of using such mediational means in terms of one's own microgenetic growth, and an ability to manage such means within interactional operations ultimately shape the extent of learning in the ZPD (see also Wells, 1999).

Conclusion

Immersion teacher education can be conceived in different ways, depending on how the nature of the world and the role of the teacher are framed. The ideological framework of immersion contains not only educational imperatives but also political, social, and cultural ones as well. In terms of each new immersion endeavor, the characteristics and nature of such contexts must be evaluated in terms of the effects of such endeavors, and in relation to our current knowledge of immersion practices as a whole. If one accepts the view that teaching and learning is a situated construction, one ceases to talk in terms of a good immersion teacher or good immersion teaching (Krashen, 1984) as some type of empirically tested or theoretically canonized and prescriptive entity. Rather, one needs to accept that immersion pedagogy is located in a range of sociopolitical, cultural, economic, and educational debates. One must then ask oneself whether different practicum models are required to graduate immersion teachers with the necessary competencies to meet specifically local needs. Obadia asserts that this is the case in saying that "French immersion is a unique Canadian phenomenon that needs its own self-analysis" (1985, p. 415).

Notes

1. For studies exploring the nature and levels of language maintenance of immersion graduates after secondary schooling, see Harley (1994), Hart, Lapkin, Swain and Howard (1991), Wesche (1985, 1993), Wesche, Morrison, Ready, and Pawley (1990) for a comprehensive review.

2. When immersion was originally implemented in Catalonia, authorities were faced with a serious teacher education problem. Many teachers were non-Catalan speakers and, of those who were, few were qualified to teach the language (Siguán, 1986, cited in de Mejía, 1994): "After experiments with various forms of short-term in-service training schemes, the Catalan government decided in 1989 to initiate 30-day immersion teacher training cycles for primary school teachers working in immersion programmes. These courses were designed [to be delivered through immersion] both to improve teachers' language fluency as well as to provide them with first hand experience of immersion programmes" (de Mejía, 1994, p. 21).

ANNOTATED BIBLIOGRAPHY

Day, E., & Shapson, S. (1996a). French immersion teachers and their professional needs. *Studies in immersion education.* (pp. 117–131). Clevedon. Multilingual Matters.

Chapter 6, presenting results of a survey commissioned by the Canadian Association of Immersion Teachers (CAIT) regarding the professional development needs of immersion teachers in Canada is particularly important because of the large number of respondents (n = 2000) and issues raised. Response rates ranged from 29.7 percent (Quebec) to 90 percnet (Northwest Territories).

Erben, T. (2001b). *Student-teachers' use of microteaching activity to construct sociolinguistic knowledge within a Japanese immersion initial teacher education program in Australia.* Unpublished Ph.D. dissertation. United Kingdom: Lancaster University.

This study attempted to investigate the nature of dialogic knowledge construction within one component of an immersion teacher education program, namely, microteaching. What is abundantly clear is that the process of teacher development may be seen as a continuing conversation among multiple actors. In this study, not only were immersion student teachers able to generate new understandings about their L2 and how to use the L2 in a JFL teaching context, but their strategic regulation of this knowledge was very much dependent on the quality of their mediated collaborative engagements with other student teachers in the group.

Johnson, R. K., & Swain, M. (Eds.). (1997). *Immersion education: International perspectives.* Cambridge: Cambridge University Press.

This edited book comprises articles from a range of stakeholders engaged in immersion education. Particularly interesting is the international perspectives it provides. All accounts of immersion practices are contextualized within the specific social, historical, educational, and political conditions of each country under focus.

Tedick, D. (Ed.). (in press). *Teacher education for second or foreign language contexts: International perspectives on research and practice.* Mahwah, NJ: Erlbaum.

The chapters in this collection represent the current thinking of some of the most respected teacher education scholars in the fields of ESL, EFL, FL, BE, and immersion education from around the world. The perspectives that teachers are professionals, not technicians; that teachers must construct their own knowledge (rather than someone else providing it to them); that knowledge construction occurs through collaboration; and that teachers need to be at the center of their own professional development are cutting edge positions that language teacher educators around the world are struggling to realize.

OTHER REFERENCES

Allen, P., Swain, M., Harley, B., & Cummins, J. (1990). Aspects of classroom treatment: Toward a more comprehensive view of second language education. In B. Harley, P. Allen, J. Cummins, & M. Swain (Eds.), *The development of second language proficiency* (pp. 57–81). Cambridge: Cambridge University Press.

Bartlett, L., & Erben, T. (1995). *An investigation into the effectiveness of an exemplar model of LOTE teacher-training through partial immersion*. A report for the Innovative Languages Other Than English Project (ILOTES), Department of Employment, Education and Training. Canberra: Australian Government Printing Service.

Bartlett, L., Erben, T., & Singh, M. G. (1996). Teacher identity formation through language immersion in an initial-teacher-education curriculum. *Asia Pacific Journal of Teacher Education, 24* (2), 173–196.

Bernhardt, E. (Ed.). (1992). *Life in immersion classrooms*. Clevedon: Multilingual Matters.

Brine, J. M., & Shapson, S. (1989). Case study of a teacher retraining program for French immersion. *The Canadian Modern Language Review, 45,* (3), 464–477.

Buchberger, I. (2000, April). *Struggle for diversity in a harmonising European context: New tasks for teacher education*. Paper presented at the American Educational Research Association Conference, New Orleans, LA [ED442773].

Day, E. M., & Shapson, S. M. (1993). French immersion teacher education: A study of two programs. *The Canadian Modern Language Review, 49* (3), 446–465.

Day, E. M., & Shapson, S. M. (1996b). A national survey: French immersion teachers' preparation and their professional development needs. *The Canadian Modern Language Review, 52,* 248–70.

de Mejía, A. M. (1994). *Bilingual teaching/learning events in early immersion classes: A case study in Cali, Columbia*. Unpublished Ph.D. dissertation, Lancaster University.

Erben, A. (1993). The importance of the practicum in teacher development. What happens in an immersion teacher training program? *Australian Association of Language Immersion Teachers. 1* (1), 16–29.

Erben, T. (1995, October). *LACITEP: A bachelor of education degree program through immersion in Japanese. Perspectives on planning, pedagogy, research, administration, assessment and teacher training*. A poster presentation presented at the conference Research and Practice in Immersion Education: Looking Back and Looking Forward. Center for Advanced Research on Language Acquisition: University of Minnesota.

Erben, T. (1999). Constructing learning in a virtual immersion bath: LOTE teacher education through audiographics. *WorldCALL*. Amsterdam: Zwetlinger.

Erben, T. (2001a). Sustainable foreign language teacher education. In G. Bräuer (Ed.), *Pedagogy of language learning* (pp. 195–221). New York: Ablex.

Erben, T. (2002). Immersion teacher education through audiographics. *American Council on Immersion Education ACIE Newsletter*, 5 (3) 10–13. Minneapolis, MN: Center for Advanced Research in Language Acquisition, University of Minnesota.

Erben, T. (in press). Teacher education through immersion and immersion teacher education. In D.Tedick (Ed.), *Teacher education for second or foreign language contexts: International perspectives on research and practice.* Mahwah, NJ: Erlbaum.

Erben, A., Cox, R., & Phillips, S. (1993, July). Primary teacher training through immersion; Multiskilling our LOTE teacher-force. *Babel*, a journal of the Australian Federation of Modern Language Teachers' Associations. *15*, 31–45 [special issue].

Erben, T. & Bartlett, L. (1997, July). Mediated interaction and the management of learning in an initial teacher education language immersion classroom. In T. Gale, T. Erben, & P. Danaher (Eds.), *Diversity difference and discontinuity: Proceedings of the Australian Teacher Education Association conference*, Yeppoon, Queensland, Australia. Available: http://atea.cqu.edu.au/content/ soc_base/erbart.html.

Erben, T., & Bartlett, L. (1998). *Managing Japanese immersion through audiographics, Teachers networking instruction in an initial teacher education LOTE program.* Volume 1 (pp. 1–100). A Commonwealth curricula project for the Committee for the Advancement of University Teaching (CAUT). Canberra: Department of Employment, Education, and Training and Youth Affairs.

Freeman, D. (1996). "To take them at their word:" Language data in the study of teachers' knowledge. *Harvard Educational Review*, *66* (4), 732–761.

Freeman, D., & Richards, J. C. (1993). Conceptions of teaching and the education of second language teacher. *TESOL Quarterly*, *27* (2), 193–217.

Frisson-Rickson, F., & Rebuffot, J. (1986). *La formation et le perfectionnement des professeurs en immersion: pour des critères nationaux* [Initial preparation and further training for immersion teachers: Toward national criteria]. Ottawa: Association Canadienne des Professeurs d'Immersion.

Guefrachi, H., & Troudi, S. (2000). Enhancing English language teaching in the United Arab Emirates. In K. E. Johnson (Ed.), *Teacher education: Case studies in TESOL practice series* (pp. 189–204). Alexandria, VA: TESOL.

Harley, B. (1994). After immersion: Maintaining the momentum. *Journal of Multilingual and Multicultural Development,15* (2 & 3), 229–244.

Hart, D., Lapkin, S., Swain, M., & Howard, J. (1991). *French immersion at the secondary/ postsecondary interface: Toward a national study.* A report submitted to the Department of the Secretary of State. Toronto: Modern Language Centre, OISE.

Johnson, R. K. (1997). The Hong Kong education system: Late immersion under stress. In R. K. Johnson & M. Swain (Eds.), *Immersion education: International perspectives* (pp. 171–

189). Cambridge: Cambridge University Press.

Koshiyama, Y. (1994). *A study of the current state and the needs of teacher training in Japanese immersion education in the United States*. Unpublished Ph.D. dissertation, University of Southern California.

Krashen, S. (1984). Immersion: Why it works and what it has taught us. *Language and Society, 12*. Ottawa: Commissioner of Official Languages.

Lapkin, S., Swain, M., with Shapson, S. (1990). French immersion agenda for the 90's. *Canadian Modern Language Review, 46* (4), 638–674.

Lim Swee Eng, A., Gan, L., & Sharpe, P. (1997). Immersion in Singapore preschools. In R. K. Johnson and M. Swain (Eds.), *Immersion education: International perspectives* (pp. 190–210). Cambridge: Cambridge University Press.

Majhanovich, S. (1990). Challenge for the 90s: The problem of finding qualified staff for French core and immersion programs. *Canadian Modern Language Review, 46* (3), 454–468.

Majhanovich, S., with Gray, J. (1992). The practicum: An essential component in French immersion teacher education. *Canadian Modern Language Review,48* (4), 682–696.

Majhanovich, S., & Fish, S. (1988). Training French immersion teachers for the primary grades. An experimental course at the University of Western Canada. *Foreign Language Annals, 21*, 311–320.

Martin, M., Obadia, A., & Rodríguez, F. (1993). *Enquête nationale sur les programmes dê formation en immersion française au Canada* [National survey of teacher preparation for French immersion in Canada]. Necean, Ontario: L'association canadienue des professeurs d'immersion.

Met, M., & Lorenz, E. (1998). Recruitment, preparation, and supervision of immersion teachers. In C. A. Klee, A. Lynch, & E. Tarone (Eds.), *Research and practice in immersion education: Looking back and looking ahead — Selected conterence proceedings* [from the inaugural conference on immersion education, Oct. 1995]. University of Minnesota: CARLA Working Papers Series #10.

Nuttal, C., & Langham, D. (1997). The Molteno project: A case study of immersion for English-medium instruction in South Africa. In R. K. Johnson & M. Swain (Eds.), *Immersion education: International perspectives* (pp. 210–239). Cambridge: Cambridge University Press.

Obadia, A. A. (1984). Le professeur d'immersion, le pivot du nouveau bilinguisme au Canada [The immersion teacher, linchpin of the new bilingualism in Canada]. *Modern Canadian Language Review, 41* (2), 376–387.

Obadia, A. A. (1985). La formation du professeur d'immersion française au Canada: Une conception philosophique et pédagogique en devenir ou à la recherche d'une troisième voie [The formation of the immersion teacher in Canada: A philosophical and predagogical conception under development, or the search for a third way]. *Canadian Journal of*

Education. 10 (4), 415–426.
Richards, J. C. (1990). The dilemma of teacher education in second language teaching. In J. C. Richards & D. Nunan (Eds.), *Second language teacher education* (pp. 3–16). Cambridge: Cambridge University Press.
Sadtono, E. (1995, April). *The standardization of teacher trainees in EFL countries*. Paper presented at the International Conference on Language in Development: The Stakeholders' Perspectives. Bali, Indonesia [ED388105].
Shiozawa, T. (1993). Social and administrative parameters in methodological innovation and implementation in post-secondary language schools in Japan. *Journal of International Studies, 12* (11), 109–139.
Siguán, M. (1986). Education and bilingualism in Catalonia. *Journal of Multilingual and Multicultural Development, 1* (3), 231–242.
Takahashi, E. (1998). Language development in social interaction: A longitudinal study of a Japanese FLES program from a Vygotskan approach. *Foreign Language Annals, 31* (3), 392–406.
Tardif, C. (1984). La formation des enseignants en situation d'immersion. *Canadian Modern Language Review, 41* (2), 365–375.
Tarnopolsky, O. B. (1996, September). *Intensive immersion ESP teaching in the Ukraine: Theoretical foundations and practical results.* Paper presented at the European Conference on Immersion Programs. Barcelona, Spain [ED409707].
Tharp, R., & Gallimore, R. (1988). *Rousing minds to life.* New York: Cambridge University Press.
Warschauer, M. (1998). Online learning in a sociocultural context. *Anthropology and Education Quarterly, 29* (1), 68–88.
Wells, G. (1999). *The zone of proximal development and its implications for teaching and learning.* Retrieved October, 2002, from http://www.oise.utoronto.ca/ ~gwells/zpd. discussion.txt.
Wesche, M. B. (1985). Immersion and the universities. *Canadian Modern Language Review, 41* (5), 931–940.
Wesche, M. B. (1993). French immersion graduates at university and beyond: What difference has it made? In J. M. Alatis (Ed.), *The Georgetown Roundtable on Languages and Linguistics 1992* (pp. 208–239). Washington, DC: Georgetown University Press.
Wesche, M. B., Morrison, F., Ready, D., & Pawley, C. (1990). French immersion: Post secondary consequences for individuals and universities. *Canadian Modern Language Review, 46* (3), 430–451.
Wilton, F., Obadia, A., Roy, R., Saunders, A. B., & Tafler, R. (1984). *National study of French immersion teacher training.* Ottawa: Canadian Association of Immersion Teachers.

CONTRIBUTOR BIODATA

Diane D. Belcher, Associate Professor of Applied Linguistics at Georgia State University. coedits the journal *English for Specific Purposes* as well as a teacher reference series, the *Michigan Series on Teaching Multilingual Writers.* She has coedited two special issues of the *Journal of Second Language Writing* and several books, including *Reflections on Multiliterate Lives* (with Ulla Connor; Multilingual Matter, 2001) and *Linking Literacies: Perspectives on L2 Reading-Writing Connections* (with Alan Hirvela; University of Michigan Press, 2001).
Contact information: dbelcher1@ gsu. edu

Colleen Brice is Assistant Professor of English at Grand Valley State University, where she teaches undergraduate and graduate courses in applied linguistics and TESOL. With Tony Silva and Melinda Reichelt, she compiled the *Annotated Bibliography of Scholarship in Writing , 1993—1997.* Her work has appeared in *International Journal of English Studies, Language,* and *TESOL Journal;* forthcoming work will appear in *Second Language Writing Research: Perspectives on the Process of Knowledge Construction* (edited by Paul Kei Matsuda and Tony Silva). Her research interests include issues in second language writing, teacher response, teacher education, and writing program administration.
Contact information: bricec @ gvsu. edu

Richard Donato is Associate Professor of Foreign Language Education at the University of Pittsburgh, where he directs the graduate programs in foreign language education and TESOL. With coauthors G. Richard Tucker and Janis Antonek, he is the recipient of the Paul Pimsleur Award for Excellence in Foreign Language Teaching Research from the *Modern Language Journal* and the American Council on the Teaching of Foreign Languages. He also received the Freeman Award from the Northeast Conference on Language Teaching and the French Institute of Washington Award for the outstanding ariticle on foreign language teaching published in the *French Review* in 2002. Editor of *Foreign Language Teaching, Journey of a Lifetime,* he developed the book *Stories Teachers Tell* for the 1998 Northeast Conference on Foreign Language Teaching, which he chaired. His research interests include foreign language learning in the elementary school and classroom language learning from a sociocultural perspective.
Contact information: donato+ @ pitt. edu

Tony Erben is Assistant Professor of Foreign Language Education/ESOL at the University of South Florida. He has been involved on postsecondary immersion teacher education for the past 15 years. His work centers in uses of technology, the practicum, and mediational tools from a sociocultural theoretical perspective in immersion teacher education settings. He established the world's first preservice teacher education degree program through Japanese immersion in Australia and received the Australian University Teacher of the Year Award in 1998 for his efforts in this area. He has been Secretary of the Australian Association of Language Immersion Teachers and has published, presented, and given numerous workshops in the North America, Australia, and Asia related to immersion teacher education. Contact information: terben @ tempest. coedu. usf. edu

Sandra Fotos is Professor of English in the School of Economics, Senshu University, Tokyo, Japan. Her research interests include grammar instruction, bilingualism, and computer assisted Language learning (CALL). She has published in a variety of journals, is past editor of *JALT Journal*, the research journal of the Japan Association for language Teaching, and is a past member of the editorial advisory board of *TESOL Quarterly*. She is currently on the editorial boards of *JALT Journal* and *The Japan Journal of Multilingualism and Multiculturalism* and the editorial board of the ESL and Applied Linguistics Professional Series, published by Erlbaum.
Contact information: sfotos @ gol. com

William Grabe is Professor of English at Northern Arizona University where he teaches in the MA-TESL and doctoral program in Applied Linguistics. He is interested in all aspects of reading and writing abilities. L1 and L2, child and adult, and theory and practice. He is also interested in issues pertaining to literacy, written discourse analysis and applied linguistics more generally. He has recently coauthored *Teaching and Researching Reading* (with Fredricka Stoller; Longman, 2002). Editor of the *Annual Review of Applied Linguistics* from 1991 to 2000, he was President of the American Association for Applied Linguistics during 2001—2002.
Contact information: William. Grabe @ nau. edu

Jennifer Jenkins is Senior Lecturer in the Department of Education and Professional Studies, King's Colleg, London University, where she directs the masters program in

English Language Teaching and Applied Linguistics and teaches sociolinguistics, world Englishes, and phonology/phonetics at undergraduate and postgraduate levels. Her research interests since the late 1980s, beginning with her doctoral work, have been concerned with the implications of the international spread of English, initially from a phonological perspective and more recently in relation to language attitudes. She has contributed numerous articles on this topic to journals and edited collections, and is the author of two books: *The Phonology of English as an International Language* (Oxford University Press, 2000) and *World Englishes* (Routledge, 2003).
Contact information: jennifer. jenkins @ kcl. ac. uk

Dorit Kaufman is Director of the Professional Education Program at the State University of New York, Stony Brook. Her research interests include native language attrition with a special emphasis on the psycholinguistic and sociolinguistic processes that trigger progressive decline in Hebrew in an English-dominant context; emergent literacy and narrative development in bilingual and attrition contexts; and the impact of interdisciplinary collaboration and constructivist pedagogy on language teacher candidates' professional growth. Related articles on these topics have appeared in journals and edited volumes. She is coeditor (with Jodi Crandall) of *Content-Based Instruction in Higher Education Settings* (TESOL, 2002) and the forthcoming *Content-Based Instruction in P-12 Education Settings* (TESOL). She is the recipient of the 2001 R. Neal Appleby Outstanding Teacher Educator Award in New York State and the 2002 State University of NewYork President's and Chancellor's Awards for Excellence in Teaching.
Contact information: dkaufman @ notes. cc. sunysb. deu

Richard Kern is Associate Professor of French and Director of the French language program at the University of California at Berkeley. Currently he is Director of the UC Education Abroad Study Centers in Lyon and Grenoble, France. His research interests include reading and writing in a foreign language and the use of networked computers to facilitate communicative language use. His most recent book, dealing with the theory and practice of reading and writing in a foreign language is *Literacy and Language Teaching* (Oxford University Press, 2000). With Mark Warschauer, he coedited *Network-Based Language Learning: Concepts and Practice* (Cambridge University Press, 2000).
Contact information: kernrg @ socrates. berkeley. edu

Michael McCarthy is Emeritus Professor of Applied Linguistics, University of Nottingham, UK, Adjunct Professor of Applied Linguistics, Pennsylvania State University, and Adjunct Professor of Applied Linguistics, University of Limerick, Ireland. He is author of *Discourse Analysis for Language Teachers* (Cambridge University Press, 1991), *Language as Discourse* (Longman, 1994; with Ronald Carter), *Exploring Spoken English* (Cambridge University Press, 1997; with Ronald Carter), *Vocabulary: Description, Acquisition and Pedagogy* (coedited with Norbert Schmitt, Cambridge University Press, 1997), *Spoken Language and Applied Linguistics* (Cambridge University Press, 1998), *Exploring Grammar in Context* (with Ron Carter and Rebecca Hughes, Cambridge University Press, 2000) and *Issues in Applied Linguistics* (Cambridge University Press, 2001). He is author of more than 50 academic papers. From 1994 to 1998 he was coeditor of *Applied Linguistics* (Oxford University Press). He is codirector (with Ronald Carter) of the 5-million word CANCODE corpus project.

Mary McGroarty, Editor-in-Chief of *ARAL*, is a Professor in the Applied Linguistics Program in the English Department at Northern Arizona University and a past President of the American Association for Applied Linguistics (1997-98). A Woodrow Wilson Fellow, she has also received Fulbright and Mellon awards. Her articles have appeared in *Applied Linguistics*, *Canadian Modern Language Review*, *Language Learning*, *TESOL Quarterly*, and several anthologies. She has served on the editorial boards of *Applied Linguistics*, *ARAL*, *Journal of Language, Identity, and Education*, *Second Language Instruction and Acquisition Abstracts*, and *TESOL Quarterly*. Her research interests include theoretical and pedagogical aspects of language learning and teaching, bilingualism, language policy, and assessment of second language skills.
Contact information: mary . mcgroarty @ nau. edu

Hossein Nassaji is Assistant Professor of Applied Linguistics in the Linguistics Department at the University of Victoria, British Columbia, Canada. His teaching and research interests include second language acquisition, communicative focus on form, and L2 written and oral discourse. His work has been published in a variety of journals, including *Applied Linguistics*, *Applied Psycholinguistics*, *Language Learning*, *Modern Language Journal*, *TESOL Quarterly*, *Canadian Modern*

Language Review, and *Language Teaching Research*. With coauthor Gordon Wells, he received the twenty-first annual Kenneth W. Mildenberger Prize of the Modern Language Association of America for their article, "What's the Use of Triadic Dialogue?: An Investigation of Teacher-Student Interaction."
Contact information: nassaji @ uvic. ca

Anne O'Keeffe is Lecturer in Applied Linguistics at Mary Immaculate College (MIC), University of Limerick, Ireland, where she is founder and coordinator of the Inter-Varietal Applied Corpus Studies (IVACS) Research Center. Her research interests centre on spoken corpora, their description and pedagogical applications, and their application in the study of language in the media. She has also been involved in the building of the Limerick Corpus of Irish English (L-CIE) with her colleagues at the University of Limerick. She has recently published a number of papers in edited volumes on corpus linguistics and (with Fiona Farr) in *TESOL Quarterly*. She has also coedited a forthcoming special issue of *Teange* (the Irish Yearbook of Applied Linguistics) on corpora, language varieties, and the language classroom.
Contact information: anne. okeeffe @ mic. ul. ie

John Read is Senior Lecturer in the School of Linguistics and Applied Language Studies at Victoria University of Wellington, New Zealand, where he teaches courses in language testing and assessment, research methodology, the social context of language learning, and academic writing. His research interests include second language vocabulary assessment and the testing of proficiency in English for academic purposes. He is the author of *Assessing Vocabulary* (Cambridge, 2000), and his articles have appeared in *Language Testing*, *English for Specific Purposes*, the *Journal of English for Academic Purposes*, and the *RELC Journal*. In addition, he is currently the coeditor of *Language Testing*.
Contact information: john. read @vuw. ac. nz

Barbara Seidlhofer is Professor of English Linguistics/Applied Linguistics in the English Department at the University of Vienna. Coeditor of the International Journal of Applied Linguistics and President of the Austrian Association for Applied Linguistics, VerbAL, she is the Director of VOICE, the Vienna-Oxford

International Corpus of English. Her publications include *Pronunciation* (with Christiane Dalton; Oxford University Press, 1994), *Approaches to Summarization: Discourse Analysis and Language Education* (Narr, 1995), *Principle and Pratice in Applied Linguistics* (coedited with Guy Cook; Oxford University Press, 1995), *Language Policy and Language Education in Emerging Nations* (coedited with Robert de Beaugrande and Meta Grosman; Ablex, 1998) and *Controveisies in Applied Linguistics* (Oxford University Press, 2003). She is currently working on a book on the conceptualization, description, and pedagogy of English as a lingua franca.
Contact information: barbara. seidlhofer @ univie. ac. at

Tony Silva is Associate Professor of ESL at Purdue University, where he directs the ESL Writing Program and teaches undergraduate and graduate courses for ESL students and ESL teachers. With Ilona Leki, he founded and edits the *Journal of Second Language Writing;* with Paul Kei Matsuda, he founded and hosts the Symposium on Second Language Writing and edited *Landmark Essays on ESL Writing and on Second Language Writing* (both pubished by Erlbaum, 2001); and with Colleen Brice and Melinda Reichelt, he compiled the *Annotated Bibliography of Scholarship in Writing*. He currently serves on the editorial boards of *Assessing Writing*, *Journal of Basic Writing*, *TESL Canada Journal*, and *Writing Program Administration*.
Contact information: tony @ purdue. edu.

Hazel Simmons-McDonald is Senior Lecturer in Applied Linguistics at the Cave Hill Campus of the University of the West Indies in Barbados. Her research interest include second language acquisition by creole and creole-influenced vernacular speakers as well as the development of literacy by these speakers within the formal context of school. She recently completed a literacy survey of primary school children in the Windward Islands and Barbados and has presented results as technical reports to the sponsoring govenments. For several years, she served as the Secretary -Treasurer of the Society for Caribbean Linguistics. At present, she is also Dean of the Faculty of Humanities and Education at Cave Hill and coordinates the university's Cultural Studies Initiative.
Contact information: hsimmac @ uwichill. edu. bb

Fredricka L. Stoller is an Associate Professor of English at Northern Arizona University, where she teaches in the MA-TESL and doctoral program Ph. D. in Applied Linguistics. She is coauthor of *Teaching and Researching Reading* (with William Grabe; Longman, 2002) and coeditor of *A Handbook for Language Program Administrators* (with Mary Ann Christison; Alta, 1997). She has published numerous articles on content-based instruction and gave a plenary address on the topic at the 2002 international TESOL Convention in Salt Lake City. Coeditor of the 2001 specital topics issue of the *TESOL journal* (v. 10, n. 2/3) on sustained-content language teaching, she has introduced teachers to different approaches to content-based instruction and other methodologies in the United States. and abroad, most recently (2002-2003) as a Senior Fulbright Lecturer in Turkey.
Contact information: Fredricka. Stoller @ nau. edu

Larry Vandergrift is Associate Professor in the Second Language Institute of the Faculty of Arts at the University of Ottawa, where he teaches courses in French as a second language, English as a second language, and second language acquisition. He has published articles in *Language Learning*, *Canadian Modern Language Review*, *Modern Language Journal*, *Foreign Language Annals*, and the *French Review*. His current research interests include second language listening comprehension, listening processes, learning strategies and the role of metacognition and motivation in the self-regulation on language learning. He is also coeditor of the *Canadian Modern Language Review*.
Contact information: lvdgrift @ uottawa. ca

Paige D. Ware earned her doctorate from the University of California at Berkeley in 2003. She has taught EFL in Spain and Germany and college-level writing to second language studens. Her research interests include technology and language learning; writing and second language development; multimedia technologies and literacy; and university, school, and community collaborations. She has worked on research projects examining the use of Web-based writing to promote cultural understanding; the multimedia literacy practices of elementary and middle-school childen; and teacher research in technology-integrated classrooms. She is currently a Research Assistant Professor at Southern Methodist University in Dallas, Texas.
Contact information: pware @ mail. smu. edu

Mark Warschauer is Vice Chair of the Department of Education at the University of California, Irvine, and an Associate Professor of Education and of Information and Computer Science. Previously, he taught and conducted research at the University of Hawai'i, Charles University in Prague, and Moscow Linguistic University, and also served as director of educational technology for a USAID project in support of English language teaching in Egypt. His new books include *Electronic Literacies* (Erlbaum, 1999), *Network-Based Language Teaching* (coedited with Richard Kern; Cambridge University Press, 2000), and *Technology and Social Inclusion* (MIT Press, 2003). His current research examines students' literacy practices using laptop computers in school and home environments. Contact information: http://www.gse.uci.edu/markw

图书在版编目(CIP)数据

剑桥应用语言学年度评论.2004:语言教育学的进展＝
Annual Review of Applied Linguistics 2004·Advances
in Language Pedagogy:英文/(美)玛丽·麦克格罗蒂
(Mary McGroarty)主编.—北京:商务印书馆,2016
(剑桥应用语言学年度评论)
ISBN 978-7-100-12501-7

Ⅰ.①剑… Ⅱ.①玛… Ⅲ.①应用语言学—研究—
英文 Ⅳ.①H08

中国版本图书馆 CIP 数据核字(2016)第 196779 号

所有权利保留。
未经许可,不得以任何方式使用。

剑桥应用语言学年度评论 2004·语言教育学的进展
Annual Review of Applied Linguistics 2004·Advances in Language Pedagogy

主编 〔美〕Mary McGroarty
导读 彭宣维

商 务 印 书 馆 出 版
(北京王府井大街36号 邮政编码100710)
商 务 印 书 馆 发 行
北京市松源印刷有限公司印刷
ISBN 978-7-100-12501-7

2016 年 12 月第 1 版　　开本 880×1230　1/32
2016 年 12 月北京第 1 次印刷　　印张 14⅝

定价:43.00元